LET'S GO

■ THE RESOURCE FOR THE INDEPENDENT TRAVELER

"The guides are aimed not only at young budget travelers but at the indepedent traveler; a sort of streetwise cookbook for traveling alone."

—*The New York Times*

"Unbeatable; good sight-seeing advice; up-to-date info on restaurants, hotels, and inns; a commitment to money-saving travel; and a wry style that brightens nearly every page."

—*The Washington Post*

"Lighthearted and sophisticated, informative and fun to read. [Let's Go] helps the novice traveler navigate like a knowledgeable old hand."

—*Atlanta Journal-Constitution*

"A world-wise traveling companion—always ready with friendly advice and helpful hints, all sprinkled with a bit of wit."

—*The Philadelphia Inquirer*

■ THE BEST TRAVEL BARGAINS IN YOUR PRICE RANGE

"All the dirt, dirt cheap."

—*People*

"Anything you need to know about budget traveling is detailed in this book."
—*The Chicago Sun-Times*

"Let's Go follows the creed that you don't have to toss your life's savings to the wind to travel—unless you want to."

—*The Salt Lake Tribune*

■ REAL ADVICE FOR REAL EXPERIENCES

"The writers seem to have experienced every rooster-packed bus and lunar-surfaced mattress about which they write."

—*The New York Times*

"Value-packed, unbeatable, accurate, and comprehensive."

—*The Los Angeles Times*

"[Let's Go's] devoted updaters really walk the walk (and thumb the ride, and trek the trail). Learn how to fish, haggle, find work—anywhere."

—*Food & Wine*

LET'S GO PUBLICATIONS

TRAVEL GUIDES

Australia 8th Edition
Austria & Switzerland 12th edition
Brazil 1st edition
Britain & Ireland 2005
California 10th edition
Central America 9th edition
Chile 2nd edition
China 5th edition
Costa Rica 2nd edition
Eastern Europe 2005
Ecuador 1st edition **NEW TITLE**
Egypt 2nd edition
Europe 2005
France 2005
Germany 12th Edition
Greece 2005
Hawaii 3rd edition
India & Nepal 8th edition
Ireland 2005
Israel 4th edition
Italy 2005
Japan 1st edition
Mexico 20th edition
Middle East 4th edition
Peru 1st edition **NEW TITLE**
Puerto Rico 1st edition
South Africa 5th edition
Southeast Asia 9th edition
Spain & Portugal 2005
Thailand 2nd edition
Turkey 5th edition
USA 2005
Vietnam 1st edition **NEW TITLE**
Western Europe 2005

ROADTRIP GUIDE

Roadtripping USA **NEW TITLE**

ADVENTURE GUIDES

Alaska 1st edition
New Zealand **NEW TITLE**
Pacific Northwest **NEW TITLE**
Southwest USA 3rd edition

CITY GUIDES

Amsterdam 3rd edition
Barcelona 3rd edition
Boston 4th edition
London 2005
New York City 15th Edition
Paris 13th Edition
Rome 12th edition
San Francisco 4th edition
Washington, D.C. 13th edition

POCKET CITY GUIDES

Amsterdam
Berlin
Boston
Chicago
London
New York City
Paris
San Francisco
Venice
Washington, D.C.

PERU

ASHLEY E. ISAACSON EDITOR
LINDSAY CROUSE ASSOCIATE EDITOR

RESEARCHER-WRITERS
MAX ARBES
JAIME DAVILA
DIANE DEWEY
IRIT KLEIMAN
SARITHA KOMATIREDDY

NICHOLAS KEPHART MAP EDITOR
TERESA ELSEY MANAGING EDITOR

ST. MARTIN'S PRESS ✠ NEW YORK

HELPING LET'S GO. If you want to share your discoveries, suggestions, or corrections, please drop us a line. We read every piece of correspondence, whether a postcard, a 10-page email, or a coconut. **Address mail to:**

Let's Go: Peru
67 Mount Auburn Street
Cambridge, MA 02138
USA

Visit Let's Go at **http://www.letsgo.com,** or send email to:

feedback@letsgo.com
Subject: "Let's Go: Peru"

In addition to the invaluable travel advice our readers share with us, many are kind enough to offer their services as researchers or editors. Unfortunately, our charter enables us to employ only currently enrolled Harvard students.

Maps by David Lindroth copyright © 2005 by St. Martin's Press.

Distributed outside the USA and Canada by Macmillan, an imprint of Pan Macmillan Ltd.
20 New Wharf Road, London N1 9RR
Basingstoke and Oxford
Associated companies throughout the world
www.panmacmillan.com

ISBN: 0-312-33566-0
EAN: 978-0312-33566-0
First edition
10 9 8 7 6 5 4 3 2

Let's Go: Peru is written by Let's Go Publications, 67 Mount Auburn Street, Cambridge, MA 02138, USA.

Let's Go® and the LG logo are trademarks of Let's Go, Inc.
Printed in the USA.

CONTENTS

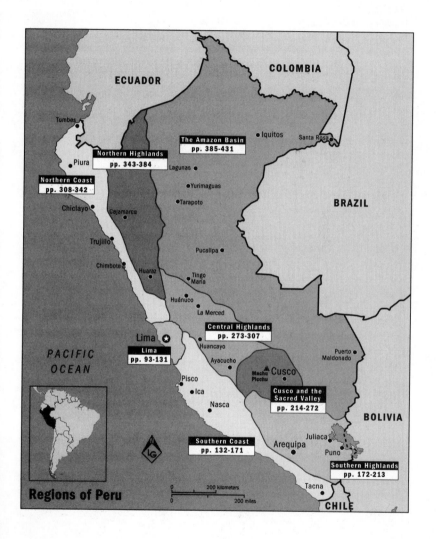

ECUADOR

COLOMBIA

Tumbes

Iquitos

Santa Rosa

The Amazon Basin
pp. 385-431

Piura

Northern Highlands
pp. 343-384

Lagunas

Northern Coast
pp. 308-342

Yurimaguas

Tarapoto

Chiclayo

Cajamarca

BRAZIL

Trujillo

Pucallpa

Chimbote

Huaraz

Tingo
María

Huánuco

La Merced

Central Highlands
pp. 273-307

Lima

Huancayo

Lima
pp. 93-131

Puerto
Maldonado

Ayacucho

PACIFIC
OCEAN

Machu
Picchu

Cusco

Pisco

Cusco and the
Sacred Valley
pp. 214-272

Ica

Nasca

BOLIVIA

Juliaca

Southern Coast
pp. 132-171

Arequipa

Puno

Southern Highlands
pp. 172-213

Tacna

Regions of Peru

200 kilometers

0

0   200 miles

CHILE

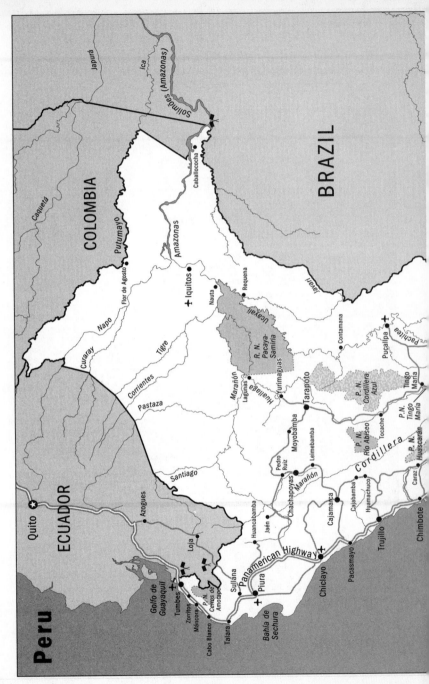

Peru

ECUADOR

COLOMBIA

BRAZIL

Quito

Japurá

Caquetá

Ica

Solimões (Amazonas)

Putumayo

Amazonas

Caballococha

Flor de Agosto

Napo

Iquitos

Requena

Nauta

Tigre

Ucayali

Curaray

Corrientes

Pastaza

R. N. Pacaya-Samiria

Javarí

Contamana

Pachitea

Pucallpa

Marañón

Lagunas

Huallaga

Yurimaguas

Tarapoto

P. N. Cordillera Azul

Tingo María

Santiago

Moyobamba

Leimebamba

P. N. Tingo María

Tocache

P. N. Río Abiseo

Azogues

Pedro Ruiz

Chachapoyas

Marañón

Cordillera

P. N. Huascarán

Caraz

Loja

Huancabamba

Jaén

Cajabamba

Cajamarca

Huamachuco

Chimbote

Sullana

Piura

Panamerican Highway

Chiclayo

Pacasmayo

Trujillo

Golfo de Guayaquil

Tumbes

Zorritos

Máncora

P. N. Cerros de Amotape

Cabo Blanco

Talara

Bahía de Sechura

VIII

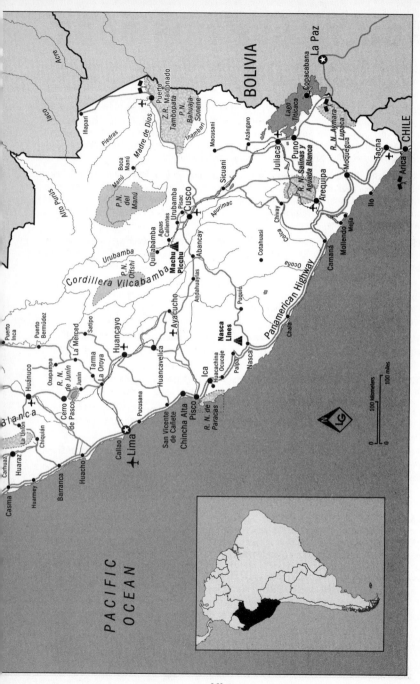

PACIFIC OCEAN

BOLIVIA

CHILE

La Paz
Copacabana
Lago Titicaca
Puno
Juliaca
Azángaro
Macusani
Sicuani
Apurimac
CUSCO
Pisac
Urubamba
Aguas Calientes
Quillabamba
Machu Picchu
Abancay
Cotahuasi
Andahuaylas
Ayacucho
Puquio
Nasca Lines
Nasca
Ocucaje
Huacachina
Ica
Pisco
Chincha Alta
San Vicente de Cañete
Pucusana
R. N. de Paracas
Chala
Panamerican Highway
Coca
Camaná
Ocoña
Chivay
Arequipa
R. N. Salinas y Aguada Blanca
Moquegua
R. N. Aymara-Lupaca
Tacna
Arica
Ilo
Mejía
Mollendo
Callao
Lima
Huacho
Barranca
Huarmey
Casma
Huaraz
Carhuaz
Cordillera Blanca
Chiquián
La Unión
Huánuco
Oxapampa
Cerro de Pasco
Junín
R. N. de Junín
La Oroya
Tarma
La Merced
Satipo
Huancayo
Huancavelica
Puerto Inca
Puerto Bermúdez
Alto Purús
Acre
Iñaco
Iñapari
Piedras
Boca Manú
P.N. del Manú
Manú
Urubamba
Cordillera Vilcabamba
P.N. del Otishi
Madre de Dios
Puerto Maldonado
Z.R. Tambopata
P.N. Bahuaja-Sonene
Inambari

100 kilometers
100 miles

IX

HOW TO USE THIS BOOK

This book begins with general information about Peru, then launches into strategically ordered chapters divided by region. The black tabs on the side of the book should help you navigate.

COVERAGE LAYOUT. We begin in Lima, then trace an S-shape through the country beginning in the most touristed areas: the Southern Coast, the Southern Highlands, and then Cusco and the Sacred Valley. From there, we cross the Central Highlands on our way to the Northern Coast and the Northern Highlands, ending with coverage of the Amazon Basin from north to south.

TRANSPORTATION INFO. Transportation information is at the beginning of major city writeups, and at the end of small towns. Directions are generally given from major cities or transportation hubs to smaller destinations. Transportation listings include information in parenthesis that tells the duration, departure time, and price of trips, in that order.

ESSENTIALS. All the practical information involved in traveling can get downright pesky. Flip to this section to get the quick and easy guide to Peru, including getting there, getting around, finding a place to stay, and staying safe.

LIFE AND TIMES. This chapter holds the answers to all your burning questions about Peru. Was anyone around before the Incas? What is Quechua? Is the Shining Path still active? Are rodents really considered a delicacy? History, literature, culture—it's all here.

ALTERNATIVES TO TOURISM. Take home Spanish fluency instead of that cheesy alpaca sweater—Peru offers many opportunities for study abroad, volunteering, and other alternatives to tourism.

SCHOLARLY ARTICLES. We hired the experts to share information on Peru's religious history (p. 71), literary giants (p. 306), and study abroad opportunities (p. 89).

FEATURES. Find interesting stories, local lore, recent news items, hidden deals, big splurges, major celebrations, regional cuisine, and researchers' tales from the road in our black sidebar features throughout the book.

PRICE DIVERSITY. Our researchers list establishments in order of value from best to worst. Our absolute favorites are denoted by the Let's Go thumbs-up (🖐). Since the best value does not always mean the cheapest price, we have incorporated a system of price ranges for food and accommodations (see opposite page and inside the back cover). These are indicated by ❶❷❸❹❺ symbols in the text.

LANGUAGE AND OTHER QUIRKS. The appendix (p. 432) includes a handy reference for Spanish pronunciation, a list of frequently-used Spanish phrases, and a glossary of Spanish words that appear in this book. Some essential Quechua and Aymara phrases also make an appearance.

A NOTE TO OUR READERS. The information for this book was gathered by *Let's Go* researchers from May through August of 2004. Each listing is based on one researcher's opinion, formed during his or her visit at a particular time. Those traveling at other times may have different experiences since prices, dates, hours, and conditions are always subject to change. You are urged to check the facts presented in this book beforehand to avoid inconvenience and surprises.

PRICE RANGES>>PERU

Our researchers list establishments in order of value from best to worst; our favorites are denoted by the Let's Go thumbs-up (☑). Since the best value is not always the cheapest price, however, we have also incorporated a system of price ranges, based on a rough expectation of what you'll spend. For **accommodations,** we base our range on the cheapest price for which a single traveler can stay for one night. For **restaurants** and other dining establishments, we estimate the average amount a traveler will spend on a meal. The table tells you what you'll *typically* find in Peru at the corresponding price range; keep in mind that no system can allow for every individual establishment's quirks, and you'll get more for your money in some places than in others. In other words, expect anything.

ACCOMMODATIONS	RANGE	WHAT YOU'RE *LIKELY* TO FIND
❶	under s/11	Campsites or basic budget hostels with running water, dorm-style beds, shared baths, and probably some insect friends. The lucky few may be blessed with hot water, TV, private bath, or a fan.
❷	s/11-24	Hostels in this range are cleaner and probably prettier. Likely to include hot water and other amenities. TV for the fortunate. Perhaps an insect—it just wants to be your friend.
❸	s/25-38	Similar to ❷, but with more amenities and usually in a quieter part of town. Often cleaner and more attractive, with perks like TVs, private baths, and kitchen access. Some offer tourist services, Internet, and breakfast.
❹	s/39-59	A resort- or business hotel-style accommodation, often in touristy areas. Usually excellent service, all the amenities, and prime location. The staff may also provide tourist services.
❺	s/60+	Jungle lodges, resorts, or very, very, very nice hotels. The sky's the limit. If it's a ❺ and doesn't have what you want, you've paid too much.
FOOD	RANGE	WHAT YOU'RE *LIKELY* TO FIND
❶	under s/8	Eat-and-run places with basic lunch *menús*, stir-fries, sandwiches, roasted chicken, and other generic fare.
❷	s/8-14	Local joints, sometimes hole-in-the-wall establishments, but most have seating. You might see *ceviche* gracing some menus, but count on pastas, salads, and set *menús*.
❸	s/15-21	All the typical dishes in a more pleasant or unique setting. An infinite array of new and exciting gastronomic options.
❹	s/22-35	More exotic or international dishes, and likely to be better prepared—or at least appear to be. Often cater to tourists.
❺	s/36+	The freshest meat and fish cooked to perfection. Excellent service should be a part of the experience. It better be worth writing home about.

RESEARCHER-WRITERS

Max Arbes   *Northern Amazon and Northern Highlands*

The mysterious transportation schedules and otherwise unpredictable nature of Amazonian life keep everyone guessing, but Max dove right in. This social studies student from Atlanta, GA is no stranger to the developing world, having spent last year in West Africa. An avid photographer and writer in his spare time, Max had no shortage of worthwhile fodder for his art as he perused Peru's jungle and the mountains of the North.

Jaime Davila   *Lima, Northern Coast, and Lake Titicaca*

This anthropology student from New Canaan, CT embodies the history buff—and the romantic—inside us all. After living in Mexico City, Jaime was ready for Lima; after three weeks there, he was ready for the sunny North. A turn of events soon found Jaime cruising around Lake Titicaca with admirable efficiency. Everyone, from his editors to the stranded ladies to whom he gave his bus seat, got a glimpse of his heart of gold.

Diane Dewey   *Southern Coast and Arequipa*

After summiting Mt. Kilimanjaro and Mt. Rainier, Diane chose Peru's Southern Coast for her next adventure. This outgoing biochemistry student and water polo player from Seabrook, TX made friends in every town and found two new passions: *pisco* sours and sandboarding. A brief stint in the highlands found her sipping cocoa in Arequipa's cafes as she drafted flawless copy. Diane's self-assured grace and dedication made her our hero.

Irit Kleiman   *Central Highlands and Central Amazon*

Only the best go to the Central Highlands, and Irit proved her mettle. This keen observer and experienced traveler from Evanston, IL put her brand-new Ph.D in French Literature on the shelf in favor of unpredictable transportation schedules, riots in old Shining Path country, and a diet of exactly five bazillion varieties of potatoes. Irit captured this and more with unparalleled confidence and accurate, imaginative writing.

Saritha Komatireddy   *Cusco, Sacred Valley, and Southern Amazon*

Everywhere Saritha went, people told her about dark-haired Sarita Colonia, a miraculous figure so powerful in Peruvian tradition that robbers will high-tail it out of a house if they see an altar to Sarita. Our own Saritha was no less miraculous. This art-lover and government student from Poplar Bluff, MO was a brave thrill-seeker with endless good humor and an appetite for new things that translated into dozens of beautiful new pages.

CONTRIBUTING WRITERS

Scott E. Isaacson, J.D. is the Executive Director of Fellows at the International Center for Law and Religion Studies at Brigham Young University.

José Antonio Mazzotti, Ph.D is the Gardner Cowles Associate Professor in Romance Languages and Literatures at Harvard University.

Alexandra Moss is the Editor of *Let's Go: Spain and Portugal 2005*.

ACKNOWLEDGMENTS

TEAM PERU THANKS: Teresa, who knows everything; Diane, Saritha, Irit, Jaime, and Max; the SAM pod (August, Dan, and Luke) and affiliates; llamas; typists and proofers, for your heroic patience; Prod; Jeremy, for food, folks, and fun; Emma, Kirkie, Anne, and Bob, for your help and support.

ASHLEY THANKS: Teresa Editrix Darcy, for being calm, happy, and comma-happy; Lindsay, I saw the color-coded edits in your application and knew you were dedicated—thanks for all the P1s and for taking half the GI; Nick, for accepting messy edits on neon paper; China, for keeping me company at 7am; the Jane Austen group, for reminding me how fun it is to be a girl; Mom, who taught me grammar, and Dad, who took us to South America.

LINDSAY THANKS: Ashley, whose calm, efficient attitude held the book together and kept us on track—you are an amazing editor; Teresa, for your pictures on paper edits, helpful suggestions, and knowing everything; August, for "sharing" me and keeping things moving over in Ecuador; Luke and Dan for making work so fun; Emma for helping everyone out; Nick for patiently churning out amazing maps; my family; and Mike for making this summer fun.

NICK THANKS: Ashley and Lindsay for correcting all my accent marks, for the fascinating stories they relay from the RWs, and for the time spent figuring out cartographic strategies. Thanks also go out to Jaime for his awesome job puddlejumping around the country, Saritha for the priceless glossy map of Cusco, Diane for her sweet job along the Southern Coast, Irit for the details she put into the Central Highlands, and Max for the new maps.

Editor
Ashley E. Isaacson
Associate Editors
Lindsay Crouse
Managing Editor
Teresa Elsey
Map Editor
Nicholas Kephart
Typesetter
Amelia Aos Showalter

Publishing Director
Emma Nothmann
Editor-in-Chief
Teresa Elsey
Production Manager
Adam R. Perlman
Cartography Manager
Elizabeth Halbert Peterson
Design Manager
Amelia Aos Showalter
Editorial Managers
Briana Cummings, Charlotte Douglas,
Ella M. Steim, Joel August Steinhaus,
Lauren Truesdell, Christina Zaroulis
Financial Manager
R. Kirkie Maswoswe
Marketing and Publicity Managers
Stef Levner, Leigh Pascavage
Personnel Manager
Jeremy Todd
Low-Season Manager
Clay H. Kaminsky
Production Associate
Victoria Esquivel-Korsiak
IT Director
Matthew DePetro
Web Manager
Rob Dubbin
Associate Web Manager
Patrick Swieskowski
Web Content Manager
Tor Krever
Research and Development Consultant
Jennifer O'Brien
Office Coordinators
Stephanie Brown, Elizabeth Peterson

Director of Advertising Sales
Elizabeth S. Sabin
Senior Advertising Associates
Jesse R. Loffler, Francisco A. Robles, Zoe
M. Savitsky
Advertising Graphic Designer
Christa Lee-Chuvala

President
Ryan M. Geraghty
General Manager
Robert B. Rombauer
Assistant General Manager
Anne E. Chisholm

LET'S GO

ABOUT LET'S GO

GUIDES FOR THE INDEPENDENT TRAVELER

At Let's Go, we see every trip as the chance of a lifetime. If your dream is to grab a machete and forge through the jungles of Brazil, we can take you there. If you'd rather bask in the Riviera sun at a beachside cafe, we'll set you a table. We write for readers who know that there's more to travel than sharing double deckers with tourists and who believe that travel can change both themselves and the world—whether they plan to spend six days in London or six months in Latin America. We'll show you just how far your money can go, and prove that the greatest limitation on your adventures is not your wallet, but your imagination. After all, traveling close to the ground lets you interact more directly with the places and people you've gone to see, making for the most authentic experience.

BEYOND THE TOURIST EXPERIENCE

To help you gain a deeper connection with the places you travel, our researchers give you the heads-up on both world-renowned and off-the-beaten-track attractions, sights, and destinations. They engage with the local culture, writing features on regional cuisine, local festivals, and hot political issues. We've also opened our pages to respected writers and scholars to hear their takes on the countries and regions we cover, and asked travelers who have worked, studied, or volunteered abroad to contribute first-person accounts of their experiences. We've also increased our coverage of responsible travel and expanded each guide's Alternatives to Tourism chapter to share more ideas about how to give back to local communities and learn about the places you travel.

FORTY-FIVE YEARS OF WISDOM

Let's Go got its start in 1960, when a group of creative and well-traveled students compiled their experience and advice into a 20-page mimeographed pamphlet, which they gave to travelers on charter flights to Europe. Four and a half decades later, we've expanded to cover six continents and all kinds of travel—while retaining our founders' adventurous attitude toward the world. Our guides are still researched and written entirely by students on shoestring budgets, experienced travelers who know that train strikes, stolen luggage, food poisoning, and marriage proposals are all part of a day's work. This year, we're expanding our coverage of South America and Southeast Asia, with brand-new *Let's Go: Ecuador*, *Let's Go: Peru*, and *Let's Go: Vietnam*. Our adventure guide series is growing, too, with the addition of *Let's Go: Pacific Northwest Adventure* and *Let's Go: New Zealand Adventure*. And we're immensely excited about our new *Let's Go: Roadtripping USA*—two years, eight routes, and sixteen researchers and editors have put together a travel guide like none other.

THE LET'S GO COMMUNITY

More than just a travel guide company, Let's Go is a community. Our small staff comes together because of our shared passion for travel and our desire to help other travelers see the world. We love it when our readers become part of the Let's Go community as well—when you travel, drop us a postcard (67 Mt. Auburn St., Cambridge, MA 02138, USA) or send us an e-mail (feedback@letsgo.com) to tell us about your adventures and discoveries.

For more information, visit us online: www.letsgo.com.

DISCOVER PERU

From trail-weary trekkers to lifelong *Iquiteños*, everyone agrees that this corner of South America is a land of extremes. Peru pulsates with a rich cultural heritage, whirls under head-spinning political fluctuations, and dazzles the imagination with some of the world's most astounding geographical diversity. To the east, chilly Andean slopes plummet into the humid Amazon Basin, while in the west, those snow-crowned peaks fall to the driest desert on earth. Indeed, this is a region brimming with superlatives. One of the most extensive empires in history called Peru home. The world's highest navigable lake laps Peruvian shores. Some of the world's longest and tallest waves crash onto Peru's beaches. UNESCO has named no fewer than ten World Heritage Sites in Peru. Offering myriad opportunities for the adventurous of heart and the inquisitive of mind—from sandsurfing to jungle-tripping, museum-hopping to llama-spotting—Peru has many secrets to share.

Of course, a look at the media makes Peru appear even more extreme than it is in some ways: a nausea-inducing roller coaster of riots, political scandal, and economic instability. In reality, once one leaves the major urban centers, life progresses calmly, coolly, and slowly. Peru is a place where everything gets done in its own time—if not today, then *mañana, sin falta*.

DIGITS AND DATA

SPECIES OF BIRDS: 1804

PERCENTAGE OF AIRPORTS WITH UNPAVED RUNWAYS: 65

KILOMETERS OF UNPAVED ROAD PER KILOMETER OF PAVED ROAD: 8.23

FAVORITE RODENT CONSUMED: Guinea pig

AMONG THE TOP 10 DRIEST PLACES ON EARTH: Ica (#5), Callao (#10)

WORLD'S 2ND-MOST-PROLIFIC COCAINE PRODUCER: Peru

LONGEST MOUNTAIN RANGE ON EARTH: The Andes

AMONG THE TOP 10 HIGHEST CITIES ON EARTH: Cusco (#6), Huancayo (#7)

WHEN TO GO

Despite its proximity to the equator, Peru spans three disparate climates (coast, *sierra*, and jungle) that keep everyone guessing. There are two distinct seasons: the **dry winter** from June to September and the **wet summer** from December to March. Along Peru's Pacific **coast**, mild winters give way to sweltering summer heat that reflects tropical norms minus the rain. Bring a sweater or twelve for trips into the **sierra;** the best time to visit the highlands is during the winter, when clear skies make for drier and happier hiking. The **jungle** (called the Amazon Basin), on the other hand, is always wet and warm, with at least 77% humidity even in the dry season. The jungle can become utterly impenetrable during the rainy months (Dec.-Apr.). For more specifics, see the climate chart (p. 19).

Local **festivals and holidays** are another seasonal variation to keep in mind when planning your trip. Go for some crazy fun, but be prepared for crowded accommodations and lots of people. The most important nationwide holidays are Christmas (December 25), Semana Santa (the week of Easter), Inti Raymi (June 24), and Independence Day (July 28-29). For a calendar detailing area festivals, see p. 78 or visit the official website of PromPeru (www.peru.org.pe).

WHAT TO DO

From surfing to skiing, resorts to ruins, sea lions to mountain lions, and pubbing to clubbing, Peru offers something for everyone. The sections below highlight a few of the reasons to visit; for more specific regional attractions, see the **Highlights** box at the beginning of each chapter.

FROM RICHES TO RUINS

As the sky grows light behind them, the Andean foothills appear haloed. Up by the Sun Gate, a weary band of trekkers holds its breath, and the new day's sun carries away the shadows that had obscured the valley below. For many, this is why they came to Peru. This is **Machu Picchu** (p. 266), the Incas' incomparable city. Few places can match Machu Picchu's dramatic setting, but the nearby fortresses of **Ollantaytambo** (p. 257), **Pisac** (p. 250), and **Sacsayhuamán** (p. 245) give it a run for its money. Up north, the ruins of **Chavín de Huántar** (p. 352) sheltered eight generations of the Chavín people within the Cordillera Blanca. Where the mountains meet the rainforest, the Chachapoyas constructed the huge, limestone fortress that is **Kuélap** (p. 382). The exhumed graves of **Sipán** (p. 328) housed a mummy hailed as the "Peruvian King Tut." Farther up the coast, outside Trujillo, **Chan Chan** (p. 320), once the capital of the Chimú Empire, is the largest preserved mud-brick city in the world. Evidence of Peru's splendid ancient past is everywhere: even fast-paced, modern **Lima** (p. 93) has its own pre-Columbian ruins.

THE HIGH AND MIGHTY

The Andes—the highest tropical peaks in the world—cut a swath through the middle of Peru, offering great opportunities for both hiking and trekking. A trekker in Peru should first consider the stunning **Inca Trail** (p. 260), much of which follows an Inca stone road. The walk begins near Ollantaytambo and passes several ancient *tambos* (rest stops) before reaching Machu Picchu. To the southeast, crystal-clear **Lake Titicaca** (p. 195) enchants visitors as the highest navigable lake on earth. The adventurous can join throngs of Arequipans who scale the slopes of the active volcano **El Misti** (p. 191). Farther north, the Cordillera Blanca's **Parque Nacional Huascarán** (p. 349) has an extensive set of fantastic trails and guards Peru's highest peak. If you'd rather not brave the chilly air and conspicuous lack of oxygen that characterize those upper elevations, never fear: Peru's low spots are just as inviting. Lovers of lush rainforest vegetation and giant insects hack their

TOP TEN RUINS

You've seen Machu Picchu, but so has everyone else. Insatiable ruins-junkies still have dozens of archaeological sites to choose from. Some *Let's Go* favorites:

1. Moray and Las Salineras (p. 260), near Cusco. These agricultural innovations span pre-Inca and Inca times.

2. Huaca del Sol (p. 320), near Trujillo. Like many sites in northern Peru, the ceremonial capital of the Moche Empire has yet to be fully excavated by archaeologists.

3. Chavín de Huantar (p. 352), near Huaraz. The Chavín lived and worshiped here for a millennium.

4. Tambo Colorado (p. 143), near Pisco. The adobe walls of this Inca fortress still retain some of the original paint.

5. Ollantaytambo (p. 257), near Cusco. A picture-perfect fortress, with pristine stone walls in the foreground and valley vistas in the background.

6. Chan Chan (p. 320), near Trujillo. The mud-and-brick citadels housed the Chimú rulers before and after death.

7. Puruchuco (p. 129), near Lima. Take a peek at daily life in an ancient dwelling.

8. Tipón (p. 247), near Cusco. Extensive terraces may have been used for experimental agriculture.

9. Pachacamac (p. 131), near Lima. The pyramids of this sacred city honored the creator god.

10. Pikillacta and Rumicolca (p. 248), ruins of a fort and aqueducts, two of the little-known sites southeast of Cusco.

way through jungle expanses all along Peru's eastern border, particularly near **Iquitos** (p. 386) or in **Parque Nacional del Manú** (p. 422). Near Arequipa, to the south, hikers can plumb the depths of **Colca Canyon** (p. 188), once thought to be the deepest ravine in the world, or the lesser-known **Cotahuasi Canyon** (p. 193), which actually claims the title. The table below lists the best of Peru's multi-day hikes; dayhikes also abound and are covered through this book.

◪ HIKE NAME	REGION	LENGTH	DIFFICULTY
Colca Canyon (p. 188)	Southern Highlands	2-9 days	Medium-Difficult
El Misti (p. 191)	Southern Highlands	2 days	Medium
Valle de los Volcanes (p. 192)	Southern Highlands	1-3 days	Easy
Cotahuasi Canyon (p. 193)	Southern Highlands	4-5 days	Varies
Chicón and San Juan Glaciers (p. 254)	Cusco and the Sacred Valley	2-3 days	Medium-Difficult
The Inca Trail (p. 260)	Cusco and the Sacred Valley	2-4 days	Medium
Salkantay (Alternative Inca Trail; p. 264)	Cusco and the Sacred Valley	5 days	Medium-Difficult
Santa Cruz (p. 356)	Northern Highlands	3-4 days	Easy-Medium
Alpamayo (p. 357)	Northern Highlands	10-12 days	Medium-Difficult
Olleros to Chavín (p. 358)	Northern Highlands	3 days	Easy
Cordillera Huayhuash (p. 360)	Northern Highlands	3-12 days	Medium-Difficult
Parque Nacional del Manú (p. 422)	Amazon Basin	Varies	Varies

URBAN EXPLOITS

Hiking boots are not a prerequisite for adventure. While bushwhacking through jungle brush with a machete is certainly appealing, there's also much to explore in the best-beaten tracks around: big cities. **Lima** (p. 93) and its suburbs offer world-class dining and nightlife, magnificent museums and colonial architecture, and the pre-Inca ruins of Huacas Huallamarca and Pucllana. There's colorful and charming—if touristy—**Cusco** (p. 215) and its calmer look-alike in the north, **Cajamarca** (p. 371). High up in the *sierra* sits erudite **Ayacucho** (p. 299), once thought lost to the Shining Path. A lively cultural vibe draws visitors to **Chincha Alta** (p. 138), home of Afro-Peruvian fusion. **Arequipa** (p. 173) is Peru's refined "White City" between the coast and the highlands. Jungle-bound **Iquitos** (p. 386) manages to be cosmopolitan despite its remote location, and **Trujillo** (p. 314) is often described as Lima's good points packaged and placed farther north.

EXOTIC EATS

Once again, variety is the name of the game, as Peru seems to outdo itself with a vast number of culinary options. Dietary staples include more varieties of **choclo** (corn) and **papas** (potatoes) than you'll find anywhere else. But experiments of the tastebud kind can be adventures in and of themselves. Locals adore **cuy** (guinea pig) splayed, spiced, and fried or roasted. The world-famous **ceviche** (raw fish marinated in lemon) graces many a menu. Central Peru's **Ayacucho** (p. 299) might make meat a little more digestible with its **mondongo** (soup with lamb or pork boiled overnight with peeled corn) or **puca picante** (spicy sauce and potatoes with rice and fried meat). Resist that carnivorous impulse in **Huancayo** (p. 285), home of **papas a la huancaína** (potato smothered in a dressing of butter, milk, and cheese). Check out **manjar blanco** in Northern Peru's **Caraz** (p. 364)—the concoction combines milk, sugar, and cinnamon in scrumptiously sinful ways. For more on Peru's dining delights, see **Food and Drink,** p. 70.

WET AND WILDLIFE

If wet's what you want, your best bet's probably either surfing or rafting. **Puerto Chicama** (p. 323) has the world's longest waves; down by **Punta Hermosa** (p. 132), South America's tallest wave (up to 7.3m) rolls in April through May. Hard-core surfers hang out in **Máncora** (p. 341), and for rafting, the **Río Cañete**, by Lunahuaná (p. 136), is a sure thing. The **Río Apurímac** (p. 243) has Class V rapids, and of course there's always **Lake Titicaca** (p. 195), whose clear water looks more inviting than its temperature feels—so stick to rowing or kayaking your way through its oh-so-blue waters. The mighty **Amazon River** (p. 385) and its tributaries are the main highway through the jungle, and no visitor to the rainforest will lack opportunities to explore its winding waterways.

Nothing compares to the **Reserva Nacional de Paracas** (p. 144) and the **Islas Ballestas** (p. 146) for wildlife, where you can spot sea lions, flamingos, and Humboldt penguins. If birds are your bag, you'll have many options. Among the best spotting sites are the lake that will never escape Titicaca's shadow, Peru's second-biggest, **Lago de Junín** (p. 281), and the macaw licks around **Puerto Maldonado** (p. 424) and **Parque Nacional del Manú** (p. 422). Manú is also home to some 1300 species of butterfly. Jungle tours always include the possibility of spotting **pumas, snakes,** or any of Peru's 32 varieties of **monkeys.** Last but not least, with any luck you'll come across those adorable llamas and their camelid cousins grazing on the highland slopes of the **Salinas y Aguada Blanca Reserve** (p. 188). For more about Peru's animal and plant life, see **Flora and Fauna,** p. 59.

■ LET'S GO PICKS: THE BEST OF PERU

BEST HIGHS: Lake Titicaca, the world's highest navigable lake; **Lima-Huancayo Train,** the world's highest standard-gauge railway; **Pico Alto,** South America's tallest wave; **Cerro Blanco,** one of the world's tallest sand dunes; **Cusco,** one of the highest cities on earth.

BEST LOWS: Colca Canyon and **Cotahuasi Canyon,** the deepest on earth.

BEST MISNOMERS: Pisco, an alcohol actually from Ica; **Vilcabamba,** ruins that were actually Machu Picchu. (That last one has been straightened out.)

BEST CULTURAL INTERPRETATIONS: According to paintings in **Cusco,** Christ ate **cuy** (guinea pig) for his Last Supper; according to a statue in **Huánuco,** San Sebastián had **smallpox;** according to chess sets in **Cusco,** Inca knights rode **llamas** instead of horses.

BEST HIGH-FLYING: Paragliders, who ride the winds over the Sacred Valley; **hang gliders,** who cruise the Callejón de Huaylas; **condors,** who soar over Colca Canyon.

BEST USE OF HOUSEHOLD ITEMS: Scissors-dancing, a fast-paced ritual display of dexterity and physical prowess.

BEST SURFING SANS THE SURF: Huacachina, where you can hang ten down the giant sand dunes of a natural oasis.

BEST EIFFEL NON-TOWERS: The **Fountains** in Moquegua and Tacna; the **Iron House** in Iquitos. It seems Gustave got around.

BEST LANDSCAPING: The **Nasca lines.** The mystery remains: who was *their* gardener?

BEST HIGHLAND EATS: Cow heart **antichucos,** marinated and grilled; **sheep's head soup**—for breakfast!

BEST VIRTUAL GALAPAGOS: Islas Ballestas, the "poor man's Galapagos," Peru's own biodiversity wonderland.

BEST DUBIOUS CLAIMS TO FAME: Cerro Blanco, a sand dune which some claim to be the world's biggest. (There are larger ones in Africa.) **Lago de Junín,** supposedly the world's highest lake. (Actually, the highest one is on the Bolivia-Chile border.)

BEST JUNGLE JUICE: Chicha, a potent concoction of yucca plant fermented by wads of spittle—the Amazonian drink of choice. Cheers!

SUGGESTED ITINERARIES

the mysterious geoglyphs of the Nasca lines before your stop in **Ica** (p. 146, 2 days), home to totally tubular sandboarding at the oasis of **Huacachina** (p. 152, 1 day). Sample the beaches on your way back to Lima, but don't dawdle—you've got a flight to catch up to the steamy jungles of **Iquitos** (p. 386, 4 days) for a quick rainforest fling before it's back to foggy Lima and your flight home.

THE BEST OF PERU (1 MONTH). Fly into **Lima** (p. 93, 3 days), where you can ease into South American life. Then join hordes of foreigners headed to **Cusco** (p. 215, 3 days). Charming, European, and gringo-filled, this city may be the best thing since sliced bread. But wait! There's more. Now it's time to hike the **Inca Trail** (p. 260, 4 days) to **Machu Picchu** (p. 266). Hop on a train to **Puno** (p. 197, 1 day), on the shores of glistening **Lake Titicaca** (p. 195, 2 days). Next, a quick flight from Juliaca will take you to the gleaming white city of **Arequipa** (p. 173, 3 days). Take in its pale churches and fascinating Santa Catalina Monastery, but leave time to watch condors soaring over the fathomless **Colca Canyon** (p. 188, 2 days). Wave goodbye to the Andean heights as you descend to the parched desert coast. Hop on a bus to points north—namely **Nasca** (p. 153, 2 days), where you can ponder

CHOOSE YOUR OWN ADVENTURE (2 WEEKS). Fly into **Lima** (p. 93, 1 day) and spend one day perusing the city and one night experiencing true Peruvian nightlife. Recover from your wild night on an early flight to **Cusco** (p. 215, 1 day), the tourist center of the country and one of the most beautiful cities in Peru. Take a day to explore the city (or lounge in its cafes), and a day for the **Sacred Valley** (p.

DISCOVER

249); then you'll be acclimated and itching for more. Wake up early and head out on the **Inca Trail** (p. 260, 3 days) to **Machu Picchu** (p. 266, 1 day). Despite the hordes of tourists, watching the sun rise over the Sacred City is an unforgettable experience. But time is scarce. Upon returning to Cusco, hop on the 12hr. overnight train to **Puno** (p. 197, 1hr.). You'll wake up to the incomparable blue of **Lake Titicaca** (p. 195), stretching out to the horizon. Puno's not the best place from which to see it, however; head down to the port and take a boat to **Islas Taquile and Amantaní** (p. 205, 2 days), where you can stay with a Quechua family and have Titicaca on all sides. Then get thee to a nunnery—a long bus ride or a quick flight away, the vast **Santa Catalina Monastery** is like a city within another city—**Arequipa** (p. 173, 2 days). But no Peruvian visit is complete without a look at the **Nasca lines** (p. 153, 2 days), so make a stop in there on your long ride back to Lima. Or, replace your Nasca voyage with a flight through Lima to **Iquitos** (p. 293, 3 days), where you'll have just enough time to stroll along the Amazon and enjoy a 2-day jungle trek before heading back home.

THE STUNNING SOUTH

THE STUNNING SOUTH (1 MONTH).
Start in **Lima** (p. 93, 1 day), but why linger in this gray urban wilderness when the tranquility of the beaches awaits? Catch a taxi or combi south to **Punta Hermosa** (p. 132, 1 day) where you can sip a cool drink and watch the tide come in. Get ready to shake your hips Afro-Peruvian-style in **Chincha Alta** (p. 138, 2 days), but not before you experience **Lunahuaná** (p. 136, 2 days). It takes some doing to get there, but you'll likely be rewarded with sunny weather, free wine, and the sound of running water and squawking birds. But for wildlife, even this lap of lushness can't compare to **Pisco** (p. 140, 2 days), or rather, to the **Reserva Nacional de Paracas** (p. 144, 1 day) near Pisco. **Ica** (p. 146, 1 day) awaits you farther south but, as with Pisco, you're better off saving your expectations for the nearby attractions. Ica's *bodegas* are nice, but nearby **Huacachina** (p. 152, 1 day) is the stuff dreams are made of. Take a dune buggy to

the top and sandboard your way down to the oasis below. A short jaunt south brings you to **Nasca** (p. 153, 3 days), where you can soar above the mysterious etchings in the sand. From here it's a long bus ride to white-walled **Arequipa** (p. 173, 3 days), but once you're there you're free to enjoy one of the most refreshing cities in the world. To choose from among the area's many **hikes** (p. 188, 3 days), just decide whether canyons or volcanoes are your thing. Back in Arequipa, a quick flight to Juliaca will put you near **Puno** (p. 197), on the high shores of **Lake Titicaca** (p. 195, 3 days), where you can paddle around in a canoe, visit the artisan markets on the floating islands, hike through the hills, or just kick back and enjoy the view at your leisure. Catch a train to colorful **Cusco** (p. 215, 3 days), the culmination of your journey. Camp out on the **Inca Trail** (p. 260, 4 days) as you ascend to **Machu Picchu,** then high-tail it back to Lima for your flight home. Yes, this is as good as it gets.

TREMENDOUS TREKKING

been hiking for the past three weeks, and delve into the heart of Parque Nacional Huascarán via the **Santa Cruz Loop** (p. 356, 5 days). After you gaze at the tallest mountain in Peru, head to **Caraz** (p. 364, 1 day) for a dayhike to watch the Puya Raymondi plant bloom. Escape those ubiquitous backpackers and head south to **Chiquián** (p. 358, 1 day), an outlet to the less popular but equally beautiful **Cordillera Huayhuash** (p. 359, 5 days). You came, you saw, you conquered.

JUNGLE FEVER (1 MONTH, GIVE OR TAKE). For most visitors to Peru, a quick trip to Iquitos or Puerto Maldonado will sate those jungle cravings. Only the truly adventurous or the truly insane brave the, shall we say, unpredictable transportation of the less touristed areas of the Amazon Basin. But if you're a fan of long days on sporadic river boats and long, long bus rides, then by all means grab a hefty sup-

JUNGLE FEVER

TREMENDOUS TREKKING (1 MONTH). Embark upon your journey in **Cusco** (p. 215, 1 day), the tourist center of Peru. At over 3400m, this high-altitude city is the perfect place to acclimate. Warm up with the oh-so-well-trodden Inca Trail to **Machu Picchu** (p. 266, 4 days), then grab your ice picks and crampons and get off the tourist track to ascend to the **Chicón Glacier** (p. 254, 1 day). Sign up for a tour of **Parque Nacional del Manú** (p. 422, 5 days) deep in the simmering Amazon, where you can watch butterflies daintily flitter by as you hack your way through the underbrush. Back in Cusco, hop on a plane to **Arequipa** (p. 173, 1 day)—the ideal gateway for descending into the depths of **Colca Canyon** (p. 188, 5 days) and climbing the volcano **El Misti** (p. 191, 3 days). Relax on the long bus ride north to **Huaraz** (p. 343, 1 day), the hiking mecca of Peru. Tear yourself away from the debaucheries of the city, laugh at everyone who hasn't

DISCOVER

ply of bug spray, strap on that backpack, and hitch a flight to **Iquitos** (p. 386, 5 days), a convenient base for exploring the rainforest. A 3-day boat trip south will land you in **Pucallpa** (p. 409, 1 day) from which prosaic locale you can hop buses until you get to **Puerto Bermúdez** (p. 417, 1-10 days) and the Albergue Humboldt, one of the most popular jungle experiences in Peru. If you plan ahead, the owners will take you on their 10-day boat trip to Cusco. Or, make a shorter jungle trek with them and then head back to Pucallpa. Fly to Lima and then to **Puerto Maldonado** (p. 424, 4 days) to see the monkeys and macaws at Tambopata-Candamo. Your guided tour of **Parque Nacional del Manú** (p. 422, 5 days) will land you in **Cusco** (p. 215, 1 day), where you can hop on a plane back to Lima. Remember to pack that machete in your checked luggage for your flight back home.

HISTORIC PERU (3 WEEKS). Every corner of Peru has its own traces of history, but you can easily take in some of the highlights. Begin your scholarly perusal of the area by taking a bus north to **Huaraz** (p. 343, 2 days) to see the 3000-year-old ruins of **Chavín de Huántar** (p. 352). From there, a long bus ride will get you to **Trujillo** (p. 314, 3 days), surrounded by shining remnants of ancient civilizations including **Chan Chan** (p. 320) and **Huacas de Sol y de la Luna** (p. 320). Not far north, you'll find the tomb of the **Señor de Sipán** near **Chiclayo** (p. 324, 2 days). Catch a flight back to **Lima** (p. 93, 2 days), where you can take in both the surrounding ancient archaeological sites as well as Lima's colonial architecture and impressive nightlife. A quick flight will find you in **Cusco** (p. 215, 2 days), the heart of Peru's historical heritage. From here you can easily explore the **Sacred Valley** (p. 249, 2 days) and hike the **Inca Trail** to **Machu Picchu** (p. 266, 3 days). Fly to **Arequipa** (p. 173, 2 days) to capture some colonial culture, then it's homeward-bound on a bus toward **Lima.** Stop over in **Nasca** (p. 153, 3 days) to check out the mysterious lines in the sand, and make it back to Lima in time for your flight.

BEACH BUMMING (2 WEEKS). Leave everything behind in Lima: for now, it's just you and the waves. Fly north to **Tumbes** (p. 336, 1 day) and spend a little time discovering the mangrove swamps at **Puerto Pizarro.** Heavenly surfing awaits, so skip Zorritos and head straight to **Máncora** (p. 341, 1 day). Pull out that Hemingway novel you brought and skim it during your down time at **Cabo Blanco** (p. 342, 1 day). Farther south, surfing at the beaches near **Chiclayo** (p. 324, 1 day) is a gentle warm-up for the real thrills farther south. Find your way to **Trujillo** (p. 314, 1 day), note the city's cleanliness, colonial architecture, and other virtues, and move on to the serene beach town of **Huanchaco** (p. 126, 1 day) and then to that magic mecca of surfing known as **Puerto Chicama** (p. 323, 1 day). Take a bus—or better yet, fly—back to Lima, where a short taxi ride leaves you on the desert hills that

BEACH BUMMING

COLOMBIA

ECUADOR

Tumbes &
Puerto Pizzaro

Máncora &
Cabo Blanco

Chiclayo

Huanchaco &
Puerto Chicama

Trujillo

PERU

BRASIL

Punta
Hermosa

Pucusana

Pisco &
R.N. Paracas

Huacachina

PACIFIC
OCEAN

CHILE

surround the record-breaking waves of
Punta Hermosa (p. 132, 2 days). Make
friends with some fishermen in **Pucasana**
(p. 135, 1 day) before taking a bus to
your second-to-last stop, **Pisco** (p. 140, 1
day) and the nearby critter haven of the
Reserva Nacional de Paracas (p. 144, 1
day). Say goodbye to the water, because
your next stop gives new meaning to the
word "surfing." The desert dunes of **Huacachina** (p. 152, 2 days) will test the limits of your newly-polished surfing skills,
leaving you covered in sand for your ride
back to Lima and your flight home.

ESSENTIALS

PLANNING YOUR TRIP

BEFORE YOU GO

Passport (p. 11). Required for all visitors except citizens of Bolivia, Chile, and Ecuador visiting certain regions.

Visa (p. 12). Visas are not required for citizens of Australia, Canada, New Zealand, the UK, and the US for stays of under 90 days.

Work Permit (p. 12). Required for all foreigners planning to work in Peru.

Recommended Vaccinations (p. 23). There are no required vaccinations, but Hepatitis A and B, measles, rabies, tetanus-diptheria, typhoid, and yellow fever are strongly recommended, especially for those traveling to more rural and humid parts of the country.

Other Health: Malaria pills are recommended for those traveling to malaria risk areas (p. 26). If your regular **medical insurance policy** (p. 23) does not cover travel abroad, you may wish to purchase additional coverage.

EMBASSIES AND CONSULATES

PERUVIAN CONSULAR SERVICES ABROAD

Peru's embassies and consulates abroad include:

Australia: Embassy of Peru in Canberra: 43 Culgoa Circuit, O'Malley ACT 2606 (☎02 6286 9507 or 6286 9105; www.embaperu.org.au). **Consulate-General:** 30 Clarence St., 3rd fl., Sydney NSW 2000 (☎02 9262 6464; c-sydney4@conper.com.au). **Consular Section in Canberra:** 40 Brisbane Ave., Ste. 8, Ground fl., Barton ACT 2600 (☎02 6273 8752; consular@embaperu.org.).

Canada: 130 Albert St., Ste. 1901, Ottawa K1P 5G4 (☎613-238-1777; emperuca@maqi.com). **Consulate:** 505 Burrard St., Ste. 260, Vancouver, B.C., V7X 1M3 (☎604-662-8880, emergencies 762-0948; conperva@direct.ca). Open M-F 9am-3pm.

Ireland: The nearest embassy is in London. See UK.

New Zealand: Cigna House, Level 8, 40 Mercer St., P.O. Box 2566, Wellington (☎04 499 8087 or 04 499 8057; www.embassyofperu.org.nz). Open M-F 9am-5pm.

UK: 52 Sloane St., London SW1X 9SP (☎020 7235 1917 or 7235 1917; www.peruembassy-uk.com). Open M-F 9:30am-5pm.

US: 1700 Massachusetts Ave. NW, Washington, D.C. 20036 (☎202-833-9860; www.peruvianembassy.us). **Consulates** (www.consuladoperu.com) can be found in most major US cities, including: **Boston:** 20 Park Plaza, Ste. 511, Boston, MA 02116 (☎617-338-2227). Open M-F 9am-1pm. **Chicago:** 180 N. Michigan Ave., Ste. 1830, Chicago, IL 60601 (☎312-782-1599). Open M-F 9am-1pm. **Denver:** 1001 S. Monaco Pkwy., Ste. 210, Denver, CO 80224 (☎303-355-8555). Open M-F and some Sa 9am-3pm. **Hartford:** 350 D Main St., Hartford, CT 06106 (☎860-548-0266 or 548-0337). Open M-F 8:30-3:30 and the last Sa of every month 9am-3pm. **Houston:** 5177 Richmond Ave., Ste. 695, Houston, TX 77056 (☎713-335-9517 or 335-9438). Open M-F 9am-4pm and some Sa 8am-1pm. **Los Angeles:** 3450 Wilshire Blvd., Ste. 800, Los

Angeles, CA 90010 (☎213-252-5910 or 252-9795). Open M-F 8am-2pm. **Miami:** 444 Bricknell Ave., Ste. M-135, Miami, FL 33131 (☎305-374-1305 or 374-8935). Open M-F 8:30am-2:30pm and some Sa 9am-1pm. **New York:** 241 E. 49th St., New York, NY 10017 (☎646-735-3828 or 735-3847, emergency 447-1781). Open M-F 9am-3pm, Sa 9am-1pm. **Paterson:** 100 Hamilton Plaza, Ste. 1220 fl. 12, Paterson, NJ 07505 (☎973-278-3324 or 278-2221). Open M-F 9am-3pm. **San Francisco:** 870 Market St., Ste. 1067, San Francisco, CA 94102 (☎415-362-5185 or 362-5647, emergencies 730-3126). Open M-F and some Sa 9am-3pm. **Washington, D.C.:** 1625 Massachusetts Ave. NW, Ste. 605, Washington, D.C. 20036 (☎202-462-1081 or 462-1084). Open M-F 9am-1pm.

CONSULAR SERVICES IN PERU

Embassies and consulates of other countries in Peru are all in Lima.

Australia, Victor Andrés Belaúnde 147, Vía Principal 155, Edificio Real 3, of. 1301, San Isidro (☎222 8281; www.australia.org.pe). Open M-F 9am-1pm and 2-5pm.

Canada, Libertad 130, Miraflores (☎444 4015, emergency 613-944-1310; www.dfait-maeci.gc.ca/peru). Open M, Tu, Th, F 8am-12:30pm and 1:15-5pm; W 8am-1pm.

Ireland, Angamos Oeste 340, Miraflores (☎446 3878). Open M-F 9am-1pm.

Israel, Natalio Sánchez 125, Edificio Pacífico Washington, 6th fl., Santa Beatriz (☎433 4431; http://lima.mfa.gov.il). Open M-Th 10am-1pm, F 10am-12pm.

New Zealand, Los Nogales 510, 3rd fl., San Isidro (☎422 7491 or 9940 0353). Visa services are available at the British embassy.

UK, Larco 1301, Torre Parque Mar, 23rd fl., Miraflores (☎617 3000; www.britemb.org.pe). Open M-Th 8am-1pm and 2-5pm, F 8:30am-noon.

US, Encalada Block 17, Surco (☎434 3000; http://lima.usembassy.gov). Open M-F 8am-5pm.

TOURIST OFFICES

PromPeru, the central Peruvian tourist agency, has information in English and is especially helpful in highly touristed areas (Cusco, Lima, and Southern Peru). The central office in Lima is PromPeru, Commission for the Promotion of Peru, Edificio MITINCI, 14th fl., Calle 1 Oeste No. 50, San Isidro, Lima (☎01 224 3131; www.peru.org.pe). Smaller offices are found in most cities, but while most tourist offices can provide maps, brochures, and basic information, only the most popular will have English speakers.

The non-profit **South American Explorers (SAE)** is widely recognized as the ultimate source of travel information on Peru. This well-respected outfit (with club-houses in Lima and Cusco, and Ithaca, New York) provides information about outdoor experiences in the region, discount airfares, trip planning, and travel conditions. Contact them at 126 Indian Creek Rd., Ithaca, NY 14850, USA (☎607-277-0488; www.samexplo.org) or at the Lima (p. 101) or Cusco (p. 219) locations.

DOCUMENTS AND FORMALITIES

PASSPORTS

REQUIREMENTS

Citizens of Australia, Canada, Ireland, New Zealand, the UK, and the US need valid passports to enter Peru and to re-enter their home countries. Travelers should review their passports in advance to verify that they will not expire during travel; returning home with an expired passport is illegal, and may result in a fine.

ESSENTIALS

NEW PASSPORTS
Citizens of Australia, Canada, Ireland, New Zealand, the UK, and the US can apply for a passport at any passport office and at many post offices and courts of law. Any new passport or renewal applications must be filed well in advance of the departure date, although most passport offices offer rush services (about 2 weeks) for a very steep fee.

PASSPORT MAINTENANCE
Photocopy the page of your passport with your photo, as well as your visas, traveler's check serial numbers, and any other important documents. Carry one set of copies in a safe place, apart from the originals, and leave another set at home. Consulates also recommend that you carry an expired passport or an official copy of your birth certificate in a part of your baggage separate from other documents.

If you lose your passport, immediately notify the local police and the nearest embassy or consulate of your home government. To expedite its replacement, you will need to know all information previously recorded and show ID and proof of citizenship. In some cases, a replacement may take weeks to process, and it may be valid only for a limited time. Any visas stamped in your old passport will be irretrievably lost. In an emergency, ask for immediate temporary traveling papers that will permit you to re-enter your home country.

VISAS, INVITATIONS, AND WORK PERMITS

VISAS
Citizens of all English-speaking countries and most countries of Latin America and the EU do not need visas for entrance into Peru for stays shorter than 90 days. Individuals entering the country for work or extended study or who plan to stay in Peru longer than 90 days must obtain a visa. Visas cost US$30 and can be purchased from Peruvian consulates abroad (p. 10), which often provide forms and instructions online. Citizens of countries in Africa, Asia, and parts of Eastern Europe may require visas in addition to a valid passport for entrance into Peru.

Double-check entrance requirements at the nearest embassy or consulate of Peru before departure. US citizens can also consult www.pueblo.gsa.gov/cic_text/travel/foreign/foreignentryreqs.html.

WORK AND STUDY PERMITS
Admission as a visitor does not include the right to work, which is authorized only by a work permit. Entering Peru to study requires a special visa. For more information, see Alternatives to Tourism (p. 88).

IDENTIFICATION
When you travel, always carry at least two forms of identification on your person, including a photo ID; a passport and a driver's license or birth certificate is usually adequate. Never carry all of your IDs together; split them up in case of theft or loss, and keep photocopies of all of them in your luggage and at home.

STUDENT, TEACHER, AND YOUTH IDENTIFICATION
The **International Student Identity Card (ISIC)**, the most widely accepted form of student ID, provides discounts on some sights, accommodations, food, entertainment, shopping, and transport; access to a 24hr. emergency helpline; and insurance benefits for US cardholders (see **Insurance**, p. 23). Applicants must be full-time secondary or post-secondary school students at least 12 years of age. Because of the proliferation of fake ISICs, some services (particularly airlines) require additional proof of student identity.

The **International Teacher Identity Card (ITIC)** offers teachers the same insurance coverage as the ISIC and similar but limited discounts. For travelers who are 25 years old or under but are not students, the **International Youth Travel Card (IYTC)** also offers many of the same benefits as the ISIC.

Each of these identity cards costs US$22 or equivalent. ISIC and ITIC cards are valid through the academic year in which they are issued; IYTC cards are valid for one year from the date of issue. Many student travel agencies (see p. 30) issue the cards; for a list of issuing agencies or more information, see the **International Student Travel Confederation (ISTC)** website (www.istc.org).

The **International Student Exchange Card (ISE)** is a similar identification card available to students, faculty, and youth aged 12 to 26. The card provides medical benefits, access to a 24hr. emergency helpline, and the ability to purchase student airfares. The card costs US$25; call US ☎ 800-255-8000, or visit www.isecard.com.

CUSTOMS

Upon entering Peru, you must declare certain items from abroad and pay a duty on the value of those articles if they exceed the allowance established by the Peruvian customs service. Note that goods and gifts purchased at **duty-free** shops abroad are not exempt from duty or sales tax; "duty-free" merely means that you need not pay a tax in the country of purchase. Upon returning home, you must likewise declare all articles acquired abroad and pay a duty on the value of articles in excess of your home country's allowance. In order to expedite your return, make a list of any valuables brought from home and register them with customs before traveling abroad, and be sure to keep receipts for all goods acquired abroad. Coca leaves are not generally appreciated by customs officials; **coca leaves are illegal in the US.**

MONEY

CURRENCY AND EXCHANGE

The Peruvian currency is the Nuevo Sol (s/). The currency chart below is based on August 2004 exchange rates between local currency and Australian dollars (AUS$), Canadian dollars (CDN$), European Union euros (EUR€), New Zealand dollars (NZ$), British pounds (UK£), and US dollars (US$). Check the currency converter on websites like www.xe.com or www.bloomberg.com or a large newspaper for the latest exchange rates.

NUEVO SOL (s/)	
AUS$1 = 2.39 SOLES	1 SOL = AUS$0.42
CDN$1 = 2.58 SOLES	1 SOL = CDN$0.39
EUR€1 = 4.09 SOLES	1 SOL = EUR€0.24
NZ$1 = 2.20 SOLES	1 SOL = NZ$0.45
UK£1 = 6.07 SOLES	1 SOL = UK£0.16
US$1 = 3.38 SOLES	1 SOL = US$0.30

As a general rule, it's cheaper to convert money in Peru than at home. While currency exchange will probably be available in your arrival airport, it's wise to bring enough foreign currency to last for the first 24 to 72 hours of your trip.

When changing money abroad, try to go only to banks or *casas de cambio* that have at most a 5% margin between their buy and sell prices. In big cities like Lima, **grocery stores** often have the best exchange rate. Since you lose money with every transaction, **convert large sums** (unless the currency is depreciating rapidly), **but no more than you'll need.**

If you use traveler's checks or bills, carry some in small denominations (the equivalent of US$50 or less) for times when you are forced to exchange money at disadvantageous rates, but bring a range of denominations since charges may be levied per check cashed. Store your money in a variety of forms; ideally, at any given time you will be carrying some cash, some traveler's checks, and an ATM and/or credit card. All travelers should also consider carrying some US dollars (about US$50 worth), which are often preferred by local tellers, upper-end urban hostels, and large tour companies.

 THE BUCK STOPS HERE. The easiest, although not the safest, way to change dollars in Peru is with the numerous money changers who gather on the streets near banks and plazas. If you use their services, be sure to check **every** bill you receive, no matter how small. Familiarize yourself with the multiple watermarks, paper, quality, etc. that distinguish legitimate currency before going to a money changer, as counterfeits are frequently of very high quality. It is also a good idea to habitually check bills received as return change, even at large stores. Counterfeit bills are a problem for Peruvians as well, but foreigners make easy—and therefore, likely—targets.

TRAVELER'S CHECKS

Traveler's checks are one of the safest and least troublesome means of carrying funds. American Express and Visa are the most recognized brands. Many banks and agencies sell them for a small commission. Check issuers provide refunds if the checks are lost or stolen, and many provide additional services, such as toll-free refund hotlines abroad, emergency message services, and stolen credit card assistance. They are readily accepted at most banks and *casas de cambio*, but it can be difficult to exchange them elsewhere, especially in rural areas, so always have other forms of currency when visiting small towns. Ask about toll-free refund hotlines and the location of refund centers when purchasing checks, and always carry emergency cash. In order to collect a **refund for lost or stolen checks,** keep check receipts and a record of which checks you've cashed separate from the checks themselves. Also leave a list of check numbers with someone at home. Never countersign checks until you are ready to cash them and always bring your passport with you when you plan to use the checks.

American Express: Checks available with commission at select banks, at all AmEx offices, and online (www.americanexpress.com; US residents only). American Express cardholders can also purchase checks by phone (☎800-721-9768). AAA (p. 38) offers commission-free checks to its members. Checks available in Australian, Canadian, Euro, Japanese, British, and US currencies. For purchase locations or more information contact AmEx's service centers: in Australia ☎800 68 80 22; in New Zealand 0508 555 358; in the UK 0800 587 6023; in the US and Canada 800-221-7282; elsewhere, call the US collect at +1 801-964-6665.

Visa: Checks available (generally with commission) at banks worldwide. For the location of the nearest office, call Visa's service centers: in the UK ☎0800 51 58 84; in the US 800-227-6811; elsewhere, call the UK collect at +44 173 331 8949 (www.visa.com). Checks available in Canadian, Japanese, Euro, British, and US currencies.

Travelex/Thomas Cook: Checks available from 2000 locations worldwide. Locations can be found online or by calling in the US and Canada ☎800-287-7362; in the UK 0800 62 21 01; elsewhere, call the UK collect at +44 1733 31 89 50 (www.travelex.co.uk).

CREDIT, DEBIT, AND ATM CARDS

Credit cards are generally accepted only in very touristy or urban areas of Peru. Where they are accepted, credit cards often offer superior exchange rates—up to 5% better than the retail rate used by banks and other currency exchange establishments. Credit cards may also offer services such as insurance or emergency help, and are sometimes required to reserve hotel rooms or rental cars. **MasterCard** (a.k.a. EuroCard or Access in Europe) is the most welcome, and **Visa** (a.k.a. Carte Bleue or Barclaycard) is often frequently accepted; **American Express** cards work at some ATMs and at AmEx offices and major airports.

ATMs are widespread in Peru. Depending on the system that your home bank uses, you can most likely access your personal bank account from abroad. ATMs get the same wholesale exchange rate as credit cards, but there is often a limit on the amount of money you can withdraw per day (usually around US$500). There is typically also a surcharge of US$1-5 per withdrawal.

Debit cards are a form of purchasing power that are as convenient as credit cards but have a more immediate impact on your funds. A debit card can be used wherever its associated credit card company (usually MasterCard or Visa) is accepted, yet the money is withdrawn directly from the holder's checking account. Debit cards also function as ATM cards and can be used to withdraw cash from associated banks and ATMs throughout Peru. Ask your local bank about obtaining one.

The two major international money networks are **Cirrus** (US ☎800-424-7787 or www.mastercard.com) and **Visa/PLUS** (US ☎800-843-7587 or www.visa.com). Most ATMs charge a transaction fee that is paid to the bank that owns the ATM.

ESSENTIALS

GETTING MONEY FROM HOME

If you run out of money while traveling, the easiest and cheapest solution is to have someone back home make a deposit to the bank account linked to your credit card or ATM card. Failing that, consider one of the following options. The online **International Money Transfer Consumer Guide** (http://international-money-transfer-consumer-guide.info) may also be of help.

WIRING MONEY

It is possible to arrange a **bank money transfer**, which means asking a bank back home to wire money to a bank in Peru. This is the cheapest way to transfer cash, but it's also the slowest, usually taking several days or more. Note that some banks may only release your funds in local currency, potentially sticking you with a poor exchange rate; inquire about this in advance. Money transfer services like **Western Union** are faster and more convenient than bank transfers—but also much pricier. Western Union has many locations worldwide. To find one, visit www.westernunion.com, or call in Australia ☎800 501 500, in Canada 800-235-0000, in the UK 0800 83 38 33, or in the US 800-325-6000. Emergency travel funds are also available through **American Express** at Travex, Santa Cruz 621, Miraflores. (☎01 690 0900; fax 690 0922; info@travex.com.pe. Open M-F 8:30am-6pm, Su 9am-1pm.)

US STATE DEPARTMENT (US CITIZENS ONLY)

In serious emergencies only, the US State Department will forward money within hours to the nearest consular office, which will then disburse it according to instructions for a US$30 fee. If you wish to use this service, you must contact the Overseas Citizens Service division of the US State Department (☎317-472-2328; nights, Sundays, and holidays 202-647-4000).

COSTS

The cost of your trip will vary considerably, depending on where you go, how you travel, and where you stay. The most significant expenses will probably be your round-trip (return) airfare to Peru (see **Getting to Peru: By Plane,** p. 29), any domestic flights and bus fares, and major tours. Before you go, spend some time calculating a reasonable daily budget.

PERU	❶	❷	❸	❹	❺
ACCOMM.	to s/10	s/11-24	s/25-38	s/39-59	s/60+
FOOD	to s/7	s/8-14	s/15-21	s/22-35	s/36+

STAYING ON A BUDGET

To give you a general idea, a bare-bones day in Peru (camping or sleeping in hostels/guesthouses, buying food at supermarkets) would cost about US$5 (s/17); a slightly more comfortable day (sleeping in hostels/guesthouses and the occasional budget hotel, eating one meal per day at a restaurant, going out at night) would cost US$18 (s/65); and for a luxurious day, the sky's the limit. Don't forget to factor in emergency reserve funds (at least US$200) when planning how much money you'll need.

TIPS FOR SAVING MONEY

Some simple ways include searching out opportunities for free entertainment, splitting accommodation and food costs with trustworthy fellow travelers, and doing laundry in the sink (unless you're explicitly prohibited from doing so). You can save a surprising number of soles by purchasing food at the supermarket, ordering the daily *menú* when you eat out, treating your own water rather than buying bottled water, and eating breakfast at bakeries rather than at restaurants. That said, don't go overboard. Though staying within your budget is important, don't do so at the expense of your health or a great travel experience.

 CASH CARRIED. Carry cash in small bills and change rather than in large bills. Many establishments in Peru do not have the means to change large notes, and drivers and vendors will become annoyed if you try to use them. Most banks will change them for you.

TIPPING AND BARGAINING

Some fancier restaurants include a small (5-10%) tip on the bill. On occasion it is appropriate to tip for maid service or for a guide or porter; in many cases, these people count on a small bonus. Tips are expected on some tours. Tips are not expected for taxis.

In some places it's okay to **bargain,** and a little practice can make it worth the effort. Bargaining for rooms works best in the low season and it's not hard to get prices lowered at markets or by street vendors. It is also acceptable to bargain with taxi drivers, though an excessively low first bid may send the *taxista* on his way without you. Advertised prices in restaurants and shops are generally non-negotiable.

TAXES

Upscale restaurants, hotels, and shops often charge a sales tax (IVA), which you should expect to appear on the bill. The real whammy, though, hits the traveler on the way out—there are airport departure taxes from regional airports (US$10) and from Lima (US$25).

THE ART OF THE DEAL. While bargaining is the norm in certain situations, travelers need not bargain down to a price that is clearly unreasonable. In countries where the cost of living is already dirt cheap, the discount of pennies or a dollar received by a foreigner might mean a lot more in the pocket of a local vendor. That said, some vendors may offer high prices just to take advantage of you. With the following tips and some finesse, you might be able to impress even the most hardened hawkers:

1. **Bargaining needn't be a fierce struggle laced with barbs.** Quite the opposite: good-natured wrangling with a cheerful face may prove your best weapon.

2. **Use your poker face.** The less your face betrays your interest in the item the better. If you touch an item to inspect it, the vendor will be sure to "encourage" you to name a price or make a purchase. Coming back again and again to admire a trinket is a good way of ensuring that you pay a ridiculously high price. Never get too enthusiastic about the object in question; point out flaws in workmanship and design. Be cool.

3. **Know when to bargain.** In most cases, it's quite clear when it's appropriate to bargain. Most private transportation fares and things for sale in outdoor markets are all fair game. Don't bargain on prepared or pre-packaged foods on the street or in restaurants.

4. **Never underestimate the power of peer pressure.** Bargaining with more than one person at a time always leads to higher prices. Alternately, try having a friend discourage you from your purchase—if you seem to be reluctant, the merchant will want to drop the price to interest you again.

5. **Know when to turn away.** Feel free to refuse any vendor or driver who bargains rudely, and don't hesitate to move on to another vendor if one will not be reasonable about the final price he offers. However, to start bargaining without an intention to buy is a major *faux pas*. Agreeing on a price and declining it is also poor form. Turn away slowly with a smile and "thank you" upon hearing a ridiculous price—the price may plummet.

PACKING

Pack lightly: lay out only what you absolutely need, then take half the clothes and twice the money. The less you have, the less you have to lose (or carry on your back). Weather in Peru is extremely variable and elevation dependent. Be prepared for frigid nights in the highlands and extreme humidity in the jungle.

The Travelite FAQ (www.travelite.org) is a good resource for tips on traveling light. The online **Universal Packing List** (http://upl.codeq.info) will generate a customized list of suggested items based on your trip length, the expected climate, your planned activities, and other factors. If you plan to do a lot of hiking, also consult **Camping and the Outdoors,** p. 46.

Luggage: If you plan to cover most of your itinerary by foot, a sturdy **frame backpack** is unbeatable. (For the basics on buying a pack, see p. 48.) Toting a **suitcase** or **trunk** is fine if you plan to live in one or two cities and explore from there, but not a great idea if you plan to move around frequently. In addition to your main piece of luggage, a **daypack** (a small backpack or courier bag) is a must.

Clothing: No matter where or when you're traveling, it's a good idea to bring a **warm jacket** or wool sweater, a **rain jacket** (Gore-Tex® is both waterproof and breathable), sturdy shoes or **hiking boots,** and **thick socks.** Because temperatures can fluctuate significantly on the coast and in the highlands, prepare for both heat and cold by dress-

ESSENTIALS

ing in layers. Long underwear is a good idea in mountainous areas. **Flip-flops** or water-proof sandals are must-haves for grubby hostel showers. You may also want one outfit for going out, and maybe a nicer pair of shoes. Female travelers should dress conservatively to avoid unwanted attention. If you plan to visit religious or cultural sites, you'll need something besides a tank top and shorts to be respectful.

Converters and Adapters: In Peru, electricity is normally 220 volts AC, enough to fry any 120V North American appliance (though there are some 110V outlets as well). Americans and Canadians should buy a **converter** (changes the voltage; US$20-30). Everyone should buy an **adapter** (changes the shape of the plug; US$5). Don't make the mistake of using only an adapter (unless appliance instructions explicitly state otherwise). For more on all things adaptable, check out http://kropla.com/electric.htm.

Toiletries: Toothbrushes, towels, cold-water soap, talcum powder (to keep feet dry), deodorant, razors, tampons, and other personal supplies are often available, but may be difficult to find; bring extras. **Contact lenses** are likely to be expensive and difficult to find, so bring enough extra pairs and solution for your entire trip. Also bring your glasses and a copy of your prescription in case you need emergency replacements. If you use heat-disinfection, either switch temporarily to a chemical disinfection system (check first to make sure it's safe with your brand of lenses), or buy a converter to 220/240V. It's also essential to carry a small roll of toilet paper with you, as many places don't provide it.

First-Aid Kit: For a basic first-aid kit, pack bandages, pain relievers, antibiotic cream, a thermometer, a Swiss Army knife, tweezers, moleskin, decongestant, motion-sickness remedy, diarrhea or upset-stomach medication (Pepto Bismol or Imodium), an antihistamine, sunscreen, insect repellent, burn ointment, and a syringe for emergencies (get an explanatory letter from your doctor). Any sharp items should be packed in your checked luggage rather than in your carry-on.

Film: Less serious photographers may want to bring a disposable camera or two. Despite disclaimers, airport security X-rays can fog film, so buy a lead-lined pouch at a camera store or ask security to hand-inspect it. Always pack film in your carry-on luggage, since higher-intensity X-rays are used on checked luggage. Film and photo developing are usually quite cheap in Peru (s/12 to develop one roll of 24-exposure 35mm film).

Important Documents: Don't forget your passport, traveler's checks, ATM and/or credit cards, adequate ID, flight tickets, and photocopies of all of the aforementioned in case these documents are lost or stolen (see p. 12). Also check that you have any of the following that might apply to you: a hosteling membership card; driver's license (see p. 12); travel insurance forms; ISIC (p. 12), and/or rail or bus pass.

Other Useful Items: For safety purposes, you should bring a **money belt** and small **padlock.** Basic **outdoors equipment** (plastic water bottle, compass, waterproof matches, pocketknife, sunglasses, sunscreen, hat) may also prove useful. **Quick repairs** of torn garments can be done on the road with a needle and thread; also consider bringing electrical tape for patching tears. If you want to do laundry by hand, bring detergent, a small rubber ball to stop up the sink, and string for a makeshift clothes line. **Other things** you're liable to forget are an umbrella; sealable **plastic bags** (for damp clothes, soap, food, shampoo, and other spill-ables); an **alarm clock;** safety pins; rubber bands; a flashlight; earplugs; garbage bags; and a small **calculator.** A **cell phone** can be a lifesaver (literally) on the road; see p. 41 for information on acquiring one that will work at your destination. You might also want to bring along a novel (which you can trade at hostel book exchanges when you're through), an MP3 player with just a few CDs, or some other way to entertain yourself on long bus rides.

TEMP. (°C/°F) PRECIP. (MM)	JANUARY			APRIL			JULY			OCTOBER		
	°C	°F	mm	°C	°F	mm	°C	°F	mm	°C	°F	mm
Arequipa	15.2	59.4	29	15	59	2.1	14	57.2	0.3	15.3	59.5	0.2
Cusco	13.1	55.6	148.7	12.5	54.5	37.9	10	50	3.5	13.6	56.5	47.2
Iquitos	26.3	79.3	267.7	25.9	78.6	301.3	25.2	77.4	162.6	26.5	79.7	230.6
Lima	22	71.6	1.2	20.4	68.7	0.4	16.6	61.9	4.4	17.3	63.1	1.7
Trujillo	20.8	69.4	1.4	20.5	68.9	0	17.7	63.9	0	17.2	63	0.2

SAFETY AND HEALTH

GENERAL ADVICE

In any type of crisis situation, the most important thing to do is stay calm. Your country's embassy abroad (p. 10) is usually your best resource when things go wrong; registering with that embassy upon arrival Peru is often a good idea. The government offices listed in the Travel Advisories box (p. 21) can provide information on the services they offer their citizens in case of emergencies abroad.

LOCAL LAWS AND POLICE

Most cities have police stations, often (but not always) in green or pale green buildings. Major tourist cities have designated "tourist police" who speak English. Tourist police are not law enforcement officers, but they are useful sources of information and support for foreigners.

DRUGS AND ALCOHOL

A meek "I didn't know it was illegal" will not suffice. Remember that you are subject to the laws of Peru, and it is your responsibility to familiarize yourself with these laws before leaving. Those caught in possession of drugs can expect extended **pre-trial detention** in poor prison conditions and a **lengthy prison sentence** if convicted. If you carry **prescription drugs** while you travel, it is vital to have the prescriptions themselves and a note from a doctor, both readily accessible at country borders. Also be aware that some prescription drugs and traditional herbal remedies readily available in Peru may be illegal in your home country. **Coca-leaf tea,** for example, though easy to acquire in Peru, is illegal in many nations, including the US. The hallucinogenic **ayahuasca** is common in the jungle, but use of it can pose serious health risks and is not recommended (see **Jungle Tripping,** p. 412).

Drinking in Latin America is not for amateurs; non-tourist bars are often strongholds of *machismo*. When someone calls you *amigo* and orders you a beer, bow out quickly unless you want to match him glass for glass in a challenge. Female travelers should also be wary of people who offer to buy them drinks. Avoid public drunkenness; it can jeopardize your safety and earn the disdain of locals.

SPECIFIC CONCERNS

NATURAL DISASTERS

EARTHQUAKES. Peru experiences frequent earthquakes, most too small to be felt. If a strong earthquake does occur, it will last only one or two minutes but will likely be followed by aftershocks. Open a door to provide an escape route and protect yourself by moving underneath a sturdy doorway, table, or desk. In coastal or mountainous areas, tidal waves and landslides may follow quakes.

FLOODS. Heavy summer (Nov.-Feb.) rainfall brings flooding and landslides in the Amazon Basin and mountainous regions. These can cause transportation delays and cancellations. This phenomenon is significantly worsened during the sporadic worldwide climate disturbance known as El Niño. For information about El Niño, visit http://meteora.ucsd.edu.

DEMONSTRATIONS AND POLITICAL GATHERINGS

Strikes and demonstrations occur frequently in urban areas and are usually announced in advance. They can significantly affect transportation as well as banks and other establishments, so follow the news and talk to locals if you are on a set schedule. Protests are usually peaceful, but they can sometimes escalate into violent confrontations with police. Where possible, avoid cities in which demonstrations are occurring; if you find yourself in such a city, the safest option is usually to stay in your hostel until the protest subsides.

 THE WRITING ON THE WALL. When it comes to predicting strikes and demonstrations, local radio stations are often more informative than the national press. If you don't have access to a radio, you might learn about these events in another way: in some places, calls for strikes are painted on the walls in prominent or roadside locations.

TERRORISM

The Shining Path (Sendero Luminoso) terrorist group has not engaged in large-scale terrorist activity in the last decade, due perhaps to the arrest of many of the group's leaders. In recent years, however, isolated violent incidents have occurred in the interior provinces of Ayacucho, Huancavelica, Huánuco, Junín, and San Martín. Although the group has staged kidnappings and other armed violence against civilians, roadblocks and armed confrontations between terrorist cells and Peruvian police are most common. Those planning to travel to remote areas of Peru should research their country's current travel warnings. The box on **travel advisories** (below) lists offices to contact and webpages to visit to get the most updated list of your home country's advisories about travel.

> **TRAVEL ADVISORIES.** The following government offices provide travel information and advisories by telephone, by fax, or via the web:
>
> **Australian Department of Foreign Affairs and Trade:** ☎ 13 00 555135; faxback service 02 6261 1299; www.dfat.gov.au.
>
> **Canadian Department of Foreign Affairs and International Trade (DFAIT):** In Canada and the US call ☎ 800-267-8376, elsewhere call ☎ +1 613-944-4000; www.dfait-maeci.gc.ca. Call for their free booklet, *Bon Voyage...But.*
>
> **New Zealand Ministry of Foreign Affairs:** ☎ 04 439 8000; fax 494 8506; www.mft.govt.nz/travel/index.html.
>
> **United Kingdom Foreign and Commonwealth Office:** ☎ 020 7008 0232; fax 7008 0155; www.fco.gov.uk.
>
> **US Department of State:** ☎ 202-647-5225, faxback service 202-647-3000; http://travel.state.gov. For *A Safe Trip Abroad*, call ☎ 202-512-1800.

ESSENTIALS

PERSONAL SAFETY

EXPLORING AND TRAVELING

Foreigners, especially those of the gringo variety, will find it nearly impossible to blend in, but respecting local customs (in many cases, dressing more conservatively than you would at home) may placate would-be hecklers. Familiarize yourself with your surroundings before setting out and carry yourself with confidence. If you need to check your map, duck into a shop or restaurant rather than doing it on the street. If you are traveling alone, be sure someone at home knows your itinerary, and never admit that you're by yourself. When walking at night, stick to busy, well-lit streets and avoid dark alleyways. If you ever feel uncomfortable, leave the area as quickly and directly as you can.

There is no sure-fire way to avoid all the threatening situations you might encounter while traveling, but a good **self-defense course** will give you concrete ways to react to unwanted advances. **Impact, Prepare, and Model Mugging** can refer you to local self-defense courses in the US (☎ 800-345-5425). Visit the website at www.impactsafety.org for a list of nearby chapters. Workshops (1½-3hr.) start at US$75; full courses (20-25hr.) run US$350-400.

Traveling within Peru can be dangerous. Roads are seldom paved and are often in very poor condition. Potholes, sharp curves, lane ends, and construction sites are often unmarked. Avoid taking night buses; travel only by day if possible and use bus companies that take special precautions, such as frequent driver-changing, to ensure your safety. The extra money you pay to travel with slightly better bus lines could be the most important investment you make.

If buses are an adventure, driving can be downright foolhardy. Think twice before braving the roads and never drive alone in rural areas. Call for taxis rather than flagging them down in the street, and use only licensed taxis from reputable companies. *Let's Go* does not recommend hitchhiking under any circumstances, particularly for women. For more info on the perils of hitchhiking, see p. 38.

POSSESSIONS AND VALUABLES

Visitors to Andean countries often return with tales of unexpected theft: handbags carefully slit and emptied of valuables, bags stolen from under restaurant tables, cameras vanished into thin air. Lima and Cusco have the worst reputations, but theft can occur virtually anywhere. While most victims of robbery are not physically harmed, almost everybody sustains wounded pride. When packing, weigh the necessity of each object against the anguish you'll experience should it be taken.

PROTECTING YOUR VALUABLES. There are a few steps you can take to minimize the financial risk associated with traveling. First, bring as little with you as possible. Second, buy a few combination **padlocks** to secure your belongings either in your pack or in a hostel or train station locker. Third, never, ever leave your belongings unattended. Fourth, carry as little cash as possible. Keep your traveler's checks and ATM/credit cards close to your body in a **money belt**—not a "fanny pack"—along with your passport and ID cards. Fifth, keep a small **cash reserve** separate from your primary stash. This should be about US$50 sewn into or stored in the depths of your pack, along with your traveler's check numbers and important photocopies.

You'll sleep better if you leave electronic devices like laptop computers at home. If you must travel with electronics such as a laptop or a PDA, check whether your homeowner's insurance covers loss, theft, or damage when you travel. If not, you might consider purchasing a low-cost separate insurance policy. **Safeware** (☎ US 800-800-1492; www.safeware.com) specializes in covering computers and charges $90 for 90-day comprehensive international travel coverage up to $4000.

CREDIT CARD COMMON SENSE. One form of robbery unfortunately involves holding travelers hostage while their credit cards are used. Most travelers are released unharmed, but it is wise to carry credit cards that have PINs known to you—captors may not be so "nice" if they think you are lying when you tell them your card has no PIN or that you forgot it.

CON ARTISTS AND PICKPOCKETS. In large cities **con artists** often work in groups, and children are among the most effective. Beware of certain classics: sob stories that require money, rolls of bills "found" on the street, mustard spilled (or saliva spit) onto your shoulder to distract you while they snatch your bag. **Don't ever let your passport and your bags out of your sight.** Beware of **pickpockets** in city crowds, especially on public transportation. Also, be alert in public telephone booths: if you must say your calling card number, do so very quietly; if you punch it in, make sure no one can look over your shoulder. If you have arranged for transportation from an airport with your accommodations, verify the name of your hotel with your driver before you get in his car—thieves have been known to copy names down on their own placards to make it look as though they were sent for someone. And always beware of conmen who pose as taxi drivers.

TAXI SAFETY. Police report that some tourists who hail taxis have been abducted and robbed. They recommend that you ask your hotel or restaurant to call a taxi rather than hailing one from the street. If you have no choice but to hail a taxi, take a few precautions: First, find out beforehand as specifically as possible how to get to your destination. If for any reason the taxi driver diverges from these directions, demand to get out no matter his excuse. Second, leave valuables, passports, and credit cards in the lockbox of your hotel. This doesn't prevent a robbery, but does prevent you from being held while your credit cards are put to use. Third, lock the doors as you get in. This may obstruct plans for criminals to jump in the car. Finally, ask the name of the taxi driver and ask to see his identification. If he doesn't have identification, do not get in the taxi. The bottom line: if for any reason you feel like the situation is unsafe, get out immediately. It's worth the extra sol to find another taxi.

ACCOMMODATIONS AND TRANSPORTATION. Never leave your belongings unattended; crime occurs in even the most demure-looking hostel or hotel. Remember that hostel owners always have access to your room, so valuables are not secure. Always keep important documents and other valuables on your person. However, most thefts occur when travelers are in transit. Carry your backpack in front of you where you can see it and don't trust anyone to "watch your bag for a second." If at all possible, avoid storing luggage on the roof of a bus or underneath it. When traveling in pairs, sleep in alternating shifts; when alone, don't sleep unless you can hold onto your valuables.

 BUS SAFETY. Buses are a notoriously good place to lose your bag. Try to keep all of your luggage with you; there have been incidents of baggage stolen from luggage compartments, both while the bus was stopped and while the bus was moving. If you must put your bag under or on top of the bus, make sure you get a luggage claim ticket and remove all valuables from the bag before storing it. Then whenever the bus stops, look out the window to make sure that your bag isn't leaving with another passenger.

PRE-DEPARTURE HEALTH

In your **passport,** write the names of any people you wish to be contacted in case of a medical emergency, and list any allergies or medical conditions. Matching a prescription to a foreign equivalent is not always easy, safe, or possible, so if you take prescription drugs, consider carrying up-to-date, legible prescriptions or a statement from your doctor stating the medication's trade name, manufacturer, chemical name, and dosage. While traveling, be sure to keep all medication with you in your carry-on luggage. For tips on packing a basic **first-aid kit** and other health essentials, see p. 18.

IMMUNIZATIONS AND PRECAUTIONS

Take a look at your immunization records before you go. Travelers over two years old should make sure that the following vaccines are up to date: MMR (for measles, mumps, and rubella); DTaP or Td (for diphtheria, tetanus, and pertussis); IPV (for polio); Hib (for haemophilus influenza B); and HepB (for Hepatitis B). Adults traveling to the developing world on trips longer than four weeks should consider the following additional immunizations: Hepatitis A vaccine and/or immune globulin (IG), an additional dose of polio vaccine, typhoid and cholera vaccines, particularly if traveling off the beaten path, as well as a meningitis vaccine, Japanese encephalitis vaccine, rabies vaccine, and yearly influenza vaccines. While yellow fever is only endemic to parts of South America and sub-Saharan Africa, many countries may deny entrance to travelers arriving from these zones without a certificate of vaccination. For recommendations on immunizations and prophylaxis, consult the CDC (see below) in the US or the equivalent in your home country, and check with a doctor for guidance. Theoretically, travelers arriving from countries currently infected with yellow fever are required to have a certificate of yellow fever vaccination that is between 10 days and 10 years old. However, this rule is sporadically enforced; see www.cdc.gov/travel for more information.

INSURANCE

Travel insurance covers four basic areas: medical/health problems, property loss, trip cancellation/interruption, and emergency evacuation. Though regular insurance policies may well extend to travel-related accidents, you may consider purchasing separate travel insurance if the cost of potential trip cancellation, interruption, or emergency medical evacuation is greater than you can absorb.

INOCULATION REQUIREMENTS AND RECOMMENDATIONS.
The Centers for Disease Control (CDC) maintains a very comprehensive and detailed database of information for people traveling abroad. As of July 2004, they recommend protection against the following diseases:

Hepatitis A: Ask your doctor about Harvix or an injection of **immune globulin.**
Hepatitis B: If you might be exposed to blood, have sexual contact, stay more than 6 months in the region, or be exposed through medical treatment. The vaccine is also now recommended for all infants and children ages 11-12 who did not complete the series as infants.
Malaria: Travelers to the coast, jungle, or rural areas may want to take weekly **prescription anti-malarial** drugs.
Rabies: If you might be exposed to animals through your work or recreation.
Tetanus-diptheria and **measles:** Booster doses as needed.
Typhoid: Particularly if you are visiting rural areas.
Yellow fever: If you will be traveling outside urban areas.

Prices for travel insurance purchased separately generally run about US$50 per week for full coverage, while trip cancellation/interruption may be purchased separately at a rate of US$3-5 per day depending on length of stay.

Medical insurance (especially university policies) often covers costs incurred abroad; check with your provider. **US Medicare** does not cover foreign travel. **Canadian** provincial health insurance plans increasingly do not cover foreign travel; check with the provincial Ministry of Health or Health Plan Headquarters for details. **Homeowners' insurance** (or your family's coverage) often covers theft during travel and loss of documents (passport, plane ticket, etc.) up to US$500.

ISIC and **ITIC** (p. 12) provide basic insurance benefits to US cardholders, including US$100 per day of in-hospital sickness for up to 60 days and US$5000 of accident-related medical reimbursement (see www.isicus.com for details). Cardholders have access to a toll-free 24hr. helpline for medical, legal, and financial emergencies overseas. **American Express** (US ☎ 800-528-4800) grants most cardholders automatic collision and theft car rental insurance and ground travel accident coverage of US$100,000 on flight purchases made with the card.

INSURANCE PROVIDERS
STA (p. 30) offers a range of plans that can supplement your basic coverage. Other private insurance providers in the US and Canada include: Access America (☎ 800-284-8300; www.accessamerica.com); Berkely Group (☎ 800-323-3149; www.berkely.com); Globalcare Travel Insurance (☎ 800-821-2488; www.globalcare-cocco.com); Travel Assistance International (☎ 800-821-2828; www.europ-assistance.com); and Travel Guard (☎ 800-826-4919; www.travelguard.com). Columbus Direct (☎ 020 7375 0011; www.columbusdirect.co.uk) operates in the UK and AFTA (☎ 02 9264 3299; www.afta.com.au) in Australia.

USEFUL ORGANIZATIONS AND PUBLICATIONS
The US **Centers for Disease Control and Prevention** (**CDC;** ☎877-FYI-TRIP; fax 888-232-3299; www.cdc.gov/travel) maintains an international travelers' hotline and an informative website. The CDC's comprehensive booklet *Health Information for International Travel* (The Yellow Book), an annual rundown of disease, immunization, and general health advice, is free online or US$29-40 via the Public Health Foundation (☎877-252-1200; http://bookstore.phf.org). Consult the appropriate government agency of your home country for consular information sheets on health, entry requirements, and other issues for various countries (see the listings

in the box on **Travel Advisories,** p. 21). For quick information on health and other travel warnings, call the **Overseas Citizens Services** (☎888-407-4747 M-F 8am-8pm; after-hours ☎202-647-4000; ☎317-472-2328 from overseas), or contact a passport agency, embassy, or consulate abroad. For information on medical evacuation services and travel insurance firms, see the US government's website at http://travel.state.gov/medical.html or the **British Foreign and Commonwealth Office** (www.fco.gov.uk). For general health info, contact the **American Red Cross** (☎800-564-1234; www.redcross.org).

STAYING HEALTHY

Common sense is the simplest prescription for good health while you travel. Travelers complain most often about their feet and their gut, so take precautionary measures: drink lots of fluids to prevent dehydration and constipation; wear sturdy, broken-in shoes and clean socks; and use talcum powder to keep your feet dry. Also, be wary of removing shoes outdoors as your feet can be a doorway for certain unpleasant organisms looking to take up residence in your body.

ONCE IN PERU

ENVIRONMENTAL HAZARDS

High altitude: The extreme variation in altitude in Peru means that **altitude sickness** (*soroche*) is a risk. Travelers to high altitudes must allow their bodies several days to adjust to lower oxygen levels in the air before exerting themselves. Note that alcohol affects the body more intensely and UV rays are stronger at high elevations. Symptoms of altitude sickness include headaches, nausea, sleeplessness, and shortness of breath, even while resting. It is best treated with rest, deep breathing, and moving to a lower altitude. Glucose tablets and coca tea are local remedies for *soroche*. If the symptoms persist or worsen or if the victim begins to turn blue, **immediately descend to a lower altitude** and proceed to a hospital if necessary. Those planning to climb some of the region's taller peaks should take a week in the *sierra* to adjust to the altitude before attempting the climb.

Heat exhaustion and dehydration: Heat exhaustion, characterized by dehydration and salt deficiency, can lead to nausea, excessive thirst, fatigue, headaches, and dizziness. Avoid it by drinking plenty of fluids, eating salty foods (e.g., crackers), and abstaining from dehydrating beverages (e.g., alcohol, coffee, tea, and caffeinated soda). Continuous heat stress can eventually lead to **heatstroke,** characterized by a rising temperature, severe headache, delirium, and cessation of sweating. Victims should be cooled off with wet towels and taken to a doctor.

Sunburn: Always wear sunscreen (SPF 30 is good) when spending time outdoors. If you are planning on spending time near water, in the desert, or in the snow, you are at a higher risk of getting burned, even through clouds. If you get sunburned, drink more fluids than usual and apply an aloe-based lotion. Severe sunburns can lead to sun poisoning, a condition that affects the entire body, causing fever, chills, nausea, and vomiting. Sun poisoning should always be treated by a doctor.

Hypothermia and frostbite: A rapid drop in body temperature is the clearest sign of overexposure to cold. Victims may also shiver, feel exhausted, have poor coordination or slurred speech, hallucinate, or suffer amnesia. **Do not let hypothermia victims fall asleep.** To avoid hypothermia, keep dry, wear layers, and stay out of the wind. When the temperature is below freezing, watch out for frostbite. If skin turns white or blue, waxy, and cold, do not rub the area. Drink warm beverages, get dry, and slowly warm the area with dry fabric or steady body contact until a doctor can be found.

INSECT-BORNE DISEASES

Many diseases are transmitted by insects—mainly mosquitos, fleas, ticks, and lice. Be aware of insects in wet or forested areas, especially while hiking and camping. **Mosquitos**—responsible for malaria, dengue fever, and yellow fever, among others— can be particularly dangerous in wet, swampy, or wooded areas. They dominate the jungle and are most active from dusk to dawn. Wear long pants and long sleeves, tuck your pants into your socks, and buy a mosquito net. Use insect repellents such as DEET and soak or spray your gear with permethrin (licensed in the US for use on clothing only). To stop the itch after being bitten, try Calamine lotion or topical cortisones (like Cortaid) or take a bath with a half-cup of baking soda or oatmeal. **Ticks** can be particularly dangerous in rural and forested regions. Pause periodically while walking to brush off ticks using a fine-toothed comb on your neck and scalp.

Malaria: Transmitted by *Anopheles* mosquitos that bite at night. The incubation period varies anywhere between 10 days and 4 weeks. Early symptoms include fever, chills, aches, and fatigue, followed by high fever and sweating, sometimes with vomiting and diarrhea. See a doctor for any flu-like sickness that occurs after travel in a risk area. To reduce the risk of contracting malaria, use mosquito repellent, particularly in the evenings and when visiting forested areas. Make sure you see a doctor at least 4-6 weeks before a trip to a high-risk area to get up-to-date malaria prescriptions and recommendations. A doctor may prescribe oral prophylactics, like **mefloquine** or **doxycycline**. Be aware that mefloquine can have very serious side effects, including paranoia, psychotic behavior, and nightmares.

Dengue fever: An "urban viral infection" transmitted by *Aedes* mosquitos, which bite during the day rather than at night. The incubation period is 3-14 days, usually 4-7 days. Early symptoms include a high fever, severe headaches, swollen lymph nodes, and muscle aches. Many patients also suffer from nausea, vomiting, and a pink rash. If you experience these symptoms, see a doctor immediately, drink plenty of liquids, and take fever-reducing medication such as acetaminophen (Tylenol). **Never take aspirin to treat dengue fever.** There is no vaccine available for dengue fever.

Yellow fever: A viral disease transmitted by mosquitos; derives its name from one of its most common symptoms, the jaundice caused by liver damage. While most cases are mild, the severe ones begin with fever, headache, muscle pain, nausea, and abdominal pain before progressing to jaundice, vomiting of blood, and bloody stools. While there is no specific treatment, there is an effective vaccine that offers 10 years of protection.

Other insect-borne diseases: Lymphatic filariasis is a roundworm infestation transmitted by mosquitos. Infection causes enlargement of extremities and has no vaccine. **Leishmaniasis,** a parasite transmitted by sand flies, usually occurs in rural rather than urban areas. Common symptoms are fever, weakness, and swelling of the spleen, as well as skin sores weeks to months after the bite. There is a treatment, but no vaccine. **CHAGAS disease (American trypanomiasis)** is another relatively common parasite transmitted by the cone nose and kissing bug, which infest mud, adobe, and thatch. Its symptoms are fever, heart disease, and later on an enlarged intestine. There is no vaccine and limited treatment. Protecting yourself from insect bites will help protect against these diseases.

FOOD- AND WATER-BORNE DISEASES

Prevention is the best cure: be sure that your food is properly cooked and the water you drink is clean. Peel fruits and vegetables. Beware of food from markets or street vendors that may have been cooked in unhygienic conditions. Other culprits are raw shellfish, unpasteurized milk, and sauces containing raw eggs. Avoid tap water; remember that tainted water sometimes disguises itself in the form of ice cubes, juices, fountain drinks, and anything washed in tap water, like salad. Buy bottled water, or purify your own by bringing it to a rolling boil or treating it with **iodine tablets;** note, however, that some parasites such as *giardia* can resist iodine treatment, so boiling is more reliable. If you do use iodine, also use an "absolute 1-micron or less" filter, available at camping stores. Always wash your hands before eating or bring a quick-drying purifying liquid hand cleaner.

 ICE, ICE, BABY. When ordering at a juice bar, always provide the vendor with your own purified water and say "sin hielo" ("no ice"). The water and ice used to make fruit drinks are a frequently forgotten source of contamination.

Traveler's diarrhea: Results from drinking contaminated water or eating uncooked and contaminated foods. Symptoms include nausea, bloating, urgency, and malaise. Try quick-energy, non-sugary foods with protein and carbohydrates to keep your strength up. Over-the-counter anti-diarrheals (e.g., Imodium) may counteract the problems. The most dangerous side effect is dehydration; drink 8 oz. of water with ½ tsp. of sugar or honey and a pinch of salt, try uncaffeinated soft drinks, or eat salted crackers. If you develop a fever or your symptoms don't go away after 4-5 days, consult a doctor. Consult a doctor immediately for treatment of diarrhea in children.

Dysentery: Results from a serious intestinal infection caused by certain bacteria in contaminated food or water. The most common type is bacillary dysentery. Symptoms include bloody diarrhea (sometimes mixed with mucus), fever, and abdominal pain and tenderness. Bacillary dysentery generally only lasts a week, but it is highly contagious. Amoebic dysentery, which develops more slowly, is a more serious disease and may cause long-term damage if left untreated. A stool test can determine which kind you have; seek medical help immediately. Dehydration can be a problem; be sure to drink plenty of water or eat salted crackers. Dysentery can be treated with the drugs norfloxacin or ciprofloxacin (commonly known as Cipro). If you are traveling in high-risk (especially rural) regions, consider obtaining a prescription before you leave home.

Cholera: An intestinal disease caused by a bacteria found in contaminated food. Symptoms include severe diarrhea, dehydration, vomiting, and muscle cramps. See a doctor immediately; if left untreated, it may be deadly, even within a few hours. Antibiotics are available, but the most important treatment is rehydration. There is no vaccine available in the US.

Hepatitis A: A viral infection of the liver acquired primarily through contaminated water, including through shellfish from contaminated water. Symptoms include fatigue, fever, loss of appetite, nausea, dark urine, jaundice, vomiting, aches and pains, and light stools. The risk is highest in rural areas and the countryside, but it is also present in urban areas. Ask your doctor about the Hepatitis A vaccine (Havrix or Vaqta) or an injection of immune globulin (IG; formerly called gamma globulin).

Giardiasis: Transmitted through parasites (microbes, tapeworms, etc. in contaminated water and food) and acquired by drinking untreated water from streams or lakes. Symptoms include diarrhea, abdominal cramps, bloating, fatigue, weight loss, and nausea. If untreated it can lead to severe dehydration. To prevent parasites, boil water, wear shoes, and eat only cooked food.

Typhoid fever: Caused by the salmonella bacteria; **common in villages and rural areas in Peru.** While mostly transmitted through contaminated food and water, it may also be acquired by direct contact with another person. Early symptoms include a persistent, high fever, headaches, fatigue, loss of appetite, constipation, and sometimes a rash on the abdomen or chest. Antibiotics can treat typhoid, but a vaccination (70-90% effective) is recommended.

Leptospirosis: A bacterial disease caused by exposure to fresh water or soil contaminated by the urine of infected animals. Able to enter the human body through cut skin, mucus membranes, and through ingestion, it is most common in tropical climates. Symptoms include a high fever, chills, nausea, and vomiting. If not treated it can lead to liver failure and meningitis. There is no vaccine; consult a doctor for treatment.

ESSENTIALS

ESSENTIALS

OTHER INFECTIOUS DISEASES

Rabies: Transmitted through the saliva of infected animals; fatal if untreated. By the time symptoms (thirst and muscle spasms) appear, the disease is in its terminal stage. If you are bitten, wash the wound thoroughly, seek immediate medical care, and try to have the animal located. A rabies vaccine, which consists of 3 shots given over a 21-day period, is available and recommended for developing world travel, but is only semi-effective. Rabies is found all over the world, and is often transmitted through dogs.

Hepatitis B: A viral infection of the liver transmitted via blood or other bodily fluids. Symptoms, which may not surface until years after infection, include jaundice, loss of appetite, fever, and joint pain. It is transmitted through activities like unprotected sex, injections of illegal drugs, and unprotected health work. A 3-shot vaccination sequence is recommended for health-care workers, sexually active travelers, and anyone planning to seek medical treatment abroad; it must begin 6 mo. before traveling.

Hepatitis C: Like Hepatitis B, but the mode of transmission differs. IV drug users, those with occupational exposure to blood, hemodialysis patients, and recipients of blood transfusions are at the highest risk, but the disease can also be spread through sexual contact or sharing items like razors and toothbrushes that may have traces of blood on them. No symptoms are usually exhibited, but if there are any, they can include loss of appetite, abdominal pain, fatigue, nausea, and jaundice. If untreated, Hepatitis C can lead to liver failure.

AIDS and HIV: For detailed information on Acquired Immune Deficiency Syndrome (AIDS) in Peru, call the US Centers for Disease Control's 24hr. hotline at ☎800-342-2437, or contact the Joint United Nations Programme on HIV/AIDS (UNAIDS), 20, ave. Appia, CH-1211 Geneva 27, Switzerland (☎+41 22 791 3666; fax 22 791 4187).

Sexually transmitted diseases (STDs): Gonorrhea, chlamydia, genital warts, syphilis, herpes, and other STDs are more common than HIV and can cause serious complications. Hepatitis B and C can also be transmitted sexually. Though condoms may protect you from some STDs, oral or even tactile contact can lead to transmission. If you think you may have contracted an STD, see a doctor immediately.

OTHER HEALTH CONCERNS

MEDICAL CARE ON THE ROAD

The country-wide emergency medical assistance number in Peru is ☎105, and most hospitals provide 24hr. emergency service. Most towns have clinics where medical help is available; **Es Salud** is a common one. The price of consultations is usually minimal (around s/10). Often, 24hr. services are available, but the clinicians on duty after business hours may have less experience. Medical care in Lima and other major urban areas is likely to be better than in rural regions, and private institutions are superior to public ones (and more expensive). Anyone needing serious medical treatment or surgery should return to Lima as soon as possible.

 PRICEY PHARMACEUTICALS. When buying drugs in Peru, be aware of the significant difference in price between patented commercial versions and generic brands. For example, Cipro (an antibiotic used to treat stomach infections and diarrhea) can cost s/70 while its generic counterparts (such as ciproflaxin) cost as little as s/5. Although choosing generic brands can save you some serious soles, there is a trade-off: generic drugs are not as well regulated as name-brands, especially if you are buying in the developing world.

If you are concerned about obtaining medical assistance while traveling, you may wish to employ special support services. The *MedPass* from **GlobalCare, Inc.,** 6875 Shiloh Rd. East, Alpharetta, GA 30005, USA (☎800-860-1111; fax 678-341-

1800; www.globalcare.net), provides 24hr. international medical assistance, support, and medical evacuation resources. The **International Association for Medical Assistance to Travelers** (**IAMAT;** US ☎ 716-754-4883, Canada ☎ 519-836-0102; www.cybermall.co.nz/NZ/IAMAT) has free membership, lists English-speaking doctors worldwide, and offers detailed info on immunization requirements and sanitation. If your regular **insurance** policy does not cover travel abroad, you may wish to purchase additional coverage (see p. 23).

Those with medical conditions (such as diabetes, allergies to antibiotics, epilepsy, heart conditions) may want to obtain a **Medic Alert** membership (first year US$35, annually thereafter US$20), which includes a stainless steel ID tag, among other benefits, like a 24hr. collect-call number. Contact the Medic Alert Foundation, 2323 Colorado Ave, Turlock, CA 95382, USA (☎ 888-633-4298; outside US ☎ 209-668-3333; www.medicalert.org).

WOMEN'S HEALTH

Women traveling in unsanitary conditions are vulnerable to **urinary tract (including bladder and kidney) infections,** which cause a burning sensation and painful (sometimes frequent) urination. Over-the-counter medicines can sometimes alleviate symptoms, but if they persist, see a doctor. **Vaginal yeast infections** may flare up in hot and humid climates. Wearing loosely fitting trousers or a skirt and cotton underwear will help, as will over-the-counter remedies like Monostat or Gynelotrimin. Bring supplies from home if you are prone to infection, as they may be difficult to find on the road. **Tampons** are almost impossible to find in Peru, and **pads,** although not hard to find, are of the thick, uncomfortable type. Chances are, your preferred brand won't be available, so you might want to take supplies along. **Reliable contraceptives** may also be difficult to find in some areas. **Abortion** is not legal in Peru unless the woman's health is at risk.

OTHER CONCERNS

TOILETS. Peruvian toilets are prone to flood if you try to flush toilet paper. Most restrooms have wastebaskets nearby in which to dispose of used tissue. In most areas, wastebaskets have covers and are cleaned every day. Always carry a small roll of toilet paper with you, as it may not be provided.

GETTING TO PERU

BY PLANE

When it comes to airfare, a little effort can save you a bundle. If your plans are flexible enough to deal with the restrictions, courier fares are the cheapest. Tickets bought from consolidators and standby seating are also good deals, but last-minute specials, airfare wars, and charter flights often beat these fares. The key is to hunt around, to be flexible, and to ask persistently about discounts. Students, seniors, and those under 26 should never pay full price for a ticket.

AIRFARES

Airfares to Peru peak between mid-June and early September; holidays are also expensive. The cheapest times to travel are January to March and September to November. Midweek (M-Th morning) round-trip flights run US$40-50 cheaper than weekend flights, but they are generally more crowded and less likely to permit frequent-flier upgrades. Not fixing a return date ("open return") or arriving in and departing from different cities ("open-jaw") can be pricier than round-trip flights.

Patching one-way flights together is the most expensive way to travel. Flights to Lima will tend to be cheapest. **Fares** for roundtrip flights to Lima from the US or Canada cost US$700-1500, US$500-900 in the low season; from the UK, UK£850-1000/UK£700-900; from Australia AUS$3200-3500/AUS$3100-3400; from New Zealand NZ$2800-3500/NZ$2700-$3400.

If Peru is only one stop on a more extensive globe-hop, consider a round-the-world (RTW) ticket. Tickets usually include at least five stops and are valid for about a year; prices range US$3400-5000. Try **Northwest Airlines/KLM** (US ☎ 800-447-4747; www.nwa.com) or **Star Alliance,** a consortium of 22 airlines including United Airlines (US ☎ 800-241-6522; www.staralliance.com).

BUDGET AND STUDENT TRAVEL AGENCIES

While knowledgeable agents specializing in flights to Peru can make your life easy and help you save, they may not spend the time to find you the lowest possible fare—they get paid on commission. Travelers holding **ISIC** and **IYTC cards** (p. 12) qualify for big discounts from student travel agencies. Most flights from budget agencies are on major airlines, but in peak season some may sell seats on less reliable chartered aircraft.

CTS Travel, 30 Rathbone Pl., London W1T 1GQ, UK (☎ 0207 209 0630; www.ctstravel.co.uk). A British student travel agent with offices in 39 countries, including the US: Empire State Bldg., 350 Fifth Ave., Ste. 7813, New York, NY 10118 (☎ 877-287-6665; www.ctstravelusa.com).

STA Travel, 5900 Wilshire Blvd., Ste. 900, Los Angeles, CA 90036, USA (24hr. reservations and info ☎ 800-781-4040; www.sta-travel.com). A student and youth travel organization with over 150 offices worldwide (check their website for a list, including US offices in Boston, Chicago, Los Angeles, New York, San Francisco, Seattle, and Washington, D.C. Ticket booking, travel insurance, railpasses, and more. Walk-in offices are located throughout Australia (☎ 03 9349 4344), New Zealand (☎ 09 309 9723), and the UK (☎ 0870 1 600 599).

Travel CUTS (Canadian Universities Travel Services Limited), 187 College St., Toronto, ON M5T 1P7 (☎ 416-979-2406; www.travelcuts.com). Offices across Canada and the US including Los Angeles, New York, Seattle, and San Francisco.

usit, 19-21 Aston Quay, Dublin 2 (☎ 01 602 1777; www.usitworld.com). Ireland's leading student/budget travel agency. 22 offices throughout Northern Ireland and the Republic of Ireland. Offers programs to work in North America.

COMMERCIAL AIRLINES

The commercial airlines' lowest regular offer is the **APEX** (Advance Purchase Excursion) fare, which provides confirmed reservations and allows "open-jaw" tickets. Generally, reservations must be made seven to 21 days ahead of departure, with seven- to 14-day minimum-stay and up to 90-day maximum-stay restrictions. These fares carry hefty cancellation and change penalties (fees rise in summer). Book peak-season APEX fares early. Use **Microsoft Expedia** (msn.expedia.com) or **Travelocity** (www.travelocity.com) to get an idea of the lowest published fares, then use the resources outlined here to try to beat those fares. Low-season fares should be appreciably cheaper than the high-season (mid-June to Aug.) ones listed here.

TRAVELING FROM NORTH AMERICA

Latin American, US, and a few European commercial airlines fly to Peru. While the US and European airlines are typically more expensive, they offer a wider variety of flight options, although the cheapest flights involve connections through one of the major hubs (Atlanta, Dallas, Houston, Los Angeles, Miami, New York, and sometimes Newark). Standard commercial carriers like American and United will proba-

FLIGHT PLANNING ON THE INTERNET. The Internet may be the budget traveler's dream when it comes to finding and booking bargain fares, but the array of options can be overwhelming.

Many airline sites offer special last-minute deals on the Web. **American** (www.aa.com); **Continental** (www.flycontinental.com); **Delta** (www.delta.com); **United** (www.ual.com); **Northwest/KLM** (www.klm.com); **Iberia** (www.iberia.com); **Lan Chile** (www.lanchile.com); **Avianca** (www.avianca.com); **Varig** (www.varig.com.br); **Copa** (www.copaair.com); and **Grupo Taca** (www.grupotaca.com) all fly to Peru.

STA (www.sta-travel.com) and **StudentUniverse** (www.studentuniverse.com) provide quotes on student tickets, while **Orbitz** (www.orbitz.com), **Expedia** (www.expedia.com), and **Travelocity** (www.travelocity.com) offer full travel services. **Priceline** (www.priceline.com) lets you specify a price, and obligates you to buy any ticket that meets or beats it; **Hotwire** (www.hotwire.com) offers bargain fares, but won't reveal the airline or flight times until you buy. Other sites that compile deals for you include www.bestfares.com, www.flights.com, www.lowestfare.com, www.onetravel.com, and www.travelzoo.com.

Increasingly, there are online tools available to help sift through multiple offers; **SideStep** (www.sidestep.com; download required) and **Booking Buddy** (www.bookingbuddy.com) let you enter your trip information once and search multiple sites.

An indispensable resource on the Internet is the **Air Traveler's Handbook** (www.faqs.org/faqs/travel/air/handbook), a comprehensive listing of links to everything you need to know before you board a plane.

ESSENTIALS

bly offer the most convenient flights, but they may not be the cheapest, unless you manage to grab a special promotion. The major US carriers that fly to Peru are: **American** (☎800-433-7300; www.aa.com); **Continental** (☎800-231-0856; www.flycontinental.com); **Delta** (☎800-241-4141; www.delta.com); and **United** (☎800-241-6522; www.ual.com). You will probably find flying one of the following Latin American airlines a better deal, if any of their limited departure points is convenient for you:

Avianca Airlines (US ☎888-337-7342; www.avianca.com). A Colombian airline with inexpensive flights to Lima, and many other Latin American destinations, although most have a connection through Bogotá.

Copa Airlines (US ☎800-359-2672; www.copaair.com). A Panamanian airline with discount fares and is affiliated with Continental Airlines.

Grupo Taca (US ☎800-535-8780; www.grupotaca.com). A reputable alliance of major Latin American airlines, including Lasca, Aviateca, Nica, Taca, and Taca Peru.

Lan Peru (US ☎212-582-3250, Lima (01) 213 8200; www.lan.com). Part of one of the largest airlines in Latin America, serving 6 continents.

Varig Airlines (US ☎800-468-2744; www.varig.com.br). A Brazilian airline with inexpensive flights from London, Mexico City, Los Angeles, and Miami to Lima, with connections in São Paulo.

TRAVELING FROM EUROPE, AUSTRALIA, AND NEW ZEALAND

Most European, Australian, and New Zealand flights have connections through North America. **Northwest/KLM** (London office ☎08705 074 074; www.klm.com) offers service from the UK and Australia to Lima through Amsterdam. **Iberia** (London office ☎084 5601 2854; www.iberia.com) goes to Lima, London, and Dublin, but most flights connect through Madrid.

TICKET CONSOLIDATORS

Ticket consolidators, or **"bucket shops,"** buy unsold tickets in bulk from commercial airlines and sell them at discounted rates. The best place to look is in the Sunday travel section of any major newspaper (such as the *New York Times*), where many bucket shops place tiny ads. Call quickly, as availability is typically extremely limited. Not all bucket shops are reliable, so insist on a receipt that gives full details of restrictions, refunds, and tickets, and pay by credit card (in spite of the 2-5% fee) so you can stop payment if you never receive your tickets. For more info, see www.travel-library.com/air-travel/consolidators.html.

Travel Avenue (☎800-333-3335; www.travelavenue.com) searches for the best available published fares and then uses several consolidators to attempt to beat that fare. Also try **Rebel** (☎800-732-3588; www.rebeltours.com) and **Cheap Tickets** (☎800-652-4327; www.cheaptickets.com). Yet more consolidators on the web include **Flights.com** (www.flights.com) and **TravelHUB** (www.travelhub.com). Keep in mind that these are just suggestions to get you started in your research; *Let's Go* does not endorse any of these agencies. As always, be cautious, and research companies before you hand over your credit card number.

CHARTER FLIGHTS

Charters are flights a tour operator contracts with an airline to fly extra loads of passengers during peak season. Charter flights fly less frequently than major airlines, make refunds particularly difficult, and are almost always fully booked. Schedules and itineraries may also change or be cancelled at the last moment (as late as 48 hours before the trip, and without a full refund), and check-in, boarding, and baggage claim are often much slower. However, they can also be cheaper.

Discount clubs and fare brokers offer members savings on last-minute charter and tour deals. Study contracts closely; you don't want to end up with an unwanted overnight layover.

BY BUS

Some also enter Peru over land, from the border nations Ecuador, Colombia, Brazil, or Chile. **Ormeño Expreso Internacional,** Javier Prado Este 1059 (☎01 472 1710), sends buses to Peru from Bogotá, Buenos Aires, Caracas, Guayaquil, Santiago, and Quito. For more information, see **Getting Around Peru: By Bus,** p. 33.

GETTING AROUND PERU

BY PLANE

Flying is a convenient option for efficient travel within Peru, as bus travel takes a very long time over dirt roads. Though flights are more expensive than bus or train travel, they are also quicker and more comfortable. Flying to Cusco, and then traveling overland back to Lima, is a particularly common itinerary.

The US government has sanctioned Aero Continente (now sold to its workers and known as Nuevo Continente) for involvement in narcotics trafficking. As of August 2004, US citizens are not allowed to do business with Nuevo Continente. Check with your nearest embassy or consulate for updated information.

Peru's largest national airline, **Nuevo Continente** (US office ☎310-323-4815; www.nuevocontinente.com.pe), has offices in every major city (see the **Practical Information** section of each city). **Lan Peru** (Lima ☎01 213 8200, US ☎800-735-5590;

www.lan.com) is the national division of Lan Chile. Both airlines offer flights to many domestic cities and destinations throughout South America. **TANS** (☎01 213 6030; www.tans.com.pe) and **Aero Cóndor** (☎01 614 6000; www.aerocondor.com.pe) also have flights in many parts of the country. As a general guideline, purchase tickets a few days before departure (at least a week ahead of time for flights between major destinations) and call to confirm the booking 72 hours before the flight. **Arrive at least two hours early for both domestic and international flights.** Often, flights are overbooked and, despite holding a *billete* (ticket), a passenger may be bumped off the flight for not having *cupo* (roughly translated as "a reservation"). Ask the ticketing agent if you have both. If you don't have *cupo*, it's still possible to fly standby if you arrive three hours early and hope for the best. Airlines often offer lower "promotional fares" from November to March. For specific flight, airline, and airport information, see the **Practical Information** section in individual cities with airports.

 AIRCRAFT SAFETY. The airlines of developing world nations do not always meet safety standards. The *Official Airline Guide* (www.oag.com) and many travel agencies can tell you the type and age of aircraft on a particular route. This can be especially useful in Peru, where less reliable equipment is often used for internal flights. The **International Airline Passengers Association** (US ☎800-821-4272, UK ☎020 8681 6555) provides region-specific safety information. The **Federal Aviation Administration** (www.faa.gov) reviews the airline authorities for countries whose airlines enter the US. **US State Department** travel advisories (☎202-647-5225; travel.state.gov/travel_warnings.html) sometimes involve foreign carriers, especially when terrorist bombings may be a threat. Peru's history of civil unrest, combined with its proximity to politically unstable Colombia, makes checking such advisories advisable.

BY BUS

While bus travel is the cheapest and most reliable way to get around Peru, it can still be daunting. Buses along the well-paved Panamerican Highway (Panamericana), which hugs the Peruvian coast, promise a reasonably tame journey. Elsewhere, prepare for anything. Coaches crammed with people and luggage whip around hairpin turns through thick clouds on the edges of cliffs. And once you muster up enough courage to open your eyes again, another bus coming in the opposite direction swerves past on a one-lane dirt highway overlooking oblivion. Because of the mountainous terrain, there are virtually no paved highways inland and the quality of dirt roads varies from smooth to non-stop bumps.

 Night buses are common in Peru, but think twice before hopping on. Most bus accidents occur at night, either because of adverse conditions or because bus drivers fall asleep. Whenever possible, opt for the daytime trip. It may be the most important decision you'll ever make.

Buses leave town from the **terminal terrestre** (bus station) or from a particular street with a high density of bus companies. Buses run between most destinations frequently enough that it is practical just to show up at the terminal and board the next bus headed your way. On very popular routes (e.g., Lima-Cusco), it is wise to buy a ticket at least one day in advance. In more rural places it may be necessary to flag down a passing bus—this is the only time when bargaining is necessary, as unpublished prices are up to the discretion of the person taking the money. In Peru you pay after you board, so it's wise to ask the other passengers what they are paying to avoid giving the driver a week's salary advance. The vehicles themselves vary greatly in quality, from open-air trucks to sparkling new Mercedes-Benz mega-buses. A general guideline: the longer the route, the nicer the bus will be, so it may be worthwhile to board a long-distance bus even if you plan to get off before the final destination. Some bus companies, like Cruz del Sur, offer different classes of travel, ranging from: the most basic; to middle-of-the-line with videos, bathrooms, and air conditioning; to the most luxurious with reclining seats and meals (sometimes referred to as "imperial service" or "royal service").

One peculiar aspect of bus travel is that the buses are rarely "full." Drivers are often happy to pack as many passengers/chicken crates as they can into the aisles or even hanging out the doors and windows. Keep your bags and belongings with you if at all possible, although luggage is usually stored on the roof or below the bus. Use your judgement—storing your luggage out of your sight makes it vulnerable to robberies. If you do store luggage, make sure to get a baggage claim ticket.

TRICKY TRANSPORT TERMINOLOGY.

auto: Car.

coche: Also car.

carro: A loosely used term, generally applied to buses. It's not a car.

combi: Looks like a van, acts like a bus. The clown car of Peruvian transport. Typically seen with someone hanging out the window, yelling the destination.

colectivo: Leaves when full or when someone pays the extra fare rather than wait.

camioneta: A pickup truck. Can act like either a combi or a colectivo, depending on the location and passenger flow.

taxi: Just like in English, except this doesn't have a meter—fix a price before you get in.

mototaxi: A Frankensteinian motorcycle/tricycle/taxi hybrid. Best for short distances only. Occasionally known to haul goats.

micro: Small bus. Well, when you compare it to an aircraft carrier, it's micro.

autobús: Bus. Reserved for the big boys, the intercity transcontinental types.

económico: Your standard, cheap, no-nonsense bus.

bus cama: The opposite of *económico*. Luxury bus featuring reclining seats, a bathroom, and a movie. Usually direct from city of departure to destination.

especial: Halfway between *económico* and *bus cama*. The platypus of the bus world.

You can also travel by **colectivo**, often a VW van that travels regular routes and picks up numerous passengers, falling in between taxis and buses in price, speed, and size. The destination is usually indicated on the bus or car itself and advertised by a man yelling the town's name over and over again. There are no scheduled stops on colectivos; when you want to get off, shout *"bajo aquí"* repeatedly.

BY TAXI

Taxis can be a convenient way to get around, especially when you are in a hurry or traveling to places where buses don't venture. They are commonly used for travel between towns or to outlying destinations. It is usually cheaper to arrange for a taxi to drop you off and pick you up at an out-of-the-way spot than it is to rent a car yourself. When taking a taxi, always agree on the price before getting in—few, if

BACKSEAT DRIVER: COLECTIVO CONSEJOS. The most common form of transport in Peru is the colectivo. Colectivos serve as taxi shuttles, whether within a large city like Lima or, more often, between towns anywhere from 1 to 10hr. apart. The catch is that colectivos can sometimes resemble those circus acts where 4137 midget clowns clamber out of a Nissan Sentra. Moreover, the speed limit for colectivos rivals that of the Starship Enterprise. A few simple rules, applied firmly despite any bullying from driver or fellow passengers, can make life—or at least that uphill hairpin turn on a dirt road with a 3000m cliff ahead and an oncoming truck—a lot more comfortable.

1. Do not sit in the front. In colectivo parlance, there are two front passenger seats; the second is invisible except where it squishes into the first. This means no seatbelt for anyone up front. On a less vital note, it also means adding "contortionism" to your list of circus acts.
2. Three to four people will squeeze into the backseat. Tell or mime for the driver that vomiting is sure to ensue if you are squished onto the middle hump. Be firm. Insist on a window-side seat, and put on that seatbelt.
3. Paying on arrival or at mid-journey is standard practice. If you are unsure how much to pay, watch what other passengers give to avoid paying for everyone's ride. Note that those up front sometimes pay less. (But see again Rule #1.)
4. Here is one situation where paranoia doesn't pay. If there is a trunk in the car, by all means, backpacks fit better there than on your knees.
5. Relax and enjoy the music. Oh, no earplugs?

NAVIGATING THE COMBIS.
1. Always keep small change on you as when you ride between towns and sights. Most drivers cannot make change for bills larger than s/10 and will be angry if you try at the end of a trip.
2. Ask a passenger on the combi for the fare rather than the driver. If you look like a tourist, you may get charged higher prices.

any, taxis have meters, and drivers often charge more for unsuspecting tourists. Be extremely careful to **only get in authorized taxis** (with a yellow and black checkerboard on the side). Also beware of advice given by taxi drivers—they are often in cahoots with particular establishments and receive commissions. In the jungle the regular taxi is replaced by the mototaxi—a motorcycle which has a 2- or 3-person open-air cart attached to the back. These tend to be cheaper, and in smaller cities they are the only option.

BY BOAT

Large **cargo ships** travel the rivers that connect many towns in the jungle. These usually have two decks: a lower one for cargo and an upper one for passengers. The latter features a few toilets and showers, several cramped and windowless cabins (bedding is not provided), and often a canteen selling biscuits, soda, toilet paper, and other "necessities." The **kitchen** can be found below, where the cook often scoops water straight from the river to prepare the rice, fish, or soup—many passengers become ill from the food, so it may be wise to bring your own. Either way, you'll need your own bowl and utensils as well as enough water to last you more days than the captain projects. Every passenger also makes use of his or her own **hammock** and hanging rope, which are best

ESSENTIALS

installed as far from the bathrooms, the engine, and the lights, as possible. Hammocks are available in markets all over the jungle, in both string and cloth varieties. The cloth sort—though somewhat more expensive—provides far greater protection against intrusive elbows or feet. Other useful items include toilet paper, a chain with which to attach your bag to a pole while you sleep, a clothesline on which to hang wet towels, and a sleeping bag or blanket—constant wind makes sleeping on deck quite chilly at night.

Boats accepting passengers hang **chalkboards** from their bows, announcing their intended destination and departure times. However, while most reach their destination, few depart on time. They often hang around the port for weeks, stuffing themselves with cargo; the boat that looks most ready to sink under the weight of its load will probably be the next to leave. There's no need to arrange a "ticket" ahead of time, as these boats don't take reservations; but it may be a good idea to establish a price with the captain. Someone will collect the passage fee (which depends on length of journey and usually includes 3 meals per day) once the boat has embarked. The fee may be reduced if you wish to bring your own food. However, a tiny private cabin will raise the price—again, arrangements should be made with the captain before departure. It's also worth going down to the port beforehand to search for a boat without your backpack; travelers who arrive at the ports with their luggage often find themselves being pulled in every direction by touts. And should your chosen vessel not depart the day you board, sling your hammock anyway and spend the night in port. The first people on board may have to wait the longest, but they also receive first choice in hammock location.

Although cargo boats are a more romantic mode of travel, **speedboats** connect some destinations in a much more practical time frame (and at a much higher price). Speedboats often serve meals with their own version of a "flight attendant."

BY TRAIN

Railroad travel is not the most convenient, cheapest, or quickest way to get around, but it can be a more comfortable alternative to buses. However, train travel has been almost completely suspended to several major cities, including Lima. For information on train travel, see the **Practical Information** sections of cities with rail access, including Cusco, Puno, and Huancayo. Buy tickets a day in advance at the station window.

BY CAR

Don't even contemplate driving in Peru until you have lived there for many years. In case you do need to rent a car, rent a driver, too—he'll cost peanuts compared to the car and gas.

RENTING

Car rental costs between US$30-80 per day, but few rental companies exist outside of big cities. If you do need to rent, a motorbike may be a better option. Such rentals are popular in more heavily touristed rural areas like the Sacred Valley. If you do so, be sure to wear a helmet. If renting a car, make sure yours has safety features like seatbelts and airbags. Check the windshield wipers and brakes, and familiarize yourself with the controls on the car before driving. Cheaper cars tend to be less reliable and harder to handle on difficult terrain. Less expensive 4WD vehicles in particular tend to be more top heavy, and are more dangerous when navigating particularly bumpy roads.

RENTAL AGENCIES

Most Peruvian rental agencies require drivers to be 25, though some rent to ages 21-24 for a US$5 surcharge if they present a valid credit card. Policies and prices vary from agency to agency. Small local operations occasionally rent to people under 21, but be sure to ask about the insurance coverage and deductible, and always check the fine print.

You can generally make reservations before you leave by calling major international offices in your home country. However, occasionally the price and availability information they give doesn't jive with what the local offices in your country will tell you. Try checking with both numbers to make sure you get the best price and accurate information. For home-country numbers, call your toll-free directory. Car rental agencies all have offices at the Lima airport; ask ground transportation officials for guidance to the car-rental desks (see **Car Rental**, p. 101). Dollar and Budget often have good specials.

COSTS AND INSURANCE

Compact and stick-shift cars are US$40-50 per day. Expect to pay more for larger cars and for 4WD. Many rental packages offer unlimited kilometers. Return the car with a full tank of gasoline to avoid high fuel charges at the end. Be sure to ask whether the price includes **insurance** against theft and collision. Remember that if you are driving a conventional vehicle on an **unpaved road** in a rental car, you are almost never covered by insurance; ask about this before leaving the rental agency. Beware that cars rented on an **American Express** or **Visa/MasterCard Gold or Platinum** credit cards in Peru might *not* carry the automatic insurance that they would in some other countries; check with your credit card company. Insurance plans almost always come with an **excess** (or deductible) of around $20 for conventional vehicles. This means you pay for all damages up to that sum, unless they are the fault of another vehicle. The excess you will be quoted applies to collisions with other vehicles; collisions with non-vehicles, such as trees ("single-vehicle collisions") will cost you even more. The excess can often be reduced or waived entirely if you pay an additional charge.

ON THE ROAD

Seatbelts are required to be worn in the front seats, though they are not commonly found in backseats. The speed limit is 35km/hr. on main roads connecting cities, and they peak at 50km/hr. on larger highways. **Gasoline** prices vary, but average about s/10 per gallon.

 DRIVING PRECAUTIONS. When traveling in the summer or in the desert, bring substantial amounts of water (a suggested 5L of **water** per person per day) for drinking and for the radiator. For long drives to unpopulated areas, register with police before beginning the trek, and again upon arrival at the destination. Check with the local automobile club for details. When traveling for long distances, make sure tires are in good repair and have enough air, and get good maps. A **compass** and a **car manual** can also be very useful. You should always carry a **spare tire** and **jack, jumper cables, extra oil, flares, a flashlight (torch),** and **heavy blankets** (in case your car breaks down at night or in the winter). If you don't know how to **change a tire,** learn before heading out, especially if you are planning on traveling in deserted areas. Blowouts on dirt roads are exceedingly common. If you do have a breakdown, **stay with your car;** if you wander off, there's less likelihood trackers will find you.

DANGERS. Many Peruvian roads, particularly in rural areas but also in cities, are unpaved and difficult to navigate. Likewise, speed limits are often not enforced or simply nonexistant. Mountain driving is fraught with hairpin turns and extremely narrow roads—use caution. Drivers tend to cross over the yellow median and drive in the middle of the road if it seems clear. Especially in the South, be prepared to stop for the occasional errant herd of llamas, vicuñas, or alpacas. Near small towns, stray dogs often linger in the streets as well. Summer rains can make jungle roads difficult for cars. Traffic also increases during holidays and festivals. For more information about road travel, a good resource is the **Association for Safe International Road Travel** (www.asirt.org).

DRIVING PERMITS AND CAR INSURANCE

If you plan to drive while in Peru, you must be over 18 and have an **International Driving Permit (IDP)**. These are especially helpful in cases (e.g., an accident or stranded in a small town) where the police do not know English; information on the IDP is printed in ten languages, including Spanish. Your IDP, valid for one year, must be issued in your own country before you depart. To apply, contact the national or local branch of your home country's automobile association.

Most credit cards cover standard insurance. If you rent, lease, or borrow a car, you will need a **green card**, or **International Insurance Certificate**, to certify that you have liability insurance and that it applies abroad. Green cards can be obtained at rental agencies, car dealers (for those leasing cars), some travel agents, and some border crossings. Rental agencies may require you to purchase theft insurance.

BY THUMB

Let's Go never recommends hitchhiking as a safe means of transportation, and none of the information presented here is intended to do so.

Because buses in Peru go nearly everywhere, you shouldn't have the need to hitchhike. However, there are still some remote areas where buses don't travel. In such places, trucks will often pick up passengers to make a little extra money. Usually they cost about the same as taxis, but they may charge a little more; settle on a price before getting in. If hitchhiking, use common sense and go with your gut; if something does not feel right or safe, chances are you're better off waiting.

BORDER CROSSINGS

Make sure that your passport is stamped at every border crossing.

TO BOLIVIA. Most tourists cross into Bolivia near Lake Titicaca, either at Yungayo on the way to Copacabana or at Desaguadero on the way to La Paz (see **Puno,** p. 197). However, the adventurous may head to Puerto Maldonado, where there is little infrastructure as you cross the border at Puerto Pardo/Puerto Heath (see **Puerto Maldonado,** p. 424).

TO CHILE. Cross into Chile at Tacna, Peru where huge American sedans pass the border en route to Arica, Chile (see **Tacna,** p. 167).

TO BRAZIL AND COLOMBIA. Entering Brazil and Colombia requires a long boat ride, but is remarkably worry-free at the neutral, tri-national zone of Tabatinga, Brazil; Leticia, Colombia; and Santa Rosa, Peru (see **Iquitos,** p. 386).

TO ECUADOR. Although it is much easier to enter Ecuador via bus from Piura, Peru to Loja, Ecuador (see **Piura,** p. 330), most tourists opt for the more difficult crossing between Tumbes, Peru and Huaquillas, Ecuador (see **Tumbes,** p. 336).

KEEPING IN TOUCH

BY MAIL

SENDING MAIL HOME FROM PERU

The mail system in Peru is privatized, and largely monopolized by the company **Serpost.** Post offices abound in Peru, and almost every village has one. **DHL** and **Federal Express** are also available. There are few mailboxes, so get mail stamped at the post office and send it from there. **EMS (Express Mail Service),** available at most Serpost offices, provides certified mail service around the world. Documents up to 250g in weight take 1-3 days and cost s/50-78, depending on the destination city. Purchase stamps at the post office.

Mailing letters from Peru can be a slow and inconsistent process, but it is generally reliable if you send your letter "recomendado" or "certificado"; it will take just 7-10 days to reach its destination (about 8 days to reach the US). **Airmail** is the best way to send mail home from Peru. **Aerogrammes,** printed sheets that fold into envelopes and travel via airmail, are available at post offices. Write "airmail," "par avion," or "por avión" on the front. Most post offices will charge exorbitant fees or simply refuse to send aerogrammes with enclosures. **Surface mail** is by far the cheapest—though also the slowest—way to send mail. It takes one to two months to cross the Atlantic and one to three to cross the Pacific—good for heavy items you won't need for a while, such as souvenirs or other articles you've acquired along the way that are weighing down your pack.

SENDING MAIL TO PERU

To ensure timely delivery, mark envelopes "airmail," "par avion," or "por avión." In addition to the standard postage system whose rates are listed below, **Federal Express** (www.fedex.com; Australia ☎ 13 26 10; Canada and US 800-463-3339; Ireland 1800 535 800; New Zealand 0800 733 339; UK 0800 123 800) handles express mail services from most countries to Peru; for example, they can get a letter from New York to Lima in 1-2 days for US$50, and from London to Peru in 1-2 days for UK£57. Sending a postcard within Peru costs s/4.50. Domestic mail is more reliable in urban areas.

Australia: Allow 6-7days for regular airmail to Peru. Postcards and letters up to 20g cost AUS$1; packages up to 0.5kg AUS$12, up to 2kg AUS$45. EMS can get a letter to Peru in 5-6 days for AUS$27. www.auspost.com.au/pac.

Ireland: Postcards and letters up to 20g cost €0.32; packages up to 0.5kg €8.50, up to 2kg €28.30. www.letterpost.ie.

New Zealand: Allow 5-10 days for regular airmail to Peru. Postcards and letters up to 20g cost NZ$1.80-6; packages up to 0.5kg NZ$15, up to 2kg NZ$39. International Express can get a letter to Peru in 2-5 days for NZ$2. www.nzpost.co.nz/nzpost/inrates.

UK: Allow 5 days for regular airmail to Peru. Letters up to 20g cost UK£0.30; packages up to 0.5kg UK£2.22, up to 2kg UK£8.22. Airsure delivers letters a day faster for UK£4.00 more. www.royalmail.co.uk/calculator.

US: Allow 4-7 days for regular airmail to Peru. Letters up to 1 oz. cost US$0.80; packages up to 1 lb. US$9.25, up to 5 lb. US$15. US Express Mail takes 2-3 days and costs US$17. http://ircalc.usps.gov.

RECEIVING MAIL IN PERU

There are several ways to arrange pickup of letters sent to you by friends and relatives while you are abroad. Mail can be sent via **Poste Restante** (General Delivery; Lista de Correos) to almost any city or town in Peru with a post office, and it is generally reliable. Address *Poste Restante* letters like so:

Simón BOLÍVAR
Lista de Correos
City, Peru

The mail will go to a special desk in the city's post office, unless you specify a post office by street address or postal code. It's best to use the largest post office, since mail may be sent there regardless. It is usually safer and quicker, though more expensive, to send mail express or registered. Bring your passport (or other photo ID) for pickup; there may be a small fee. If the clerks insist that there is nothing for you, have them check under your first name as well. *Let's Go* lists post offices in the **Practical Information** section for each city and most towns.

BY TELEPHONE

CALLING HOME FROM PERU

A **calling card** is probably your cheapest option. Calls are billed collect or to your account. You can frequently call collect without even possessing a company's calling card just by calling their access number and following the instructions. To **call home with a calling card**, contact the operator for your service provider in Peru by dialing the appropriate toll-free access number.

You can usually also make **direct international calls** from pay phones, but if you aren't using a calling card, you may need to drop your coins as quickly as your words. Where available, prepaid phone cards and occasionally major credit cards can be used for direct international calls, but they are generally less cost-efficient. Placing a **collect call** through an international operator is even more expensive, but may be necessary in case of emergency. You can place collect calls *(llamadas con cobro revertido)* through most service providers even if you don't have one of their phone cards.(See **Placing International Calls,** below, for directions on how to place a direct international call.)

CALLING WITHIN PERU

PLACING INTERNATIONAL CALLS FROM PERU. To call home from Peru, dial:

1. The **international dialing prefix,** 00.
2. The **country code** of the country you want to call: **Australia,** 61; **Canada** or the **US,** 1; **Ireland,** 353; **New Zealand,** 64; the **UK,** 44.
3. The **city/area code.**
4. The **local number.**

Telephones are relatively easy to work in Peru, where the Spanish firm **Telefónica del Perú** has the monopoly on service. The simplest way to call within the country is to use a coin-operated phone. Coin-operated telephones may be the only option in smaller cities, but are rare in big cities. If you use a calling card with a coin-operated phone, it may be necessary to insert s/1 to connect, although the s/1 will be returned at the end of the call.

Prepaid phone cards (available at Telefónica stores, newspaper kiosks, and in drugstores), which carry a certain amount of phone time depending on the card's denomination, usually save time and money in the long run. About 34 minutes costs s/20. To call the US, choose Incatel or Holaperú. The computerized phone will tell you how much time, in units, you have left on your card. Another kind of prepaid telephone card comes with a Personal Identification Number (PIN) and a toll-free access number. Instead of inserting the card into the phone, you call the access number and follow the directions on the card. These cards can be used to make international as well as domestic calls. Phone rates typically tend to be highest in the morning, lower in the evening, and lowest on Sunday and late at night. To make a calling card call, keep your eyes peeled for the newer blue **public phones** that often have slots for both phone cards and coins. These public phones are a better bet than the telephone offices, which sometimes only have old phones unable to cope with the concept of toll-free calls. Before settling on a calling card plan, be sure to research your options in order to pick the one that best fits both your needs and your destination.

CALLING PERU FROM HOME. To call Peru from your home country, dial:

1. The **international dialing prefix.** To call from **Australia,** dial 0011; **Canada** or the **US,** 011; **Ireland, New Zealand,** or the **UK,** 00.
2. The **country code** of Peru, 51.
3. The **city/area code.** *Let's Go* lists the city/area codes for cities and towns in Peru opposite the city or town name, next to a ☎. If the first digit is a zero (e.g., 01 for Lima), omit the zero when calling from abroad (e.g., dial 011 51 1 from Canada to reach Lima).
4. The **local number.**

CELLULAR PHONES

It is not impossible today to be on a canoe in the middle of a remote lake, only to have the serene silence abruptly shattered by the incessant chime of your tour guide's cell phone. These devices are growing in popularity and prevalence in Peru, and are not very expensive. Some businesses don't have office phones, relying solely on cell phones. **TIM** (www.tim.com.pe) is the major Peruvian cell phone company. However, email remains the most cost-effective way to stay in touch from Peru, and cell phones only make sense if you plan to remain in cities for the majority of your time in Peru (something that few travelers do).

The international standard for cell phones is **GSM,** a system that began in Europe and has spread to much of the rest of the world. To make and receive calls in Peru you will need a **GSM-compatible phone** and a **SIM (subscriber identity module) card,** a country-specific, thumbnail-sized chip that gives you a local phone number and plugs you into the local network. Many SIM cards are **prepaid,** meaning that they come with calling time included and you don't need to sign up for a monthly service plan. Incoming calls are frequently free. When you use up the prepaid time, you can buy additional cards or vouchers (usually available at convenience stores) to get more. A SIM card from TIM costs about s/100. For more information on GSM phones, check out www.orange.co.uk, www.roadpost.com, www.t-mobile.com, or www.planetomni.com. Companies like **Cellular Abroad** (www.cellularabroad.com) rent cell phones that work in a variety of destinations around the world, providing a simpler option than picking up a phone in-country.

GSM PHONES. Just having a GSM phone doesn't mean you're necessarily good to go when you travel abroad. The majority of GSM phones sold in the United States operate on a different **frequency** (1900) than international phones (900/1800) and will not work abroad. Tri-band phones work on all three frequencies (900/1800/1900) and will operate through most of the world. As well, some GSM phones are **SIM-locked** and will only accept SIM cards from a single carrier. You'll need a **SIM-unlocked** phone to use a SIM card from a local carrier when you travel.

TIME DIFFERENCES

Peru is five hours behind **Greenwich Mean Time (GMT),** and does not observe Daylight Saving Time.

The following table applies from late October to early April.

4AM	5AM	6AM	7AM	8AM	NOON	10PM
Vancouver Seattle San Francisco Los Angeles	Denver	Chicago	**LIMA** New York Toronto	New Brunswick	London	Sydney Canberra Melbourne

This table is applicable from early April to late October.

4AM	5AM	6AM	7AM	8AM	NOON	9PM
Vancouver Seattle San Francisco Los Angeles	Denver	**LIMA** Chicago	New York Toronto	New Brunswick	London	Sydney Canberra Melbourne

BY EMAIL AND INTERNET

The Internet may be the easiest way to keep in touch. Internet cafes have infiltrated every large city in Peru, and can be found sneaking into smaller cities and rural areas as well. Internet access runs s/1-2 per hr. in Internet cafes, depending on the cafe and the time of day, and more in more rural areas. Also, XP operating systems are increasing in prevalence.

Though in some places it's possible to forge a remote link with your home server, in most cases this is a much slower (and thus more expensive) option than taking advantage of free **web-based email accounts** (e.g., www.hotmail.com and www.yahoo.com). **Internet cafes** (about s/1.50 per hr.) are listed in the **Practical Information** sections of major cities. For lists of additional cybercafes in Peru, check out www.cybercaptive.com.

Laptops are a popular target for petty thieves, so for your peace of mind, it's best to leave them at home. However, traveling laptop users can call an Internet service provider via a modem using long-distance phone cards specifically intended for such calls. They may also find Internet cafes that allow them to connect their laptops to the Internet. And most excitingly, travelers with wireless-enabled computers may be able to take advantage of an increasing number of Internet "hotspots," where they can get online for free or for a small fee. Newer computers can detect these hotspots automatically; otherwise, websites like www.locfinder.net can help you find them. For information on insuring your laptop while traveling, see **Personal Safety: Possessions and Valuables,** p. 21.

ACCOMMODATIONS

HOTELS AND HOSTELS

Most budget accommodations in Peru are basic, family-owned hotels and hostels. Names do not correspond to quality, but rather to size. In general, an establishment with one to six rooms is a "hospedaje familiar"; six to 20 rooms is a "hostal"; and more than 20 rooms is a hotel. An average single room will cost about US$4-8, but bigger establishments (i.e., hotels) are generally more luxurious, and consequently can be more expensive.

Rooms are usually small and simple, bathrooms may be private or communal, and there is often a lounge area or courtyard. Many accommodations offer **matrimonials**—rooms for two people with a double or queen-sized bed rather than two twin beds—that often cost less than a traditional double. Hostels with dorm-style accommodations are rarely found outside of large cities. Budget accommodations generally include sheets, blankets, and that's about it—bring your own towels. In the chilly Andes, you can generally expect wool blankets. Both hotels and hostels may offer laundry service for a fee (usually around s/3-6 per kg.) or may have a place where guests can do their own laundry (sometimes a washtub and a clothes line), or there may be no laundry facilities at all. It is expected everywhere that you **throw your toilet paper into the waste basket**—*not* the toilet.

Hostel and hotel owners frequently require guests to present a passport number upon checking in. There is occasionally a lockout time before which you must return to the hotel or hostel. If you get locked out, you can try to wake the owner or receptionist, but don't expect a cheerful greeting. **Hot water** can be something of a luxury, especially in small towns. **Electric showers** usually provide a short (about 1min.) burst of hot water (and occasionally minor shocks), available 24hr. **Thermal showers** have a separate hot-water knob and a set time (usually early morning) when you can take a shower. Most hostels over s/20 will have 24hr. hot water. Reservations are generally only necessary for big festivals and in cities with a large number of tourists.

BOOKING HOSTELS ONLINE. One of the easiest ways to ensure you've got a bed for the night is by reserving online. Click to the **Hostelworld** booking engine through **www.letsgo.com,** and you'll have access to bargain accommodations from Argentina to Zimbabwe with no added commission.

HOSTELLING INTERNATIONAL

Hostelling International (HI) is a federation of national hosteling associations around the world. HI members receive discounts for stays at affiliated hostels. There are only a few HI hostels scattered throughout Peru, so it's probably not cost-effective to join HI just for your visit, but if you are already a member you can save a few soles. HI's umbrella organization's web page (www.hihostels.com), which lists the web addresses and phone numbers of all national associations, can be a great place to begin researching hosteling in a specific region.

OTHER TYPES OF ACCOMMODATIONS

JUNGLE LODGES

Jungle lodges are the predictable, luxurious way to see the jungle. Many of the affordable ones sit quite close to cities and offer trails, swimming pools, and excursions into the jungle.

HOME EXCHANGES AND HOSPITALITY CLUBS

Home exchange offers the traveler various types of homes (houses, apartments, condominiums), plus the opportunity to live like a native and to cut down on costs, though there are limited opportunities for this kind of accommodation in Peru. For more information, contact HomeExchange.Com, P.O. Box 787, Hermosa Beach, CA 90254 USA (☎800-877-8723; www.homeexchange.com).

Hospitality clubs link their members with individuals or families abroad who are willing to host travelers for free or for a small fee to promote cultural exchange and general good karma. In exchange, members usually must be willing to host travelers in their own homes; a small membership fee may also be required. **Global-Freeloaders.com** (www.globalfreeloaders.com) and **The Hospitality Club** (www.hospitalityclub.org) are good places to start. **Servas** (www.servas.org) is an established, more formal, peace-based organization, and requires a fee and an interview to join. An Internet search will find many similar organizations, some of which cater to special interests (e.g., women, GLBT travelers, or members of certain professions.) As always, use common sense when planning to stay with or host someone you do not know.

CAMPING AND THE OUTDOORS

Camping is possible in Peru, but it is most frequently an option for hikers along trails or in national parks for free or a minimal fee, rather than in established campsites in towns. It is possible to camp in some small towns or on beaches, often for free, but there are usually no real resources—make sure you have all the necessary supplies before leaving. Some parks and reserves have designated camping areas and some more frequently climbed mountains have *refugios* (rustic shelters) at various elevation levels. Closer to town, some tourist recreation centers have space for camping next to pools, restaurants, and discos. Some landowners may allow camping on their property, but be sure to ask. Be cautious when camping in non-designated spots, especially in isolated areas.

The **South American Explorers (SAE)** is a good resource for information about possible outdoors itineraries (see **Tourist Offices,** p. 11).

LEAVE NO TRACE. *Let's Go* encourages travelers to embrace the "Leave No Trace" ethic, minimizing their impact on natural environments and protecting them for future generations. Trekkers and wilderness enthusiasts should set up camp on durable surfaces, use cookstoves instead of campfires, bury human waste away from water supplies, bag trash and carry it out with them, and respect wildlife and natural objects. For more detailed information, contact the **Leave No Trace Center for Outdoor Ethics,** P.O. Box 997, Boulder, CO 80306, USA (☎800-332-4100 or 303-442-8222; www.lnt.org).

USEFUL PUBLICATIONS AND RESOURCES

A variety of publishing companies offer hiking guidebooks to meet the educational needs of novice or expert. For information about camping, hiking, and biking, write or call the publishers listed below to receive a free catalog.

Automobile Association, Contact Centre, Carr Ellison House, William Armstrong Drive, Newcastle-upon-Tyne NE4 7YA, UK. (☎0870 600 0371; www.theAA.com).

Sierra Club Books, 85 Second St., 2nd fl., San Francisco, CA 94105, USA (☎415-977-5500; www.sierraclub.org). Publishes general resource books on hiking, camping, and women traveling in the outdoors.

The Mountaineers Books, 1001 SW Klickitat Way, Ste. 201, Seattle, WA 98134, USA (☎ 206-223-6303; www.mountaineersbooks.org). Boasts over 600 titles on hiking, biking, mountaineering, natural history, and conservation.

NATIONAL PARKS

Peru has ten national parks—Bahuaja-Sonene, Cerros de Amotape, Cordillera Azul, Cutervo, Huascarán, Manú, Otishi, Río Abiseo, Tingo María, and Yanachaga-Chemillén. In addition to certified National Parks, protected areas of Peru have several other categories of distinction—nine national reserves, six national sanctuaries, four historical sanctuaries, six protected forests, two game reserves, and many community reserves and other reserved areas to protect the nation's delicate and diverse ecosystems, as well as its wealth of ancient ruins and other historical sites. Machu Picchu is a historical sanctuary, while the mangrove swamp forest Manglares de Tumbes is a national sanctuary. Together, these protected areas comprise about 10% of Peru. The largest of the parks is the Reserva Nacional Pacaya-Samiria (p. 399), a tropical forest in northern Peru of 2,080,000 hectares.

If visiting a national park, remember that these are essentially wild areas, with many sections under little if any official regulation. Though they were created to combine conservation, research, and, in some cases (as with the Inca Trail) regional tourism, many areas still see little outside influence, and are completely undeveloped and difficult to access any more than superficially. Generally, travelers must pay the entrance fee to the park at a hut or cabin, where they receive a slip that may or may not be checked upon leaving. Depending upon whether the entrance and exit are at the same point, you may have to sign in and then later sign out. Because each protected area has different entrance fees and regulations, see the **Practical Information** section of each destination for details.

WILDERNESS SAFETY

THE GREAT OUTDOORS

Staying **warm, dry, and well hydrated** is key to a happy and safe wilderness experience. For any hike, prepare yourself for an emergency by packing a first-aid kit, a reflector, a whistle, high energy food, extra water, raingear, a hat, and mittens. For warmth, wear wool or insulating synthetic materials designed for the outdoors. Cotton is a bad choice since it dries painfully slowly.

Check **weather forecasts** often and pay attention to the skies when hiking, as weather patterns can change suddenly. Always let someone, either a friend, your hostel, a park ranger, or a local hiking organization, know when and where you are going hiking. Know your limits and do not attempt a hike beyond your ability. See **Staying Healthy,** p. 25, for information on outdoor ailments and medical concerns.

WILDLIFE

Some of the world's biggest, baddest, most eager-to-suck-your-blood **mosquitos** buzz just about everywhere along the river system, particularly in the jungle, but also in the south near Cusco and Arequipa. Wear 100% DEET bug spray and long clothes, but be resigned to the fact that these ravenous warriors are known to bite right through them. **Snakes** and **alligators** also live in the Amazon, but most wild animals keep to themselves. Stay out of the rivers, unless you're certain that your presence won't pose a threat to wildlife and they won't pose a threat to you.

ESSENTIALS

CAMPING AND HIKING EQUIPMENT

WHAT TO BUY

Good camping equipment is both sturdy and light. North American suppliers tend to offer the most competitive prices.

Sleeping Bags: Most sleeping bags are rated by season; "summer" means 30-40°F (around 0°C) at night; "four-season" or "winter" often means below 0°F (-17°C). Bags are made of **down** (warm and light, but expensive, and miserable when wet) or of **synthetic** material (heavy, durable, and warm when wet). Prices range US$50-250 for a summer synthetic to US$200-300 for a good down winter bag. **Sleeping bag pads** include foam pads (US$10-30), air mattresses (US$15-50), and self-inflating mats (US$30-120). Bring a **stuff sack** to store your bag and keep it dry.

Tents: The best tents are free-standing (with their own frames and suspension systems), set up quickly, and only require staking in high winds. Low-profile dome tents are the best all-around. Worthy 2-person tents start at US$100, 4-person at US$160. Make sure your tent has a rain fly and seal its seams with waterproofer. Other useful accessories include a **battery-operated lantern,** a plastic **groundcloth,** and a nylon **tarp.**

Backpacks: Internal-frame packs mold well to your back, keep a lower center of gravity, and flex adequately to allow you to hike difficult trails, while **external-frame packs** are more comfortable for long hikes over even terrain, as they carry weight higher and distribute it more evenly. Make sure your pack has a strong, padded hip-belt to transfer weight to your legs. There are models designed specifically for women. Any serious backpacking requires a pack of at least 4000 in^3 (16,000cc), plus 500 in^3 for sleeping bags in internal-frame packs. Sturdy backpacks cost anywhere from US$125 to US$420—your pack is an area where it doesn't pay to economize. On your hunt for the perfect pack, fill a prospective model with something heavy, strap it on correctly, and walk around the store to get a sense of how it distributes weight. Either buy a **rain cover** (US$10-20) or store all of your belongings in plastic bags inside your pack.

Boots: Be sure to wear hiking boots with good **ankle support.** They should fit snugly and comfortably over 1-2 pairs of **wool socks** and a pair of thin **liner socks.** Break in boots over several weeks before you go to spare yourself blisters.

Other Necessities: Synthetic layers, like those made of polypropylene or polyester, and a pile jacket will keep you warm even when wet. A **space blanket** (US$5-15) will help you to retain body heat and doubles as a groundcloth. Plastic **water bottles** are vital; look for shatter- and leak-resistant models. Carry **water-purification tablets** for when you can't boil water. Although most campgrounds provide campfire sites, you may want to bring a small **metal grate** or **grill.** For those places that forbid fires or the gathering of firewood, you'll need a **camp stove** (the classic Coleman starts at US$50) and a propane-filled **fuel bottle** to operate it. Also bring a **first-aid kit, pocketknife, insect repellent,** and **waterproof matches** or a **lighter.**

WHERE TO BUY IT

The mail-order/online companies listed below offer lower prices than many retail stores. A visit to a local camping or outdoors store will give you a good sense of the look and weight of certain items. However, be sure to purchase camping gear before embarking on your trip, as very few outdoor-supply shops exist outside of major tourist destinations like Cusco (see **Cusco: Local Services,** p. 221). Pack everything you need before your trip, and never count on being able to pick up extra or replacement supplies on the road.

Campmor, 28 Parkway, P.O. Box 700, Upper Saddle River, NJ 07458, USA (US ☎888-226-7667; www.campmor.com).

Discount Camping, 880 Main North Rd., Pooraka, South Australia 5095, Australia (☎08 8262 3399; www.discountcamping.com.au).

Eastern Mountain Sports (EMS), 1 Vose Farm Rd., Peterborough, NH 03458, USA (☎888-463-6367; www.ems.com).

L.L. Bean, Freeport, ME 04033 (US and Canada ☎800-441-5713; UK ☎0800 891 297; www.llbean.com).

Mountain Designs, 51 Bishop St., Kelvin Grove, Queensland 4059, Australia (☎07 3856 2344; www.mountaindesigns.com).

Recreational Equipment, Inc. (REI), Sumner, WA 98352, USA (US and Canada ☎800-426-4840, elsewhere 253-891-2500; www.rei.com).

YHA Adventure Shop, 19 High St., Staines, Middlesex, TW18 4QY, UK (☎1784 458625; www.yhaadventure.com).

TREKKING AND HIKING

There are three ways to explore the Andes: join a tour group, hire an *arriero* (a local muleteer who acts as guide and porter), or set out alone. While each way has its own distinct feel, all three options ultimately tend to be similar in price.

JOINING A GROUP. Tour groups abound in the major hiking cities of Peru, and this may be the most practical option for solo travelers. Many tour agencies offer similar services at similar prices (US$40-70 per day). It's important to ask specific questions and get all answers in writing. Inquire about group size (more than 20 people is a bad sign); food (some agencies only supply bread and water); porters' responsibilities (most budget companies have you carry your own pack); equipment (you'll probably have to supply a sleeping bag—make sure it's a warm one); and a guide with experience and language ability.

HIRING A GUIDE. Hiring a guide may be the only option in many smaller hiking towns. *Arrieros* (US$10-15 per day) can serve as guides, porters, or both. Know in advance exactly what services your guide will provide. Some guides will only take groups of 3 or more people. Make arrangements with the guide at least a day or two in advance so that the guide can prepare. It is occasionally possible to hire a *burro* (US$4-5 per day), a cook (US$20 per day), and/or a horse (US$4-5). Know what the *arriero* is providing so that you can make up the difference—most will provide tents but only cooks provide food. If you are not returning to the departure city, you must also pay for the *arriero's* return transportation.

GOING IT ALONE. Don't do it, especially if you're a woman. For the stubborn among you: bring a good compass and an even better map.

WHAT WE WOULD BRING:

CLOTHING	EQUIPMENT
boots or running shoes	sleeping bag
camp shoes or flip-flops	water bottle
lots of socks (polypropylene and wool)	flashlight, batteries
down jacket	insulated mat, if camping
woolen shirt	backpack and daypack
shorts/skirt	toilet paper and hand trowel
long trousers	lighter
raingear and umbrella	sunblock and lip balm
cotton T-shirts or blouses	towel
thermal underwear	water purification system
gloves	sewing kit with safety pins
sun hat and wool hat	small knife
snow gaiters	first-aid kit
snow goggles/sunglasses	ziploc bags

ESSENTIALS

JUNGLE TOURS

Tours in the Amazon Basin typically last 2-25 days and include treks through rainforests, canoe rides, visits to remote indigenous communities, and overnight stays in *cabaña* outposts or jungle lodges. However, reaching anything even resembling untouched jungle requires lots of money and time. When arranging a trip, you should visit several different agencies and guides. Ask them to explain exactly what you will be doing and exactly how many will be going (larger groups tend to see fewer animals). Before signing, make sure you know what's included—food, speedboat transport, daytrips, and lodging are standard. Major jungle cities generally have a variety of guides who speak Spanish and English and occasionally other European languages. Finally, try bargaining—most people book these trips from home at set rates, but walk-in customers have far more leverage.

HIRING AN INDEPENDENT GUIDE. After deciding which area you want to explore, you must make the equally important decision of who will guide you through it. Freelance guides can offer less crowded, more adventurous, and more flexible trips than those based in lodges, and their services are often cheaper than a lodge if there's a group to split costs. However, not all guides are created equal. You might end up having an excellent time with a tour guide who knows what he's doing, points out interesting wildlife, and respects the land and the people, or you could go along silently as your guide mentally counts his profits and stares out into a jungle he doesn't know much about. Ask to see any potential guide's license and national ID card to check that the names coincide; then head to the tourist office to inquire about his record. Keep in mind, though, that the majority of guides do not have licenses because licenses cost upwards of US$1000. A license may mean that a guide is reliable, but the lack of one does not dictate that he is not.

JUNGLE LODGES. The pampered way to see the rainforest. Some lodges' trips have strict schedules, while others can accommodate customers' interests.

ORGANIZED ADVENTURE TRIPS

Organized adventure tours offer another way of exploring the wild. Activities include hiking, biking, skiing, canoeing, kayaking, rafting, climbing, photo safaris, and archaeological digs. Tourism bureaus often can suggest parks, trails, and outfitters. Organizations that specialize in camping and outdoor equipment, like REI and EMS (p. 48), are also good sources of info. Tours usually offer all necessary equipment and meals; always bring your own water. Trips arranged in Peru tend to be less expensive than trips arranged from abroad, but they can also be a bit riskier. When planning any type of organized trip, verify the reputability of the company with a tourist office or ask other travelers before you go. SAE (see **Tourist Offices,** p. 11) can be an invaluable resource in evaluating guides and companies; they provide trip reports with recommendations and warnings.

AmeriCan Adventures & Roadrunner, P.O. Box 1155, Gardena, CA 90249, USA (☎800-TREK-USA or 310-324-3447; UK ☎01 295 756 2000; www.americanadventures.com). Organizes group adventure camping and hosteling trips (transportation and camping costs included).

Specialty Travel Index, 305 San Anselmo Ave., #309, San Anselmo, CA 94960 (US ☎800-624-4030, elsewhere 415-455-1643; www.specialtytravel.com).

SPECIFIC CONCERNS

SUSTAINABLE TRAVEL

As the number of travelers on the road continues to rise, the detrimental effect they can have on natural environments becomes an increasing concern. With this in mind, *Let's Go* promotes the philosophy of **sustainable travel.** Through a sensitivity to issues of ecology and sustainability, today's travelers can be a powerful force in preserving and restoring the places they visit.

Ecotourism, a rising trend in sustainable travel, focuses on the conservation of natural habitats and using them to build up the economy without exploitation or overdevelopment. Travelers can make a difference by doing advance research and by supporting organizations and establishments that pay attention to their impact on their natural surroundings and strive to be environmentally friendly. Such travel is of particular value in Peru, where much of the unprotected rainforest continues to suffer from clearing for farmland. Ecotourism lodges frequently practice sustainable agriculture and actively work to preserve their surrounding ecosystems. Guests at these lodges often eat organic meals, and activities include hikes into the surrounding land. **Volunteers** at such establishments can often live at lodges for extended periods at reduced rates in exchange for helping run the establishment. Also, the profits of many rainforest lodges flow directly back into the indigenous communities who run them. Thus ecotourism has many benefits, as it not only directly funds preservation, but it enriches local communities, giving them an incentive to preserve the environment rather than exploit its resources or destroy it for farmland. For more information on conservation-themed travel opportunities, visit http://www.bigvolcano.com.au/ercentre/assoc.htm, www.planeta.com, www.earthfoot.org, or see **Alternatives to Tourism,** p. 81.

ECOTOURISM RESOURCES. For more information on environmentally responsible tourism, contact one of the organizations below:
The Centre for Environmentally Responsible Tourism (www.c-e-r-t.org).
Earthwatch, 3 Clock Tower Place, Ste. 100, Box 75, Maynard, MA 01754, USA (☎800-776-0188 or 978-461-0081; www.earthwatch.org).
International Ecotourism Society, 733 15th St. NW, Washington, D.C. 20005, USA (☎202-347-9203; www.ecotourism.org).

RESPONSIBLE TRAVEL

The impact of tourist dollars on the destinations you visit should not be underestimated. The choices you make during your trip can have potent effects on local communities—for better or for worse. Travelers who care about the destinations and environments they explore should become aware of the social and cultural and political implications of the choices they make when they travel.

Community-based tourism aims to channel tourist dollars into the local economy by emphasizing programs that are run by members of the host community and that often benefit disadvantaged groups. An excellent resource for general information on community-based travel is *The Good Alternative Travel Guide* (UK£10), a project of **Tourism Concern** (☎020 7133 3330; www.tourismconcern.org.uk).

With the rise in interest in indigenous communities, many rural areas of Peru have become target destinations for forays into the Amazon jungle. Foreign influences have already dramatically altered the lifestyle in such areas, where the definition of "traditional" is distinctly different from its meaning just 50 years ago, before this phenomenon. While several indigenous communities, mostly deep within restricted areas of national parks, are legally protected from outside contact, many other such communities now have integrated foreign tourism into their daily lives. Often, such tourism offers these communities a profitable way to maintain their cultural traditions. However, some tour companies exploit the communities they visit, in the quest to provide paying foreigners with an "authentic" cultural experience.

Further, responsible travel involves treating the environment and local people who work for you during your travels with respect and consideration. Tip individuals such as trail guides—they need and deserve it. Ensure that tour companies adequately pay and care for their employees. For example, for a trek through the Cordillera Blanca, check that your guide, cook, and porters get to sleep in a tent, not a cave. Also make sure that your activities respect the local environment and cultures. Be wary of establishments that have caged animals for tourist viewing, and do not patronize establishments that degrade the environment or exploit local people as cultural exhibitions. Hire ecologically conscious guides, as they also tend to be the most knowledgeable. If visiting indigenous communities, make sure that your tour company does so with those communities' consent, and that the communities also profit from your visit in a constructive way.

TRAVELING ALONE

There are many benefits to traveling alone, including independence and greater interaction with locals. On the other hand, solo travelers are more vulnerable targets for harassment and street theft. As a lone traveler, try not to stand out as a tourist. Look confident, and be especially careful in deserted or very crowded areas. Never admit that you are traveling alone. Maintain contact with someone at home who knows your itinerary. For more tips, see *Traveling Solo* by Eleanor Berman (Globe Pequot Press, US$18), visit www.travelaloneandloveit.com, or subscribe to **Connecting: Solo Travel Network,** 689 Park Rd., Unit 6, Gibsons, BC V0N 1V7, Canada (☎ 604-886-9099; www.cstn.org; membership US$28-45).

WOMEN TRAVELERS

Women exploring on their own inevitably face some additional safety concerns, but it's easy to be adventurous without taking undue risks. If you are concerned, consider staying in hostels which offer single rooms that lock from the inside or in rooms for women only. Stick to centrally located accommodations and avoid solitary late-night treks or bus rides.

Always carry extra money for a phone call, bus, or taxi. **Hitchhiking** is never safe for lone women, or even for two women traveling together. Look as if you know where you're going and approach older women or couples for directions if you're lost or uncomfortable. Generally, the less you look like a tourist, the better off you'll be. Dress conservatively, especially in rural areas. Wearing a conspicuous **wedding band** sometimes helps to prevent unwanted overtures.

In cities, you may be harassed no matter how you're dressed. *Machismo* is very common among Peruvian men and they will often express their manliness with a kind of stuttered hissing or, sometimes, by yelling vulgarities. Your best answer to verbal harassment is no answer at all; feigning deafness, sitting motionless, and staring straight ahead at nothing in particular will do a world of good that reactions usually don't achieve. The extremely persistent can sometimes be dissuaded by a firm, loud, and very public "*¡Déjame en paz!*" (DEH-ha-me en pas, "Leave me in peace!") or "*¡No me moleste!*" (no may mole-EST-ay, "Don't bother me!"). If need be, turn to an older woman for help; her stern rebukes will usually be enough to embarrass the most determined jerks. Don't hesitate to seek out a police officer or a passerby if you are being harassed. Memorize the emergency numbers in places you visit (Peru's country-wide number is ☎105), and consider carrying a whistle on your keychain. A self-defense course will both prepare you for a potential attack and raise your level of awareness of your surroundings (see **Self Defense,** p. 23). Also be aware of the health concerns that women face when traveling (see p. 29).

GLBT TRAVELERS

Homosexuality is not openly accepted in Peru. The derogatory term *"maricón"* is used more frequently than the proper *"homosexual,"* and homosexuals may be subject to ridicule. However, Lima is slowly becoming more tolerant of gay, lesbian, bisexual, and transgendered (GLBT) individuals. To avoid hassles at airports and border crossings, transgendered travelers should make sure that all of their travel documents consistently report the same gender. Listed below are contact organizations, mail-order bookstores, and publishers that offer materials addressing some specific concerns. **Out and About** (www.planetout.com) offers a bi-weekly newsletter addressing travel concerns and a comprehensive site addressing gay travel concerns. The online newspaper **365gay.com** also has a travel section (www.365gay.com/travel/travelchannel.htm).

Gay's the Word, 66 Marchmont St., London WC1N 1AB, UK (☎+44 20 7278 7654; www.gaystheword.co.uk). The largest gay and lesbian bookshop in the UK, with both fiction and non-fiction titles. Mail-order service available.

Giovanni's Room, 1145 Pine St., Philadelphia, PA 19107, USA (☎215-923-2960; www.queerbooks.com). An international lesbian/feminist and gay bookstore with mail-order service (carries many of the publications listed below).

Movimiento Homosexual de Lima (MHOL), Mariscal Miller 822 Jesús María (☎(01) 433 6375; http://mhol.tripod.com.pe/mhol), in Lima. Works for the acceptance and integration of homosexuals into mainstream Peruvian society.

FURTHER READING: GLBT TRAVEL.

Spartacus 2003-2004: International Gay Guide. Bruno Gmunder Verlag (US$33).

Damron Men's Travel Guide, Damron Accommodations Guide, Damron City Guide, and *Damron Women's Traveller.* Damron Travel Guides (US$11-19). For info, call ☎800-462-6654 or visit www.damron.com.

Ferrari Guides' Gay Travel A to Z, Ferrari Guides' Men's Travel in Your Pocket, Ferrari Guides' Women's Travel in Your Pocket, and *Ferrari Guides' Inn Places.* Ferrari Publications (US$16-20).

The Gay Vacation Guide: The Best Trips and How to Plan Them. Mark Chesnut. Kensington Books (US$15).

TRAVELERS WITH DISABILITIES

Traveling with a disability through Peru may be difficult. The more upscale hotels will generally be able to meet your needs, but public transportation systems and most hostels are ill-equipped for wheelchairs. Those with disabilities should inform airlines and hotels of their disabilities when making reservations; some time may be needed to prepare special accommodations. Call ahead to restaurants, museums, and other facilities to find out if they are handicapped-accessible.

USEFUL ORGANIZATIONS

Accessible Journeys, 35 West Sellers Ave., Ridley Park, PA 19078, USA (☎800-846-4537; www.disabilitytravel.com). Designs tours for wheelchair users and slow walkers. The site has tips and forums for all travelers.

Directions Unlimited, 123 Green Ln., Bedford Hills, NY 10507, USA (☎800-533-5343). Books individual vacations for the physically disabled; not an info service.

Mobility International USA (MIUSA), P.O. Box 10767, Eugene, OR 97440, USA (☎541-343-1284; www.miusa.org). Provides a variety of books and other publications containing information for travelers with disabilities.

Society for Accessible Travel & Hospitality (SATH), 347 Fifth Ave., #610, New York, NY 10016, USA (☎212-447-7284; www.sath.org). An advocacy group that publishes free online travel information and the travel magazine *OPEN WORLD* (annual subscription US$13, free for members). Annual membership US$45, students and seniors US$30.

MINORITY TRAVELERS

Nearly all of the population of Peru is Caucasian, indigenous, or a mixture of the two. This general homogeneity means that any foreign traveler—regardless of skin color—is bound to stick out and attract substantial attention, particularly when traveling in rural or less touristed areas. In general, light-skinned travelers are viewed as wealthier and therefore are more likely to be the targets of petty crime. In less urban areas, travelers of African or Asian ancestry will likely attract attention from curious locals and their gawking children, who may giggle, point, or stare. Asians are called *chinos*, while blacks are often called *morenos* or *negros*. Usually these words are not meant to be offensive; to natives of this region they are simply descriptive terms. In many rural areas, non-Spanish speakers may be viewed as a threat.

DIETARY CONCERNS

Vegetarians are rare in mainstream Peru, and vegans are almost unheard of. In larger cities, vegetarians shouldn't have too much trouble finding amenable cuisine. However, in smaller towns—where every restaurant seems to serve a fixed *menú*—vegetarians may have to resort to a monotonous diet of rice. Still, many restaurants will serve a vegetarian dish upon request—a *sandwich de queso* (cheese sandwich) or eggs, usually in the form of a *tortilla* (omelette), are a popular option. *Sopas de verduras* (vegetable soups) are sometimes available, but inquire first because they are often served with a big chicken bone in the middle for flavoring. In the jungle, plantains and yuccas abound. When ordering, request a dish *sin carne* (without meat). Another option is to visit the local market and stock up on fruits and vegetables. The travel section of the Vegetarian Resource Group's website, at www.vrg.org/travel, has a comprehensive list of organizations and websites that are geared toward helping vegetarians and vegans traveling abroad. For more information, visit your local bookstore or health food store, and consult *The Vegetarian Traveler: Where to Stay if You're Vegetarian, Vegan, Environmentally Sensitive*, by Jed and Susan Civic (Larson Publications; US$16). Vegetarians will also find numerous resources on the web; try www.veg-dining.com and www.happycow.net, for starters.

Travelers who keep kosher should contact synagogues in larger cities for information on kosher restaurants. If you are strict in your observance, you may have to prepare your own food on the road. A good resource is the *Jewish Travel Guide*, edited by Michael Zaidner (Vallentine Mitchell; US$18). Travelers looking for halal restaurants may find www.zabihah.com a useful resource.

OTHER RESOURCES

Let's Go tries to cover all aspects of budget travel, but we can't put *everything* in our guides. Listed below are books and websites that can serve as jumping-off points for your own research.

USEFUL PUBLICATIONS

Hippocrene Books, Inc., 171 Madison Ave., New York, NY 10016, USA (☎718-454-2366; www.hippocrenebooks.com). Publishes foreign language dictionaries and language learning guides.

Hunter Publishing, P.O. Box 746, Walpole, MA 02081, USA (☎800-255-0343; www.hunterpublishing.com). Has an extensive catalog of travel guides and diving and adventure travel books. **Latin American Travel Advisor,** P.O. Box 17-17-908, Quito, Ecuador (fax (32) 562 566; www.amerispan.com/lata/). Publishes quarterly newsletter on 17 countries in Latin America, focusing on the public safety, health, weather, natural phenomena, travel costs, politics, and economy of each country. US$39 for one-year newsletter subscription. Sells road, city, and topographic maps. Organizes small-group expeditions and multilingual private guides. Complete travel information service.

Rand McNally, P.O. Box 7600, Chicago, IL 60680, USA (☎847-329-8100; www.randmcnally.com). Publishes road atlases.

Specialty Travel Index, 305 San Anselmo Ave., #313, San Anselmo, CA 94960, USA (☎415-459-4900 or 800-442-4922; www.specialtytravel.com). Published bi-annually, this is a listing of specialty travel opportunities through adventure tour operators. One-year subscription (2 copies) US$10 (US$15 to Canada and US$20 overseas), but information is also available for free on the website.

WORLD WIDE WEB

Almost every aspect of budget travel is accessible via the web. In 10min. at the keyboard, you can make a hostel reservation or find the price of a bus from Lima to Arequipa. Listed here are some regional and travel-related sites to start off your surfing; other relevant sites are listed throughout the book. Because website turnover is high, use search engines (such as www.google.com) to strike out on your own. Embassy and consulate websites also offer helpful information and regional advisories for travelers to Peru (see **Practical Information** in big cities).

 WWW.LETSGO.COM. Our freshly redesigned website features extensive content from our guides; community forums where travelers can connect with each other and ask questions or advice—as well as share stories and tips; and expanded resources to help you plan your trip. Visit us soon to browse by destination, find information about ordering our titles, and sign up for our e-newsletter!

THE ART OF TRAVEL

How to See the World: www.artoftravel.com. A compendium of great travel tips, from cheap flights to self defense to interacting with local culture.

Travel Library: www.travel-library.com. A fantastic set of links for general information and personal travelogues.

Travel Intelligence: www.travelintelligence.net. A large collection of travel writing by distinguished travel writers.

World Hum: www.worldhum.com. An independently produced collection of "travel dispatches from a shrinking planet."

BootsnAll.com: www.bootsnall.com. Numerous resources for independent travelers, from planning your trip to reporting on it when you get back.

INFORMATION ON PERU

AllExperts: www.allexperts.com. If you have a question, they'll find you an answer. An online question answer service providing advice about Peru.

Atevo Travel: www.atevo.com/guides/destinations. Detailed introductions, travel tips, and suggested itineraries.

CIA World Factbook: www.odci.gov/cia/publications/factbook/index.html. Tons of vital statistics on Peru's geography, government, economy, and people.

Foreign Language for Travelers: www.travlang.com. Provides free online translating dictionaries and lists of phrases in Spanish.

Geographia: www.geographia.com. Highlights, culture, and people of Peru.

Latinworld: www.latinworld.com. Provides information on Latin America with links to specific countries including Peru, Ecuador, and Bolivia in English and Spanish.

World Travel Guide: www.travel-guides.com. Helpful practical info.

Peru Newspapers: www.onlinenewspapers.com/peru. Provides a comprehensive index of the websites of local and national Peruvian newspapers (most are in Spanish).

PlanetRider: www.planetrider.com. A subjective list of links to the "best" websites covering the culture and tourist attractions of Peru.

South American Explorers: www.samexplo.org. All you'll ever need to know and more about South America. See **Tourist Offices,** p. 11.

LIFE AND TIMES

Most travelers come to Peru with a few images in mind: Machu Picchu clinging perilously to the edge of a barren mountain; women in traditional dress herding llamas across the countryside; a young man rowing down the Amazon in a hand-made canoe. While these scenes certainly exist, they are only a few of the marvels this incredible land has to offer. From desert to mountains to rainforest, Peru's three distinct zones—*costa*, *sierra*, and *selva* (coast, highlands, and jungle)— offer unbelievable geographical diversity. In some areas, it's possible to travel from a barren coastal desert, through the awe-inspiring Andes, to a hot, humid jungle in less than a day.

Peru is a country that continually flaunts its millennia-long history. As the largest ancient culture in South America—indeed, as the largest ancient empire south of the equator—the Inca realm at one time extended from Colombia to Chile. However, before the Incas, hundreds of other cultures called the area home and left behind impressive evidence of their stays. Sites like Chan Chan (p. 320), Túcume (p. 329), and Chavín de Huántar (p. 352) show the sophisticated level of technology Peruvians had achieved centuries before the Incas.

Peru still bears the mark of its indigenous peoples. With eleven million *indígenas*, nearly half of whom speak Quechua, Aymara, or other dialects, this Andean country is in no danger of forgetting its heritage. The struggle for these *indígenas* (and for Peru) lies not in simply protecting the traditions of the past, but in adapting them to coexist with the modern world. More and more rural villagers move to Lima in an effort to secure a consistent income, and now over one-fourth of Peru's inhabitants live in the sprawling, modern metropolis—a far cry from the images of natural beauty one might see in a brochure. More than 70% of the population of Peru lives in urban areas. The relationship between *indígenas* and those of European descent has not always been peaceful, but the election of Alejandro Toledo, Peru's first indigenous president, symbolizes that Peru can simultaneously respect its history and push toward modernity. It remains a unified country—one colorful natural and human mosaic that begs to be explored.

PERU FACTS AND FIGURES

PRESIDENT: Alejandro Toledo.

POPULATION: 25.7 million.

AREA: 1,285,215 sq. km.

PRINCIPAL EXPORTS: Gold, copper, fish.

VARIETIES OF POTATOES: 3500.

ONLY VEGETABLE NAMED AFTER A SOUTH AMERICAN CITY: Lima beans.

NUMBER OF BUTTERFLY SPECIES IN MANÚ BIOSPHERE: 1300.

LAND

Tourists travel to Peru from all over the globe to bask on Pacific beaches, scour Andean peaks, and float along Amazon tributaries. The extraordinary geography composing this nation has lured foreigners for centuries.

THE COAST

Between the towering Andes to the east and the Pacific Ocean on the west lie the scorched foothills of the Peruvian coast. Peru's parched beaches stretch from the **Sechura desert** in the north down the length of the country, encompassing at its southern tip part of Chile's **Atacama desert,** the driest on earth. The forces of nature combine from all sides to keep the rain away. Warm tropical air from the east drops its moisture on the Andes before it ever reaches the coast; the Pacific offers little relief, as the cold **Humboldt current** sweeps up from Antarctica to create a persistent, chilly fog that evaporates like dew. The seemingly relentless desert is cut in a few places by **fertile valleys** that offer lush havens like Lunahuaná, but for the most part, the coast is dramatically dry and barren. The stark desert is a stunning backdrop for the beaches that play host to both the world's longest and South America's tallest **waves,** attracting surfers from around the world. Temperatures range from 12°C (54°F) in the winter (Apr.-Oct.) to 30°C (86°F) in the summer (Nov.-Mar.). In valley areas, humid air can cause the temperatures to feel colder or warmer than they actually are. The northern coast, on the other hand, sees 300 days of sunshine a year and warm temperatures year-round.

THE HIGHLANDS

The highlands of Peru are dominated by the Andes, the longest mountain chain in the world. The Andes run from north to south along the entire western coast of South America, from the wet tropical regions of Venezuela in the north to Chile's frigid Patagonia in the south. This is a geologically young range—wind and water have not yet worked their erosive magic on the rugged peaks. Youth is relative for mountains, though—the prehistoric tale of the birds and the bees that created the Andes began over 70 million years ago, when the oceanic Nazca and the South American **tectonic plates** collided. Lava spurts from **volcanoes** like **El Misti** (near Arequipa) and occasional earthquakes are evidence that the Andes are still growing, as the Nazca plate continues to be subducted under South America. All along the Andes, active and extinct volcanoes mingle with long stretches of arable highlands **(sierra),** which are cultivated with barley, wheat, and corn.

The wet, cold **páramo** (high, bleak tableland) dominates the upper reaches of the northern Peruvian Andes. Seemingly barren, this area's short, shrubby bushes burst into color from September to November, revealing its dormant beauty. The **Cordillera Blanca,** in the north, is home to the towering **Mount Huascarán** (6768m) and other peaks that draw trekking enthusiasts. The southern Peruvian Andes are no less spectacular, hosting **Cotahuasi Canyon** and its brother **Colca Canyon,** which, at a depth of 3400m, puts the Grand Canyon to shame. Farther south in Peru, the rugged Andean peaks and valleys morph into desolate high-altitude plains, called **altiplano** or **puna.** Despite its barren appearance, the *altiplano* is highly populated and supports **Lake Titicaca,** the world's highest navigable lake.

The dry season (Apr.-Oct.) is the ideal time to visit the highlands, as there are frequent rain showers in the wet season (Nov.-Mar). Daytime temperatures vary through the year, but nights are always cold; it is not unheard of for weather to plunge from a warm and sunny 24°C at midday to -3°C that night.

THE JUNGLE

Peru is home to the headwaters of the mighty **Amazon River,** which snakes its way from the Andes through the eastern regions of the country. Hot and humid, the **Amazon Rainforest** is part of the largest river basin in the world, which carries 20-25% of all fresh water on the earth's surface. This part of Peru is divided into two parts: the subtropical **cloud forest,** and the **lowland forest,** which is ideal for tourism in the dry season (Apr.-Oct.), as temperatures remain very warm and the level of the river recedes. During the wet season, many roads become damaged and much of the Amazon becomes impenetrable. The high jungle is the choice climate for growing coca, a sacred crop since Inca times, but lately also used for less holy purposes—to produce cocaine for export. Coffee and bananas also thrive here. Much of South America's world-renowned natural biodiversity prospers in this area. Increases in oil fields, cattle ranches, and slash-and-burn agriculture slowly threaten the flora and fauna, but recent efforts to preserve the ecological diversity throughout Peru seem to be making positive progress.

FLORA AND FAUNA

Peru works hard to maintain its status as one of the most ecologically diverse countries on earth: 13% of its territory is set aside as natural reserves. The diversity of Peru's flora, particularly in the Amazon Basin, is difficult to overestimate. Some of the earth's rarest flowers bloom in Peru's cloud forests, including **bromellas** and **giant begonias.** The massive **Puya Raymondi** plant, which blooms only once in its 100-year life, grows at Andean heights of around 4000m (see **Flower Power**, p. 352). Scientists have identified 3000 varieties of **orchids** that flourish here. Peru is also home to more practical plants: corn, potatoes, *ají* chili peppers, lima beans, yucca, manioc, cotton, squash, pineapples, avocado, coca, and enormous quantities of rice. Many of these native crops were unknown in Europe until the Spanish exploration and conquest.

No less impressive than its vegetation is Peru's animal wildlife. Peru has 1800 species of birds alone, from its 50 species of **parrots** and **macaws** to the Andean **condors** and **cocks-of-the-rock** to the **flamingos** and **Humboldt penguins** that inhabit the cool coastal islands. The coast of Peru has 33 species of marine mammals, most notably the two species of **sea lions** that are frequently seen along the southern coast, especially in the area of the Islas Ballestas and the Reserva Nacional de Paracas. Marine otters *(chingungos)*, whales, sperm whales, and dolphins inhabit Peru's waters and are visible to varying degrees. Around 32 species of **monkeys** live in the Amazon Basin. More than 1300 species of **butterflies** have been identified within the boundaries of Parque Nacional del Manú—estimates for the total number of butterfly species in Peru reach an astonishing 4200. Perhaps the most unforgettable of Peru's fauna, however, are its **camelids,** the long-necked beasts gracing travel brochures and tourists' imaginations. **Llamas** are the most common camelids and also the strongest, making them the most popular beasts of burden. **Alpacas** stand a little shorter than their llama cousins; alpaca wool is commonly used to make textiles, though it is not as fine nor as valued as the wool of the tiny **vicuña.** The **guanaco** stands nearly as tall as the llama, but has not been domesticated.

THE LOCAL STORY

COCA: SACRED AND PROFANE

In most countries, the *coca* plant is notorious for one reason—it is the base element in the production of cocaine. However, this stigma doesn't extend to Peru, where coca in its original form is used commonly for a wide variety of purposes. Many tourists drink **coca tea** *(mate),* which helps alleviate altitude sickness and regulate breathing. The *indígenas* of these countries use *coca* to cure everything from toothaches to indigestion and diarrhea.

Coca has long been used in the Andean region for **spiritual purposes.** Anthropological evidence dates use of the leaf back to 1300 BC. The Incas used it as a sign of nobility, as well as a tribute to the sun god, **Inti.** Later, the Spanish restricted access to the plant, deciding that *coca* and its sacramental practice did not conform to Christian spiritual values. *Coca* took on a whole new connotation when, in 1880, the concept of *coca* **addiction** was discovered. But since *coca* needs no care, the crop continued to be fruitful, growing on the steep fields of the Andes and producing six harvests per year. By the mid-1970s, cocaine consumption created an incredibly profitable *coca* market. Today, Peru is the world's second-largest producer of this **oro blanco** (white gold), second only to Colombia.

4000 BC
The development
of agriculture leads
to more
established tribes.

2000 BC
The introduction of
pottery marks the
start of the Lower
Formative Period.

1000-300 BC
The city of
Tiahuanaco springs
up along the
shores of Lake Titi-
caca.

The Chavín culture
thrives in the north-
ern regions, then
vanishes:
mysterious disap-
pearance #1.

200 BC-AD 700
The Mochica
develop complex
irrigation systems.

600 BC-AD 1172
A diversity of tribes
reduces to two:
Huari and
Tiahuanaco. In AD
1172, the
Tiahuanaco vanish.

AD 1000
The Lake Titicaca
region falls into
Aymara hands.

1150-1450
The Chimú produce
Chan Chan and
avocados.

1200
Birth of a nation—
Manco Cápac
spawns his ■ **Inca**
Empire near
Cusco.

Most of these animals are tranquil and won't bother you unless you bother them; however, the Peruvian jungle does have its share of vicious critters. The **desmodus "vampire" bat** (one of the few bats that can walk) feeds on sleeping or unconscious mammals. An **anaconda,** on the other hand, won't get to you without your noticing. People who know rainforests often advise that you watch what you touch, as snakes can resemble vines, branches, or—in the case of the anaconda—full-grown tree trunks. But perhaps the **candirú acu,** more commonly called the **orifice fish,** wins the prize for **Most Frightening Jungle Animal.** This miniscule, almost invisible river catfish, is the number-one reason bathers should never, ever go skinny-dipping in the Amazon.

HISTORY OF PERU

LIFE BEFORE THE INCA

REALLY ANCIENT HISTORY (18000-1000 BC)

Long before the Incas settled Cusco or built Machu Picchu, early peoples prospered in Peru's highlands and coastal regions. The first hunter-gatherers seem to have arrived around 18000 BC—a time when northern Europe was locked in an ice age, and the world had not yet invented farming or animal-herding. Early **cave paintings** near Tacna (7600 BC) and evidence of houses near Lima (5800 BC) are the most notable remnants of these early inhabitants. The origin of these early peoples is uncertain, though archaeological evidence reveals that they stood about a meter and a half high and had broad faces with tapered skulls. Some scholars hypothesize (though the theory is currently under fire) that the ancestors of these early peoples had journeyed across the Bering Strait and made their way down the coast of the Americas.

PROLIFIC PROGENITORS

The advent of maize (a steady annual crop) and irrigation systems (developed around the 13th century BC) revolutionized the ancient peoples' potato-and-adobe lifestyle. The development of agriculture led to stable settlements and, subsequently, to the development of ceremonial activities, textiles, ceramics and metallurgy. Archaeologists cite a ruin in Caral, 125 miles north of Lima, as the first urban center in the Americas. Its unnamed inhabitants built a 60 ft. pyramid in 2627 BC and dominated the area for more than 600 years. By 1000 BC, the **Chavín**—usually regarded as the earliest Peruvian civilization—had settled the area of Ancash and built the temple of **Chavín de Huantar** (p. 352). The Chavín were best known for their stylized religious iconography. Other early civilizations had various specialties that often reflected remarkable adaptation to environmental conditions. The **Paracas** (700 BC) culture of southern Peru was known for its textiles, the **Mochica** (Moche; AD 100) of the north left behind intricately detailed ceramics, and the **Tiahuanuco** (AD 300) bequeathed to future generations the innovation of terraced agriculture. Besides Chavín de Huantar, the most visible remnants of early civilizations include the striking and enigmatic drawings in the desert known as the **Nasca lines** (AD 300; p. 157), built by the people of the same name, who also developed a system of aqueducts to bring water from the mountains to the parched desert. Throughout this period, there were many independent tribes living in the jungle, but these peoples tended to be less technologically advanced than their neighbors.

NOT-SO-ANCIENT HISTORY

By AD 600, the many native groups had boiled down to two main ones—the **Tiahuanaco** (Tiwanaku) in the south and the **Huari** (Wari) in the central region. The Tiahuanaco empire originated near the Bolivian side of Lake Titicaca, and became the first great Andean empire—spanning Bolivia, Peru, Chile, and Argentina, before disappearing mysteriously in AD 1172. The Huari settled near Ayacucho and developed an antagonistic military system similar to that which would later be established by the Inca Empire.

Remnants of the Tiahuanaco and Huari splintered into various smaller tribes. The **Chimú** built the great city of **Chan Chan** (p. 320), which still stands outside Trujillo and was once home to about 100,000 residents, and the **Chachapoyas** people built the fortress of **Kuélap** (AD 800; p. 382). These early cultures maintained autonomy for over 1000 years, but that independence ended with the rise of an overwhelming military force based in southern Peru: the Inca.

THE INCA EMPIRE

At its height, the Inca Empire controlled nearly one-third of South America and more than 10 million people. At the time, it was the largest empire in the world. It all started around 1438 in Cusco (or *Qosqo*, in the Inca tongue of Quechua).

Contrary to popular belief, the word "Inca" does not refer to the citizens of the Inca Empire, who are more correctly called "Quechua People." The only true "Inca" was the ruler of the empire, who generally lived in Cusco and controlled every aspect of society, from military conquest to the complicated food system. The patrilineal order meant that there were only 11 true Incas before the power structure began to disintegrate in the 16th century. The origin of the first Inca is much disputed. Some say that the first Inca, Manco Cápac, arose from Lake Titicaca. Others say that he was merely a well-dressed native. Regardless, he was considered to be the son of the sun, and accepted as leader of the Quechua people.

A DAY IN THE LIFE

The Inca Empire is most renowned for its conquests, but before its rapid expansion it consisted of an extremely successful civilization centered in Cusco. The people were divided into smaller citizen groups (usually organized along kinship lines) called **ayllus.** Within each *ayllu*, land was distributed to each family according to size, and a portion of the crop was donated

1200-1400
The Quechua people live a relatively peaceful life.

circa 1300
"With this shoe, I thee wed."
Quechua people exchange shoes for wedding vows.

1438
The sixth Inca, Cápac Yupanqui, comes into power and begins rapidly expanding his empire.

1470
An Aymara uprising against Inca rule is quickly put down.

1500
After less than a century of expansion, the Inca Empire covers 775,000 sq. km and includes 16 million inhabitants.

1526
Huayna Cápac, the last Inca prior to conquest, dies (possibly from measles introduced by pesky Europeans).

1528-32
Sibling rivalry wreaks civil war upon the Inca Empire.

1532
Spanish *conquistador* Francisco Pizarro lands on Peruvian shores near Tumbes.

LIFE AND TIMES

1532
Pizarro and his cronies capture the Inca Atahuallpa in Cajamarca.

1533
While Atahuallpa is being held prisoner in Cajamarca, he watches the Spaniards play chess and soon learns the rules of the game. Before long, the Inca is ■ **beating the pants off** his European captors—some regard this as the real reason for his murder.

1533
The Spanish take Cusco.

1533-40
By this time the inhabitants of Machu Picchu have vanished: mysterious disappearance #2.

1536
The Spanish put down the only widespread indigenous rebellion.

1541
Followers of Almargo assassinate Pizarro.

1548
The Spanish fight amongst themselves until the crown takes power.

1572
Túpac Amaru, the real "last Inca," is executed in Cusco.

to the Inca as a form of tribute called the **mita**. The tribute served as a welfare system, as the Inca stored the crops and then distributed his stores to the people in times of hunger. The Quechua people also performed mandatory duties for the Inca, serving in various capacities from mine laborers to concubines. Polygamy was common, but only among the upper classes, as special permission from the Inca was necessary to take multiple wives. The Inca were one of the most religious cultures in history; for them, nearly everything in nature had a spiritual essence (see **Divine Demographics,** p. 71), whether a god or a divine spirit. This deep religiosity is evident in the massive stone temples the Incas built—a feat even more remarkable considering that the Incas never developed the wheel. Extensive roads and agricultural terraces attest to this engineering skill. Although they never developed writing, the Incas used a complicated system of knotted cords called **quipus** to keep records.

IMPERIALISM 101

Although many Incas attempted minor expansion, the first to undertake serious military conquests was **Inca Cápac Yupanqui,** in the middle of the 15th century. His successes grew as he moved both north into Ecuador and south into Bolivia (conquering the Aymara) until he reached Chile and suffered his first defeat. Several tribes attempted to resist Inca expansion, but within 50 years both the *sierra* and the coast had been conquered. In 1493, **Huayna Cápac,** grandson of Pachacuti Inca Yupanqui and son of a Cañari princess, became the ruler of the entire empire, known as **Tawantinsuya** ("four corners" in Quechua), which spanned from present-day northern Chile to southern Colombia.

A few aspects of life among the conquered tribes, such as their traditional religious beliefs, were left largely intact, but most areas of society were significantly changed by the conquering Incas. In addition to new foods (such as yucca, sweet potatoes, and peanuts), languages (such as Quechua), and agricultural techniques (such as irrigation and terracing), the conquered were forced to adopt the Inca system of *ayllus* and to pay the *mita*. The final Inca before the conquest of the empire by the Spanish, Huayna Cápac, focused on consolidating his widespread empire and traveled all over, putting down uprisings and strengthening unions whenever he could—sometimes by marriage, other times by replacing troublesome populations with colonists from more peaceful parts of the empire. These colonizations spread the traditional Inca language of Quechua, which is still widely spoken today in many indigenous communities throughout South America.

THE BEGINNING OF THE END

Although Huayna Cápac is generally considered one of the better Incas, he made one fatal mistake. Rather than leaving the empire to a sole heir, he divided his land between two sons: newly-acquired Quito was left to **Atahuallpa,** his favorite son (although born to a lesser wife), while the remainder of the empire was left to **Huáscar,** a son by Huayna Cápac's sister, and therefore the legitimate heir. Not surprisingly, civil war ensued, and in 1532, Atahuallpa decisively defeated Huáscar near Riobamba in central Ecuador. Though the internal fighting was over, it left the empire weakened and divided, unprepared for the arrival of the Spanish conquistadors a few months later.

THE SPANISH ARRIVE

In 1530, Spanish explorer Francisco Pizarro arrived in South America as part of an expedition to Ecuador. In 1532, he embarked on an expedition of his own. He landed in Tumbes, Peru, then made his way up the Andes to Cajamarca, where an unsuspecting Inca Atahuallpa was going about his usual business of lounging in the Baños del Inca (p. 375). Although aware of the foreigners' arrival, Atahuallpa failed to recognize the threat they represented. Fearing that the Spanish planned to unseat him in favor of his brother, he ordered the execution of Huáscar and many of Huáscar's supporters. Ironically, this action devastated the Inca Empire and facilitated the oncoming Spanish conquest. Thus, after a fierce and unbalanced battle (180 Spaniards vs. 5000-6000 Quechua), Pizarro defeated the Quechua people and captured Atahuallpa. Pizarro offered to free Atahuallpa if he could raise a **king's ransom,** filling his prison cell once with gold and twice with silver (yielding nearly 15,000kg of precious metals). Atahuallpa complied, but instead of releasing him, the Spanish killed the Inca.

The remaining strength and cohesion of the Inca nation died with Atahuallpa. Nevertheless, the conflict continued. Pizarro and his army continued south to Cusco, where they bestowed power upon **Manco Cápac II** (half-brother of Atahuallpa). This surprising alliance ended when Cápac realized that he was simply a puppet of the Spanish. When Pizarro's co-leader Diego de Almagro traveled to Bolivia, Cápac led the Quechua people in rebellion. But although they had superior numbers, the Inca forces were unable to eject the conquistadors. Cápac retreated to Vilcabamba, a town deep in the rugged Andean interior, and established a new Inca kingdom. He continued to rule until 1544, when he was assassinated. In 1570 **Túpac Amaru**, Cápac's son and the legitimate heir, became the real last Inca and served until Vilcabamba was raided by the Spanish in 1572.

THE COLONIAL ERA

CHURCH AND STATE

After Pizarro and Almargo finally stopped fighting amongst themselves, the Spanish crown officially claimed all of South America (except Brazil) as the Viceroyalty of Peru, centered in Lima. Power shifted frequently for a decade until **Pedro de la Gasca** became the first viceroy to hold power for a significant amount of time. With the Spanish came another European institution—Christianity. The official religion of Peru was Catholicism, and missionaries from many orders came to convert the *indígenas* and build schools and medical facilities.

1719
Thousands of indigenous people die of European diseases during a great epidemic.

1736
In an attempt to revive mining revenues, the Spanish decrease indigenous tax rates from 20% to 10%.

1780
Túpac Amaru II leads an indigenous rebellion near La Paz. They lose, and he is executed in Cusco in 1781, sharing the fate of his namesake.

September 1820
General San Martín arrives from Chile and attacks Pisco in the name of "liberation."

July 1821
San Martín declares Peruvian independence.

1822
San Martín is forced to leave the country in disgrace.

August 1824
Simón Bolívar proves who the real liberator is, winning the battle of Junín.

December 1824
■ Peruvian independence, at last.

LIFE AND TIMES

1829-1834
Agustín Gamarra is the most stable leader of the era—although that's not saying much.

1845
Ramón Castilla becomes president and holds office until 1862.

1840s
The exportation of *guano* leads to 9% annual economic growth.

1859-60
Peru and Ecuador have a border war: border dispute #1.

1860
Castilla creates the first Republican constitution.

1863
Spain rocks the boat by claiming the Chincha Islands.

1866
Peru fights Spain and wins.

1872-76
Good-bye military— Manuel Pardo is the first civilian president.

1879
Spain finally recognizes Peru's independence.

1879-83
The War of the Pacific devastates Peru's economy.

INDIGENOUS "LIFE"

During this time, the native population was grossly exploited. The most blatant abuse of power came through the **encomienda** system, by which the crown granted land to conquistadors and allowed them to use the natives for slave labor. In exchange, the Spanish settlers were obligated to "Christianize" the natives. Laborers were sometimes paid, but these earnings were immediately "offered" as tributes to the Crown. As treacherous as the *encomienda* system was, these farmers were fortunate compared to their highland counterparts. *Indígenas* from all over the region were sent to work in colonial mines, facing brutal conditions in dark and dangerous quarries to unearth the rich mineral deposits. The *encomienda* system re-established the **mita,** but with a new angle. The *mita* that had once served as a system of reciprocal altruism was transformed, under Spanish rule, into a system of forced mine labor and high taxes. By the 18th century, these taxes constituted a large source of income for the Spanish government, increasing by one million pesos each year.

Of all the threats presented by the Spanish, perhaps the most devastating was one no one intended: disease. **Smallpox** and **measles,** brought by the colonists, virtually wiped out the coastal population and drastically reduced that of the *sierras*. In the first century of Spanish rule, Peru's native population was reduced by 80%.

RESURRECTION 'N' REBELLION

Tense relations between *indígenas* and the Spanish led to much unrest. As the availability of land decreased and taxes rose in the 18th century, small rebellions became more frequent. In 1780, a man named **Túpac Amaru II,** who claimed to be a descendant of the last Inca, executed a Spanish official and started a rebellion of 60,000 natives that lasted until 1783, two years beyond his death in a Cusco plaza (like his predecessor). Despite his death and the suppression of the revolt, this remains the most successful indigenous rebellion to date.

WARS OF INDEPENDENCE

IMPORTED INDEPENDENCE (1820-1824)

In 1808, Napoleon continued his expansion in Europe and took over the Spanish throne. Across the Atlantic, **Simón Bolívar** of Colombia and General **José de San Martín** of Argentina seized the opportunity of tumultuous times and spearheaded independence movements. After successfully liberating their own countries, the great cavaliers moved to Peru.

This came as a surprise to the large Spanish population in Lima, whose members feared that pursuing independence from Spain would cause an indigenous rebellion. Unfortunately for them, they had no choice: San Martín came up from Chile with 5000 men, attacked Pisco, moved to Lima, and declared Peruvian independence. The Peruvians never warmed to Chilean rule, however, and it took Bolívar to finish the job. The great

South American liberator took over, winning the Battle of Junín and the Battle of Ayacucho, and finally declared independence on December 9, 1824.

FALTERING FIRST STEPS (1824-1840)

After independence, power transferred from the *peninsulares* (Spanish mainlanders) to the elite Peruvian *criollos* (people of European descent born in Peru). However, the country was still plagued by tension between the *criollos* and the *indígenas*. Following liberation, Simón Bolívar maintained power for two years before returning to Bogotá. Bolívar schemed about uniting all the Spanish-speaking countries of South America in one nation, but his dream was never realized and Peru became an independent country. Afterwards, a series of military leaders grappled for power, averaging a new president every nine months, which caused significant political instability, further aggravated by losses in brief wars with Bolivia, Colombia, and Chile. Bolivia invaded its weakened neighbor in 1836 and forced it into the hated **Peru-Bolivia Confederation,** which lasted until Chile ended the alliance by military force in 1839.

EXCRETION-BASED ECONOMICS (1840-1863)

Things began to calm down around 1840, as Peru experienced a "guano boom." Over the next few decades Peru accrued close to US$600 million by exporting the potent fertilizer *guano* (Quechua for "bird droppings") from the Chincha Islands. Meanwhile General **Ramón Castilla** rode the *guano* economic tide to power and used his popular support to end the factional conflict that had racked Peru since independence. During the blissful **"Age of Castilla,"** Peru abolished remaining vestiges of slavery, established a school system, terminated native tribute, and repaid Peru's internal and external debt. Unfortunately, Castilla and his successors committed a number of economic policy blunders and failed to capitalize on the opportunities presented by the *guano* boom. In 1862 Castilla left office.

ALL GOOD THINGS MUST COME TO AN END (1863-1886)

Real problems ensued in 1863 when Spain claimed the Chincha Islands and Peru lost its source of ever-valuable *guano*. The Peruvian government proceeded to spend US$180 million constructing elaborate railroads, and this venture, in addition to the worldwide depression of 1873 and two successful but costly wars against Ecuador and Spain, forced Peru to default on its foreign debt. The **War of the Pacific** (1879-83), a conflict with Chile over the nitrate-rich Atacama Desert, dealt the final blow. Peru suffered a humiliating defeat and was forced to sign the **Treaty of Ancón,** which ceded economically important provinces to Chile, only half of which were returned 10 years later.

GROWING PAINS (1886-1914)

After the war, Peru was in financial ruin and political chaos. General **Andrés Mariscal Cáceres** (1886-90, 1894-95), created a relatively successful program for initiating export-led eco-

1919
Strikers in Lima ask for more humane working conditions.

1924
Haya de la Torre founds the Alianza Popular Revolucionaria Americana (APRA) with an ideology combining Marxism and fascism.

1933
General Benávides is elected the next dictatorial leader.

1939
Peru aligns itself with the allies in World War II.

1941
Ecuador appears again, for border dispute #2.

1946
José Luís Bustamante becomes the president of Peru.

1963-68
Belaúnde unsuccessfully attempts a leftist government.

1968
The military takes over again.

1970
An extremely strong earthquake in the north kills 50,000.

LIFE AND TIMES

66 ■ LIFE AND TIMES

1980
After 12 years of military rule, Peru is pretty much in its worst condition to date.

1980
Belaúnde shows up again and takes another stab at the presidency.

1981
Defining the phrase "history repeats itself," Ecuador and Peru engage in border dispute #3.

1985
Inflation rises to 163% per year.

1990
Alberto Fujimori, "El Chinito," is elected president.

1992
President Fujimori creates a new constitution that allows him to run for a second term amid accusations of "dictator."

1992
Fujimori captures Abimael Guzmán, leader of the Shining Path terrorist group.

1995
Peru and Ecuador clash yet again, causing border dispute #4.

1996
Partyers at the Japanese embassy in Lima are taken hostage.

nomic growth, encouraging the rubber boom in the Amazon and industrialization in Lima. In the **Revolution of 1895, José Nicolás Piérola** (1890-99) seized power and led the country to rapid economic and structural development. He was followed by **José Pardo** (1904-08), who encouraged public education. The civilian-ruled "Aristocratic Republic" lasted until WWI, when an economic slump sent the more humane leaders tumbling to the ground. The economic development of the early 1900s propelled mass migration from rural areas in the *sierra* to urban centers along the coast. This massive influx of rural poor into the cities helped facilitate the rise of mass-based labor and social-reform movements.

SOCIALISM STUDIES (1914-1930)

Imports decreased, prices rose, and strikes ensued during WWI. As a result, the post-WWI period marked a rise in worker's movements and socialist ideas. The most lasting result was the **Alianza Popular Revolucionaria Americana** (American Popular Revolutionary Alliance; APRA; the most important acronym in Peruvian history), founded by Haya de la Torre. Writers and thinkers advanced new, liberal thought and helped increase awareness of and sympathy for the extreme poverty of rural Peru. This push for radical social change and greater equality became known as the **Indigenista movement**.

Augusto Leguía (1908-12, 1919-30) seized power once again in 1919. He attempted reforms (including a fight against yellow fever and a new program providing loans to farmers), but these accomplishments were overwhelmed by his extreme corruption. During his rule, Leguía dissolved Congress, rewrote the constitution, and created a dictatorship, running unopposed in the 1924 and 1929 elections. Eventually he did achieve some economic prosperity, but the wealthiest classes reaped the greatest rewards. In the face of temporary economic decline engendered by the **Great Depression** of 1930, Leguía's political career came to an abrupt halt with one swift military coup.

THE POPULISTS VS. THE MILITARY (1930-1968)

Beginning in 1930, Peruvian politics constantly pitted the military against the APRA. A series of conservative dictators attempted to banish APRA but were unsuccessful. The most prominent president of the era, conservative **Manuel Prado** (1939-45, 1956-62) tried to reach a middle ground with the leftist group, but most of his achievements were overruled by subsequent dictators. Consequently, economic power continued to shift toward the rich elites on the Pacific Coast. Haya de la Torre did win one election in 1962, but he was quickly overthrown (in typical Peruvian fashion) by the sore-losing military. **Fernando Belaúnde** of a newer party, **Acción Popular (AP)**, took advantage of general frustration with the APRA to gain power in 1963. Despite attempted reforms, both Belaúnde and the AP proved too moderate for their own constituency and in 1968 a group of military officers committed to radical change decided the time was ripe for a new order.

RADICAL MILITARY REGIMES (1968-1980)

General **Juan Velasco Alvarado** (1968-75) became the newest military president and instituted a revolutionary socialist program that was nationalistic, reformist, and anti-oligarchic. But good intentions went bad as Velasco's program soon lead to over-bureaucratization, corruption, economic stagnation, and soaring inflation. General **Francisco Morales Bermúdez Cerrutti** (1975-80) reversed much of Velasco's legislation, but proved incapable of halting the downward spiral.

ATTEMPTS AT NORMALCY (1980-1990)

Acknowledging the failure of their program, the military arranged for democratic elections in 1980. Remarkably, Peru began holding elections regularly every five years. The relatively conservative ex-president **Fernando Belaúnde** (1980-85) emerged victorious and began laying the foundations for a return to a free-market system. Unfortunately, some misguided policies, several natural disasters, and a dire international economic situation triggered soaring inflation. As a result, leftist terrorist guerrilla organizations such as the **Sendero Luminoso** (Shining Path) and the **Túpac Amaru Revolutionary Movement** began emerging in the Central Highlands (see **Guerrillas in the Mist,** p. 68).

The 1985 election went to the APRA's **Alan García Pérez** (1985-90). For the first time in its history the APRA ruled the country, and it managed temporarily to curtail inflation and mitigate the trade imbalance. In 1987, however, with the economy already severely stressed, García nationalized the country's banking system, causing private investment to plummet. Inflation continued its upward swing, and by the 1990 election the economy lay in ruin and García was dismissed as a failure.

FUJIMORI AND SUCCESS (1990-1995)

In 1990, the APRA was eliminated in the first round of elections. Conservative **Mario Vargas Llosa** (p. 75), a prominent writer, and **Alberto Fujimori** (1990-2000), a dark-horse university president of Japanese descent, remained for a runoff; the latter finally won thanks to support from a grass-roots campaign conducted by **Cambio '90** (Change '90). "El Chinito," as Fujimori was called, was able to capitalize on his seeming integrity and departure from the status quo.

The most pressing concern for the newly elected Fujimori was Peru's skyrocketing inflation, and he responded with an economic shock policy that came to be known as **"Fujishock."** The program involved a tax increase on public services to repay external debt, price deregulation and trade liberalization, labor market deregulation, and better control over tax collection. Fujishock was largely successful: inflation fell from 2300% to 10% from 1990 to 1992. Growth was very uneven, however, and Fujishock resulted in severe hardship for the nation's poorest. Despite these adverse consequences, broad support for the new president continued long after his election.

Responding to divisions within the government, Fujimori staged a successful coup—the **autogolpe**—on April 5, 1992, dissolving the Congress and suspending the constitution to

1997
El Niño sweeps through Peru, leaving havoc in its wake.

1998
The Ecuador-Peru border dispute is finally settled.

2000
Fujimori bends the rules of his own constitution to run for a third term.

2001
Alejandro Toledo is the first *indígena* to be elected president of Peru.

2001
Fujimori flees the country after a major financial scandal disgraces his administration.

2001
A 7.9 earthquake rocks Peru.

2004
Toledo's approval ratings drop as scandal simmers and unemployment rises.

2004
Geologists warn that Machu Picchu may succumb to a devastating landslide, making it all the more precious to visitors and archaeologists.

LIFE AND TIMES

THE LOCAL STORY

GUERRILLAS IN THE MIST

The bombing of ballot boxes on May 17, 1980, in Chuschi, Peru, was the first of many terrorist acts committed by the **Sendero Luminoso** (Shining Path). Founded and led by Abimael Guzmán, a philosophy professor at the University of Huaymanga, the group directed a brutal campaign against capitalism, claiming to advance a Maoist, communist ideology.

Throughout the 1980s, the Shining Path swept through highland villages, arming peasants and executing government officials in the name of a better life. The Peruvian army returned fire with secret missions and death squads. Citizens found themselves caught in a horrifying predicament: families of even modest means were targets for the Shining Path's anti-capitalist fervor, and all others were assumed to be sympathizers by the Peruvian army. The total carnage—over 30,000 dead or missing in Ayacucho alone—left a deep scar on the country. It also radically transformed Peru's socioeconomic landscape, as villagers fled to the anonymity of bigcity shantytowns.

Guzmán was captured in 1992, and after a much-televised manhunt authorities also captured his successor, Oscar Alberto Ramírez Durand (a.k.a. Feliciano). Since then, Peruvians have reclaimed security and rebuilt their lives.

rule by personal decree. But unlike earlier dictators, Fujimori was quickly forced to restore democratic rule. In November 1992, he held elections for an entirely new Congress composed of 80—instead of the previous 240—members. The new Congress quickly drafted a new **constitution,** which, in accordance with the president's wishes, centralized power, increased presidential authority, and allowed a single person to hold the presidency for two terms. Fujimori then continued to promote his conservative economic policy.

FUJIMORI AND FAILURE (1995-2000)

In 1995, with a growing economy and a high approval rating, Fujimori easily won a second term. Critical victories included the arrest of **Abimael Guzmán,** leader of the Sendero Luminoso, and the recovery of all 72 hostages taken from the Japanese embassy on December 17, 1996. In October 1998, Fujimori negotiated with Ecuadorian president Jamil Mahuad for a peace treaty ending the long-standing border dispute with Ecuador. Finally, Fujimori's war against drug cultivation and export was considered one of Latin America's most successful anti-drug campaigns.

Problems arose in 2000 when Fujimori began a re-election campaign, after again amending Peru's constitution in 1996 to allow a president to seek a third term. A heated race against **Alejandro Toledo** of the "Possible Peru" party left neither candidate with a majority of votes, but Toledo boycotted the runoff elections, claiming electoral fraud. Although officially out of the race (with Fujimori running unopposed), Toledo amassed 25.67% of the vote, and another 29.93% of the ballots were left blank or defaced in protest, meaning that if the ballots had been counted, the race would have been close. Because only complete ballots were counted, Fujimori was declared the winner; **mass protests** resulted.

THE TURN OF THE CENTURY (2000-2001)

Fujimori held power until September 16, 2001, when a shocking video apparently showed **Vladimiro Montesinos,** Fujimori's chief adviser and head of national intelligence, bribing an opposing congressman. Chaos ensued: Fujimori stepped down and fled the country, Congress was publicly discredited, and only the military had true power. Head congressman Valentín Paniagua served as interim president while Montesinos was pursued in Panama and Fujimori hid in Japan. Charges of corruption pursued Fujimori and Montesinos wherever they hid.

TODAY

Special elections in April 2001 came down to two familiar faces—Alejandro Toledo, and economy-destroyer of the 1980s **Alan García.** Once again runoff elections were necessary, and in a surprisingly close (and unsurprisingly dirty) race held in May, Toledo won, and García gracefully accepted defeat. In August 2001, Congress officially accused the still-exiled Fujimori of crimes against humanity for reportedly ordering death squads in the fight against terrorism. Toledo's election marked hope for a new era in Peru with his plans to integrate *indígenas* into mainstream society and eradicate the poverty that they face. Efforts have been made to raise the status of human rights and investigate those responsible for the crimes allegedly committed under Fujimori through the Commission of Truth and Reconciliation. Steps are also being taken to restructure the judiciary and armed forces, which were among the state institutions subjected to Montesinos's coercion and control. By 2004, Toledo's approval ratings had dropped amid scandal and high rates of unemployment. Peru's progress continues to be held back by widespread corruption and by the difficulty of balancing prudent long-term economic policy with immediate demands for more spending on social programs. Yet Peru remains a potentially wealthy country with remarkable natural resources and a growing tourism industry that are the keys to its future.

PEOPLE

DEMOGRAPHICS

The majority of Peru's population descends from the native Quechua line and inhabits the *sierra* region. Officially, Peruvian society is 45% indigenous, 37% *mestizo* (some combination of indigenous and Spanish), 15% Spanish, and 3% other (primarily of Japanese, Chinese, and African descent), but these categories are difficult to define as many people choose to designate themselves as *mestizo*.

Most of the indigenous people of Peru are in the lowest socio-economic and political tier, earning their income largely from agricultural work, mining, and heavy industrial labor. Illiteracy levels among indigenous communities are high due to lack of regular or properly administered education, reducing the possibilities for social advancement. Since 1919 the government has been attempting, at least marginally, to integrate indigenous groups more fully in society. In 1926, 59 indigenous communities were officially recognized, a number that steadily increased throughout the next several decades. A significant step came in 1979 when a new constitution eradicated the **literacy requirement** to vote, enfranchising a huge number of indigenous people. The 2001 election of a president of indigenous descent, Alejandro Toledo, who was born in a small town in the *sierra*, is evidence of growing opportunities for native populations. However, despite the gains of the last few decades, racial division continues to be a crucial issue in Peruvian society, as those of European descent hold most of the wealth and positions of political influence.

LANGUAGE

About 80% of the population speaks **Spanish,** the first official language of Peru. However, **Quechua,** spoken by 16% of Peruvians, became the second official language of the country in 1975. **Aymara,** although unofficial, is still spoken by a small percentage of the indigenous population, particularly in the south. Many indigenous people speak their native tongue at home, while speaking Spanish in public. Indigenous populations in the jungle speak 38 different dialects belonging to no fewer than 15 different language families.

RELIGION

Peru provides for religious freedom in its constitution. Nevertheless, the population is predominantly **Roman Catholic,** a faith brought to Peru with the Spanish conquest. In many cases, indigenous populations have not abandoned their own traditions but have incorporated Catholicism into earlier belief systems. The resulting **syncretized religions** intertwine the properties of indigenous gods and spirits with those of Catholic saints. In a given situation, offerings may be made to a certain saint rather than an indigenous spirit, but some traditions managed to weather the years of colonial rule and globalization—many *indígenas* in the Andes still worship the mountains where the mighty spirits (or *apus*) that control fertility and rain reside, and in some areas, **shamans** *(curanderos* or *chamanes)* are still called upon to cure the sick.

Missionary activities during the 20th century created a small population of **Protestants** and other non-Catholic Christians, which comprise about 7% of the population. In recent years, missionaries from **The Church of Jesus Christ of Latter-day Saints** ("Mormons") and **Seventh Day Adventists** have won increasing numbers of converts in the region (see **Divine Demographics,** p. 71).

CULTURE

FOOD AND DRINK

Although it has yet to become a widespread international delicacy, the food of Peru will not leave you unsatisfied. The staples of the region are enhanced with delectable spices and careful preparation. Peruvian food consists mainly of rice, potatoes, chicken, rice, pork, rice, lamb, fish, and rice. **Ají** (hot pepper) makes any meal standard, but the more daring can try some Peruvian specialties: **cuy** (guinea pig), **ceviche** or **cebiche** (raw seafood marinated in lemon juice, which partially cooks the meat, with cilantro and onion), and **papas a la huancaína** (potatoes covered in a spicy cream sauce). Potato-lovers should also try **papa rellena** (potato patties stuffed with meat). For something a bit heartier, try **anticuchos de corazón** (cow heart kebab) or **cau cau** (tripe served with potatoes and vegetables in sauce). Anyone near Lake Titicaca will be overwhelmed by the quality and abundance of **trucha** (trout). Equally scrumptious is **encocado de mariscos** (seafood in coconut milk), often served in a coconut shell. If you don't have the cash to eat these delicacies, sample a **bistec a lo pobre** (steak mixed with bananas and egg). One national specialty is **tacu tacu,** a dense mix of mashed beans and rice served with anything and everything: don't leave Peru without trying it, but do leave room for dessert—**picarones** (deep-fried bread in a golden syrup) and **mazamora** (a sweet purple pudding) are some local favorites.

The most common restaurants are small, family-owned local diners, sometimes referred to as **comedores.** Unequivocally the most economical way to acquire your daily sustenance, and certainly the most popular way to eat out among locals, is the **menú del día** (meal of the day). Sometimes referred to as *el almuerzo* (lunch) during the day or *la merienda* or *la cena* (dinner) at night, this is a set platter at a set price, usually with two courses, a drink, and various extras. If the *menú* doesn't do the trick or gets monotonous, try **a la carte** selections. These usually cost more and provide less nourishment, but sometimes it's worth the extra cash just to choose your own meal.

To diversify your diet you may decide to dine at one of three other types of restaurant that are both inexpensive and abundant. **Chifas** (Chinese restaurants), present in even the smallest of towns, are generally clean and serve scrumptious and filling **chaufas** (fried-rice dishes). **Cevicherías** (sometimes called *picanterías*)

Religious Life in Peru

I live in a place where stones still keep ancient ritual messages of gods that have ordered the land, of rivers with channels so deep that they inspire the idea of bleeding wounds over our nation, and of mountains with unreachable heights in whose perpetual snows senile gods decide the fate of our people. —Carlos Valerrama Adriansén, Reflections on the Right to Religious Freedom in Peru

Peru's religious history can be divided into three eras: the ancient period culminating with the Incas, the Hispanic or Catholic period, and the modern pluralistic period. However, Peru has always been remarkably syncretic, blending various religious traditions.

Some say that the ancient peoples of Peru worshipped their dead, others that they revered the sun, and others that they had no "gods" in the modern sense of the word. The Incas did keep mummified remains of their leaders, which they dressed and paraded about on festival occasions, and to which they offered food and drink. But this treatment does not sound quite like "worship"; it is probably more accurate to say that, to them, their ancestors were not dead at all. They were not exactly gods, but they were supernatural, spiritual, and holy.

Peru's ancient peoples considered many things to be supernatural, although that word implies a distinction they probably would not recognize. They believed that there were multiple manifestations of gods or spirits tied to their physical surroundings. Practically anything, from small stones to great rivers and mountains, could be *huaca:* a person, place, or thing with sacred associations. We should not rush to romanticize this belief system; the certainty that the dead were not really dead made room for horrific rituals of human sacrifice. Still, this ancient tradition of holiness makes Peru a major destination for "New Age" spiritual seekers who share the sense of sacredness in the surroundings.

When the Spanish arrived in the 16th century, they brought their Roman Catholic religion with them. Because so many things were sacred to the native people, it was not difficult to accept new gods in the form of the Holy Trinity and the saints. The Spanish established a firm union of Church and State, in which each organization used the other for its own ends: the Spanish monarchy relied upon the Church to provide order, stability, and public services, especially in far-flung areas, while the Church relied upon the Crown for funds and to protect its position as the sole legitimate religion. This theocracy was not entirely different from the Incas' fusion of political and religious power.

Indeed, although Peru became "Catholic," the role of religion did not fundamentally change.

When the 19th-century revolution threw off the yoke of Spanish rule, there was again little change in the religious situation. The Republic stepped into the position previously held by the Crown in its close relationship with the Church. This was in startling contrast to the United States, for example, in which separation of Church and State and the free exercise of religion were built into the Constitution early on. Peruvian constitutions from 1829 on stated that the only religion of the Republic was the Roman Catholic Church—to the exclusion of any other. This prohibition of religious pluralism lasted until 1915, when the first Freedom of Worship law was adopted. In spite of this law, various constitutions of the 20th century, including the current Constitution of 1993, have continued to affirm the State's legal and financial support of the Catholic Church.

Progress toward pluralism continues nonetheless. During the last 30-40 years there has been significant growth in newer religious movements, such as various Evangelical churches, Seventh-day Adventists, and The Church of Jesus Christ of Latter-day Saints (the Mormons). For example, the Mormons now count almost 400,000 members in Peru. In 2003 the Ministry of Justice established a Department of Non-Catholic Religions, the first Peruvian government agency to recognize such religious groups. This new religious fervor in Latin America contrasts sharply with trends in Europe. At the same time that the number of Christians attending church in Europe has fallen drastically, the number of Peruvians participating in weekly religious activity has greatly increased.

There are many theories to explain this spiritual revolution. It is surely a multifaceted phenomenon, but factors probably include the very deep personal experience and broad commitment expected by these new religions. In this regard, the growth of new movements may actually hearken back to the all-encompassing spiritualism inherent in the ancient heritage of the Peruvian people.

Scott E. Isaacson, J.D. is the Executive Director of Fellows at the International Center for Law and Religion Studies at Brigham Young University.

ON THE MENU

AN UNCOMMON KOLA

The fluorescent yellow glow envelops the country; the sweet aroma of bubble gum hangs in the air. As any visitor to Peru will soon discover, the omnipresent Inca Kola (also spelled "Inka Cola" or "Inka Kola") is more than a soda; it's a national symbol. After hitting the markets in 1935, Inca Kola has dominated Peruvian soda culture for decades, never once altering its secret, fruity formula. The overwhelmingly artificial drink may be an acquired taste, but it instills a sense of national pride in the many Peruvians who gulp it by the liter. In fact, Peru is one of the few countries where Coca-Cola is challenged as the leading soft drink. For years, Inca Kola officials claimed that they dominated the market, while, not surprisingly, the folks at Coke said that their product was slightly in the lead.

These days, however, both colas face another threat: Kola Real, a cheap and convincingly Coke-like drink encroaching on Latin American beverage markets. Coca Cola and Inca Kola are teaming up to defeat the newcomer. In 1999, Coca Cola acquired the Inca Kola trademark everywhere except Peru, and in 2004 the owner of Inca Kola purchased an 80% share in the Peruvian Coca Cola bottler. There's some comfort for Peruvians: like Inca Kola, Kola Real is based in Peru, so no matter the results of the battle, Peru will always have a fizzy source of national pride.

serve seafood, especially *ceviche*. **Pollerías** serve scrumptious **pollo a la brasa** (roasted chicken). Larger and more touristed cities also offer all the fast food, international food, and vegetarian options you're accustomed to at home.

Breakfast food can be found in most any *comedor*, though *desayuno* (breakfast) is usually light. Most common are bread, juice, coffee, eggs, and sometimes rice and beans, as well as plantain dishes such as **chirriados** in certain regions. Well-touristed areas may offer a *desayuno americano*, which includes a bit more food for the more voracious appetite. If you don't mind a light breakfast (or want a midday snack), a quick and easy way to grab a bite is to buy fruit at the local **mercado** (market) or visit a **panadería** (bakery).

Juices made from the region's abundant exotic fruits are common and delicious, especially closer to the jungle. **Coffee,** however, is not as good as it should be, considering that the beans come from the region. It is usually served as *esencia* (boiled-down, concentrated grinds mixed with water or milk). You might also be served hot water with a can of Nescafé instant coffee. *Mate de coca* (coca tea) is a good cure for altitude sickness, and a local specialty. A favorite dairy drink is **yogur,** a drinkable combination of milk and yogurt.

If you're looking for something more intoxicating, never fear. South American liquor is cheap and abundant. Any Peruvian will be quick to tell you that food is always followed by a drink, and another drink…and another. Many a tasty brew is made from **aguardiente,** an extremely potent sugarcane alcohol. And then, of course, there's the omnipresent **chicha,** a liquor made from the yucca plant and fermented with the saliva of the women who brew it. Look for it in houses that fly white or red flags over their doors. The Peruvian drink of choice is the traditional **chicha morada,** a sweet purple beverage made from corn. **Non-alcoholic chichas** (also non-saliva) come in myriad varieties throughout the region, and are occasionally served straight out of a plastic bag. Local favorites are usually named after parts of the country itself, so drinking could be considered a form of travel: **pisco,** clear white brandy with a tequila-like kick, most often comes in the form of a **pisco sour—** mixed with lemon juice, egg whites, and sugar. Another favorite is the **Peru libre,** a combination of Coca-Cola and *pisco*. The most popular beers are also tied to cities—**Cusqueña** and **Arequipeña** dominate their respective regions while **Cristál** is a more general interloper. However, when sobriety is a priority, opt for **Inca Kola** (see **An Uncommon Kola**).

Unless urgent visits to the nearest restroom are your idea of fun, **avoid drinking tap water.** Water advertised as *purificada* (purified) may have only been passed through a filter, which does not necessarily catch all of those **diarrhea-causing demons.** Water that has been boiled or treated with iodine is safe to drink; otherwise, **bottled water** is best. Watch out for *refrescos* and other water-based juices and avoid freshly-washed fruit. Also use bottled water when brushing teeth.

CUSTOMS AND ETIQUETTE

WOMEN AND MEN. Foreign visitors to Latin America are often shocked by the culture of **machismo.** Women are frequently subject to whistling, catcalls, or other advances on the street, most of which are harmless if ignored. Women in bars—and foreign women in general—are often regarded as promiscuous. Females who drink and act rowdy, or even just express their opinions in a public setting, will shock men who expect and prize meekness in women. Whether you're male or female, be sensitive to rising testosterone levels. Never say anything about a man's mother, sister, wife, or girlfriend. On the flip side, men are generally courteous, especially to older women (see **Machismo Defined,** p. 164).

APPEARANCE. Personal hygiene and appearance are often difficult to maintain while traveling, but they are very important. Clean-shaven men with short hair and women who don't show much skin are more likely to receive respect than scruffy mop-heads or bra-less women. Men should remove hats while indoors. When entering churches, cathedrals, or other houses of worship, women's shoulders should be covered and they should avoid wearing short skirts or very short shorts.

COMMUNICATION AND BODY LANGUAGE. Latin Americans hold politeness in high esteem, among both acquaintances and strangers. When meeting someone for the first time, shake hands firmly, look the person in the eye, and say *"Mucho gusto de conocerle"* ("Pleased to meet you"). When entering a room, greet everybody, not just the person you came to see. Females often greet each other with a peck on the cheek or a quick hug. Sometimes men shake hands with women in a business situation, but the standard greeting between a man and a woman—even upon meeting for the first time—is a quick kiss on the cheek. **Salutations** are considered common courtesy in small towns. *"Buenos días"* in the morning, *"buenas tardes"* after noon, and *"buenas noches"* after dusk should be said to anyone with whom you come into contact. It is also customary to say *"buen provecho"* ("enjoy your meal") to those with whom you dine.

When signaling for people, don't use one finger pointed upward; simply motioning with your hand in a sweeping motion is more polite. The American "OK" symbol (a circle with the thumb and forefinger) is considered vulgar and offensive. Spitting is perfectly acceptable in this region—but beware of the burp, as it is considered rude in public.

TIME. Punctuality isn't as important in Peru as it is in Europe and the US (as bus schedules will quickly confirm), but there are, of course, limits. A different perspective on time is apparent during meals, which are rarely hurried. After a big meal, enjoy the ingenious tradition of *siesta*, a time in the afternoon when it's just too hot to do anything but relax, have a drink, or nap; don't expect much to happen during the mid-afternoon, as banks and shops often shut their doors.

PHOTOGRAPHY. Be sensitive when taking photographs. If you must take pictures of locals, first ask permission—they may object strongly to being photographed, and if they don't, they may ask for a tip.

THE ARTS

ARCHITECTURE

While Peru is home to some of the most spectacular architectural achievements in history, many of the country's ruins no longer stand, either because of the forces of nature or because the Spanish destroyed or co-opted their buildings. The new has remained intimately connected to the old; a number of important towns are built on the rubble of the Inca civilization, and in many cases, the Spaniards even reused Inca building stones. Many hilltop colonial churches were built over the foundations of Inca temples.

Colonial architecture is a blend of the Old and New Worlds: Spaniards commissioned works to be done in the Baroque style, but *indígenas* who executed the works added their own distinctive cultural touches. Religious institutions have the aesthetic upper hand—churches and convents in older towns are decorated with intricately carved facades, ornate interiors sparkling with gilt, and leafy stone vines wrapping around classically styled columns. Municipal buildings and private residences are usually more modest two-story buildings with high ceilings, interior courtyards, covered verandas, and large wooden doors. The region's urban centers were built more for walking than looking, as evidenced by the blocky concrete buildings that dominate the downtown areas of most larger cities. Most of these buildings were erected in the 20th century, when architects were primarily concerned with keeping building costs low.

ART

Although the most famous examples of pre-conquest artistic expression in Peru are architectural (Machu Picchu, Chan Chan), beautifully decorated ceramics and textiles reveal the richness of ancient art. Much of this pre-Columbian art was destroyed in the conquest, however, including the priceless gold and silver pieces acquired by the Spaniards as Atahuallpa's ransom.

In the 16th century, Spanish colonization brought European art to the New World. Flemish, Italian, and Spanish religious paintings were used to illustrate the teachings of Christianity. By the 17th century, newly converted natives who had been trained in contemporary styles of painting began to add local touches to their works of art. The tradition that developed, known as the **Cusco School,** reflects the mixture of European and Peruvian influences. For example, a famous painting of *The Last Supper* by acclaimed artist **Marcos Zapata** depicts the well-known religious scene with a distinctly Andean twist—the subjects of the painting are feasting on *cuy* (guinea pig).

In the late 19th and early 20th century the tide turned as the celebration of indigenous culture was all the rage and the Spanish influence was abandoned. This **indigenista movement** was reflected in the work of artists such as Cajabamba native **José Sabogal.** After traveling through Europe, Sabogal returned to Cusco, rejected the Old World, and devoted his life to painting the people and places of Peru.

Modern Peruvian art has tended toward the abstract, but varies greatly, as seen in the multitude of museums throughout the country. Inca heritage and indigenous culture continue to be influential, as demonstrated by the world-renowned **Usko-Ayar Amazonian School of Painting** in Pucallpa (p. 413). The works produced by founder and visionary painter **Pablo Amaringo** and his students celebrate the flora, fauna, and culture of the Amazon and its native peoples.

LITERATURE

The lack of a written language prior to the conquest greatly limited "Peruvian literature," but traditional stories and historical accounts were passed down to future generations in oral and pictographic forms. After the Spanish Conquest, a rich body of literature developed out of the folklore and history of the region. The most popular colonial writer was **El Inca Garcilaso de la Vega,** the son of an Inca princess and a Spanish conquistador who spent much of his professional life in Spain. One of his famous books, *Comentarios Reales de los Incas* (1609), recorded the last days of the Inca Empire. Other colonial works consisted primarily of Spanish missionaries's extremely biased accounts of native life.

The first independently Peruvian literary movement, known as **costumbrismo** and developed in the 19th century, centered around glorifying or condemning the various elements of Peruvian history, the indigenous and the Spanish. Notable *costumbrismo* author **Ricardo Palma** (1833-1919) was famous for his satires collected in *Peruvian Traditions*. The most celebrated Peruvian poet, **César Vallejo** (1892-1938), wrote modernist works dealing with issues of humanity and historical realism. His most notable collections are *Los Heraldos Negros* (1918), *Trilce* (1922), and *Poemas Humanos* (1939).

The 20th century brought new ideas and two internationally renowned authors. Easily the most famous—and most notorious—Peruvian writer is **Mario Vargas Llosa.** His first novel, *La Ciudad y los Perros* (1963), commented indirectly on political injustice. Many of his works, such as *La Casa Verde* (1969), have been stylistically experimental as well as controversial. In 1990 Llosa unsuccessfully ran against Alberto Fujimori for the presidency of Peru (see **Fujimori and Success,** p. 67). The election has not affected the quality of his writing—one of his newer works, *Lituma en los Andes* (1993), is regarded as one of his best. Less famous, but also noteworthy, **José María Arguedas** (1911-1965) took a break from his day job as an anthropologist to explore the complexities of Andean cosmopolitanism. Arguedas's claim to fame lies in his incorporation of Quechua words into his work (see **José María Arguedas,** p. 306).

LIFE AND TIMES

MUSIC

The traditional music of Peru is a fresh combination of Spanish and pre-Hispanic musical styles. Traditional instruments and harmonies influence modern pop music, but also form an important genre in their own right. Although these traditional tunes may not make the Top 40 charts, they are an important (and exportable) part of Peruvian culture.

The most recognizable Andean instrument is the **panpipe** or *rondador*, made from cane and believed to be over 2000 years old. Its relative, the **zampoña,** comes from the southern Andes and has two rows of pipes instead of one. This instrument, along with the five-note scale on which the tunes are based, gives Andean music its distinctively haunting sound. In addition to pipes, two flutes are often used—the larger **quena,** which resembles a recorder, and the smaller **pingullu.** The panpipes and flutes, along with percussive instruments like bells, drums, and **maracas** (rattles made from gourds), are all indigenous innovations.

Traditional music also uses instruments of European origin like the **guitar** and its smaller relative, the **charango,** which often combine with the mandolin. All these have evolved into their own unique Peruvian varieties. Along the southern coast, Afro-Peruvian bands play *música negra* using unique instruments like the **quijada,** a percussion instrument made from the jawbone of a donkey.

ARTESANÍA

Folk art is fundamental to Peruvian culture and to many Peruvians' way of life. The highlands in Ayacucho and Huancayo (including the surrounding Río Mantaro region) are jewels of the Peruvian **textile** industry, and Lake Titicaca's **Isla Taquile** is also famous for its fine-spun products. Most textiles use sheep, llama, or alpaca wool, while more expensive items entail softer vicuña wool, a much rarer find.

Woodwork is also a trademark of the Andes, ranging from intricate wooden boxes to sculptures to furniture, all made and often sold out of artisans' homes. In Peru's Río Mantaro region, **gourds** known as *matés burilados* carved with scenes of farming life make popular gifts. Peru also has its share of reputable **ceramics** influenced heavily by indigenous cultures. Not all folk art needs to be built to last, though; some of the most fleeting art is the most beautiful, like the carpets of flower petals **(alfombras de flores)** that often adorn plazas during festivals, or the decorated **t'anta wawas** breads depicting children or animals.

TRADITIONAL CLOTHING

Traditional Peruvian dress is the result of a fusion of brilliant native color and fabric with the more dour European styles brought by the Spanish. Red is a common color, but colors and patterns are often unique to regions; for example, the heavy ponchos that men wear in Cusco might be short with black designs against a red background, but in Puno they are longer and dyed crimson for special occasions. Women wear any number of variations on a theme: black or multicolored skirts with colorful decorative belts over layers of intricately embroidered petticoats and blouses. Straw hats might be used to keep out the sun in warm areas; brightly-colored woolen caps, often with earflaps, keep out the chill high in the Andes. The *cushma* is a loose unisex tunic sewn up both sides worn in some jungle tribes. These styles are generally only found in rural areas; city-dwellers and younger parts of the population dress more or less like inhabitants of any Western city.

POPULAR CULTURE

MUSIC

Despite the abundance of American pop, Peru does have its own modern music. In the highlands, the most popular genre, **Huayno,** incorporates high-pitched voices, traditional flutes, and an unchanging beat. Some of the most famous Huayno titles include *Valicha, Mamita Corazón,* and *El Picaflor.*

Toward the jungle, traditional music takes on a more Brazilian flavor, with drums at center stage. Especially prominent are the **Semiotic drums,** created by the Bora natives. These drums are made from tree trunks and were originally used for long-distance communication.

Traditional music is prevalent and popular, but so is rock and roll. The most notable rock group in Peruvian history is **Arena Hash,** four male teenagers who attended high school near Lima in 1987. The band was a huge hit throughout Peru, and their song *Cuando la cama me da vueltas* was distinguished by Panamericana as "the most popular rock single among Peruvian and foreign artists." The band broke up, but bassist **Christian Meier** dropped his last name and launched a successful solo career in the mid-90s. Other popular groups include **Agua Bella, Grupo Karakol, Agua Marina, Rossy War,** and **Pepe Vásquez.**

FILM

These days the best-known film in Peru might be the one that recorded the corruption of Vladimiro Montesinos, ending the Fujimori administration in 2001 (see **The Turn of the Century,** p. 68). Still, Peru has made significant contributions to the Latin American film scene. The current director of note in Peru is Tacna native **Francisco Lombardi,** who first achieved notoriety with **La Ciudad y los Perros** (*The City and the Dogs;* 1985), an adaptation of the Mario Vargas Llosa novel. **La Boca del Lobo** (*The Mouth of the Wolf;* 1988) brought international attention to the conflict between the Shining Path and the Peruvian military. Lombardi followed this success with another highly acclaimed film, **Caídos del Cielo** (*Fallen from Heaven;* 1990), in which he tries to address philosophical issues like the meaning of life; his most recent film, **Tinta Roja** (*Red Ink;* 2000), shows two aspiring journalists in Lima. Other Peruvian directors include Alberto Durant, who directed 1991's **Alias, La Gringa** and whose film **Coraje** (*Courage;* 1998) offers a rare look at issues facing Peruvian women. Augusto Tamayo San Ramón has also met with international success: his **Anda, Corre, Vuelva** (*Walk, Run, Return;* 1995), debuted at the 1996 Hispanic Film Festival, and traces three young Peruvians facing terrorism and violence in Lima.

TELEVISION

The most popular shows in Peru are **soccer,** soccer, and soccer. During any *fútbol* game everyone in town flocks to the nearest TV. Televisions are prevalent throughout Peru, and even poor rural families will splurge for this vicarious entertainment. When there is no soccer match occurring, Peruvians turn to talk shows and **telenovelas** (soap operas). Three national television stations broadcast out of Lima via more than 60 local stations, but most shows are cheesy foreign imports or dubbed American sitcoms.

NEWSPAPERS

Almost every town in Peru with any significant population has a small daily paper, but the principal Peruvian papers come out of Lima. **El Comercio** and **La República** are the two most influential. Operating since 1825, **El Peruano** is one of the oldest papers in the Americas. Others include **Liberación, El Ojo,** and **Expreso.** Although the press has theoretically been free from government control since 1980, newspapers are notoriously partial and openly demonstrate a strong political bias during elections. Smaller newspapers focus on specific topics like sports (*fútbol* maybe?).

SPORTS AND RECREATION

Like most of Latin America, Peru treats soccer—known everywhere but the US as "football" or **fútbol**—as a national passion and pastime. Distant runners-up include **basketball** and **volleyball,** which have become quite popular in recent years.

If the courts don't do it for you, the slightly more adventurous can experience the thrills of the Andes. The mountain range is home to some of the best **trekking** and **mountaineering** in the world. With dozens of peaks over 5000m high, Peru has become a prime destination for serious mountain climbers from across the globe. The Cordillera Blanca provides phenomenal snow-capped peaks and has attracted growing numbers of **skiers** and **snowboarders.** If water's your thing, there is excellent **whitewater rafting** and **kayaking** through raging rivers from the mountains to either the Pacific or the tropical Amazon Basin. Be sure to find out which rivers are safe during the rainy or dry seasons and plan your trip accordingly. **Surfing** has also emerged in the region, with truly bodacious waves up and down Peru's coast. Hate the water, but want to surf? Try **sandboarding** in Huacachina: "surf" shops there will rent out sandboards and wax, and even give you your first lesson on the enormous dunes. For more sedate activity, the valleys created by volcanic peaks provide perfect conditions for short- or long-distance **hikes** through pristine countryside.

BULLFIGHTING

Bullfighting is not just for Spaniards. Peru leads the charge of Latin American bullfighting's popularity, holding various *ferias* (fairs) throughout the year. Unlike European bullfighting, where matches are held seasonally, Latin America holds *ferias* year-round, and fans consistently fill the stadiums. Lima is the season's pilot location, holding the **Feria del Señor de los Milagros,** the oldest fair in South America. The *feria* takes place in **Plaza del Acho,** the continent's oldest bullring.

FESTIVALS AND HOLIDAYS

Peruvians like to party, and often; even if you don't plan to attend any festivals, you'll probably stumble across at least one. Take note of festival dates, as hotels fill up quickly and banks, restaurants, stores, and museums may close, leaving you homeless, broke, and hungry. When traveling on or around major festival days, reserve accommodations well in advance. Local tourist offices can provide information about regional festivals, and **PromPeru** (p. 11) maintains a calendar of festivals throughout the country on its website (www.peru.org.pe).

Semana Santa (Holy Week), immediately preceding Easter, brings the most parties in these Andean nations. Ayacucho and Cusco are regarded as the best places to experience this celebration. However, large festivals can be found in most cities, especially in the Highlands. As one might expect, **Navidad** (Christmas), on December 25, is another important religious holiday, but instead of a commercial onslaught of pine trees and Santa-inspired clearance sales, processions of the Christ child dominate. **Carnaval** celebrations occur the week before Lent. In Cajamarca and other highland cities, townspeople run around flinging water, paint, oil, and other liquids at each other (and at gawking tourists). **Día de los Difuntos** (Day of the Dead; Nov. 2) combines the Catholic tradition of All Souls' Day with *indígena* burial rituals. Offerings of food, along with little bread renditions of people and animals, are laid on top of the graves of relatives. Many Highland towns also hold a **Corpus Christi** (Body of Christ) celebration in early June.

Not all regional celebrations are rooted in Catholicism; especially in the highlands and in the jungle regions, locals continue to celebrate holidays honoring non-Christian deities. The most famous of these is the festival of **Inti Raymi** ("Festival of the Sun" in Quechua), celebrated in Cusco on June 18-24. A tribute to the Inca sun god Inti, this solstice festival involves colorful parades, traditional dances, live music, and an oration in Quechua given at the archaeological complex of Sacsayhuamán. Hordes of tourists come to the city, helping to make it the second largest festival in Latin America.

Most towns celebrate an **Independence Day** associated with the date on which they were liberated from Spain. Peruvians go all out for their **Fiestas Patrias** on July 27-29; even in the smallest towns, schoolchildren begin practicing weeks in advance for the parades.

DATE	FESTIVAL	DESCRIPTION
January 1-6	El Año Nuevo	New Year's Day, with festivals throughout the week
January 6	Bajada de Reyes	Festival of the Three Kings (Epiphany)
January 18	Aniversario de la Fundación de Lima	Anniversary of the Founding of Lima
February 1-7	Fiesta de la Virgen de la Candelaria	Festival of the Virgin of the Candelaria (Puno)
mid-February	El Año Nuevo de China	Chinese New Year (Chinatown, Lima)
mid-February	Festival de Arroz	Rice Festival (Camaná)
late February	Verano Negro	Black Summer (Chincha)
February 30	Festival de Celebración y Festejo	Festival of Celebration and Festivity
early March	Carnaval	Carnival (throughout South America)
early March	Fiesta de la Uva, el Vino y el Canotaje	Festival celebrating wine (Lunahuaná)
mid-April	Semana Santa	Holy Week
mid-April	El Día de Pascua	Easter

DATE	FESTIVAL	DESCRIPTION
May 1	Día del Trabajador	Labor Day
May 1	Virgen de Chapi	Virgin of Chapi (Arequipa)
June 19	Corpus Christi	Body of Christ
June 24	Fiesta de San Juan/Inti Raymi	Saint John the Baptist's Day/Festival of the Sun (largest celebration in Cusco)
June 29	Festividad de San Pedro y San Pablo	Saint Peter's and Saint Paul's Day
July 14-16	Celebración de la Virgen del Carmen	Celebration of the Virgin of Carmen
late July	Semana de Huaraz	Huaraz Week (Huaraz)
July 27-29	Fiesta del Sol Fiestas Patrias	Festival of the Sun (Huánuco) National Holidays (Independence Day)
throughout July	Semanas Turísticas	Tourist weeks (throughout Peru)
mid-August	Aniversario de la Fundación de Huánuco	Anniversary of the founding of Huánuco
August 15	Aniversario de la Fundación de Arequipa	Anniversary of the founding of Arequipa
August 30	Fiesta de Santa Rosa de Lima	Celebration of Santa Rosa, patron saint of Lima
October 4	Virgen del Rosario	Virgin of the Rosary
October 18-28	El Señor de los Milagros	Lord of the Miracles (Lima)
November 1-2	Día de los Santos y de los Difuntos	All Saints' and All Souls' Day
November 1-7	Semana de Puno	Puno Week (Puno)
December 8	Día de la Inmaculada Concepción	Day of the Immaculate Conception
December 25	La Navidad	Christmas Day
December 28	Los Santos Inocentes	All Fools' Day
December 31	Incineración del Año Viejo	New Year's Eve

LIFE AND TIMES

ADDITIONAL RESOURCES

What follows is a list of our favorite books about (in one way or another) Peru—in print, available in English, and never, ever dull:

GENERAL INFORMATION

Art of the Andes: From Chavín to Inca, by Rebecca Stone-Miller. This book and its 185 photographs detail the history of every kind of art in Andean regions, from mummies to murals, textiles to ceramics, stonework to shamanism.

Machu Picchu, by Barry Brukoff. Breathtaking color photographs are interspersed with verses from Pablo Neruda's epic poem, "Alturas de Machu Picchu."

Peru In Focus, by Jane Holligan de Díaz Límaco. A no-nonsense overview of all things Peruvian. A concise resource for travelers.

The Peru Reader: History, Culture, Politics, by Orin Starn, Carlos Ivan Degregori, and Robin Kirk. An introduction to various aspects of the country.

HISTORY

The Ancient Kingdoms of Peru, by Nigel Davies. The author, an expert in all things Inca, offers new insights into the civilizations of pre-Hispanic Peru.

Born in Blood and Fire: A Concise History of Latin America, by John Charles Chasteen. A thorough yet concise introduction to South American history.

The Conquest of the Incas, by John Hemming. This new book vividly describes the turbulent end of the Inca Empire and the subsequent amalgamation of Spanish and native cultures, using firsthand accounts to shed light on this time period.

The Incas, by Terence Daltroy. A synthesis of the most recent research into Inca history, culture, politics, and ideology.

The Incas and their Ancestors: The Archaeology of Peru, by Michael E. Moseley. Detailed drawings and explanations of important archaeological sites in Peru, along with a brief history of the relevant ancient civilizations.

The Incas: People of the Sun, by Carmen Bernard. This 190-page history of the Inca Empire reads like a grade-school textbook, complete with big print, glossy paper, and tons of pictures. A perfect introduction to the ancient empire.

Machu Picchu: Unveiling the Mystery of the Incas, edited by Richard L. Burger and Lucy C. Salazar. This illustrated book was written to accompany an exhibition of Inca artifacts sponsored by Yale, and includes Hiram Bingham's original account of the 1911 Yale Expedition that discovered Machu Picchu.

The Shining Path: A History of the Millenarian War in Peru, by Gustavo Gorriti Ellenbogen et al. One of the most recent accounts of the savage rise and fall of the Shining Path Terrorist movement.

FICTION AND NON-FICTION

The Celestine Prophecy: An Adventure, by James Redfield. Controversial best-seller. Purports to be the true story of the "author's" spiritual self-discovery in Peru.

Death in the Andes, by Mario Vargas Llosa. Peru's most famous author and one-time presidential candidate recounts a surreal and haunting story of an isolated Andean village plagued by avalanches and Shining Path terrorists.

The Other Path: The Economic Answer to Terrorism, by Hernando de Soto. This captivating book investigates Lima's so-called "informal" economy, revolutionizing the study of some of Latin America's deepest social and economic problems in terms it doesn't take an economist to understand.

Royal Commentaries of the Incas and General History of Peru, by El Inca Garcilaso de la Vega. The rise and fall of the Incas as told by the most famous early Peruvian writer, the 16th-century son of a conquistador and an Inca princess.

The Storyteller, by Mario Vargas Llosa. A modern fable that weaves cultural questions into an engrossing mystery about indigenous people in the Peruvian Amazon.

Sweat of the Sun, Tears of the Moon: A Chronicle of an Incan Treasure, by Peter Lourie. The captivating true story of a treasure hunt in the Andes.

'Tambo: Life in an Andean Village, by Julia Meyerson. The journal of the author's stay in a small Peruvian village while her husband, an archaeologist, was doing fieldwork.

The White Rock: An Exploration of the Inca Heartland, by Hugh Thompson. The author—also a documentary film maker—recounts his successful 1982 expedition to find the lost Inca city of Llactapata, weaving Inca history and 45 black-and-white photographs into his narrative.

ALTERNATIVES TO TOURISM

A PHILOSOPHY FOR TRAVELERS

Let's Go believes that the connection between travelers and their destinations is an important one. Over the years, we've watched the growth of the "ignorant tourist" stereotype with dismay, knowing that many travelers care passionately about the communities and environments they explore—but also knowing that even conscientious tourists can inadvertently damage natural wonders and harm cultural environments. With this "Alternatives to Tourism" chapter, *Let's Go* hopes to promote a better understanding of Peru and enhance your experience there.

In the developing world, there are several options for those who seek to participate in alternatives to tourism. Opportunities for **volunteering** abound, both with local and international organizations. **Studying** can also be instructive, either in the form of direct enrollment in a local university or in an independent research project. *Let's Go* discourages **working** in the developing world due to high local unemployment rates and weak economies.

As a **volunteer** in Peru, you can participate in projects from researching parrots in the rainforest to teaching special-needs children in remote villages in the Andes, either on a short-term basis or as the main component of your trip. Peru's biologically diverse regions are increasingly the subject of conservation efforts, especially as the nation moves to develop its great potential in the ecotourism industry. Its many bio-reserves welcome help in studying and preserving the country's threatened flora and fauna. Simultaneously, the demand has grown for English classes in rural areas and cities alike, where the language is a useful tool for developing ecotourism and business. Teaching Peruvians English equips them with a tool to help them better participate in the global community. Many programs, particularly those in urban areas, offer the opportunity to volunteer, participate in a homestay, learn Spanish, and tour different areas of the nation. Other volunteerism organizations offer multiple options for service, ranging from building trails in remote areas to helping out in orphanages. While many programs do not require fluency in Spanish, familiarity with the language is useful, and many organizations provide opportunities to learn, both formally and informally. Later in this section, we recommend organizations that can help you find the opportunities that best suit your interests, whether you're looking to pitch in for a day or a year.

Studying at a college or language program is another option. There are many language schools in Peru, geared toward students of all ages. Most are flexible in terms of their period of study, ranging from several weeks in the summer to over a year. Many help coordinate further travel or volunteerism projects for students, as well. Programs generally include homestays, which encourage further cultural immersion. Other students choose to live in apartments in urban areas, often in group settings. Studying in Peru incorporates the student into a world that a tourist might have more difficulty discovering. Besides having the opportunity to develop personal relationships with Peruvians in an academic setting, international students in Peru also experience the nation's dynamic culture.

Start your search at ■ **www.beyondtourism.com,** *Let's Go*'s brand-new search-able database of Alternatives to Tourism, where you can find exciting feature arti-cles and helpful program listings divided by country, continent, and program type.

VOLUNTEERING

Peru, a country rich in culture and history, also boasts natural diversity and great potential for economic and social development. Unfortunately, Peru also has sig-nificant contemporary concerns in areas such as rainforest conservation and clos-ing the economic gap that currently exists between those living in urban and in rural areas. Volunteering opportunities in Peru range from helping indigenous communities develop their economies to working on a butterfly farm in the Ama-zon, one of the most ecologically rich areas of the world. Volunteering can be one of the most fulfilling experiences you have in life, especially if you combine it with the thrill of traveling in a new place. Volunteering in any developing country can be dangerous for a foreigner, and Peru is not immune to the threats of crime and environmental risks less common in the developed world. However, the rewards of giving your time and energy to causes that improve Peru, and which in many cases have global impact, are enormous.

People who volunteer in Peru often do so on a short-term basis, at organizations that make use of drop-in or once-a-week volunteers. Most participants in short-term work in Peru choose to work in cities like Lima and Cusco, where they can combine living in a major metropolitan area with community service. Others choose to head to the jungle, engaging in conservation activities. Much short-term volunteer work involves working on reserves in rainforest conservation, or work-ing with vulnerable children in cities. Try to research potential programs before committing—talk to people who have participated and find out exactly what you're getting into, as living and working conditions can vary greatly. Different programs are geared toward different ages and levels of experience, so avoid tak-ing on too much or too little. The more informed you are and the more realistic your expectations, the more enjoyable the program will be.

Many volunteer services charge you a fee to participate. These costs can be sur-prisingly hefty (although they frequently cover airfare and most, if not all, living expenses). Most people choose to go through a parent organization that works out logistical details and frequently provides a group environment and support sys-tem. There are two main types of organizations—religious and non-sectarian—although there are rarely restrictions on participation for either.

GENERAL COMMUNITY SERVICE

These parent organizations coordinate volunteer placements in a wide variety of fields. International service groups often have programs in several nations, including Peru. Peruvian programs place international volunteers in many different types of ser-vice, without emphasizing a specific area. These are run by Peruvians themselves, many of whom are members of the communities which their programs serve. From planting trees to building houses, these organizations offer something for everyone.

American Jewish World Service, 45 W. 36th St., 10th fl., New York, NY, 10018, US (☎212-736-2597 or 800-889-7146; www.ajws.org). Projects in Peru include working for *Solas y Unidas,* an empowerment group for women affected by HIV/AIDS, and with a reproductive health and rights education program with Asháninka women. Volunteers must be 25+.

Cross-Cultural Solutions, 47 Potter Ave., New Rochelle, NY 10801, US (☎800-380-4777 or 914-632-0022; www.crossculturalsolutions.org), provides short- and long-term humanitarian placements in health care, education, and social development. Fees range US$2100-4200.

Elderhostel, Inc., 11 Av. de Lafayette, Boston, MA 92111-1746, US (☎877-426-8056; www.elderhostel.org), sends volunteers 55+ around the world to work in construction, research, teaching, and many other projects. Costs average US$100 per day plus airfare.

Global Routes, 1 Short St., Northampton MA 01060, US (☎413-585-8895; www.globalroutes.org), has high-school programs focused on construction and college teaching internships throughout the world; both involve homestays. Programs cost US$4000, excluding airfare.

Habitat for Humanity International, 121 Habitat St., Americus, GA 31709, US (☎229-924-6935 ext. 2551; www.habitat.org), organizes volunteers to build houses in over 83 countries. Programs last 2 weeks-3yr. Short-term programs US$1200-4000.

InterExchange, 161 6th Ave., New York, NY 10013, US (☎212-924-0446; www.interexchange.org). 8-week program places volunteers (23+) in 4 weeks of intensive Spanish classes in Cusco, and then 4 weeks of service. Volunteer placements are available in social work, healthcare, culture, education, and tourism. Volunteers live with host families for the first 4 weeks, and in student residences for the last 4. US$1450.

i-to-i, 190 9th Ave., Ste. 320, Denver, CO 80203, US (☎800-985-4864 or 303-765-5325; www.i-to-i.com). Volunteers (18+) can work on teaching projects in a Lima orphanage, teaching tour guides in the Amazon jungle, conservation projects on the Pacific coast, or historical preservation. Programs typically last 9-12 weeks.

Peace Corps, Office of Volunteer Recruitment and Selection, 1111 20th St. NW, Washington, D.C. 20526, US (☎800-424-8580; www.peacecorps.gov). Opportunities in 70 developing nations, including Peru. For US citizens 18+, 2-year commitment required.

Service Civil International Voluntary Service (SCI-IVS), SCI USA, 3213 W. Wheeler St., Seattle, WA 98199, US (☎/fax 206-350-6585; www.sci-ivs.org), arranges placement in Peruvian work camps for those 18+. Registration US$65-125.

Volunteers for Peace, 1034 Tiffany Rd., Belmont, VT 05730, US (☎802-259-2759; www.vfp.org), arranges placement in work camps in Peru. Membership required for registration. Annual *International Workcamp Directory* US$20. Programs average US$200-500 for 2-3 weeks.

ENVIRONMENTAL CONSERVATION

Conservation is one of the most critical issues in Peru. Preserving the vast array of flora and fauna in this biodiversity hotspot is the goal of numerous programs. From protecting tropical rainforests to managing organic farms, there's an organization for every cause.

INTERNATIONAL PROGRAMS

Earthwatch, 3 Clocktower Pl., Ste. 100, Maynard, MA 01754, US (☎800-776-0188 or 978-461-0081; www.earthwatch.org). Arranges 1- to 3-week programs throughout Peru to promote conservation of natural resources. Fees vary based on program location and duration, but average US$1700 excluding airfare.

ProWorld Service Corps, 264 E. 10th St., No. 5, New York, NY 10009, US (☎877-733-7378; www.proworldsc.org). Volunteers (18+) work at the Manú Rainforest Nature Reserve in anthropology, biological research, community development, environmental issues, and reforestation. Other opportunities in health care and teaching in the Sacred Valley of the Incas.

LOCAL PROGRAMS

AEDES, Cooperativa John Kennedy A1, Arequipa (☎054 43 0794; www.aedes.com.pe). Tourists can volunteer in the Bustamante y Rivero district, an ecological association specializing in ecotourism.

Casa Ecológica Cusco, Triunfo 393, Cusco (☎25 5646), in a hippie-feeling *plazoleta.* Organizes reforestation efforts in the jungle that can be done as daytrips from Cusco. Open M-Sa 10am-8pm, Su 4-8pm.

Mosoq Kausay, Shakra de Efrain, Arin, Cusco (www.travatools.com/mosoqkausay). Volunteers of any age interested in permaculture and sustainable agriculture work on conservation and organic farming projects in the Sacred Valley. The program seeks to promote the economy of the local people while allowing them to share the agricultural skills and customs of their ancestors with international volunteers. Activities include learning to plow with oxen and practicing Quechua stonewalling.

Pilpintuwasi Butterfly Farm, Iquitos (☎23 2665; pilpintuwasi@hotmail.com). Austrian Gudrun Sperrer's butterfly farm shows off over 40 species of the most colorful (and least dangerous) insects of the Amazon. Opportunities are available for volunteers seeking to help out and learn more about raising the insects. (See p. 393.)

Tambopata Reserve Society (TReeS), 488 Calle Lambayeque, Puerto Maldonado (☎84 57 2788; www.geocities.com/treesweb). Volunteers (18+) work on 3 separate teams: 1 for mammals, 1 for birds, and 1 for reptiles. Teams spend 2 weeks at each of 5 lodges. English spoken.

RURAL DEVELOPMENT

The rural areas of Peru see little of the comparative wealth found in the country's cities. Child malnutrition and infant mortality are twice as high in rural areas as in the cities. Aboriginal groups in particular lack adequate education, healthcare, and nutrition. Volunteers help educate children and teach rural populations of Peru about sustainable agriculture to help develop their economies.

INTERNATIONAL PROGRAMS

Amigos de las Americas, 5618 Star Ln., Houston, TX 77057, US (☎800-231-7796; www.amigoslink.org). Sends high-school and college students in groups of 2-3 to work in rural Latin American communities for up to 8 weeks. 1yr. of previous Spanish instruction required. Costs average US$3500, including airfare.

Foundation for Sustainable Development, 59 Driftwood Ct., San Rafael, CA 94901, US (☎415-482-9366; www.fsdinternational.org). Supports grassroots development in rural communities. Volunteers work as interns to promote legal and human rights. Most volunteers are college students, graduate students, and professionals who desire practical work experience with a local nonprofit organization. Accommodations are generally homestays. The Peru program is based in Puno. US$2100 for 9 weeks, June-Aug.

LOCAL PROGRAMS

Mundo Verde Spanish School, Calle Nueva Alta 432-A, Cusco (☎84 22 1287; http://mundoverdespanish.com). Spanish school supports a conservation project in the Peruvian rainforest, developing sustainable resource management in 3 villages. Volunteers (15+) teach English to village children or work on rainforest conservation. In-person interview required. 20hr. of lessons US$150.

Socio Adventures, Bambamarca 273, Cajamarca (☎76 83 1118; www.socioadventures.com). A 5-day trek to the Cadmalca community near Cajamarca to build a cooking stove. Ages 18+ (under 18 must be supervised).

Tambopata Education Center (☎82 80 3306 or 57 3935; www.geocities.com/tambopata_language), in Madre de Dios. Center offers English classes to locals and Spanish classes for international students. Volunteer projects include assistant teaching in local schools, working on a reforestation lodge, and helping set up a lodge in the jungle. Volunteers ages 18-80 (children must be with family or in groups). US$10 per night; US$27 per night with 4hr. of Spanish classes daily.

Tinkuy Peru, La Florida 280, Huancayo (☎64 21 3028; www.tinkuyperu.com). Volunteer in the Peruvian Highlands, teaching English to local children or tourist police, or working in an orphanage. Program can accommodate skilled workers like medical professionals. Ages 21+. 10 excursions to tourist sites outside Huancayo included.

URBAN ISSUES

While the rural areas of Peru are very poor, there is also a great deal of poverty in the cities, particularly in Lima. Programs in urban areas of Peru often focus on improving child welfare and health conditions.

INTERNATIONAL PROGRAMS

Health Volunteers Overseas, 1900 L St. NW, Ste. 310, Washington, D.C. 20036, US (☎202-296-0928; www.hvousa.org). Program invites medical professionals to work in Peru's Social Security Health System, *Empresa de Seguros de Salud (Es Salud)* hospital system, which has 2 million paid subscribers providing coverage for 6 million people. Housing and in-country transportation provided.

LOCAL PROGRAMS

Apuperu, Diego Ferre 355, Miraflores, Lima (☎11 445 8338). Volunteer to be a sports trainer for at-risk youth in Lima with TEMA, a group of students and alumni from local *Universidad Pontífica.* 20hr. per week. Volunteers ages 18-30. Spanish proficiency, first aid knowledge, and climbing experience required.

New Family (Mosoq Ayllu), San Carlos 859, Huancayo (☎64 21 5913; www.geocities.com/mosoq_ayllu). Doctors, dentists, nurses, and medical students ages 18+ work alongside their Peruvian counterparts to learn and teach medical practices in local health centers. 1-month min. commitment. Functional level of Spanish required.

YOUTH AND COMMUNITY

Urban youth in Peru face many challenges, particularly in the areas of health, safety, and education. While there are many programs to help such children, most organizations are critically understaffed and underfunded. Volunteers working in Peru have the opportunity to directly impact at-risk youth in Peru's cities, often working with entire families.

INTERNATIONAL PROGRAMS

Alliance Abroad Group, Inc., 1221 South Mopac Expressway, Ste. 250, Austin, TX 78746, US (☎888-6-ABROAD; www.allianceabroad.com). Volunteers 18+ spend 1-3 months working with youth, aiding medical clinics, or working with indigenous communities. Intermediate level of Spanish required. Group housing is in apartments/flats. Participants work independently.

Global Vision International, Nomansland, Wheathampstead, St. Albans AL4 8EJ, UK (☎44 0 870 608 8898; www.gvi.co.uk). Volunteers ages 18-65 complete community projects in and around Cusco. Includes 2 weeks of intensive language programs and cultural activities. 1-month min. stay. US$1480, does not include airfare.

Global Volunteers, 375 East Little Canada Rd., St. Paul, MN 55117, US (☎800-487-1074; www.globalvolunteers.org). Organizes orphanage and child care projects for homeless and impoverished children and their families in Lima. Volunteers live in a hotel. Approx. US$2000 for 2 weeks, excluding cover airfare.

LOCAL PROGRAMS

Kiya Survivors (☎01 640 9404; www.kiyasurvivors.org). Work in the Andean village of Urubamba in a small center for special-needs children. Programs last 2-6 months, and can include tours throughout Peru.

Fundación Paz Holandesa, Jorge Chávez 527, Arequipa (☎54 20 6720; www.pazholandesa.com). Dutch-founded program established in Arequipa coordinates free medical aid from doctors and administrative volunteers for impoverished Peruvian children.

ARCHAEOLOGICAL DIGS

Peru is rich with artifacts from the many ancient civilizations that once inhabited its diverse regions. Each year, many groups excavate Incan ruins, particularly in the Sacred Valley.

Archaeological Institute of America, 656 Beacon St., Boston, MA 02215, US (☎617-353-9361; www.archaeological.org). The *Archaeological Fieldwork Opportunities Bulletin* (US$20 for non-members) lists field sites in Peru and around the world. Purchase the bulletin from Kendall/Hunt Publishing, 4050 Westmark Dr., Dubuque, IA 52002, US (☎800-228-0810).

Projects Abroad, 19 Cullen Dr., West Orange, NJ 07052, US (☎973-324-2688; www.projects-abroad.org). Work in the historic town and battlefield of Ollantaytambo, excavating religious, astronomical, administrative, and urban sites of the ancient Incas.

ESSAY CONTEST WINNER!

beyondtourism.com

Last year's winner, Eleanor Glass, spent a summer volunteering with children on an island off the Yucatan Peninsula. Read the rest of her story and find your own once-in-a-lifetime experience at **www.beyondtourism.com!**

"... I was discovering elements of life in Mexico that I had never even dreamt of. I regularly had meals at my students' houses, as their fisherman fathers would instruct them to invite the nice gringa to lunch after a lucky day's catch. Downtown, tourists walked the streets and spent too much on cheap necklaces, while I played with a friend's baby niece, or took my new kitten to the local vet for her shots, or picked up tortillas at the tortilleria, or vegetables in the mercado. ... I was lucky that I found a great place to volunteer and a community to adopt me. ... Just being there, listening to stories, hearing the young men talk of cousins who had crossed the border, I know I went beyond tourism." - Eleanor Glass, 2004

LG LET'S GO

University of Missouri Field School, Columbia, MO 65211, US (☎573-882-4731; http://web.missouri.edu/~nad2b1/BuenaVista), sends students to study at the site of Buena Vista in the Chillón Valley June-July. Outside students welcome. US$2000 for students registering for UM credit, US$2500 for other students. Excludes tuition, personal expenses, airfare, and insurance.

TEACHING ENGLISH

Teaching jobs abroad, with the exception of some elite American private schools, are rarely well paid. Volunteering as a teacher, though, is nevertheless a popular option. Volunteer teachers often get some sort of a daily stipend to help with living expenses. Although salaries at private schools might be low compared to the US, a low cost of living makes it much more profitable. In almost all cases, you must have at least a bachelor's degree to be a full-time teacher, although undergraduates can often get summer positions teaching or tutoring.

Opportunities for teaching abound in Lima, Cusco, and other major cities, where English-speaking businesses have a distinct advantage. If you want to teach in rural areas, volunteering is the most common option, often in exchange for room and board. Teachers are required to have a work visa, which must be sent to you from Peru before your departure, which is sometimes difficult. Often, a free 90-day visitor's visa will suffice.

Many schools require teachers to have a **Teaching English as a Foreign Language (TEFL)** certificate. Not having this certification does not necessarily exclude you from finding a teaching job, but certified teachers often find higher-paying jobs. Native English speakers working in private schools are most often hired for English-immersion classrooms where no Spanish is spoken. Those volunteering or teaching in public, poorer schools are more likely to be working in both English and Spanish.

Placement agencies or university fellowship programs are the best resources for finding teaching jobs. Alternatively, you can make contact directly with schools or just try your luck once you get there. If you are going to try the latter, the best time to look is several weeks before the start of the school year.

The following organizations may be helpful placing teachers in Peru.

INTERNATIONAL PROGRAMS

Amity Institute, Amity Volunteer Teachers Abroad Program, 10671 Roselle St., Ste. 100, San Diego, CA 92121-1525, US (☎858-455-6364; www.amity.org). Offers both full-year and semester-long positions. US$25-50 processing fee and US$500 placement fee. For anyone with at least 2-3 years of teaching experience, **AVTA** also offers positions with **Teacher Workshops Abroad,** a program that conducts pedagogical workshops for local teachers. Same fees apply.

International Schools Services (ISS), 15 Roszel Rd., Box 5910, Princeton, NJ 08543-5910, US (☎609-452-0990; www.iss.edu). Hires teachers for more than 200 overseas schools including schools in Huaraz and Lima. Candidates should have experience teaching or with international affairs. 2-year commitment expected.

Nepal Kingdom Foundation and Muirs Tours, Nepal House, 97A Swansea Rd., Reading, Berkshire RG1 8HA, UK (☎44 0 118 950 2281; www.nkf-mt.org.uk/volunteer_Peru). Programs in Cusco and Huancayo allow anyone with experience in TEFL to teach English in poor or rural areas for a minimum of 5 weeks. Includes a trek to Machu Picchu and other sightseeing tours.

Office of Overseas Schools, US Department of State, Room H328, SA-1, Washington, D.C. 20522, US (☎202-261-8200; www.state.gov/m/a/os). Maintains a current list of schools abroad and agencies that place Americans in teaching positions abroad.

REGIONAL PROGRAMS

Centro Cultural Peruano Norteamericano, Melgar 109, Arequipa (☎89 1020), hires foreigners to teach English. The center was established in 1955 in a *casa antigua,* and now offers English classes and cultural events year-round.

El Británico, Larco 500, Trujillo (☎938 6987). Volunteers with min. 6 months verified English-teaching experience may teach general English classes for both children and adults for 3-6 months. Benefits include a monthly stipend of US$150 and board with a local family.

ESDIT, the Escuela de Idiomas y Turismo, Jerusalén 400 and Melgar 105, Arequipa (☎20 6626), hires foreigners to teach English for 2 months min. Ask for Elba Oviedo.

IncaEduca, Nueva Baja 560, Cusco (☎22 7526; www.inca-educa.org), welcomes volunteers to teach English to underprivileged young people 15-25 in the Cusco area for 3, 6, or 9 months.

Inglés Megasistema Marconi ASDI, Rivero 414, Arequipa (☎21 5634). Hires foreigners to teach English. Call to inquire.

Translex (☎40 5184; translexQP@hotmail.com) seeks native English speakers to teach conversational English classes. 1-month min. commitment. No experience needed.

STUDYING

 VISA INFORMATION. You will need a student visa for stays longer than 90 days in Peru. To get a student visa from the Embassy of Peru, you must show proof of economic solvency, be enrolled in a Peruvian educational institution, have a recommendation letter written by yourself and another issued by the Peruvian consul, a letter of moral and economic guarantee from a Peruvian citizen, a medical examination certificate (takes 4 weeks to get and costs US$10), and four photos (front and side). Student visas are only obtainable prior to entering Peru. You can also get one in immigration at one of the borders.

Study abroad programs range from basic language and culture courses to college-level classes, often for credit. In order to choose a program that best fits your needs, research as much as you can before making your decision—determine costs and duration, as well as what kind of students participate in the program and what sort of accommodations are provided. Most students in Peru live in homestays or in group living arrangements in apartments in cities.

In programs that have large groups of students who speak the same language, there is a trade-off. You may feel more comfortable in the community, but you will not have the same opportunity to practice a foreign language or to befriend other international students. For accommodations, dorm life provides a better opportunity to mingle with fellow students, but there is less of a chance to experience the local scene. If you live with a family, there is a potential to build lifelong friendships with Peruvians and to experience day-to-day life in more depth, but conditions can vary greatly from family to family.

UNIVERSITIES

Most university-level study-abroad programs are conducted in Spanish, although many programs offer classes in English and beginner- and lower-level language courses. Those relatively fluent in Spanish may find it cheaper to enroll directly in a university abroad, although getting college credit may be more difficult. You can

BEYOND BOOKS
Studying in Peru makes culture a living reality

The women surrounded me and wrapped me in a skirt that looked more like an onion than an article of clothing. They cinched my waist with a rainbow-colored band and draped a heavy black *mantilla* over my head. I protested loudly and vehemently in Spanish, but they either didn't understand or didn't really care. After all, they had been paid to do this to me. I stepped out of the metal-roofed house onto the rugged, sloping ground of the island of Taquile, in the middle of Lake Titicaca, and tried to look up at the stars. I had admired them earlier that evening. I had found the Southern Cross for the first time and thought about how far I was from anything familiar. I was surprised by how much I noticed the sky when its normal pattern was missing. Now, though, draped in this heavy shawl, I couldn't even lift my head to look into the eyes of the islanders around me, let alone to see the heavens. My ribs ached when I tried to breathe, and the layers of my skirt slowed me when I tried to walk too quickly.

My short stay on Taquile was one of the most memorable experiences I had during the summer I spent in Peru on a study abroad program centered in Cusco. If I had not been in the company of a dozen other students and two professors, I probably would not have gotten into these circumstances. If I had been on Taquile alone, I might never have hiked up to the top of the mountain on the barest etching of a trail and reveled in the sun as it set over the peaks on the other shore. I might never have eaten a meal of fried trout, eggs, quinoa, black fingerling potatoes, and *chicha* at the home of the village leader. I certainly would not have paid his wife and daughters to dress me in their costume, lead me down to the town hall in the absolute darkness of night on an island with little electricity, and teach me traditional dances. I probably would have come on the boat from Puno and stayed for just a few hours like every other tourist, ready to catch the bus to my next destination and move on, to see another place, add it to my collection, maybe snap some photos. I would have decided the dance was just a spectacle performed for tourists, a waste of money.

But I wasn't there alone, and I was not a backpacker, but a student. I had decided on a whim to take a trip across the Equator with a dozen other students from my university—after all, Latin America did interest me, but my heart had always been in Spain. Yet Peru, with all its ancient glory and modern complexity, wooed me away from Iberia. The courses I took in Cusco on Andean history and Latin American literature were meaningful not just because of my engaging professors or my natural interest in the material, but because they animated my understanding of my surroundings and encouraged me to analyze my interactions with the people of Peru in light of what I was learning.

If I were merely a tourist, I could still have gone to Cusco's Plaza de Armas and Sacsayhuamán on Inti Raymi, lost myself in a crowd that smelled of roasting guinea pig, and watched people tear the heart out of a llama on a concrete slab, but I would not have understood the history and implications behind the ceremony; I would not have known that the Spanish had banned this winter solstice celebration as subversive and heretical, and that it had only been resurrected in the past century. This same phenomenon was true of my visits to Machu Picchu, Ollantaytambo, and Pachacamac—even of modern Lima, where we spent a week. I could have visited the same places and seen the same sights if I had been backpacking. I could even have met many of the same people. I could have spoken to Peruvians and had them tell me exactly what they thought about my country and the process of globalization. But I certainly would not have had the opportunity to become so well acquainted with the women of Taquile, or to meet Hugo Blanco, the revolutionary hero and *compadre* of Che Guevara who happened to be a friend of my professor. In any event, I would not have had the same understanding of the society I had entered, and it would not be imprinted in my memory as deeply as it is. I might still have remembered the women of Taquile, but I wouldn't have had such powerful feelings for them.

Alexandra Moss is the Editor of Let's Go: Spain and Portugal 2005. *She studied with the Harvard Summer School in Cusco in 2002.*

search www.studyabroad.com for various semester-abroad programs that meet your criteria, including your desired location and focus of study. Another good resource for finding programs that cater to your particular interests is the **South American Explorers Club** (p. 11). The following organizations can help place students in university programs abroad, or have their own branch in Peru.

AMERICAN PROGRAMS

Council on International Educational Exchange (CIEE), 7 Custom House St., Portland, ME 01410, US (☎800-40-STUDY/800-40-78839; www.ciee.org/study). Sponsors work, volunteer, academic, and internship programs in Peru.

Rainforest and Reef, 417 Watson St., Coopersville, MI 49404, US (☎877-769-3086; www.rainforestandreef.org). Offers field courses in rainforest and marine ecology for universities, community colleges, high school groups, and individuals, both professionals and tourists. Courses last approx. 2 weeks.

School for International Training, College Semester Abroad, Admissions, Kipling Rd., P.O. Box 676, Brattleboro, VT 05302, US (☎800-257-7751 or 802-257-7751; www.sit.edu). Runs the **Experiment in International Living** (☎800-345-2929; fax 802-258-3428; www.usexperiment.org), 3- to 5-week summer programs that offer high-school students cross-cultural homestays, community service, ecological adventure, and language training in Peru and cost US$1900-5000.

PERUVIAN PROGRAMS

Universidad del Pacífico, International Relations Of., Bldg. E 4th Fl., Salaverry 2020, Lima 11 (☎219 0100, ext. 2275; www.up.edu.pe). This private university specializes in economics and business administration, and has a foreign-student exchange program.

Universidad Peruana de Ciencias Aplicadas, Prolongación Primavera 2390, Monterrico (☎313 3333; www.upc.edu.pe). Allows foreign students to study for up to 2 semesters while immersing themselves in Peruvian culture. Applicants should be regular students enrolled in a foreign institution at the university level. 2 terms: Mar.-July and Aug.-Dec.

LANGUAGE SCHOOLS

Language schools can be independently run international or local organizations or divisions of foreign universities. Their programs rarely offer college credit, but they are a good alternative to university study if you desire a deeper focus on the language or a slightly less rigorous courseload. These programs are also good for younger high school students who might not feel comfortable with older students in a university program.

INTERNATIONAL PROGRAMS

A2Z Languages, 5112 N. 40th St., Ste. 103, Phoenix, AZ 85018, US (☎800-496-4596; www.a2zlanguages.com), offers 1-week to 6-month language programs for all levels. Also arranges educational and cultural tours.

AmeriSpan Unlimited, P.O. Box 40007, Philadelphia, PA 19106, US (☎800-879-6640 or 215-751-1100; www.amerispan.com). 1-week to 6-month language immersion programs in Peru. Also offers educational travel and volunteer and internship opportunities.

International Association for the Exchange of Students for Technical Experience (IAESTE), 10400 Little Patuxent Pkwy., Ste. 250, Columbia, MD 21044-3510, US (☎410-997-2200; www.aipt.org). 8- to 12-week programs in Peru for college students who have completed 2 years of technical study. US$25 application fee.

Languages Abroad, 413 Ontario St., Toronto, Ontario M5A 2V9, Canada (☎800-219-9924 or 416-925-2112; www.languagesabroad.com). 2- to 12-week language programs in Peru for beginning to advanced levels.

LOCAL PROGRAMS

▨ **AMAUTA Spanish School,** Suecia 480, Cusco (☎26 2345; www.amautaspanish.com), up Suecia from the Plaza de Armas at the top of the hill. The largest Spanish school around, AMAUTA offers language programs in Cusco, Manú, and Urubamba. Group classes (max. 6 people) US$98 per week, private classes US$184 per week; packages include 20hr. of class, free Internet access, and activities like salsa dancing, seminars on Peruvian culture and society, city tours, and Peruvian cooking lessons. Full immersion programs and a variety of special-interest programs such as Peruvian culture and a volunteer program (4-8 weeks) are also available. Individual classes may be taught on a per-hour basis (US$10.50 per hr.). Classes run daily 8:30am-12:30pm or 2:30-6:30pm, with placement exam on first day at 8am. AMAUTA also offers accommodation (US$114 per week, Su-Sa) either with a Peruvian host family (3 meals per day) or in the school's Student Guest House (breakfast included, kitchen access). Office open M-F 8am-6pm, Sa 9am-noon, informational meeting Su 4pm. AmEx/MC/V.

▨ **Amigos Spanish School,** Zaguán del Cielo Mz. B23, Cusco (☎24 2292; www.spanish-cusco.com), up Sunturwasi from the Plaza de Armas, right on Choquechaca, and left on Recoleta. The school's motto is "In our school, to learn means to help"; this nonprofit language school channels its revenues toward the education and upbringing of 16 disadvantaged Cusco kids. Group classes (max. 4 people) daily 8am-noon, US$5 per hr.; private classes US$8 per hr. 10% discount for students. Courses include salsa and merengue lessons and tours. Amigos also offers family accommodations (US$110 per week, all meals included). Office open daily 8am-7pm. No credit cards.

Academia El Sol, Grimaldo del Solar 469, Miraflores, Lima (☎242 7763; http://elsol.idiomasperu.com). Offers group instruction at 5 levels. Courses start any Monday for 20hr. per week and can continue for any period of time. Intensive program is about US$1400 for 8 weeks (does not include accommodation).

Academia Mayor de La Lengua Quechua, Sol 103, of. 107, Cusco (☎25 1944; www.unsaac.edu.pe/runasimi), inside the Galerías Turísticas. Teaches Quechua, the language of the Incas, still spoken by 16% of Peru's population. s/120 per month (classes daily 4-7pm). No credit cards.

Excel Language Center, Cruz Verde 336A, Cusco (☎23 2272; www.excel-spanishlanguageprograms-peru.org). Offers Spanish lessons to all age levels, including children. Provides extracurricular activities and cultural immersion. Group lessons US$3-5 per hr., private lessons US$7 per hr. Open M-F 9am-noon and 3-8pm.

Incas del Perú, Giraldez 652, Huancayo (☎22 3303; fax 22 2395), adjacent to Restaurante La Cabaña. Run by the charismatic Lucho Hurtado, who speaks near-flawless English. Dedicated to promoting authentic cultural experiences in Huancayo and the Río Mantaro Valley, Lucho offers crash courses in Spanish, Quechua, weaving, and the pan flute. Ask about **volunteer programs,** which include Spanish lessons and homestays. Open daily 9am-1pm and 2:30-7pm. SAE and student discounts. AmEx/DC/MC/V.

Peru For You, Solano 308, Huancayo (☎21 7276 or 991 1976; www.peruforyou.com), in San Carlos, across the street from the side of the Picchus church. Natalia Rivera Gómez and Aldo Tineo Velita have flexible programs doing volunteer teaching and community outreach or studying Spanish while living with a local family begin year-round; length of stay varies from 1 week to 1 year.

San Blas Spanish School, Tandapata 688, Cusco (☎84 24 7898; www.spanish-schoolperu.com). 2 schools, 1 in Cusco and the other in small colonial Cai Cay, offer classes of no more than 4 people. In addition to classes, offers volunteer projects in both locations for 2 weeks or more. Also offers salsa dancing lessons and cooking classes. Homestay.

FOR FURTHER READING ON ALTERNATIVES TO TOURISM

Alternatives to the Peace Corps: A Directory of Third World and U.S. Volunteer Opportunities, by Joan Powell. Food First Books, 2000 (US$10).

How to Live Your Dream of Volunteering Overseas, by Collins, DeZerega, and Heckscher. Penguin Books, 2002 (US$17).

International Directory of Voluntary Work, by Whetter and Pybus. Peterson's Guides and Vacation Work, 2000 (US$16).

Invest Yourself: The Catalogue of Volunteer Opportunities, published by the Commission on Voluntary Service and Action (☎718-638-8487).

LIMA

Lima may seem an overwhelming urban jungle for travelers arriving in Peru with fantasies of the highlands. With nine million inhabitants (over one third of the Peruvian population), Lima's streets are alive with fruit carts and rainbow-colored buses, religious processions and socialist rallies, traffic jams and enthusiastic *limeños* happy to meet a foreign friend. Although Lima may not be as cosmopolitan as other capital cities, its distinctly Peruvian nature means that there's no better place to get a feel for the country's rich and diverse history. Ancient pyramids, *casas antiguas*, ornate churches, and some of the country's finest museums pop-

Lima Overview

MUSEUMS

Museo Arqueológico Rafael Larco Herrera, **1**
Museo de la Historia Natural, **4**
Museo de la Nación, **5**
Museo de la República, **3**
Museo de Oro del Perú y Armas del Mundo, **6**
Museo Nacional de Antropología, Arqueología, e Historia, **2**

SEE LIMA CENTRO DETAIL MAP pp. 96-97

SEE MIRAFLORES & SAN ISIDRO DETAIL MAP p. 100

SEE BARRANCO DETAIL MAP p. 127

ulate the city. Though the city can seem a foggy, relentless barrage to the unprepared, those who persevere will be rewarded with memorable adventures and an enriched understanding of Peru, both ancient and modern.

HIGHLIGHTS OF LIMA

EXPLORE the ruins at **Puruchuco** to experience life in an Inca palace (p. 131).

TRACE the history of all the civilizations that have lived in Peru at the extensive archaeological exhibits of the **Museo de la Nación** (p. 119).

BALANCE on cliffs that fall to the Pacific Ocean in glitzy **Miraflores** (p. 125), home to Lima's rich and famous, as well as fine shops and the famous **LarcoMar** (p. 118).

DANCE 'til dawn in the suburb of **Barranco**—Lima's **nightlife** (p. 125) puts the rest of the country's to shame.

LIMA   ☎ 01

Lima began as the relatively quiet home of various pre-Hispanic cultures on the banks of the Río Rímac. With the great Inca expansion of the 15th century, it soon became the residence of affluent members of society. Though the center of the empire was far away in Cusco, Lima did house large quantities of gold and silver and some architectural masterpieces. When the Spanish conquered the area, they recognized its strategic potential as a prime coastal location, stripping it of its gold and destroying most of the Inca buildings. Francisco Pizarro established the new colonial capital here in 1534.

Following an earthquake in 1746, Lima was forced to re-create itself. The result was the elaborate buildings and immense plazas now present in Lima Centro, fashioned in an ornate style leaders hoped would mirror that of European cities. In 1821, Lima became the capital of the newly independent nation of Peru, and the destruction of the old city walls in 1872 helped to join all the suburbs to Lima Centro. Lima prospered during the 19th century as Peru's main port, but the good times couldn't last forever. In the last half of the 20th century, Lima suffered from political and economic crises, rising poverty, and overly rapid urbanization.

However, with the new millennium settling in, Lima's fortunes are again on the rise. The restoration of the historic center, a renewed emphasis on job training and education, and plans to build an aquarium and more beachside hotels indicate that Peru is looking to the future with Lima leading the way.

⬛ INTERCITY TRANSPORTATION

FLIGHTS
Aeropuerto Internacional Jorge Chávez is 14km north of Lima Centro, on Elmer Faucett in the suburb of Callao (☎595 0666 for automated flight information; ☎517 3500 or 517 3502 for flight information from a live person; www.lap.com.pe). **Currency exchange** booths in the international terminal change US dollars, but since most transportation options into Lima take American currency, avoid the high exchange rates here and change your money in the city. **ATMs** (24hr. MC/V) are in the domestic terminal; there is also one on the right in the baggage claim area immediately after exiting customs. Ask the people in blue suits behind the ground transportation desk for help finding your best transportation option. They can also provide directions to the bus service into the city, the "Urbanito" (US$8). There are colectivos (s/1-1.50) along Benavides, Brasil, and Javier Prado that stop at the airport's outside gate and run into town. However, the safest and fastest way to get to the city has traditionally been the "Official Taxi Distributor" outside the international

terminal. Be prepared to pay US$9-10 to either Lima Centro or Miraflores. As in most of Lima, taking an unofficial taxi can save you a couple of bucks, but such taxis are not closely regulated and can be dangerous.

 Transportation schedules and routes in Peru change frequently, so call or check websites before planning your trip to confirm that the times and prices listed below are still correct.

INTERNATIONAL AIRLINES

AeroMexico, Vía Principal 180, Centro Empresarial Real, San Isidro (☎421 3500; www.aeromexico.com). Flies to **Mexico City.**

Alitalia, Calle Mártir Olaya 129, Miraflores (☎447 3899 or 242 9667; www.alitalia.com). Flies daily to **Italy** (either Milan or Rome, 10:30am).

American, Canaval y Moreyra 390, 1st fl., San Isidro and Larco 687, Miraflores (☎211 7000 for reservations; www.aa.com). Flies daily to **Dallas** (1:30am), and **Miami** (7:30am, 10:40pm).

Continental, Victor Andrés Belaúnde 147, Edificio Real 5, Of. 101, San Isidro (☎222 7080; www.continental.com). Flies to **US** cities.

Copa, Canaval y Moreyra 480, Of. 105, San Isidro (☎610 0808; www.copaair.com). Flies to many destinations in Latin America including **Santo Domingo, Bogotá, Panama City, Buenos Aires,** and **Mexico City.** US$400-700.

Delta, Vía Principal 180, Centro Empresarial Real, San Isidro (☎211 9211; www.delta-air.com). Flies daily to **Atlanta** (12:00am).

Iberia, Camino Real 390, 9th fl., San Isidro (☎411 7800; www.iberia.com). Flies daily to **Amsterdam, Brussels,** and **Frankfurt.**

KLM, José Pardo 805, Miraflores (☎213 0200; http://peru.klm.com). Flies to **Amsterdam** (Tu-Su 8:35pm).

LanChile, José Pardo 513, 2nd fl., Miraflores (☎213 8300; www.lanchile.com). Flies to **Buenos Aires** (W, Su 1:30); **Los Angeles** (1:05am); **Miami** (7:00am); **New York** (11:50pm); and **Santiago** (4 per day).

Lufthansa, Jorge Basadre 1330, San Isidro (☎442 4455; www.lufthansa.com). Flies to most **European** destinations.

Varig, Camino Real 456, 8th fl., San Isidro (☎221 0527; www.varig.com.pe). Flies daily to **Brazil** (1:55pm).

DOMESTIC AIRLINES

Lan Peru, José Pardo 513, Miraflores (☎213 8300; www.lan.com). Flies to: **Arequipa** (1½hr.; daily 6am, 6:25pm; M, Su 9am; Th also 4pm; US$81); **Chiclayo** (1½hr., M 2pm; Tu, Th, Sa 5:45pm, Su 4:50pm; US$65) also via **Trujillo** (45min.; M, W, F, Su 4pm; US$65); **Cusco** (1¼hr., 2-5 per day, US$81); **Puerto Maldonado** (2½hr.; Tu, Th, Sa 9:40am; US$65); **Tarapoto** (1hr., daily 6am, US$74).

Nuevo Continente, Torrico 981, Lima Centro (☎431 6700 or 819 3743), and Pardo 605, Miraflores (☎242 4260; reservations in Lima ☎431 6700; www.nuevocontinente.com.pe). Both open M-F 9am-7pm, Sa 9am-5pm. Flies to: **Arequipa** (1¼hr.; daily 6:10, 9am, noon, 5:30pm); **Chiclayo** (1hr.; daily 6am, 5pm); **Cusco** (1hr.; daily 5:50,

 The US government has sanctioned Aero Continente (now sold to its workers and known as Nuevo Continente) for involvement in narcotics trafficking. As of August 2004, US citizens are not allowed to do business with Nuevo Continente. Check with your nearest embassy or consulate for updated information.

TO CERRO
SAN CRISTÓBAL

300 meters
300 yards

RÍMAC

BARRIOS ALTOS

Huánuco

Jauja

Cangallo

Junín

PL.
ITALIA

Miro Quesada

Cusco

Castenata

PL. DE
ACHO

9 de Octubre

Hualgayoc

Museo Taurino
de Acho

Río Rímac

García Hurtado de Mendoza

Marañón

Julián Piñeiro

Castilla

Trujillo

Cajamarca

Palta

Ayabaca

García Ribeyro

Conde de Superunda

Casa de
Oquendo

Santo
Domingo

Santuario
de Santa Rosa

Las
Nazarenas

Ica

Callao

Huancavelica

Cañete

Añaraes

Tejadas

Sancho de Rivera Bravo

Oroya

Enrique Meiggs

TO
(11km)

Villa Mar

PL.
CASTILLA

Caqueta

Dansey

Huarochiri

PL.
2 DE MAYO

Colonial

Ugarte

Venezuela

Uruguay

García

Velarde

Garcilaso de la Vega

Torrico

Belén

Pachitea

Cornejo

Parque
Universitario

Lampa

Apurímac

Azángaro

Cusco

Miro Quesada

Ancash

Amazonas

Amazonas

Casa de Trece Monedas

Rodríguez

PL.
BOLÍVAR

Congress
Building

Museo de la
Inquisición

BARRIO
CHINO

Capón

Andahuaylas

Mercado
Central

PL.
GASTAÑETA

Ayacucho

Huallaga

Paruro

Instituto
Cultural Peruano-
Norteamericano

Convento de
San Francisco

Train
Station

Palacio del
Gobierno

Casa de
Aliaga

Palacio
Municipal

Sta. Rosa

Santa
Rosa

Queenland
Adventures

San
Agustín

Casa de
Riva Agüero

PL.
MAYOR

La Catedral
de Lima

Junín

Banco de
Crédito

Banco Central
de Reserva
del Perú

Palacio
Torre Tagle

Biblioteca
Nacional

Iglesia de
San Pedro

Dancey

Abancay

CENTRO

Iglesia de
La Merced

Banco
Wiese

Western
Union

Interbank

Ucayali

Ira

Ica

Puno

Carabaya

La Unión

Ocoña

Camaná

Callloma

Moquegua

Torrico

Tacna

Nicolás de Piérola

Inclán

Peñaloza

Zepita

Quilca

Dávalos

Ilo

Carhuaz

Chacas

Pomabamba

Colonial

Pillitos

Borda

Museo Nacional
de la Cultura Peruana

Museo de Artes
y Tradiciones
Populares

Hospital Arzobispo
Loayza

PL. SAN
MARTÍN

New
Continente

Nuevo
Continente

Hipermercado
Metro

Emancipación

RÍMAC

Lima Centro

▲ ACCOMMODATIONS
Hospedaje Plaza Mayor, 5
Hostal de Los Artes, 29
Hostal Iquique, 28
Hostal Roma, 2
Hostal San Francisco, 9
Hostal Santa Rosa, 4
Hotel España, 10
Hotel Europa, 8
Hotel La Casona, 7
Hotel Wiracocha, 7
Machu Picchu Guest House, 31
Pensión Familia Rodríguez, 17
Pensión Ibarra, 1

● FOOD
El Mesón del Almirante, 12
L'Eau Vive, 25
Los Balcones de Olaya, 6
Los Frutales, 11
Los Manglares de Tumbes, 19
Natur, 20
Norky's, 22
Restaurante Paraíso, 3
Salón de Los Espejos, 14
Wa Lok, 27

★ ENTERTAINMENT
Cine Club BCR, 15
Cine Excelsior, 21
Cine Planet, 24

♪ NIGHTLIFE
Cafe Teatro "Palais Concerto," 23
Las Brisas del Titicaca, 30
Rincón Cervecero, 26
Sagitario Disco, 16

■ SHOPPING
Saga Falabella, 13

LIMA

BREÑA
LA VICTORIA
SANTA BEATRIZ
JESÚS MARÍA

Parinacochas
Lucanas
La Mar
Huamanga
TO PACHACAMAC, EMPRESA MERCED, EXPRESO HUAMANGO
Misti
Cañete
Huanta
Jardín Botánico
Abtao
Raimondi
Centro Deportivo Experimental
N. de Piérola
Inambari
Buses to Pachacamac, Pucusana
Buses to Chosica, Cañete, Chincha, Ica
Montevideo
Leticia
Ormeño
Flores
Carlos Zavala
Colmenares
Sandía
Aljovín
Cuadros
Ríos
García Naranjo
28 de Julio
León de Huánuco
Bausate y Meza
Andahuaylas
Renovación
Pizarro
Huascarán
Manco Cápac
Iquitos
Canta
Galvez
Antonio Raimondi
Grau
Misti
PL. MANCO CÁPAC
Sáenz Peña
Humboldt
Unanue
Barranca
San Cristóbal
Isabela Católica
Flores
Cruz del Sur
Vía Expresa
Paseo de la República
TO SAN ISIDRO, MIRAFLORES (10km)
Estadio Nacional
Madre de Dios
Parque de la Reserva
Díaz
Petit Thouars
Velarde
Corpancho
Saco Oliveros
Arequipa
Arenales
Chile
Larrabure
Sánchez
Nazca
Paseo de la República
Gran Parque de Lima
PL. GRAU
Museo de Arte
Museo de Arte Italiano
Washington
Bolivia
Chota
Portugal
Iquique
España
Arica
Breña
Paraguay
9 de Diciembre
Clínica Internacional
Lavandería K10
Immigration Office
Tarma
Huancayo
Chincha
Yauyos
Guzmán Blanco
Walkuski
Cervantes
Gaspar
Gálvez h
Brasil
TO (1.3km)
PL. BOLOGNESI
PL. JORGE CHÁVEZ
Av. de la Peruana
Salaverry
Campo de Marte
Goethe-Institut
Roosevelt
Roma
Roma
Abtao

6, 9, 9:20am); **Iquitos** (1¾hr.; daily 6:45am, 6:30pm); **Juliaca** (2¼hr.; daily 6am, noon); **Pucallpa** (2hr., daily noon); **Puerto Maldonado** (2hr., daily 9am); **Piura** (2hr.; daily 7am, 5pm); **Tacna** (2hr., daily 5:30pm); **Tarapoto** (1hr., daily 3:15pm); **Trujillo** (1hr.; daily 7am, 4, 7pm); **Tumbes** (2hr., 6:20am); **Yurimaguas** (1¼hr., Su 2:45pm). All flights US$64, except Cusco and Arequipa (US$74), if purchased in Peru.

TANS, Arequipa 5200, Miraflores (reservations ☎213 6000; www.tansperu.com.pe). Open M-F 9am-7pm, Sa 9am-5pm. Flies to: **Cusco** (1hr.; daily 5:45, 9am); **Iquitos** (2¼hr.; daily 7:30am, 1:10pm; Tu, F, Su also 4:30pm); **Pucallpa** (1hr., daily 1:10pm); **Puerto Maldonado** (2hr., daily 9am); **Tarapoto** (1hr., daily 7:30am). All flights cost US$65-81, depending on dates purchased.

TRAINS

Train service from Lima to most destinations has been suspended indefinitely. On certain weekends, limited train service is available to San Bartolomé and Huancayo. **Ferrocarril** (☎361 2828; www.ferroviasperu.com.pe) offers round-trip day excursions to San Bartolomé Sundays from April to November. Trains leave in the morning from the station at Central de Desamparados, Ancash 201, behind Presidential Palace, and return in the late afternoon. The famous Lima-Huancayo train (see **Natural Highs,** p. 286) usually departs the last Sunday of each month during the dry season (Apr.-Oct.; roundtrip US$30). Purchase tickets in the red TeleTicket booth of any E-Wong Supermarket, located throughout Lima. **PeruRail,** Armendariz 397, Miraflores (☎444 5025; www.perurail.com), no longer serves Lima.

BUSES

There is no central terminal in Lima; buses leave from individual agencies instead. Many agencies are around Carlos Zavala, just north of Grau in Lima Centro, although most agencies serving central Peru are around Luna Pizarro in La Victoria. Check with agencies for current prices and schedules. Buy tickets in advance for popular routes like Cusco and Arequipa. Prepare to pay about s/20-50 extra for added leg room, meals, snacks, and reclining seats; *imperial* or *especial* seats offer a more comfortable—but more expensive—ride.

Cruz del Sur, 531 Quilca, Lima Centro (☎424 1005; www.cruzdelsur.com.pe), at the corner of Carlos Zavala 211 and Montevideo. To: **Arequipa** (15hr.; daily 12:30, 3, 5, 7, 9pm); s/40); **Ayacucho** (13hr., daily 9:30pm, s/50); **Cajamarca** (14hr., daily 7pm, s/70); **Chiclayo** (10hr., daily 8:45pm, s/50); **Huancayo** (4hr.; daily 7:45am, 1:30, 10:45, 11:30pm; s/35); **Huaraz** (8hr.; daily 9:30am, 10pm; s/40); **Ilo** (17hr., daily 3:45pm, s/90); **Piura** (15hr., daily 9:30pm, s/75); **Sullana** (17hr., daily 3:45pm, s/40); **Tacna** (18hr., daily 10:30am, s/55); **Trujillo** (8hr., daily 10:30pm, s/45); **Tumbes** (18hr., daily 4:30pm, s/95).

Empresa La Merced, Luna Pizarro 255, La Victoria (☎423 3667). To: **La Merced** (8hr.; daily 8, 11am, 9, 9:30, 10pm; s/20) via **Tarma** (6hr., s/17); **Oxapampa** (12hr., daily 5pm, s/28).

Flores, Paseo de la República 637 (☎424 3276) and Montevideo 523 (☎426 3623). To: **Arequipa** (14hr.; daily 9am, 1:30, 3:30pm; s/36) via **Nasca** (8hr., s/26); **Chiclayo** (10hr., daily 1pm, s/31); **Cusco** (29hr., daily 5pm, s/71); **Piura** (15hr.; daily 1, 3:15pm); **Tacna** (18hr., daily 10:15pm, s/40); **Trujillo** (8hr., daily 2:15pm, s/60); **Tumbes** (18hr., daily 4pm, s/85).

León de Huánuco, 28 de Julio 1520 (☎424 3893), La Victoria. To: **Huánuco** (8hr.; daily 8:45, 9:45pm; s/23-28); **La Merced** (7hr., daily 9:30pm, s/15); **Pucallpa** (20hr., daily 3, 6pm; s/40); and **Tingo María** (12hr., daily 7:30am, s/30).

Ormeño, Carlos Zavala 177, Lima Centro (☎427 5679; www.grupo-ormeno.com). To: **Arequipa** (15hr., daily 9pm, s/30); **Ayacucho** (13hr.; daily 6:30am, 9pm; s/30); **Chiclayo** (10hr., daily 8pm, s/25); **Cusco** (29hr., daily 4pm, s/140); **Huancayo** (4hr., daily 11pm, s/20); **Huaraz** (8hr.; daily 6:30am, 9pm; s/17); **Ica** (5hr., daily every hr. 6:30am-10pm, s/10); **Juliaca** (20hr., daily 9am, s/210); **Nasca** (7hr., daily 6:30am-9:15pm, s/17); **Pisco** (4hr.; daily 7:30, 9:15am; s/8); **Piura** (15hr., daily 4pm, s/30); **Trujillo** (8hr.; daily 8am, 4, 8, 10:30pm; s/20).

Ormeño Expreso Internacional, Javier Prado Este 1059 (☎ 472 1710). Passengers may take up to 20kg of luggage, US$1-3 for each additional kg. Visa. To: **Bogotá** (3 days; M 1pm, Tu 5pm; US$130); **Buenos Aires** (4 days; Tu, Th, Su 1pm; US$110); **Caracas** (4 days, M 1pm, US$150); **Guayaquil** (1 day, daily 3pm, US$40); **Santiago** (2½ days; Tu, Sa 1:30pm; US$80); **Quito** (1½ days; M 1pm, Tu 5pm; US$50).

■ ORIENTATION

Given Lima's size, it's definitely worth your soles to buy a map. Many bookstores sell *Lima 2000x4* (s/75), which includes four maps. Purchase a basic Lima map for s/15; it will provide much of the same information and save you some soles. Taxis and colectivos are invaluable for traveling efficiently throughout the city.

The main tourist districts are **Lima Centro** and, to the south, **San Isidro, Miraflores,** and **Barranco.** The primary landmark in Lima is the **Plaza Mayor,** the main square, bounded by the streets **La Unión, Junín, Carabaya,** and **Huallaga.** In Lima Centro, streets running from east to west change names when they cross La Unión. Streets in the historic center are generally labeled with plaques on the side of corner buildings showing the colonial name in fancy script, while the more popular name (necessary for navigation) appears in smaller letters above or below. Heading southwest from Plaza Mayor, La Unión's busy **pedestrian walkway** leads to the Centro's second largest square, **Plaza San Martín.** This intersects with one of Lima Centro's biggest streets, **Nicolás de Piérola.** Another major roadway, **Garcilaso de la Vega,** runs north-south a few blocks west of Plaza San Martín. Most east-west streets in this area change names when they cross Garcilaso de la Vega. Heading south, both Piérola and G. de la Vega intersect the east-west thoroughfare, **Grau.** Most of the long-distance colectivos and buses depart from just north of Grau, between Iquitos (which turns into Carlos Zavala) and Piérola. In Lima Centro, the areas west of **Tacna** and east of **Abancay** are generally considered unsafe for tourists after sunset, so be cautious.

The fastest way to head south from Lima Centro is the **Paseo de la República,** parallel to G. de la Vega, which quickly turns into the appropriately named **Vía Expresa.** This highway travels all the way to Barranco. The southern continuation of G. de la Vega, **Arequipa,** ends at the Óvalo in Miraflores, where **Larco** (Arequipa's southern continuation), **José Pardo,** and **Diagonal** all intersect. Diagonal (also known as Oscar R. Benavides, but not to be confused with Alfredo Benavides a few blocks south of the Óvalo) is the easiest direct route down the Miraflores cliffs to the beach. When streets in San Isidro or Miraflores have an "Este" or "Oeste" suffix, it means that that portion of the road lies east or west of Arequipa. To reach Barranco from Miraflores, head south on Larco until it meets the seaside LarcoMar shopping center, then bear east as it merges into Armendariz; Armendariz leads to San Martín, which continues south to Barranco's main **Parque Municipal.**

▐ LOCAL TRANSPORTATION

Public Transportation: Lima's streets are crowded with **buses** and **colectivos** (s/1.20-1.50), which are the cheapest, albeit not usually the fastest, way to travel between 6am and 1am. Colectivos (also called combis) are easy to identify: stickers on their windshields specify destinations, and routes are painted on the vehicles' sides. Boarding can be challenging, as many colectivos race down the street to be the first to reach the awaiting passengers, pushing your chosen bus out of the way. The drivers stop for only a few seconds, so get onboard quickly before the bus speeds away. Stops are not fixed, but shouting "bajo aquí" will allow

LIMA

Miraflores and San Isidro
SEE LEGEND, p. 101

TO 🏛 (1blk), CONTINENTAL (1blk), PROMPERU (3blk)

TO 🏛 (1blk) Australia

TO ⭐ 🏛 2 (4blk)

TO 3 (3blk)

27 DE NOVIEMBRE

TO LIMA CENTRO

TO DHL (6blk)

TO UNIÓN ISRAELITA SHARON, 4 (8blk)

Choque huanca

Rosario
Miro Quesada
Huaca Huallamarca
Toribio
Andes
Espejo
Arequipa
Petit Thouars
Fuente
Villarán
El Parque

Campo de Golf

LetterExpress
Placencia
Conquistadores
República
Cavero
Real
Monclova
Esquilache
Aqua Sport
Paillardelle
SAN ISIDRO
Chacarilla
Capio
Florida
Baños Tivoli
Aramburú

Pezet
Cervantes
Eguiguren
Samanez
Roosevelt
Calderón
Camino
Real
Libertadores
Paz Soldán
Vargas
Los Incas
Morales de la Torre
Arce
Santa Cruz
Arenales
Arequipa
Asunción
Chumbi
Petit Thouars
Sevilla
Águilas
Garzas
Palomas

Teatro Cultural PUCP
Willa Dasso
Bustamante
Pardo y Aliaga
Parro
Rossel
Ángeles
Suárez
Orue
Recavarren
Codornices
Dante

Parque la Redonda
Tudela y Varela
Salazar
Clinica Anglo-Americana
Covendeia
American Express
Santa María
Teruel
Liona
Tenaúd
Huáscar

Cochrane
Zapata
Nelson
Carrión
Herrera
García Calderón
Tacna
Junín
Santa Rosa

Enrico Poli Museum
Vandeghan
Santa Cruz
E. Wong
ÓVALO GUTIÉRREZ
Bellido
5
Montero
Angamos Oeste
Sucre
Meiges
6
Mabich
7
Huaca Pucllana
Entrance
8
José Antonio Sarrio
Tarapacá
Elías
11

Pq. Villena
Llano
Larco Herrera
9

Pq. Palacios
La Mar
Museo Amano
Chiclayo
Rosario
Arica
Borgoño
10
Instituto Cultural Peruano-Norteamericano
Flores
Angamos Este
San Carlos
El Cármen

27 de Noviembre
Chacaltana
Varela
Torre Tagle
Iglesias
Espinar
Aguirre
Piura
PL. SOLARI
Atahualpa
Aguero
Parque Miranda
Huáscar
Santa Rosa
San Agustín
San Miguel

La Mar
Enrique Palacios
Independencia
Inclán
🛈
South American Explorers
Ugarte
Paseo de la República
Gonzales Prada
Leoncio Prado

2 de Mayo
MIRAFLORES
15
TANS
Colina
Colina
San Diego

Túpac Amaru
Moore
PL. MORALES BARROS
12 (2blk)
14
Napanga
León
Roma
Bolognesi
Grau
José Pardo
Lan Peru
Camino
16
Baños Pardo
ÓVALO MIRAFLORES
Bonilla
Esperanza
Palma
Cáceres

Zavala
Galvez
Berlin
18
FedEx
Olaya
Botica Fasa
Parque Central
Cantuarias
Diez Canseco

Francia
Chávez
Recavarren
Fajardo
Canadá
19
21
22
20
Parque Kennedy
Larco
Banco Wiese Sudameris
33
Silva
Trujillo
Alfaro
36

17
PL. BOLOGNESI
Revett
23
24
26 27
Schell
Tarata
31
Servirap Laundry
35
Odiolo
Qicaí
Ulloa

Madrid
Italia
PerúFly
37
Tripoli
25
Interbank $
30
29
32
34

Malecón Cisneros
Balta
Q. Benavides (Diagonal)
San Martín
39
Santa Isabel
Bolívar
40
A. Benavides
Parque Reducto
15 de Enero
Chariarse
Ribeiro

PLAYA COSTA VERDE
Venecia
38
Oupen Sauna
Colón
Western Union $
La Paz
Solar
Reducto

Parque Raimondi
41
Parque del Amor
Mis. 28 de Julio
Lavalle
Buenos Aires
Porta
Ocharán
42
Gonzales
43
Teatro Auditorio Miraflores
Av. 28 de Julio
Manco Cápac

Fanning
Ferre
Larco
Delfas
Alcanfores
Santa Isabel
San Fernando
Núñez de Balboa
TO 14 (2blk)
Castillo

La Paz
La Rosa Náutica
UK
Aljovín
Armendáriz
TO BARRANCO

LarcoMar
45 46 47 48
Mosca Azul

Ignacio de Loyola
Parque Porras

0   400 meters
0   400 yards

Miraflores and San Isidro

SEE MAP, p. 100

🏠 ACCOMMODATIONS

Casa del Mochilero, 13
Eurobackpackers Hostel, 43
Explorers House, 14
Friend's House, 42
HomePeru, 5
International Youth Hostel, 36
Pensión José Luís, 44
Residencial El Castillo, 35
Youth Hostel Malka, 3

🍴 FOOD

Delicatessen Minimarket
  Kosher, 4
El Peruanito, 11
El Señorío de Sulco, 12
Govinda, 34
La Bodega de la Trattoria, 8
Las Brujas de Cachiche, 17
Las Tejas, 31
Makoto Sushi Bar, 45
Namaskar, 7
Palachinke, 24
Palacio Beijing, 40
Punta Sal, 38
Restaurant
  Bircher-Benner, 33
Segundo Muelle, 41
Siham's Rincón
  Árabe-Latino, 9
Sí Señor, 37
Tropicana, 30
Vivaldino, 46
Vrinda, 2

☕ CAFÉS

Café Café, 20
Café Haiti, 22
Gelatería Laritza D., 6
Quattro D, 10
Tarata Café, 29

⭐ ENTERTAINMENT

CineBar, 47
Cine Club Miraflores, 39
El Pacífico, 16
Julieta, 23
Orrantia, 1
UVK Multicines, 48

🍺 NIGHTLIFE

Bierhaus, 21
The Brenchley Arms, 15
Downtown Vale Todo, 25
Freheit Bier & Bar, 26
Legendaris, 18
Los Altos de San Ramón, 19
Murphy's Irish Pub, 32
Tequila Rock, 27

you to disembark. The main colectivo route is **Arequipa/Tacna/Wilson** from Larco in Miraflores, along Arequipa through San Isidro, to Lima Centro. To return to San Isidro or Miraflores from Lima Centro, catch a colectivo marked "Todo Arequipa" on Garcilaso de la Vega. The **Brasil/La Marina/Faucett** route runs from Parque Kennedy in Miraflores to the market on La Marina, and then to the airport. Buses marked **Barranco/Chorrillos** go to the southern nightlife district in Barranco via Arequipa or Larco. Many colectivos also run east-west along Javier Prado from La Molina to San Isidro and Magdalena del Mar.

Taxis: Generally cheap and easy to use, taxis in Lima are never hard to find, but there are no meters, so negotiate a price before entering any cab. A ride should cost s/6-8 from Lima Centro to Miraflores, and s/5-6 within the Miraflores/San Isidro/Barranco area. Tips are not expected. Official taxis are yellow, but regular cars with taxi stickers in their windows are cheaper, usually by a couple of soles. Unofficial taxis are not well regulated and can be extremely dangerous; always call a cab or take a marked taxi. To go outside city limits or to the airport, it's best to call a cab. The following companies operate 24hr.: **Taxi Real,** Los Geránios 438, Lince (☎470 6263); **Taxi Móvil,** Petit Thouars 3970, San Isidro (☎422 6890); and **Taxi Lima** (☎271 1763).

Car Rental: Avis (☎434 1111), **Budget** (☎575 1674), **Dollar** (☎444 3050), **Hertz** (☎445 5716), and **National** (☎433 3750) are all at the airport; ask ground transportation officials for guidance to the car-rental desks. Rental agencies are also located throughout Lima. Compact and stick-shift cars are US$40-50 per day. Dollar and Budget often have specials as low as US$33-35 per day. Most of the companies rent to drivers over 25, but younger drivers can usually rent for a US$5 surcharge if they present a valid credit card.

🔢 PRACTICAL INFORMATION

TOURIST AND FINANCIAL SERVICES

Tourist Offices:

South American Explorers (SAE), Piura 135, Miraflores (☎/fax 445 3306; www.saexplorers.org). The small plaque outside the door is easy to miss, but finding it yields a goldmine of friendly advice and information on all things Peruvian and South American. English spoken. Good collection of maps. Message boards. Book exchange and library. Equipment storage. Membership required for full use of facilities. US$50 per year, but discount available with ISIC. Open M-Tu and Th-F 9:30am-5pm, W 9:30am-8pm, Sa 9:30am-1pm.

Tourist Office, Paseo de los Escribanos 145 (☎427 6080, ext. 222), behind the Plaza Mayor, Lima Centro. This small office provides basic (though not necessarily up-to-date) information on attractions and tour companies. English spoken. Open M-F 9am-6pm, Sa-Su 11am-3pm.

PromPeru, 610 José Basadres (☎574 8000; www.peru.org.pe), right next to the huge Telefónica building in San Isidro, has more up-to-date tourist info, and helpful general advice. Open M-F 9am-1pm and 2:30-5pm.

Instituto Geográfico Nacional, Aramburu 1190 (☎ 475 3030), near the 9th block of República de Panamá in Surquillo, sells a wide selection of **maps.** ID required. Open M-F 9am-5pm.

Tours:

Intej, San Martín 240, Barranco (☎ 247 3230; www.intej.org), 5 blocks up from the park. Not only will they sell you an ISIC, but they'll arrange tours, travel packages, work, study, homestays, or volunteer opportunities (see **Alternatives to Tourism,** p. 81). Fines for changing travel dates must be paid in cash. Open M-F 9:30am-12:30pm and 2-6pm, Sa 9:30am-1pm.

Lima Tours, Belén 1040 (☎ 424 7560; www.limatours.com.pe), runs good city tours.

Peru Smile, Valdemar Mosser 435 (☎ 9 997 1349; perusmile@yahoo.com). Tours of Lima and multi-day trips to northern or southern Peru. Open 24hr.

Queenland Adventures, Callao 144 (☎ 426 5945 or 427 5780), has reasonably- priced tour packages to all parts of the country.

Embassies and Consulates: For Peruvian embassies abroad, see p. 10.

Argentina, 28 de Julio 828, Lima Centro (☎ 433 3381). Open M-F 10am-12:30pm.

Australia, Victor Andrés Belaúnde 147, Edificio Real 3, Of. 1301, San Isidro (☎ 222 8281; fax 221 4996). Open M-F 9am-noon.

Bolivia, Los Castaños 235, San Isidro (☎ 422 8231 or 442 3836; fax 222 4694). Open M-F 9am-1pm.

Brazil, José Pardo 850, Miraflores (☎ 421 5660; consular@embajabrazil.com.pe). Open M-F 9:30am-12:30pm.

Canada, Libertad 130, Miraflores (☎ 444 4015; fax 444 4347). Open M-F 8:30-11:30am and Tu, Th 2-4pm.

Chile, Victor Andrés Belaúnde, San Isidro (☎ 147 611 2211; eglimape@mail.cosapidata.com.pe). Open M-F 9am-1pm.

Colombia, Jorge Basadre 1580, San Isidro (☎ 441 0530; fax 441 9806), on the 4th block of Eucaliptos. Open M-F 9am-1pm.

Ecuador, Las Palmeras 356, San Isidro (☎ 440 9941; fax 442 4182), off the 6th block of Javier Prado Oeste. Open M-F 9am-1pm and 3-6pm.

Ireland, Angamos Oeste 340, U.R.B. Aurora, Miraflores (☎ 446 3878; mgperu@pol.com.pe). Open M-F 9am-1pm.

Israel, Natalio Sánchez 125, 6th fl., Santa Beatriz (☎ 433 4431; fax 433 8925; emisrael@terra.com.pe), facing Plaza Washington. Open M-F 9am-noon.

Mexico, Jorge Basadre 710, San Isidro (☎ 221 1100 or 221 1173). Open M-F 9am-1pm.

Netherlands, Principal 190, 4th fl., Santa Catalina, La Victoria (☎ 476 1069; negovlim@hys.com.pe). Open M-F 9am-noon.

New Zealand, Natalio Sánchez 125, 4th fl. (☎ 433 8923; reya@nzlatam.com). Open M-F 8:30am-2pm.

South Africa, Victor Andrés Belaúnde 147, San Isidro (☎ 440 9996; saemb@post.cosapidata.com.pe). Open M-F 9am-noon.

UK, Larco 1301, Torre Parque Mar 22nd fl., Miraflores (☎ 617 3000; fax 617 3100). Open M-F 8:30am-noon.

US, Encalada Block 17, Monterrico (☎ 434 3000; http://lima.usembassy.gov). Open M-F 8am-5pm.

Immigration Office: Dirección de Inmigración, España 700, 3rd fl., Breña (☎ 330 4114 or 330 4074), 2 blocks west of Ugarte at Huaraz. 30-day visa extension (US$20 plus s/24), up to 3 times per year. New tourist card s/12. Open M-F 9am-1:30pm.

Currency Exchange: Casas de cambio and money changers are all over the city. The best place to do street banking is in central Miraflores on **Tarata,** the pedestrian walkway 1 block south of Schell, or on La Unión in Lima Centro, where the **money changers** (distinctly identifiable in bright yellow, blue, and green vests) are regulated, so you're less likely to be ripped off. To change money indoors, visit **LAC Dollar,** at Camaná 779 (☎ 427 3906) and La Paz 211 (☎ 242 4085) for good rates. Open M-Sa 9:30am-6pm. However, for the best exchange rates in Lima, nothing beats local grocery stores.

Banks: Banco de Crédito, Lampa 499, Lima Centro (☎427 5270), or Larco 1099, Miraflores (☎442 8642). Changes and sells AmEx and Visa traveler's checks, makes Visa cash advances, and has Plus/V **ATMs.** Open M-F 9am-6pm, Sa 9am-12:30pm. **Banco Wiese,** Carabaya 545, Lima Centro; Alfonso Ugarte 1292, Breña; Larco 642, Miraflores (☎211 6000). Gives MC cash advances. Changes AmEx, Citicorp traveler's checks. All open M-F 9:15am-6pm, Sa 9:30am-noon. **Interbank,** La Unión 600 at Huancavelica, Lima Centro; Larco 690 at Benavides, Miraflores (☎219 2000; www.interbank.com.pe). Exchanges AmEx, Citibank, Thomas Cook, and Visa traveler's checks. No commission if exchanging for soles, US$5 commission for US dollars. They also sell AmEx and Citicorp traveler's checks at a 1% commission. Open M-F 9am-6pm.

ATM: Most **Red Unicard** ATMs accept Cirrus, Maestro, MC, PLUS, and Visa; some will accept only Visa and Plus. 24hr. machines at **Banco de Comercio,** Lampa and Ucayali, Lima Centro; **Banco Wiese Sudameris,** Larco at Tarata, Miraflores; **Banco de Lima,** Grau 422, Barranco.

American Express: Prado and Aliaga, San Isidro (☎441 4794). Sells AmEx traveler's checks, but does not exchange them for cash. Open M-F 9am-5:30pm, Sa 9am-1pm.

Western Union: Locations include Carabaya 693, Lima Centro (☎428 7614); Larco 826 at 28 de Julio, Miraflores (☎/fax 241 1220); and the main office at Petit Thouars 3595 (☎422 0014). Many more throughout the greater Lima area; ☎422 0014 or www.westernunion.com can find the one nearest you.

LOCAL SERVICES

English-Language Bookstores: Mosca Azul, Malecón de la Reserva 713, Miraflores (☎241 0675), next to Kentucky Fried Chicken on the east side of LarcoMar, sells used non-Spanish books, mostly of the Harlequin romance variety (s/5-9). Open M-Sa 10am-9pm, Su 3-10pm. **Librería Época,** Belén 1072, has guide books and a small foreign language section. Open M-F 10am-7pm and Sa 10am-1:30pm. **South American Explorers** (p. 101) has a variety of English and foreign language books for exchange and an extensive library with 2-week check-out for members only.

Library: Biblioteca Nacional, 4th block of Abancay, Lima Centro (☎428 7690; http://binape.perucultural.org.pe). In-depth collection about Lima's history (Spanish only). A 1-year library card (s/8, necessary even for a 1-day visit) requires a valid passport. Open M-Sa 8am-8pm, Su 9am-1pm.

Cultural Centers: Find newspapers, magazines, film screenings, and cultural events from various countries at the **Instituto Cultural Peruano-Norteamericano** (ICPNA), Cusco 446, Lima Centro (☎428 3530), or Angamos Oeste 160 at Arequipa, Miraflores (☎241 1940; http://icpnacultural.perucultural.org.pe); the **British Council,** Alberto Lynch 110 (☎221 7552), near the Óvalo Gutiérrez at the Miraflores-San Isidro border, offers resources for English speakers; Germans can visit the **Goethe-Institut,** Nasca 722, Jesús María (☎433 3180; open M-F 9am-8pm).

Jewish Centers: 3 synagogues: conservative **Unión Israelita Sharon,** 2 de Mayo 1815, San Isidro (☎440 0290), by the 18th block of Javier Prado; reform **Sociedad de 1870** (☎445 1009); and an **orthodox congregation,** 581 Enrique Bira (☎471 7230). Also: **Club Hebraica** (☎437 2395), outside the city; **Delicatessen Minimarket Kosher,** Pezet 1472, San Isidro (☎264 2187), around the corner from the Israelita Sharon.

Gay and Lesbian Organizations: Movimiento Homosexual de Lima, Mariscal Miller 828, Jesús María (☎433 6375; fax 433 5519), has lots of info. Discussion groups 7:30-9:30pm: M women, Sa men, F mixed groups. Open M-F 9am-1:30pm and 4-9pm. See http://gaylimape.tripod.com for more current information on events and gay-friendly hostels and clubs.

Laundromat: Common in Miraflores, but more scarce in Lima Centro. Available at many hostels. A good price is s/12-14 per 4kg. **Servirap,** Schell 601, Miraflores (☎241 0759), at Solar, will wash everything you can cram into their big baskets for s/16; same-day service s/20. Dry-cleaning 4 shirts s/12. Open M-Sa 8am-10pm, Su 10am-6pm. **Lavandería K10,** España 481, Lima Centro (☎332 9035). For loads over 4 kg, s/3 per kg. Open daily 7am-8pm.

Pharmacies: Well-stocked **Boticas Fasa** has two 24hr. locations: La Unión 616, Lima Centro (☎222 2662); and Larco 129, Miraflores (☎444 0511), on Parque Central. Many other locations around the city; call ☎619 0000 for the nearest and free delivery.

EMERGENCY AND COMMUNICATIONS

Emergency: Police ☎105. Fire ☎116.

Police: Miraflores ☎445 4216; San Isidro ☎421 1627; Barranco ☎477 0088; Breña ☎424 4263. **Tourist police,** Pasaje Tambo de Mora 104 (☎424 2053), and at the corner of Belén and Uruguay.

Tourist Protection Bureau: INDECOPI, La Prosa 138, San Borja (☎574 8000, 24hr. hotline), works to protect tourists' consumer rights. Helps tourists in the event of lost or stolen documents and valuables. English spoken. Open M-F 8:30am-4:30pm.

Medical Services: Clínica Internacional, Washington 1471, Lima Centro (☎433 4306), between 9 de Diciembre and España. Consultations s/70-100, depending on doctor. Open M-F 8am-8pm, Sa 8am-2pm for consultations, 24hr. for emergencies. **Clínica Anglo-Americana** (☎221 3656), on the 300 block of Salazar, San Isidro, has the best selection of immunizations (though no typhoid). Consultations s/125-200. Open M-F 8am-8pm and Sa 9am-noon. Both clinics have English-speaking doctors. **Hospital del Niño,** Brasil 600, Breña (☎330 0066) specializes in children's health.

Telephones: You can dial home-country operators from most **Telefónica del Perú** phones, found on many street corners (s/0.50). For regular international calls, dial ☎108 to reach an operator. Local calls s/0.50, but an increasing number of pay phones only accept phone cards. Telefónica del Perú or Telepoint cards are sold in most small markets and pharmacies (s/5-50) and on street corners. **Directory assistance** ☎103. **National Operator Assistance** ☎109. **Telefónica del Perú,** La Unión 620 (☎433 1616), allows collect calls. Open daily 8am-11pm.

Internet Access: Plentiful all over the city, especially in Lima Centro on La Unión Block 8, one block north of Plaza San Martín, and in Miraflores on Tarata, the pedestrian walkway just off Larco. s/2-4 per hr. in Lima Centro, s/1.50-2 per hr. in Miraflores. Most open daily 8am-10pm; some on Tarata open 24hr. If you see incredibly low prices posted in the window, they may only be valid during off-peak hours. Die-hard cheapskates can get 1hr. free Internet access at the Congress building (☎426 0769), at Junín and Lampa, 2 blocks east of Plaza Mayor in Lima Centro. You must book in advance and bring a foreign passport.

Post Offices: Correo Central (☎427 0370), on Pasaje Piura, half a block from Plaza Mayor. Open M-F 8am-8pm, Su 9am-3:30pm. Main **Miraflores** office, Petit Thouars 5201 (☎445 0697; www.serpost.com.pe). Open M-Sa 8am-8pm. Main **Barranco** branch, Grau 610, of. 101 (☎477 5837), in the Galerías Gemina complex. Open daily 8:30am-5:45pm. The **Poste Restante** (Lista de Correos) office is around the corner from Correo Central at Camaná 189; address letters to: (name), Poste Restante, Lima 1, Peru. Open M-Sa 8am-8:30pm.

Express Mail: It's quicker and more secure to send packages via an express mail service like **DHL,** Los Castaños 225, San Isidro (☎517 2500). Open M-F 8:30am-9pm, Sa 9am-5pm, Su 9am-1pm. **LetterExpress,** Libertadores 199 (☎444 4509), San Isidro. Open M-F 9am-1pm, Sa 10am-1pm. **FedEx,** Mártir Olayo 260 (☎242 2280), Miraflores. Open M-F 8:30am-6pm.

▐ ACCOMMODATIONS

ACCOMMODATIONS BY PRICE

B Breña **LC** Lima Centro **SMB** San Isidro, Miraflores, and Barranco

UNDER S/11 (❶)		Residencial El Castillo (109)	SMB
Explorers House (108)	SMB	Youth Hostel Malka (108)	SMB
Hostal San Francisco (106)	LC		
		S/25-38 (❸)	
S/11-24 (❷)		HomePeru (108)	SMB
Casa del Mochilero (107)	SMB	▨ Hospedaje Plaza Mayor (105)	LC
Eurobackpackers Hostel (108)	SMB	Hostal de Los Artes (107)	B
▨ Friend's House (107)	SMB	▨ Hostal Iquique (106)	B
Hostal Santa Rosa (106)	LC	Hotel La Casona (106)	LC
▨ Hotel España (105)	LC	Pensión José Luís (107)	SMB
Hotel Europa (106)	LC	▨ The Point (107)	SMB
Hotel Wiracocha (106)	LC		
Machu Picchu Guest House (107)	B	**S/39-59 (❹)**	
Pensión Familia Rodríguez (106)	LC	▨ Hostal Roma (105)	LC
Pensión Ibarra (106)	LC	International Youth Hostel (HI) (107)	SMB
		Mochilero's Backpackers (108)	SMB

LIMA CENTRO

Staying in Lima Centro is convenient for visiting most of Lima's tourist attractions, but the area is older and noisier than its southern neighbors San Isidro, Miraflores, and Barranco. It may feel a little worn, but there's no better place to get a real sense of how the capital's colonial history blends with contemporary culture. *Casas antiguas* (rambling 17th-century mansions that have been converted into hotels) are by far the most attractive and affordable options in Lima Centro. If you look beyond the eccentric decor, uneven floorboards, and occasional errant paint chip—focusing instead on the elaborately-painted ceilings and arched doorways—your time here may prove remarkable. Even hostels in buildings that have been stripped of their colonial hearts by years of renovations have the advantage of a historic, central location. Lima's chilly winter mist makes the ubiquitous hot showers a luxury you are bound to appreciate. As in most of Peru, expect to pay significantly more for a private bath.

▨ **Hostal Roma,** Ica 326 (☎ 427 7576; www.hostalroma.8m.com). Stand in Roma's bright and airy tiled courtyard and leave the gray monotony of Lima Centro behind. The hostel's comfortable rooms are all clean but vary greatly in attractiveness—look for one with a skylight or windows. Simple 2-level coffee shop serves breakfast. Rides from the airport available on request. Internet s/3 per hr. 24hr. hot water. TV lounge w/cable. Singles US$13, with bath and breakfast US$16; doubles US$20, with bath and breakfast US$25; triples US$28, with bath and breakfast US$33. Prices 20% lower Jan.-May and Nov. to mid-Dec. 7-10% SAE discount. ❹

▨ **Hotel España,** Azángaro 105 (☎ 427 9196; hotel_espana@hotmail.com). This statue-filled colonial house echoes with the commotion of enthusiastic backpackers. The roof-top garden and cafe (open daily 8am-11pm) double as an aviary. Request a room with a balcony or window to avoid dark rooms. Airport transportation for groups of 2 or more (US$2-3). Internet s/2 per hr. (9am-10pm). Telefónica in lobby. Message board. 24hr. hot water. Locked storage facilities (bring your own padlock). Laundry service. Check-out noon. Curfew 1:30am. Dorms US$3; singles without bath US$6; doubles US$9; triples US$12; quads US$14. Discounts available for longer stays. ❷

▨ **Hospedaje Plaza Mayor,** Callao 125 (☎ 426 7487; www.hospedajeplazamayor.com). Just half a block from its namesake, this modern hostel stands out from the many *casas antiguas* typical of the area. Most rooms have carpeted floors and private baths, and all have their own TVs, making this one of the best values in Lima Centro. Airport transportation available. 24hr. hot water. Discounts for stays of 15 days or more. Singles s/30; doubles s/20 per person. ❸

Hostal San Francisco, Azangaro 127-125 (☎436 2735; hostalsf.lanpro.com.pe), a few blocks away from the Plaza Mayor. Spacious and very comfortable, this modern establishment is a quiet, welcoming respite from the chaos of downtown. Each bed includes a desk lamp for late-night reading. Internet (s/2 per hr.) and TV lounge. Storage facilities (bring your own lock). Hot water. Dorms s/10; doubles s/30, with bath s/42. ❶

Pensión Ibarra, Tacna 359, No. 1402 and 1502, 14th and 15th fl. (☎/fax 427 8603). If you can find this family-owned hideaway (there's no sign), you'll be rewarded with impressive views of Lima. This home-away-from-home provides laundry facilities and full kitchen access. Noise from the busy street dies down in the late evening, but if you plan to get much sleep you might as well ask for a room off the street. No private bathrooms. Hot water either in the morning or at night—check with the proprietress. Dorms and singles US$7; doubles s/25; triples s/40. 10% discount on stays of 10 days or more. 10% SAE discount. ❷

Pensión Familia Rodríguez, Nicolás de Piérola 730, 2nd fl. apartment #3 (☎423 6465; jotajot@pol.com.pe). This simple apartment, equipped with a 6-person dorm room, a matrimonial, and a triple, provides a family atmosphere and small, yet comfortable, quarters. The clientele is limited to non-Peruvians, consisting primarily of European and North American travelers. 24hr. hot water. Breakfast included. Reservations recommended, especially June-Aug. Dorms US$6. ❷

Hotel Europa, Ancash 376 (☎427 3351). This massive, labyrinthine *casa antigua* could use some windows in its large, sparsely-decorated bedrooms; nonetheless, its relatively peaceful location across from a beautiful convent remains backpacker-friendly. Restaurant. TV lounge. Hot water. Luggage storage. Singles s/16; doubles s/23; triples s/30. Rooms available with private baths. ❷

Hostal Santa Rosa, Camaná 218 (☎427 8647), a few steps from the tourist office. This centrally-located hostel's rooms vary significantly in size. Still, all provide a peaceful, if basic, retreat from the crowds and noise of the surrounding area. Hot water. Singles s/14, with bath s/20; doubles s/25, with bath s/35. Discount with payment up front. ❷

Hotel La Casona, Moquegua 289 (☎/fax 426 6552). This *casa antigua*'s wide, beautiful courtyard, and elegant marble staircase recall Lima's rich colonial past. Though the rooms seem a bit tired, they are all carpeted, with antique wooden furniture and hot water. Courtyard restaurant open 8am-8pm. Singles s/25, with breakfast or TV s/28; doubles s/30, with breakfast or TV s/35; triples s/40, with breakfast or TV s/54. Discounts available for longer stays and groups of 10 or more. ❸

Hotel Wiracocha, Junín 284 (☎427 1178), half a block from Plaza Mayor. For such a large place with a central location, the quiet—if characterless—rooms feel surprisingly private. TV lounge. Hot water. Singles s/20, with bath s/25; matrimonials s/25, with bath s/30; doubles s/35, with bath s/40; triples, with bath s/54. No credit cards. ❷

BREÑA

Though not exactly smack in the middle of the action, Breña hotels are a short 20min. walk from the sights of Lima Centro. Hotels here offer more substance for your soles; rooms are generally cleaner, quieter, larger, and better decorated than those in Lima Centro.

■ **Hostal Iquique,** Iquique 758 (☎433 4724; http://barrioperu.terra.com.pe/hiquique). The common baths, lined with plants and decorative tiles, are spotless in this recently renovated hostel. Some rooms have telephone/TV; most are spacious and have a table. 24hr. hot water. Kitchen access. Book exchange. Lobby TV. Internet s/2 per hr. Airport transportation US$13. Singles US$7, with bath US$10; matrimonials US$9, with bath US$13; doubles US$10, with bath US$16. ❸

Hostal de Los Artes, Chota 1460 (☎433 0031; artes@terra.com.pe), near the Museo de Arte. A beautiful, though sparsely decorated, Dutch-owned and operated *casa antigua*. Spacious rooms with unbelievably high ceilings, and 1 awesome 2-story triple. Plenty of hot water, extra blankets, and towels. Helpful staff. Small but growing book exchange. Check-out 11am. Singles s/30; doubles with bath s/50; triples s/60. ❸

Machu Picchu Guest House, Juan Pablo Fernandini 1015 (☎/fax 424 3479), parallel to Brasil Block 10. This narrow hostel is a long walk from Lima Centro (with easy access by bus from Brasil), but its unrivaled friendliness makes it worth the trek. Ample rooms and comfy TV lounge with videos and cable. Laundry service. Common kitchen. English spoken. Breakfast included (8am-noon). Reservations recommended. Dorms s/12; doubles s/24; triples s/36. ❷

SAN ISIDRO, MIRAFLORES, AND BARRANCO

Hotels increase in modernity as you move south from Lima Centro; dorm-style rooms are more prevalent in the many family-owned places that welcome the independent traveler with the comforts of home. Such comforts generally come at a price. For example, kitchen access is much more common in these areas, though paying to use the stove and oven is sometimes required. Generally speaking, San Isidro, Miraflores, and Barranco rooms are more secure, peaceful, and pristine than the ones in Lima Centro. Staying in the suburbs offers proximity to Lima's exciting nightlife, and to a wider variety of restaurants as well. Know your destination's address in advance, as most establishments lack prominent signs.

Friend's House, Manco Cápac 368, Miraflores (☎446 6248), 2 blocks to the right of Larco (when facing the ocean). The location of this little teal-colored *casa* is ideal—right off busy José Larco and a few blocks from LarcoMar. Time here passes over the foosball table, in front of the cable TV, in the small living room, or in the kitchen. Dorms are tightly packed, but very comfortable. Rides from the airport US$10. Communal hot baths. Free bicycle use. Breakfast included. Dorms US$6; doubles US$12; triples US$18. Discounts for longer stays. ❷

The Point, Malecón Junín 300, Barranco (☎247 7997 or 247 7709; www.thepointhostel.com), off San Martín and Ugarte. This self-proclaimed "by backpackers, for backpackers" hostel is a gem amid the many similar lodging options of Miraflores and Barranco. Come for the young and hip atmosphere, the house-owned guests-only pub, ping pong, book exchange, hammocks, and oceanside locale. Very popular, so call ahead. Internet s/3 per hour. Cable TV. Kitchen. 24hr. hot water. US$7-9 per person. ❸

Pensión José Luís, Francisco de Paula Ugarriza 727, Miraflores (☎444 1015; www.hoteljoseluis.com), off 28 de Julio between República de Panamá and Paseo de la República. Walk into this richly decorated house and delight in the elegant living room and peaceful front patio. Each simple room has its own bath. Kitchen. Reading rooms. Cable TV. Book exchange. Telephones on each floor. Airport service US$10. Breakfast included. Reservations required. US$10 per person. ❸

International Youth Hostel (HI), Casimiro Ulloa 328, Miraflores (☎446 5488; fax 444 8187), off Alfredo Benavides. The largest hostel in the area, in a quiet, mainly residential neighborhood. There is nothing particularly authentic or charming about this clean, modern, well-furnished hostel, but it does offer hotel-like amenities including a lobby and sitting rooms. In-house Telefónica and Internet (s/4 per hr.). Laundry facilities. Kitchen access (s/2 for stove). TV lounge. Full travel desk (open M-F 9am-5pm). Luggage storage. Check-out 12:30pm. Dorms US$12.50, with HI membership US$10.50; doubles with bath US$28.50, with HI membership US$26. ❹

Casa del Mochilero, Cesareo Chacaltana 130-A, Miraflores (☎242 2409 and 445 5219; mochilerosinn@hotmail.com), the red house off the circle at the 10th block of José Pardo. The large sign is a blessing, as are the leather armchairs around a cable TV with DVD player, and warm family atmosphere. You'll find all the necessities here—hot water, clean

A MATCH MADE IN INDIA?

You can't take a combi ride in Peru without stumbling over a Hare Krishna restaurant. Most Hare Krishnas are ethnic Peruvians, many raised Catholic, who converted to this form of Hinduism as adults. The tradition originated in India, and the first Hare Krishna center in Lima opened in 1977. Over the years, the movement grew, attracting terrorism-scarred Peruvians with its non-violent philosophy. Today, the Peruvian Hare Krishna population numbers in the thousands and adheres to a few basic principles: strict vegetarianism, no drugs, and no attachment to material objects. Though they revere the Hindu god, Krishna, devotees emphasize that they are not Hindus, but merely adherents to Krishna consciousness."

To at least one "scholar," the Hare Krishna craze in Peru makes perfect sense. On a trip to Peru, Indian architect V. Ganapati Sthapati discovered that Machu Picchu conforms exactly to the design principles prescribed by the Vastu Shastras of India, as does the Sacsayhuamán complex in Cusco. After finding the same similarities in other Latin American architectural masterpieces, Sthapati theorized that Mayan, the creator of Indian architecture, descended from the Maya people of Central America, and that the Hindu planning principles actually originated centuries ago, in Latin America.

rooms, and cheap prices. A bit far from the action, but the extra quiet provides a good night's sleep. Locked storage facilities in rooms. Kitchen access. Tight, but comfortable, 5-person dorms US$4. ❷

HomePeru, Arequipa 4501 (☎241 9898; www.home-peru.com), at Junín. From the outside, this hostel simply looks like any other house lining the busy street, but inside, you'll find one of the most spacious hostels in all of Lima. The lovely garden and authentic tiled patio all contribute to the charm of this centrally-located establishment. Free Internet and cable TV. Hot water 24hr. Kitchen access (US$2 for stove use). Storage facilities. Dorm US$8; private rooms US$10, with bath US$12 per person. ❸

Youth Hostel Malka, Los Lirios 165, San Isidro (☎442 0162; www.youthhostelperu.com). From Arequipa, head 4 blocks up Javier Prado Este, turn right on Las Camelias (just before Bembo's Burgers), then right on Los Lirios. This popular hostel's slightly obscure location only adds to its peaceful atmosphere. Malka offers comfortable rooms at good rates, complete with a lush green garden with a small climbing wall and ping-pong table. Cable TV/DVD with Playstation. Internet. Manager speaks English. Common bathrooms. Hot water. Luggage storage. Cafeteria (breakfast US$3). Laundry service (US$1 per kg.). Single-sex dorms US$6, with ISIC US$5. ❷

Eurobackpackers Hostel, Manco Cápac 471, Miraflores (☎791 2945; www.eurobackpackers.com), right off Larco. This simple, comfortable hostel offers city tours as a part of the room rate. Hammock. Free Internet. Cable TV. Breakfast included. Kitchen access. Laundry service. Hot water 24hr. Dorm US$7, with extras (Internet, breakfast, and city tour) US$10; doubles US$17, with extras US$20. ❷

Mochilero's Backpackers, Pedro de Osma 135, Barranco (☎477 4506; www.backpackersperu.com), 1 block from Parque Municipal, where buses leave for all parts of the city. This converted mansion has a giant open foyer, a cable TV room, board games, hot common baths, and a fully stocked kitchen. The adjoining pub, **Mochilero's,** gets rowdy on weekends (M-Sa 7pm-3am). Close to nightlife. Lockers (bring your own lock). Breakfast US$1. Dorms US$10, with ISIC US$9; singles with breakfast US$15; doubles with breakfast US$25. ❹

Explorers House, Alfredo Leon 158, Miraflores (☎241 5002; explorers_house@yahoo.es). Just a few blocks from the beach, Explorers House is the cheapest bed and breakfast in Miraflores and still manages to be quite comfortable. English-speaking owner. Kitchen access. 24hr. hot water. Cable TV with DVD player. Laundry service. Dorms US$5. ❶

Residencial El Castillo, Diez Canseco 580 (☎446 9501). Quiet, antique-filled mini-mansion with a tranquil backyard. Simple but sufficient rooms. 24hr. hot water. Dorms US$12; doubles US$24; triples US$30. Discounts for longer stays. ❷

◨ FOOD

FOOD BY TYPE

LC Lima Centro SMB San Isidro, Miraflores, and Barranco			
CAFES		Tropicana (113)	SMB ❶
Café Café (112)	SMB ❶	Quattro D. (4-D) (112)	SMB ❷
Café Haiti (112)	SMB ❹	**INTERNATIONAL**	
📷 Gelatería Laritza D. (112)	SMB ❶	Café Haiti (112)	SMB ❹
Quattro D. (4-D) (112)	SMB ❷	📷 El Mesón del Almirante (110)	LC ❷
📷 Tarata Café (112)	SMB ❸	Namaskar (111)	SMB ❹
CHINESE (CHIFAS)		Siham's Rincón's Árabe-Latino (112)	SMB ❷
Salón de Los Espejos (110)	LC ❸	Sí Señor (111)	SMB ❸
Palacio Beijing (111)	SMB ❸	**SEAFOOD AND CEVICHERÍAS**	
Wa Lok (114)	LC ❹	Los Manglares de Tumbes (110)	LC ❸
CRIOLLO		Makoto Sushi Bar (111)	SMB ❸
📷 El Mesón del Almirante (110)	LC ❷	Punta Sal (111)	SMB ❹
📷 Manos Morenas (113)	SMB ❹	📷 Segundo Muelle (110)	SMB ❹
Restaurante Paraíso (113)	LC ❶	**TRADITIONAL PERUVIAN**	
Salón de Los Espejos (110)	LC ❸	El Peruanito (113)	SMB ❶
Vivaldino (114)	SMB ❹	El Señorío de Sulco (114)	SMB ❺
EUROPEAN		Javier (111)	SMB ❸
Antica Trattoria (111)	SMB ❹	La Bodega de la Trattoria (111)	SMB ❸
📷 L'Eau Vive (109)	LC ❷	Las Brujas de Cachiche (114)	SMB ❹
Palachinke (110)	SMB ❹	Las Tejas (111)	SMB ❸
FAST FOOD		Los Balcones de Olaya (113)	LC ❶
D'nnos Pizza (113)	LC/SMB ❶	Restaurante Paraíso (113)	LC ❶
Norky's (113)	LC ❶	**VEGETARIAN AND VEGETARIAN-FRIENDLY**	
GELATERÍAS AND JUICES		Govinda (113)	SMB ❶
📷 Gelatería Laritza D. (112)	SMB ❶	Natur (113)	LC ❶
Los Frutales (113)	LC ❶	Restaurant Bircher-Benner (111)	SMB ❷
		📷 Vrinda (112)	SMB ❶

LIMA CENTRO

While Lima Centro's lunch *menús* (s/3.50-6) offer the most bang for your *sol*, their conspicuous lack of variety can get old fast. Still, nowhere else provides such a wide selection of inexpensive eateries in so small an area. A few particularly cheap places line Azángaro and some of the other avenues surrounding the Plaza Mayor. Food stalls line Lima Centro's streets, particularly at night, and offer cheap Peruvian treats—s/0.50 can buy a delicious *empanada*. **Hipermercado Metro,** at Venezuela and Ugarte in Breña, is one of the few mega-markets near Lima Centro. (Open M-Sa 9am-10pm, Su 9am-9pm.)

📷 **L'Eau Vive,** Ucayali 370 (☎427 5612), a few blocks from Plaza Mayor and 1 block west of the Biblioteca Nacional. Most travelers come here for their 3-course lunch *menú* (s/12), but skip that option—it's just like any *menú* in town. Ordering a la carte gets you carefully prepared French delicacies that can't be found for such a bargain anywhere else in Peru. Dinner is a splurge, but delicious. L'Eau is run by friendly Carmelite nuns who donate all profits to charity. A la carte lunch s/8-12. Pasta s/10. Dinner entrees s/ 25-50. Open M-Sa 12:30-3pm and 7:30-9:30pm. Visa accepted at dinner. ❷

🍽 **El Mesón del Almirante,** Huancavelica 151 (☎427 5971). This 2-story haven for businessmen and older tourists specializes in an array of *criollo* and international dishes to suit every palate. The hearty and delicious *parihuela* soup (s/14), a seafood stew, will keep you cozy-warm for the rest of the afternoon. *Menú* with meat and chicken options s/9. Chicken entrees s/12-18. Seafood and meat entrees s/18-21. Open M-Sa 8am-5pm. s/20 min. to use DC/MC/V. ❷

Los Manglares de Tumbes, Moquegua 266 (☎427 1494). Nothing's subtle at this rowdy combination of fisherman's wharf and Las Vegas showroom. Bamboo shoots painted in psychedelic colors reflect off mirrors as disco lights spin, creating a bright escape from Lima's dreary weather. The salsa band, which arrives at 2pm, helps you forget the cramped dining area. The huge menu, available in English, offers tasty seafood dishes like mixed *ceviche* (s/18). Entrees s/12.50-25. Open Tu-Th 10am-10pm, F-Sa 10am-midnight, Su 9am-7pm. ❸

Salón de Los Espejos, in Hotel Murray, Ucayali 201 (☎428 8188). The aptly-named Salón de Los Espejos (Hall of Mirrors) offers high-quality *criollo* and *chifa* specialities served in a palatial French-style banquet room. Lavish *criollo* all-you-can-eat buffet every Friday (s/25). The space may be reserved for afternoon tea (desserts, sandwiches, and tea; s/30) by calling ahead. *Criollo* or *chifa menú* s/14. Entrees s/25. Open daily noon-4pm. AmEx/DC/MC/V. ❸

SAN ISIDRO, MIRAFLORES, BARRANCO

With a few exceptions (mostly listed below), there are four types of restaurants in the San Isidro-Miraflores-Barranco area: cheap fast food, economical but unexceptional *chifas*, expensive international cafes, and excellent *criollo* restaurants and *cevicherías*. Though traditional Peruvian food is less common than in Lima Centro, the quality is often superior. International restaurants offer rarities like sushi or samosas, though at higher prices. In Miraflores, San Ramón is a popular and exciting street radiating from Diagonal on the west side of Parque Kennedy, and houses a plethora of nearly identical Italian restaurants (large pizzas around s/ 25). Most popular dining options lie in Miraflores, as Barranco contains more nightlife and residential areas, and San Isidro lacks variety. Most establishments cater to a clientele of upper-class families and accept credit cards. Numerous supermarkets in the area provide an alternative dining option. Try **Santa Isabel,** Benavides 481, Miraflores (☎444 0087), one block east of Larco, and José Pardo 715, Miraflores (☎446 5931), or **E. Wong,** Santa Cruz 771, Miraflores (☎422 3300), at Óvalo Gutiérrez, and Paseo de la Republic 2440, San Isidro (☎421 0999), just north of Javier Prado in the Centro Comercial. (All open daily approx. 9am-9pm; Santa Isabel's Benavides location open 24hr.)

🍽 **Segundo Muelle,** Malecón Cisneros 156, Miraflores, and other various locations (☎241 2517; www.segundomuelle.com), in front of Parque del Amor. This popular seafood restaurant is packed with preppy well-to-do families in khakis and sweaters enjoying the afternoon in front of a striking oceanside view. Serves what is possibly the yummiest *ceviche* in all of Lima. Try the creamy *ceviche segundo muelle* (s/28) and taste perfection. Most dishes average around s/25-30. Open daily noon-5pm. AmEx/MC/V. ❹

Palachinke, Schell 120, Miraflores (☎447 2601), on Parque Kennedy; also in Surco at the Centro Comercial El Polo (☎437 7764; open daily 1pm-midnight). A cozy restaurant reminiscent of a Swiss chalet, with friendly staff. Sit at one of the tables covered in blue-checkered cloth near the open kitchen to watch the cooks frying up the best crepe-style pancakes in town. The *mediano* size is easily large enough for a meal (s/14-18). Lunch *menú* until 5pm s/14. Open M 3-11pm, Tu-Su noon-11pm. AmEx/MC/V. ❸

Punta Sal, Malecón Cisneros Block 3, Miraflores (☎445 9675), across from Parque del Amor; also at Conquistadores 948, San Isidro (☎441 7431). It's no surprise that this place is famous among *Limeños* for its fresh, authentic *ceviche* (s/28). The Miraflores location has fast and friendly service, with a great ocean view. Entrees around s/24. Both open daily 11am-5pm. Miraflores location open F-Sa 11am-11pm. MC/V. ❹

Antica Trattoria, San Martín 201, Barranco (☎247 3443). There may be an abundance of Italian restaurants in Lima, but few can claim a chef trained in Italy. Hardwood floors, rustic tables, and a brick oven near the entrance are reminiscent of an authentic Italian villa. Given the quality of the food and romantic, elegant atmosphere, higher prices aren't surprising. Pasta s/20-28. Risotto s/26-30. Open daily 12:30-4pm and 7:30pm-12:30am. AmEx/MC/V. ❹

Javier, Bajada de Baños 403-B, Barranco (☎477 5339). Take the stairs to the left of Puente de los Suspiros down a stone walkway for about 3min.; it's in a yellow building on the left. Rooftop tables at this packed restaurant offer a breathtaking view, especially at sunset. The slightly bland decor is balanced by the otherwise romantic atmosphere; bring a date and join the hordes of lovestruck youngsters lining the walkway nearby, enjoying the views and soothing lull of the Pacific. *Ceviche* s/12. *Anticuchos* (skewered cow heart) s/7. Open M-Th 4pm-1am, F-Su noon-4am. ❷

La Bodega de la Trattoria, General Borgono 784 (☎241 6899), across from entrance to Huaca Pucllana. This ritzy restaurant with outdoor seating offers a wide menu, specials listed on the chalkboard, marble tables, and wonderfully warm terra-cotta-colored walls. Gaze onto the peaceful plaza or the stunning Huaca in a relaxed atmosphere. Entrees s/15-25. Open daily 8:30am-2am. AmEx/MC/V. ❸

Palacio Beijing, Alfredo Benavides 768-B, Miraflores (☎444 3569), between Solar and Paseo de la República. Palacio lives up to its imperial name with unpretentious elegance and enormous meals, serving up delicious and cheap food. The multilingual manager has been said to entertain guests with piano solos. Vegetarian-friendly. Delivery. Filling 3-course meal s/11-12. Dinner for 2 s/25-30. Open daily noon-11pm. ❸

Makoto Sushi Bar, on the bottom level of LarcoMar, Miraflores (☎444 5030), and on Las Begonias 522 in San Isidro. Though Peru is famous for another form of raw fish, Makoto is a suitable fix for the sushi junkie. The interior emulates a Japanese rock garden, complete with a soothing water feature. Rolls s/12-15. Sashimi for 2 s/39. Open M-Th 12:30pm-midnight, F-Sa 12:30pm-1am, Su 12:30-11pm. AmEx/MC/V. ❸

Las Tejas, Diez Canseco 340, Miraflores (☎444 4360). Right off Larco. Don't be fooled by the red-tiled floor and wrought-iron fence; this is no Spanish *tapas* bar, serving typical Peruvian food instead. Enjoy the *ceviche* (s/27) or some *antichuchos* (s/15) sitting below street-level. Open daily noon-midnight. MC/V. ❸

Restaurant Bircher-Benner, Diez Canseco 487, Miraflores (☎444 4250), between Larco and Paseo de la República. Founded by a vegetarian German immigrant in 1972, Bircher-Benner is dedicated to providing a wide array of scrumptious, high-quality—though pricier—vegetarian options. Next to the brightly colored, elegant dining room is one of the best health food stores in all of Lima. Individual pizzas s/18-24, omelettes s/16-19. *Menú* noon-1pm s/10-11. Open M-Sa 8:30am-10:30pm. AmEx/MC/V. ❷

Namaskar, Espinar 651 (☎445 8174). Namaskar's owner, born and bred in Delhi, welcomes herbivores and carnivores alike with authentic Indian dishes in this simple and pleasant site hidden on a street filled with fast-food outlets. Samosas s/6-8. Entrees s/ 18-40. Open daily 11am-3pm and 6-11pm. AmEx/V. ❹

Sí Señor, Bolognesi 706, Miraflores (☎/fax 445 3789), also 598 Angamos Oeste. A festive *cantina* serving Mexican favorites of average quality (tacos s/18-22, burritos s/24). The real draw is the bar. Come ready to show your allegiance to José Cuervo (tequila shots s/5-8) and get carried away with the Mexican vibe. Happy hour 5-9pm. Open daily 5pm-midnight. AmEx/MC/V. ❸

Siham's Rincón Árabe-Latino, Independencia 633, Miraflores (☎447 5229), 1 block off Angamos. Palestinian-born owner Siham Giha has been cooking Middle Eastern favorites at this small restaurant for 30 years. Falafel s/7. Hummus s/7.50. Schwarma s/8.80. Stuffed grape leaves s/13. Open daily 11am-10pm. AmEx/MC/V. ❷

CAFES

Feast your eyes—not your stomach—at Miraflores's posh, overpriced cafes. A slice of tasteless quiche will cost more than a full meal in Lima Centro, but the espresso is affordable and generally authentic, and the Italian-style *gelato* (ice cream) is to die for. The cosmopolitan European atmosphere and decor is hard to find anywhere else in Lima. **Óvalo Gutiérrez,** where Comandante Espinar, Conquistadores, and Santa Cruz converge, has several pricey, yuppified gathering places. More coffee-oriented cafes are near Parque Central. **Pasaje Nicolás de Rivero** (also called Pasaje de los Escribanos), a pedestrian street off the west end of the Plaza de Armas, is a little slice of Miraflores cafe culture transplanted into Lima Centro.

▧ **Gelatería Laritza D.,** Comandante Espinar 800, off Óvalo Gutiérrez, Miraflores (☎447 0689); also at LarcoMar in the center of the bottom floor (☎242 6443). This popular hangout serves the best *gelato* in Lima (s/5.50 for 2 scoops). Flavors are so enticing you'll want to try everything from *guanábana* fruit to the lusciously creamy *manjar blanco* (whole milk flavor). Open Su-Th 8am-midnight, F-Sa 9am-1am. ❶

▧ **Tarata Café,** Pasaje Tarata 260, Miraflores (☎446 6330). Pretend you're dining outdoors—minus the chill Lima weather—amid the extraneous patio umbrellas that fill this hidden cafe's interior. Feast on full meals of salad, french fries, and steak (*lomo argentino;* s/25), or sip a delicious cappuccino in front of the big-screen TV. Entrees s/16-28. Open daily noon-10pm, extended hours F and Sa. ❸

Quattro D. (4-D), Angamos Oeste 408, Miraflores (☎447 1523). Quattro feels more European than its counterparts, perhaps due to the combination of higher prices and smaller chairs. This place really serves it all—tasty *gelato*, rich desserts, and decent espresso drinks. Pleasant interior filled with potted and hanging ferns, and a great view of the busy street outside. *Gelato* cones s/6. *Tiramisu* s/12. Open M-F 7:30am-12:15am, Sa-Su 8:30am-12:15am. ❷

Café Café, Mártir Olaya 250, Miraflores (☎447 9220 or 445 1165; open M-W 8:30am-1am, Th 8:30am-2am, F-Sa 8:30am-3am), off Parque Kennedy; also at LarcoMar on the 2nd floor (☎445 9499; open Su-Th 8:30am-1am, F-Sa 8:30am-3am). At these cafes brimming with Lima's young and moneyed, the fabulous coffee and pastries from their 6-page English/Spanish menu are sure to suit your palate. Each location has its own feel: Mártir Olaya is supremely popular among chic 20-somethings, while LarcoMar boasts a stunning ocean panorama. Cappuccino and espresso s/4-8. AmEx/MC/V. ❶

Café Haiti, Diagonal 160 (☎446 3816), 2 doors down from Cinema El Pacífico. A posh favorite and an ideal people-watching spot, this international cafe has underwhelming food and lackluster service. Very European, right down to the cross-stitch detail on the wicker chairs and the sophisticated clientele, juxtaposed with some interesting Haitian-inspired dishes. Entrees average s/35. Open 24hr. ❹

REALLY CHEAP EATS

Travelers on shorter stays or with thinner money belts will find the greasy lunch *menús* and street snacks the cheapest—though not the most interesting or healthy—option in Lima. Many of Lima's other cheap food options are fast food joints. Here are a few notable exceptions.

▧ **Vrinda,** Javier Prado Este 185, San Isidro (☎421 0016), off the overpass at the 30th block of Arequipa. Serves a daily vegetarian *menú* (s/5) and arranges Sunday excursions to "ecological communities" for yoga sessions (s/25). Open M-Sa 9am-9pm. ❶

Los Balcones de Olaya, Pasaje Olaya 110, Lima Centro (☎426 4037), across from the Palacio del Gobierno. Though the *menús* (s/5-8) and other entrees (s/15-20) are similar to others in the area, what distinguishes this mezzanine restaurant is its magnificent view of the Plaza Mayor from the large, open balcony. On chilly days, sip some rich house coffee (s/4-5) to warm up as you people-watch. Open daily 8am-8pm. ❶

Norky's, La Unión 426, Lima Centro (☎428 5763); Abancay 210, Miraflores (☎521 0526); on José Pardo at Bellavista; and at endless other locations. This popular, mall-style place features bright neon lights and slow-roasting rotisserie chicken. Chicken combo meals s/4-9.50. Open daily 11am-11pm. ❶

El Peruanito, Angamos Este 391, Miraflores (☎241 2175), near the Vía Expresa. According to some carnivores, El Peruanito has the best sandwiches (s/3-6) and *menús* (s/4-5) in Lima. Open daily 7am-midnight. ❶

Los Frutales, Camaná 337, Lima Centro (☎427 7477), 3 blocks from the Plaza Mayor. Not to be confused with the carnivore haven by the same name next door. A wide selection of juices (s/3-4) and other health-conscious fare abounds at this small restaurant. Enjoy a meal among the murals inside, or just visit the counter and purchase all the teas, soy, or vitamins your healthy heart desires. Salads s/2.50-4.50. Specials from the glass display case s/5-7. Open daily 9am-9pm. ❶

Restaurante Paraíso, Camaná 244, Lima Centro (☎428 1106), 1 block off the Plaza Mayor near the tourist office. This Europeanesque restaurant serves typical *criollo* and Peruvian delights; the real draw is the view of the cathedral from the tables facing outside. *Menú* s/5. Entrees s/15. Open M-Sa 8am-8pm. ❶

Tropicana, Schell 492, Miraflores (☎444 5626), at La Paz. Low-key, tropical-hut-style eatery. Great for meals or snacks on the go. Juices are extra fresh and extra good. *Menú* s/6. Sandwiches s/6-8. Open M-Sa 8am-11pm. ❶

Govinda, Schell 630, Miraflores (☎444 2871). The flagship location of this Hare Krishna chain. Govinda's healthful, imaginative vegetarian cuisine offers an alternative to standard meat and fish fare. For those who prefer their flounder swimming in the ocean, Govinda offers a tofu *ceviche* that should please any animal-lover. Also visit the shop next door for Indian goods and garb. Entrees s/6-9. Lunch *menú* s/6-7. Open M-Sa 11:30am-7pm, Su 11am-4pm. A smaller branch, Garcilaso de la Vega 1670, Lima Centro (☎433 2589), serves snacks and a limited lunch *menú*. Open daily 11am-8pm. ❶

Natur, Moquegua 132, Lima Centro (☎427 8281), 1 block off La Unión. A diverse selection of vegetarian and vegan cuisine in a friendly, but uninspiring, setting. The restaurant has a wide range of different honeys, which employees will mix into any juice for a sweet, refreshing drink (s/3). A few shelves stock a limited selection of soy products for purchase. Specials noted on the chalkboard. English menu. Soups s/6. Vegetable stir-fries s/6-7. Open M-Sa 8am-9pm, Su 10am-5pm. ❶

D'nnos Pizza, (☎242 0606). If you're in the mood to order in, D'nnos has some of the freshest slices around. Large pizzas s/30-40. Free delivery. ❷

THE BIG SPLURGE

It's definitely worth visiting one of the expensive *criollo* restaurants to sample Peru's signature cuisine. If you're missing culinary luxuries from home, extra soles can also bring better service and free bread.

◼ **Manos Morenas,** Pedro de Osma 409, Barranco (☎467 0421). This fusion of Peruvian and Italian culinary delights is *criollo* food at its best, in a 19th-century mansion near the ocean. Risotto-lovers will enjoy Manos's special recipe. Live *criollo* music and dance Th-Sa after 10:30pm (s/35 cover). Entrees s/20-40. *Ceviche* s/35. Open daily 12:30-4:30pm, Th-Sa also open 7pm-midnight. AmEx/MC/V. ❹ If you want to chow on their *cau-cau* (a fish stew) but lack the cash, stop by their **stand** at the LarcoMar food court s(*ceviche* s/20). ❸

El Señorío de Sulco, Malecón Cisneros 1470 (☎441 0183; www.senoriodesulco.com), at the end of José Pardo, with ocean views. The Incas would have been obese had their food been anything like Señorío's. Only traditional tools (earthen pots, etc.) are used to prepare regional meat, chicken, and fish specialties (s/30-45). Open M-Sa 10am-midnight, Su 10am-6pm. ❺

Las Brujas de Cachiche, Bolognesi 460, Miraflores (☎444 5310), at Plaza Bolognesi. Gourmet elegance reigns inside this sophisticated haunt, bewitching the clientele with traditional Andean platters. Lunch buffet US$29. *Menú* US$26. Entrees s/20-40. Live *peña* band F-Sa night. Open M-Sa 12:30pm-1am, Su 12:30-4pm. ❹

Wa Lok, Paruro 864-878, Lima Centro (☎427 2656), to the right at the end of Capón; also Angamos Oeste 700 (☎447 1329). Generally considered the finest of Lima's many *chifas*, but skip the fried rice and go straight for the *dim sum*, served all day (around s/7.50). Entrees average s/32. Open daily 9am-11pm. AmEx/MC/V. ❹

Vivaldino, Malecón de la Reserva 610, Miraflores (☎446 3859), at LarcoMar on the 2nd level. Candlelight, tuxedo-clad waiters, and a bar stocked with the finest liquors provide the backdrop for a sumptuous *criollo* dining experience in this restaurant on the sea. Pasta, chicken s/20-30. Meat, seafood s/25-40. Open daily 5pm-midnight. ❹

◉ SIGHTS

Most of Lima's historic plazas, *casas antiguas*, museums, and churches cluster in Lima Centro. This district—bounded roughly by 28 de Julio to the south, Alfonso Ugarte to the west, Río Rímac to the north, and Abancay to the east—was built on top of an old Inca city, though today almost nothing remains of that pre-Hispanic architecture. A small part of Lima's historical center spills over into Rímac north of the river, across the 17th-century bridge, the Puente de Piedra. Tromping from one sight to the next in such a crowded and busy section of Lima can wear out any traveler; the area immediately around the Plaza Mayor can give you a sense for Lima Centro's colonial history with minimal walking time. However, those who brave the packed streets and lengthy distances will be rewarded by a wealth of interesting and beautiful sites.

LIMA CENTRO

PLAZAS

PLAZA MAYOR. Where an Inca temple and the last palace of the Inca prince once stood, Lima's main square now glorifies Spanish culture. The Plaza has been the city's administrative and political center since its founding and has witnessed some of the most important events in Peru's history: it was where victims of the Inquisition were hanged in the 16th century, where the zealous priest Francisco de Ávila burned a huge cache of sacred Inca objects in 1609, where the festivities honoring new Spanish viceroys were held, where Peruvians declared their independence in 1821, where bullfights once thrilled the masses, and where citizens recently protested the corruption of Peru's former head of secret service, Vladimiro Montesinos. Flanked by colonial-style buildings with elaborately carved cedar balconies, the Plaza revolves around a bronze **fountain** topped by a trumpeting angel, crafted by legendary artisan Pedro de Noguera in 1651. This fountain is actually the oldest standing object in the square—all of the surrounding buildings are 20th-century replicas of the originals, which collapsed in various earthquakes. A newly built fountain topped with the Peruvian flag now resides on the Plaza's northeast corner, where a statue of Francisco Pizarro once dominated. A granite **monument** to the last pre-Hispanic ruler of this valley, Inca leader Tauri Chusko, is set aside on Pasaje Santa Rosa, a pedestrian sidewalk across from the cathedral.

The two most spectacular buildings on the plaza are the **Catedral de Lima** on the east side (see **Churches,** below) and the **Palacio de Gobierno** on the northern end. The Palacio, a replica of Pizarro's residence, which once occupied this spot, today houses the Peruvian president, and is open to citizens and tourists alike. Make a reservation 24-48hr. in advance with the Departamento de Actividades. *(Jr. de la Unión, Plaza Pizarro, of. 201; ☎311 3908; www.presidencia.gob.pe. English tours available.)* You'll get a glimpse of some of the most opulent rooms in all of Lima Centro—complete with some of the highest security. Watch the changing of the guard up close and personal from within the gates themselves, but for the best view, stand in front of the gates, directly in the middle. The 30min. show takes place Monday though Saturday at 11:45am. The **Palacio Municipal,** or City Hall, across the Plaza from the cathedral, has a small Pancho Fierro **art gallery** that highlights the work of colonial Peruvian artists. *(Open M-F 10am-4pm. Free.)* Since the privatization of the postal system, Lima's **Correo Central,** just off the Plaza on Conde de Superunda, has become more a stamp collector's **museum** than an important mail center; for a break from exhibits focused on history, check out the Star Wars stamp. *(Museo Postal y Filatélico del Perú, open M-Su 8:30am-6:45pm. Free.)*

OTHER PLAZAS. Plaza Mayor sits at the northern end of the hectic pedestrian mall La Unión; at La Unión's southern end is Lima's other main square, **Plaza San Martín.** This plaza was inaugurated on July 28, 1921, to celebrate Peru's centennial. Peruvians congregate amid the French Baroque architecture to stroll, sit, and protest; tourists who want a glimpse of the day's political cause can often find some sort of demonstration here when there's nothing in the Plaza Mayor. Grassy **Plaza Bolívar,** at Abancay and Junín, serves as front yard to the Parliament Building. **Plaza Grau,** at the end of Paseo de la República, offers little more than a park between the Sheraton Hotel and Palacio de Justicia with flowers and life-size animal statues. Three smaller plazas with similar equestrian statues lie along Alfonso Ugarte (from south to north): **Plaza Bolognesi,** where Ugarte meets 9 de Diciembre and Brasil; **Plaza 2 de Mayo,** where Ugarte and Piérola intersect; and **Plaza Castilla.**

ily Chronicle

IN RECENT NEWS

CONQUERING THE CONQUEROR

Travelers who have been in Lima before will notice something different about the magnificent Plaza Mayor. The statue of Francisco Pizarro, conqueror of the Incas, is gone.

The history of the statue is shrouded in legend and controversy. Arrayed in full *conquistador* attire, Pizarro sat upright upon an equally well-armored horse in the center of the Plaza Mayor, facing away from the cathedral. The statue was soon relocated to a corner of the Plaza—local legend holds that because the horse's backside faced the church, the priests were offended by what they had to stare at. The new location, soon named the Plaza Pizarro, was just northeast of the Plaza Mayor and east of the Palacio de Gobierno, where Pizarro himself had lived and been assassinated in 1541. The statue then faced an acceptable southwest.

In 2003, the statue was again removed. Why another change? Many vocal Peruvians objected to the statue because Pizarro represented the subjugation of their ancestors and the seizure of their property long ago. Efforts to erase the memory of the statue continue: its location is kept under wraps, and the plaza has been renamed Plaza Perú. Travelers wishing to see the legendary statue will have to go to Trujillo, Spain (Pizarro's birthplace), where an identical copy exists.

CHURCHES

The Spanish quest to save Inca souls resulted in the construction of numerous visible reminders of the three great motivators: gold, glory, and God. Lima's churches are artistic masterpieces filled with ornate wood carvings, elaborate gold- and silver-plated altars, and ethereal religious paintings. Most of the churches close 12:30-3pm, so spend either the morning or late afternoon enjoying them.

CONVENTO DE SAN FRANCISCO. One of the finest examples of viceroyal architecture in Peru, this 17th-century church holds priceless colonial treasures: a Franciscan library containing over 25,000 rare books (including the first dictionary published by the Royal Spanish Academy); an old dining room with a Peruvian take on the Last Supper, where Jesus and his apostles feast on *cuy* (guinea pig); a main cloister inlaid with Sevillian tile; and beautiful murals illustrating the life of St. Francis of Assisi. Most visitors rush through these religious riches to visit a different sort of stash—the famous **catacombs,** narrow underground passageways containing the skulls and bones of over 25,000 bodies. Discovered in 1943, this morbid attraction is the highlight of a visit to the convent. Until the city cemetery was opened in 1808, locals tossed the corpses produced by natural disasters and epidemics into this subterranean crypt, although today the whitewashed bones are arranged in neat, photogenic patterns. *(Ancash 471, at Lampa, a 5min. walk from the Plaza de Armas. ☎ 427 1381 and 423 7377. Open daily 9:30am-5:45pm. s/5, students s/2.50. Free guided tours in English every hr. M-F 10am-noon and 3-5pm, and every 15-20min. Sa-Su.)*

LA CATEDRAL DE LIMA. Lima's central cathedral was first constructed in 1555, completely destroyed by a severe earthquake in 1746, then faithfully rebuilt shortly after in the same spot. The Catholic cardinal has his office in the attached Palacio Arzobispal, and his Sunday mass at 11am is broadcast to the entire country. The glass coffin in the sacristy, on the right upon entering the cathedral, contains human remains that, after years of debate and DNA testing, are now generally regarded as those of the conqueror **Francisco Pizarro,** who died in Lima in 1541. Visitors should also see the crypt, where Lima's archbishops now rest for eternity, or the attached **Museo de Arte Religioso,** which contains wooden furniture and choir stalls carved by master artisan Pedro de Noguera, and a large collection of gilt-encrusted 17th- and 18th-century paintings. *(On the east side of the Plaza de Armas. ☎ 427 9647 ext. 6. Museum and cathedral s/5 M-F 9am-4:30pm, Sa 10am-4:30pm. Discounts for students and children.)*

IGLESIA DE SAN PEDRO. The Jesuit-built, 17th-century church harbors gorgeous golden naves and gilded altars with Moorish-style balconies, rendering its interior the most beautifully decorated in all of Lima Centro. At its construction in 1638 it was named after St. Paul, but after the Jesuits' expulsion from the church in 1772 it was renamed after St. Peter. To the left upon entering, see the Cruz de Baratillo, a cross once owned by a local saint. Look for "La Abuelita," the oldest bell in Lima. *(Azángaro 451, at Ucayali. ☎ 428 3017. Open daily 10am-noon and 5pm-6pm. Free.)*

IGLESIA Y CONVENTO DE SANTO DOMINGO. This 16th-century church houses the skulls of Lima natives San Martín de Porres (the first black Catholic saint), the ever-virginal Santa Rosa (see **Santuario de Santa Rosa,** below), and the body of lesser-known San Juan Masias. All are down the right aisle off the entrance. Inside the monastery, well-preserved Sevillian tile mosaics represent the life of Santo Domingo de Guzmán, founder of the Dominican order. Dark cloisters and a magnificent, blooming central garden offer a pleasant retreat from the bustling streets outside. The church also houses a private chapel dedicated to San Martín de Porres. *(Camaná 170, across from the Correo Central. ☎ 427 6793. Open M-Sa 9am-1pm and 3-6pm, Su 9am-1pm. Free. Guided tours in English and Spanish; s/3-4 tip expected.)*

SANTUARIO DE SANTA ROSA. Constructed over the site where Isabel Flores de Oliva (better known as Santa Rosa de Lima) was born in 1586, this courtyard sanctuary commemorates the life of Peru's only female saint. See the small adobe meditation and prayer hut that she and her brothers built by hand, the room where she secluded herself from her family and slept on a tree-trunk bed, the remnants of the lemon tree with which she cast away Satan, and the well where she tossed the key to her chastity belt to pledge her devotion to God. The church has paintings of Santa Rosa. *(On the 1st block of Tacna. ☎ 425 1279. Open daily 9am-1pm and 3-6pm. Free.)*

IGLESIA DE LA MERCED. Home to the massive, much-kissed silver cross of miracle-worker Padre Pedro Urraca, this church boasts an impressive, elaborately carved stone facade, Lima's most beautiful by far. First built in 1534, before the city's founding, this church was the site of Lima's first mass. It has since been destroyed twice by earthquakes and once by fire, but the current incarnation (built in the 18th century) mimics its original appearance. *(La Unión and Huancavelica. ☎ 427 8199. Open daily 7:30am-12:30pm and 4-9pm. Free.)*

LAS NAZARENAS. Las Nazareñas contains one of the oldest—and some say, most miraculous—walls in Lima. During the colonial era, many freed Africans lived in this area of town, then known as Pachacamilla. When the original church crumbled in a 1655 earthquake, one wall with a large mural of Jesus on the cross, painted by a former slave, survived unharmed. Since then, a cult has formed around the image, known as **El Señor de los Milagros** (Lord of the Miracles). In mid-October, purple-clad devotees lead processions through the streets with a replica of the painting and cover the Plaza de Armas with huge quilts made of flowers. Oddly enough, the wall itself is not visible in the church; the image above the altar is actually a painted copy of the real thing. *(At Huancavelica and Tacna. ☎ 423 5718. Open M-Sa 6:30am-noon and 4:30-9pm, Su 6:30am-1pm and 4-9pm. Free.)*

SAN AGUSTÍN. The order of St. Augustine arrived in 1551 and began to build on this site in 1573. Although earthquakes have ravaged much of Lima's architecture, this church's facade has been preserved since the early 18th century, and is beautifully representative of Lima's Baroque-style architecture. *(At the corner of Ica and Camaná. ☎ 427 7548. Open daily 8:30am-noon and 3-5pm. Free.)*

OUTSIDE LIMA CENTRO

CERRO DE SAN CRISTÓBAL. A large twinkling cross stands on the top of the San Cristóbal hill, about 420m above the city center. Many *limeños* head to the Cruz de San Cristóbal to light candles and pray for loved ones. The top of the hill offers visitors the best views of the city, especially at night, when young lovers often make the trip. The perpetual fog can hinder the view, especially in winter, but the drive up should still provide incredible views of the busy city below. *(Buses to the Cerro (30min., 10am-7pm, s/2.50) leave from the Plaza Mayor. People wearing "Urbanito" signs around their necks serve as on-board tour guides, often in both English and Spanish. To avoid waiting for the infrequent buses from the Plaza, take a cab for about s/8. There is a museum and restaurant at the top.)*

BARRIO CHINO. Lima's small **Chinatown** *(Barrio Chino)* is in the eastern part of the city center, mainly along Calle Capón, and is reminiscent of other Chinatowns worldwide. While the term *chino* has come to refer to anyone of Asian descent (President Fujimori, whose parents were born in Japan, was known as "El Chino"), a sizable Chinese population has existed in Peru since the mid-19th century, when landowners first brought Chinese laborers to the country. While generally assimilated into Peruvian life, today's Chinatown community maintains its distinct ethnic identity. A massive, newly renovated traditional gateway arches over street tiles illustrating the animals of the zodiac. The **Chinese New Year,** in late January or early to mid-February, adds a lively parade and fireworks to the mix. *(Capón is at the eastern end of Ucayali. Chinatown begins 2 blocks east of Abancay.)*

PARQUE DE LEYENDAS ZOO. Every weekend families flock to the somewhat shabby **Parque de Leyendas** and zoo, where you can listen to Amazon birds chirp, watch llamas graze, and hear desert monkeys yelp, all without leaving the decidedly urban bustle of metropolitan Lima. Exhibits represent Peru's three regions: the Amazon, the *sierra*, and the coast. An international section boasts the same old lions and elephants you remember from childhood. The park also has botanical gardens and a few *huacas* (pre-Inca ruins) that you can explore on horseback (s/2). *(☎451 8696. Parque de las Leyendas in San Miguel. Take a colectivo along La Marina to reach the zoo, or take a taxi from Miraflores for about s/8.)*

MIRAFLORES

Miraflores fills the land between San Isidro and the Pacific coastline with modern high-rises, glittering casinos, and well-kept oceanside parks. To many of Lima's poor, its name is synonymous with wealth, although many of Miraflores's residential areas are more populated by middle-class families than by San Isidro's young, wealthy professionals. Much of Miraflores was either built or rebuilt in the last two decades, and its wide modern streets, lined with cafes and international shops, display Lima's cosmopolitan flair.

Óvalo Miraflores, the traffic circle at the end of Arequipa, marks the northern end of the district's activity. It is flanked by a large cinema complex, El Pacífico, and every fast-food joint under the sun. Just south of the Óvalo, **Parque Central** and **Parque Kennedy,** busy with vendors selling all manner of homemade goods, are prime spots for people-watching, cafe-lounging, and partying. You'll have to head farther south along **Larco** to lose your money in a **casino,** although the street's trendy clothing shops and shoe stores could eat it up just as easily. ■**LarcoMar** (www.larcomar.com), at the southern end of Larco, is a three-story, open-air shopping mall. Built into the side of an ocean-front cliff, the center is nearly undetectable from the street above. Beyond the myriad trendy shops, restaurants, bars, and movie theaters, the complex offers breathtaking views of the sea, an underground bowling alley, and a pleasant escape from Lima's congested streets.

The beach along the southern end of Miraflores, **Playa Costa Verde,** is packed with sunbathers, swimmers, and surfers from December to April, despite the rocky shore and murky water. It's easiest to descend the seaside cliffs and access the ocean via **Diagonal,** which runs along the west side of Parques Central and Kennedy. Surfers head a few km north to **Playa Waikiki,** or south to **Herradura,** which has the largest swells (2-5m) in the area. If you'd rather admire the water than enter it, parks along **Malecón Cisneros** provide the vistas that keep postcard companies in business. Right off this coastal avenue is **Parque del Amor,** known for its enormous statue of lovers embracing, real-life couples mimicking the statue, and mosaics inscribed with love poems. Farther up the Malecón, flowers in **Parque Maria Reiche** (see **The Reiche Stuff,** p. 158) grow in patterns resembling the famous Nasca Lines. *(Taxi from Lima Centro s/6-8. Or, catch a colectivo marked "Todo Arequipa" from Lima Centro or San Isidro and hop off at the Óvalo.)*

BARRANCO

A century ago, Barranco was an isolated seaside enclave accessible only by train and populated mainly by artists, writers, and the marginalized mistresses of the elite. Over the years, however, suburban sprawl has transformed the no-man's-land to the north into vibrant Miraflores, and Barranco is now fully connected to the rest of Lima. In the meantime, its reputation has shifted from bohemian to bacchanalian; with the highest concentration of clubs and bars in

the city, this district is nightlife central. The old mansions and seaside promenades that fan out from **Parque Municipal** are pleasant for walks during the day,
but the crowds really come out at night to drink and dance. A few vestiges of
Barranco's artsy past remain, thanks to artisans who sell their wares at the far
end of Parque Municipal and artists' workshops (many of which are open to
the public) on the blocks between the park and the ocean. **Juanito's** (see **Nightlife,** p. 125) still offers foreigners a chance to knock one back with Lima's
bearded and bespectacled intelligentsia. Facing the parkside church, Barranco's walkway to the water starts behind the smaller plaza to the left and
leads down the stone steps and over the **Bajada a los Baños** walkway via the
Puente de los Suspiros (Bridge of Sighs), so named for the lovelorn who sigh as
they gaze at the twinkling lights below (in reality, the name may be borrowed
from Venice's famous bridge, named for a very different kind of sighs, those of
prisoners who got their last glimpse of freedom from the bridge). In somber
contrast, **La Cruz del Morro** stands on the edge of the cliff separating Barranco
from Chorillos. Originally constructed from the debris of terrorist bombings
(see **Guerrillas in the Mist,** p. 68), the brightly lit, enormous cross (visible from
Miraflores at night) serves as a conspicuous reminder of the country's recent
bloodshed. The walk along the beach from Miraflores to Barranco takes about
15min., but at night the area below the cliffs (except for the luxurious **La Rosa
Náutica** restaurant on the pier) is dark and deserted. *(Taxi from Miraflores s/3-4. Or,
catch a colectivo marked "Chorrillos" or "Barranco" and jump off at the gas station at Grau and
Piérola, 5 blocks north of the park (a 10min. walk). Returning is easier; colectivos marked "Todo
Arequipa," on Grau along the park, go all the way to Lima Centro via Miraflores and San Isidro.)*

RUINS

HUACA HUALLAMARCA AND HUACA PUCLLANA. Although urbanization has
taken over most ancient ruins, two pre-Inca centers of administration and ceremony of the Cultura Lima (AD 200-700) remain in the city. Showing two diverse
periods in this culture, both sites merit a visit, if only for the magnificent views
they provide from the tops of the temples. The Lima people eventually abandoned
Huallamarca as a religious center in order to use it as a cemetery; there you can
see the Princess of Huallamarca, the mummified remains of a noblewoman with
2m of beautifully-preserved hair. The Lima built their new administrative and religious center at Pucllana, and the developments in building techniques between the
two structures are clear. Accessible through a free guided 1hr. tour. *(Huallamarca,
201 El Rosario, at Nicolás de Riviera in San Isidro. ☎424 4124. Open Tu-Su 9am-5pm. s/5.
Huaca Pucllana is off the 4th block of Angamos in Miraflores, entrance on Borgoño. ☎445 8695.
Open M and W-Su 9am-5pm. Free. 45-60min. tour.)*

🏛 MUSEUMS

Lima is home to some of the country's finest and most diverse museums. Most
have an archaeological slant, focusing on the history and handicrafts of various
pre-Columbian civilizations living in Peru. When that thousandth piece of ceramic
becomes too much—and it will—there are museums of fine art and other specialized museums to take the edge off. If you know what to look for in each museum,
you'll find many fascinating exhibits guaranteed to thrill the casual observer and
impress even the most erudite connoisseur of history and art.

■ MUSEO DE LA NACIÓN. If you visit no other museum, visit this one. This
museum's four very modern floors offer an excellent overview of Peru's very un-
modern archaeological heritage, tracing the various civilizations that have inhabited the area over the centuries. The staggering collection of pre-Columbian arti-

facts dates to 10,000 BC, and the fact that the Inca relics don't begin until the top floor emphasizes just how much history Peru has. Tour guides can point out the highlights and supplement the few explanatory signs. Don't miss the detailed replicas of Peru's archaeological highlights, including the Man of Sipán and murals from Huaca de la Luna. Scale models of the Nasca Lines, Machu Picchu, and ancient Cusco give newcomers to Peru a taste of what's to come. *(Javier Prado Este 2465, San Borja. From Arequipa, take a colectivo marked "Todo Javier Prado" toward Jockey Plaza.* ☎ *476 9878 or 476 9873. Open Tu-Su 9am-5pm. s/6, university students and senior citizens s/3, children s/1.60. Guided tours (1hr.) in English leave every hr., s/10.)*

MUSEO NACIONAL DE ANTROPOLOGÍA, ARQUEOLOGÍA, E HISTORIA. Though some of its best items were lost to the Museo de la Nación, this museum still retains an impressive collection of ceramics and other archaeological finds, and coupled with the attached Museo de la República, it provides an excellent history of Peru, from many centuries BC until the mid-19th century. The titillating paleontology room features trepanated and other freakily deformed skulls (see **Beauty is Only Skull Deep,** p. 145), as well as a mummy demonstrating that tuberculosis existed in the Americas before 1492. The fantastic scale model of Machu Picchu gives viewers a basic idea of how this wonder of the world was used by its inhabitants. The adjoining **Museo de la República** was once the home of Bolívar and San Martín, two of Peru's great liberators, and today features colonial furniture, weapons, and paintings of many of the men memorialized in the city's street names. Don't miss the tree supposedly planted by Bolívar while he resided here. *(On Plaza Bolívar, Pueblo Libre. From Museo Herrera, follow the blue line painted on the ground through a couple of neighborhoods and past the supermarket (10min. walk).* ☎ *463 5070. Open Tu-Su 9am-5pm. s/10. Guided tours (80min.) available in English, s/10.)*

MUSEO ARQUEOLÓGICO RAFAEL LARCO HERRERA. Opened in 1927, this museum holds the world's largest private collection of pre-Columbian Peruvian art. Nearly 45,000 pieces reside in this beautiful, early 18th-century colonial mansion, including gold and silver jewelry, textiles, and vaults crammed with thousands of ceramic pieces (mostly from the Moche and Chimú cultures) showing just how much ancient Peruvians loved to play with clay. All the displays have explanatory signs in English and French. Downstairs, hidden from the view of visiting elementary school groups, is the popular **Sala Erótica,** a collection of adult-themed ceramics. *(Bolívar 1515, 12 blocks from the Plaza Bolívar, Pueblo Libre.* ☎ *461 1312. Open daily 9am-6pm. s/21, students s/11. Guides s/15.)*

MUSEO DE LA INQUISICIÓN Y DEL CONGRESO. This peek into Peru's past is not for the faint of heart. Here you can see the dark, cramped cells and torture chambers—some with mannequins strapped in for demonstration—of the Spanish Inquisition, which lasted about 250 years. Historical records show that of the 1474 alleged heretics accused by the tribunal, only 10% were actually tortured—most confessed after lashings—and 32 were killed. The somewhat incongruous upstairs portion of the museum houses a brief history of the national congress, with an interesting display of past Peruvian flags. *(Junín 548, off Abancay, in Lima Centro. Colectivos from Miraflores marked "Arequipa-Tacna-Wilson" take you to the Centro, and the museum is a 10min. walk from the Plaza Mayor.* ☎ *311 7801; www.congreso.gob.pe/museo.htm. Open daily 9am-5pm. Free guided tours every 30min. in English, French, Portuguese, and Spanish.)*

MUSEO DE ARTE. Dedicated solely to art created by native Peruvians, this collection spans over 3000 years of history. The museum houses everything from Chavín ceramics and textiles to colonial silverware in a huge 19th-century palace. The paintings' style and subject matter evolve drastically over time, from 17th- and 18th-century religious themes (excellent examples of the Cusco School), to 19th-century upper-class portraits, to more abstract 20th-century scenes of everyday life in Andean villages. Downstairs, the **Sala de Arte Contemporáneo** contains abstract art from the past 50 years, much of which is political in nature. The museum also offers films and has short-term classes in subjects from singing to sculpture to computer literacy. *(Paseo Colón 125, at Garcilaso de la Vega and Grau, in the unmistakable palatial building. Colectivos from Miraflores marked "Arequipa-Tacna-Wilson" pass in front of the museum. ☎423 4732 or 423 5149. Open M-Tu and W-Su 10am-5pm. s/12, students s/6. Free some M, call to confirm.)*

MUSEO DE ORO DEL PERÚ Y ARMAS DEL MUNDO. This aptly named museum displays an overwhelming collection of gold from Peru and weapons from all over the world. The basement vault overflows with an impressive variety of pre-Columbian gold—jewelry, ornate metal-plated capes, *tumis* (ceremonial knives), and even earplugs—as well as pottery, masks, and mummies. Upstairs, the walls are packed with guns, swords, and cannons that together form the world's largest collection of firearms. *(Alonso de Molina 1100, off Primavera Block 18, in Monterrico, Surco. Taxis s/10-12. ☎345 1292. No cameras. Open daily 11:30am-7pm. s/30, children s/15. Guides s/40 per group; English-language catalog s/50.)*

MUSEO DE LA HISTORIA NATURAL. The number of stuffed birds, fossils, monkeys, and fish in this small museum is astounding, and the dinosaur room provides a detailed representation of Peru's own velociraptor. *(Arenales 1256, San Isidro. ☎471 0117. A taxi from Miraflores should cost s/5, or take a colectivo marked "Todo Arequipa" from Lima Centro or Miraflores to Arequipa block 12. Open M-F 9am-5pm, Sa-Su 9am-1pm.)*

CASAS ANTIGUAS (HISTORIC HOUSES). Although most old mansions in Lima Centro have gradually rotted away or been converted into cheap hotels, some have been preserved in their original grandeur. Built in 1735, the **Palacio Torre Tagle**, Ucayali 358 (☎427 3860) is widely considered the finest example of colonial architecture in Peru, and retains its glory as the headquarters of the Ministry of Foreign Affairs. However, it is unfortunately closed to the public. The **Casa de Aliaga,** La Unión 224 (☎424 5110), built in 1535, is the oldest standing colonial house in Lima today, though it may also be difficult for tourists to enter. The **Casa de las Trece Monedas,** Ancash 536, is currently being renovated. **Casa Oquendo** (or **Casa Osambela**), Conde de Superunda 298 (☎427 7987; open M-F 9am-4pm); and **Casa de Riva Agüero** (also the **Museo de Arte Popular**), Camaná 459 (☎427 9275; open M-F 10am-1pm and 2-8pm) are also impressive and open to the public.

THE LOCAL STORY

PREHISTORY AND PABLO PICASSO

When is ancient art more than a museum piece? How about when it inspires a major modern art movement?

When Peruvian art historians took sculptures and masks from the ancient Huari culture (AD 800-1300) to display at the 1900 World's Fair in Paris, never did they imagine that they would inspire one of the greatest artistic movements in European history. And yet, legend has it that it was at that very fair that **cubism** put down roots, finding inspiration in the geometric motifs of the Huari images.

Art critic Louis Vauxcelles (1869-1948) suggested that the dominant phase of cubism from 1907-1914, led by George Braque and Pablo Picasso and characterized by fragmented, planar patterns, was inspired by these artists' frequent exposure to forms of primitive Peruvian artwork. Braque is said to have commented that primitive art opened visions of new possibilities for him, and that what he saw in the Peruvian masks represented manifestations of subtle human instincts that contrasted with the false traditions he despised in art. Perhaps, then, those ancient instinctive manifestations are what we see re-manifested in early 20th-century cubism.

BANK GALLERIES. Small galleries seem to be the accessory of choice for Lima banks. **Banco Central de Reserva del Perú** has a permanent ceramics collection that is worth the trip if only for the rare explanations of the techniques and styles of each culture. Upstairs is a restful gallery of Peruvian art. *(Ucayali 271, at Lampa, Lima Centro. ☎ 427 6250. Open Tu-F 10am-4:30pm, Sa-Su 10am-1pm. Free with passport.)* The **Museo Numismático del Banco Wiese** is a coin collector's dream. *(Cusco 245, Lima Centro. ☎ 428 6000. Open M-Sa 10am-8pm. Free.)*

OTHER MUSEUMS. Smaller art museums are scattered throughout the city. The **Museo de Arte Italiano** houses a collection of 18th- to 20th-century Italian paintings and sculptures in an imposing Neoclassical building. *(Paseo de la República 250, across from the Sheraton. ☎ 423 9932. Open M-F 10am-5pm. s/3, students s/2.)* The **Museo de Artes y Tradiciones Populares** displays weavings, dolls, and other folk art by 20th-century Peruvian artisans. *(Camaná 459, 2nd fl., Lima Centro. ☎ 427 9275. Open Tu-Su 10am-1pm and 2-7:30pm. s/2, students s/1.)* Barranco's **Museo de Arte Colonial Pedro de Osma** focuses on paintings, sculptures, furniture, and *artesanía* from colonial Peru. *(Pedro de Osma 421, Barranco. ☎ 467 0063. Open Tu-Su 10am-1:30pm and 2:30-6pm. s/10, students s/5 with guide.)* The **Museo de la Electricidad** goes into detail about the history of electricity in Lima. *(Pedro de Osma 105, Barranco 105. ☎ 447 6577. Open daily 9am-5pm. Free.)* The **Enrico Poli Museum** contains some incredible gold and archaeologically notable pieces. *(Lord Cochrane 466, Miraflores. ☎ 422 2437. Open Tu-Th by appointment. US$15.)* **Museo Amano** specializes in pieces from the Chancay culture. *(Retiro 160, off Angamos Oeste Block 11, Miraflores. ☎ 441 2909. Free. Tours in Spanish M-F 3 and 5pm by appointment.)* The **Museo Taurino de Acho** displays relics from bullfights of Lima's past, as well as a few paintings. *(Hualgayoc 332, Rímac. ☎ 481 1467. Open M-Sa 9am-6pm. s/7.)* The **Museo Nacional de la Cultura Peruana** offers a smallish mix of pre-Columbian archaeological finds and contemporary art. *(Alfonso Ugarte 650, Lima Centro. ☎ 423 5892. Open M-Sa 9am-4:30pm. s/3, students s/2.)*

🎜 ENTERTAINMENT

Lima is an entertainment haven, but figuring out what's happening when can be a bit of a challenge for travelers. The newspaper *La República* has a Friday supplement, *Viernes Sábado Domingo*, which lists the upcoming weekend's concerts, sporting events, plays, films, and other diversions. The *Luces* section of *El Comercio* lists current movies, concerts, and shows. Catch a movie, watch a play, or bungee off a hot air balloon; the foggy sky's the limit.

SPORTS

FÚTBOL. Soccer is more than a sport in Peru—it's a religion with the power to empty streets, halt traffic, and drag even policemen from their work. The **Estadio Nacional,** off blocks 7-9 of Paseo de la República, and the nearby **Estadio Alianza Lima** host most of the important games. Matches between the two Lima-based teams, reigning champion **Universitario** (or simply "la U"; www.universitario.com) and bitter rival **Alianza** (www.alianzalima.com) are all but guaranteed to get rowdy; no one can innocently wear off-white or blue to matches. If you can't make the match, listen to it in a colectivo, park, or any other venue with a loudspeaker. To get tickets, you must visit the stadiums one day in advance, or the morning before the game. (National match seats s/25-45. Professional match seats from s/10.) **Volleyball,** also played in the Estadio Nacional, comes in a distant second.

ANIMAL ANTICS. When you've tired of watching humans, turn to the animals: bullfighting, cockfighting, and horse racing are popular spectator events. **Plaza de Acho,** Hualgayoc 332, across the bridge from Lima Centro, in the northern suburb of

Rímac, hosts bullfights during the **Fiestas Patrias** in the last week of July, as well as from October to November. (☎481 1467. Check *El Comercio* for exact dates and times. Tickets from s/20.) Roosters battle to the death in **La Chacra**, at the end of Tomás Marsano in Surco, at **Coliseo Sandia**, on Paseo de la República 6500 in Barranco (☎477 0834; M-Tu and Th 8pm), and **Coliseo El Rosedal**, in Rímac (tickets s/10 for national championships). Horses run in circles at the **Hipódromo de Monterrico**, on Javier Prado Este at the Panamericana Sur. (☎435 1035. Races Sa-Su 1:30pm, Tu and Th 2pm. Tickets s/2. Minimum bet s/1.)

OTHER THRILLS. If spectator sports aren't your thing, create the spectacle yourself. **PerúFly**, Jorge Chávez 658, in Miraflores, offers anything and everything in the way of extreme sports. You can **bungee jump from a hot air balloon** 100m over the ocean, or **paraglide** with an instructor over the Miraflores beach. To paraglide solo, you'll have to take their six-day course (US$350), which includes practice runs over sand dunes and the Pachacamac ruins. (☎444 5004; www.perufly.com. Tandem paraglide flights daily. Office open M-Sa 9am-5pm.) You can also organize **diving** excursions with **Aqua Sport**, Conquistadores 645, San Isidro. (☎221 1548; www.aquasport.com. Open M-F 9:30am-8pm. One tank dive US$60.) Rent a bike at **Bike Móvil**, Aviación 4021, Surco, which also organizes a few excursions. (☎449 8435; bikemovil@terra.com.pe. Open M-Sa 8am-8pm.) Popular trips on **horseback** include outings to Pachacamac with **Cabalgatas**, Francisco Alyaza y Paz Soldán 456, Miraflores. (☎440 8821; informes@cabalgatas.com.pe. Call a few days ahead.)

FILM

High-budget Hollywood movies (in English with Spanish subtitles) are relatively inexpensive in Lima (s/6-15). It's harder to find theaters that show Spanish-language films. Most movies take three to six months after their US release to make it to Peru, though blockbusters usually make it in a few weeks. Screenings and times are listed daily in the *Luces* section of *El Comercio*. The best movie experience is undoubtedly **CineBar,** Sala 12 in UVK Multicines LarcoMar (p. 118). Viewers sit in plush armchairs around cafe-style tables, receive a free beer or soda, and can press a buzzer during the movie to call a waiter over and order more food or drinks. (M and W s/16, Tu s/13.50, Th-Su s/21.) Other theaters (with the largest screens, cleanest seats, and best sound quality) include: **El Pacífico,** José Pardo 121, on Parque Kennedy, Miraflores (☎445 6990; s/12, Tu s/6); **Orrantia,** Arequipa 2701, at Javier Prado, San Isidro (☎221

PERUVIAN PIRACY

You won't go far in Peru before you run into a market—be it one specializing in cow heart kebabs or traditional medicine. Recently, however, another type of market has captured the public's attention. A walk through Lima Centro, a drive through Miraflores, or a visit to the markets around San Miguel will undoubtedly introduce you to some of Peru's most prominent and controversial goods—bootlegged CDs and DVDs. Many Peruvians purchase these goods, as they are incredibly cheap compared to their legal counterparts.

This branch of the "informal" market does not sit well with Peruvian officials. Not only have they lost millions of dollars in tax revenue, but they are also increasingly hassled by movie companies and record labels who want them to crack down. In one drastic response, in April 2003, Peruvian government officials used a steamroller to destroy 50,000 bootlegged CDs.

At the heart of this problem, however, lies another, graver issue. The government recently required that all bootlegged software be removed from government computers by 2005, suggesting that even some officials weren't entirely above board. In the battle for legal integrity in the market, it's clear that Peru still has a long way to go.

6000; M-W s/5, Th-Su s/8); **Excelsior**, La Unión 780, Lima Centro (☎ 426 3547; s/6.50); **Cine Planet**, La Unión 819, Lima Centro (additional location at Santa Cruz 814, Miraflores; ☎ 452 7000; M and W s/5, Tu s/4.50, Th-Su s/7.50); **Cinemark**, in Jockey Plaza, Javier Prado 4200, Monterrico (☎ 437 0222); and **UVK Multicines LarcoMar**, in the LarcoMar shopping center in Miraflores (☎ 446 7336; M and W s/10, Tu s/7.50, Th-Su s/15).

Older, international art house films (in both English and Spanish) are shown at *cine clubes* (film clubs) such as: **Julieta**, Pasaje Porta 134, on the south side of Parque Kennedy, Miraflores (☎ 444 0135; s/6, Tu s/3); **Filmoteca de Lima**, in the Museo de Arte, Lima Centro (see **Museums**, p. 120; ☎ 331 0126; s/6, students s/5); **Cine Club BCR**, Ucayali 279, Lima Centro (☎ 427 6250); and **Cine Club Miraflores**, Larco 770 (☎ 446 3959) in the Centro Cultural Ricardo Palma.

THEATER

Weekly theater performances are listed in the *Luces* section of *El Comercio*. Most plays are in Spanish, though there are occasionally a few English productions; most of these are at the **Instituto Cultural Peruano-Norteamericano** (see **Local Services**, p. 103). The **British Council** also puts on frequent plays in English. Spanish-language theater, often with local actors, takes place at: **Teatro Cultural PUCP**, Camino Real 1075, San Isidro (☎ 222 6809); **Teatro La Plaza Usil**, LarcoMar, Miraflores (☎ 620 6400; 50% discount Th); **Teatro Auditorio Miraflores**, Larco 1150, Miraflores, in the basement (☎ 447 6861; children's theater in the afternoon, adult shows on weekends); and **Auditorio de San Miguel**, La Marina 2554, San Miguel (☎ 447 1135). The **Teatro Mocha Graña**, Saenz Peña 107, Barranco (☎ 247 6292) puts on local plays.

☐ SHOPPING

The city's glitziest shopping centers are **Jockey Plaza** (also called Centro Comercial El Polo) in Monterrico, and **LarcoMar** in Miraflores (see **Miraflores**, p. 118); both are filled with goods imported from the US and Europe. (To get to Jockey Plaza, take a colectivo marked with the same name down Javier Prado Este. LarcoMar is at the end of Larco, the southern continuation of Arequipa; take a "Todo Arequipa" colectivo heading to Miraflores.) Alternatively, you can find imported merchandise galore under one roof at the South American department store chain **Saga Falabella**, 571 La Union. (☎ 428 6246. Other locations on the second block of La Unión in Lima Centro and at the Centro Camino Real in San Isidro. Prices commensurate with US prices. Open daily 11am-10pm.) There are also a number of trendy clothing stores around Parque Kennedy and down Larco in Miraflores.

For more local character and better bargains, head to the pedestrian street **La Unión** which runs between Plaza San Martín and Plaza Mayor. This crowded mall teems with street performers, tattoo parlors, and vendors selling everything from shoes to more shoes. Get the best deals on electronic goods, watches, brand-name tennis shoes (Pumas US$50) and hiking boots, t-shirts, sweatshirts, and just about anything else at the **Polvos Azules flea market**. Leave your valuables at home and keep your money close to your body, or you might find your watch on a sales table. (Just off the Vía Expresa at 28 de Julio, slightly south of Lima Centro. Open daily 9am-9pm.) For some real local flavor, head to the bountiful fresh food markets, including **Mercado Modelo de Frutas**, 1404 Circunvalación, La Victoria (open 24hr.) and **Jorge Cháves Food Market**, on the 5th block of Nicolás Allyon. Like most outdoor markets, these areas are safer to visit during the day.

◪ ARTESANÍA

Lima markets feature **artesanía** from all over Peru, and tourists flock to them on last-minute shopping sprees. As a rule of thumb, the markets in the goods' places of origin usually have wider selections and lower prices. If you don't want to go all the way to the *sierra* to buy a sweater, though, the best *artesanía* markets in Lima lie along blocks 700 to 900 of **La Marina** in San Miguel. As always, the quality of the alpaca sweaters, woven wall hangings, and gold, silver, and turquoise jewelry varies. None of the prices are fixed and bargaining is expected. (From Lima Centro, take a colectivo marked "La Marina" from Javier Prado. Most booths open M-Sa 9:30am-8pm, Su 10:30am-6pm.) Other artisans appear at more expensive (and convenient) markets in Lima Centro, near Plaza Mayor at Carabaya 319 (open M-Sa 10am-9pm, Su 10am-6pm); and in Miraflores, around the 5200 to 5400 blocks of Petit Thouars, north of Gonzales Prado (open M-Sa 9am-8pm, Su 10:30am-7pm).

◪ NIGHTLIFE

Every night but Sundays and Mondays, Lima comes alive and stays wide-eyed until 5 or 6am. Parks, large and small, fill with strolling families, skateboarding teenagers, smooching couples, and attentive snack sellers. Clubs blare all varieties of music while the energetic clientele salsa the night away and the sedentary imbibe one pitcher of beer or *pisco* sour after another. Nightlife and liveliness can be found all over the city, though most is centered in Miraflores and Barranco.

LIMA CENTRO

If you have your heart set on partying in Lima Centro, there are a few places to try, but take a cab and know the club's address, as the area can be unsafe after dark.

Rincón Cervecero, Jr. de la Unión 1045-A (☎428 1422), just south of Plaza San Martín. Enter this long pub-esque bar and unwind from a long day of touring historic Lima. This relaxed and comfortable bar offers awesome 80s tunes, barrel tables, and various glasses for imbibing your favorite Peruvian beer—a drink from a curvaceous *kero* cup is s/9.50. Pitchers s/16. Finger food s/13. Open M-Th 5pm-1am and F-Sa 5pm-3am.

Las Brisas del Titicaca, Walkuski 168 (☎332 1881; www.brisasdeltiticaca.com). Look for a blue house off the 1st block of Brasil. A relatively inexpensive and extremely popular *peña* bar that attracts folk, Andean, and *criollo* acts. Mostly caters to an older, well-dressed crowd. Shows W-Sa 9:30pm. Cover s/25-30. Open W-Sa 9pm-3am. V.

Cafe Teatro "Palais Concerto," Jr. de la Unión 706, 2nd fl. (☎428 9831; palais_concert@hotmail.com). This interesting exhibition hall by day, theater by afternoon, and club by night is one of Lima Centro's only nightclubs. Rock to some hot dance beats in this *casa antigua* that boasts no cover, a tiled dance floor, and cheap drinks. Pitchers s/10. Other drinks from s/4. Open Tu-Su 7pm-3am.

MIRAFLORES

Slick locals clad in designer attire swarm to Miraflores to groove into the wee hours; others spend their weekend nights loitering at the outdoor LarcoMar shopping center. Real nightlife centers around **Parque Kennedy,** where a few prime dance floors supplement a superfluity of relaxed and comfortable bars. Peruvians seem to have inherited something from the Spanish besides their language: their nightlife hours. Most of the bars start getting packed with a younger crowd around midnight and don't calm down until late the next morning. In addition, most of Lima's gay and lesbian nightlife, lauded by some as the best nightlife in all of Lima, is here as well (see **Gay and Lesbian Nightlife,** p. 128).

■ **Murphy's Irish Pub,** Schell 627 (☎242 1212), at Solar. Fulfills all the duties of an Irish pub with Guinness—though not always on tap (can s/15)—hearty meat and potatoes to sate the appetite, and sports on the huge TV. Pool table. Drinks s/10-12. Pitchers of beer s/18. Happy hour 7-10pm. Live music W-Sa. Cover s/10 on live music nights. Open M-Sa 6pm-4am.

■ **Freheit Bier & Bar,** Lima 417, 2nd fl. (☎835 8085; www.freiheitperu.com), off El Parque D'Onofrio on Parque Kennedy. This spacious wood tavern provides both a low-key atmosphere for travelers looking to kick back with a cold brew and a spacious dance floor so you can burn some of those recently imbibed calories. Pitcher of beer s/10. Cocktails s/10-12. Live music some Thursday nights. F-Sa cover s/10 starting at 10:30pm. Open W-Th 8pm-12:30am and F-Sa 8pm-5am. AmEx/V.

Treff Pub Alemán, Alfredo Benavides, C.C. Los Dueños 571-104 (☎444 0148). Not quite as Germanic as its name would suggest, Treff still mingles medieval and modern with its wide-open doorway leading from the cobblestoned streets into a pub complete with TV and soccer banners from around the world. Relax in the mellow atmosphere, or challenge a friend to a quick game of pool. Beer s/7. Shots s/7-10. Cocktails s/8-13. Pitchers s/20. Open daily 7pm-late. AmEx/MC/V.

Bierhaus, Berlin 192 (☎09 818 7305), at the intersection of Bellavista and Berlin. Finding an empty table may be hard if you come late, but this extremely popular bar keeps the beer flowing into the wee hours of the morning. Cover s/10, includes 1 beer. Drinks s/10-15. Pitchers s/15. Open daily 10pm-late.

Tequila Rock, Diez Canseco 146 (☎444 3661), near Parque Kennedy. A slightly older, more touristy crowd frequents this place. Dancing with one's reflection in the mirror is the groove of choice. Lots of standard bump and grind music, including some American favorites. Drinks s/16-18. Cover Th-Sa s/20 after 9:30pm. Ladies only after 2am. Open daily 8:30pm-7am. AmEx/MC/V.

The Brenchley Arms, Atahualpa 174 (☎445 9680), off José Pardo, near the Óvalo. Enter the wrought-iron gates and approach the English-style cottage that houses this painstakingly British pub. An ideal place to wind down at the well-stocked bar or eat a hearty meal in the comfortable wooden booths. Pitchers s/18. Drinks s/12.50-17. *Piqueros* s/11-16. Entrees s/13-25. Open M-Sa 6pm-3am. AmEx/DC/MC/V.

Los Altos de San Ramón, San Ramón 8, 2nd and 3rd fl. (☎9 818 0304), off Parque Kennedy. Food on the 2nd fl., Latin beats in a tight dance space on the 3rd. Pitchers of beer s/18, or with a serving of *antichuchos* s/20. Cocktails s/10-12. V.

BARRANCO

With so many nightlife options in this seaside suburb, the only challenge is sifting through them to find the one that suits your tastes. **Pasaje Sánchez Carrión,** just off the park, is a pedestrian walkway lined with nothing but bars and discos. They all play identical dance hits, normally have no cover, and often offer cheap beer (pitchers as low as s/10). Most also lack a distinctive character, but there are still plenty of cafes and bars off the walkway that value substance. Cross the **Puente de los Suspiros,** and pounding surf replaces the usual strains. Bars near this nautical lookout are more romantic (and expensive) than elsewhere. Hungry late-night revelers can always find a sandwich (s/5) along the first and second blocks of Piérola, a few blocks up Grau at the traffic light.

■ **Puka Tayta,** Sánchez Carrión 104, 2nd fl. (☎247 4193), at the corner of Grau in the yellow building overlooking Parque Municipal. Caters to a mature crowd ready to chill and enjoy some of the Cuban *trova* music or 80s rock by live acoustic performers (Th-Sa 11pm). Snag a table on the balcony for a prime view or sit at the bar and let Ernesto prepare you one of the best *pisco* sours in town (s/12). Drinks s/10-15. Pitcher of beer s/18. Sa all of the 13 *pisco*-based drinks are s/8. Open daily 8pm-3am. V.

La Posada del Ángel has 3 locations: Pedro de Osma 164 and 222 (☎247 0341), and San Martín 157 (☎247 5544). Decorated with antiques a la Victorian era, this bar draws an intellectual bunch looking for a comfortable place to chat. All the locations attract a tranquil crowd of young and old alike. Live Cuban folk music. There's often a wait for a table on weekends. Pitcher of *sangría* s/26. Open daily 7pm-3am. AmEx/V.

Wahio's, Plaza Espinosa 111, Boulevard de los Bomberos (☎477 4110 or 247 2592), off Bolognesi. This wide bar is packed both inside and out; there's no better reggae beat around. Pick a table near the windows if you're not a fan of smoke. Pitchers of beer s/10. Drinks s/10-15. Open W-Sa 9pm-4am.

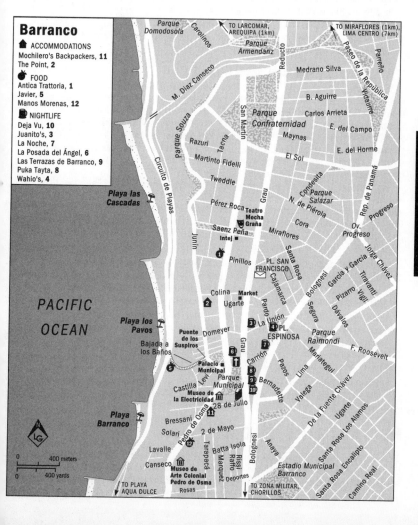

Barranco

🏠 ACCOMMODATIONS
Mochilero's Backpackers, **11**
The Point, **2**

🍴 FOOD
Antica Trattoria, **1**
Javier, **5**
Manos Morenas, **12**

🌙 NIGHTLIFE
Deja Vu, **10**
Juanito's, **3**
La Noche, **7**
La Posada del Ángel, **6**
Las Terrazas de Barranco, **9**
Puka Tayta, **8**
Wahio's, **4**

LIMA

La Noche, Bolognesi 307 (☎277 2186; www.lanoche.com.pe), at the far corner of Sánchez Carrión, ironically close to the Centro Familial Cristiano (Christian Family Center) next door. Whether you feel like dancing, listening to live bands, or engaging in a round of toasts, this enormous 3-story bar has the room. Frequent poetry readings and art shows. Pitcher of beer s/ 15. Drinks s/10-17. Live music M-Sa 11pm-2am. Open M-Sa 7pm-4am. AmEx/MC/V.

Las Terrazas de Barranco, Grau 290 (☎247 1455), off Parque Municipal. This triple-whammy of the Barranco scene—restaurant, bar, and club—gets hectic at night, so come early or prepare to wait outside. Pop hits, flashing lights, tiled mirror decor, and Peruvian MTV. Drinks s/10-15. Pitchers s/18. Open daily 9pm-3am. DC/MC/V.

Juanito's, Grau 274, an unlabeled doorway next to Domino's Pizza. Founded in 1937, this touristless hole-in-the-wall is the oldest bar in Barranco and the legendary watering spot of various Peruvian artists. The real reason to come is El Famoso Cucharita, who can do the unimaginable with beer bottles, teaspoons, and cigarettes (performances nightly around 10pm-midnight). Sandwiches s/6. Pitcher s/14. Open daily 11am-3am.

Deja Vu, Grau 294 (☎247 6989; www.dboleto.com), off Parque Municipal. Salsa dancing with a mixed crowd of tourists and locals. Live *criollo* music. Pitchers s/20. Cocktails s/10-15. Open daily 9pm-late. AmEx/DC/MC/V.

GAY AND LESBIAN NIGHTLIFE

Although homosexuality isn't widely accepted in Peru, Lima is home to the most visible gay community in the country. The capital has some excellent resources (see **Local Services,** p. 103) and great nightlife. For the latest in Lima's ever-changing gay scene, check out http://gaylimape.tripod.com. When looking for gay-friendly night-life, the key phrase is *"al ambiente."* Many of the buildings are unmarked on the outside but rocking inside, and most are not exclusively frequented by gays or lesbians. Indeed, the gay nightlife scene is often acknowledged to be better than the rest.

Gay men also often meet in the city's private **Baños Turkos** (saunas), though not all baths are exclusively homosexual. The most popular mainly-gay baths are **Baños Pardo,** José Pardo 182, Miraflores (☎446 8582; s/38; open daily); **Oupen Sauna,** 28 de Julio 171, Miraflores (☎242 3094; s/30, M-Th before 6pm s/ 25); and **Baños Tivoli,** Petit Thouars 4041, San Isidro (☎222 1705; M and W-Su s/ 25, Tu s/20), popular after 6pm.

Legendaris, Berlin 363, Miraflores (☎446 3435; www.gayperu.com/legendaris), off Parque Kennedy. One of the hippest gay clubs in town with a misty jungle-themed dance floor, a classy lounge upstairs, and 80s tunes. Drinks s/12-16. Cover F after midnight and Sa 11pm-midnight s/1, Sa after midnight s/15. Open W-Sa 10:30pm-6am.

Downtown Vale Todo, Pasaje Los Pinos 168, Miraflores (☎444 6433; www.gay-peru.com/downtownvaletodo). A very popular mixed gay and lesbian spot. Awkward paintings line the walls as Go-Go boys and patrons dance in cages on the bar and karaoke blares. The VIP room offers a nice view of the dance floor and a private bar. Drinks s/10-15. Cover F s/13, VIP s/18; Sa s/18, VIP s/23. Open M-Sa 10:30pm-late.

Sagitario Disco, Wilson 869 (☎424 4383). One of the only exclusively gay spots in Lima Centro. Recently renovated and boasts A/C. The area can be unsafe at night, so take a taxi there and back. Drinks s/12-15. Open M-Sa 10pm-late.

⚡ DAYTRIPS FROM LIMA

The area around Lima was once inhabited by many ancient cultures, including the Chancay (AD 1200-1450), whose ruins still lie scattered about the region. Three main routes offer escape from the dismal fog and urban bustle of Lima: north to the beaches of Ancón; east and inland to Chosica and the ruins at Puruchuco, Cajamarquilla, and San Pedro de Casta; or south to the Pachacamac ruins.

RESERVA NACIONAL LOMAS DE LACHAY

Reaching this site can be challenging without hiring a taxi or another form of private transportation. Take the bus to Huacho (leaves every 15min. from Parque Universitaria, s/16) and ask to be let off at the "Reserva de Lachay." From there, walk about an hour in the sierra to the ticket booth, and another hour to the information center. Walk back to the Panamericana to flag a bus back to Lima. Entrance fee s/5.

Simon and Garfunkel could not imagine a better sound of silence than the one here, where hearing nothing is a welcome escape from the constant noise of taxis, buses, or blaring street music. The nature reserve is home to a bountiful cornucopia of ecological delights, just a 2hr. shot from the capital. This is a great way to see Peru's astounding geographic diversity—from the **mirador** (a 20min. trek from the information center), you can see both the green *lomas* and the vast *sierra* in the background. *Limeños* enjoy grilling their lunches at the picnic areas and hiking the 2hr. trail around the expensive reserve lodge. The Reserve also offers great **camping sites,** a rarity in the Lima area (s/10 per person, bring your own equipment). If you're lucky, you might see deer or foxes. Visit in the summer months (Dec.-Mar.) to see more plants in full bloom, but this little slice of nature provides peace and quiet with amazing *vistas* year-round.

PURUCHUCO

Take a colectivo marked "Chosica" from Plaza Grau. Ask the driver to stop at "las ruinas de Puruchuco" (45min., s/1.50), and look for the "zona arqueológica" sign on the right. To avoid the long hike from the colectivo stop to the site, contact a tour company or hire a cab for US$5-10. ☎ 494 2641. Open daily 9am-5pm. s/5-6.

The **ruins** of Puruchuco (Quechua for "plumed helmet") consist of an adobe dwelling that was once the home of an Inca noble. The recent discovery of 2000 mummies, including a pregnant woman, has brought more attention to this site. Visitors enjoy free rein to explore each poorly lit chamber of the labyrinth where the chief and his servants lived. Though restored perhaps a little too well in the 1960s—the floor and many of the walls have been plastered with smooth concrete, and some of the ancient bedrooms

ily Chronicle

IN RECENT NEWS

WHAT LIES BENEATH

Guerrilla activity in the late 1980s forced many Peruvians to flee their countryside homes for the relative safety of Lima, resulting in the upsurge of numerous shanty towns like Túpac Amaru. Unbeknownst to the residents of Túpac Amaru, they had plopped down directly atop what was once an Inca cemetery, called Puruchuco.

In 1999, after mummy remains and artifacts kept cropping up mysteriously throughout the settlement, the villagers contracted a team of local scientists assisted by funds from National Geographic, to begin an archaeological exploration of the area. Two years later, a total of 2000 mummies had been excavated from beneath the shantytown. Among the finds were many "mummy bundles"—groupings of seven mummies tied together in layers of fine textiles. Forty of these bundles were adorned with *cabezas falsas* (false heads), elaborately decorated masks used to symbolize the status of the Inca elite after death. Mummies are still being uncovered in the area, and archaeologists believe that under Túpac Amaru lies the most extensive collection of Inca artifacts ever found in the Andean region. Local residents have proved vital to the excavation effort by guarding the graves from looters. What started as a trickle of ceramics and mummy masks has turned into a flood of Inca history.

now have electrical outlets— Puruchuco offers a convincingly authentic glimpse of ancient life. The complex also contains a small but informative **museum** and a small scale model of the site called "puruchucito."

ANCÓN

Colectivos (45-90min., s/1.50) run from Plaza 2 de Mayo. The beach is a downhill walk from the final stop.

Normally a quiet seaside town on the peaceful Peruvian shore, Ancón brims with visitors in the summertime (Dec.-Mar.). The town was once a popular escape for wealthy urbanites. Today, however, a curious mix of opulent yachts and dilapidated buildings sporting 1950s beach resort-style architecture serve as testaments to its previously ritzy status. Ancón's oceanfront is divided into two parts by the huge Fuerza Aérea del Perú, Escuela de Supervivencia en el Mar (Air Force of Peru, School of Ocean Supervision), and you can watch the seamen practicing along the coast. To reach a wide stretch of sand, head right from the Fuerza Aérea, facing the water. To the left, the area is more commercial, lined with oceanfront buildings and beautiful yachts. The **beaches** are relatively clean, but ask around the **Paseo Turístico**—a little dock extending from the beach—for water conditions. Also from the dock, you can take a 30min. boat trip (s/2) around the Ancón coast, or sample some fresh *ceviche* (s/5-10) at the numerous stands lining the area.

Numerous **pre-Inca ruins** lie in the Chillón Valley near Ancón, but they are undeveloped and difficult to visit. Visit the **Museo de Sitio de Ancón**, on a little hill behind the town center, to see pictures of the coast's development over the past century, as well as funerary displays and replicas of ceramic pieces (s/1).

CHANCAY

Buses labeled "Huaral Turismo" leave from Plaza de Acho in Lima (1½-2½hr., 15 per day, s/3.50). In Huaral, you can take a bus (from the dirt parking lot between the river and the freeway) to Chancay. To reach the seaside restaurants, take a mototaxi in Chancay (s/1-2). Those short on time might consider hiring a driver. The Ecotruly Ashram is right off Km65 of the Panamericana Norte, but ask at Chancay for more specific information on how to get there. It's about a 30min. walk from the highway.

The Chancay Valley harbors a wealth of rarely visited ruins, but they have yet to be developed for tourists. Start off the day at Chancay, a typical coastal town, known for great seaside restaurants with amazing views of the crashing ocean below. **El Castillo de Chancay ❷** boasts two restaurants, with seafood and *comida típica*. (Cover s/6. Entrees s/10-13.) El Castillo also has a small museum containing textiles, mummies, and approximately 1000 ceramic pieces from the Chancay culture. The **Ecotruly Ashram Hare Krishna temple** next to the Pacific Ocean serves organic vegetarian meals cooked in a traditional mud or solar oven. The guided tour (s/3) reveals adobe huts and organic gardens, as well as the *Templo de Filosofía*. The temple also offers meditation space and rooms for longer stays. Be on the lookout for interesting tree sculptures along the main entrance. Call in advance to visit. (☎ 444 4747 or 470 8804; www.vrindavan.org/trulys.)

CHOSICA

Colectivos marked "Chosica" (1-1½hr., s/1.50-3.50) run inland from Plaza Grau in Lima Centro. The temple is about 5km from town, at Km32 of the Carretera Central. Open daily 9am-8pm. Ask the colectivo to drop you off at the pink Hare Krishna temple, or take a mototaxi from the central plaza (s/1).

Chosica, nicknamed "Villa del Sol," sees sun nearly 365 days of the year, making it a choice spot for weekend getaways. The town itself boasts few sites, and is best done as a quick visit for those continuing east. Off the central plaza is the **Christo Blanco** (White Christ), a large statue of Jesus with open arms. Also off this plaza, you'll see the **Camino de las Banderas** (flag walkway), a small park bordered by national and international flags. By far the town's most interesting site, the **Hare Krishna temple** (the religion's primary place of worship in Peru), was constructed in 1991 and has painted domes and a beautiful garden that recalls India's sacred places. Visitors are welcome, and monks give free tours. Every Saturday at noon the temple hosts a festival with music and vegetarian food, free to the public. Enjoy the quaint vegetarian **restaurant ❶** (*menú* and entrees s/3), and the small store selling books and teas.

CAJAMARQUILLA

*One of the more remote and less secure sites unless visited through a private tour company (**Peru Smile** costs about US$10 per hr.; see p. 102). If visiting independently, get off at Km10 of the Carretera Central and walk to the ruins. Buy your ticket in advance at the Puruchuco Office to save time. (Entrance fee s/3. Open daily 9am-5pm.)*

Tucked away between some refinery mills and a new *pueblo jóven* (shantytowns built to accommodate the city's burgeoning population), this former Huari city-state, one of the largest in ancient Peru, is today a small remnant of its former self. Construction of the five primary **pyramids** and six secondary pyramids is estimated to have begun around AD 400, while it was deserted around AD 1400. There is no site better than Cajamarquilla for witnessing first-hand the impact (or lack thereof) of the development of sites for tourism. With crumbling walls and little information around the ruins themselves, the area is practically abandoned and quite different from its counterparts like Puruchuco. Travelers can visit both sites together on the same day. Be very careful here; avoid traveling alone.

PACHACAMAC

Colectivos marked "Lurín" (1hr., s/2) run frequently, heading east on Grau in Lima Centro. Others that pass Pachacamac (1hr., every hr. 5am-10pm, s/2.70) also leave from the corner of Montevideo and Andahuaylas. Be sure to ask the driver for "las ruinas"; if you say "Pachacamac," you may be dropped off at a small town about 1km past the entrance to the ruins. Ruins and museum open daily 9am-5pm. s/6. English-speaking guides s/15.

Limeños head south for the beaches, but tourists head south for another reason—the Pachacamac ruins, which locals have transformed into quite an attraction. On the way there, colorful makeshift huts dot the hillsides of Lima's southern outskirts, constituting Villa El Salvador, the most famous of Lima's *pueblos jóvenes* (shantytowns). Pachacamac (roughly translated as "creator of land and time") was a Huari god who represented both genders and had the power to destroy the world through earthquakes and to see the past as well as the future—hence the two faces, one on either side of his head. The site was first built between AD 200 and 600 as a sacred city to this deity, and around AD 650 the Huari added pyramids, accessible by huge stone ramps. When the Incas razed the remaining Huari settlement in 1470, they feared the sacredness of this complex so much that they left it intact. In fact, the Incas associated Pachacamac with their own creator-god, and added a Temple of the Sun to the complex. When the Inca emperor Atahuallpa tried to convince the Spanish to set him free by tempting them with tales of his kingdom's treasures, he named two gold-laden spots in particular: the sun temples in Cusco and Pachacamac. Hernando Pizarro (Francisco's brother) led an unsuccessful expedition to Pachacamac in 1533. Since then, most of the complex has fallen into disrepair, but the largest structures—the Huari pyramids and the Inca

THE SOUTHERN COAST

Welcome to the desert. Stark and dusty, the Southern Coast of Peru is one of the driest places in the world. It is a land of extremes, claiming the world's driest desert (Atacama), one of the earth's tallest sand dunes (Cerro Blanco), and the tallest wave in South America (Pico Alto). The dry expanses between small towns draw scientists, desert junkies, and, more recently, sandboarders to their unforgiving hills, but only for a visit—almost no one calls the desert home. Those who do live here inhabit desert oases and fertile valleys fed by Andean rivers. The ancient cultures that ruled these lands, the Paracas and Nasca, were migratory and ingenious in their ability to thrive here. Their mysterious remains add further drama to the already intriguing landscape: huge lines in the desert, skulls with deformed heads, and eerily preserved mummies.

In addition to the ancient cultures that settled here, foreign influences have been strong along the coast. The resulting regional character, a blend of everything from European-influenced architecture to African-influenced festivals, is very different from the rest of Peru. Southern Coastal Peru is well touristed and unmistakeably modern, with the conveniently paved Panamericana providing easy transport through the harsh climate to the gems that dot the coast. Still, outside of tourist offices, gringo cafes, and hotels is Peru as usual: charming, urban, and unpredictable. Just leave your raincoat behind.

HIGHLIGHTS OF THE SOUTHERN COAST

HANG TEN on the tallest wave in South America at **Punta Hermosa** (p. 132), or the sand dunes of the picture-perfect desert oasis of **Huacachina** (p. 152).

WIND DOWN at one of the many *bodegas* of fertile **Lunahuaná** (p. 136).

CHILL with penguins and sea lions at the **Reserva Nacional de Paracas** (p. 144) and the **Islas Ballestas** (p. 146).

SPECULATE about the meaning of the **Nasca lines** (p. 157), anciently etched in the sand and only discernible from an airplane.

PUNTA HERMOSA   ☎01

Surrounded by stark desert hills, the rocky beaches of Punta Hermosa (pop. 4000) offer a pleasant respite just 45km away from the madness of metropolitan Lima. During the quiet winter months (June-Sept.) the town is a haven of serenity for locals as well as for the most devout wetsuit-clad surfers. The summer months (Dec.-Mar.) see the opening of the restaurants, discos, and hotels that sit boarded up and empty during the rest of the year. In the summer, the town serves mainly as a getaway for the wealthy urbanites whose luxurious beach houses line the coast along the **Playa Blanca.** Thousands of Lima residents longing for a day of sun join the throngs of surfers who come for Punta Hermosa's famous waves. While the north coast of Peru has the world's longest wave, Punta Hermosa boasts **Pico Alto,** South America's tallest wave, which reaches an incredible 7.3m (the biggest swells arrive Apr.-May). Surfers also pilgrimage here for **Punta Rocas,** a beach legendary for churning out 5m rideable waves 365 days of the year.

⌨ TRANSPORTATION AND PRACTICAL INFORMATION. Punta Hermosa is 2km off the Panamericana; all buses traveling this part of the Panamericana pass through Punta Hermosa, but most drop passengers right next the highway, where frequent **combis** provide service into town. Make sure your bus or colectivo is going to the beach, not just dropping you off on the side of the highway. The most direct are the brown-striped combis marked "Lurín" (1½ hr., frequent departures 6am-8pm, s/3), leaving from Plaza Bolognesi in Lima Centro; they drop passengers off at **El Complejo**, on the top of a hill 200m from the beach. **Taxis** from Lima will also take passengers to Punta Hermosa. There is **no bank and no hospital** in the town. Limited services include the **police,** Comisaría Punta Hermosa, Libertad Block 2 (☎230 7066), near the top of the stairs that lead down to the beach, and **Telefónica del Perú,** the blue booths scattered throughout the town. **Internet** (s/1 per hr.) and **postal services** can be found at El Complejo.

⌨ ACCOMMODATIONS AND FOOD. Since the majority of Punta Hermosa's visitors are either day-trippers or vacation home owners, the hotel selection is limited and generally expensive. The white stucco ▩**Casa Barco Hostal ❸**, Av. Punta Hermosa 340, provides clean rooms for any budget in the quiet neighborhood of Playa Norte. The bright gardens, breezy lounge and restaurant, and unbeatable sunset views make Casa Barco a hit. (☎230 7081; www.casabarco.com. Breakfast included. Dorm-style beds with shared bath s/20; balcony rooms overlooking the beach up to s/65.) ▩**Luisfer ❹**, Miramar Mz. L Lote 13, on Calle 7, is a surfer's paradise. The price includes three hot meals a day, which guests praise as the best food in town. Operated by national surfing champion Luís Fernando and his

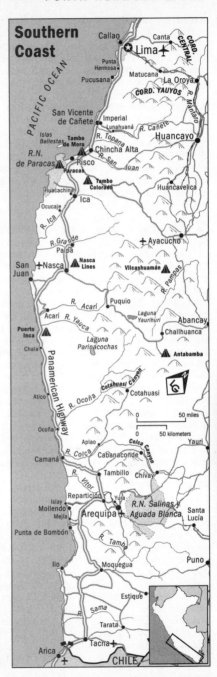

Southern Coast

wife, the hostel also provides a swimming pool, free rides to Punta Rocas, and a variety of old surfboards for lend. The hostel arranges rides from Lima with prior notice. (☎230 7280; luisfersurf@terra.com.pe. Cable TV/VCR. 3- to 4-bed dorms, private rooms, and doubles all US$16.) The thatch-roofed **La Rotunda ❷**, also a restaurant, offers pleasant rooms right on the Malecón. (☎230 7390. Dorms with bath s/25; private rooms with ocean view US$20-40.)

Restaurants in Punta Hermosa vary greatly in price depending on the location. Along the Malecón and the Panamericana, restaurants are generally overpriced and closed during the off season (Apr.-Nov.). A short walk a few blocks off the beach or the Panamericana means a good meal for s/3-6. **La Rotunda ❸**, Bolognesi 530, has excellent seafood that is worth the price. (☎584 3701. Entrees s/18-22. Seafood s/20-27. Open daily Apr.-Dec. 9am-7pm; Jan.-Mar. 8am-11pm.) A colorful tile floor distinguishes **Restaurant Central III ❸**, located a few blocks toward the Panamericana from El Complejo. *Ceviche* and *pescados* run s/18-25. (☎334 3025. V.) **Restaurant Carmencita ❶**, right above the beach, serves juicy hamburgers (s/6) and *pollo* (s/4-5) to weary surfers.

◪ BEACHES. Punta Hermosa boasts more than ten beaches, all easily accessible by foot or by the little brown buses marked "Lurín" that arrive at El Complejo (s/0.50 to El Silencio). North of Punta Hermosa is **El Silencio**, whose calm waters bring hordes of tourists followed by hordes of local vendors to cater to their every whim. *Heladerías* and tourist restaurants line the Panamericana at Km43, the gateway to the beach. Just south of El Silencio are the **Señoritas** and **Caballeros** beaches, divided by a spectacular rock precipice—the best place in Punta Hermosa to watch the sun set over the Pacific. Continuing south is the famous **Pico Alto,** where those less daring than the hard-core surfers can experience the thrill of Pico's 7.3m waves from a thatched-roof veranda far above the beach. Just around the corner from Pico Alto is **Playa Norte,** the playground of wealthy locals, followed by **La Isla,** a huge rock formation accesible via a walkway from the mainland. The **Malecón** and **Playa Negra,** directly in front of Punta Hermosa proper and distinguished by black sand, are popular spots with locals. Condos, summer homes, and Punta Hermosa's classy **Club Náutico** are located on the exclusive **Playa Blanca.** Without a doubt, the most popular destination for surfers is **Punta Rocas,** 2km south of Punta Hermosa, the only place in the world where you can catch well-formed waves up to 5m high all year long. Punta Rocas has become an international surfing destination, drawing both national and international competitions to Punta Hermosa's beaches in recent years.

◪ NIGHTLIFE. Nightlife in Punta Hermosa centers around the bars lining the Malecón. During the summer, many locals simply bring coolers of beer to drink on the beach. For dancing, Punta Hermosa itself has few options, but the surrounding area boasts *discotecas* that are popular enough to draw tourists from Lima and elsewhere. **Home,** at Panamericana Km43.5, draws huge crowds of locals and tourists each weekend during the summer—explaining its size—but is closed during the low season. (Drinks s/2-3. Cover s/20-30. Open F-Sa 11pm-dawn.) **South,** a few blocks to the north (go figure), is a smaller but equally popular club open only on Saturdays from January to March. (Cover s/20-30.) There are also several options in San Bartolo, 4km south of Punta Hermosa, accessible via the little brown combis from El Complejo. **El Huayno Discoteca,** 150m from the entrance to San Bartolo, under the huge red Cristal sign, pumps dance music onto an open-air dance floor. (Cover s/5. Open Dec.-Mar. F-Sa 11pm-6am.) **La Rumba,** at Panamericana Km48, does the same but with more Latin spice. (☎247 3280. Cover s/10, includes one beer. Open Dec.-Mar. Sa 11pm-6am.)

PUCUSANA ☎03

Since 1876, the inhabitants of the Chilca region have been fishing the fertile waters near Pucusana (pop. 10,000). Nowadays, Pucusana is a colorful coastal village sandwiched between dramatic desert hills and the clear bay that is the source of its livelihood. During the summer season (Jan.-Mar.), Pucusana draws tourists from Lima and elsewhere to its many beaches. Wealthy Peruvians and tourists alike wade in the **Playa de las Ninfas** (located behind the intersection of Malecón and Las Ninfas), a well-protected lagoon secluded from the vast Pacific by the steep surrounding hills. The **Isla Galápagos,** 20m from the mainland, is both an exclusive residential neighborhood with about a hundred residents and a spectacular secluded beach. When the water is low, it is possible to wade to the island; otherwise you will need to take a short boat ride (s/1). Fishermen on the port give a 45min. tour of all of Pucusana's beaches for s/15. For a less touristy experience, take a fishing trip (all fishing gear included) on one of the brightly-colored boats (s/15 per hr.). The **Museo de los Delfines,** Calle Jorge Chávez N. 302, has limited exhibits about the marine life of Pucusana. (☎430 9228. Open Sa-Su 10am-noon and 2:30-6pm.) If you'd rather just sit back and relax, climb to the **Mirador de Pucusana,** high above the port, to enjoy a *pisco* sour and the stunning views of the port, the Isla Galápagos, and the desert hills.

Accommodations in Pucusana are clustered along the Malecón San Martín and are generally quite simple. One exception is the **Mirador de Pucusana ❸,** Porto Velho 54-01, which offers 24hr. hot water, Internet, a restaurant, and the best views in the area. Getting there is quite a climb up the hill in front of Salón Blanco, but well worth the effort. (☎430 9228. s/25 with shared bath; up to s/40 with private bath.) At the end of Malecón San Martín, **Salón Blanco ❷** offers simple rooms, some with great views of the port (☎430 9452; salonblancos@hotmail.com. s/20 with shared bath; up to s/40 with private bath.) **Restaurante El Sol ❷,** Billingduth 220, offers some of the best food in Pucusana. Diners can savor *pescados* and *mariscos* in sight of the turbulent waters of the El Boquerón lagoon. (☎430 9072. *Ceviche* s/11. *Menú* s/8-10. Open 9am-6:30pm.) For cheap and tasty pizza, try **Antonella Pizza and Pasta ❶,** one block from Malecón San Martín on Leoncio. (Slices s/2.50. Whole pizzas s/10.)

To reach Pucusana from points northward, take the little brown **combis** marked "Lurín" found all along the Panamericana Vieja to San Bartolo (10 min., s/1.50). Near the entrance of San Bartolo (under the arch), wait for a white **bus** marked "Pucusana." Pucusana is the last stop (30 min., s/2). Walk down the hill to the **Malecón San Martín,** which lines the port and houses many restaurants and the majority of the town's accommodations. The **police** (☎430 9005) and **hospital** (☎430 9053) can be found two blocks from Malecón on Lima. There is **no bank** in Pucusana, but there is an **ATM** (MC/V) in the Salón Blanco restaurant on the end of Malecón San Martín closest to La Playa Ninfas.

SAN VICENTE DE CAÑETE ☎014

San Vicente de Cañete (pop. 160,000; elev. 54m), or just "Cañete," is a hectic town just 2½hr. outside of Lima that serves tourists primarily as a gateway to the rural adventures of Lunahuaná. The noisy, crowded streets may deter some from spending time in Cañete, but those looking to experience a piece of Peruvian urbana less overwhelming than the capital city will find Cañete a colorful stop.

Hostal La Casona ❸, Bolognesi 222, on the Plaza de Armas, is the best value by far in Cañete, with concrete walls that are brightened by Peruvian wall hangings and pictures of tourist attractions. (Singles s/25; doubles s/40.) Cheap and filling fare can be found all along the Plaza de Armas. For a good *menú* (s/5) try **La Estancia ❶,** 2 de Mayo 657, which serves standard *criollo* fare, fresh juices, and cold beer. (☎581 1328. Open daily 8:30am-10pm.)

All buses heading north to Lima or south from Lima on the Panamericana pass through Cañete. From Lima Centro, direct buses for Cañete (2½hr., s/5) leave from Montevideo between Iquitos and Abancay. There are frequent **buses** from Cañete to Lima (2½hr., every 5min., s/7) and Pisco (1hr., s/3-5). At the intersection of the Panamericana and 2 de Mayo, across the street from the various bus terminals, you can catch colectivos to Imperial (20min., s/0.50), where you can continue on to Lunahuaná (40-50 min., s/2.50). The **Plaza de Armas** lies on 2 de Mayo, a few blocks inland from the bus stop on the Panamericana. **Interbank,** 2 de Mayo 451, has a **24hr. ATM.** (Open M-F 9am-1pm and 4-6:15pm, Sa 9:15am-12:30pm. MC/V.) **Police** (☎581 2083) are at 2 de Mayo on Plaza San Martín. There is a **24hr. pharmacy** at **Hospital Rezola** (☎581 2010), at the opposite end of 2 de Mayo from the buses. **Internet** access is available at **Informáticas,** Sepúlveda 231, on the Plaza de Armas. (☎581 3384. s/1.50 per hr. Open 8am-11pm.)

LUNAHUANÁ   ☎034

Two things bring visitors to lush Lunahuaná (pop. 5000; elev. 480m): wine and whitewater, both of which are celebrated at the **Fiesta de la Uva, el Vino y el Canotaje** (Festival of Grapes, Wine, and Rafting) during the first weekend in March. Highlights of the *fiesta* include free wine tastings and communal grape stomping, when the townspeople shed their shoes and jump into an enormous vat of grapes. While the high season for wine and rafting runs roughly December through March, both can be enjoyed year-round. The many *bodegas* (vineyards) in the area are always open for tours and tastings, and during the low season (May-Dec.) the rapids of the Rio Cañete become more beginner-friendly. If there's anything that Lunahuanans are more proud of than their local *pisco*, it's the sun that purportedly shines every day of the year. In fact, scenic Lunahuaná—just an hour side trip off the Panamericana—is one of the most under-appreciated gems of the Southern Coast.

 TRANSPORTATION. There is no direct bus service from Lima to Lunahuaná—you'll have to pass through Cañete. Take a **colectivo** from the bottom of 2 de Mayo to the small village of Imperial (10-20min., s/0.50); from there, catch another colectivo to Lunahuaná (40min., s/2.50). From Lunahuaná, white **buses** marked "Lima" provide direct service back to the capital (3hr). Frequent **combis** (every 15min. during the day, every 30min. at night; s/1) travel the main road between the *poblados*. Combis will drop you at any *poblado* or in the Plaza de Armas.

 ORIENTATION AND PRACTICAL INFORMATION. Lunahuaná isn't so much one town as it is a series of small *poblados* (neighborhoods) spread out along **Grau,** the road that runs above the **Río Cañete.** The name of the road changes in each neighborhood, so in Jita it is called "Jita" and in Uchupampa it is named "Uchupampa." The largest *poblado* is called Lunahuaná, and its **Plaza de Armas**—where most of the events take place during the Festival de la Uva, el Vino y el Canotaje—sits two blocks above the main road.

The **tourist office,** one block from the Plaza de Armas on Grau in Lunahuaná, provides pamphlets on local tours, restaurants, and vineyards; **Lunahuaná Valley Tours** (☎9673 8041; lunvalleytours@terramail.com.pe), in the tourist office on Grau, offers inexpensive tours that cover the Ruins of Incahuasi, the *bodegas*, the Iglesia Colonial, the *mirador*, and other sights (3hr.; 9, 11am, 1, 3pm; s/15). Other services include: **Banco de la Nación,** on Grau (☎284 1007; open 8am-2:30pm); **police** (☎284 1007), on the corner of the Plaza de Armas; and a **hospital,** one block from the Plaza on Calle de los Andes, including a 24hr. walk-in **Centro de Salud.**

⛱☕ ACCOMMODATIONS AND FOOD. It's worthwhile to pay a little more for a hotel in Lunahuaná—dirt-cheap ones lie in the main *poblado*, but the quality of the rooms usually plunges severely with the price. Some of the hotels along Grau offer unbelievable views of the river and surrounding mountains and are well worth the extra cash. The best bang for your buck is the ■**Restaurant Hostal Campestre Mi Rosedal ❸**, on the main road in the Uchupampa *poblado* at Km41.7. Rooms are clean and welcoming and include hot baths. (☎284 1177. Singles s/30; matrimonials s/35; doubles s/50.) The **restaurant ❷** downstairs woos customers with its shrimp specialties and its breezy patio, one of the prettiest in Lunahuaná. (*Chupe de camarones* s/4. Entrees s/7-16. *Menú* s/7.50. Open daily 8am-9:30pm. MC/V.) Wooden cabanas, pleasant balconies, and tastefully decorated rooms are only the beginning at **Las Viñas ❹**, at Km41.50 in nearby Condoray; the hostel also rents **campsites ❶** and organizes horseback rides, kayak lessons, and rafting trips. (Mobile ☎01 437 3187. Campsites s/10, with tent rental s/15; singles s/45; matrimonials s/70; doubles s/90. AmEx/V.) **El Guanabo ❶,** in the Juta *poblado*, has campsites with river views. (s/10; with tent rental s/20.) Magnificent views from ■**Restaurant Campestre ❷**, on Grau at Km52 in the Catapalla *poblado*, reveal the nearby mountains, river, and the precarious-looking *puente colgante* (hanging bridge). (☎536 4180. *Sopa cholla* s/12; *camarones* s/16.) **Restaurant Embassy Río ❸** in Uchupampa offers tasty, high-quality meals (☎479 9127; *menú de camarones* s/20), as does **El Pueblo ❸** in Lunahuaná (*ceviche* s/16).

◩⛰ SIGHTS AND OUTDOOR ACTIVITIES. There are several *bodegas* along Grau that give tours and sell their local wines and *piscos*. The oldest and most popular is **La Reyna de Lunahuaná,** in the Catapalla *poblado*. (☎449 9917. Information in English. Open Sa-Su 9am-6pm. Bottle of wine s/10. *Pisco* s/20.) The tourist office near the Plaza de Armas maintains a complete list of Lunahuaná's *bodegas*.

During the high season for **whitewater rafting** (Jan.-Mar.), rapids on the Río Cañete reach Class IV and sometimes Class V (expert), inducing some tour agencies to require prior experience. The rest of the year, the rapids are Class II-III—good for beginners. Most rafting trips (Apr.-Dec. US$10-15; Jan.-Mar. US$20) last just over 1½hr. including instruction time. Many hotels, restaurants, and agencies around the Plaza de Armas offer whitewater rafting trips. **ALDEA** (Asociación Latinoamericana de Deportes de Aventura), on Grau in San

THE BODEGAS OF LUNAHUANÁ

In 1630, an enterprising Spaniard named Francisco Caravantes discovered that the fertile valley of Lunahuaná was perfect for cultivating grapes. Ever since, the valley has prided itself on its local wines and *piscos*, produced and sold in *bodegas* along Grau and marketed all over Peru. Today, the *bodegas* do much more than produce wine; they are also full-service tourist destinations with restaurants, stores, and free tours. Between February and April, tourists can kick off their shoes, roll up their pants, and literally jump right into the wine pressing. Arrive early—grape stomping takes place in the morning. Although tours of the *bodegas* are undoubtedly the highlight, the stores sell liquors for unbeatable prices: bottles of wine s/8-10, *pisco* s/15-20.

The best time to visit is during the **Fiesta de la Uva, el Vino y el Canotaje,** in early March. The *bodegas* come together in celebration of the river and its gifts to Lunahuaná, and grape-stomping takes center stage in the Plaza.

The tourist office has a list of all the *bodegas* in Lunahuaná. **La Reyna de Lunahuaná,** across the river in the Catapalla *poblado* (7km from town), is the oldest and best-known. (☎449 9917 English info. Open Sa-Su 9am-6pm.) Also popular (and closer) is **Viña Los Reyes,** in Condoray (☎284 1206. Tours in English and German. Open 7am-7pm.)

NEAR CHINCHA ALTA: LA CASA-HACIENDA SAN JOSÉ

The **Casa-Hacienda San José** ❺, dating back to 1688, originally produced sugar and honey but added cotton in the late 18th century. At its peak, more than 1000 enslaved Africans worked at the *hacienda*, and in 1879, they organized a revolt in which they murdered the son of their owner on the steps of the house. Cotton, asparagus, and citrus fruits are still harvested in the fields, but the San José of today is primarily a resort hotel. Breathtaking grounds [ ] swimming pool, horse stables, tennis courts, and *sapo* (a traditional game similar to horseshoes). Guided tours include a candlelit excursion into the catacombs where past owners reside. Open daily 9am-5pm. 30min. tours in Spanish only, s/10.) **Combis** marked "El Carmen" (45min., leave when full about every 5min., s/2) bring you from the corner of Caqueta and Italia, on the opposite side of Chincha's market from the bus terminals, or you can take a **taxi** (20min., s/13-15). Return combis leave from the main entrance. The **hotel** isn't exactly "budget," but its all-inclusive packages cram a lot of bang into every buck. A cheaper option is to stay one night, have breakfast, and do all the tours. (☎22 458 or 01 444 5242; www.haciendasanjose.com.pe. Guided tours s/10-15. Rooms US$26-41; 2- and 3-day packages US$51-31. AmEx/MC/V.)

Jerónimo (Km39), is a nationally respected company that was the first to organize guided trips down the Cañete River. ALDEA's tours come complete with English-speaking guides upon request. **Valley Tours** (☎9673 8041), a smaller operation in the tourist office just off the Plaza de Armas, also boasts English-speaking guides at slightly lower prices. **Kayaking** is also possible if you can convince the agencies that you know what you're doing; there is no kayak instruction.

The Lunahuaná region offers a few sites of interest beyond wine and whitewater. A 20min. walk from the Plaza de Armas up into the hills above Lunahuaná will take you to the **Mirador de San Juan**, which offers views of the entire Chilca Valley. The cross was constructed in 1901 in remembrance of Saint John the Baptist. The **Iglesia Colonial** in the Plaza de Armas was constructed in 1690, and its interesting architecture deserves a glance. The Inca **Ruins of Incahuasi** lie outside the city near the town of Socsi (Km29), accessible via combis from Lunahuaná.

CHINCHA ALTA   ☎056

Chincha Alta (pop. 80,000; elev. 101m), or just "Chincha," was the central hub of an ancient culture whose stubborn resistance to Inca conquest caused the Inca Pachakuteq to enter into a pact of non-violence and cooperation with the Chinchas. Today Chincha is best known for another union, **Afro-Peruvian,** that began in the early days of the Spanish conquest when the Spanish brought African slaves to work on the *haciendas*. After slavery was abolished in the 18th century, many people of African descent remained, and their culture continues to add a rare flair to this one-of-a-kind city.

🮲 **TRANSPORTATION. Ormeño** (☎26 1301), in the *plazuela*, sends **buses** to: Arequipa (14hr., 6 per day, s/35) via Camaná (6hr., s/25); Lima (3hr.; 2:30, 5:30, 7:30pm; s/6); Marcona (5½hr., 3 per day, s/13) via Nasca (4hr.; 4, 10:30pm; s/10); Ica (1½hr., every 1½hr., s/4); Palpa (3½hr., 5 per day, s/10); Pisco (30min.; 10am, 4:30, 6pm; s/2); Tacna (19-20hr., 12:30, 6pm, s/50). Other bus companies and **colectivos** leave from the same area.

🮲 🮲 **ORIENTATION AND PRACTICAL INFORMATION.** Chincha Alta's main street is the busy **Mariscal Benavides,** which runs between the tree-laden **Plaza de Armas** and the bus-laden **Plazuela Bolognesi. Mariscal Castilla** runs perpendicular to Benavides two blocks from the bus station. The **Municipalidad** (☎26 5914), on the Plaza de Armas, houses a **tourist office** that provides information on the town and local tours. The **Banco de Crédito,** near the bus station on Benavides, will exchange traveler's checks and has a **24hr. ATM** outside. (☎26 1221. Open daily 10am-4pm.)

Internet access (s/1-5 per hr.) is plentiful in Chincha, especially along Benavides. **Serpost** is on the Plaza de Armas. (☎26 1114. Open M-F 8am-2pm, Sa 8am-4pm.) Other services include **police** (☎26 1261), on the Plaza de Armas, and **Hospital San José** (☎26 9006 or 26 1232), on Alva Maúrtua at the corner of San Martín, away from the Panamericana.

🛏🍴 ACCOMMODATIONS AND FOOD. Chincha is rife with cheap rooms and expensive ones, but there is little in between. The good news is that the water is hot just about everywhere in the city. **Hotel Sotelo ❷,** Benavides 260, near the Plaza and the bus station, has three floors of basic but clean pale blue rooms off long hallways. (☎26 1681. TV s/5. Singles s/12, with bath s/18; doubles s/20, with bath s/30.) Next door, get something twice as nice for twice the price at **Hostal Sumar ❹,** Benavides 242, where you can relax in the welcoming lounge and sleep under a thatched roof. (☎84 4501. Singles s/40; doubles s/60. MC/V.) **Hostal Bicerrel ❸,** Mariscal Castilla 232, one block off Benavides, provides very basic rooms, but the owners deserve credit for trying to create ambience with their downstairs bar and lounge. (☎26 1260. Singles s/25. Cable TV upon request.)

When in Chincha, eat as *chinchanos* do; a local favorite is *tacu tacu* (a scramble of rice, beans, onions, meat, and spicy *ají*). **Restaurante Cevichería Costa Marina ❷,** Plaza de Armas 147, right next to Serpost, is good for seafood and traditional *chinchana* cuisine. (☎838 5512. *Tacu tacu* s/16. *Menú* s/6. Entrees s/10-20. Open daily 9am-9pm, later on weekends.) By far the cheapest and most interesting way to eat in Chincha is to visit the **mercado** on Benavides near the bus station, which sells sweets, fruits, nuts, whole chickens, fish, and other local dishes. (Opens when the first vendors arrive, usually around 8am.)

📷🎵 SIGHTS AND ENTERTAINMENT. Modern Chincha is Peru's capital of African folklore and art, characterized by traditional *chinchana* cuisine and the Afro-Peruvian music and dance that energize Chincha's streets and nightclubs. All this celebration of Afro-Peruvian heritage culminates in the annual festival of **Verano Negro,** in late February. The 🔷**Casa Hacienda San José,** a former plantation home of the Cilloniz family, offers a glimpse into the region's cultural history, complete with Afro-Peruvian dance lessons. Tourists come en masse to Chincha during the **Semana Turística** in late October to celebrate the birthday of the province of Chincha with parades, music, and dance. Also of note in Chincha is the dramatic palm tree-lined **Plaza de Armas** and the busy **mercado** on Benavides.

VERANO NEGRO

The ancestors of most Afro-Peruvians were brought to Peru as slaves during the 16th century. Slavery ended in the 19th century, but the Africans stayed. Each year, from February 20-29, Afro-Peruvians celebrate their diverse cultural heritage during a festival in Chincha Alta called **Verano Negro,** or Black Summer. Near the beginning of the festival, food vendors storm the city for the **Gran Festival de la Gastronomía Peruana,** bringing dishes either of African origin or mixtures of African and Peruvian cuisines. Each night, Afro-Peruvian music blasting in the Plaza de Armas signals that start of a party that rarely stops before dawn. During the day, exhibitions of art from prominent Afro-Peruvian artists dot the city and are generally free of charge. Afro-Peruvian dances like the *festejos* and *alcatraz* are performed in the Plaza de Armas. Several prominent Afro-Peruvian speakers take the stand to talk about Afro-Peruvian history and current issues. Competitions in sports like basketball, swimming, and water polo are staged all over Chincha. The **Gran Bicicletada** is a bicycle procession from Chincha to El Carmen, the home of the first Africans in Peru. On the last night of the festival, locals throw a massive dance party in El Carmen known as **Pena Negra.**

PISCO
☎ 056

The word *pisco* is more often associated with the locally-produced, powerful white brandy than the small coastal town from which its name derives. Nonetheless, Pisco (pop. 160,000) tries its best to be interesting, and the effort is paying off—Pisco is one of Peru's most touristed cities, second only to Cusco. Most come to visit the wildlife at the Islas Ballestas (Peru's "poor man's Galápagos"), the beaches in the Reserva Nacional de Paracas, and the ruins of Tambo Colorado. Then they go home and celebrate with a *pisco*.

☞ TRANSPORTATION

Only buses with Pisco as a final destination go directly to town. However, any bus heading beyond Pisco can drop you at the turnoff (tell the bus driver, *"Bajo en la cruce para Pisco"*). From there, frequent **colectivos** leave for the town center (10min., s/0.50). The remarkably pleasant station of **Ormeño**, San Francisco 259 (☎53 2764), at Ayacucho, sends **buses** to: Arequipa (12hr., 6pm, s/30); Ayacucho (8½hr., 9am, s/20); Lima (3½hr.; 2, 4:45pm; royal class only, s/30); Nasca (4½hr.; 9am, 1:30pm; s/17); Tacna (17hr., 1pm, s/40). The larger **Ormeño terminal** (called San Clemente), Libertadores 101 (☎54 3388), sends buses to farther destinations: Arequipa (12hr.; noon, 4, 7pm; s/40); Ayacucho (8½hr., 6pm, s/30); Tacna (15hr., 12:30pm, s/50). To get to San Clemente terminal, take a **colectivo** from the *mercado* (10min., s/1). **Transportes Saky**, Pedemonte 190 (☎53 4309), on the corner (no sign), sends frequent buses to Ica (1hr., every 20min. 6am-8pm, s/2.50). Colectivos to Paracas (30min., leave when full, s/1) leave from the market area at Fermín Tanguis and B. de Humay. Colectivos to Chincha (1hr., s/2) leave from two blocks south of Plaza Belén on Comercio, away from the pedestrian walkway.

✳ ☷ ORIENTATION AND PRACTICAL INFORMATION

The **Plaza de Armas** hosts most services, while **San Francisco**, running north of the Plaza, has most travel agencies. On the southwest side of the plaza, the pedestrian walkway Comercio (called **Boulevard** by locals) leads to the smaller **Plaza Belén.**

Tours: Everywhere you look, especially on San Francisco between Ormeño and the Plaza, agencies advertise trips to the Islas Ballestas, Paracas Reserve, and (less frequently) Tambo Colorado. Tour agencies are notorious for hassling visitors with offers of over-priced tours as they enter the bus station. Instead, arrange tours at the tour offices themselves or ask for advice at your hotel. Most credible companies offer tours to Islas Ballestas for s/25, Ballestas and Paracas for s/35, and Tambo Colorado for s/40-50.

■ **Ballestas Travel,** San Francisco 249 (☎53 3095; jpacheco113@yahoo.com or jpache-cot@terra.com.pe). As the oldest tour company around, Ballestas Travel offers thorough tours of the sights with highly knowledgeable and entertaining guides. English and French spoken. Open daily 10am-10pm.

Zarcillo Connections, San Francisco 111 (☎53 6543; www.zarcilloconnections.net), not to be confused with **Zarcillos Tours** down the street, rents bicycles (US$10/hr.), provides sand dune buggy tours through Paracas (US$15). Tours to Ballestas US$10, Paracas US$10, and Tambo Colorado US$15. English and French spoken. Open daily 10am-10pm.

Sea Lion Tours, San Francisco 120 (☎54 5134; sealiontours@latinmail.com), is in Hostal Pisco.

Bank: Banco de Crédito, Pérez Figuerola 162 (☎53 2340), on the Plaza, changes traveler's checks (AmEx/V). 24hr. **ATM** accepts AmEx/MC/V. Open M-F 10am-6pm, Sa 9am-12:30pm.

Laundromat: Lavandería Iris, Pedemonte 170, has next-day service. s/5 per kilo. Open daily 8am-2pm.

Pisco

🏠 ACCOMMODATIONS
Hostal La Portada, 1
Hostal San Isidro, 2
Hostal Villa Manuelita, 5
Hotel Pisco, 4
Hotel Posada Hispana, 3
Hotel San Jorge Suite, 11

🍎 FOOD
Don Manuel, 12
La Catedral, 7
Mr. Ronald, 13
Restaurant Turístico
D'Reyes, 10

⭐ ENTERTAINMENT
Libertador Cinema, 6

🍺 NIGHTLIFE
Catamarán, 9
Dragon Pub, 8

Emergency: ☎ 105.

Police: San Francisco, Mz. 2 (☎ 53 5343), on the Plaza de Armas.

Hospital: Hospital San Juan de Dios (☎ 53 2332), 3 blocks from the Plaza de Armas on San Juan de Dios. Emergency room and pharmacy both open 24hr.

Telephones: A few **Telefónica del Perú** booths lie around the Plaza de Armas. For more privacy, head to **ServiFast E.I.R.L.**, Progreso 123 (☎ 53 6286), on the Plaza de Armas. Open daily 8am-2am.

Internet Access: Internet is abundant in Pisco, especially around the Plaza de Armas, usually for no more than s/1 per hr.

Post Office: Serpost, Callao 176 (☎ 53 2272), 1½ blocks from the Plaza de Armas. Open M-Sa 9am-5pm.

ACCOMMODATIONS

The large number of budget travelers who pass through Pisco ensures the existence of many clean, comfortable, and low-priced options, usually with hot water. Camping on the Paracas Reserve requires only the park entrance fee (s/5 per day; discounts for multiple days), but bring your own supplies because there are no places to rent or buy them there or even in Pisco. While camping on the beaches in the Paracas Reserve is common and well regulated, the police advise against camping on the Pisco beach.

▨ **Hostal San Isidro,** San Clemente 103 (☎ 53 6471; www.sanisidrohostal.com), 2 blocks north of the cemetery; take a left where Bolognesi ends. Clean and cheerful rooms include TVs upon request, while the spacious courtyard sports a cozy bar, billiards, and pool. Owners provide free coffee in the morning—perfect for 8am tours. Breakfast s/7. Singles s/20, with bath s/25; doubles with bath s/50; triples with bath s/75. ❸

Hostal Villa Manuelita, San Francisco 227 (☎ 53 5218; hostalvillamanuelita@hotmail.com), a block off the Plaza de Armas. Decorated in exquisitely detailed Spanish style, this residence boasts walls painted in warm tones illuminated by black-grate chandeliers, a pleasant patio, impeccable service, and, last but not least, hot water. Breakfast included. Doubles US$25; triples US$30. ❸

Hotel Posada Hispana, Bolognesi 236 (☎ 53 6363; www.posadahispana.com), 1 block from the Plaza. Castilian owner and a cadre of young staff members are as cheerful and friendly as its bright yellow exterior. 2-story dorms and private rooms are immaculately maintained and include bath. A backyard garden adds to the charm. Breakfast s/7. Internet included. US$25 per person. ❷

Hotel San Jorge Suite, Comercio 187 (☎ 53 4200), on the pedestrian walkway. It doesn't take much eye-squinting to imagine you're living in luxury here. All rooms have TVs and baths with soap and towels. Singles US$12; doubles US$25. MC/V. 5-10% discount if you own Let's Go. ❷

Hostal La Portada, Alipio Ponce 250 (☎ 53 2098; hostallaportada@terra.com), 3 blocks from the Plaza de Armas, behind the police station. Those longing for a bit of home will love Mamá Gloria's small, bed-and-breakfast-style hostal. Rooms are clean and handsomely decorated. Breakfast (s/5-7) served each morning in Mamá Gloria's living room. Laundry service included. No single rooms. Doubles s/45; triples s/65. ❷

Hotel Pisco, San Francisco 120 (☎ 53 6669; hostalpisco@latinmail.com or hotelpisco@terra.com), in a colorful refurbished colonial house on the Plaza de Armas. Comfy wicker chairs surround cable TVs near the bar. Breakfast s/5-6. 24hr. hot water. Dorms s/10; singles with bath s/15; matrimonials and doubles s/35; doubles with bath s/40; triples s/45. ❷

▊ FOOD

The tourist industry has made a substantial impact on Pisco's food offerings. Pizza is nearly as common as *ceviche*, and is (not surprisingly) more expensive. Spanish, Haitian, Italian, and American restaurants line the Plaza de Armas along with the traditional *cevicherías*. Alternatively, the **Shopping Market Belén** is a good place to stock up on basics if you're feeling inspired to make use of your hostel's kitchen. The market is located on the Belén Plaza on the side nearest the Plaza de Armas and is open daily 10am-7pm.

La Catedral, Pérez Figuerola 200 (☎ 53 5611), on the corner of the Plaza de Armas across from the Banco de Crédito. A variety of international favorites, from local *ceviche* to Italian lasagna. Hanging plants, ceiling fans, and twinkling lights animate the restaurant's interior. Entrees s/8.50. *Ceviche* s/18. Open daily noon-4pm and 6-10pm. ❷

Mr. Ronald, Pérez Figuerola 200 (☎ 53 4273), on the corner of the Plaza de Armas, next to La Catedral. As the name might suggest, Mr. Ronald serves cuisine more or less à la Ronald McDonald. Big burgers, fries, pizza, and fried chicken dominate the menu. Entree plus a side and ice cream s/4.90. Spaghetti s/3.90. Open noon-6pm. ❶

Don Manuel, Comercio 187 (☎53 2035), next door to the Hotel San Jorge, is the last word in upscale Pisco dining. The posh *menú* (s/15) includes a complimentary *pisco* sour, several seafood options, and drinks in a classy indoor dining room. *Ceviche* s/9-25. *Conchas de abanico* (scallops) s/16.50. Pasta, chicken, fish entrees s/10-20. Open daily 10am-11pm. ❷

Restaurant Turístico D'Reyes, Comercio 167 (☎53 5288), on the pedestrian boule-vard. Simpler than its neighbors, D'Reyes attracts a lot of tourists and serves tasty food at low prices, including fresh-squeezed orange juice for breakfast. *Menú* s/8. Vegetarian *menú* s/10. Entrees s/10-20. Open daily 7am-7pm. ❷

◉ SIGHTS

Besides the pleasant Plaza de Armas and the nearby ■**Reserva Nacional de Paracas** (p. 144), the other thing worth seeing near Pisco is the ruins of **Tambo Colorado,** built in 1450 AD. This Inca fortress about 45km and a s/50 cab ride from Pisco was known by the Incas as Pucahuasi, meaning "red" in Quechua. The name fits even today because, unlike the arguably more majestic ruins in Cusco, the adobe walls still retain some of the original red, yellow, and white paint from hundreds of years ago. The ruins boast a sacrificial altar, baths, and dozens of unique rooms all over-looking the fertile Pisco Valley. Although commonly passed over by tourists, the ruins of Tambo are some of the best preserved in Peru and should not be missed. (s/7. Open daily 9am-5pm.) A small **museum** (free) near the entrance displays reconstructions of Pucahuasi as it existed under Inca Pachakuteq, 550 years ago. Sporadic colectivos run to Tambo from Pisco on the corner of B. de Humay and 4 de Julio, starting at around 7am and leaving when full (1hr., s/5). The best way to experience Tambo, however, is with a tour (US$15-20 depending on the number of people). Try **Zarcillo Connections** (p. 140) in Pisco for a good deal.

◉ ♪ NIGHTLIFE AND ENTERTAINMENT

Pisco nightlife converges along **Comercio.** By day, Comercio brims with locals and travelers alike; by night, they ascend to second-floor bars with open-air balconies. **Catamarán,** Comercio 162, is one of the most popular bars and features dark wood, twinkling lights, and music from all over the world. (☎53 3547. *Pisco* sours s/7.70. Margaritas, daquiris, and piña coladas s/10. No cover. Open until 2am.) Those feel-ing footloose head to **Dragon Pub,** Pérez Figuerola 263, half a block from the Plaza de Armas, for cool interior lighting, Asian flair, and karaoke. (☎53 5527. Liter of beer, sangria or *pisco* sour s/11. Must be 18+. Open daily 8pm-dawn.)

For the travel-weary, there is a small movie theater on the Plaza de Armas in the back of the **Libertador** shopping center, next to **La Catedral,** which shows two Amer-ican movies a day, dubbed into Spanish. (Shows daily 5:30 and 7:30pm. s/3.)

EL CHACO   ☎056

El Chaco has two industries, fishing and tourism, and not much else. Fishermen donning yellow boots and carrying pails of pungent fish cruise the waters of Para-cas Bay in small fishing boats, the only kind that the government allows in the port. Otherwise, El Chaco's role as a gateway to the Islas Ballestas and Paracas Reserve is the only thing that rescues it from sleepy oblivion. Vendors sell their wares to the hundreds of tourists that pass through the town every day.

Accommodations in Chaco are nice, but generally expensive, as they usually take the form of full-service resorts that provide room, board, and guided tours to the Islas Ballestas and Reserva Nacional de Paracas. Most backpackers opt to stay in Pisco (p. 140); however, there are a few budget-friendly options here.

El Amigo ❸, Alan García Mz. D Lote 10, has pleasant views of Paracas Bay and the Chaco port from its roof-top terrace (which doubles as a dance floor at night) and from some of its well-kept rooms. (☎54 5042. Hot water. All rooms with private bath. Singles s/35; doubles s/40-60; all prices negotiable.) The cheapest place to sleep in Chaco is **Hostal Fiorella ❷,** Paracas Mz. A Lote 4. Ask for a room with a view. (☎54 5134. Hot water. Doubles only, s/30.) Nearly identical tourist restaurants abound around the port, as do vendors selling everything from Paracas visors to chocolate-flavored lollipops. For a good *menú,* try **Juan Pablo ❷.** (Entrees s/10-20. Open 7am-9pm.) **Colectivos** leave for Chaco from Pisco's market area at Fermín Tanguis and B. de Humay (every 30min., leave when full, s/1). There is **no bank, no medical service** and **no Internet** in Chaco; the nearest services are 25km away in Pisco. The **police** are on Paracas, on top of the hill where the colectivo stops (☎54 5076).

▧ RESERVA NACIONAL DE PARACAS

The Reserva Nacional de Paracas is the beauty of Peru's southern coastline, along with its sister attraction, the Islas Ballestas. Home to over 200 different marine species—from sea lions to sea spiders—Paracas rivals the Galápagos in terms of the diversity of aquatic life forms to be found here. Massive sand dunes and awe-inspiring rock formations along the coast, plus deformed mummies housed in the desert museum, draw tourists from all over the world. Altogether, Paracas ranks high on the list of southern Peru's natural wonders.

AT A GLANCE

AREA: 3350 sq. km; 35% land, 65% water.

CLIMATE: Temperate year-round; almost no rain. Dec.-Mar. is the best time to see whales. High winds in the late afternoon.

HIGHLIGHTS: Highest concentration of birds in the world, including flamingos.

GATEWAY: Pisco.

CAMPING: Permitted and free.

FEES AND HOURS: Park entrance s/5, includes a **map** of the park. Museum ("Centro de Interpretación") s/5, open daily 8am-6pm.

▤ TRANSPORTATION

Colectivos leave regularly from the market on B. de Humay in Pisco for the port of El Chaco, just outside the entrance to the reserve (20-25min., every 10 min. 6am-8pm, s/1). **Taxis** from Pisco to El Chaco cost around s/8. You can walk the 7km from El Chaco to the museum—stick close to the water, and you'll probably see some flamingos in the bay—or take a taxi (s/10, round-trip s/13). Since there is no public transportation within the reserve, you'll have to rely on taxis to reach distant sights and beaches. Even the most independent travelers must resign themselves to a guided tour in a 12-passenger **motorboat** if they wish to visit the Islas Ballestas, as it is nearly impossible to secure a spot on any of the privately owned boats that regularly visit the islands.

◧ ▨ ORIENTATION AND PRACTICAL INFORMATION

The Reserva Nacional de Paracas, Carretera Pisco, Puerto San Martín Km27, extends down more than 25km of coastline, encompassing the Paracas Peninsula and a whole lot of ocean. The Islas Ballestas, not technically part of the reserve, lie about 5km northwest of the peninsula, 29km from El Chaco.

Supplies: There are unfortunately no places to rent tents or other camping gear in Pisco, but food and flashlights are available from any store in town.

Tours: The only way to visit the Islas Ballestas is with a guided tour. Although it is possible to visit the Paracas Reserve alone, the wide desert expanse between sites convinces most visitors to come as part of a tour. The most economical packages visit the Islas Ballestas in the morning and the reserve in the afternoon, making a full day of it (s/35). Tours to only the peninsula involve three main stops: the **Tello Museum** and **Centro de Interpretación, La Catedral,** and **Lagunilla** beach. Tours to just the islands usually last 2-3hr., cost s/25, and leave early (7-8am), since morning is the best time to see the wildlife. Sign up with an agency the night before to reserve a spot, and wear layers because the temperature varies. For specific agencies, see **Tours,** p. 140.

ACCOMMODATIONS

Camping on the Paracas Peninsula is free and does not require a permit (those staying three or more days are required to pay a fee of s/10 in addition to the s/5 to enter the reserve). Although the reserve is considered safer than other beaches, never camp alone; the local police in Pisco recommend pitching tents in groups of four or more. Sites for camping within the park include **Atenas** beach, 8km from the entrance beside the Julio C. Tello Museum (2km). Most travelers looking to avoid camping stay in Pisco, though limited options are also available in El Chaco.

SIGHTS

■ **THE PENINSULA.** In 1975, the Reserva Nacional de Paracas was established to protect the ecological and archaeological splendor of the Paracas peninsula and the Islas Ballestas. The Paracas peninsula's human history begins with the arrival of the region's first inhabitants some 9000 years ago; these people thrived from around 500 BC to AD 200. Their remains can be seen at the **Julio C. Tello Museum** in the reserve (open daily 9am-5pm, s/7), named for the man often referred to as the "father of Peruvian archaeology." Tello (1880-1947) led excavations at the sites of **Cerro Colorado** and **Cabezas Largas** in Paracas from 1924 to 1930, unearthing much of what we now know about the Paracas culture.

Detailed information about the climate, food chain, and taxonomic groups of marine life inhabiting the Islas Ballestas and the waters surrounding the peninsula can be found in the **Centro de Interpretación,** the

THE LOCAL STORY

BEAUTY IS ONLY SKULL DEEP

Archaeological investigations in the Reserva Nacional de Paracas have revealed that the Paracas culture had some ideas about physical beauty and health that today seem rather unusual. Skulls unearthed in the region suggest that infants of upper-class birth had boards tied around their foreheads so that as they grew, their skulls became elongated. A long, sloped cranium probably signaled ethnic identity, beauty, and prestige. In addition to cranial elongation, the Paracas people also practiced an early form of brain surgery known as **trepanation.** The procedure involved removing a piece of the skull to relieve pressure on the brain following a severe head trauma. However, the large number of trepanated skulls discovered in Paracas suggests that this practice was used not just to cure head trauma, but also to treat psychological or behavioral problems, perhaps by providing an escape route for evil spirits thought to be residing in the brain. Astonishingly, the survival rate for these procedures was over 50%, as evidenced by signs of healing around the holes. A modified form of this procedure is still used worldwide in emergency situations when a neurosurgeon is unavailable.

first stop on tours to the park, located right next to the Tello Museum, 2km from the park's entrance. About 200 yards behind the Centro de Interpretación, toward the ocean, stands a **bird-watching tower** for viewing the famous Paracas flamingos. According to legend, when the Argentine General San Martín came to liberate Peru from Spanish control in 1921, he dreamt of the red and white flamingos of Paracas, thus inspiring the flag of the new republic that is adorned with their colors.

After the museums and flamingo watching, the next point of interest in the reserve is **La Catedral,** 12km from the entrance. This natural rock formation, located alongside the coast where the desert sand dunes meet the sea, resembles the dome of a religious sanctuary, giving the formation its name. Sailors prefer to describe the formation as a condor gazing over the Pacific. **Lagunilla** beach, the final stop on tours through the park, is home to three seafood restaurants that, like the rest of Paracas, are without electricity, but serve up fresh fish along with higher prices. All three restaurants serve some of the best *ceviche* in the area, but the best value is **Tía Peli ❷,** overlooking the port and the beach. (*Ceviche* s/18. Entrees s/10-20.) There is also a small swimming hole at Lagunilla where tourists can cool off. If you're not interested in purchasing an overpriced lunch, be sure to pack one before your tour and bring it along for a picnic on the beach.

EL CANDELABRO AND THE ISLAS BALLESTAS. Before reaching the Islas Ballestas, tours stop in front of El Candelabro, a geoglyph that resembles an Olympic torch etched in sand on the northeast side of the Paracas Bay. The three-pronged figure is 177m high, 54m wide, and up to 60cm deep. Its creators and its significance remain a mystery, but some believe that it dates back to the Paracas culture (circa 700 BC) and represents a hallucinogenic kind of cactus that was used in religious ceremonies. Others believe that the figure was constructed by 17th-century sailors to aid in navigation, as the design points directly south. However, given the fact that the earliest record of El Candelabro dates from just after the arrival of the Argentine General José de San Martín in the early 1820s, the most accepted theory is that the symbol was constructed in celebration of Peru's liberation from Spain. With many theories and no definitive answers, the mysterious origins of the geoplyph only add to the attraction.

The highlight of the tour is not El Candelabro itself, but the 300 million-year-old islands, which provide an up-close-and-personal view of thousands of birds, including **Peruvian boobies, Inca terns, pelicans, turkey vultures,** three types of **cormorants,** and **Humboldt penguins.** The Peruvian government forbids industrial fishing here, ensuring an abundant supply of fish in order to attract the highest concentration of birds on earth. In addition, the islands house marine life including **sea lions and dolphins,** as well as **sea spiders, starfish,** and other crustaceans—216 marine species in all. **Whales** also frequent the coast from December through March.

The Islas Ballestas are not contained within the Paracas Reserve because they are valuable to Peruvians for more than just ecotourism. **Guano,** the excrement of the Guanay and Cormorant birds which inhabit the islands, is the finest form of natural fertilizer in the world. Every five to seven years, an expedition of Peruvian mountain men spends three months collecting the precious droppings, which are then exported to Europe and the US in 50 kg bundles worth US$80 each.

ICA   ☎ 056

A major transportation hub and desert capital of the Ica region, the city of Ica (pop. 346,019; elev. 406m) may be a little rough around the edges, but don't head south just yet. The city sits above the coastal fog and enjoys more sun than any of its neighbors. And, judging from the business suits and briefcases making their way through the well-groomed Plaza de Armas, Ica enjoys more than that. The cli-

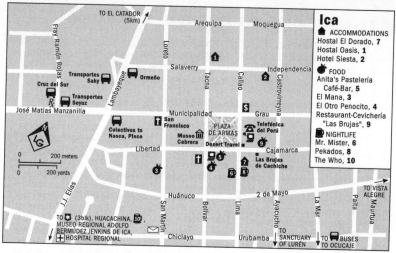

mate is perfect for the cultivation of asparagus, but also, more importantly, of wine. Ica boasts almost 90 *bodegas*, which together produce more wines and *piscos* than any other part of the country. During the second week of March, Ica celebrates the **International Wine Festival** with the Queen of the Harvest, grape stomping, a horse exhibition, and cockfights. Ica's most significant service to tourists is in funneling them to awesome adventure activities in the nearby desert oasis of **Huacachina,** complete with 1000m tall sand dunes and some of the most interesting museums in the region. However, only a block or two away from the Plaza de Armas the splendor degenerates into unkempt, dusty neighborhoods that remind tourists to be wary of petty crime. That said, don't clutch your bag and run. There is much to see and do in Ica, and as any Ican will boast, there is no better place in the world to enjoy a (real) *pisco* sour.

TRANSPORTATION

Flights: Aero Cóndor runs a small, private **airport** (☎52 2424), from which you can take expensive flights over the Nasca lines (US$100-200). Inquire at tour agencies on the Plaza de Armas for more information (see **Tours**).

Buses: Transportes Soyuz, Matías Manzanilla 130 (☎22 4138), sends buses to **Lima** (4hr., every 6 min., s/16). **Cruz del Sur,** Fray Ramón Rojas (☎22 3333), just behind the gas station at Municipalidad, goes to: **Arequipa** (12hr.; 5 per day starting at 5:30pm, s/35; imperial 9pm, s/55); **Moquegua** (15hr., imperial 7:45pm, s/90); **Tacna** (17hr.; 3:30, 6, 9:45pm; s/40, imperial s/90). **Ormeño** (☎21 5600), at Lambayeque and Salaverry, serves: **Cusco** (22hr., 7:30pm, s/130); **Lima** (4hr., 15 per day 6:30am-7:45pm, s/35); **Nasca** (3hr.; 9:15, 10:45am, 3, 10pm; s/6). **Transportes Saky,** Lambayeque 219, across from Ormeño, sends buses to **Pisco** (1hr., every 25min., 6am-8:30pm, s/2.50). **Colectivos** also leave when full for **Nasca** (s/4) and **Pisco** (s/2) from the intersection of Lambayeque and Municipalidad.

! Ica suffers from more petty crime than many of the surrounding areas. Exercise considerable caution with all of your belongings, especially around bus terminals and near the river. Also beware of violent crime in the vicinity of the river.

✦🛈 ORIENTATION AND PRACTICAL INFORMATION

As in most large Peruvian cities, Ica's **Plaza de Armas** is the center of activity, bordered by **Municipalidad** to the north and **Libertad** to the south. Most bus terminals are on **Lambayeque** near its intersection with **Municipalidad**, which leads to the north side of the Plaza de Armas. Streets running north-south change names after Municipalidad, while those running east-west switch names after **Callao**, which forms the Plaza's eastern border. **Tacna** borders the Plaza on the west.

Tours:

Las Brujas de Cachiche, Cajamarca 100, just off the Plaza de Armas. Offers 4-5hr. city tours (9am, s/25) and tours of the 4 most popular *bodegas* (4hr., 9am, s/25). Tour price includes all entrance fees. English guides. Open 9am-10pm. MC.

Roberto Penny Cabrera, inquire at **El Otro Penocito** (see **Food;** ☎62 4868; icadeserttrip@yahoo.esp). This khaki-clad local icon, known to some as "Desert Man," leads expeditions in search of fossilized shark teeth and other evidence that the Ica desert was once the bottom of the ocean. This is no flimsy trip, but a once-in-a-lifetime real desert adventure. US$100 per day; prices negotiable. Reserve 2-3 days in advance; prior to the outings, the tour operator requires meetings to arrange for supplies and 1 day's rest.

Desert Travel, Lima 171 (☎23 4127; desert_travel@hotmail.com), in **Tejas Don Juan** on the Plaza de Armas. Tours of Ica that include Huacachina, the *bodegas,* the Museo Regional, the Santuario de Lurén, and sandboarding for s/35-40. Also offers flights over Nasca, US$50-70 depending on the size of the group. Free information about other tours and hotels in Ica and hotels. MC.

Currency Exchange: Banco de Crédito (☎22 2726), on the Plaza de Armas, will change AmEx and V traveler's checks with a US$5 charge on anything more than US$100. 24hr. AmEx/MC/V **ATM.** Open M-F 10am-6pm, Sa 9:30am-2:30pm.

Emergency: ☎105 or 22 7343.

Police: J.J. Elías Mz. 5 (☎22 4553).

Pharmacy: Bóticas Universitarias, at the corner of Manzanilla and Rojas next to the gas station. Open 24hr.

Hospital: Hospital Regional (☎23 5101), on Prolongación Ayabaca. Open 24hr. for emergencies.

Telephone: Telefónica del Perú, Lima 149 (☎21 7350), on the Plaza de Armas. Open daily 8:30am-10pm. Also has **Internet** access (s/1 per hr.).

Internet Access: LMN Services, Bolívar 211. Look for the purple building. Open daily 8:30am-midnight.

Post Office: Serpost, 556 San Martín (☎23 3881). Open M-Sa 8am-8:30pm.

🏠 ACCOMMODATIONS

Most backpackers choose to snooze in **Huacachina** (p. 152) rather than in Ica proper, avoiding the variable hot water, dark hallways, and noisy rooms that characterize Ican budget accommodations. Most hotels, therefore, cater to locals. Still, staying in the city means more choice and an escape from the tourist loop.

Hostal El Dorado, Lima 251 (☎21 5015), in the hip bar district of Calle Lima. The prospect of stumbling only a few feet to get home is only half the attraction. El Dorado is the best deal in Ica, with a neon lobby, huge beds, and even huger TVs. Hot water in every room. Most rooms have windows to the street. Singles s/30; matrimonials s/40; doubles s/60. No credit cards. ❸

Hostal Oasis, Tacna 216 (☎23 4767). Rooms are open, airy, and clean, with TVs. All rooms have baths blessed with toilet paper and hot water. Singles s/25; matrimonials s/35; doubles s/35. No credit cards. ❷

Hotel Siesta, Independencia 194 (☎23 4633). Dim hallways lead to rooms that are spartan, but clean, and have views of the busy streets below. Hot water. Private baths. Laundry service. Singles s/25; doubles s/30; triples s/50. No credit cards. ❷

🍴 FOOD

Ica isn't known for its cuisine, but a handful of restaurants offer good grub.

El Otro Penocito, Bolívar 225 (☎23 3921), 1 block from the Plaza de Armas. Doubling as an art gallery for up-and-coming Peruvian artist Reynaldo Santos Uribe, El Otro Penocito serves colorful international and vegetarian entrees that echo the classy bohemian interior. By day, it's the hippest eatery in town, populated with young professionals. By night, it's the best place to share a *pisco* sour with lively local denizens such as owner and bartender Harry Hernandez Rosas, artist Uribe himself, or the khaki-clad "Desert Man" (see **Tours,** p. 148). *Criollo* dishes s/12-15. Seafood entrees s/24. Open daily 11am-4pm and 6pm-2am. No credit cards. ❷

Restaurant-Cevichería "Las Brujas," Cajamarca 118 (☎22 7665). This romantically lit restaurant entices locals and foreigners alike with great prices, traditional Andean food, and live guitar music between noon and 1pm. *Menú* with lots of variety s/9. Breakfast s/3-4.50. *Ceviche* s/9. Open daily 7:30am-8pm. ❶

Anita's Pastelería Café-Bar, Libertad 133 (☎21 8582), on the Plaza de Armas. Delicious sweets on display, giant sandwiches, a diverse menu, and a cafe-style setting make Anita's a popular lunch stop for Ica's professionals. Breakfast s/3-12.50. Sandwiches s/4-9. *Criollos* s/11. Pastries s/0.50-4.50. Open 8am-2am. No credit cards. ❷

El Mana, San Martín 248, serves heaps of tasty vegetarian fare for excellent prices. *Menú* s/3.50-4. Open daily 7am-10pm. No credit cards. ❶

👁 SIGHTS

MUSEO REGIONAL ADOLFO BERMÚDEZ JENKINS DE ICA. This museum displays artifacts from the Paracas, Nasca, Huari, Chincha, and Inca periods of Ica's regional history. Most shocking is the "bioanthropology hall" that displays mummies as well as deformed skulls (including an unforgettable clay diorama depicting a man undergoing trepanation, an early form of brain surgery), and the so-called "trophy heads" that were worn on the belt after a successful battle. There are also interesting

ON THE MENU

LAS TEJAS

Ica's Plaza de Armas is lined with shops selling **las Tejas,** sweets wrapped in colorful paper. Street vendors carry twelve varieties, from *limón* (lemon) to *pecana* (pecan). It all started in the late 19th century, when women gathered to make the treats as a social event. At first, *las Tejas* were only of one type: lemon covered with white sugar. The women who made them soon began to include some of the most abundant regional fruits: *naranjas* (oranges), *pecanas,* and *pasas borrachas* (fermented raisins). However, the *las Tejas* explosion didn't occur until the late 20th-century advent of **choco-Tejas,** covered in white or milk chocolate and filled with creamy *dulce de leche* (caramel) and another of several fillings, with new flavors emerging each year. The sweets are still handmade and wrapped individually in brightly covered foil. Each one costs around s/1, but it's cheaper to buy them in variety packs of 3-6. Although every store along the Plaza de Armas claims to be the oldest producer of *las Tejas,* **Helena Chocolates and Tejas** (☎23 1293; www.helenachoco-latier.com) produces the finest in Ica and sells them worldwide. At their **factory** (Nicolás de Ribera El Viejo 227, near the Santuario de San Lurén), you can watch the sweets being made, but a more delicious (and informative) trip is to the elegant store on the Plaza at Cajamarca and Lima.

THE LOCAL STORY

A CASE OF MISTAKEN IDENTITY

Pisco sours may go down easy, but the history of the drink hasn't been such a smooth ride. As native as *pisco* may seem to Peruvians today, the pre-Columbian societies actually didn't have white grapes. It was the Spanish, scouring the Peruvian coastline in the early 1500s in search of the right spot to cultivate the home wines they missed so much, who deemed the dry, fertile Ica Valley vine-worthy. The powerful brandy (45 proof, stronger than most rum or vodka) was invented later in the century—not as a drink, but as a disinfectant or the conquistadors to treat their wounds—that is, until they ran out of things to drink.

Before long, the Spanish settlers wanted to send their new concoction home to be sampled by friends and family. When the first barrels went out, they were stamped with the name of the port from which they departed, Pisco. The name on the barrels stuck, despite the fact that *pisco* had been born and bred in the Ica Valley. Ica residents held a grudge for years, but now they have a bigger problem on their hands: Chilean cultivators have far surpassed Peruvians in *pisco* production and export, and many are now promoting the drink overseas as their own homegrown invention.

explanations of the processes of mummification and burial. Colonial paintings adorn the upstairs, and behind the museum is a 1:500 scale model of the Nasca lines, complete with a tiny *mirador*. Many exhibits have English explanations. *(On the 8th block of Ayabaca, a short taxi ride (s/2) from the Plaza de Armas. ☎23 4383. Open M-F 8am-7pm, Sa 9am-6pm, Su 9am-1:30pm. Adults s/10, with ISIC s/5, children s/1. Camera permit s/5.)*

MUSEO CABRERA. Brilliant scholar or deranged lunatic? You be the judge. The now-deceased **Dr. Javier Cabrera,** who held a degree in medicine from Lima's prestigious Universidad de San Marcos, claimed that his collection of over 17,000 stones— ranging from baseball-sized rocks to boulders weighing over a ton—provides conclusive evidence that the pre-Incas performed such amazing feats as brain transplants, domestication of dinosaurs, and discovery of the theory of relativity. Although locals confessed to having carved the petroglyphs themselves, Dr. Cabrera always insisted on the authenticity of his collection despite never having the stones carbontested to determine exact ages. Nevertheless, in the words of renowned archaeologist Maria Reiche, they are "engraved by some of the most talented artisans of our time," and Dr. Cabrera's eloquent explanations of the rocks' significance are worth consideration. *(Bolívar 170, on the Plaza de Armas. ☎21 3026. US$10, includes a 1hr. guided tour conducted in Spanish by Dr. Cabrera's widow or daughter. Call first to make a reservation.)*

SANCTUARY OF LURÉN. Honoring Ica's patron saint, this neoclassical structure stands out among the city's primarily colonial-style cathedrals. The church was built in 1556 in the settlement of Villa Verde, predating the city's founding by seven years. Today, locals celebrate Señor de Lurén during Holy Week and on the evening of the third Sunday in October. A candle-lit procession moves through the streets of Ica to the Sanctuary, where thousands of flowers are thrown onto the ground and dancing and music ensues. (On the 10th block of Ayacucho, at Piura. Open M-Sa 6:30am-1pm and 4-8:30pm, Su 6am-1pm and 4-8:30pm. Free.)

◢ BODEGAS

Considering that Ica is, or claims to be, the true home of the national liquor, pisco, it isn't surprising that greater Ica is littered with *bodegas*, each offering tours and free samples. The *bodegas* are divided into two groups: the *bodegas mecanistas* (by machine), and *bodegas artesanales* (by manual labor). The largest and most popular *bodegas* are the *mecanistas*, although the *artesanales* still do old-fashioned grape-stomping in the summer (Jan.-Mar.).

The oldest bodega in Ica and the largest in the country is **Vista Alegre,** Camino a la Tinguiña at Km2, a *bodega mecanista* established in 1857. Located at the entrance to Ica, Vista Alegre boasts a rich history that weaves the Picasso family's story with the emergence wine-making in Peru. Forty-five minute tours of the vineyard are free and provide samples of the *bodega's* products, including *pisco* and more than nine types of wines and champagnes. A 5min. taxi ride from the Plaza de Armas costs s/2. Do not walk, as the trip takes you through a rough part of Ica. (☎23 2919; bvalegreica@viabcp.com. Open daily 9am-6pm.) The most popular *bodega artesanal* is **El Catador,** in the Subtanjalla district 5km north of town. El Catador was founded in 1985 by the González family, who invite visitors to come between January and March, kick off their shoes, and help with the grape stomping. The complex also houses a restaurant and weekend disco. Taxis from Ica are s/5. Infrequent colectivos (s/2) leave from the mercado on the corner of Moquegua and Amazonas. (☎40 3427; el_catador@peru.com. Open daily 8am-8pm. Tours in Spanish only. Restaurant open 10am-6pm.)

NIGHTLIFE

The hottest bars and *discotecas* around are in nearby **Huacachina** (p. 152; 5km, s/4 for a taxi at night), but if you have your heart set on heading downtown, there are a few hotspots. Bars are concentrated along **Calle Lima** between Cajamarca and 2 de Mayo. The most popular is **Mr. Mister,** Lima 282, playing international rock every night from 8pm until dawn. (Drinks s/5-6.) **Pekados,** Lima 255 (☎21 4026), sports a cool mirrored interior and karaoke. (Drinks s/5-6. No cover. Open nightly at 8pm.) For dancing, **The Who** (disco and karaoke), in the Hotel Real Ica near the Museo Regional, buzzes all weekend long with the Ican under-20 crowd, playing everything from reggae to rap to rock. (Cover s/15, one beer included.)

DAYTRIPS FROM ICA

OCUCAJE
Blue sedans with white tops serve as colectivos to Ocucaje (30min., leave when full, s/3). Microbuses also provide service to Ocucaje (1hr., leave when full, s/2). From the Plaza de Armas, walk 2 blocks up Cajamarca, then turn right onto La Mar and continue another 3 blocks, going 1 block to the right of Plaza Barranca.

Ocucaje (pop. miniscule; elev. 420m) is translated as "between hills" from the Aymara, but it could also mean "in the middle of nowhere." A 30min. drive from Ica (including some off-road maneuvering through sand dunes), this small desert town is best known for its winery, **Fond de Cave,** the most traditional and scenic of Ica's three industrial *bodegas*. In addition to the standard *pisco*, the Ocucaje winery has produced a variety of white, red, dry, and sweet wines since 1898. Some of their older brews have been aging since 1940. Legend has it that a pregnant woman who drinks the wines of Fond de Cave is guaranteed to give birth to twins, though modern science frowns upon using alcohol as a fertility drug. (1hr. tours leave M-F 11am and 3pm, Sa noon. s/12.50 per person.) Ocucaje also boasts the beautiful **Hotel Ocucaje ⑤,** next door to the winery, featuring a large swimming pool, horseback riding, tennis courts, ping-pong, foosball, and pool tables. All-inclusive package deals, including a tour of the winery, sandboarding tours, and meals, are worth the splurge if you can afford it. (☎40 8001. 1-night stay with winery tour M-Th US$64; 3-day M-Th US$100; 3-day F-Su US$130; 4-day M-Th US$130.) Even for non-guests, the hotel provides a unique way to get the adrenaline pumping, with 1hr. stints on *areneros* (4x4 dune buggies) over dunes as high as 25m, as well as a couple of sandboarding runs. (☎40 8001; www.hotelocucaje.com. US$25. Trips leave every 90min. Reservations recommended.)

HUACACHINA   ☎056

Surf's up! But where are the waves? Although Huacachina (pop. 300; elev. 420m) is technically contained within Ica's municipality, it is undeniably distinct from its noisy neighbor. Perched among sand dunes more than 1000m tall, this picture-perfect oasis feels miles away from noisy, urban Ica. Lovely Huacachina serves as both a place to sleep and to party for most backpackers who choose to daytrip to Ica rather than the other way around. Huacachina offers many thrills of its own. Here, the sport of choice is **sandboarding**, an exhilarating experience that will leave you sand-covered and breathless.

TRANSPORTATION AND PRACTICAL INFORMATION. Getting to Huacachina is easy. There are no colectivos, but **mototaxis** travel the 8km between Ica and Huacachina (10min.; s/2 during the day, s/4 in the morning or late at night). A short walk around the lagoon offers a view of (almost) the entire town. Services in Huacachina are limited. There is **no bank, no ATM,** and **no internet.** There is a small **tourist police** kiosk near the entrance to Huacachina. The nearest **hospital** is 3km away in Ica, the **Hospital Regional** (p. 148).

ACCOMMODATIONS AND FOOD. The very pink, very fancy **Mossone Hotel** (☎21 3630), located directly on the *laguna*, offers a swimming pool for s/15, including a free sandwich and drink, but better accommodations can be found elsewhere. For travelers in search of peace and tranquility, the new, classy, and quaint **Hotel Suiza ❷**, situated on the *laguna* at the far end from the entrance to Huacachina, offers cozy rooms with billowing curtains, sparkling bathrooms, continental breakfast, and Sinatra echoing from the stereo behind the bar. The Swiss owners strive to make their hotel seem like a home for guests. (☎23 8762. Singles US$20; doubles or matrimonials US$30; triples US$45; quadruples US$70.) Most backpackers find a haven at **Hostal Rocha ❶**, a stately house across the street from the *laguna*, on the small circle with the chapel as you enter Huacachina. Along with its big rooms, even bigger lounging terraces, and free kitchen and bike use, Rocha also rents sandboards and sports a popular bar in back. The hostel also allows camping in its backyard. (☎22 2256. Singles s/10, with hot water bath s/15; doubles s/20-40. Campsites s/5 per person per night with access to all facilities. No credit cards.) The serene **Hostel del Barco ❷**, Balneario de Huacachina 180, features a popular bar, laundry service, hot water, and an inviting porch complete with hammocks. (☎21 7122; hospedajedelbarco@hotmail.com. Singles s/15; matrimonials s/25; triple with bath s/30. No credit cards.) Lakeside **camping** is free, but lock away your belongings at a sandboard rental agency for the night. **Restaurant Morón ❷** sits literally on the lagoon and serves up excellent *ceviche* (s/8) and *pescado ajo* (fish cooked in garlic; s/12). The restaurant features live music on its patio during the evenings. (☎80 5203. Open daily 9am-9pm.) **La Sirena ❷**, on the Balneario de Huacachina, directly across the *laguna*, also has views of the lake. (☎21 3239. Breakfast s/5. Fish entrees s/13-15. *Menú* s/7. Open daily 7am-10pm.)

▓ **NIGHTLIFE.** During the week, "nightlife" in Huacachina is limited to the couples strolling along the edge of the lagoon. But Huacachina's vibrant nightlife brings tourists and locals alike to its bars and *discotecas* on the weekends. The most popular hotspot is the **La Duna** *discoteca*, above the lagoon with the entrance facing the street. Because La Duna is the hippest that Ica has to offer, locals flood the doors each weekend night. (Drinks s/5-6. Cover s/10-15. Open F-Sa 8pm-dawn.) The backyard bar of **Hostal Rocha** is popular with backpackers who dig the bonfire and tiki lamps. (☎22 2256. Drinks s/5-6. No cover. Open until 5am.) The all-night pool and weekend bar of **La Casa de Arena,** Perotti 120, off the *laguna*, draws the heartiest partyers of the backpacking crowd to its thatched-roof interior. (Mixed drinks s/5. Beer s/6. No cover. Closes early on weeknights.)

▣ **OUTDOOR ACTIVITIES.** The thrill of the dunes is the main attraction in Huacachina. **Sandboards** can be rented at the slopes or at **Hostal Rocha** (s/3 per hr., s/5 per day). Ask for free instruction, then huff and puff your way up the enormous dunes, stick your feet in the loops, and take off down the steep slopes. Rental agencies can provide a safe place to store valuables. Alternatively, take an adrenaline-pumping ride in a **dune buggy** that twists and turns and speeds over the dunes to the best sandboarding slopes in the desert. Dune buggies can be rented at any hotel or at ▓**Desert Adventures,** at the entrance to Huacachina, for around US$12 per person. (☎22 8458; desert_adventures@hotmail.com or desertadvent@yahoo.es. Office open 8am-7pm.) Those looking for relaxation can lounge around **Laguna Huacachina,** a small lake with allegedly curative properties, or putter around in pedal boats (s/7 for 30min.) or rowboats (s/10 per person.)

NASCA
☎**056**

It's impossible to speak of Nasca (pop. 85,000; elev. 580m) without mentioning the **Nasca lines,** the geoglyphs that draw hordes of tourists for a brief stint in a puddle-jumper soaring above the desert floor. Likewise, it's impossible to speak of the Nasca lines without mentioning **María Reiche,** the German mathematician who spent 40 years in Nasca studying the mysterious figures in the sand. Her work garnered international attention, which turned this somewhat forgettable city into Peru's second-most-frequented tourist attraction. Nascans are forever grateful; her name graces buildings and streets, and is even written in the desert. The area is littered with other sites of interest, archaeological and otherwise; Nasca huddles in the shadow of one of the tallest sand dunes in the world, **Cerro Blanco** (2078m). Since the town depends mainly on the influx of foreign cash, tourist agencies accommodate visitors at every corner. Beyond these services, however, life in Nasca moves along at a snail's pace. According to a local saying, as it takes two eyes to see the Nasca lines, it takes two *cervezas* to understand them.

⌐ TRANSPORTATION

Flights: The small **airport** (☎52 2688) in Nasca is primarily used for flights over the Nasca lines, but it is possible to charter expensive flights between Lima and Nasca on **Aero Cóndor,** Lima 187 (☎52 2424; www.aerocondor.com.pe). To get to the airport, hire a taxi (5min., s/3) or catch a colectivo at the corner of Lima and Bastidas near the Ormeño station (s/0.50).

Buses: Most buses into the town arrive and depart on Lima. Tickets sell out quickly during July and Aug. **Ormeño,** Lima 253 (☎52 2058) serves: **Arequipa** (9hr., 3 per day, s/75); **Ica** (2hr., 6 per day starting at 6am, s/5); **Lima** (7hr., 6 per day 7:15am-11pm, s/17); **Pisco** (3½hr., 1:30pm, s/40); **Tacna** (11hr., 8pm, s/50). **Transportes Wari,** a 5min. taxi ride on the road to the airport, sends buses to **Cusco** (13hr.; 7, 9, 11pm; s/50). Colectivos to **Chala** (3hr., s/10) leave from in front of the Civa bus station; those running to **Ica** (2½hr., s/5) via **Palpa** (45min., s/2.50) leave from the corner of Lima and Bastidas near the Ormeño station.

■✶🛈 ORIENTATION AND PRACTICAL INFORMATION

The small city has a simple layout: Lima is the only diagonal street in the city grid. Hotels and restaurants are on Lima and Bolognesi, which splits off from Lima and heads to the Plaza de Armas.

Tourist Office: There is no official tourist office in Nasca, so you'll have to rely on private tour agencies.

Tours: Prices are similar at most agencies: US$40-50 June-Sept. and US$35-40 Oct.-May, plus a departure tax of s/10, for a 30min. flight over the lines. Tours coupled with trips to the cemetery are generally US$5-10 more and include a stop at the artisan shops in Nasca. The following tour agencies are considered reputable.

Alegría Tours, Lima 186 (☎52 3775; www.nazcaperu.com), run by the owner of Hotel Alegría I, which is just next door (see **Accommodations,** below), has the greatest variety of tours to nearby sights. Make arrangements directly through Efraín Alegría (☎52 3431), who speaks several languages including English, French, and Italian. Tours to the Nasca lines (30min., US$35-50), cemetery (3hr., US$5), and Cerro Blanco (7½hr., US$30). AmEx/MC/V.

Nasca Trails Travel Agency, Bolognesi 550 (☎/fax 52 1402; nascatrails@terra.com.pe), on the Plaza de Armas. English-, German-, French-, and Italian-speaking Juan Tohalino Vera runs a helpful, straightforward agency and hostel (see **Accommodations,** below). Offers flights over the lines (30min., US$35-50), cemetery of Chauchilla (4hr., US$30), and the aqueducts (2½hr., US$8).

AeroParacas, Lima 185 (☎/fax 52 1027; aeroparacas@wayna.rcp.net.pe), a few blocks from the bus station. Offers tourist information at no charge. Runs the gamut of tours, including flights over the Nasca lines in one of their private planes (30min., US$40), the cemetery of Chauchilla (3hr., US$7, 3 people min.), the aqueducts (2hr., US$7), and daytrips to the Reserva to see *vicuña* (3 people US$60). Open daily 8am-9:30pm. Guides speak English, French, and Italian. AmEx/V.

Currency Exchange: Banco de Crédito (☎52 2455), on the corner of Lima and Grau, changes AmEx, CitiCorp, and Visa traveler's checks, gives Visa cash advances, and has the only 24hr. Plus/V **ATM** in town. Open M-F 10am-4pm, Sa 9:30am-12:30pm. **Money changers** wander the streets.

Police: (☎52 2105), on Lima, across from the Ormeño station.

Emergency: ☎105.

Hospital: Hospital Apoyo de Nasca (☎52 2010, emergencies 52 2586), on Callao at Morsesky. Open 24hr. for emergencies.

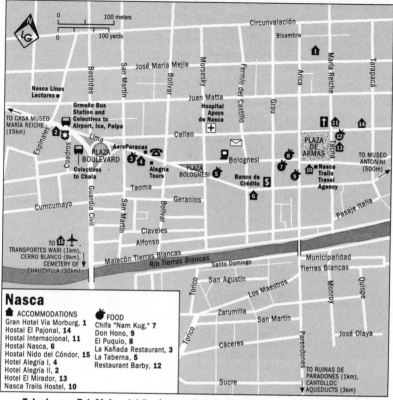

Nasca

⌂ ACCOMMODATIONS
Gran Hotel Vía Morburg, **1**
Hostal El Pajonal, **14**
Hostal Internacional, **11**
Hostal Nasca, **6**
Hostal Nido del Cóndor, **15**
Hotel Alegría I, **4**
Hotel Alegría II, **2**
Hotel El Mirador, **13**
Nasca Trails Hostel, **10**

🍴 FOOD
Chifa "Nam Kug," **7**
Don Hono, **9**
El Puquio, **8**
La Kañada Restaurant, **3**
La Taberna, **5**
Restaurant Barby, **12**

Telephones: Telefónica del Perú, Lima 359 (☎52 2737; fax 52 2232). Booths around town permit local and international calls. Open daily 7am-11pm.

Internet Access: Bolognesi is lined with Internet cafes, including **Centro Informático Mundo Virtual,** Bolognesi 395 (☎52 1048), in a spacious yellow building. s/2 per hr. Open daily 8am-midnight.

Post Office: Fermín del Castillo 379 (☎52 2016). Open M-F 9am-1pm and 2-5:30pm, Sa 8am-3:30pm.

🏠 ACCOMMODATIONS

For those in a hurry, it's possible to arrive in Nasca early, take a flight over the Nasca lines, tour the cemetery, and leave town that evening. However, you'll get a better deal if you arrive in town the night before. Hotels often offer a special package deal with a certain airline or travel agency.

Hotel Alegría II (☎/fax 52 2497; shernandezc3@hotmail.com), across from the Ormeño station. Inviting gardens, free coffee, hot water, laundry service, and Internet access. The attached restaurant is a great place to hang out while waiting for your bus (hearty *menú* s/8; open 7am-noon and 7-10pm). Camping in the garden includes access to all services. Singles s/10; doubles s/20. Campsites s/5 per tent. No credit cards. ❶

Hotel Alegría I, Lima 168 (☎52 2702). More expensive than its sister hotel, but very popular. If you take a tour with Alegría Tours you can use the hotel's services—including luggage storage, hot shower, laundry service, and book exchange—even if you don't spend the night. Singles US$10; doubles with bath and TV US$30. ❸

Nasca Trails Hostel, Bolognesi 550 (☎52 2858; nazcalinesperu.com), behind the Nasca Trails Tours office on the Plaza de Armas. Friendly English-speaking owner Juan Tohalino Vera provides free pickup from the bus station, straightforward tour advice in his front office (see **Tours,** above), and some of the most comfortable beds in Nasca. All rooms have private baths with hot water. Singles s/15; doubles s/25. ❷

Hostal Internacional, Maria Reiche 112 (☎52 2744; hostalinternacional@hotmail.com). Internacional's rooms may be less attractive than their bungalows, but they're also less expensive. All rooms have hot baths. Bungalows have cable TV. Laundry service and a *cafetería/pollería* (open 7am-9:30pm). Singles s/30; doubles s/35. Single bungalows s/45; double bungalows s/60. No credit cards. ❸

Gran Hotel Vía Morburg, José María Mejía 108 (☎/fax 52 2566 or 52 2141; hotmailviamorburg@yahoo.es or hotelviamorburg@hotmail.com), 4 blocks up Arica from the Plaza. A small pool and rows of exotic plants decorate this soothing hotel. All rooms have huge beds and hot baths. Cushy common room with TV. Restaurant (breakfast s/4; open 7am-11pm). Singles s/20; doubles s/30; triples s/45. No credit cards. ❸

Hostal Nido Del Cóndor, Panamericana Km447 (☎52 1168; www.aerocondor.com.pe), directly across from the airport, is a classy combination of a hotel, a campground and a resort. Swimming pool, courtyard, spacious open-air restaurant, and a grassy camping knoll with BBQ grill (bring your own tent). All rooms have private bath and TV. Good for families. Also offers flight packages in conjunction with **Aero Cóndor,** Nasca's oldest and most respected flight service. Breakfast included. Laundry service. Singles US$25; doubles US$35; triples US$50. Campsites s/10 per person. AmEx/MC/V. ❺

Hotel El Mirador, Tacna 436 (☎/fax 52 3741 or 52 3121). This unmistakably modern, glossy building on the Plaza de Armas has a luxurious feel and a rooftop restaurant with a great view. The rooms themselves may be nothing to write home about, but they come with TV, fan, phone, hot bath, and some of the most comfortable beds in Nasca. Breakfast included. Singles s/40; doubles s/50; matrimonials s/60. ❹

Hostal El Pajonal, Callao 911 (☎52 1011), 1 block from the Plaza de Armas. In addition to spacious rooms with cable TV (s/5) and hot baths, El Pajonal offers tour advice even though it has no connections with an agency. Small kitchen, laundry areas, and free luggage storage. Singles s/20; doubles and matrimonials s/25; triples s/35. ❶

Hostal Nasca, Lima 424 and 438 (☎/fax 52 2085). New rooms with private hot baths supplement the original concrete rooms and cold water common baths. Congenial owners maintain a calm atmosphere, and the pleasant courtyard is good for picnics. The hostel has two claims to fame: it's the oldest hotel in Nasca, and apparently Maria Reiche once lived here. Free Internet. Breakfast included for rooms with private baths (restaurant opens at 7am). Singles s/9 per person; doubles with bath s/50. MC/V. ❶

◗ FOOD

As Nasca's economy is based entirely on tourists who arrive and leave the same day, it is not surprising that restaurants here feature good selection at high prices. However, affordable set *menús* are easy to find as well.

▣ **La Kañada Restaurant,** Lima 160 (☎52 2917; info@nanasca.com), next to Hotel Alegría I. Builds romance nightly with a thatched roof, candlelit back patio, and live music (7-8pm). It also boasts one of the most diverse menus in town, with a mixture of typical Peruvian dishes and comforting international fare. The wide array of scrumptious *criollo* entrees come with a complimentary *pisco* sour. Entrees s/15-25. *Menú* s/6.50, vegetarian s/7. Open daily 7:30am-midnight. AmEx/MC/V. ❷

Don Hono, Arica 251 (☎52 3066), just off the Plaza de Armas. A small, simple spot that serves only the freshest fruit and fish. Don't pass up their juice made with mineral water (s/3). Fruit salad with yogurt, honey, and cereal s/5. Catch of the day s/10-15. Milkshakes and banana splits s/7. Open daily 9am-10pm. ❷

La Taberna, Lima 321 (☎80 6783), between Morsesky and Fermín de Castillo. Serves a wide selection of pasta, meat, and fish in a dining room covered with multilingual graffiti. Grab a marker and add your own signature or sketch of the Nasca lines. Entrees s/13-17. *Menú turístico* s/7.50. Open daily 8am-4pm and 6-11pm. ❶

Restaurant Barby, at Tacna and Callao, next to El Mirador on the Plaza de Armas, with a colorful overhang. This no-frills establishment is popular with locals, and for good reason—it has a tasty, filling *menú* for s/3. The *menú* offers 5 options daily, including 1 vegetarian. Open daily 7am-10pm. ❶

El Puquio, Bolognesi 481 (☎52 2137; pizzeria_elpuquio@hotmail.com). This pizzeria doubles as a video pub—at night patrons can rent a movie from the shop next door (s/3) and owner Raúl will happily screen it on the big TV. Pizzas (small s/8, medium s/17) and pasta (s/5-10) are of average quality, but the atmosphere and a few *cervezas* are enough to even the score. Open daily 11am-3pm and 6-11pm. ❷

Chifa "Nam Kug," Bolognesi 448 (☎52 2151). Serves surprisingly tasty Chinese fare over red tablecloths. If you squint just a bit at the mirrored walls and Chinese adornments, you can imagine yourself back at home at your neighborhood Chinese buffet. The "English" menu is strangely similar to the Spanish version, since the entrees are all in Chinese. Entrees s/4.50-6.50. *Menú* s/4-6. Open 10am-4pm and 6-11pm. ❶

👁 SIGHTS

THE NASCA LINES

*Flights leave regularly on 3- to 5-person planes. You can arrange a trip at the airport or through a group in town for about the same price (see **Tours**, p. 154). It's best to go in the morning, as cooler air ensures a smoother ride. If you don't have money—or just want a different perspective—you can see 2 figures from a mirador built by Maria Reiche on the Panamericana in 1976. Take any northbound bus or colectivo out of Nasca (15min., s/1.50). Taxi s/25, includes highway toll.*

THE LOCAL STORY

HOW THE NASCA VALLEY WAS BORN

As tourists arrive daily by the busload to ponder the strange features of the Nasca valley (the dunes, the colored hills, the geoglyphs, and the staggering absence of rain), a local legend explains how it all came to be.

After Wiraccocha, the Quechua sun god, had finished creating the universe, a group of angels came to tell him that there were materials left over. Wiraccocha noted the abundance of mountains, llamas, wolves, condors, and hummingbirds, and set out to create one last new place on earth. The barren coastal desert of South America was a perfect canvas for his final masterpiece.

He began by marking the place with a huge pile of sand so the angels could find it. The angels then bordered the area with mountains of many colors and shapes. They filled the valley with animals so that the people could eat and have companions. The people were so pleased that they built a temple called Cahuachi, and carved huge pictures in the desert celebrating Wiraccocha's generous gifts. In return, Wiraccocha promised that the sun would shine every day over the precious lands, and that it would never rain so that the impressive pictures would last forever. The Nascans celebrated at Cahuachi, and then built tunnels for water so that they could survive the coming drought.

THE REICHE STUFF

German mathematician **Maria Reiche** was undeniably obsessed with the enigmatic **Nasca lines.** From her first glance in the 1940s, Reiche saw a mystery so great that it consumed all her energies until the day she died. Reiche spent years alone in the desert, measuring the lines and cleaning off debris that obscured the designs. She became the major advocate of the **astronomical calendar theory,** which posits that the lines marked celestial paths or copied the designs of constellations and were used by farmers when planting their crops.

Reiche is now regarded as a national hero. In addition to wrestling with ancient puzzles, she became Nasca's fiercest guardian, thwarting plans to irrigate the desert for agriculture, construct highways through the plain, or reconstruct" the lines. Revenues from Reiche's published works supported research projects and the hiring of guards to patrol the grounds. In June 1998, at the age of 95, Maria Reiche died of ovarian cancer, leaving many to wonder who could possibly continue her work. Since then, the occasional disturbance of the lines by careless tourists and treasure hunters has heightened fears. However, locals revere her memory through streets, museums, and schools—some have even suggested that the Nasca site be renamed the Reiche Lines.

Mysteriously etched into the desert over 1000 years ago by the removal of rocky surface soil to reveal the white-colored dirt beneath, the Nasca lines are Peru's second-biggest tourist attraction. In 1994, they were named a UNESCO World Heritage Site. The lines, which have been attributed to both the Paracas and the Nasca cultures, are best described as **geoglyphs,** drawings that represent birds, hands, monkeys, sharks, spiders, flowers, and elongated trapezoids. These geoglyphs have remained nearly unchanged due to the desert's unique thermal air cushion and its location in one of the driest places on earth (it receives only a few minutes of rain each year). Due to unique wind patterns, even a footprint in this desert would survive 1000 years. Amazingly, the numerous designs extend hundreds of feet in length, making them indiscernible except from above. Because of this, the lines did not gain international attention until the 1930s, when one of the figures (a lizard) had already been cut in half by the Panamericana. Since then, many theories have been advanced, but the origin of the lines remains highly disputed.

ARCHAEOLOGY. Theory One: The most esteemed authority on Nasca was **Maria Reiche,** who lived at the site for over 50 years, and believed that the lines were intended to map the movements of celestial bodies as a way of directing land cultivation. She posited that the **Nasca culture** used long ropes and sophisticated mathematics to create the extraordinarily straight figures and then magnify their designs to a gargantuan scale. Some designs seem to depict constellations, and Reiche demonstrated that many lines point toward where the sun and moon would have risen and set 1000 years ago. However, some scholars have shown that this correspondence doesn't occur frequently enough to be statistically significant.

Theory Two: British documentary-maker Tony Morrison theorizes that the lines were a predecessor to the Inca zodiac system called **ceque.** The Incas conceived of a great conceptual wheel centered on the **Qorikancha** in Cusco (p. 232), with sight lines radiating out toward the horizon. Each line ran through some sacred spot, or **huaca.** Similarly, the Nasca lines may have indicated shrines of great importance.

Theory Three: Anthropologist Johan Reinhard, best known for his work in the Arequipa area, believes that the lines were connected to a mountain/water/fertility cult, and that the straight paths led to spots where fertility rites were performed. Each of the animal figures somehow symbolically relates to water. Reinhard argues that the artists designed the lines in their particular sizes and shapes in order to be seen by deities residing on the nearby mountaintops.

Viktoria Nikitzi, who worked with Maria Reiche for many years, gives lectures about these theories with a scale model of the Nasca lines. *(Espinales 300, 1 block past the Ormeño station. In English, min. 4 people. 2hr., nightly 7pm. s/10.)*

ALIENS. The incredible notion that an ancient people with no aeronautical technology would spend so much time and energy constructing something they would never be able to see has led some observers to other, slightly more off-beat, hypotheses. In 1969, Erich von Daniken asserted that the lines were actually constructed by extraterrestrial life forms who wished to mark a landing site for their aircraft. Since then, many have regarded Nasca as an otherworldly energy center, attracting mystics who sometimes try to camp directly on the lines in order to absorb some of their power. (This is prohibited, and incredibly stupid. Driving or walking over the lines will destroy them permanently) Critics of the alien theory include those who are offended by the assumption that the indigenous people could not have had the intelligence to build the formations themselves.

OTHER SIGHTS

CEMETERY OF CHAUCHILLA. A 25min. bus ride from Nasca proper, the cemetery houses mummies with bones and skulls bleached white by the sun. Nasca's dry climate has preserved the bodies—including their still-attached hair, skin, and cotton textiles—for over 1000 years. In fact, many of the well-preserved textiles were looted by the poor during the depression of the 1930s for use as clothing. The bones' placement in the deep tombs is not quite as authentic. When *huaqueros* (grave robbers) looted artifacts from these tombs, they left the bodies scattered around the desert. Only seven years ago, archaeologists returned them to the graves as they might have originally been placed—crouched in the fetal position and facing eastward, toward the rising sun. A visit to the reconstructed graves offers an eerie glimpse into ancient Nascan culture. *(Round-trip taxi s/30, often included in flights over the lines. Tours from Nasca US$5. Admission s/5.)*

CANTALLOC AQUEDUCTS. Built between AD 400 and 600, these ingenious underground canals tap subterranean rivers coming from the *sierra* in order to irrigate the fields of the dry Nasca Valley. Their careful construction reduces evaporation in transportation from the Andes, filters the water, and keeps it at a surprisingly cool temperature. Some of the aqueducts are still used by local farmers, and work as well as (if not better than) any modern system of irrigation. The blowholes located every few kilometers, called *ojos* (eyes), allow people to enter the aqueducts for annual cleaning. Some guides allow tourists to climb down into the canals during dry season (Apr.-Dec.), but low oxygen levels can make this risky during rainy season. While there are more than 30 aqueducts in the Nasca Valley, each beautifully lined with small stones, the **Cantalloc** is the most frequently visited. The nearby **Ruinas de Paradones** are well-preserved walls from an ancient administrative center. *(Taxi ride 5-10min. to the site. Round-trip taxi s/20. Tours from Nasca 7am-5pm, US$7-$8. Entrance fee s/3.)*

CAHUACHI. *Cahuachi* is derived from the Quechua word "hahuachi," meaning "a place to see." Archaeologists believe that the 24 sq. km Cahuachi ruins, although not the best-preserved in Peru, were once Nasca's largest religious ceremonial center and pilgrimage site, and some believe that Cahuachi holds the key to the mysterious Nasca lines. The site was constructed between 500 BC and AD 200 and abandoned around AD 359, perhaps because of a strong earthquake. Which specific temples and pyramids are open to the public varies from month to month, as archaeologists generally re-bury their excavations to protect them from high winds. Tours include visits to **Pueblo Viejo,** ruins of a residential settlement from the pre-Nasca Paracas culture (800 BC-AD 100), and the **Estaquería,** a mysterious grouping of *huarango* tree trunks placed over adobe brick platforms. *(The only way to visit these sights is with a guided tour from Nasca (see **Tours**, p. 154). US$10 per person with a group, US$15 per person with 2 people.)*

MUSEO DIDÁCTICO ANTONINI. This museum provides an extensive introduction to the archaeological and anthropological wonders of the region. It charts the progression of the various excavation projects in the region from Pueblo Viejo to Cahauchi, with vivid color photographs and detailed explanations in Spanish. The museum also features excellent displays of ceramics and textiles, reconstructions of dwellings, and an authentic Nasca aqueduct in the back. *(Av. de la Cultura 600, a 10min. walk down Bolognesi from the Plaza de Armas, past the school on the right and the fire station on the left. ☎ 52 3444; fax 52 3100. Call 1-2hr. in advance to reserve an English-speaking guide. Open daily 9am-7pm. s/10, includes guide. Photography permit s/5.)*

CERRO BLANCO. Touted as the tallest sand dune in the world (though there are probably larger ones in Africa), at an incredible 2078m, Cerro Blanco offers novice sandboarders newly arrived from Huacachina a chance to put their skills to the test. The hike to the top of the monstrous dune takes 3½-4hr., a climb rewarded with views of the entire Nasca Valley—not to mention the trip down on a board, which takes an astonishing 2-3hr. *(Taxi s/25 to the base; Alegría Tours offers transport, board, and continental breakfast at the top for US$30.)*

OTHER SIGHTS. Casa Museo Maria Reiche, on the Panamericana 26km north of town, is the local legend's former home. Her grave is out back, and the house displays a small collection of charts and artifacts. Besides an intimate glimpse at Reiche's obsession manifest in the hundreds of drawings on the walls, the museum is overly interesting. *(Catch an Ica-bound bus and ask to be let off at the site, about 20min. north of Nasca.)* Three hours out of town, the **Pampas Galeras Reserve** is one of the best places in Peru to see *vicuñas* (llama-like animals). True lovers of the camelid won't want to miss the **Vicuña Festival,** June 22-24, where llamas and their cousins are celebrated through costume, dance, and, of course, *pisco*. *(Hop on an early bus heading north to Puquio or Cusco, or take a guided tour from Nasca, US$35-50.)*

PALPA   ☎ 034

Legend holds that the ancient inhabitants of Palpa (pop. 18,000; elev. 347m) once captured the sun and would only agree to release it on two conditions: that it would always shine on Palpa, and that the town's oranges would be the best in the country. It seems the sun kept its promise on both counts—Palpa is now known as *"la tierra del sol y las naranjas"* (the land of sun and oranges). However, Palpa officials still work hard to lure tourists. An official city map marks 28 sights that might be of interest to travelers, including geoglyphs (lines in the earth) and petroglyphs (lines in rock) that archaeologists consider to be as important as their counterparts in Nasca (if you don't believe it, check out Palpa's web page, www.concytec.gob.pe/palpa-ica/index.htm). It seems that Palpa only lacked a Maria Reiche to bring the nearby archaeological sites international attention. A visit to the Palpa Valley provides an escape from the tourist circuit and a chance to experience sites untainted by access roads and multilingual souvenir shops.

📑📰 TRANSPORTATION AND PRACTICAL INFORMATION. Due to its small size, Palpa is not a regular stop on any bus route. **Colectivos** to Ica depart from in front of the Ormeño station in Nasca; ask the driver to drop you off in Palpa (45min., leave when full, s/2.50). The town's limited services include: a **Telefónica** booth in the middle of the Plaza; a **post office,** Progreso 158, on your way from the bus drop-off to the Plaza de Armas (open daily 8am-6pm); police (☎40 4040), on the Panamericana a few blocks from the bus stop in the opposite direction from Nasca; and the **hospital**, on Independencia (☎40 4053), four blocks from the Plaza.

█ █ ACCOMMODATIONS AND FOOD. The accommodations options in Palpa are spartan. **Posada del Río ❷**, Panamericana Km396 (☎40 4386; posadadelrio@hotmail.com), features huge rooms with hot water and private baths in a restored colonial house, complete with squawking resident lovebirds and white wicker patio chairs (s/20 per person). The **Hostal San Francisco ❶**, Lima 181, one block north of the Plaza de Armas, offers simple rooms and cold baths. (☎40 4043. Singles s/10, with bath s/15; doubles s/15, with bath s/20.) On the next block is the comparable **Hostal Villa Sol ❶**, Lima 200, with common baths only. (Singles s/8; doubles s/16.) A good place to eat is the hospitable **El Monterrey ❷**, Grau 118, on the Panamericana next to the Mobil station. (☎40 4126. Entrees s/8-17. *Menú* s/5. Open daily 6am-10pm.)

█ SIGHTS. The sights most worthy of a visit are the **Petroglifos de Chichictara**, anthropomorphic figures carved into volcanic rocks scattered across a mountainside, 11km east of Palpa. The petroglyphs are believed to be the work of the Chavín, a pre-Paracas culture, and have various astrological and religious meanings. Take a taxi to the rocks (round-trip s/20) or go with a knowledgeable guide who can explain the significance of the different designs and symbols. Ask for **Manuel Ángel Casiles Ventura** (☎40 4416 or 40 4488) in the Municipalidad building, Portal de Escribanos 145, on the Plaza de Armas. Call Manuel in advance to make arrangements if possible. Also impressive are the **Palpa lines**, constructed between 100 BC and AD 600 (earlier than the Nasca lines), which, like those in Nasca, were studied by Maria Reiche. **Aero Cóndor** flies a combination flight over the Palpa lines, the Nasca lines, and the Cantalloc aqueducts, which leaves from the Nasca airport (1hr., US$75; see **Tours**, p. 154). The **Reloj Solar** (s/7, students s/2), a large, double-lined spiral, possibly used as a sundial, is visible from a *mirador* 3km from town (a steep climb by foot; taxi s/6). Outside Palpa, you can visit the lost city of **Huayuri**, ruins from the Nasca period with influences from the Paracas culture. At its entrance stands **El Árbol Milenario** ("The Millennium Tree"), a famous *huarango* tree over 1000 years old that has come to serve as a symbol of ancient medicine (taxi s/20). An ancient cemetery, **Las Moñas**, is located in the hills 4km from Palpa, across the hair-raising **puente colgante** (hanging bridge). Here, unlike in Nasca, there are no reconstructions and no mummies, as they are whisked away to museums as soon as they are discovered. To see the tombs and scattered bones that do remain, it is best to take a guided tour from Nasca or Palpa. Full-day tours of all the sites, including transportation and guide (min. 2 people, US$40), can be arranged at the Municipalidad in Palpa or through an agency in Nasca. You can also design your own guided tour by looking through a book of the sites and arranging to visit to only those that interest you.

CHALA AND PUERTO INCA   ☎ 054

Three hours south of Nasca, Chala (pop. 5000) is a one-road town (the one road being the Panamericana) with a large, clean beach. Just north of town is Puerto Inca, home to remarkable oceanside **Inca ruins** relatively unknown among tourists but well loved by regional archaeology buffs. Constructed from AD 1300 to 1500, these structures were an Inca seaport as well as a ceremonial center and favorite resort. It is no mystery why the Inca chose to vacation here: the rugged, cliff-lined, black beaches are breathtaking. A road (still visible in places) linked the resort to Cusco, 240km away. Today, there are many trails that hug the cliffs, passing small circular caves *(chulpas)* around the complex that were used to store fish and agricultural products. The ruins themselves are beside the Puerto Inka Hotel (2km from the Panamericana), which is responsible for the upkeep of the site, but smaller ruins are visible along the trails that lead variously to a sacrificial altar, several *miradores*, and an entertaining penguin rock (45min. each from the hotel). The cliff-lined coast is also perfect for exploring in a **kayak** (for rent from Hotel Puerto Inka for s/10 per hour), with a **snorkel** (s/10 per hour), or on a **jet ski** (US$45 per hour). Hotel Puerto Inka also rents **body boards** (s/10 per hour).

The best value for accommodations are the campgrounds of **Hotel Puerto Inka ❶,** Panamericana Sur Km603, which guarantee proximity both to the ruins and to many affordable activities including jet-skiing, snorkeling and kayaking. (☎55 1055; fax 27 2663. s/5 per person. Hot showers s/5. No tent rental.) The hotel also offers **bungalow-style rooms ❺** with hot showers (US$24 per person, 2-day packages US$26.50, 3-day packages US$51; AmEx/MC/V), and a beachside **restaurant ❸** (entrees s/15-24; open 7am-10pm). In Chala, there are several cheap hotels, including the basic **Hostal Grau ❷,** on Comercio, one block north of the market. (☎55 1009. No hot water. s/12 per person; s/20 for private bath and ocean views.) **Restaurant Chimony ❶,** near the market in Chala, is favored by locals. (☎55 1079 or 80 5698. Entrees s/6-12. *Menú* s/4.50. Open 8am-10pm.) Residents also frequent **Pulpo ❶,** just next door, because of its delicious and filling *menú* (s/5) and its fresh seafood entrees. (☎55 1250. Seafood s/17. Open 7am-3:30pm and 7-10:30pm.)

Colectivos to Chala (3hr., leave when full, s/12; to Puerto Inca s/13) depart from in front of the Civa bus station, across the Panamericana from the Ormeño station in Nasca. **Buses** along the Panamericana also pass through town. **Caminos del Inca,** whose offices are near the bus stop in Chala, sends buses to **Arequipa** (7hr.; 1, 7pm; s/15) via **Camaná. Taxis** and **combis** heading to the ruins depart from the market area, a 5min. walk down the Panamericana toward Arequipa (s/15 each way). When coming from the north, you can get off at the turn-off to the ruins and walk 2km down the long winding road. The center of town is a 5min. walk along the **Panamericana** toward Arequipa. All services are on the Panamericana and most do not have street numbers. The only bank, **Banco de la Nación,** is a block away from the bus station toward Nasca. (Open M-F 8am-2:30pm.) There is **no ATM.** Other services include: the **police** (☎55 1163), two blocks from the bus station in the direction of Nasca; a 24hr. **hospital** and clinic, **Es Salud** (☎55 1016), toward Arequipa, near Hostal Grau; and **Serpost,** past the hospital (open M-F 9am-4pm).

CAMANÁ   ☎054

Five hours south of Chala is Camaná (pop. 55,000), the "Cuidad Hermosa" whose main attractions are its beaches. Locals, however, take more pride in their agricultural feats than in their recreational achievements. Camaná's soil produces the largest quantity of rice per hectare in the world, a feat celebrated at the **Festival de Arroz** (Festival of Rice) in mid-February. The even more boisterous **Festival de Camarón** (Festival of Shrimp) takes place on the second Sunday in November. Camaná was thrust into the spotlight in 2001, when a tsunami pounded the town and destroyed many buildings. The city has recovered now, and besides these festivals, the only thing that distinguishes Camaná from the rest of the southern coast are its bicycle taxis. It's a clean city and a nice place to rest en route to Arequipa.

The brand new **Hotel de Turistas ❷,** Lima 138, is expensive, but the amenities justify the price: steaming hot showers, cable TV, telephones, two swimming pools, a poolside bar, an excellent continental breakfast included, laundry service, and a huge, scruffy resident dog. (☎57 1740; hotelturcamana@terra.com.pe. Singles US$19; doubles US$25; triples US$35. V.) The cheaper **Hostal Lima ❷,** Lima 306, the small red door next to the pharmacy, has hot showers and cable TV in rooms with private bath. (☎57 2901. Singles s/12, with bath s/20; doubles s/18, with bath s/30; triples s/27. No credit cards.) **Pollos Willy ❶**, Lima 137, offers an inexpensive chicken combo (s/5.50) and an even cheaper junior combo (s/3.50) that both manage to be more than filling. (☎57 1028. Open daily 3:30pm-midnight.) For a taste of the northern coast, head to the **Rinconcito Trujillano ❷**, Pizarro 304, near Castilla, with friendly owners, delicious food, and an airy rooftop seating locale. The owner arranges local trips for tourists. (☎57 1252. Entrees s/10-25. Open daily 9am-7pm.)

Transportes Cromotex, Lima 301 (☎57 1752), sends buses to Arequipa (3hr., 13 per day starting at 4am, s/10) and Lima (12hr.; 7, 9pm; s/50). **Flores**, Lima 319 (☎57 1013), sends buses to **Arequipa** (3hr., 16 per day 5:30am-6:30pm, s/10). The main streets in Camaná are **Lima** and **Mariscal Castilla**, neither of which borders the fairly quiet **Plaza de Armas.** Heading south, Lima becomes the pedestrian walkway **28 de Julio**, which runs into the Plaza de Armas. **Tourist Information** is available in the Municipalidad building, Puente Grau 122, on the Plaza de Armas. (☎57 1044. Open M-F 7:30am-2:30pm.) **Banco de Crédito**, 9 de Noviembre 139, also on the Plaza, changes dollars and traveler's checks and has an AmEx/V **24hr. ATM**. (☎57 3029. Open M-F 9:30am-1pm and 3:30-6pm, Sa 9:30am-12:30pm.) In an **emergency** dial ☎105 or the **police**, Castilla 600 (☎57 2988). The **post office** is at Castilla 223. (☎57 1157. Open M-Sa 8am-1pm and 4-7pm.)

MOLLENDO ☎054

During the summer (Jan.-Mar.), Arequipans flock to Mollendo (pop. 35,000) for its attractive beaches and calm currents. The rest of the year, the town is reduced to a stopping point en route to the nearby Mejía bird sanctuary. No matter the season, Mollendo is an attractive town in its own right, with sloping streets and two lime-green churches. Mollendo's beach, **Primera Playa**, is inviting and convenient, and has a beachfront water park (open Jan.-Mar. s/4). **Nightlife** around the plazas can get rowdy on summer weekends, especially when young naval officers stationed nearby come to party.

▐▌ TRANSPORTATION AND PRACTICAL INFORMATION. Buses enter and leave from the new **terminal terrestre** outside of town. (**Taxis** to the town center s/3; colectivos s/1. Taxis to the beach should cost s/2.50.) Both **Santa Úrsula** and **Del Carpio** send buses from Mollendo to Arequipa (2½hr., every 30min. 4:30am-7:30pm, s/6). To head south along the coast, you must take a combi marked "Valle" at the Grifo Tito (Mariscal Castilla, 6 blocks from the Plaza Bolognesi) to Cocachacra (30min., s/2). At Cocachacra, take a colectivo to Fiscal (20min., s/3), a gas station where buses to Moquegua, Tacna, and Ilo often stop.

The city center has two plazas, **Plaza Grau** and **Plaza Bolognesi.** Grau is on the beach at the southern edge of town, and Bolognesi is two blocks up. Two main streets run downhill to the beach: **Mariscal Castilla** is lined with hostels, and **Arequipa** with street vendors. **Banco de Crédito**, Arequipa 330, has an AmEx/V ATM. (☎53 4260. Open M-F 10am-6pm, Sa 9:30am-12:30pm.) The hospital, **Es Salud**, is five blocks up from the Plaza Bolognesi on Mariscal Castilla. (☎53 3689. Open 24hr. for emergencies.) Other services include: **police**, Plaza Grau 140 (☎53 4242), at the end of Comercio; **Farmacia María Inmaculada**, Arequipa 509 (☎53 3265; open daily 8am-1pm and 4-9pm); **telephone office**, Arequipa 390 (☎53 3375; open daily 9am-11pm); **Internet Starnet**, Arequipa 327 (s/2.50 per hr.; open daily 8am-1am); and **Serpost**, Arequipa 530 (☎53 2264; open M-Sa 8am-1pm and 4-7pm).

▐▌ ACCOMMODATIONS AND FOOD. Hostal La Cabaña ❷, Comercio 240, 2nd fl., on Plaza Bolognesi, offers stellar rooftop views. The rooms that have private baths also have phones and TVs. (☎/fax 53 4671. Singles s/25; doubles s/35; triples

FROM THE ROAD

MACHISMO DEFINED

Unfortunately for the Ican colec-tivo driver, his sedan passengers consisted entirely of elderly Peruvian ladies, with the exception of myself. Packed into the sedan like so many sardines, we watched while our chubby *chofer* lazily picked at his breakfast sandwich, hooting at the pretty young girls walking by. The sun was beating down on the car while we sweated, with our laps full of backpacks or big bags of bread or palm fronds. Mutiny ensued. The women began by yelling out the window, "*oye, gordito, vamanos!*" ("hey fatty, let's go!"). When he still ignored our pleas, one woman got out of the car muttering something under her breath, stormed over, and swatted him with her palm frond while the rest of the colectivo broke out into laughter. Needless to say, we were on the road in less than two minutes.

If there's one thing that I was warned about as a woman travel-ing alone through Peru, it was the cultural phenomenon of *machismo*. I had interpreted *machismo* as being some sort of unequal and degrading system, far from the liberalities afforded to women in the Western world. I soon realized that I didn't have it quite right.

It first hit me while navigating the combis through the *poblados* of Lunahuaná. There, combis careen through the curving roads, barely stopping for passengers

s/40.) **Hostal la Casona ❸,** Arequipa 188, has a down-stairs lounge area and cafeteria (open 7am-11pm) along with private baths, hot water, and cable TV. (☎53 5160. Apr.-Nov. s/25 per bed; Dec.-Mar. s/35.) **Hostal Villa ❺,** Castilla 366, four blocks uphill from Plaza Bolognesi, is the most attractive place in town, but the added luxury comes at a price. Inviting rooms have baths, telephones, cable TV, and large windows. (☎53 2700. Singles s/69; doubles s/79; triples s/99.)

As far as food goes, Mollendo's fresh fish wins hands down. The best dive hangout is **Cabellita del Mar ❶,** on the first block of Arequipa, overlooking the beach. Only one entree is served daily (s/3.50), but the views, beer, and fishnets hanging from the ceiling make this a local favorite. (Food served daily 8am-4pm; only beer after 4pm.) There are lots of sea-food restaurants around Plaza Bolognesi, but the best is **Restaurant Marco Antonio ❷,** Comercio 258. *Corvina* (s/17) is the real delicacy, but the fish of the day (s/11) is tasty too. (☎53 4258. Entrees s/10-20. Open daily 8am-6pm. AmEx/V.) **La Brisa Pollería ❶,** Arequipa Block 3, serves generous portions of chicken and fries cooked in wood-burning ovens. (☎53 3104. ¼ chicken and fries combo s/7. Open daily noon-midnight.)

▣ DAYTRIP FROM MOLLENDO: MEJÍA. Mejía is the self-proclaimed "Pearl of the Pacific," though that may be a bit of an exaggeration. Its sole attraction is the ▣**Santuario Nacional Lagunas de Mejía** (Mejía Lakes National Bird Sanctuary), 3km south of town, which is reason enough to visit the area. The 8km strip of unspoiled coastal marshlands is home to 157 species of birds, including the protected *parihuana* (Andean flamingo), the Peruvian pelican, and the American kestrel. The best time to visit is when migratory flocks come en masse from the western coast of North America (Jan.-Mar.), a journey of over 2500 miles. Call the **visitors center** in advance to reserve a guide for the seven *lagunas* and various *miradores*. The center also provides **maps** for those interested in independent exploration. A walk through the park takes 3-4hr.; bikes, motorcycles, and cars are permit-ted as well. There is no public transportation within, but the park lies alongside the Panamericana, where cars to Mejía and Mollendo pass frequently. **Combis** from Mollendo to **Mejía** (marked "El Valle") leave from the Grifo Tito's gas station at the traffic circle, 6 blocks up Mariscal Castilla from Plaza Grau (30min., s/1.50). The sanctuary is 4km past Mejía. Get off 1km past the sign at the visitors center, the brown building on the left. (☎80 0004. Open daily sunrise-sunset, but call ahead to make sure. s/5. Guide service included, Spanish only. Tip expected.)

In addition to the bird sanctuary, the warm waters off Mejía's beaches are usually serene. Recently, the huge **Club Mejía** resort, where rich Arequipans come to relax between January and March, has dominated the sand, but you can catch your rays and save your soles at the agreeable **Hostal El Chunchito Jr. ❶**, Tambo 406, at Bolívar. The place is surprisingly quiet for being so close to the Panamericana. (☎55 5061. Singles s/10; doubles s/20.)

MOQUEGUA ☎053

Moquegua (pop. 64,000; elev. 1410m) lives up to its Quechua name, which means "quiet place." Life here is relaxed, with locals picnicking around the shady Plaza de Armas on slow afternoons. The cobblestone streets are lined with colonial houses, making Moquegua a pleasant place to wander. Locals are enormously proud of their town and its history, and, most of all, of the strange fountain in the center of the Plaza de Armas designed by Gustave Eiffel himself. Despite the sense of calm here, Moquegua isn't lazy; each morning the **Catedral Santo Domingo** rings its thundering bells promptly at 6:30am, and the "quiet place" begins to buzz with activity. At seven, the markets are already full of vendors selling local specialties (avocados and olives) and the many local *bodegas* open their doors for the day. Moquegua's proximity to Atacama, the driest desert in the world, and its altitude high above the coastal fog keep it both sunny and dry. This extreme climate preserves ancient artifacts incredibly well, making Moquegua a fascinating destination for both archaeologists and tourists.

⌗⧄ TRANSPORTATION AND PRACTICAL INFORMATION. The bus terminal for **Ormeño**, La Paz 524 (☎76 1149), is at the traffic circle. Ormeño sends buses to: Arequipa (4hr., 5pm, s/15); Lima (18hr.; 3, 4:15, 7pm; s/35); Tacna (2½hr.; 6, 11:30am, 4:30pm; s/6). The terminals for **Flores** and **Cruz Del Sur** (☎76 2005) lie 5min. farther down La Paz. Buses go to: Arequipa (3½hr., 19 per day 4:45am-12:30am, s/20); Ilo (1hr., 10 per day 6:30am-10pm, s/10); Lima (18hr.; 5, 6, 9pm; s/35); Tacna (2hr., 12 per day 6am-9pm, s/12). **Colectivos** to Ilo and Tacna converge around the Flores and Cruz del Sur stations.

The fountain of water-spitting frogs, designed by Gustave Eiffel, in the **Plaza de Armas** marks the center of town. **Ayacucho, Moquegua, Ancash,** and **Tacna** border the Plaza. Two blocks to the left of the Plaza (facing downhill), **Piura** leads down to the traffic circle, where its name changes to **La Paz**. The **tourist office,** Ayacucho 1060, distributes maps and informative

who manage to throw their bags of *maize* on top and jump into the vehicle that has inevitably already begun to accelerate. So after I had managed to get my backpack and myself safely into the car, I was surprised to see the combi come to a complete stop. Off in the distance was a woman carrying a baby, sauntering toward the combi at an unhurried pace. The driver stopped the car, ran to take her bag, and waited patiently as she climbed into the car and painstakingly chose the perfect seat near the back.

Certainly my young skin and *gringa* freckles precipitated catcalls and a few extra "*buenos días.*" I had been right in one thing, that *machismo* involves brazen flirting that could be considered degrading in the United States. However, my experiences dissolved any preconceived notions I had of Peruvian women forced into subjection. Rather, while young women certainly receive unsolicited and unwanted attention while walking down the street, they also often receive a level of respect, and even perhaps chivalry, that's not seen in many cultures. And if there's anyone you want on your side in a sticky situation, it's an elderly Peruvian lady.

–Diane Dewey

Spanish brochures. (☎76 2236. Open M-F 7:30am-3:30pm.) **Banco de Crédito,** Moquegua 861, has the only 24hr. AmEx/V **ATM.** (☎76 1325. Open M-F 8am-4pm, Sa 9:30am-12:30pm.) Other services include the **police,** at Ayacucho 808 (☎76 1391, emergency 105), and **Es Salud** hospital, on Urbanización Villa Hermosa (☎76 3990 or 76 1565; open 24hr. for emergencies). **Cafe Internet,** Moquegua 478, is on the corner of the Plaza de Armas. (☎76 1245. s/2 per hr. s/5 for the whole night F-Sa. Open daily 9am-11pm.) **Serpost,** Ayacucho 560, is also on the Plaza de Armas. (☎76 2551. Open M-Sa 8am-noon and 3-5:30pm.)

🏠🍴 ACCOMMODATIONS AND FOOD. Moquegua's accommodations come in all shapes and sizes. **Hostal Piura ❸,** Piura 255, offers handsome rooms with comfy mattresses, oriental rugs, mirrors, hot baths, and cable TV. (☎76 1159 or 76 3827. Singles s/30; doubles s/40; triples s/55. July-Nov. prices drop s/5.) **Hotel los Limoneros ❹,** Lima 441, one block from the Plaza de Armas, boasts the prettiest grounds in town around a restored colonial mansion. The rooms aren't quite as spectacular as their views of the desert hills, but they have hot water and cable TV. (☎76 1649. Singles s/40; doubles s/55.) On the lower end of the spectrum is **Hostal Carrera ❷,** Lima 320, with bare but adequate rooms. (☎76 2113. Singles s/12, with bath s/15; doubles s/24, with bath s/27.)

Moqueguan restaurants serve the local specialties—*palta* (avocado), wine, and *pisco*—and a surprising amount of Italian food. Cheap daily *menús* (s/2.50-3) abound in the nearly identical eateries along Balta near the traffic circle. For more upscale dining, **La Alameda Restaurante Espectáculo ❶,** Lambayeque 132, features three floors of black-and-white tiled floors, colored hanging lamps, 3-D murals, and live music all day. A long list of offerings includes *comida típica* (s/5-7), *ceviche* (s/12-17), and *pisco* sours (s/6). (☎76 1273. Open daily 10am-11pm.) The delicious smell of *empanadas* (s/0.50) and other breads and pastries (s/0.50) emanating from the **Panificadora el Obrero ❶,** 270 Piura, is almost as good as the breads themselves. (Open daily 7am-2pm.) The **Mercado Mariscal Nieto,** on Calle Grau, one block from the traffic circle, has a large selection and more fresh chickens than you could hope for. (Open daily 6am-4pm.)

👁 SIGHTS. The dry desert has perfectly preserved the relics (and sometimes the bodies) of the people of earlier cultures, making Moquegua an area of intense archaeological interest. **Museo Contisuyo,** Tacna 294 (entrance on the Plaza), is a great source of regional information. Its interactive exhibit (with unusually accurate English translations) traces cultural development since the Archaic period, 12,000 years ago. (☎/fax 76 1884; muscont@terra.com/pe. Open M and W-Su 10am-1pm and 3-5:30pm, Tu 10am-noon and 4-8pm. s/1.50.) The museum can arrange a visit to the **Paleolithic Caves of Toquepala,** the site of invaluable Stone Age cave paintings believed to date from 10,000 years ago. (Guided trips in Spanish, with public transportation. Call in advance to arrange a guide and prices.) At the Ayacucho corner of the plaza, the impressive **Catedral Santo Domingo** holds the remains of 13th-century Italian martyr Santa Fortunata, whose legacy is honored with fireworks every October 14. Built in 1652, the cathedral doubled as a convent until it was destroyed by an earthquake in 1784. It was then completely rebuilt through the support of local families, who marked each stone with their family inscriptions, still visible today. (Open daily 6:30am-noon and 3-7:30pm.) Also on the Plaza de Armas is the **Casa Tradicional de la Flor Angulo,** directly across from the Museo Constisuyo, a restored colonial house that is furnished exactly as it might have been during the 18th century. To visit, knock on the door and the current resident will give a brief tour (free). **Cerro Baúl** ("Storage Trunk Hill"), named for its boxy appearance, lies 12km from town, where the pre-Inca Huari constructed a city in AD 600-750 that, among other things, was the center of distribution for corn beer.

The city's ruins (it burned down mysteriously around AD 950) sit on the summit. The excursion involves an uphill hike (1½hr.), most pleasant in th e morning when it's cooler. Frequent **colectivos** headed for "Torata" leave from the corner of Balta and Tacna, 2 blocks downhill from the Plaza de Armas, and pass Cerro Baúl (get off at "El Cruce Torata y Cahone," 45min., s/2).

TACNA

☎052

Tacna (pop. 238,653; elev. 562m), Peru's southernmost city and principal crossing point into Chile, lies only 36km from the border. In Quechua, its name means "I rule in this place," and its history reflects this concern with sovereignty. Lost to Chile in the 1879 War of the Pacific, Tacna's citizens voted themselves back into Peru on August 28, 1929, earning the city the nickname "Heroic Tacna." Residents celebrate this day each year with the **Procesión de la Bandera** (Flag Parade), followed by a week-long celebration featuring farm, livestock, and handicraft fairs along with music and dance. Yet despite this patriotic zeal, on the surface, Tacna's well-maintained streets, excellent universities, and relatively high prices seem to have more in common with Chile than Peru. It is a place where tourism takes a back seat to business as usual; tourists aren't considered intruders, but they are far from the center of attention. Tacna is a city of its own making and proud of it: clean, well dressed, and fiercely patriotic.

▐ TRANSPORTATION

Flights: Aeropuerto Carlos Ciriani Santa Rosa (☎84 4503 or 84 4939), 5km south of town. Taxi s/10. **Nuevo Continente,** Apurimac 265 (☎74 7300), flies to **Arequipa** (30min., 8:10am, US$34) and **Lima** (2hr.; 8:10pm; US$64). **TANS** also flies to **Arequipa** (1hr., 8:10pm, US$34.50) and **Lima** (1½hr.; 2:30, 8:10pm; US$74), but they have no office in Tacna, so tickets must be purchased through a travel agency.

Trains: Estación Ferroviaria (☎72 4981), at Albarracín and 2 de Mayo. Follow Blondell beyond the cathedral in the Plaza de Armas, turn right onto Dagnino just before the railroad tracks, and continue until it ends. As of June 2004, passenger service has been temporarily suspended. Service between Tacna and Arica should resume August 2004.

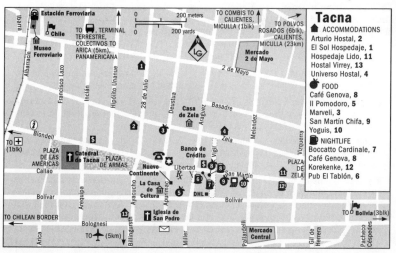

SOUTHERN COAST

Tacna

▲ ACCOMMODATIONS
Arturio Hostal, **2**
El Sol Hospedaje, **1**
Hospedaje Lido, **11**
Hostal Virrey, **13**
Universo Hostal, **4**

🍴 FOOD
Café Genova, **8**
Il Pomodoro, **5**
Marveli, **3**
San Martín Chifa, **9**
Yoguis, **10**

🍸 NIGHTLIFE
Boccatto Cardinale, **7**
Café Genova, **8**
Korekenke, **12**
Pub El Tablón, **6**

Buses: *Terminal terrestre,* a 20min. walk north of the Plaza de Armas on Hipólito Unanue. Taxi from town s/2. **Cruz del Sur** (☎72 5759) provides service to **Arequipa** (6hr.; 5am, noon, 8pm; s/15) via **Moquegua**. **Ormeño** (☎72 3292) has service to: **Arequipa** (6hr.; 2:30, 10pm; s/15) via **Moquegua** (2hr., s/5); Lima (20hr.; 2, 4:30, 9:30pm; s/40). **Flores** (☎72 6691) has frequent service to: **Arequipa** (6hr.; 8:30am, 12:30, 3, 6:30, 9:45pm; s/20); **Lima** (20hr.; noon, 7:20pm; s/40); **Moquegua** (2hr.; 3, 6, 8pm; s/8).

International Colectivos: Sedans to **Arica, Chile** (1hr., leave when full 6am-11pm, s/3.5-7) leave from near the bus terminal.

BORDER CROSSING: TACNA TO ARICA, CHILE. The Chilean side of the border is open M-Th and Su 7am-midnight and F-Sa 24hr. The best way to cross the border is in one of the giant 1970s American sedans that leave when full from either the international bus terminal in Arica or the Tacna bus terminal (1hr., leave when full 6am-11pm, s/3.5-7). All you should need to cross the border is a passport, but you should also have your tourist card, terminal departure tax ticket (s/1) to verify that you're a visitor, some money (about US$30) as proof that you have means to travel, and patience. Don't be alarmed if the driver takes possession of your passport during the ride; it's standard procedure for him to present all passports to customs. Expect to be asked why you're entering Chile. Chilean customs officials are meticulous—they may search your bags. The worst time to cross is on the weekends and early mornings, when traffic is heaviest; the best time is during the afternoon *siesta*. The process is quicker for tourists than Peruvian citizens, but plan on a 15-20min. wait depending on your method of transport. The Peruvian side of the border is open 24hr. Entering Peru is quicker and easier because officials usually do not search luggage. International buses heading deeper into the two countries also cross the border, but are often slower in crossing as more people need to have their papers and luggage checked.

✴ 🛈 ORIENTATION AND PRACTICAL INFORMATION

The main street in town, **San Martín,** houses most of Tacna's tourist services. San Martín intersects the **Plaza de Armas,** where it splits into **Callao** to the left and **Blondell** to the right. Another major street, **Bolognesi,** runs parallel to San Martín two blocks to the south. **Hipólito Unanue,** which intersects San Martín at the Plaza de Armas, runs north to the **bus terminal** and the Panamericana.

Tourist Office: Blondell 50, 4th fl. (☎/fax 74 6944; tacna@mincetur.gob.pe), in the municipal building behind the cathedral. Information and **maps.** Open daily 8am-1pm.

Consulates: Bolivia, Bolognesi 1721 (☎74 5121), about 1km east of the Plaza de Armas. Open daily 9am-3pm. **Chile** (☎72 3063), on Presbítero Andía at Albarracín, 100m past the train station. Open M-F 9am-1pm.

Banks: Banco de Crédito, San Martín 574 (☎72 2541), exchanges AmEx and Visa traveler's checks, gives Visa cash advances, and has an AmEx/V **ATM.** Open M-F 10am-6pm, Sa 9:30am-12:30pm. **Money changers** stand at San Martín and Apurimac.

Markets: Shopping opportunities abound in Tacna. The most convenient public market is the **Mercado Central,** on Bolognesi at Paillardelli. Open daily 6am-8pm. The mother of all Tacna markets is **Polvos Rosados,** on Pinto, just past Industrial, the road that intersects the bus station. Taxi s/2. Find everything from athletic shoes to chocolates, liquor to electronic goods, at prices 35-60% lower than in Lima. Open daily 8am-8pm.

Police: (☎ 72 4201), on San Martín, at the Plaza de Armas. Open 24hr.

Emergency: ☎ 105.

24hr. Pharmacy: Inka Farma, San Martín 537 (☎ 72 8080).

Hospital: Hospital Hipólito Unanue (☎ 72 3431, emergency 74 2121), on Blondell beyond the cathedral. Open 24hr. for emergencies.

Telephones: San Martín 442 (☎ 72 5254). Open daily 7am-10pm. Telefónica del Perú **pay phones** are on the Plaza.

Internet: The many cafes tend to be full, especially at night. **InfoRed Internet,** San Martín 735 (☎ 72 7573), is fast. s/2 per hr. Open daily 8am-11pm.

Post Office: Serpost, Bolognesi 361 (☎ 533 2004). Open M-Sa 8am-8pm. **DHL,** Bolívar 646 (☎ 72 4202). Open M-F and Su 8am-1pm and 3-7pm.

ACCOMMODATIONS

The highlight of Tacna's accommodations is that you'd be hard-pressed to find a TV *without* cable. On the other hand, while Tacna's hotels feature the best of amenities, they lack a bit in style. Most mid-range hotels are centered around the Plaza de Armas and up San Martín, while the bare-bones places cluster at the southern end of town, across Bolognesi. It can be difficult to find a room in mid-December, when Chileans arrive en masse to do their Christmas shopping.

Arturio Hostal, 28 de Julio 194 (☎ 71 1664). Sports well-furnished rooms with hardwood floors and lots of light. All rooms have private hot baths, cable TV, and telephones. The downstairs restaurant-cafe serves a fine continental breakfast (s/5; open 7am-noon and 4-10:30pm). Fax. Safety deposit box. Laundry service. Singles s/35; doubles s/40; triples s/55. AmEx/MC. ❸

Hostal Virrey, Ayacucho 88 (☎ 72 3061; hostalvirrey@hotmail.com), just off the Plaza de Armas. Has everything a good hotel should: nice hot showers, cable TV, big windows, telephones, a downstairs restaurant, and room service, all perhaps compensating for the conspicuous lack of charm. Singles s/25; doubles s/35; triples s/50. ❸

El Sol Hospedaje, 28 de Julio 236 (☎ 70 7382). As the name suggests, rooms with baths have sunny balconies or big windows; those without baths are smaller and darker. All are spotless and have cable TV. Hot water. Laundry service. Singles s/20; doubles with bath s/30; triples s/25. ❷

Universo Hostal, Zela 724 (☎ 71 5441). Clean, carpeted rooms in a quiet building, with an emphasis on safety and solitude. All rooms have baths, phones, and cable TV. Singles s/25; doubles s/40. ❸

Hospedaje Lido, San Martín 876-A (☎ 57 7001). Well-maintained but bare rooms include the basic amenities. Baths are hot, most rooms have cable TV, and the price is right. Singles s/23; doubles s/33; triples s/43; quads s/53. ❷

FOOD

There is no shortage of restaurants around the Plaza de Armas and along San Martín. The regional specialty, *picante a la tacneña*, is a spicy mix of potatoes, beef, and *ají* (hot pepper) sauteed in oil. Italian restaurants abound, especially on Libertad, the pedestrian street before the 600th block of San Martín.

Il Pomodoro, Bolívar 524 (☎ 72 6905). Something of a Tacna staple, this 10-year-old eatery features gourmet pizza (personal s/15, large s/30), pasta (s/12-17), and steaks (s/30-37) in a swanky little dining area with a hanging-wine-glass bar. Open daily noon-3:30pm and 7-11:30pm. AmEx/MC/V. ❸

SOUTHERN COAST

Café Genova, San Martín 643 (☎74 4809). Where sophisticated locals come to sip cocktails at outdoor tables. *Lomo saltado* s/24. Beef with asparagus, bacon, and a spicy tomato salsa s/28. *Mojitos* s/7.50. Open daily 9am-midnight. AmEx/MC/V. ❹

Yoguis, San Martín 797. Two floors of Coca-Cola paraphernalia, Charlie Chaplin posters, and loud jukeboxes. Try a couple of their special *yoguis* (corndogs, s/1.50), and finish with a cup of dreamy hot chocolate (s/2). Hamburgers s/4. Open daily 9am-1am. ❶

Marveli, Zela 495 (☎71 1037). This vegetarian restaurant has nutritional charts of each meal and plenty of soy products. Serves healthier versions of traditional Peruvian fare. *Menú* s/6-8. Open M-Th 8am-noon and 3-7pm, F 8am-noon. ❶

San Martín Chifa, San Martín 727. Chinese tapestries, candles, and small private rooms add an ambience of mystery. Kam Lu Wonton s/14. Sam Si s/17. Combination plates s/10-16. Hearty menú s/5-8. Open daily 11am-midnight. ❷

👁 SIGHTS

The city of Tacna itself is more interesting than its actual "sights," but you may find a diamond in the rough.

PLAZA DE ARMAS. The Plaza features a fountain known as the **Pileta Ornamental,** designed in the 19th century by **Gustave Eiffel** of Eiffel Tower fame (he also fashioned similar fountains for Buenos Aires, Lisbon, Paris, and nearby Moquegua). Facing the Plaza, the simple but elegant neo-Renaissance **cathedral** was finished in 1854. A giant chandelier hangs over the altar inside and small, round, stained-glass windows line the nave. *(Open daily 7am-noon and 4-6:30pm. Mass M-Sa 7:30am and 5:30pm, Su noon.)* On the other side of the Plaza, an 18m **commemorative arch** honors Miguel Grau and Francisco Bolognesi, two heroes from the War of the Pacific.

OTHER SIGHTS. The **Museo Ferroviario** consists of two exhibit rooms along the tracks at the train station displaying old newspaper clippings, route maps, collections of train stamps from all over the world, and railroad equipment and machinery. Antique locomotives are on display across the tracks and at the end of the station. The locomotives themselves are in a sad state of repair, but somehow that adds to the charm. *(Knock at the green door on 2 de Mayo 412, to the right of the clock. ☎72 4981. Open M-Sa 7am-5pm. s/1.)* **La Casa de Cultura** (or Museo Regional Histórico), above the public library, displays local pre-Inca artifacts and large oil paintings representing the War of the Pacific. *(Apurimac 202, at Bolívar. Open M-Sa 9am-1pm and 1:30-3:30pm. s/5.)* Francisco Antonio de Zela y Arizaga, who shouted the first cry for Peru's independence in 1811, lived and died in the **Casa de Zela,** one of the oldest colonial houses remaining in Tacna. The collection of military portraits and colonial furniture make the historic house worth a walkthrough. *(Zela 542. Open M-Sa 8:30am-12:30pm and 3:30-7pm. Free.)*

🎵 📷 ENTERTAINMENT AND NIGHTLIFE

Affluent residents and local university students congregate in the trendy bars and *discotecas* amidst the flashy casinos of San Martín. The pedestrian walkway **Libertad** is brimming with activity on weekend nights.

Pub El Tablón, Libertad 83, halfway down the pedestrian walkway. Live music and karaoke in a cozy, dimly lit bar room. Cocktails s/7-12. Open M-Sa 7pm-late.

Boccatto Cardinale, San Martín 631. Outdoor and indoor seating, mirrored interior, and live rock and *criollo* music every F and Sa night from 11:30pm on. A great list of drinks. Luscious orange-peach ice cream vodka s/14. Beer s/3.50. Open daily 9am-3am.

Korekenke, San Martín 841 (☎999 8573). A little pub with friendly atmosphere. The attached *discoteca* is larger and louder. Live music F-Sa nights. Cover s/10-15. Open Th-Sa 10:30pm-3am.

Café Genova, San Martín 643 (☎74 4809), next door to Boccatto Cardinale. A classy, subdued hangout. Cocktails s/6-14. "Planter's Punch" s/7. Beer s/4. Open daily 9am-midnight. AmEx/MC/V.

▶ DAYTRIP FROM TACNA: CALIENTES AND MICULLA

To get to Calientes or Miculla, take a combi marked "12" (45min., every 15min. 6am-7pm, s/2) from Tacna at Leguía and Kennedy, about 1km north of the Plaza de Armas. Walk up San Martín away from the Plaza de Armas, take a left on Patricio Melendez, and finally a left on Leguía. Combis stop right in front of the entrance of the Centro Comercial. Round-trip taxi s/25-30. Baths open daily 6am-6pm. 30 min. for 1 person s/8, for 2 s/15, for 3 s/20. Combis back to Tacna leave about every 1½hr.

Calientes's (elev. 1350m) biggest attraction is its collection of **thermal baths** (*baños termales*) nestled between the desert hills. Its incredibly tranquil vibe makes Calientes a relaxing escape from busy Tacna. The baths themselves are clean and pleasant at a steamy 38∘C. A larger (free) pool is fed by the water from the baths—the water cools off slightly by the time it makes it here. Most visitors choose to daytrip to Calientes, but the **Hospedaje Baños Termales ❸**, just above the baths, has basic rooms and includes two trips to the baths in the room price. No hot water, but who needs it here? (Singles s/30; matrimonials with private bath s/50; doubles s/60.) At **Restaurant Tradición Caliente ❶** you can munch on cheap *tamales* (s/3) and *palta a la reyna* (s/4) with views of the baths from the outdoor seating area. Three kilometers to the east, the town of **Miculla** boasts 400 **petroglyphs** that are estimated to be at least 1500 years old, with over 2000 engravings of animals and people. Robberies have been reported in the area, so it is best to make the walk in large groups. Right at the entrance of town is a large sign pointing in the direction of the petroglyphs. Follow the road 2km and across two 70m-long, 1m-wide suspension bridges—don't look down.

THE SOUTHERN HIGHLANDS

The Southern Highlands are home to one of Peru's best-known natural treasures: clear and cool, Lake Titicaca lies nonchalantly at a dizzying 3812m, making it the highest navigable lake in the world. Between these wondrous Andean heights and the barren coastal plains, magnificent Arequipa stands guard. Well above the coastal fog and surrounded by volcanoes, Arequipa is a haven for tourists who come here to relax and acclimate before moving up to Cusco. This endearing city defines the region every bit as much as Paris does France, with its distinctive white architecture and sophisticated culture. Arequipa is also a convenient base for visits to the nearby Colca and Cotahuasi Canyons—the two deepest ravines in the world. Indeed, the attractions of this region are more than compelling—they are second to none.

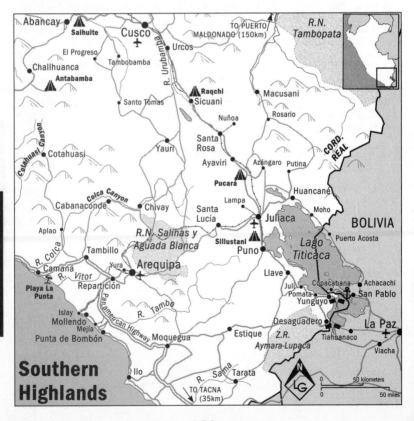

Southern Highlands

> ### HIGHLIGHTS OF THE SOUTHERN HIGHLANDS
>
> **WANDER** the serene streets of Arequipa's **Santa Catalina Monastery** (p. 181).
>
> **WATCH** condors soar over fathomless **Colca Canyon** (p. 188), glimpsing llama herds along the way at the **Reserva Nacional Salinas y Aguada Blanca** (p. 188).
>
> **WITNESS** the sunset over one of the world's highest lakes, **Lake Titicaca** (p. 195).
>
> **WEAVE** textiles with Quechua men and women on Titicaca's **Islas Taquile and Amantani** (p. 205).

AREQUIPA ✳   ☎ 054

Citizens of Arequipa (pop. 1,072,958; elev. 2335m) walk with their heads held high. The "Ciudad Blanca," or "White City," is home to some of the best universities and one of the most impressive colonial centers in Peru, and is the jumping-off point for some of the best outdoor adventures that Peru has to offer. The population of Arequipa has exploded from 300,000 to over one million in just 30 years, no doubt due to the year-round warm climate, job opportunities, and relatively stable local government. While the downside of this growth is suburban sprawl, the city's colonial center maintains its grandeur with several beautiful churches, the enormous 16th-century Santa Catalina monastery, and what is reportedly the most beautiful Plaza de Armas in Peru. Arequipa's architecture, characterized by the use of white volcanic rock known as *sillar*, has defined a new style called *Arequipeño*, which, like many things in Arequipa, obscures the distinction between Spanish and indigenous influences. European-style pastries are filled with local foods. Bullfights draw huge crowds, but pit other bulls, rather than men, against bulls. Catholic churches are resplendent with indigenous shadow-and-light ornamentation. From its beautiful plaza to the surrounding mountains and rich culture, Arequipa offers the highlights of Peru in a single package deal.

⌐ TRANSPORTATION

Flights: The **Aeropuerto Internacional Alfredo Rodríguez Ballón,** (☎44 4564; iperuarequipaapto@promperu.gob.pe), on Aviación, 7km northwest of the *centro,* has only domestic flights. Taxi from the city s/10. **Nuevo Continente,** Santa Catalina 105 A-B (☎28 8595), on the Plaza de Armas, offers flights to: **Cusco** (40min., 10:35am, US$34); **Juliaca** (30min.; 7:55am, 1:45pm; US$34); **Lima** (1¼hr.; 9:55am, 12:45, 3:45, 9pm; US$69); **Tacna** (30min.; 7:10pm; US$34). Open daily 9:30am-7:30pm. **Lan Peru,** Santa Catalina 118 (☎20 1100; fax 20 6097), goes to: **Cusco** (50min., 8am, US$34); **Juliaca** (30min., 2pm, US$44); **Lima** (1½hr; 8am, 2 or 4, 8pm; US$74).

Trains: Passenger train service from Arequipa has been suspended indefinitely. Groups of 40 or more may be able to charter trains to Lake Titicaca. The **train station** (☎21 5350; www.perurail.com), 1km down La Merced from the *centro,* is only for cargo.

Buses: There are 2 bus terminals in Arequipa, both 3km south of the *centro* (taxi s/3). The **terminal terrestre** (☎24 1735) hosts the majority of bus companies. **Cruz del Sur** (☎42 7728) sends land cruisers to **Lima** (17hr.; 7:30am, 3, 6, 9pm; s/35). **Del Carpio** sends buses regularly to **Mollendo** (2hr., every 30min. 4am-7:15pm, s/6). **Flores** sends buses to **Ilo** (5hr.; every 30min. 6:15am-8:45pm; M-F s/20, Sa-Su s/25) and **Moquegua** (4hr.; every 30min. 4:45am-8:45pm; M-F s/20, Sa-Su s/15). Long-distance and luxury coaches leave from neighboring **Terrapuerto Station** (☎42 2277). **Ormeño** (☎42 4187) goes to **Lima** (17hr., 3 per day, s/35) via **Nasca** (10hr., s/35). **San Cristóbal** (☎42 2062) goes to **Cusco** (12hr.; 5, 7pm; s/25) and **Puno** (6hr.; 6, 7, 8am, noon, 8pm; s/15) via **Juliaca** (5hr., s/15). **Transportes Reyna** (☎43 0612) sends buses to **Andagua** (10hr., 4pm, s/18) and to **Cabanaconde** (6hr., 2, 7, 11:45am) via **Chivay** (4hr., s/12). All bus-riders must purchase an **exit ticket** (*ticket embarque;* s/1 for buses to Mollendo, all others s/1.50), available from booths inside the terminals.

Taxis: Taxis are the most convenient means of transportation within the dense city. **Taxi Seguro** (☎45 0250) has 24hr. service.

TAXIS IN AREQUIPA. Despite Arequipa's reputation as a safe city, tourists hailing taxis in Arequipa after dark have been abducted and robbed, even from marked taxis. See p. 34 for important precautions when you travel by taxi.

ORIENTATION

Arequipa feels much smaller than it really is, as most services are concentrated in the intimate **centro antiguo,** the historical center of Arequipa. The centro extends north from the **Plaza de Armas,** and has three major thoroughfares that run parallel to each other and uphill from the Plaza. If you're facing the cathedral in the Plaza, **Santa Catalina** forms the left-hand border and runs past (and beyond) the Santa Catalina Monastery. The Plaza is bound on the right by **Portal de Flores,** which changes into **San Francisco** north of the Plaza. One block down and parallel is **Jerusalén,** which hosts the majority of tour agencies (careful—there are two streets called Jerusalén). Half a block north of the Plaza de Armas, just behind the church, the pedestrian walkway of **Catedral** is littered with souvenir shops. Be aware that most streets change names east of Jerusalén or south of the Plaza de Armas, and there are several streets with the same name (Jerusalén, Bolognesi). Luckily, the city's regular grid pattern prevents much confusion.

PRACTICAL INFORMATION

TOURIST AND FINANCIAL SERVICES

Tourist Office: Run by PromPeru and Inecopi (☎21 1021), Portal de la Municipalidad, on the Plaza de Armas across from the cathedral. Offers free maps and advice on getting to nearby sights. Open M-Sa 8am-7pm.

Tours: See **Guided Tours from Arequipa,** p. 186.

Consulates: Bolivia, Ejército 712, 4th fl. (☎25 9051). Open M-F 8:30am-3:30pm. **Chile,** Galerías Gameza Mercaderes 212, of. 401-A (☎21 9429). Open M-F 9am-2pm. **Germany,** Colegio Max Uhle, Fernandín (☎25 2194). Open M-F 11am-1pm. **Guatemala,** Combate Naval 108 (☎99 7767; diplomacygt@latinmail.com). Open M-F 10am-noon and 3-6pm. **Spain,** Ugarte 218 (☎21 4977). Open M-F 11am-1pm. **Switzerland,** Villa Hermosa 803 (☎25 2499). Open M-F 8:30am-1pm and 3-6pm, Sa 8:30am-1pm. **UK,** Tacna and Arica 158 (☎24 1340). Open M-F 8:30am-1pm and 3:30pm-6:30pm.

Currency Exchange: Banco de Crédito, San Juan de Dios 123 (☎21 2112), 1 block from the Plaza de Armas on the corner of San Juan de Dios and Morán. Exchanges cash and traveler's checks. Open M-F 10am-6pm, Sa 9:30am-12:30pm. 24hr. AmEx/Plus/V ATM. More **ATMs** cluster around the corner of San Juan de Dios and Morán. There are several **casas de cambio** on the 1st block of San Francisco; most charge 5% commission for cashing traveler's checks. Most open daily 9am-7pm.

Alternatives to Tourism: From ecotourism development to English teaching, many opportunities await in Arequipa. See **Alternatives to Tourism,** p. 81.

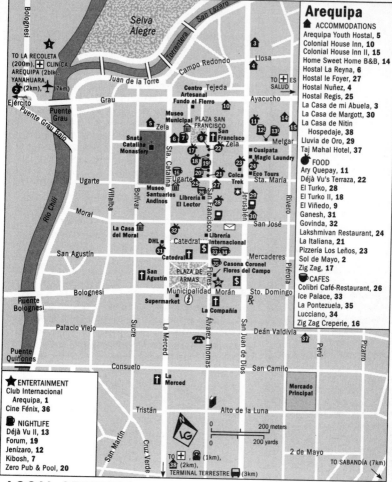

Arequipa

⌂ **ACCOMMODATIONS**
Arequipa Youth Hostal, **5**
Colonial House Inn, **10**
Colonial House Inn II, **15**
Home Sweet Home B&B, **14**
Hostal La Reyna, **6**
Hostal le Foyer, **27**
Hostal Nuñez, **4**
Hostal Regis, **25**
La Casa de mi Abuela, **3**
La Casa de Margott, **30**
La Casa de Nitin
   Hospedaje, **38**
Lluvia de Oro, **29**
Taj Mahal Hotel, **37**

● **FOOD**
Ary Quepay, **11**
Déjà Vu's Terraza, **22**
El Turko, **28**
El Turko II, **18**
El Viñedo, **9**
Ganesh, **31**
Govinda, **32**
Lakshmivan Restaurant, **24**
La Italiana, **21**
Pizzería Los Leños, **23**
Sol de Mayo, **2**
Zig Zag, **17**

☕ **CAFES**
Colibri Café-Restaurant, **26**
Ice Palace, **33**
La Pontezuela, **35**
Lucciano, **34**
Zig Zag Creperie, **16**

★ **ENTERTAINMENT**
Club Internacional
   Arequipa, **1**
Cine Fénix, **36**

▶ **NIGHTLIFE**
Déjà Vu II, **13**
Forum, **19**
Jenizaro, **12**
Kibosh, **7**
Zero Pub & Pool, **20**

LOCAL SERVICES

Outdoor Equipment: Camping gear for rent or sale abounds along the 3rd, 4th, and 5th blocks of Jerusalén. **Colca Trek,** Jerusalén 401-B (see **Outdoor Activities**), offers the best selection of tents, maps, bikes, and other gear. Open M-F 9am-1pm and 3:30-7pm, Sa 9:30am-1pm. AmEx.

Markets: Stores with high-quality but expensive **alpaca goods** can be found on Pasaje Catedral, the pedestrian street near the Plaza (see **Shopping**).

Mercado Principal, at the corner of Piérola and San Camilo, 2 blocks downhill from the Plaza de Armas and across San Juan de Dios. This hectic indoor market has exotic fruit, cheap alpaca goods, and fresh fish. Be wary of pickpockets. Open daily 6am-7pm.

Casona Coronel Flores del Campo, Portal de Flores 136, on the Plaza. Peruvian *artesanía.* Open M-Sa 9:30am-9pm, Su 10am-9pm.

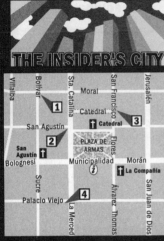

AREQUIPA'S COLONIAL MANSIONS

Arequipa is well-known for a distinctive architecture—one that combines the highly ornamental style of the Spanish with the light-and-shadow contrast of indigenous Peru, all constructed with white lava rock. Spanish colonization of Peru during the 17th and 18th centuries resulted in a series of striking colonial mansions in this style all around the city's historic center. You can read the history of these mansions on their walls: each resident family left a distinctive design in one of the facades. Casa del Moral (see Sights) is the best known, but there are many others that often escape tourists' attention because they house banks, libraries, and art galleries. Here is a list of some of the most impressive colonial mansions in Arequipa's center.

1 Casa del Moral, Moral 318 (see Sights).

2 Casa Arróspide (also called Casa Irriberry), at the corner of Santa Catalina 101 and San Agustin, was built in 1743.

Centro Artesanal Fundo El Fierro has its entrance on the right of Grau, before San Francisco, coming from Santa Catalina. *Artesanía.* Open daily 9am-8pm.

Laundromats: Magic Laundry, Jerusalén 404. Wash and dry s/4 per kg. 3hr. service. Open M-Sa 9am-7pm. **Lavanderías Chick,** Ejército 904 (☎25 9710). Wash and dry s/4 per kg. Items received by 11am finished by 6pm. Open daily 9am-6pm.

Cultural Centers: Instituto Nacional de Cultura, Alameda San Lázaro 120 (☎21 3171). Film screenings, plays, and art classes. Open M-F 8am-2:30pm.

English-language Bookstores: Librería El Lector, San Francisco 221 (☎28 8677; el_lector69@hotmail.com) has a nice selection of English books along with a book exchange. Open M-Sa 9am-9pm, Su 9am-8pm. AmEx/MC/V. **Librería Internacional,** San Francisco 125 (☎20 5317), half a block from the Plaza de Armas, has a small selection of English fiction and a larger selection of English travel books. Open daily 9am-9pm. AmEx/V.

Library: Biblioteca Municipal, Alvarez Thomas 312. Books in Spanish only. Open daily 7:30am-8pm.

emergency and communications

Emergency: ☎ 105. Fire: ☎ 116.

Police: ☎25 4020.

Tourist Police: Jerusalén 315 (☎20 1258). Open 24hr. They also provide a free brochure (with **map**) and safety information. English spoken.

24hr. Pharmacy: Botica del Pueblo, San Juan de Dios 200 and Santo Domingo (☎21 3631). AmEx/MC/V.

Hospitals:

Clínica Arequipa (☎25 3416), on Bolognesi at Puente Grau. English spoken. Open 24hr.

Es Salud (☎46 4181), on the corner of Peral and Ayacucho. Open daily 7am-9pm, 24hr. for emergencies.

Hospital General Honorio Delgado (☎23 3812), on Carrión, 1km south of the Plaza de Armas. Open 24hr.

Hospital Goyeneche, on Goyeneche (☎22 3501). Open 24hr.

Telephones: Telefónica del Perú, Alvarez Thomas 209 (☎20 0109), places international calls. Open daily 7am-8:30pm. Most public phones are inside small shops, but there's also a cluster at the corner of Ugarte and San Francisco.

Internet Access: Cybercafes are all over the place. **La Red,** Jerusalén 306 (☎28 7707), has speedy access for s/1.50 per hr. **Chips Internet,** San Francisco 202-A (☎20 3651) charges s/2 per hr. Both open daily 9am-midnight.

Post Office: Serpost, Moral 118 (☎21 5247). Open M-Sa 8am-8pm, Su 9am-1pm.

Express Mail: DHL, Santa Catalina 115 (☎22 0045). Open M-F 8:30am-7pm, Sa 9am-1pm.

⛏ ACCOMMODATIONS

It's hard to choose favorites from among Arequipa's plethora of excellent hostels, hotels, and *casas de alojamiento*, many of which inhabit well-maintained *casas antiguas* with similar central rooftop terrace layouts. A slight increase in price can mean an exponential increase in comfort and security. Prices are often negotiable. Most hostels are affiliated with a travel agency, so you can arrange Colca Canyon tours without leaving home.

▨ Colonial House Inn II, Rivero 504 (☎28 4249; colonialhouseinn@hotmail.com or colonialhouseinn@star.com.pe), 5 blocks north and east of the Plaza de Armas. The unmarked entrance opens to reveal a restored colonial house, complete with white lava-stone walls, a bright garden, and high arched ceilings in all the rooms. You'll love the quintessential *arequipeño* feel. Rustic rooftop terrace has fantastic views of the surrounding volcanoes. Amenities include 24hr. hot water, full-service breakfast (s/4-9), cable TV, book exchange, tourist info, and Internet. s/20 per person, with bath s/35. ❷

Colonial House Inn, Grau 114, 2nd fl. (☎22 3533; colonialhouseinn@hotmail.com). A *casa antigua* with 6 spacious rooms—so popular they opened a new one down the block (see **Colonial House Inn II**). English-speaking hosts provide book exchange, Internet (s/1 per hr.), rooftop terrace, cable TV, kitchen access (s/1), and breakfast omelettes (s/6). All rooms have private baths and hot water. s/25 per person. ❸

Arequipa Youth Hostal, Zela 313 (☎966 9253). This hip hostel has a spunky red interior, cool blue couches around a cable TV, and friendly, young, English- and French-speaking owners to boot. Common-bath dorms are spiced up by a garden, a small bar, hot water, luggage storage, safe-deposit box, outdoor washing facilities, kitchen access, book exchange, and breakfast (s/3-6). Dorms s/10, with continental breakfast s/14. Discounts for longer stays. ❶

Home Sweet Home Bed and Breakfast, Rivero 509A (☎40 5982 or 966 4987; www.homesweethome-peru.com), 5 blocks north and east of the Plaza de Armas. True to its name, this cute family-run hostel makes you feel at home with a hearty (and free!) breakfast of homemade crepes and eggs. The owners speak English and French. Luggage storage. Kitchen access. Dorms US$3; doubles US$5, with bath US$7. ❷

Lluvia de Oro, Jerusalén 308 (☎21 4252; lluvia_de_oro@hotmail.com). This little bed and breakfast features one of the coolest outdoor lobbies in Arequipa, complete with a palm tree and black-grate lanterns. Its proximity to the tourist police makes it espe-

Today, the magnificent residence is home to the Complejo Chávez de la Rosa and boasts a gallery featuring works of local Peruvian artists, art classes, and a small artisanal shop. Just walk right in.

🄳 Casa Tristán del Pozo, San Francisco 108, is arguably the most beautiful colonial mansion in all of Arequipa, distinguished by three patios: the first is wide and long ago welcomed visitors to the *casa;* the second is decorated with symbolic family facades and was the private patio for the residents; and the third is small and less ornamental—long ago it was the servants' hang-out. Today the *casa* houses the Banco Continental, but the small museum and site gallery (open M-F 9am-1pm and 3:45pm-6:45pm) are worth a quick peek.

🄴 Casa Goyeneche, La Merced 201, stands on what was Arequipa's busiest street when the house was built in the 17th century. Today the *casa* houses the Central Reserve Bank, but it is still decadently arrayed with original colonial furniture. Casa Goyeneche is open for visits 9am-noon and 4pm-6pm.

cially secure, and the sweet ladies who run it will bend over backward to make sure you're comfortable. Clean, simple rooms have private baths with 24hr. hot water and vaulted ceilings. Laundry service (s/6 per kg). Continental breakfast included. Singles s/30; doubles s/40; double suites s/60; triples s/60. ❸

La Casa de Nitin Hospedaje, Urbanización San Isidro F1 (☎28 4700; f_legros@yahoo.com), a 15min. walk downhill from the Plaza de Armas, beneath the Puente de Fierro. Worlds away from the clamor of Arequipa *centro*, in the leafy Vallecito neighborhood. 6 welcoming rooms with sloping wooden ceilings, bath towels embroidered with feet, and balconies overlooking the Río Chili and distant volcanoes. The walk is more than justified by the attentive owners, 24hr. hot water, cable TV, Internet (s/2 per hr.), delicious American-style breakfast (included), laundry service (s/5 per kg), minibar, and mountain-bike rental. Take a taxi after dark (s/2). Singles US$15; doubles US$30. Late June-Aug. and at Christmas, singles US$20; doubles US$30. ❹

✳ **La Casa de Margott,** Jerusalén 304 (☎22 9517; lacasademargotthostal@hotmail.com). This bright yellow *casa antigua* just 2 blocks from the Plaza de Armas is a fantasyland of Baroque *arequipeño* flair. Arching doorways, simple rooms, and palm-tree lined courtyard. Downstairs coffee shop serves breakfast (included). All rooms have private baths, 24hr. hot water, and cable TV, and there are a security box and English-speaking owners as well. Singles US$16; doubles US$25; triples US$32. ❹

Hostal La Reyna, Zela 209 (☎/fax 28 6578), at Santa Catalina. An attractive *casa antigua* reincarnated as a popular hostel. The dim reception area gives way to sunny, clean rooms around a rooftop terrace. Breakfast (s/3.50) served all day. Camping equipment rental, book exchange, laundry service (s/4 per kg), kitchen access (stove s/3), and free luggage storage. English and French spoken. s/12 per person, s/15 with bath. ❷

La Casa de mi Abuela, Jerusalén 606 (☎24 1206; www.lacasademiabuela.com or www.lacasademamayacchi.com), uphill from the *centro*. A full resort with 2 restaurants (open daily 7am-10pm), multilingual library, book exchange, Internet (s/3 per hr.), travel agency, swimming pool, ping pong table, cable TV, and nearly 50 rooms. Though all rooms are nice and have private baths, quality does vary. Breakfast s/7. English spoken. Reservations recommended. Singles US$26; doubles US$33; triples US$42; bungalow quads US$50. Dec.-May prices drop US$3. AmEx/MC/V. ❺

Taj Mahal Hotel, Deán Valdivia 212 (☎/fax 28 2221), 3 blocks from the Plaza de Armas, in the heart of the commercial district. Across from a sunny church garden, this classy hotel has all the luxuries in a cozy atmosphere. Cable TV, carpets, room service, and tourist information. Continental breakfast included. Free laundry service with stays of 5 days or more. Singles US$30; doubles US$40; triples US$54; quads US$60. ❺

Hostal le Foyer, Ugarte 114 (☎28 6473; hostallefoyer@yahoo.com). Spacious rooms open onto a sunny courtyard. Ask for a balcony with noise-proof doors. Big, new common baths. Hot water, laundry (s/5 per kg), and book exchange. Complimentary transportation to airport and bus stations. Singles with bath s/35; doubles s/35, with bath s/50; triples s/45, with bath s/60. ❸

Hostal Nuñez, Jerusalén 528 (☎21 8648; hostal_nunez@terra.com). Larger rooms have hot baths and cable TV; common baths are spartan but clean. Hairdresser and laundry services, safety-deposit boxes, and free tourist info available. English spoken. Cafeteria serves breakfast (s/5). Rooms with bath include breakfast. Singles US$7, with bath US$13; doubles US$13, with bath US$20; triples with bath US$30. ❷

Hostal Regis, Ugarte 202, 2nd fl. (☎22 6111), at San Francisco. Dramatic marble staircase, chandeliers, and elaborate balconies grace this colonial mansion; the foyer is much more extravagant than the rooms. Book exchange, video rental (s/5), and huge lobby TV. Info on nearby sights. Owner speaks English. Doubles s/35, with bath s/50; triples s/52.50, with bath s/73.50. ❷

◘ FOOD

There are an overwhelming number of great restaurants in the *centro*. Specialties include *rocoto relleno* (meat and vegetables stuffed in a spicy red bell pepper), *palta rellena* (the vegetarian version), *adobo de chancho* (a spicy pork stew), and *soltero de queso* (chunks of cheese mixed with potatoes and vegetables). Sick of eating out? Head to **El Super,** Municipal 130, next to the tourist office on the Plaza de Armas. (☎28 4313. Open daily 9am-9pm. MC/V.)

Ary Quepay, Jerusalén 502 (☎20 4583; www.aryquepay.com). This *casa antigua* serves well-prepared local specialties in a candlelit dining room and a covered courtyard. Each night features dance and folk music in 5 languages (7-9pm). Dine on house specialties like *cuy chactao* (guinea pig splayed and fried in Arequipan fashion; s/20) and *filete de alpaca* (alpaca steak; s/22). Vegetarian options s/12. Open June-Oct. 7am-midnight; Nov.-May 10am-midnight. AmEx/MC/V. ❸

Zig Zag, Zela 210 (☎20 6020). Look for the ostrich statue in the entrance. Zig Zag offers the best *carnes a la piedra* (stone-grilled meats) in the city, served sizzling from the grill to your table. House specialty is the renowned ostrich steak (s/31). Rolled spinach with Roquefort cheese sauce s/15. Salmon steaks s/24. Zig Zag's special cocktail served in an ostrich egg cup s/13. Open daily 6pm-midnight. AmEx/MC/V. ❸

Sol de Mayo, Jerusalén 207 (☎25 4148), on the street leading to Yanahuara's *mirador* (see **Outside the City Center,** p. 183). A local favorite since 1897, with a country club ambience and live music every afternoon (noon-2pm). Sol de Mayo serves succulent Arequipan appetizers (*rocoto relleno* s/12.50) and typical Peruvian entrees (s/15-32) in a beautiful outdoor courtyard. Specialty of the house is *camarones* (shrimp; s/28-32.50). Open daily 11am-10pm. AmEx/MC/V. ❹

Lakshmivan Restaurant, Jerusalén 402 (☎22 8768; www.geocities.com/lakshmivan-peru). Serves everything but meat, including vegetarian versions of local specialties. Lakshmivan is a feast for the eyes as well; its red- and orange-colored walls are resplendent with Surrealist art and murals. Breakfasts and desserts are house specialties and not to be missed. Vegan entrees also available. Entrees s/5-6.50. 5-dish buffet with soup, salad, bread, and juice offered Mar.-Dec. (s/15). Open daily 7am-10pm. ❶

El Viñedo, San Francisco 319A, 3 blocks from the Plaza de Armas. Vegetarians beware; El Viñedo serves spicy Argentine fare, including succulent sirloin (s/25) and ostrich steaks (s/22). The interior ambience is as hot as the food: colorful artwork, dark wood, and thatched-roof ceilings. Open daily 10:30am-11pm. AmEx/MC/V. ❹

La Italiana, San Francisco 303B (☎20 2080). The number of Italian entrees is amazing in and of itself. La Italiana serves everything from light fruit pizzas (s/15) to pesto *gnocchi* (s/20), and the *lasagna especial* (s/18) is ooey-gooey scrumptious. Drink it all in: the candle-lighting, the soft Italian music, and the long wine list (free drink with each order). Open daily 11am-midnight. V. ❸

Govinda, Santa Catalina 120A-B (☎28 5540; rest_govinda@yahoo.es). Offers a variety of light, healthy *menús* (s/6) and runs the gamut of fresh vegetarian specialties (buffet lunch s/10.50). Fresh juices and yogurts (s/3-6) make a great breakfast or snack. Ask the owner to play any CD from his eclectic collection. Open daily 7am-9:30pm. ❶

El Turko, San Francisco 216-A (☎20 3862). Fast, filling, and oh-so-good that they opened a 2nd one across the street. Walls are decorated with newspapers from the last decade. The chicken döner kebab (s/5) is a treat. Entrees s/10-16. Open M-W 7am-11:30pm, Th-Sa 24hr., Su 8am-11pm. ❷

El Turko II, San Francisco 315 (☎20 3862), is a more refined (and slightly more expensive) version of its predecessor. Traditional Turkish fare is prepared in plain view in brick ovens. A cool second-floor loft has the best seats in the house. Entrees s/10-20. Beer s/5.50. Open daily 8:30am-midnight. V. ❸

Pizzería Los Leños, Jerusalén 407 (☎28 9179; los_lenos@yahoo.es), at Cercado. Backpackers and locals alike savor piping-hot, brick-oven pizzas in a graffiti-decorated dining room. Large pizza s/30-50. Pasta s/10-13. Open daily 4pm-11pm. AmEx/MC/V. ❷

Ganesh, Santa Catalina 111, 2nd fl. (☎993 4498; jantje41@hotmail.com), 1 block off the Plaza de Armas. Brand-new Ganesh specializes in Asian food: Indian, Indonesian, Vietnamese, and Thai. The food is complemented by the East Asian decorations and mirrored bar (cocktails s/5), all overlooking busy Santa Catalina below. Entrees s/11-18. Open daily noon-1am. ❷

Déjà Vu's Terraza, San Francisco 319-B (☎28 3428). Lounge on a hammock on the rooftop terrace over breakfast (s/6), or admire El Misti over grilled *corvina* (s/20) any time of day. The downstairs bar has live music and dancing most Sa nights. Beer s/6. Non-alcoholic piña coladas s/8. The sister restaurant, **Déjà Vu II,** has free English movies and dancing (see **Nightlife,** p. 185). 10% ISIC discount. Open daily 8am-11pm. ❶

☕ CAFES AND SWEETS

▨ Zig Zag Creperie, Santa Catalina 208 (☎20 6620; info@zigzagrestaurant.com; www.zigzagrestaurant.com), inside Alliance Francaise. Over 100 varieties of gourmet crepes, including: crawfish and smoked trout (s/10); chilean smoked salmon with wild mushrooms (s/9); tiramisu (s/7); and warm red wine (s/5.50). The number of options is almost as incredible as the crepes themselves. While you wait, lounge in the classy bar downstairs, sprawl on the plush sofas upstairs, or sip a cold drink on the rooftop *mirador*. Bon Appetit! Open daily 8am-11pm. AmEx/MC/V. ❷

Lucciano, Mercaderes 115 (☎20 6075). Lucciano's wide display of breads and pastries draws hungry glances from nearly everyone that walks by, but pastries here are a feast for the stomach as well as the eyes. Arguably the finest in Arequipa. The empanadas (s/1.60) are flaky and buttery, the slices of cake (s/2.50-4) are immense, and the cappuccino (s/5) is strong. Chocolate lovers won't want to miss the small but deadly *borrachitos:* gooey, dense balls of chocolate cake, filled AND frosted with—you guessed it—chocolate (s/0.70). Moderation? Not here. Open daily 8am-10pm. ❶

Colibri Café-Restaurant, San Francisco 225 (21 1120), 2 blocks from the Plaza de Armas, serves sinfully sweet pastries, pies, and other goodies under a light blue fresco ceiling. Sandwiches (s/3), and a daily lunch and dinner *menú* (s/5-6.50). Cake and coffee combo makes a good afternoon snack (s/4.50). Open daily 8am-11pm. ❶

Ice Palace, Mercaderes 125. Ice cream flavors from chocolate torte to black forest to mango to mint, and all so good! 1 scoop s/2, 2 scoops 2/4, 5 flavors plus fudge s/4.90. Open daily 7:30am-11pm. ❶

La Pontezuela Café-Restaurant, Portal de Flores 100. The touristy atmosphere may make you cringe, but there's nothing like this view of the Plaza. Avoid the typical food; instead, sip a *café con leche* as you watch the sun set over the city. Entrees s/10-20, vegetarian s/10. Live folk music daily at noon, 6, and 8pm. Open daily 8am-10pm. ❷

🛍 ARTESANÍA

4000 years ago the Incas domesticated the Alpaca for their wool, the source of the incredibly fine fibers that could be woven into warm clothing. Eventually, alpaca wool was reserved for the nobility and interwoven with gold threads, gaining it the name, "gold of the andes". Today anyone can don a soft alpaca sweaters, and don them they do. Arequipa abounds with alpaca goods of all kinds. The quality is excellent for the price you pay, although prices vary across the city. The pedestrian walkway, **Pasaje Catedral,** right behind the Cathedral, has the best selection of high-end alpaca goods. Baby alpaca sweaters run s/80-200. Cheaper—albeit slightly more touristy—alpaca goods can be found on **Santa Catalina,** both on the

Plaza de Armas and a few blocks north. The best selection of cheap alpaca is found both in the **mercado principal,** at the corner of Piérola and San Camilo, and right outside the market along **San Camilo.** Sweaters here run s/20-80. An excellent selection of artisan goods is at the **Centro Artesanal Fundo El Fierro,** entrance on the right of Grau, before San Francisco, coming from Santa Catalina. (Open daily 9am-8pm.) **Casona Coronel Flores del Campo,** Portal de Flores 136, on the Plaza de Armas, also sells *artesanía.* (Open M-Sa 9:30am-9pm, Su 10am-9pm).

◉ SIGHTS

CITY CENTER

▨ SANTA CATALINA MONASTERY ⚹

Santa Catalina 301. ☎ 22 9798. Open daily 9am-4pm; last admission 5pm. Excellent 1-2hr. tours in English (s/10 tip expected), but the monastery is also navigable on your own. s/25, s/20 for Peruvian citizens.

THE PAST. A functioning Dominican convent, this enormous 20 sq. km complex of cobblestone streets, chapels, artwork, and residences seems more like a city within walls. A population of 500 (including 175 nuns, maids, and students) once dwelt here; now only 30 nuns live in a small, isolated section. Santa Catalina was first constructed in 1579, although subsequent earthquakes made many renovations necessary. Most of the nuns took their vows as teenagers and were forbidden to leave the complex for the rest of their lives. The rules were so strict that if a nun accidentally smelled a flower or saw her own reflection in water, she had to flagellate herself as penance. Only the wealthiest families could pay the expensive dowry for their daughter to "marry God," and the size of a nun's room depended on how much money her parents donated. Historically, Santa Catalina's nuns have been the best-educated women in Arequipa; as novices, they were required to learn to read and write. Many parents placed their daughters in the convent at as young as 12 years old, hoping to save the souls of the entire family; other girls entered voluntarily rather than face an arranged marriage. For the first 300 years of the convent's existence, the nuns lived in relative isolation even from each other, with personal maids to do their cooking and cleaning—tasks that would interrupt a purely contemplative life (hence the smaller cells and kitchens behind many of the larger rooms). Santa Catalina's routine was shaken up in 1871 when Madre Josefa was elected head mother; as Madre Priora, she sent the maids packing and initiated a communal lifestyle.

THE PRESENT. Guests receive free **maps** of the monastery on the back of the entrance ticket, and most rooms have explanations in English. Closest to the entrance is the **novice cloister,** restored in the early 19th century, where initiates would train for up to four years before taking their vows. A highlight of the main complex is the narrow **Calle Toledo,** the oldest and longest street in the convent. The street ends at the **Lavandería** (20 huge stone basins on an incline), where the nuns could do laundry and look out at other buildings, but where high walls kept outsiders from peering in on them. Uphill from and parallel to Toledo, **Calle Burgos** passes a beautiful flower garden before reaching a cafeteria, a good spot to grab a quiet snack. Continuing to the right, **Calle Granada** leads to the fish-filled fountain at **Plaza Socodobe,** a market area where nuns bathed and bartered for goods. Calle Granada leads to the *coro alto* and a beautiful view of Volcán Chachani. Along the way are the former quarters of **Ana de Los Ángeles Monteagudo,** beatified by Pope John Paul II in 1985 after a cancer-stricken woman was cured upon praying to her. The shrine in her room is littered with written requests for favors. Farther along, the large, curtained chapel is open to the public for daily mass at 7:30am. Tours conclude in the religious art gallery, which was once a dormitory for the nuns.

SOUTHERN HIGHLANDS

CE MAIDENS OF THE ANDES

n an expedition up the Ampato
Volcano in September 1995,
high-altitude anthropologist Johan
Reinhard and his climbing part-
ner, Miguel Zárate, noticed something strange—bright red feathers
protruding from a slope on the
summit. After excavation, they
discovered that the feathers were
attached to the headdress of a
mummified Inca sacrifice,
remarkably preserved by the sub-
freezing temperatures at the peak
of this Mt. McKinley-sized volcano. Tests revealed that the
body was that of a 13- or 14-year-
old girl killed by a severe blow to
the head over 500 years ago.

Meet **Juanita,** Ampato's premier ice maiden. Hardly one of a
kind, Juanita was one of 13 mummies exposed on the summits of
nearby mountains after heat given
off by the eruption of Volcán
Sabancaya in 1990 melted ice
caps around Arequipa. The sacri-
ices were part of the Inca ritual
Cápac Cocha, in which the purest, most beautiful pre-pubescent
girl in the empire was chosen to
be handed over to the mountain
deities in a time of crisis. Less frequently, boys or even young men
and women would be sacrificed,
sometimes in boy-girl pairs symbolic of married couples. The prerequisite seems to have been
virginity, pure and unblemished.
These chosen children were taken
from their families to live with the
ncas until the ritual.

OTHER SIGHTS

CATHEDRAL. The 17th-century **cathedral,** constructed out of white volcanic *sillar,* is the highlight of Arequipa's picturesque Plaza de Armas.
Inside the ornate interior, the marble altar was
fashioned in an Italian neo-Renaissance style with
French Baroque influences. The enormous Belgian
organ is the second-largest in South America; two
or three people can play at once. Since the construction of the cathedral, it has fallen prey to
many earthquakes and been gutted by an 1844 fire,
then rebuilt in the late 19th century. The latest
damage came in June 2001, when a severe earthquake caused one of the towers to fall, but the
tower has since been repaired. (☎ 23 2635. Open M-Sa
7-11:45am and 4:30-6pm, Su 6:30am-1:30pm and 4:30-8pm
except between 9-9:30am.)

LA COMPAÑÍA. Just off the Plaza de Armas, on the
corner of Santo Domingo and Alvarez Thomas, this
Jesuit church is an excellent example of the Baroque-
Mestizo style. Constructed in 1573 in imitation of the
contemporary popular Spanish style, its original facade
was destroyed by an earthquake and rebuilt in 1698.
Local influences are apparent in the intricately carved
sillar adorning the entrance, and even clearer in the
San Ignacio Chapel to the left of the altar. The cupola
was painted with a jungle motif in a style similar to that
of the Cusco School. Adjacent to the chapel, some **cloisters** constructed in 1738 were damaged in the 2001
quake. The remaining original cloisters now house high-
quality, high-priced *artesanía* shops, accessible
through the huge wooden doors a few shops up from La
Compañía. (☎ 21 2141. Open M-F 8:30am-noon and 3-7pm.
Daily services at noon, 6, 7pm. Free.)

LA CASA DEL MORAL. Named for the 200-year-old
moral (mulberry) tree in its central courtyard, this
casa antigua was built in 1730 for a Spanish viceroy. Its design and decoration are examples of the
fusion of colonial and *mestizo* influences, but its
distinction is the facade's designs of leopards or
snakes emerging from their mouths. When British
silver moguls Arthur and Barbara Williams bought
the house in 1948, they added *sillar* fireplaces,
personal minibars, and European and Asian furniture; tour guides can tell you which pieces are
original. The small room containing old maps of
South America shows the progression of the per-
ception of the continent. The history of the house
is written on its walls: each resident family left a
symbolic imprint above one of the doorways. (Moral
318. Open M-F 9am-5pm. s/5, students s/3. Tours in Spanish
or English included, small tip expected.)

OUTSIDE THE CITY CENTER

YANAHUARA. A pleasant 15min. walk from the town center, this suburb has a stunning *mirador* (lookout) made of *sillar* archways. Engraved with republican and revolutionary slogans, the *mirador* affords excellent views of the city center, El Misti, and Pichu Pichu. Along the small park behind the *mirador*, the **Lejo Parroquial de Yanahuara church** is noted for its elaborate facade. Below the *mirador* is a series of narrow alleys and old family orchards for which the neighborhood is known. *(To reach the mirador, cross Río Chili on Puente Grau from its intersection with Santa Catalina. Take Ejército to Jerusalén, 2 blocks after the statue of the bulls; turn right and continue uphill until you reach the park on the right. Church open M-F 9am-noon and 4-8pm, Sa 7am-1pm and 3-8pm, Su 6am-1pm and 2:30-8pm.)*

OTHER SIGHTS. Seven kilometers southeast of the city, the tranquil town of **Sabandía** is a nice break from the packed city center and a good stop on a long bicycle ride. Its main attraction is the tiny *molino* (water-powered wheat mill), which dates from 1621. The surrounding grounds are nicely decorated, and a lone alpaca patrols the grass. The brand-new **Rancho Aventura** next door features gardens, horseback riding (s/5 per 15min.), and a **restaurant ❷**, all with the best views of El Misti in greater Arequipa. *(Chincharrones for 2, s/17. Open Tu-F 11am-6pm and Sa-Su 10am-6pm.)* Nearby, in the smaller town of Huasacache (10km east), the **Mansión del Fundador** is a consummate example of a 17th-century colonial estate. The mansion provides little explanation on the history of its impressive interior and grounds, but even a superficial look reveals the contrast between this restored bit of the 17th century and the modern urban sprawl next door. *(Buses to Sabandía leave from Independencia and Paucarpata, the eastern continuation of Mercaderes. Taxis s/15 round-trip. The mill is to the right of the main road, on the same road as the El Lago Resort. Open daily 9am-5pm. s/5. Mansión del Fundador, ☎44 2460, is on Paisajista, taxi s/5 each way. Open daily 9am-5pm. s/7, students s/3.)*

🏛 MUSEUMS

MUSEO SANTUARIOS ANDINOS. This archaeological museum houses well-preserved mummies found on nearby volcano summits. Each mummy was a human offering by the Incas, an unblemished youth sacrificed to the gods. The best-preserved and most famous is **Juanita** (see **Ice Maidens of the Andes**), who often goes on tour (the museum still brags about her trip to Japan in 2000). The

Being selected for *Cápac Cocha* was one of the greatest honors possible, as the girl would live with the gods eternally, but such a privilege also demanded extreme effort. Accompanied by priests, the chosen girl first had to walk over 300 kilometers from Cusco, then climb a 6000m peak. By the time they reached the summit, most girls must have already been half-dead from exhaustion and frostbite, but the show went on: priests gave the chosen one a potent mix of alcohol and hallucinogenic drugs, performed the sacred rites, then killed her by strangulation or with a sharp blow to the head. The gift to the gods was finally put in a grave filled with objects of symbolic significance. Juanita was buried with seashells—maybe she was an offering to the sea, perhaps asking for rain.

Juanita has become an international celebrity—she toured the world like a rock star in the late 1990s. Today, despite some locals' protestations that Juanita should never have been removed from the summit, Juanita and five other mummy sacrifices have a new home—Arequipa's **Museo Santuarios Andinos**. A lifelike Juanita sits in a reclined position with a curiously relaxed look on her face, though she is obviously bracing herself against the deadly Andean cold.

BUTTING HEADS

With the introduction of bulls to Arequipa in the sixteenth century, the area quickly became the dairy and livestock capital of Peru. This business has been profitable, making the *rancheros* on the outskirts of Arequipa wealthy and proud of it. Around the late 19th century, *rancheros* here had enough excess money to begin to raise a few fighting bulls: bulls trained to fight each other rather than a matador, in a show not of cunning but of brute strength. A cow is paraded in front of two bulls standing side by side, provoking the creatures to begin a fight that lasts anywhere from a few seconds to two hours. The loser is the bull that runs away, tail between his legs, as the crowd boos and laughs.

The fighting bulls initially provided an arena to settle rivalries between neighboring towns. Each bull was given a symbolic name, and towns gathered to cheer on their champion bull in a fervent show of town pride. The situation is not much different today, as wealthy landowners fill the stands at arenas and cheer on their own's champion bulls.

None of today's bulls, however, live up to stories of local legend Melenik, a bull said to have been born to fight. Melenik simply refused to pull a plow, so his owners trained him as a fighting bull, and Melenik did not disappoint. In fact, with his unique style of fighting, stabbing the other bull in

museum screens a 20min. *National Geographic* documentary on the discovery of Juanita, followed by a wonderful 25min. tour through displays of Inca metals, ceramics, textiles, and several other mummies. *(Santa Catalina 210. ☎21 5013. Open M-Sa 9am-6pm, Su 9am-3pm. s/15, students s/5. Tours in English, Spanish, French, German, Italian. Tip expected.)*

LA RECOLETA. La Recoleta was constructed in 1648 as a Franciscan convent, and still functions today with a population of 15 monks. The convent now contains a **museum** with exhibits on missionary activity in the Amazon Basin, pre-Columbian pottery, textiles, and ceramics. It also houses an art gallery specializing in religious work, with several cells on display depicting life in the convent. Monsignor Mariano Holguin, the first archbishop of Arequipa and the president of Peru for a grand total of one day in 1931, once lived in a cell here. Most interesting is the 20,000-volume **library,** with a number of *incunables* (books printed during the 15th century) and old maps. *(Recoleta 117. In a bright red building visible from the center of Arequipa, a 10min. walk over the Río Chili. After crossing the bridge, turn left on Ejército. Entrance is in the gray building on the right just past the church. ☎27 0966. Open M-Sa 9am-noon and 3-5pm. English tours available for an extra charge depending on group size. s/5, students s/3.)*

🎵 SPORTS AND ENTERTAINMENT

If the surrounding natural highlights are not enough, the city of Arequipa itself offers plenty of diversions. The posh **Club Internacional Arequipa** has excellent sports and recreational facilities, including two swimming pools, a soccer field, a bowling alley, a sauna (open daily 1-9pm, s/6), and basketball, racquetball, and tennis courts. To get there, cross Puente Grau and turn right; the main entrance is across the river. (☎25 3384. One-day pass M-F s/10, Sa-Su s/15; 8-day pass s/50. Open daily 6am-11pm. Arrange for a pass through the office, open daily 9am-5pm.) Arequipans take great pride in their unique **bullfights** that, instead of pitting man against beast, match up two bulls of equal weight (categories range from 300 to 1500kg). Unlike traditional bullfights, these are neither excessively bloody nor lengthy. First, a fertile female is led in front of the macho males; the two *varones* go at it and the loser is the first one to run away. For details, see **Butting Heads.**

Déjà Vu II, Melgar 119-A (☎22 9755) has free nightly screenings of English-language movies with Spanish subtitles (7:30pm). **Cine Andino,** La Salle 185 (☎20

2202), also screens relatively recent international movies (s/6); many are in English with Spanish subtitles. **Cine Fénix,** Morán 104, also shows movies (s/5).

🎞 NIGHTLIFE

Arequipa may be Peru's second-largest city, but its nightlife tends to disappoint when compared to its capital counterpart or the ever-raging Cusco. Nevertheless, this city still knows how to party in its own highland manner, especially on weekends and holidays. There is a healthy assortment of *discotecas*, *peñas*, and gringo rock clubs, mostly centered around the intersection of San Francisco and Zela. If you're planning to make a night of it, it's worth your while to seek out the ubiquitous **free drink cards** distributed in hostels and touristy restaurants. Several local restaurants, especially near the Plaza de Armas, occasionally have live traditional music on weekend evenings. Some clubs charge a cover (s/8-15) on weekends.

Forum, San Francisco 317 (☎20 4294; forumrockcafe.com). Part dance club, part Copacabana wannabe, this bumping oasis includes a functioning waterfall. Starting at 1am on weekend nights nearly all of Arequipa flocks to its 6 bi-level bars and gigantic dance floor. Live Latin bands F-Sa. Pool tables. Restaurant and bar open M-Th 6pm-5am, *discoteca* open F-Sa 10pm-4am.

Déjà Vu II, Melgar 119-A (☎22 9755), near the intersection with Rivero. Nightly English-language movies with Spanish subtitles. Pool table and live music in the summer.

Jenízaro, Melgar 119. Tourists and locals dance to mostly international music. Comprehensive bar. Open Th-Sa 10pm-4am.

Zero Pub & Pool, San Francisco 317, above Forum and to the right. 2 pool tables, big booths with leather seats, Pink Floyd tunes, and juicy hamburgers. This bar lacks Latin flavor, but not good times. Open daily 6pm-2am.

Kibosh, Zela 205, is a multilevel adventure, with 4 bars inside. Popular Kibosh has lots of space to dance or just to chill. Best salsa in town. The rock music is loud, as it should be. Open Th-Sa 9pm-4am.

⛰ OUTDOOR ACTIVITIES

The region around Arequipa hits all the extremes. Hike above the clouds on the El Misti or Chachani volcanoes, or delve into the earth by trekking down the Colca and Cotahuasi canyons, the deepest in the

the neck—Melenik never lost. This was 1946; never since has a bull lived up to Melenik's reputation.

Today bullfights are as popular as ever. Locals arrive with cowboy hats, stylish boots, and fists full of *chicharrones*. The slow pace of the afternoon is all part of the experience: the event is wholly social until the final few fights. The fights between champion bulls combined with local rivalries precipitate yelling, stomping, and wild cheering from the crowd.

Bullfights take place each Sunday between April and December. The most important fights occur in April during the Bull Fighting Championship, and in August during Arequipa's anniversary. The venue rotates between three different stadiums: the Cerro Juli stadium near Sabandía (taxi s/8), the Zarracola Bolaúnde "El Azufral" near the airport (taxi s/8), and the Estadio del Campo Ferial in Characato, a town 30min. past Sabandía (taxi s/25). The fights usually run from 1 or 2pm until 5pm. Check the local newspaper for the location of the fight, or call the **Asociación de criadores, propietarios y aficionados de toros de pelea** (Association of Breeders, Owners, and Fans of Fighting Bulls, ☎42 2772).

THE MIRACULOUS VIRGIN OF CHAPI

One day during a drought, a man entered the Temple of Chapi to pray to the Virgin for water. The next day, the floor seemed strangely wet, and when locals pulled up the floorboards they found a natural spring underneath that quickly became known as "miracle water." The water not only provided sustenance during the drought, but it was also thought to be medicinal.

This is only one of the miracles Arequipans attribute to the Virgin of Chapi, their patron saint. The Virgin is portrayed as a richly-robed statue of a woman holding a baby, with mother and child wearing gigantic crowns. One legend tells of children who claimed to have been playing with baby Jesus one night. The next day, the baby in the Virgin's arms was found with mud and dirt on his shoes. Locals also claim that the expression on the Virgin's face changes, and that tears under her eyes predict bad times ahead. The most devout claim that she can heal the terminally ill; people with cancer have been inexplicably cured after praying to her.

The origins of the Virgin are uncertain. It is thought that she arrived from Seville, Spain near the beginning of the 17th century. For centuries, the Virgin was housed in her own temple outside of town. The earthquake of 2001 destroyed the temple, and she has since been moved to the Cathedral on the Plaza de Armas.

world (see **Hiking Near Arequipa**, p. 188). Get soaked in whitewater rapids, or venture into the desert to visit the Toro Muerto petroglyphs. Tour agencies in town offer nearly every kind of trip permutation, but it's possible to make most excursions on your own (see **Guided Tours**, below). If you go with guides, choose from reputable companies—traveling with a shoddy outfit in wilderness areas can put more than your pocketbook at risk. If you choose the independent option, find as many people as possible to go with you; **small groups have been assaulted on El Misti.** Also, be certain that you are acclimated and have the correct equipment—hiking at such high altitudes can be dangerous. See **Trekking and Hiking,** p. 49, for more information.

GUIDED TOURS FROM AREQUIPA

Some of the most exciting excursions around Arequipa require special equipment or the expertise of a guide. Of the many travel agencies, the following have specialized tours or represent the best in their category. All companies should be able to provide guides who speak fluent English.

■ **Colca Trek,** Jerusalén 401-B (☎20 6217; www.trekinperu.com), in the same building as Campamento Base. With possibly the best mountain equipment in Arequipa (for rental and purchase), the agency leads personalized treks in the **Colca** and **Cotahuasi** canyons and the surrounding **volcanoes, whitewater rafting** excursions, or any combination of the above. Do-it-yourself mountaineers can get maps that include trail descriptions of the volcanoes (US$12 per page) and detailed hiking advice for free from Colca Trek's knowledgeable owner, Vlado Soto. They also rent 4×4 vehicles (US$85 per day) to trekkers going alone. Standard 2-day Colca Canyon tours (US$20) include transportation, hotel, and breakfast. 3-day Colca tours (around US$80, depending on group size) include food, transportation, equipment, and donkeys. 1-day rafting excursions in the Río Majes (US$40) include a stop at the Toro Muerto petroglyphs. All prices rise US$5 July-Aug. If these activities leave you hungry for more, ask about the 6-day "Source of the Amazon" trek, which travels through all 3 regions of Peru: the jungle, the *sierra*, and the desert. Open M-F 9:30am-1pm and 3:30-7pm, Sa 9:30am-1pm. AmEx.

Cusipata, Jerusalén 408-A (☎20 3966; gvellutino@terra.com.pe). With trips led by the 3 Vellutino brothers, known as "the rafting champions of Arequipa," Cusipata leads the pack in rafting and kayaking excursions, ranging from 3hr. trips (US$25-40 per person) to 12-day journeys (US$600 per person). To kayak solo, you must take their 2-3 day course (US$120). Open M-Sa 9am-1:30pm and 3-7:30pm. V.

Eco Tours, Jerusalén 402-A (☎20 2562; ecotours@terra.com.pe). A multilingual (English, French, and German), student-oriented agency specializing in ecology. Offers the standard Colca trip (US$30) and trips to Toro Muerto (US$20) or the Reserva Nacional Salinas y Aguada Blanca (US$25). Multiple-day treks through Colca, Cotahuasi, El Misti, Chachani, and Ampato. Whitewater rafting (1 day US$20). Rental gear (bicycles US$15 per day). Spanish tutorials US$5 per hr. 10% ISIC discount. Open daily 9am-9pm. AmEx/MC/V.

Giardino, Jerusalén 604-A (☎22 1345; www.giardinotours.com), inside the Casa de Mi Abuela hotel. This well-established guide company is a full-service travel agency with its own fleet of vehicles and guides who speak English, Italian, French, and German. The most popular tour is the Caminata Giardino, a relaxed journey through the countryside that includes a country picnic (prices depend on group size). With prior arrangement, Giardino leads multiple-day treks through Colca Canyon and the surrounding volcanoes. Standard 2-day Colca tour US$40, 3 days around US$110. Office open daily 9am-1pm and 3-7pm. AmEx/MC/V.

WHITEWATER RAFTING

The Río Colca snakes for over 400km around the department of Arequipa, changing its name, direction, and rafting difficulty along the way. The rapids range from Class II-V, but all pass through gorgeous mountain scenery. The most popular trip for beginners is a 7km stretch of the **Río Chili** just north of the city center; the Class II-III rapids are navigable in the dry season (Apr.-Dec.) only. The trip includes a small stretch of Class IV rapids, which beginners can skip by walking onshore. The **Río Majes,** north of Camaná, is navigable year-round, but requires instruction first (Class II-III; full-day trip with about 3hr. on the water). Only experienced rafters should take on the **Río Colca,** in the highlands around the Colca and Cotahuasi Canyons; its rapids range from Class III-V (strongest on the stretch between Canco and Majes) and are only navigable April through December.

Kayaking is also possible on all of these rivers. While you can bring your own equipment and tackle the river independently, the lack of public transportation to the rivers and the variable river conditions convince most adventurers to go with a guide. Tour agencies can put together 3- to 12-day packages to the Río Colca. Normally, double kayaks (with a guide in one seat) are used; to take a single kayak, agencies require a 3-day course (US$120-150). As always, the larger the group, the lower the price: 4hr. trips down the Río Chili can cost as little as US$25 per person in groups of 4 or more. Groups of 2-3 cost US$35 per person. Prices are comparable for the Río Majes, and sometimes include a trip to the Toro Muerto petroglyphs. These trips are full-day and include 2-3hr. of instruction before 3hr. of actual river-running. The best guides can be found at **Cusipata** and **Colca Trek** (see **Guided Tours from Arequipa,** above).

TORO MUERTO PETROGLYPHS

Before Colca was "discovered" in 1986, this site was the original Arequipa tourist attraction, consisting of more than 5000 black volcanic rocks (remnants from eruptions 50 million years ago) engraved with images thought to be more than 1000 years old—the work of the Huari and Chuquibamba cultures. The figures include dancing people, the sun, and even dogs and snakes.

The easiest route to the petroglyphs is with a one-day tour (US$25 per person), though it's much cheaper and relatively simple to go solo. **Transportes del Carpio** (☎43 0941) sends buses from Arequipa's terminal to Corire, the closest town to the petroglyphs (3hr., every hr. 5am-6:45pm, s/10; same return times). Get off about 1.5km before town, at a sign marking the turnoff for Toro Muerto; if you miss the sign, just head from Corire on foot (30min.) or take a taxi (15min.). From the turn-off, the petroglyphs are a 1½hr. walk (entrance fee s/5). Although you can return to Arequipa the same day, it's easier to spend the night in Corire. These days, many people choose to see Toro Muerto as part of a whitewater rafting trip.

OTHER OUTDOOR ODYSSEYS

The **Reserva Nacional Salinas y Aguada Blanca** covers 367,000 hectares of highlands northwest of Arequipa. Here the alpaca, vicuña, and llama rule the roost—a drive through the reserve almost guarantees a sighting of a herd of fluffy camelids. Fortunately, government protection has left the animals largely unconcerned with humans and their cameras, giving tourists an up-close-and-personal view of their long faces and playful behavior. There is no public transportation within the reserve. Most tourists visit on the way to Colca Canyon, but it is possible to explore the reserve in-depth with a guide from Arequipa. **Eco Tours** has guides who specialize in ecology and lead one-day tours through the reserve (US$25).

The countryside around Arequipa is perfect for exploration with a **bike** (see **Guided Tours**). Most agencies rent bikes (around US$15 per day). The best routes are either east or west of the city where the terrain is green. To the west, there are great trails along Río Chili north of the city, winding along with the river through terrain that is pleasantly hilly and exerting. To the east, the country roads leading to Sabandía and Characato provide spectacular views of El Misti and Chachani with very little physical difficulty. Here it is possible to stop by the **Mansión del Fundador** (p. 183) for an afternoon break. Companies that rent bikes generally provide transportation to the trails and either a guide or explicit directions for free.

HIKING NEAR AREQUIPA

COLCA CANYON

Although no longer considered the world's deepest canyon (nearby Cotahuasi Canyon has that honor), Colca is visited much more frequently by tourists. Touted as being twice as deep as the Grand Canyon, the cavernous, 3400m deep fissure was formed by a 150km long seismic fault between the Hulca Hulca (5800m) and Bomboya (5500m) volcanoes. Incredibly, the canyon was unknown to outsiders until a Polish group explored it in 1986. It is home to some of the boldest condors in the world; watching groups of them soar up the canyon and surf the morning is a beautiful show. The best time to see them soar is between 8:30 and 10am.

AT A GLANCE	
AREA: 120km long.	**TIME:** 2-9 days.
CLIMATE: Dec.-Mar. rain damages roads and the hike becomes impossible.	**ALTITUDE:** 2100-5000m.
	DIFFICULTY: Medium-Difficult.
FEATURES: Colca Canyon (the second deepest in the world), beautiful condors.	**FEES:** US$6 entrance fee for Cruz del Cóndor.

🛈 PRACTICAL INFORMATION

Along the ridge of the canyon are a number of traditional Andean villages and scenic *miradores*, the most popular of which is the **Cruz del Cóndor.**

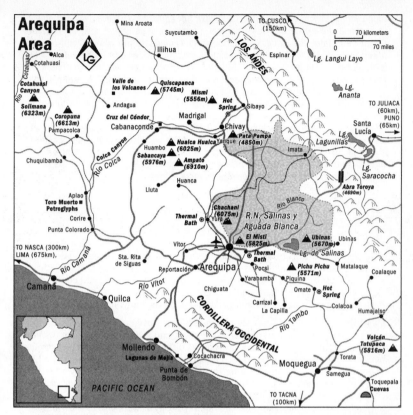

Transportation: Transportes Reyna (☎53 1090) sends buses from Arequipa to **Chivay** (4hr.; 2, 7, 11:45am; s/10) and on to **Cabanaconde** (6hr., s/12; for more information see **Chivay,** p. 194). Buses return to Arequipa from **Andagua** (4, 6pm, s/23). Tickets can be purchased in advance at Campamento Adventure Shop next to Colca Trek.

Accommodations: There are more accommodations in Chivay than in Cabanaconde. Camping zones in the canyon charge small fees (about s/5 per tent; s/8 to sleep in bungalows). There is no camping at Cruz del Cóndor.

Maps: The best **map** of the region (US$12) is available from **Colca Trek** (p. 186).

Supplies: A good sleeping bag and warm clothes are necessary for climbing at this high altitude. Bring water, as there is very little available along the way. Donkeys and donkey guides (US$10 per day per person) make the trek a bit easier. English-, French-, and Spanish-speaking guides can be found in Arequipa (US$60 per day per person or US$180 per day for a group of 14 people or fewer).

Tours: Traveling alone is not much cheaper than taking a tour, but most conventional tours of the Colca Canyon last 2 days and 1 night and do not include any hiking. If you're in a hurry, many agencies offer a 1-day trip, but it involves a night drive to view the condors, which is extremely dangerous and not recommended. A standard 2-day tour (US$20-35, depending on the quality of the hotel) leaves Arequipa before 9am and stops in the **Reserva Nacional Salinas y Aguada Blanca** to watch vicuña. To round off the day, groups visit the **La Calera hot springs** (s/5) in the late afternoon, then spend the night in Chivay. The next morning, groups depart early for **Cruz del Cóndor** and later visit small villages such as **Yanque** (with a colonial church) and **Maca,** arriving back in Arequipa around 6pm. When considering the value of the tour, find out what is included in the price: standard attractions, transportation, an English-speaking guide, entrance fee, hotel room, and/or breakfast. Regardless, take at least s/50 (to cover lunch, dinner, and admission to the hot springs), warm clothing, and a camera. Agencies also offer increasingly-popular 3-day, 2-night tours that most often include canyon hikes, equipment, food, and mules for porters, but the first night is still spent in a hotel (US$70-100 depending on hotel, equipment, and food). Agencies offering conventional tours crowd Santa Catalina in the center of Arequipa, or on the fourth and fifth blocks of Jerusalén. Trekking agencies (see **Guided Tours,** p. 186) can also arrange conventional tours, but they will be led by guides from conventional agencies, not trekking guides.

🅗 HIKING

3-DAY HIKES. If the 2-day tour is too posh, the 3-day trip includes some backpacking. The first day includes a drive through the Reserva Nacional Salinas y Aguada Blanca, an short hike to the petroglyphs inside the reserve, a quiet afternoon visit to Cruz del Cóndor, and a hotel-stay in tiny Cabanaconde. The next day, the group descends into the canyon (6hr.) accompanied by mules and cooks, then camps that night. The third and final day consists of a strenuous ascent out of the canyon (4hr.), and a long drive back to Arequipa on the canyon's opposite side.

7-DAY HIKES. If the 2- or 3-day tour is insufficient, attempt the 6- to 7-day hike that goes through the canyon, over a 5000m pass, and around the Valle de los Volcanes before returning to Arequipa. Itineraries differ, as most trekking companies are willing to put together personalized excursions, but a typical one might go like this: Day 1 is occupied with the long bus trip to Cabanaconde. Enjoy your last night in a bed, then set out directly for the canyon on Day 2. Pass through the village of Tapay and continue until you reach the base of the Río Colca (7hr. from Cabanaconde), where you camp for the night. On Day 3, walk 6hr. to the village of Choco to camp for the night. Day 4 (total 9hr. hiking) is the most difficult, as you climb over the 5500m pass and begin your descent, finding a campsite on the way down. Day 5 is relatively easy, as you continue down to the small town of Chacas (5hr.), where you camp for the night. On Day 6, climb through the Valle de los Volcanes, cross one more pass, and after about 5hr. reach the final destination, Andagua. The final day, Day 7, is a long bus ride back to Arequipa.

DAYHIKES. Cruz del Cóndor is an easy 6km (1½hr.) walk from Cabanaconde on the road back toward Chivay; buses to and from Arequipa also pass the site when traveling between the two towns. The most popular **trek** is a 2-3hr. hike from Cabanaconde to the bottom of the canyon, where small, swimmable **Sangalle oasis** makes a good camping spot (3-4hr. hike back up). To spend the day hiking around the town of Cabanaconde, there are paths leading to: **La Muralla,** a very long wall constructed by the ancients; **La Casa de Inca,** as the name suggests, an Inca house in ruins; and **El Torril,** where the bulls run during the festival. On the other side of town, a 1hr. walk from Calle Marca, lie the pre-Inca ruins of the **Huray** culture. For those interested in viewing the canyon from different angles, the **Mirador de Achachigua** is a 10min. walk west of the Cabanaconde, and the **Mirador de San Miguel** is a 20min. walk east of town. The tiny mountain village of **Petra,** Quechua for "one who brings sunshine," is a 40min. walk past Cabanaconde on the main road.

EL MISTI

Heading up toward the mountains, instead of down into the canyons, El Misti (5825m) towers conspicuously over Arequipa and is a popular two- to three-day climb. The summit affords spectacular views of Lake Salinas and Pichu Pichu, as well as the yellow sulfur bubbling in the crater below. The ascent is demanding, but can be undertaken by anyone in fair shape. Although El Misti is an active volcano, fear not—it has erupted only four times since 1454.

AT A GLANCE	
DISTANCE: 25km.	**TIME:** 2 days.
CLIMATE: Rain and snow usually make the hike impossible Feb.-Mar.	**ALTITUDE:** 3000-5800m.
	DIFFICULTY: Medium.
FEATURES: Views of nearby lakes and the volcano crater.	**FEES:** None.

🔢 PRACTICAL INFORMATION

Transportation: Buses to **Chiguata** leave from the intersection of Espinar and Sepúlveda, in the Miraflores district (45min., daily about every 30min.). Cars leave for the higher town of **Cachamarca,** saving about 30min. of climbing time. Inquire at travel agencies for departure times, which vary.

Accommodations: Be prepared to camp.

Maps: The best **map** of the region (US$12) is available from **Colca Trek** (p. 186).

Supplies: Pack warm clothes. The summit is icy, so bring an ice axe and crampons, which can be rented from **Colca Trek** (p. 186) or **Hostal La Reyna** (p. 178). 4x4 vehicles can be rented from **Colca Trek** and other agencies, US$55-85 per day.

Tours: The safest way to tackle El Misti is with a guide. **Colca Trek, Giardino,** and **Eco Tours** all offer 2-3 day treks. See **Guided Tours,** p. 186.

🥾 HIKING

There are three routes up El Misti, one of which is only easily accessed with a guide from an agency. The poor areas around the base of El Misti nearest to Arequipa can be dangerous even for groups, so consider beginning your ascent from the backside of the mountain (the Monte Blanc route begins there).

Miguel Grau: A little longer than the other 2 trails, the Miguel Grau route is usually undertaken in 3 days instead of 2. This is the only trail that can be reached via public transportation (see above). Start along the road to Chiguata and be sure to obtain a topography map from the Instituto Geográfico Militar in Lima or from Defensa Civil in Arequipa, and instructions from a guide at one of the trekking agencies, as the route is somewhat unclear.

Monte Blanc: This route, which begins at 4100m and curves around the northwest side of the volcano, is best done with a guide. The government requires hiking permits which guides will secure for you, and the trail head can only be reached in a 4x4 vehicle, which an agency will provide. The route through the Aguada Blanca is the least strenuous and can easily be done in 2 days (only 3hr. hiking the first day).

Pastores: This route, starting at Tres Cruces, also known as the Piedra Grande cemetery, is one of the most popular because it is relatively short, well traveled, and easily accessible. However, a 4×4 vehicle is necessary—in the town near the cemetery, hikers have been accosted.

VALLE DE LOS VOLCANES

More than 80 small **volcanic craters** (none of which measures more than 300m high) line the lunar landscape of this 65km valley. The craters are believed to be the cones of extinct fire-spewers that made up the legendary "Valle del Fuego," almost completely buried 2000 years ago under hardened lava from the nearby Volcán Coropuna. They can be visited on a multi-day trip with a tour from Arequipa or on your own from the town of **Andagua** (pop. 1000; also spelled "Andahua").

AT A GLANCE	
DISTANCE: 80km.	**TIME:** 1-3 days.
CLIMATE: Rain Dec.-Mar. makes paths difficult to navigate. Apr.-Dec. is generally sunny.	**ALTITUDE:** 3500-4000m.
	DIFFICULTY: Easy.
	FEES: None.
FEATURES: Volcanoes, craters, Antimarca ruins, Saquilay waterfall.	

🔋 PRACTICAL INFORMATION

Transportation: The hard way to get to Andagua is via the 5- to 7-day trek from Cabanaconde (p. 195). The easy way is by bus from Arequipa; Transportes Reyna sends daily buses from Arequipa to **Andagua** (10hr., 4pm, s/18). From Andagua, Valle de los Volcanes is a 1hr. walk.

Accommodations: There are no campsites in the Valle de los Volcanes, but there are several very basic hostels in Andagua.

Maps: Maps of the valley are nowhere to be found in Andagua, but you can purchase one at **Colca Trek** (p. 186) in Arequipa.

Supplies: No special supplies necessary, unless you plan to pitch a tent somewhere in the valley. All supplies can be rented or purchased from Arequipa agencies.

Tours: There are no standard tours to the valley offered by agencies in Arequipa, though you can visit the valley as part of a longer, 5- to 7-day Colca Canyon trekking tour (see **Colca Canyon,** p. 188). Tour agencies may also be willing to arrange personalized trips. Independent hikers can do daytrips of the valley using Andagua as a gateway (2hr. walk from Andagua to the valley).

🔋 HIKING

DAYHIKES. All hikes through the valley tend to follow the cattle paths that wind around the mountains; there are no specific trekking routes. A possible hike leading out of Andagua and through parts of the valley starts from the corner of the Plaza de Armas by Hostal Pucumarca and follows the road leading to the soccer field at the back of town. Upon reaching the soccer field, follow the cattle road leading from the far right corner, which will take you through the valley. Follow the road as it winds around the mountains to your left. Views of the **twin volcanoes** and the red-stained cliff of the Antimarca ruins in the distance will appear on your right. To return, turn around and follow the cattle road back to return to Andagua. Leaving from the other side of the plaza in Andagua, a 40min. walk along the road brings you to the ruins of **Antimarca.** Another 45min. in this direction leads you through the valley to the **Saquilay waterfall** and **lake.**

COTAHUASI CANYON

Colca Canyon may have all the publicity, but at 3354m deep, Cotahuasi narrowly beats it out for the title of deepest canyon in the world. Cotahuasi is difficult to reach, but as Colca becomes more touristy, people are making the longer trek in an effort to avoid the crowds. Because of its distance from Arequipa, it is necessary to spend the night in the town of Cotahuasi before beginning the descent into the canyon, unless you go on a tour from Arequipa (see **Guided Tours,** p. 186).

AT A GLANCE

DISTANCE: 80km.	**TIME:** 4-5 days.
CLIMATE: Rainy season Jan.-Mar.; dangerous to attempt hikes into the canyon during these months.	**ALTITUDE:** 2683-4900m.
	DIFFICULTY: Varies. All trekkers should be acclimated before exploring Cotahuasi.
FEATURES: 150m Sipia waterfall, Luichu hot springs, rock forest of Pampamarca Canyon, birds near Quincamayo, intersection point of 5 canyon rivers.	**FEES:** Camping is free everywhere in the canyon. No fees or permits are necessary.

🛈 PRACTICAL INFORMATION

Transportation: Transportes Reyna (☎ 43 0612), at the *terminal terrestre*, sends buses from Arequipa to the town of **Cotahausi**, continuing on to **Alca**.

Accommodations: The town of Cotahausi has several hostels with very basic accommodations for about s/20 per night.

Maps: Obtain maps of the area in Arequipa. **Colca Trek** (p. 186) has them for US$12.

Supplies: Tent for camping. 4x4 might be necessary for longer treks or if you plan to explore the nearby Canyon of Pampamarca.

Tours: There is no "standard package" for Cotahausi like there is for Colca Canyon—tours are tailored to individual groups.

4- TO 5-DAY HIKE. A 4- to 5-day tour of Cotahuasi led by a trekking agency in Arequipa uses the agency's private vehicles for transport. Tours generally include the Toro Muerto Petroglyphs, Laguna Payarcocha, the rock forest in Pampamarca Canyon or the exotic birds in Puica, and Peru's only dinosaur footprints.

DAYHIKE. The most popular hike (1-2 days) from the town of Cotahausi is down into the canyon to the waterfall of **Sipia.** Catch a colectivo or a taxi from town to the road that leads to the bridge (4hr. walk) for the Sipia waterfall, or take a taxi directly to the bridge. After crossing the first bridge, another 30min. hike leads down to a second hanging bridge. Walk another 1½hr. alongside the river to see the waterfall. Return along the same path to the campsites near the second bridge to camp for the night. If you choose the extended hike, **Day 2** begins with the 30min. walk back up to the first bridge. From there it's an 8hr. return along the road to Cotahuasi, although you might encounter cars heading back to town after crossing the upper bridge. Horses can be rented in Cotahuasi (about s/50 per day, includes guide); just ask around the shops in town. It is also common practice to hire a child in Cotahausi to guide you to the falls for a tip (about s/20).

CHIVAY ☎ 054

In Chivay (pop. 4052; 3633m), dogs lounge in the sun with apparently no cares in the world. In this place where the altitude almost matches the population, life is relaxed, despite its role as the capital of the Colca region, funneling tourists through its cobble-stoned streets to the more spectacular sites of Colca Canyon itself. However, with stunning scenery, opportunities for short hikes, and the **La Calera hot springs,** this town is not without its own charms.

✈ 🛈 ORIENTATION AND PRACTICAL INFORMATION

Tiny Chivay centers around the **Plaza de Armas,** where **buses** arrive and affordable restaurants and hostels congregate. **Transportes Reyna** (☎43 0612), on Grau, a block behind the market on the corner of the Plaza, sends buses from Arequipa to **Chivay** (4hr.; 2, 7, 11:45am; s/12), and from Chivay to **Cabanaconde** (3hr.; 5am, 10:30am, 3:30pm; s/3). Return buses to **Arequipa** (4hr.; noon, 3, 4:30pm; s/12) leave from the new terminal (☎53 1143), 4 blocks south of the Plaza de Armas. Information about the town and Colca Canyon is available from the **tourist police,** in the municipal building on the Plaza. (Open daily 24hr.) The **hospital,** Centro de Salud, is on the third block of Puente Inca in a bright blue building. (☎53 1074; open 24hr. for emergencies.) **Banco de la Nación** is also on the Plaza. The **post office** (☎53 1019) is inside La Pascana Restaurante on the corner of Puente Inca and Siglo XX. (Open daily 7am-9pm). Internet access can be found at **FOCS@net,** Calle Jose Caylloma 2nd block. (Open daily 8am-10:45pm; s/4 per hr.)

🍴 🛏 ACCOMMODATIONS AND FOOD

The quality of accommodations in Chivay is determined by the number of blankets, as nights are often below 0°C. **Hostal La Pascana ❷,** on the corner of Puente Inca and Siglo XX on the Plaza, features clean, rustic rooms around a pleasant courtyard. (☎53 1019; gromup@latinmail.com. Breakfast included. 24hr. hot water. Laundry service. Singles s/18; doubles s/26; triples s/39). **Hostal Anita ❷,** Plaza de Armas 607, offers simple rooms with hot baths. (☎53 1114. Singles s/18; doubles s/35; triples s/45; quads s/35.) **Pozo del Cielo ❺,** across the river on a hill overlooking the town, has adobe and dark-wood bungalows with incredible views of the canyon, as well as such priceless luxuries as heating. Watch your head—the old-school doorways force you to bow to the earth god before entering. (Continental breakfast included. Laundry. Singles US$45; doubles US$56; triples US$73. 10% discount for foreigners.) For food, **Casablanca ❷,** Plaza de Armas 705, is the oldest restaurant in Chivay and a prime choice for vegetarians, even though the house specialty is alpaca for two (s/36). (☎53 1093 or 53 1088. *Menú* s/13.50. Open daily 5am-11pm. MC/V.) **Lobo's Pub ❷,** (lobosbarcolca@terra.com.pe), Puente Inca 134, on the Plaza, specializes in brick-oven pizzas (s/10-24), a filling *menú* (s/8), and a long bar list. The hot cider and beer (s/8) are perfect for chilly Chivay nights. (lobosbar-colca@terra.com.pe. Open daily 9am-10pm. AmEx/V.)

👁 SIGHTS

The nearby **Calera hot springs** are Chivay's most popular (and relaxing) attraction. Heated by nearby volcanoes, the sulfuric springs are very warm (up to 45°C at midday, 39°C at night) and surprisingly clean. (Open daily 4:30am-7:30pm. s/10.) To get to the hot springs, catch a colectivo (5min., every 20min., s/0.50) or taxi (s/2.50) in front of the church. **Adventure Turismo,** Salaverry 117 (☎53 1073 or

53 1172; pedroscolca@hotmail.com) rents **mountain bikes** (US$10 for 3hr.), and offers a variety of tours including a full-day excursion to the **Pincholio geysers** on horseback (US$12) and trips to nearby towns, where life goes on much as it did hundreds of years ago (US$20-30).

CABANACONDE

A twisty 2hr. drive down the road from Chivay brings you to miniscule Cabanaconde (3287m), which serves as an ideal base for expeditions into the canyon. Unlike Chivay, it is within walking distance of **Cruz del Cóndor** (6km; 1½hr.), the main lookout point over Colca Canyon. There are many relaxing and scenic **hikes** from Cabanaconde, including a 10min. hike leading to a stunning view of Colca Canyon from the **Achachigua** *mirador*. Popular treks lead to the canyon bottom, where the **Sangalle oasis** (1 day), perfect for swimming, **Andagua** (5-7 days), and the spectacular **Valle de los Volcanes** (p. 192) await. For detailed hiking information, see **Colca Canyon,** p. 188. On July 14-18, the celebration of the Virgen del Carmen inspires dances, fiestas, and **bullfights** in the arena outside of town.

For information on how to get to Cabanaconde, see **Chivay,** above. Return **buses** leave from Cabanaconde's plaza for Arequipa (6hr., 5 per day 8am-9pm, s/15) via Chivay (2hr., s/3). There are a few basic accommodations offerings in Cabanaconde. **La Posada del Conde ❷** offers comfortable quarters with private hot baths and an adjoining restaurant. (☎44 0197. Singles US$8; matrimonials US$1. Prices rise during the festival.)

LAKE TITICACA

Lake Titicaca inspires epic legends, and it's easy to see why. At 3827m and extending across 8560km², it's the largest lake in South America and the largest in the world above 2000m. Traveling on its surface is like being on the open sea, except for the enormous peaks poking out of the horizon. The lake has 36 islands, not counting the floating ones made by the Uros people. Agencies herd tourists to the Uros Islands from June through August, but two more remote (natural) isles, Taquile and Amantaní, see fewer visitors and have managed to preserve centuries-old customs not witnessed anywhere else in Peru. On the Bolivian side of the lake, Isla del Sol and Isla de la Luna are the mythic birthplaces of the Sun and Moon (See **Titicaca: Cradle of Civilization**) and are usually visited from the port of Copacabana. The best time to visit the lake is just after the dry season,

THE LOCAL STORY

PERUVIAN HAT DANCE

At first glance, Yanque, the closest town to Chivay, seems fairly forgettable, but it has a few memorable quirks. Skeletons excavated from the area show that pre-Inca people here buried children under their homes as offerings to the earth god. Doorways here are tiny, forcing people to bow their heads and pay respect to the earth as they enter.

The really interesting bit of Yanque trivia, though, is that the town lies on the dividing line between two distinct cultures of the Colca Valley—in fact, the border runs right through the Plaza de Armas. To the east, the people wear wide, flat hats, and to the west, people wear rounded hats. In ancient times, the two groups actually deformed their heads to mark the difference, but the Spanish put a stop to that, and so locals resorted to hats instead. Even today, there is little mingling between the two peoples. The church, built in 1540, has segregated seating for residents of each side of town. At festival times, there is again little intermingling—dancing occurs in two groups, and often the groups compete with one another to see who can throw the best party.

To get to Yanque, take a taxi (s/8) from in front of the church in Chivay. Taxis returning to Chivay leave from the Plaza de Armas in Yanque.

TITICACA: CRADLE OF CIVILIZATION

In a time long before the Incas, the creator god Wiraccocha formed a world in shadow and populated it with clumsy giants. These huge people stumbled around in the dark, becoming more and more irritated, until they began to fight with one another. Wiraccocha erupted in anger, turning his large children to stone and flooding the world. In time, Wiraccocha's temper cooled and he decided to give this creation business another try, this time stumbling upon the notion of light. He directed the Sun and Moon and Stars to rise out of Lake Titicaca. (At the last minute, the Sun, envious of the Moon's light, scooped up a handful of ashes and cast them at the Moon, giving her a permanently dull complexion.) In time, Lake Titicaca would also spawn the first Inca and founder of Cusco, Manco Cápac.

In truth, a number of peoples preceded the Incas. The Aymara, descended from the Colla, Lupaca, and Tiahuanaco, once dominated the area. (The word "Titicaca" itself is Aymara for "gray puma.") The expansion of the Inca Empire in the 14th and 15th centuries brought Quechua customs to Titicaca, but never supplanted them. To this day, the Quechua and Aymara live apart— Quechua north of the lake and in the Peruvian highlands, Aymara in the south and into Bolivia.

September through November, when increased rainfall revives some of the lake's surrounding vegetation and clouds mitigate the nearly ceaseless sunshine.

JULIACA   ☎ 051

More of a business center and transportation hub than must-see tourist destination, frigid Juliaca offers very little for tourists to see or do, but is a necessary stop on the way to Puno (if flying from Lima) or the serene town of Lampa. Flying from Lima to Juliaca and then taking a bus to La Paz is the cheapest way to get between the two capitals. The town has adjusted well to its role as a conduit rather than a destination. Recently, the broken sidewalks have been repaired and the dirt roads are being paved, as Juliaca works to clean up its image.

If you're staying overnight in Juliaca to catch an early flight, the simple **Hostal Luquini ❸**, Bracesco 407, on Plaza Bolognesi, has firm mattresses, blankets, a nice airy courtyard, and not much else. Still, the clean, quiet rooms provide respite from the noisy Plaza. (☎ 32 1510. Singles s/15, with bath s/27; doubles s/30, with bath s/45; triples s/39, with bath s/50.) The locally recommended **Restaurant Trujillo ❸**, San Ramón 103, off Plaza Bolognesi, has a wide array of dishes—try the *lomo secado* (beef, s/13) in the bland but comfortable wood-paneled dining room. (☎ 32 1945. Entrees s/13-24. Open daily 7am-10pm.)

The cheapest way to get to Puno from **Manco Cápac airport**, 2km from Juliaca, is to take a taxi into Juliaca (s/8-10) and then a colectivo. **Nuevo Continente**, San Ramón 175 off Plaza Bolognesi (☎ 35 3004; open M-F 8am-noon and 2-6pm) has **flights** to Lima (2¼hr.; daily 8:55am, 2:45pm; US$64) via Arequipa (30min., US$34). **La Perú**, San Ramón 125, off Plaza Bolognesi (☎ 32 2228) offers flights to Lima (2hr., daily noon, US$74) via Arequipa (25min., US$50). **Ormeño**, San Martín 1230 (☎ 32 6994) has **buses** to: Arequipa (4hr., daily 4pm, s/25); Cusco (5hr., daily 4:30pm, s/25); Lima (18hr., daily 4pm, s/55). **Cruz del Sur**, Circunvalación 801 (☎ 32 2011) runs to Cusco (5hr., daily 3pm, s/20). **PeruRail**, Bolognesi 303 (☎ 32 1036; www.perurail.com) has **trains** to Cusco (9hr.; M, W, Sa 9:25am; tourist class US$17, first class US$119), departing from the train station in Plaza Bolognesi. **Colectivos** to Puno leave from Plaza Bolognesi at all hours (s/2).

All the main activity in Juliaca centers in Plaza Bolognesi, bordered by San Ramón, Mariano Nuñez, and Bracesco. You can change money and AmEx or Visa traveler's checks at the **Banco de Crédito**, Mariano Nuñez 136, off Plaza Bolognesi (☎ 32 1011, open M-F 9am-5pm, Sa 9am-noon.) Find **Internet** at **Eye**, 479 Bracesco, on Plaza Bolognesi. (☎ 32 4380. Open daily 9am-10pm. s/1.50 per hr.) The **police** (☎ 32 2793) are on Manuel Prado.

LAMPA
☎ 051

Affectionately and appropriately named the "pink city," Lampa, just 31km from Juliaca, is a charming little town whose sights and welcoming tranquility make for a worthwhile visit. Head straight to the Plaza de Armas and find the magnificent ◾**Santiago Apostle de Lampa Cathedral.** Built in 1695, this stone church has a beautiful, detailed facade, but the real highlight is inside, where you'll find a side chapel with walls covered in black Carrera marble. Here too, you will find a domed structure enclosing the grave of a prominent Lampa citizen with lines of skulls and bones—many from Spanish soldiers—covering the walls. The full hanging skeletons are a rare find anywhere in the world, but perhaps the most fascinating sight is the replica of Michelangelo's Pietà that sits atop the dome. This is so well done that when the original piece was damaged in Rome, restorators came to examine this statue. It is rumored that tunnels once connected Cusco to Lampa via the cold, dark catacombs downstairs. Though you may break into a cold sweat when the priest turns all the lights off on your tour, the dampness is actually the result of the lagoon located here during Inca times. If the cathedral is closed, proceed to the rectory to find a priest to guide you around (tip expected). After you're done at the church, head to the **Rampaq Museo,** Ugarte 472, where you will find artifacts from many of the southern pre-Inca cultures, including some basic tools. The prized piece here is a fascinating *kero* (a traditional cup) made of stone with intricate depictions of 16 Inca cosmological figures—the only *kero* of this type in the world. If the museum is closed, ask at the convenience store across the street to be let in. (Donations appreciated.)

If you take a while visiting the sights and need to spend the night, **Hospedaje Milam ❶** has clean, comfortable beds. Owner Edgardo Mendez Valdivia can arrange biking trips for groups of one to three that travel 110km to see a forest reserve, ancient ruins, and magnificent waterfalls. If interested, call at least a week in advance. (☎ 966 4187; hot water s/1.50; s/5-10 per person). Several nameless and nearly identical **restaurants ❶** serve up cheap eats (s/6-7.50) on Plaza Grau.

The Plaza de Armas is connected to Plaza Grau by the Cathedral. On Plaza Grau, head down Ugarte to find the rectory, museum, and hospital. **Colectivos** to Lampa (s/1) leave when full from Huáscar in Juliaca, next to the Mercado Santa Barbara. Colectivos to Juliaca leave when full from Tarapacá in Lampa (s/1).

PUNO
☎ 051

Referred to as the Folklore Capital of Peru, Puno (pop. 120,000) hosts a unique confluence of cultures: Aymara from the south and Quechua from the north. Though the Quechua originally named the city a "place of rest," Puno now hums with the sounds of bus drivers shouting their destinations, Quechua women enthusiastically selling their brilliantly colored crafts, and tricycle taxis careening around corners with heavy loads of tourists. Puno's lively cacophony and dusty streets contrast with its more famous (and placid) neighbor, Lake Titicaca. Puno is an excellent hub for excursions to the lake, home to many agencies that offer comprehensive and well-organized tours. Were it not for the persistent tourist agencies, Puno's self-concerned streets and late-night bars would give no hint of their proximity to such otherworldly peacefulness.

▐ TRANSPORTATION

Getting in and around Puno is easiest through one of the city's many tourist agencies, which can also handle border crossings to or from Bolivia.

Flights: The **airport** is 45km away in Juliaca (p. 196). "Aeropuerto" buses leave regularly along Tacna (45min., s/5-7) and tour agencies make trips to the airport. Most airlines have Puno offices. **Nuevo Continente,** Tacna 301 (☎ 36 7196; open M-F 8am-noon

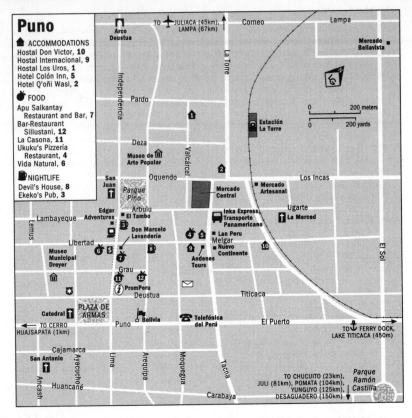

and 2-6pm) flies to **Lima** (2hr.; 8:30am, 2:45pm; US$65) via **Arequipa** (30min., US$40). **Lan Peru,** Tacna 299 (open M-F 8am-noon and 1-6pm) flies to **Lima** (2hr., noon, US$74) via **Arequipa** (30min., US$50).

Trains: Estación La Torre, La Torre 190 (☎35 1041). Open M and F 7-11am and 4-8pm, Tu-Th 7-11am and 2-6pm, Sa 7-10am, Su 4-7pm. Tickets sold 1 day in advance. **PeruRail** trains run to **Cusco** (10hr.; M, W-Th, Sa 8am; *turismo* US$17, *primera clase* US$119).

Buses: Buses to **Arequipa** and **Cusco** leave from the streets around Melgar. **Cruz del Sur,** on Tacna (☎38 2451; open 9am-9pm), runs to **Arequipa** (5hr., 3pm, s/30) and **Cusco** (6hr., 2pm, s/25). **Inka Express,** Tacna 314 (☎36 5654), runs to **Cusco** (8hr., daily 8am, US$20; includes lunch and stops at sites along the way). **Ormeño,** Titicaca 318 (☎35 2321; open 8am-10pm), runs to **Cusco** (6hr., 3:30pm, s/30) and **Lima** (19hr., 4pm, s/70) via **Arequipa** (5½hr., s/30). Many agencies arrange trips to **Copacabana** (3hr., s/15-25) with a border passport stop in **Yunguyo. Transporte Panamericano,** Tacna 245 (☎35 2001; tourpanamericano@hotmail.com; open daily 7am-5pm) has direct service to **La Paz, Bolivia** (4hr., 7:30am, s/20) and **Copacabana, Bolivia** (3hr., 7:30am, s/10-20), leaving from Av. del Sol.

Boats: Motorized *lanchas* leave regularly from Puerto Lacustre at the edge of town (taxi s/5, or a 15min. walk from the center) to **Amantaní** and **Taquile** (4hr., 7:30am, s/15) and **Los Uros** (1hr., 7:30am, s/10). Guided trips or overnight excursions to the two islands can be arranged through a tour agency or hotel and are the best way to visit. Unguided trips can be arranged with boat owners at the port, though a guide is recommended for overnight stays.

BORDER CROSSING: INTO BOLIVIA

When traveling with an agency, border crossing and money exchange are easily arranged. Daytrips to Bolivia from Peru are not an option, as all travelers crossing the border must stay for 24hr. before they are allowed back into Peru.

At Yunguyo: The most popular crossing between Peru and Bolivia, **Yunguyo** is en route to Copacabana. To get to Yunguyo from Puno, arrange a trip with one of the agencies along Tacna and Lima or take a taxi to the 14th block of Sol where you can catch an **omnibus** (departures all day, s/5). Buses drop their passengers off a few kilometers from the border, where a number of colectivos and taxis wait to shuttle individuals to the border (s/2). Both sides of the border are open 8:30am-7:30pm (though the agent may be asleep in the back). Customs officials in Kasani (on the Bolivian side) can only grant clearance for 30 days. Change money at the little stand outside the immigration office in Kasani, as banks in Copacabana do not buy soles, and rates at *casas de cambio* are unreliable. From Yunguyo, catch a colectivo for the short but bumpy ride to **Copacabana** (30min., Bs/3). There is little reason to stay overnight in Yunguyo, but if you do, **Residencial Isabel ❶,** San Francisco 110, on Grau at the corner of Plaza de Armas, has wood floors, firm beds, a public telephone, and clean rooms, even if the common bathrooms are a bit cramped. (☎85 6019. Singles s/10, with TV s/6; doubles s/20, with TV s/26.)

At Desaguadero: Those going directly to La Paz cross through Desaguadero. Desaguadero-bound omnibuses leave Puno all morning and early afternoon from the 14th block of Sol (2½hr., s/5). A cluster of people with individual tables, calculators, and piles of cash are prepared to change your money at very similar rates. At the bus stop from Puno, agencies on the Panamericana, across from the parking lot, send **buses** to many locations. **Ormeño,** Panamericana 319 (☎85 1157; open daily 8am-9pm) sends buses to **Lima** (20hr., 5pm, s/90-150) via **Puno** (3hr., s/15-25) and **Arequipa** (8hr., s/30-80). **Colectivos** to **Puno** and **Juliaca** are s/5. There is a customs office, Panamericana 302, near the parking lot, immediately before the bridge (open 8am-7pm). On the Bolivian side, colectivos run to La Paz (s/10-15). If you end up here overnight, **Hostal Corona ❶,** Panamericana 248, has a 70s-style common area with cable TV to compensate for basic rooms with rock-hard beds. (Hot shower s/2. Singles s/10, with bath s/16; doubles s/24, with bath s/35.)

✦🛈 ORIENTATION AND PRACTICAL INFORMATION

Lima, Puno's main pedestrian thoroughfare, is home to the bulk of the city's commercial activity. The center of town, along Lima, is marked by the **Plaza de Armas** at one end and the **Parque Pino,** five blocks away, at the other. Trains from Cusco drop their passengers on **La Torre,** four blocks from Lima, away from the lake. Buses stop along **Melgar,** which is perpendicular to Lima. **Lake Titicaca** is a 15min. walk from the center of town.

Tourist Office: PromPeru, Lima 549 (☎36 5088; iperupuno@promperu.goto.pe), on the corner of Deuste and Lima on the Plaza de Armas. The helpful, mostly Spanish-speaking staff provides **maps,** advice, and information on local festivals and transportation. Open daily 8:30am-7:30pm.

Tours: Andenes Tours, Tacna 300 (☎36 3383); **Edgar Adventures,** Lima 328 (☎35 3444); and **Misterios del Titicaca,** Teodoro Valcárcel 135 (☎36 7016; mystery@ec-red.com), offer tours to the **Taquile** and **Amantaní** islands (s/25-50), which include visits to Los Uros and accommodations Amantaní. **Andino Travel,** Teodoro Valcárcel 158 (☎36 8077; andinotravel@terra.com), gives lake tours with a mystical bent.

Consulate: Bolivia, Arequipa 120, 2nd fl. (☎35 1251). Visas available immediately. Open M-F 8:30am-5:30pm. Knock for emergencies if closed.

Currency Exchange: Banco Continental, Lima 402 (☎35 1080). Open M-F 9:15am-1pm and 4:30-6:30pm, Sa 9:30am-12:30pm. A number of **casas de cambio** on Lima are open mornings and afternoons and have low commissions for cashing traveler's checks and changing dollars.

ATM: The few that exist are located primarily along Lima. Try **Banco Continental** for Visa. **Interbank,** a few buildings to the left of Banco Continental, has an MC/V **ATM,** but it closes with the bank. Open M-F 9am-1pm and 4-6:15pm, Sa 9:15am-12:30pm.

Supermarket: El Tambo, Lima 361. Open M-Sa 9am-2pm and 3-11pm, Su 9am-5pm.

Laundromat: Don Marcelo Lavandería, Lima 427 (☎35 2444). Drop off clothes in the morning and they'll be ready the following afternoon. s/5 per kg. Open 24hr.

Police: Tourist police (☎35 3988), on the Plaza de Armas. Open 24hr.

Hospital: El Sol 1022 (☎35 3021 or 36 9696). Open 8am-6pm, 24hr. for emergencies.

Telephones: Public telephones are plentiful on Lima. **Telefónica del Perú** (☎36 6636), on Moquegua. Open daily 8am-6pm.

Internet Access: Numerous places line Lima and charge s/1-1.50 per hr. **SurNet,** Lima 378, has plenty of fast computers and a cheerful staff. Open daily 8am-11pm.

Post Office: Serpost, Moquegua 269 (☎/fax 35 1141). Open M-F 8am-8pm.

🛏 ACCOMMODATIONS

Even in the high season, Puno has more than enough room for visitors, ranging from four-star hotels to the most modest of hostels. When business is slow, hefty discounts are common. Rates jump (about s/10) during July and August.

■ **Hostal Don Victor,** Melgar 166 (☎36 6087), off Lima; 4 blocks down Libertad, which turns into Melgar. Bright, spacious rooms with large windows, thick blankets, clean bathrooms, TV, and 24hr. hot water. A rooftop deck provides sweeping views of the lake and town. Staff is eager to please, and the dapper Don Victor can be found strolling the grounds. Singles s/30; doubles s/50; triples s/65. Groups s/20 per person. ❸

Hotel Colón Inn, Tacna 290 (☎35 1432 or 35 7090; www.titicaca-peru.com). A well-kept *casa antigua* with beautiful dark wood molding. Visitors sip drinks in an interior garden or lounge in bed, relishing panoramic views of Puno and parts of the lake. Pizzeria, restaurant, bar, laundry service, and Internet access. Breakfast buffet included. All rooms have private, 24hr. gas-heated baths and security boxes. June-Nov. singles US$46; matrimonials and doubles US$54; triples US$70. Dec.-May singles US$39; matrimonials and doubles US$49; triples US$59. AmEx/MC/V. ❺

Hostal Los Uros, Teodoro Valcárcel 135 (☎35 2141), 1 block from La Torre. A bright stairwell leads to cozy rooms with comforters and fuzzy towels. Call ahead, since this popular hostel fills up during the high season (July-Aug.). 24hr. hot water. 24hr. emergency medic on call. Singles s/18, with bath s/21; matrimonials and doubles s/28, with bath s/34; triples s/42, with bath s/51. Traveler's checks accepted. ❷

Hostal Internacional, Libertad 161 (☎35 2109; h_internacional@latinmail.com), 2½ blocks from Lima. Comfy couches and persistently purple carpet soften any rough edges. Welcoming rooms with clean baths, cable TV, and 24hr. hot water. Small but growing multilingual book exchange. Singles s/45; matrimonials and doubles s/70. ❹

SOUTHERN HIGHLANDS

Hospedaje Q'oñi Wasi, La Torre 119 (☎36 5784; qoñiwasi@mundomail.net). Farther from the center of town, but right across from the train station. Wood-paneled walls and matching headboards give the finishing touch to this clean, well-lit hotel. Request a carpeted room for extra comfort. Owners speak English and French. Singles s/35; doubles s/25, with bath s/35. ❸

⬛ FOOD

Busy **Lima** has many overpriced restaurants, but there are some standouts, and vegetarians will find plenty of options around town, where meat and chicken take a backseat to pastas and fresh lake fish. In almost all restaurants, *trucha* (trout) and *pejerrey* (kingfish) are served zealously along with other Peruvian delicacies—daring visitors can sample some fine *alpaca*, while others thank their lucky stars for the plethora of Italian restaurants with brick-oven pizzas.

Apu Salkantay Restaurant and Bar, Lima 425 (☎36 3955). This island-style wooden shack houses one of the best dining options in Puno. Friendly staff serves a variety of hearty international dishes, with an emphasis on Italian cuisine, but the chef's special is a *saltado* made with alpaca (s/18). Large selection of coffees (s/5-8). Personal pizza s/10. Entrees s/12-18. Open daily 8am-10pm. ❷

La Casona, Lima 517 (☎35 1108; casona_peru@peru.com), off the Plaza de Armas. Serves up some of the freshest food in town—the fried *trucha* is especially good (s/18). Admire the wide range of antiques, or make friends with the tourists at the next table. Entrees s/10-20. Open daily 9am-10pm. DC/V. ❸

Vida Natural, Libertad 449 (☎36 6386), just off of Lima, away from the lake—follow the signs as you cross Libertad. In this vegetarians' paradise, food is carefully prepared and served by a certified nutritionist. Not for the hasty—cooking here is a (long) labor of love. Rice and soy patties s/9. Fresh juice s/4-5. Open M-F and Su 7:30am-8pm. ❷

Ukuku's Pizzería Restaurant, Libertad 216 (☎36 7373 or 36 9504). This popular establishment recently moved from Lima to a more subdued setting on Libertad, where it displays modern paintings of Puno's sights. Get comfortable, as the food takes a while to cook, but you can use the time to read the extensive multilingual menu, which includes fish, pasta, and brick-oven pizza. 3-course tourist *menú* s/12. Entrees s/8-16. Open Su-F 10am-10pm. ❶

Bar-Restaurant Sillustani, Arequipa 500. Thatched walls and romantically-lit interior allow for quiet conversation with the local crowd, away from the hubbub of Puno life. 2-course *menú* with tea is tasty, filling, and cheap (s/5). Open M-Sa 11am-1am. ❶

⬛ SIGHTS

Lake Titicaca—islands and excursions included—is Puno's greatest site, but there are others. The two-room **Museo Municipal Dreyer,** Conde de Lemus 289, across Deustua from the cathedral, houses a small collection of pre-Inca remains, including pots, jewelry, and some shockingly lifelike mummies. The museum also maintains a small collection of coins and documents from the Spanish colonial period. (Open M-Sa 7:30am-3:30pm. s/0.50.) The **Arco Deustua,** though a bit of a hike from the center of town, is worth its spot on the map. The arch, built in 1847, commemorates the heroes of battles at Junín and Ayacucho, while fantastic views and quiet rest spots make the walk truly worthwhile. To get there, head down Lima away from the Plaza. The **Cerro Huajsapata** has all the views plus pre-Hispanic history—this natural *mirador* includes a monument to the Inca Manco Cápac, who was born on the Isla del Sol in Lake Titicaca. Rumor has it that a series of tunnels under the hill leads all the way to Cusco.

SOUTHERN HIGHLANDS

⬛ NIGHTLIFE

The great lake isn't Puno's only allure. Those more interested in Saturday night fever than pre-Inca civilizations have plenty of opportunities to indulge. The pubs and clubs in Puno pick up early and go until all hours of the morning, celebrating rituals that would make the Incas blush. Tourist-oriented hotspots are all along Lima, while local bars await the adventurous foreigner on the outskirts. **Ekeko's Pub**, Lima 355, gives new meaning to *cuba libre*, serving free rum and coke during daily happy hour (8-10pm). This club-in-a-bar's-clothing has a balcony overlooking busy Lima. (Beer s/6. Drinks s/8-12. Open daily 5pm-5am.) **Devil's House**, Arequipa 405, one block away from Parque Pino, is a busy two-level tourist haunt. The candles and subtle lighting add intimacy to the bar. (Beer s/5; pitcher s/15. Drinks s/9-12. Open daily 7pm-3am.)

⬛ FESTIVALS

There are three major **festivals** unique to Puno. **Fiesta de la Virgen de la Candelaria** (Feb. 1-7) celebrates Puno's patron saint with spectacular traditional dance and dress. **Adoración del Sol** (June 21-23) is a religious celebration in which *brujas* (witches) from all over South America gather to perform traditional sun-worship dances all night to absorb the energy of the sun as it begins its decline into the coldest months of the year. It is also a celebration of the year to come, as the old year is symbolically sacrificed. **Semana de Puno** (Nov. 1-7), celebrates Puno's culture and people with daily parades put on by local high school and university students; it peaks on November 5.

⬛ DAYTRIPS FROM PUNO

⬛ JULI

It is possible to take a colectivo to Llave and then transfer to a Juli-bound combi, but recent unrest in Llave encourages most travelers to use a time-efficient private taxi (s/ 150-200), which includes stops at Pomata and Chucuito, or to take a Desaguadero-bound bus from El Sol (s/5) and ask to be dropped off at Juli. The second option involves more walking and waiting, but is much cheaper.

Juli is sometimes called "Pequeña Roma" (Little Rome) because of the hills around the town, the charming cafes, and the four old churches. Start off in the Plaza de Armas at the **Iglesia San Pedro**, by far the most well kept of all Juli's sights. This stone Dominican-built church has a beautiful brick dome and goldwork typical of Peruvian churches. (Open 7am-4pm.) As you leave the church, take a left and walk up Santa Cruz until you get to a dead end. Take a right and you'll see the pink **Iglesia Santa Cruz**, a completely abandoned Jesuit church. Bypass the sheep and push open the makeshift door, revealing a hauntingly beautiful interior. The roof has caved in, and bushes and small trees grow where the pews once stood. Some of the stonework details and Jesuit symbols are still visible. You may be tempted to stay awhile in this garden-like retreat, but make your way to the **Iglesia San Juan de Letrén,** one block off the Plaza de Armas on Junín. This church was abandoned much like Santa Cruz, but, unlike its neighbor, it has been somewhat protected from decay. Through the dim light, you'll see numbered objects strewn about—each and every piece has been thoroughly catalogued. Grand Italian-inspired paintings overwhelm the bland white walls, representing the religious experiences of Santa Teresa de

Ávila on the right and Saint John the Baptist on the left. The most impressive feature in this makeshift museum is the left nave, which showcases lively wooden sculptures depicting Christ being brought down off the cross. (Open 8am-5pm. s/3.) Finally, head to **Iglesia La Asunción,** a block away from the Plaza down Asunción. In addition to beautiful gold leaf and ornate detailing, this Dominican-built but Jesuit-occupied church claims to have the oldest pulpit in Peru. Each side nave reveals something about the area's religious history. When the church was founded in the 17th century, the area was dominated by Dominican friars, who left their mark on the left nave with paintings depicting their patron saints. When the Dominicans were expelled, the newly-arrived Jesuits decorated the right nave with their own portraits. Paintings on the central walls of the church are the work of Italian painter Bernado Vitti, a teacher who later inspired a great deal of Peruvian artists with his iconographic art. (Open 8am-5pm. s/3, includes guided tour in Spanish.) Before you leave Juli, notice the old house opposite San Pedro on the Plaza, known as "the prison" for its no-nonsense windows.

SILLUSTANI

The best way to see Sillustani is with a tour agency, which will pick you up at your hostel. Tours usually leave around 2:30pm and return to Puno by 6pm (s/15). They include a guided tour of the ruins (usually in Spanish and English), and in most cases, a stop at a local family's house. Alternatively, to save a few soles, take a colectivo bound for Juliaca (s/1.50) and ask to be let off at the Sillustani fork, but given the irregular schedule of transportation between the fork and Sillustani, this form of transportation is not recommended. Entrance fee s/5.

Sillustani, 34km north of Puno, is a peninsula jutting into the Laguna Umayu, a salt lake surrounded by the stark *altiplano* (plateau; see **Cry Me a River**). It was a sacred burial site of the Colla people, who constructed numerous stone tombs, called **chullpas,** in which whole families were buried with their riches. Cylindrical, square, and trapezoidal *chullpas* exhibit various stages of wear-and-tear; in some, the carved outer walls have crumbled to reveal the rougher inner layer. The path culminates at the lizard-adorned **Chullpa de Largato,** perhaps the most magnificent funerary tower. Today, Sillustani's *chamán* (shaman) performs an annual ceremony in the temple by the tombs, during which a pregnant llama is sacrificed and the fetus extracted to symbolize hope for future agricultural fertility.

THE LOCAL STORY

CRY ME A RIVER

If you look left as you pass the entrance to Sillustani, you'll notice an island in the Laguna Umayu. Today, this island is a nature reserve, home to llamas looked after by a family living in the brightly-colored house. Legend has it, though, that this hill was once a plateau where the palace of Kawillaca stood, overlooking a prosperous Inca settlement. Kawillaca, a powerful leader, had a loyal slave called Sinchi Roca whom he liked so much that he promised to give him whatever he desired after he completed a certain amount of work. Sinchi Roca, who had became infatuated with Kawillaca's daughter, Ururi, worked day and night to claim his promise from Kawillaca and marry the princess. Kawillaca was so upset when Sinchi Roca asked for his daughter's hand that he added one condition: Sinchi Roca must take the dangerous path to the North to fetch a certain flower. A worried Ururi cried for days, and finally the news came that Sinchi Roca had died. Not long after, Ururi died as well. The gods decided to punish Kawillaca's cruelty by flooding the town with Ururi's tears. Umayu was completely covered with water except for what remains today—an island. To this day, the water around the island tastes salty, an anomaly in this high-altitude freshwater region.

To visit Umayu, inquire at the entrance to Sillustani.

CHUCUITO

To get to Chucuito, take a tricycle taxi to Acora (s/1), where colectivos leave regularly for Chucuito (20min., s/1). A taxi from Puno will take you straight there (s/20-30). At Chucuito, walk down from the Plaza and turn left at the church. Look for the fenced area. Open 7am-7pm. Children will act as guides for a sol or two. Free.

Chucuito, 18km south of Puno, is a small Aymara village. Aside from two colonial churches and a nearby fish farm, Chucuito is the proud site of the **Inca Uyo,** a pre-Columbian fertility temple housing some 80 stone carvings that shock visitors with their detail of the male anatomy—the fact that children serve as guides is all the more disturbing. Legend holds that women would sit atop the stones to increase their chance of having a male baby. Many discerning observers consider the Inca Uyo a fake. Several other Inca ruins feature large erect stones, possibly with phallic significance, but never with the kind of verisimilitude seen at Chucuito. Furthermore, the Spanish settled the area in the 17th century, and likely would not have left such a temple intact. Even structures never seen by Spanish eyes—Machu Picchu for instance—don't look as complete as the Uyo. Nevertheless, locals take it quite seriously.

POMATA

Pomata is about 20min. from Juli by bus or taxi. The church is on the Plaza de Armas, about a 10min. walk up the hill from the highway. Open 8-5pm. Free.

The **Iglesia de Santiago de Romita** is Pomata's one and only sight, but what a sight it is. The pink church, whose first stone was laid in 1566, was occupied by the Dominicans until the mid-18th century. Most of the beautiful stonework, such as the magnificent facade, was done by indigenous people. Thin slabs of rose-colored marble inserted in the windows create a soft, tranquil light. Look closely at the altar—if you only see a white sheet, step to the left until you find the door to a staircase that leads to a small private chapel housing the cedar statue of the **Virgen del Rosario de Pomata.** Many of the paintings around the church show some of the miracles attributed to the statue.

LOS UROS

Tour agencies charge around s/15 for a guided tour of 2 of the 45 little islands that make up Los Uros. Tours leave around 9am and rarely last more than 2hr. Be sure to bring sunscreen, as sunlight is extreme on the islands. For a longer daytrip, a visit to Los Uros can also be combined with a trip to Isla Taquile. Tours covering Los Uros and Taquile (s/25) leave around 8am and return to Puno around 4pm.

Centuries ago, the Uros people lived along the shores of Titicaca. Faced with the gradual infiltration of the Aymara and later the Incas, the Uros saw only one means of cultural preservation: they isolated themselves by constructing islands out of the **totora reeds** that grow in the lake. Today, 32 islands still float in a cluster just a 30min. motorboat ride from Puno. The inhabitants build everything out of *totora*—houses, boats, souvenirs for tourists—and must continually stack more reeds on the surface of the islands as old reeds rot underneath. During wet season (Oct.-Feb.), this process takes place at least once, sometimes twice, a week. In the dry season, it is done about twice a month. Walking across an island is an eerie experience—the surface sinks slightly under each step.

While some Uros people still depend on the ancestral practice of fishing, their language and other aspects of their cultural heritage have essentially vanished due to intermarriage with the Aymara. Today, tourism is their major source of income. Twenty of the islands have arranged deals with tour agencies in Puno and subsist on the daily traffic of tourists who are shipped in and out within 30min., creating a strange kind of mutual exploitation in which toddlers "innocently" pose for tourist photos, then demand s/1, while adults hawk cheap souvenirs they couldn't have made on the island—such as ceramics where there is no earth. You can take a ride on a *totora* reed boat (s/3), but it's mostly a tourist gimmick, as locals use motorboats to get around. Most of the islands have small "museums" that consist of collections of stuffed birds native to Lake Titicaca. Bring small change, as islanders won't change large bills.

ISLAS TAQUILE AND AMANTANÍ

*The island of Taquile can be seen as a daytrip from Puno, but it is best seen in one of the excellently organized 2-day packages (s/50) that include 3 meals (lunch and dinner the first day, breakfast the second) as well as lodging with a family on Amantaní. Tours leave Puno around 8:30am, feature a brief stop in Los Uros, and then head to Amantaní, arriving around 2pm. They move on to Taquile (30min.) the next morning at 8am. Tours return to Puno by 4pm. Give yourself time to get acclimated before you attempt a tour, as the 20min. hike up Isla Taquile will seem a lot longer if you don't. See **Tours**, p. 200.*

ISLA TAQUILE. This small island (pop. 2000) is far enough from the shore that it has maintained a good deal of authenticity, though it has more restaurants and amenities than Amantaní. People on Taquile still speak Quechua, and some other ancient traditions have resisted the wear of time. Women wear brightly colored skirts called **polleras** and cover themselves with black headscarves, a practice instituted by the conquistadors. Men don **chullos,** floppy woolen caps indicating the marital status of the wearer—unmarried males wear caps that are red on the bottom and white on top, with the tips folded to one of the sides, while married men wear caps of solid red, with the tips folded to the back.

Taquileños support themselves with the sale of exquisitely crafted **textiles.** All around the island, women spin wool using the drop-spool method, while men do all of the knitting. During high season (June-Aug.), islanders set up stands in the Plaza de Armas to sell fine scarves, hats, belts, and gloves, and all earnings are pooled. Local women meet incoming boats to offer tourists a place to stay, but will either keep quiet or whisper their response when spoken to. Most locals speak some Spanish. Bring some small coins, as pictures with locals are never free. **Accommodations ❷** with local families tend to have no running water or electricity. If you'll be staying on the island, bring a flashlight and warm clothing or a sleeping bag. Families generally charge around s/15 for lodging and a bit more for meals; it is also customary to bring a gift of fruit to the family. Islanders are chiefly vegetarian, but a slew of restaurants will prepare seafood dishes—the **municipality-run restaurant ❷** serves excellent *pejerrey* (fish) with soup and tea (s/10).

ISLA AMANTANÍ. Amantaní (pop. 4500), the third-largest island on Lake Titicaca, is even more pristine than Taquile, though it has cut into Taquile's share of tourism. Also Quechua-speaking, Amantaní possesses its own set of customs, more strongly influenced by Aymara ancestry than those of Taquile. The residents are divided into eight distinct communities of adobe houses, separated by stone walls. Socio-politically, the island uses a kind of communalism, alternating the farming and harvesting responsibilities among communities.

Amantaní is nearly paradisiacal. Red and turquoise houses dot the rocky terrain, while eucalyptus trees watch over the expansive lake—the location will take your breath away, if the thin air hasn't already. The island is dominated by two hills, each crowned with a temple. The taller hill is devoted to the **Pachatata** (Father Earth) and the shorter to **Pachamama** (Mother Earth). No one is allowed to enter either temple except on the annual feast day (Jan. 20), when the island's population splits in two, each half gathering at its own temple. One representative from each hill runs a race from the summits to a point between them—if Mother Earth wins, the harvest will be a success; otherwise, the coming yield will be scarce. For some reason, the Pachamama side always seems to win. The hike up both hills follows a path created by Inca ancestors, under intact stone archways and over centuries-old agricultural terraces. Don't lose yourself in the views, however; night moves in quickly and the descent should not be attempted in the dark. As in Taquile, **accommodations ❷** are arranged by local families and cost about s/15; visitors should come with a gift. Few restaurants exist, so be prepared to eat whatever your family prepares. Islanders often invite their guests to participate in nightly dance shows, especially during the high tourist season.

COPACABANA, BOLIVIA   ☎ 28

Between its ancient Aymara heritage and the (relatively) recent European influx, Copacabana has developed its own unique culture. Cafes teem with local hipsters, permanent visitors, and those just passing through. Most tourists spend their time between Plaza Sucre and the lake, while locals congregate around Plaza 2 de Febrero. Still, most find themselves paralyzed by the overwhelming beauty of Titicaca's setting sun and the city's chill attitude, inspired by the lake's peacefulness.

1 SOL = 2.33 BOLIVIANOS	1 BOLIVIANO = 0.43 SOLES

BOLIVIANO (BS)		
	AUS$1 = 5.67 BOLIVIANOS	1 BOLIVIANO = AUS$0.18
	CDN$1 = 6.07 BOLIVIANOS	1 BOLIVIANO = CDN$0.16
	EUR€1 = 9.80 BOLIVIANOS	1 BOLIVIANO = EUR€0.10
	NZ$1 = 5.27 BOLIVIANOS	1 BOLIVIANO = NZ$0.19
	UK£1 = 14.5 BOLIVIANOS	1 BOLIVIANO = UK£0.07
	US$1 = 7.94 BOLIVIANOS	1 BOLIVIANO = US$0.13

◤ TRANSPORTATION

Buses: All buses to **Puno** leave from Plaza Sucre at 1:30pm. **Trans Tur** (☎62 2233; copacabana_bolivia@hotmail.com), on Plaza 2 de Febrero, opposite the cathedral. Open daily 7am-7pm. To **La Paz** (3½hr.; daily 8am; Tu 3, 6:30pm; W 10, 11:30am, 3, 5, 6:15pm; Su 3, 5, 6pm; Bs14). Make reservations 1 day in advance, though last minute tickets are sometimes available. **Grace Tours** (☎62 2160), on 16 de Julio, next to Hotel Colonial. Open daily 6:30am-6:30pm. To: **Cusco** (15hr., 1:30pm, Bs80); **La Paz** (3½hr., 1:30pm, Bs20); **Puno** (3½hr., 1:30pm, Bs15). **Colectivos** to the border (Bs2) leave when full from Plaza Sucre.

▰✳ ❼ ORIENTATION AND PRACTICAL INFORMATION

Lake Titicaca marks Copacabana's western border. **6 de Agosto** leads uphill from the lake to **Plaza Sucre** and, after a few more blocks, **Plaza 2 de Febrero.** Most accommodations and services cluster around these landmarks. Buses and colectivos drop passengers off along 16 de Julio or 6 de Agosto, near Plaza Sucre. Street numbers are rare, but Copacabana is small enough that you won't get too lost.

Tourist Office: On Plaza 2 de Febrero, across from the cathedral. Open M, W-Su 9am-noon and 2-6pm.

Tours: Grace Tours (see **Buses,** above) offers a variety of packages for seeing the islands off Copacabana, including half-day trips to Isla del Sol (Bs15) and full-day trips to both Isla del Sol and Isla de la Luna (Bs25). City tours (Bs20).

Currency Exchange: Banco Unión (☎62 2323), on 6 de Agosto. US$2 commission for up to US$200 in AmEx traveler's checks. MC/V. Open Tu-F 8am-6pm, Sa 9am-1:30pm, Su 8:30am-noon. **Cooperativa Multiactiva Virgen de Copacabana L.T.D.A.** (☎62 2116), on 6 de Agosto next to the Hotel Playa Azul, exchanges traveler's checks (1% commission). Open M-F 9am-1pm and 2:30-6:30pm, Sa-Su 9am-1pm. MC/V. You can also exchange soles around Plaza Sucre, but rates are less reliable.

ATM: There are no ATMs in town, and the bank has limited hours on weekends, so plan ahead. If you're in a bind, many of the stores that line 6 de Agosto will advance you money on a credit card for a 15% commission.

Emergency: ☎110.

Police: On Plaza 2 de Febrero, across from the cathedral.

Pharmacy: Pharmacies are harder to come by in Bolivia than in Peru, so stock up in Puno. There is one in Copacabana, **Farmacia,** on Conde de Lemos, just off 2 de Febrero, to the right of the cathedral.

Hospital: Off Felix Rosa Tejada. ☎118.

Telephones: ENTEL (☎62 2331), on Murillo, just left of the cathedral. Open daily 8am-1:30pm and 2:30-8pm.

Internet Access: Alf@-internet, 6 de Agosto, next to Hotel Colonial. Bs14per hr. Open daily 10am-10pm.

Post Office: On Plaza 2 de Febrero. **Western Union** service. Open Tu-Sa 9am-noon and 2:30-6pm, Su 9am-3pm.

PHONE CODE	The country phone code for Bolivia is ☎591.

ACCOMMODATIONS

Nearly every block of Copacabana boasts a high-flying sign for an *alojamiento*, *residencial*, or *hostal*. There are always beds, though overcrowding can be a problem, especially for some bigger hotels and on holidays. Rooms are cheaper and have more amenities than those in Puno—the only thing lacking is television, but with so many attractions nearby, who needs it?

▨ **Hotel Colonial** (☎62 2270; www.titicacabolivia.com), on 16 de Julio at 6 de Agosto. This colonial hotel right off Plaza Sucre has a plethora of rooms with stunning lake views—be sure to request one. Wood floors and large everything: rooms, beds, windows, bath. Breakfast included. 24hr. hot water. Singles Bs35; doubles Bs60; triples Bs90. ❷

▨ **Alojamiento Emperador,** Murillo 235 (☎62 2083). Walking away from the lake on 6 de Agosto, turn right at the far end of the cathedral onto Murillo. Step through the colorful open hallway into the airy yellow courtyard and find a veritable paradise for the do-it-yourself backpacker. Rooms are clean and the rooftop terrace is an ideal place for relaxing. Well-stocked kitchen. Laundry service (Bs7 per kg). Luggage storage. Singles Bs10, with bath Bs15; doubles Bs20, with bath Bs25. ❶

▨ **Chasqui de Oro** (☎62 2343), on the beach; turn left at the end of 6 de Agosto and walk about 10min., nearly to the end of the beach. Decadent and majestic, this mini-resort has up-close-and-personal views of the lake in addition to its 35 gigantic rooms, huge private baths, TVs, and a wonderful plush patio. Singles US$10; doubles US$20. ❸

Hostal Brisas del Titikaka (☎62 2178; hbrisastiticaca@hotmail.com), at the lakeside end of 6 de Agosto. One sweet triple has lake views, a private bath with 24hr. hot water, and a balcony; independent travelers will have to settle for the viewless, mid-sized rooms with common bath. Internet access (Bs15 per hr). Singles Bs35; doubles Bs70; triples Bs105. 10% HI discount. ❷

SOUTHERN HIGHLANDS

Residencial Copacabana, Oruro 555 (☎62 2220), 2 blocks down Jáuregui from Plaza 2 de Febrero. Open hallway around a glass atrium leads to bright and tranquil, if small, rooms. Clean common baths. Friendly staff can arrange transportation. Singles Bs15, with bath Bs20; doubles Bs30, with bath Bs35. ❶

Hotel Gloria, 16 de Julio 3 (☎62 2094; www.hotelgloriabolivia.com). Think yellow. Bright, clean, and panoramic, though you'll pay a pretty penny for a room with a view. In the game room, ping-pongers take periodic breaks to watch the sun set on the lake before showering in their private baths and retiring to their large, soft beds to watch TV. Paneled windows keep rooms warm. Laundry (Bs8 per kg). Viewless singles US$23; doubles US$29; triples US$36. MC/V. ❺

Hotel Utama (☎62 2013), 3 blocks from Plaza 2 de Febrero, on Perez. Terra cotta stairs lead to comfy rooms with thick beds and interesting landscape murals that make up for the lack of lake views. Sparkling clean bath. Book exchange and free water bottle upon arrival. Singles US$5; doubles US$10. 10% ISIC discount. ❷

Ambassador Hotel (☎62 2216), on Plaza Sucre at Jáuregui, in a proudly orange building. Rooms with hardwood floors surround a central patio. Bath in every room; TV in most. Breakfast included. Laundry service (Bs10 per kg). Singles Bs50; doubles Bs95; triples Bs120. Cards on the front desk provide 10% discount. ❸

Residencial Sucre, Murillo 228 (☎62 2080); take a right past the cathedral. Small, cozy rooms encircle a checkered courtyard. 24hr. hot water and color TVs. Breakfast included. Laundry (Bs8 per kg). Singles Bs35; doubles Bs70. ❷

🄵 FOOD

Copacabana offers a wide range of food, from falafel to fresh *trucha* (trout), a regional specialty. Stands on the beach serve the catch of the day, fried or lightly grilled—**Kiosk 11** ❶ is quite good (fish Bs10). Find fresh fruit at the **market,** off 2 de Febrero on Jáuregui. Many restaurants double as hangout spots after dark.

Restaurant Colonial (☎62 2160), at 6 de Agosto and 16 de Julio. Specializes in fish and outdoor relaxation—only the hungry hordes could interrupt the peaceful setting. Go for the chairs carved out of tree stumps. Entrees Bs20-28. Open daily 7am-11pm. ❷

Pacha Café (☎62 2206), on 6 de Agosto between Plazas 2 de Febrero and Sucre. Jungle is the theme in this intimate, candlelit restaurant. Wooden vines run along the walls and over the chairs. Charming courtyard and small book exchange. Delicious brick oven pizza (Bs35) and *trucha tomatada* (Bs20). Open daily 7:30am-11pm. ❷

Mankha Uta, on 6 de Agosto, toward the lake. A multimedia eating experience with live music at 8pm followed by a movie. For more sedate revelers, the roomy patio is perfect for stargazing. Look out for the diverse and cheap *menús,* including vegetarian. Bs20-22. Open daily 7am-midnight. ❷

Restaurant Vegetariano Flores, on 6 de Agosto across from Residencial Flores. This airy restaurant serves local dishes with a vegetarian twist. Patriotic tablecloths display the colors of the Bolivian flag. Omelettes Bs15. Pizza Bs30. MC/V. ❷

🄶 SIGHTS

> ❗ The area around Copacabana is not particularly well lit, and a path that's slippery or hard to find during the day will only prove more trouble after sunset. When visiting sights in the area, allow time to return before dark.

COPACABANA CATHEDRAL. In the 16th century, Franciscan missionaries forced most of Copacabana's population to convert to Catholicism. One man in particular, Francisco Yupanqui, took their lessons to heart and built a statue of the Virgin

Mary with a baby Jesus in her arms. Unfortunately, the Franciscans did not approve of his likeness—both mother and child looked Aymara—and they ordered the artist to destroy his blasphemous creation. But Yupanqui was convinced that his people needed an image in which they could truly believe, so rather than start over, he covered his statue with a layer of gold and decorated it with elaborate religious images. The missionaries welcomed the new statue and built a church to house it. In time, legends sprung up about the statue's healing powers, and the church drew worshipers from around the region. On the left side of the cathedral is a small sanctuary where worshipers come to light candles (which can be purchased outside the cathedral) in honor of the Virgen de Candelaria. A small museum presents a variety of religious artifacts and a well-kept garden. (*On 2 de Febrero, in the center of town. Open daily 6:45am-9pm. Museum open M and W-F 9am-noon and 2:30-5:30pm; Sa-Su and for festivals 8am-noon and 2:30-6pm. Tours for groups of 8 or more M-F 11am, noon, 2, 6pm; Sa 8am, noon, 2, 6pm.*)

HORCA DEL INCA. Copacabana's most prized misnomer, this figure confused the Spanish conquerors, who mistook the hilltop stone construction (shaped like a capital "H") for a gallows (*horca*). While the name has stuck, today the truth is known about Intiwatana, as the Incas called it: it is a sophisticated astronomical observatory constructed in 1700 BC. On June 21, the sun's rays pass through a series of holes and land on the Horca, marking the southern hemisphere's winter solstice, which served as the Inca new year. If the sun's rays shine on the correct area of the Horca, citizens of Copacabana celebrate the coming of a prosperous harvest; if the rays hit a dark crevice, Copacabana must begin to prepare for a barren crop—the site's caretaker can point out the significant spots. Some other large stones at the site indicate the four cardinal directions; still others (again with the help of the sun) remind people when the leap year is upon them. The view alone makes the trip worthwhile. (*Start facing the entrance to the cathedral and take Murillo out of town; when you reach a fork where the dirt paths diverge, head straight and uphill (30-40min.). Follow the arrows painted on rocks to the top. Bs10.*)

BAÑO DEL INCA. Some 1500 years ago, the Huayna Cápac community of the Inca Empire established a summer residence in Kusijata, now a tiny town in the hills of the *altiplano*. There, they tunneled 300m into the side of the mountain and tapped into a deep spring so that all members of the community could enjoy the water's mythic properties of renewal. The water flows out from the mountain and into a pipe that deposits it in a basin some few feet down the hill. Although the water is considered sweet and healing outside the mountain, once inside the basin below, it is deemed dirty and only fit for washing clothes. Trekkers find shade under the Spanish-imported eucalyptus and pine trees, but the real prize for visitors are the stunning views of the lake's farthest recesses, shared only with the occasional bemused gaze of a passing llama. In addition, a small museum holds the mummified evidence of an early Inca cesarean section. (*Follow Hugo Ballivián out of town, where it leads into a dirt path that crosses an expanse of farmland (1hr.). Ask locals for directions once out of town, since the path zigzags. The museum, in Kusijata, is on the hill in front of you, a white building tucked inside a stand of eucalyptus. If the door to the fountain is closed, just knock and a tour guide will soon appear. Bs5.*)

CERRO CALVARIO. The 14 large crosses marking the steep trek up to Cerro Calvario were constructed in 1946 with a dual purpose. The crosses were dedicated to prominent members of the Copacabana community, and also symbolized Jesus's journey to crucifixion at Calvary. Some visitors leave stones at the bases of the crosses as a testament to their faith, and although such devotions are not required, these **stations of the cross** allow excuses to stop, breathe, and watch Copacabana shrink into the shadow of the hill. On Sundays and holidays, worshipers scale the hill, purchase miniatures (including cars, houses, bags of food, laundry detergent, and more) at a merchant stand, and then sacrifice them at individual altars scattered around the park in the hopes of earning life-sized versions. Tourists perform this ritual all week long. *(The path up Cerro Calvario begins behind the Capilla del Señor de la Cruz de Colquepata, a church at the top of Bolívar.)*

INTIKALA (TRIBUNAL DEL INCA). The best one can do to understand the mysterious tribunal's purpose is to look at its Inca name, Intikala. "Inti" means sun and "kala" means rock, and if you spend an hour here on a late afternoon, you'll see a lot of both. There are seven rocks from the Inca era with what appear to be seats carved out of them, indicating that the site was probably some a sanctuary. *(From 2 de Febrero, go 2 blocks behind the cathedral on Hugo Ballivián and take a left. The site is 2 blocks up the hill, to the left of the church.)*

■ NIGHTLIFE

Don't jump out of bed the first, second, or 50th time you hear a loud bang in the night—most likely it's just a group of kids experimenting with their never-ending supply of firecrackers. Nightlife in Copacabana is alive and well, with a distinctly European flavor. Rather than questionable dance floor antics, most of the action takes places in candlelit restaurants filled with comfortable chairs and couches, board games, and espresso. **Café Bar Sol y Luna,** 16 de Julio 3, an annex of the Hotel Gloria, is the coolest spot in town, sporting lots of soft chairs, couches, a wide range of coffees (Bs4-9), delicious hot chocolate (Bs6-8), and cocktails (Bs25). There is also a digital cable feed and satellite TV, a book exchange, board games, music on request, and an English-speaking staff. (☎62 2094; open daily 6pm-late.) **Alf@-internet,** 6 de Agosto, next to the Hotel Colonial, is a general hipster hangout in the guise of an Internet cafe. After you've checked your email, enjoy the other amenities, including a wide selection of movies (Bs3 per person) and a pool table. (Open daily 10am-10pm, although closing times vary.)

■ HIKING NEAR COPACABANA: COPACABANA PENINSULA

HIKE	DISTANCE	TIME	ALTITUDE	DIFFICULTY
Isla del Sol	17km	4-5hr.	3800-4000m	Easy

As European as the town of Copacabana has become, its surrounding farmland, where *campesinos* make their living, remains frozen in time. The 4hr. trek down the Copacabana Peninsula brings hikers little more than a stone's throw away from the south end of Isla del Sol. Bring sunblock, snacks, and water or a means to purify it. Start walking out of Copacabana on Junín, then follow the dirt road that runs along the lake to **Sicuani** (3½hr.) and **Yampupata** (4-5hr.). At the strait, catch a boat to **Isla del Sol** (motorboats, sailboats, and rowboats Bs25-60). Return tickets from Isla del Sol can be purchased aboard boats leaving in the afternoon from the dock below **Escalera del Inca.**

ISLA DEL SOL, BOLIVIA

Few would guess from the currently humble lifestyle on Isla del Sol that both Manco Cápac and Mama Ocllo, who together founded the Inca Empire, were born on these rocky shores. Today, Isla del Sol is home to more than 5000 people spread out over five communities, and paths through its rocky hills afford spectacular views of Bolivia's distant snowy peaks.

⚑⚐ TRANSPORTATION AND PRACTICAL INFORMATION. Tour agencies in Copacabana offer a variety of packages to Isla del Sol. Options include half-day trips to the south end of the island (8:15am-12:30pm, Bs15) and full-day trips (8:15am-6pm, Bs26) which begin at the north end (10am) and pick you up for the return journey at the south end (4pm). There are full-day packages that include both Isla del Sol and Isla de la Luna (8:15am-6pm, Bs25), but these can be rushed, and often spend most of the day on the water. An agency mini-bus will pick you up at your hotel in the morning free of charge. Most hotel owners can make reservations. Alternatively, you can walk to the end of the Copacabana Peninsula to Yampupata and take a short boat ride to the south end of the island on your own.

⚑⚐ ACCOMMODATIONS AND FOOD. Accommodations at Isla del Sol don't have phone numbers, so make sure there are rooms available before you let the boat back to Copacabana sail into the sunset, especially June-August. The best accommodations lie on the south end of the island, though many lack running water and electricity (candles are provided, but bring a flashlight just in case). There are a few **restaurants** in town, but don't expect much variety. The small village of **Challa,** just over halfway to the north end of the island, has limited accommodations offerings. A 30-40min. walk brings you to **Challapampa,** which has a few restaurants serving breakfast and lunch. Unofficial campsites lie on the rocky shores around Challa, Challapampa, Palacio del Inca, and the western beaches.

◙ SIGHTS. The biggest attraction on Isla del Sol is the awe-inspiring **hike** from one end to the other, but there are several routes by which one can walk the length of the island. Of the two most trodden (3-3½hr. each), one follows the ridge of hills that stretches across the island, allowing for constant panoramic views of Lake Titicaca; the other treads a variable, lung-testing path on the eastern side of the island. Tour groups encourage you to take the easier, panoramic route—it's tough to make it to the boat on time if you don't. **Sheep** and their herders have carved less popular paths all over the mountain—these wind in and out of every bay and allow hikers to explore ever more rustic scenery, but require up to 6hr. to navigate. If you select one of these routes, be certain to bring water. The most common island hike runs north to south, as most hotels and restaurants are located at the southern end, making it a nicer destination than starting point.

The north's main attraction is **Palacio del Inca,** on an isthmus. This intricate network of crumbling stone rooms and 4ft. doorways provides entertainment and access to a sandy beach on the western shore. (40min., cut across the buildings to the beach, cross it, and follow the available path. Entrance fee Bs10.) If you're lucky, you might spot the **Titicaca Rock,** a gray boulder that looks like a puma when viewed from the north. **Museo Marka Pampa** houses a small collection of ruins that date back to the time of the developing Inca Empire. (Bs10, includes visit to Palacio del Inca.) On the southern edge of the island, **Escalera del Inca** is a steep stone staircase that runs from the collection of hotels and restaurants above to the main southern port below. Going down can be quite treacherous, as you must contend with loose gravel, uneven rocks, and scores of pack mules. **Fuente del Inca** is the main source of water on the island and emerges as a little waterfall in the southern port. **Templo del Sol** (Bs10) lies south of the southern commercial center. Tour groups leaving the southern port usually stop at the temple for a 30min. exploration before returning to the boat for the return to Copacabana.

For those who want to spend a full day on the lake without having to hike the length of Isla del Sol, package deals including Isla de la Luna are the best option, though they leave little time for exploration.

SOUTHERN HIGHLANDS

ISLAS SURIQUI AND KALUATA, BOLIVIA

The island community of **Suriqui,** about 35min. from the small town of Huatajata, remains true to its roots. A small entourage will most likely be waiting on the landing to show you miniature versions of **totora reed boats,** Suriqui's claim to fame. In the first half of the 20th century, Norwegian scientist Thor Heyerdahl decided to use the skills of the Suriqui people to prove his theory that ancient people of South America could have reached the Pacific Islands by means of small handmade boats still used on Lake Titicaca. A short visit to the **Centro Cultural** explains the tedious method used to create the narrow boats that are used for fishing and for collecting reeds to repair waterlogged boats.

Another 20min. from Suriqui sits **Kaluata** ("Stone House"), an island speckled with 700-year-old Aymara remains. The intricate stonework still amazes architects. Set back from the shore, the homes were constructed solely from stone; even the roof is composed of overlapping rocks. The roofs are slowly succumbing to the elements, however, and only a few remain. The Aymara who live on the other side of the island graze animals here, but refuse to enter these mysterious homes for fear of being sucked in by the same spirit forces that caused their ancestors' disappearance centuries ago. The intrigue deepens toward the center of the island where, in the hollow of the valley, barely identifiable remnants of a temple once led to an extensive tunnel. No destination or exit has ever been found, although many explorers have disappeared deep within. As a result, the entrance was blocked by stones and is now grown over. Still, local legend has it that the power of the ancient pathway is so great that those wandering too close when the heat of the midday sun strikes may be captured by the ancient inhabitants.

Buses en route to La Paz from Copacabana pass through Huatajata, from which hotel and restaurant owners can shuttle visitors to and from the islands in motorboats. Visiting both islands takes about 3hr.

TIAHUANACO, BOLIVIA

The ruins of Tiahuanaco (Tiwanaku) provide an extensive history lesson about the barren *altiplano* and fodder for archaeological, historical, pseudo-historical, occult, science fiction, and conspiracy theories of every kind—for example, some claim that the city was built by extraterrestrials, others that it is the lost city of Atlantis. The Tiahuanaco Empire (2500 BC to AD 1172) stretched through what are now Bolivia, Peru, Chile, and Argentina before mysteriously disappearing. Present-day *campesinos* living near the ruins are trying to emulate the Tiahuanaco agricultural system that once fed eight million people, about the population of modern-day Bolivia. From the ticket office, the first building you'll see as you enter the complex has exhibits in Spanish about the ancient culture's history, cosmology, and ways of life. You'll also see the **Ponce Stellae,** or Monolito Ponce—the exact significance of this figure remains unknown, but he is holding a *kero,* or ceremonial, cup. Continue on to the **Museo Regional de Tiahuanuco,** which displays relics of the great empire, including tools, elongated skulls (probably a status symbol), and a mummy in the fetal position. Outside, the ruins themselves represent three levels of the Tiahuanuco religious framework: **Pirámide de Akapana** was probably a religious temple that honored the mighty surrounding mountains. Scientists estimate that it stood 18m tall, but today it is almost completely buried. Distinctive stone heads emerge from the walls of the **Templete Semisubterráneo,** a large quadrangular temple, while a stone map of the Tiahuanuco region hides in **Kantat Hallita,** another semi-underground temple. Different theories attempt to explain the jutting heads—one claims that they represent the heads of defeated enemies, while another asserts that they are heads of all the nations of the world with whom the empire had contact when crossing the ocean in reed boats. **Kalasaya,** an enormous open-air temple, houses detailed structures that suggest that it served as an agricultural calendar. Three stone statues—**Monolito Ponce, Monolito Fraile,** and **Puerta del Sol**—probably played important roles in measuring time. Hundreds of religious designs decorate the stone floor of **Putuni,** also known as the Palacio de Los Sarcófagos (Palace of the Sarcophagi). Finally, the wondrous massive stones of **Pumapunku,** some weighing up to 130 tons, cover the site. Where they came from and how anyone moved them remains a mystery. (Open daily 8am-5pm. Bs25.)

Most travelers explore this site on their way to La Paz. From Desaguadero, take a La Paz-bound **combi** and ask to be dropped off at Tiahuanaco (Bs6)—3 massive pillars mark the entrance. Follow the pink stones all the way to the museum (about a 10-15min. walk). To get back to Desaguadero, flag down a westward-bound combi (1hr., Bs5).

CUSCO AND THE SACRED VALLEY

Inca Manco Cápac founded Cusco around AD 1100, back when his people were just one of many small Andean groups vying for control of the region. Things changed in 1438, when the soon-to-be ninth Inca Pachakuteq defeated the fierce Chanca people (a military wing of the Huari), opening the way for a massive expansion of the empire. Cusco ("Qosqo" in Quechua) became the hub of Inca Peru, the building grounds of great palaces and temples, and an administrative and religious center. Today, the name "Cusco" applies to both the city and the surrounding Sacred Valley, which includes the glorious ruins of Machu Picchu, the fascinating ancient military and agricultural sites near Pisac, and the rushing waterways of Ollantaytambo. As in Inca times, the Cusco region revolves around the city—only now, the connection is based on a thriving tourist industry. But the undeniable comforts of Cusco (the city) should not dissuade anyone from spending time in Cusco (the region).

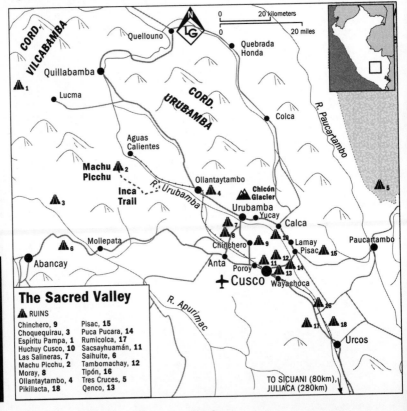

The Sacred Valley

RUINS

Chinchero, 9
Choquequirau, 3
Espíritu Pampa, 1
Huchuy Cusco, 10
Las Salineras, 7
Machu Picchu, 2
Moray, 8
Ollantaytambo, 4
Pisac, 15

Pisac, 15
Puca Pucara, 14
Rumicolca, 17
Sacsayhuamán, 11
Saihuite, 6
Tambomachay, 12
Tipón, 16
Tres Cruces, 5
Qenco, 13

Exploring the serene Sacred Valley allows visitors to observe a lifestyle that the hustle and bustle of tourism still hasn't distorted (for the most part). The term "Sacred Valley" refers to the area around the Río Urubamba (known in Quechua as the Vilcanota), which flows northeast from Cusco. With its rolling, maize-resplendent hills, the Urubamba Valley was the breadbasket of imperial Cusco, particularly after Inca engineers solved the region's landslide problem by constructing agricultural terraces. These steps, a few meters in width and height, were sculpted from the earth and retained by stone walls; thousands still exist. Another remarkable Inca achievement was the redirection of the Río Urubamba—the ancients straightened the waters near Pisac to allow for more efficient crop irrigation. The result of this labor was the longest pre-Columbian canal in the Americas. Furthermore, the Incas left a valley replete with structures that would be considered architectural masterpieces in any age: the fortresses of Pisac and Ollantaytambo and the sprawling city of Machu Picchu, among many others. It's no wonder that inhabitants of the Sacred Valley continue to take pride in their Inca heritage.

HIGHLIGHTS OF CUSCO AND THE SACRED VALLEY

DEVOUR a gourmet meal at one of Cusco's chic **restaurants** (p. 226) before you boogie with other backpackers at one of the city's **clubs** (p. 241).

RIDE the wind as you **paraglide** above the Sacred Valley (p. 244), or explore on **horseback** (p. 244).

GAZE upon the city's red rooftops from awe-inspiring **Sacsayhuamán** (p. 245).

CONQUER the **Inca Trail** (p. 260), an enchanting pilgrimage to the sacred Inca city of **Machu Picchu** (p. 266) and one of the best treks in South America.

CUSCO
☎ **084**

Cusco (pop. 300,000; 3400m) strikes a tricky balance between authentic and touristy Peruvian culture. Travelers, especially young backpackers, flock to Cusco, and the city has responded to them: trendy restaurants, Andean craft stores, Internet cafes, and the hottest discos this side of Lima litter the urban center. Meanwhile, the remnants of Inca and Spanish cultures coincide harmoniously: majestic colonial churches stand beside indigenous artisan studios, and rainbow-colored flags of the Inca Empire fly over the rooftops along modern *plazoletas*. This city, like the paint on its walls, is vibrant and ever-changing. It's a town made for people: green benches in calm plazas invite visitors to sit and relax as they enjoy the view of the mountains; curious strangers in busy cafes bring newcomers into friendly conversation; and narrow, winding streets heading off into the distance entice travelers to explore. A short walk away from the central Plaza de Armas leads to goats and llamas wandering through the streets, friends chattering away in Quechua, s/3 meals, and beautiful mountain views. Though Cusco's largest tourist attraction is nearby Machu Picchu, a traveler can spend weeks just exploring the area within the city limits. Tourists and locals alike love this city, a thriving blend of cultures nestled deep within the towering Andes.

⌐ TRANSPORTATION

Airport: Aeropuerto Alejandro Velasco Astete (☎22 2611), in the southeastern part of the city. Take a colectivo marked "Aeropuerto" along Sol (s/0.50). Taxi s/10. International departure tax s/25; national departure tax s/12. Open daily 5am-3pm.

TO SACSAYHUAMÁN (2km),
QENKO (3km), PUCA PUCARA (6km),
TAMBOMACHAY (7km)

0   200 meters

0   200 yards

N
LG

Choqechaka

Atoqsayk'uchi

Carmen Alto

2

Pumacurco

Ladrillos

1

3

South
American
Explorers

17

Don Bosco

Amauta
Spanish
School

San
Cristóbal

Arco Iris

Ese

Don Bosco

Kiskapata

Huaynapata

Ataúd

Purgatorio

Culebras

12

Coricalle

Teqsiqocha

Thesqalda

Suecia

9

11 PLAZA DE
NAZAREÑAS

13

10

14

Palacio

Hatunrumiy

Amargura

Saphi

26

27

Tourist
Police

28 29 31
30

Tigre

Procuradores

PLAZA
TRICENTENARIO

SEE PLAZA DE ARMAS
DETAIL MAP p. 224

15

16

Herales

Tambo de Montero

Santa
Teresa

Plateros

Andean
Travel Tours

32

Tucumán

La Catedral

Sunturwasi (Triunfo)

34

Sta. Catalina Ana

Santa Teresa

Panes

Carnes

PLAZA DE
ARMAS

Western
Union

Sta. Catalina

Qhapchikijlla

35

Siete Cuartones

40

Espaderos

Confitería

Comercio

Compañía

Caritos

Sta. Catalina Angosta

49

Meloc

38

Teatro Granada

42 43 44
41

San Juan de Dios

PLAZA
REGOCIJO
(COSIPATA)

Pt. Espinar

Medio

Mantas

La
Compañía

Intik'ijlla (Loreto)

iPerú, Tourist
Ticket Office

Arones

Garcilaso

45

Jerusalén

46

Heladeros

Academia Mayor
de la Lengua Quechua

ATM

Nueva Alta

39

Tordo

Márquez

Municipal
Office

La Merced

Rx

El Sol

San Bernardo

47

Almagro

Interbank

Nueva Baja

Ceniza

La Ibérica

PLAZA SAN
FRANCISCO

Mesón de la Estrella

Teatro
Municipal

Quara

San Andrés

Desamparados

San
Francisco

Ayacucho

Carmen Quilcoc

Unión

Santa Clara

Concebidayoc

Matará

Chaparro

Santa Clara

Cruz Verde

Excel
Language
Center

Teqte

Baja

San Pedro

Túpac Amaru

Nueva

Pera

Estación
San Pedro

Qascaparo

Mercado
Central

Belén

Lechugal

Tres Cruces de Oro

Pavitos

Clínica
Paredes

Cusco

SAN BLAS

TO PISAC, AMIGOS SPANISH SCHOOL (3blk)

ACCOMMODATIONS
Amaru Hostal, **20**
Casa Hospedaje Sumaq T'ikaq, **6**
El Condado San Agustín I, **51**
Hospedaje 250, **44**
Hospedaje Latino América, **1**
Hospedaje Magnolia II, **55**
Hospedaje Royal Frankenstein, **43**
Hospedaje Sambleño, **5**
Hospedaje San Blas II, **3**
Hostal Plateros, **32**
Hostal Qori Inti, **48**
Hostal Resbalosa, **9**
Hostal Tullumayo, **25**
Hostal Tumi, **40**
Hotel California, **39**
Hotel Royal Qosqo, **28**
Hotel Suecia II, **26**
Koyllur, **24**
Niños Hotel, **38**

FOOD
Al Grano, **37**
Café Cultural Ritual, **17**
El Sol, **29**
Greens, **7**
Jack's, **18**
Kin Taro, **46**
La Granja Heidi, **19**
Los Perros, **27**
Los Toldos Chicken, **47**
Macondo, **21**
MAP Café, **13**
Narguila, **30**
Pacha Papa, **23**
Tupananchis, **22**

CAFÉS
El Arbolito, **53**
Moni, **50**
π Centro, **2**
Sweet Temptation, **34**

MUSEUMS
Convento de Santa Catalina, **49**
Museo de Arte Contemporáneo, **14**
Museo de Arte Precolombino, **12**
Museo de Arte Religioso, **16**
Museo Histórico Regional, **45**
Museo Inka, **10**
Qorikancha and Iglesia de Santo Domingo, **52**

ENTERTAINMENT
Movie Net Cafe, **33**
Sunset Video Cafe, **31**

NIGHTLIFE
Fallen Angel, **11**
Fanáticos Pub, **35**
Jaguiga Bar Snooker, **42**
Mandela's Bar, **15**
The Muse, **8**
Rosie O'Grady's, **36**
Tangible Myth, **41**
Tierra del Sol, **4**

SHOPPING
Centro Artesanal Cusco, **54**

Pashaqpakana
Tandapata
Suyt'uqatu
K'urkurpata
PLAZOLETA SAN BLAS
San Blas
Carmen Bajo
Siete Ventanas
Chiwampata
Recoleta
Rulnas
Sta. Mónica
Tullumayo
Cabrakancha
San Agustín
Maruri
Romeritos
Abracitos
Pampa del Castillo
Zetas
Av. de la Cultura
Huáscar
Intiqawarina
Awaqpinta
US
Tullumayo
Mercado Wanchaq
Manco Inka
ATM
ATM
Colectivos to Aeropuerto
Buses to Urubamba
El Sol
Pantipata
Garcilaso
Garcilaso
Centro Q'osqo
DHL
Historia del Cusco
Garcilaso
Mango Chapaq
Puente Rosario
Kuychipunku
Pardo
Pachacutec
World Courier de Perú
San Miguel
Grau
Centenario
Pardo
FedEx
Regional

TO CLÍNICA PARDO (300m), HOSPITAL REGIONAL (1km), TERMINAL SANTIAGO (1.5km)

TO CLÍNICA AMERICANA (1blk)

Estación Huanchac

TO TOWER OF PACHAKUTEQ (.5km), TERMINAL TERRESTRE (1km), (4km)

CUSCO AND THE SACRED VALLEY

Nuevo Continente, Portal de Carnes 254 (☎24 3031), on the Plaza de Armas. Open M-Sa 9am-12:30pm and 2:30-6:30pm, Su 9am-2pm. Flies to: **Arequipa** (40min., daily 11:35am, US$34); **Lima** (1hr.; daily 7:30, 7:40, 11am, 12:45pm; US$69); **Puerto Maldonado** (30min., daily 10:45am, US$34).

Lan Peru, Sol 627B (☎25 5552; cuscooficina@lanperu.com.pe). Open M-F 8:30am-7pm, Sa 8:30am-6pm, Su 9am-noon. Flies to: **Arequipa** (50min., daily 9:05am, US$44); **Juliaca** (1hr., daily 9:05am, US$90); **Lima** (70min.; daily 7:45, 9:15am, 12:50, 4:30pm; US$80); **Puerto Maldonado** (50min.; Tu, Th, Sa 11:20am; US$44).

Lloyd Aero Boliviano (LAB), Santa Catalina Angosta 160 (☎22 2990). Open M-F 9am-7pm, Sa 9am-noon. Flies to **La Paz** (50min.; Tu and Sa 10am; US$98).

Taca, Sol 602B (☎24 9921; gtacuz@grupotaca.com). Open M-Sa 8am-8pm, Su 9am-2pm. Flies to **Lima** (70min.; Tu, F, Su 6:15am; US$63).

TANS, San Agustín 315 (☎24 2727; www.tansperu.com.pe). Open M-F 9am-6:30pm, Sa 9am-3:30pm, Su 9am-noon. Flies to **Lima** (1hr.; daily 7:30am, 12:30pm; US$74) and **Puerto Maldonado** (30min., daily 10:30am, US$55).

Trains: Reservations for all trains should be made at least 1 day in advance, especially June-Sept. (☎23 8722 or 22 1992; www.perurail.com).

Estación Huanchac (☎23 3593), on Pachacutec, off Sol. Ticket window open M-F 7am-5pm, Sa-Su 7am-noon. Trains leave from Huanchac to **Puno** (10½hr.; M, Tu, F, Sa 8am; *Inka First Class* one-way US$90, *Backpacker* one-way US$15).

Estación San Pedro (☎22 4552). From the Plaza de Armas, walk 7 blocks along Mantas, which becomes Márquez, then Santa Clara, then San Pedro. Ticket window open daily 5-9am. Tourists are no longer allowed on the local train to **Machu Picchu.** Tourist trains go to **Machu Picchu** (4hr.; *Vistadome* 6am, US$45 each way; *Backpacker* 6:15 and 6:35am, one-way US$35, round-trip US$60). Trains leave from San Pedro, but tickets must be purchased at Huanchac.

Buses:

Terminal terrestre, several kilometers southeast of the city center on Alameda Pachakuteq. Walk down Sol to the Pachakuteq monument, bear left past the rotary, and take the 1st right past the railroad tracks (30min.). Taxi s/3. Many bus companies offer competitive prices; walk into the station to see what's being offered that day, as times and prices change frequently. Buses to: **Abancay** (5hr.; 6, 8am, 1, 8pm; s/10-15); **Arequipa** (11hr., 8 per day, s/20-30); **Ayacucho** (24hr.; 6, 7am, 7pm; s/25); **La Paz** (15hr., every other day 10:30pm, s/80); **Lima** (22-24hr.; 2, 3, 4, 5pm; s/50-100); **Puno** (6-8hr., M-F every 30min. 7am-10pm, s/10-30); **Tacna** (20hr., M-F 4pm, s/60).

Puente Rosario, 5 blocks down Sol from the Plaza, on the right. Sends buses to **Urubamba** (1½hr., every 15min. 5am-7pm, s/3) via **Chinchero** (35min.).

Puputi sends buses to **Pisac** (50min., every 15min. 7am-7pm, s/2.50) via **Tambomachay** (30min., s/1.50). Follow Recoleta out of the city, make a right on Puputi, and follow it downhill 1½ blocks; the station will be on your left.

Terminal Santiago, on Antonio Corena. Take a cab, as the terminal is hard to find and not in the safest neighborhood (s/2 from the Plaza de Armas). Sends buses to **Quillabamba** (8hr.; M-F 3 and 4pm, Sa-Su 8am; s/15-25).

Taxis: Taxis surround the Plaza de Armas. From town, to the bus terminal s/3; to the airport s/10. Within the city center s/2, after dusk s/3. Slightly more expensive (s/5) when called ahead (☎22 2222).

Colectivos: Run along Sol, Pardo, and Tullumayo. s/0.50.

Taxis in Cusco don't have running meters, so be sure to agree on a price before departing for your destination. Always take official taxis, marked by black and yellow checkerboards on the sides of the car and polygonal yellow stickers on the windshield. Imposters can be misleading, overpriced, and dangerous.

ORIENTATION

Cusco revolves around the **Plaza de Armas.** From the Plaza's right-hand corner (facing downhill), Cusco's main avenue, **Sol,** runs toward the post office, bus terminal, Huanchac train station, and airport. **Procuradores** and **Plateros** head uphill from the Plaza de Armas and are filled with hostels, restaurants, Internet cafes, and tour companies. The streets behind the cathedral lead uphill from the Plaza to the steep, cobblestoned hills of **San Blas,** brimming with artisan shops and hip places to grab a bite. The tranquil **San Cristóbal** neighborhood, to the north of the Plaza, sits at the top of the stairs known as **Resbalosa.**

The Plaza itself is full of places to explore, eat, and relax. **Portales** (niches) are on each side of the Plaza. As you face the cathedral, in front of you and to the left is the **Portal de Carnes,** home of some of the Plaza's more trendy restaurants and clubs. To the left are **Portal de Harinas** (adjacent to Carnes) and **Portal de Panes,** with gift shops, pizzerias, and grills. Behind you are **Portal de Confituría** and **Portal de Comercio,** the touristy side of the Plaza, filled with tour agencies, *casas de cambio,* and small stores hawking cheap textiles and memorabilia. To your right (and adjacent to Comercio) is **Portal de la Compañía,** virtually empty except for a few interesting signs and occasional graffiti. Next to the Portal de la Compañía is **Portal de Carrizos,** with an expensive pizzeria and high-end luxury-item stores selling jewelry and quality textiles. In front and to the right is **Portal de Belén,** containing a few more restaurants and a supermarket.

TIP **BUT I THOUGHT THIS STREET WAS CALLED...** Cusco's streets can go from charming to frustrating if you don't understand the quirks of the naming system. A significant number of Cusco's streets are known both by their Spanish names and their Quechua ones; the meaning of the words is usually the same. Often there is no standard spelling for Quechua names—Huaynapata, for example, is sometimes written Waynapata. Also, any one street may undergo a name change as it runs between different neighborhoods.

PRACTICAL INFORMATION

TOURIST AND FINANCIAL SERVICES

Tourist Offices:

Municipal Office, Mantas 177A (☎22 2032), near the Plaza de Armas. Provides **maps** of Cusco, the Sacred Valley, and the Inca Trail. The office overflows with information about the surrounding sights and areas as well as safety advisories. Friendly staff will help with just about anything. The office also displays advertisements and local arts and crafts. **Tourist tickets** are sold 9am-noon and 3-5pm. English spoken. Open M-F 8am-7pm, Sa 8am-2:30pm.

iPerú, Sol 103, inside the Galerías Turísticas (☎25 2974; www.peru.org.pe). Maintains a 24hr. tourist information and assistance hotline (☎574 8000). Its office provides comprehensive city guides for Cusco and surrounding areas. You can also file complaints here if you are a victim of fraud. English spoken. Open daily 8:30am-7:30pm.

South American Explorers (SAE), Choquechaka 188, 4th fl. (☎24 5484; www.saexplorers.org), up Sunturwasi from the Plaza de Armas, left on Choquechaka; the office is on the right. An incredibly useful resource for English-speaking travelers, SAE provides recommendation lists, trip reports, bulletin boards, luggage storage, safety-deposit boxes, library, book exchange, updates on train schedules, a large collection of guidebooks, fieldbooks, maps, and insider advice. Membership: individual US$50, dual US$80, volunteer US$35; student discount available. English spoken. Open M-F 9:30am-5pm, Sa 9:30am-1pm. Extended hours during high season (June-Aug.) Tu-Th 9:30am-7:30pm.

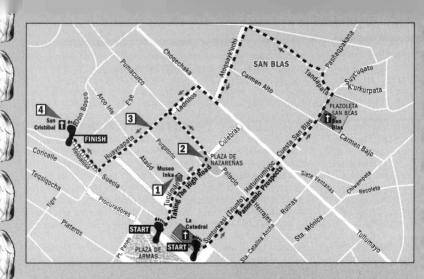

Cusco is the tourist center of Peru, and it can be tough for visitors to find a place free of foreign faces and English translations. Even locals hesitate when asked the question, "Where is the *real* Cusco, without tourists?" Well, here's what we found.

START: Plaza de Armas.

FINISH: San Cristóbal.

DISTANCE: <1km

DURATION: 1½-4hr.

WHEN TO GO: Any time

1 MUSEO INKA. Follow Cuesta del Almirante (a.k.a. Tucumán) up from the Plaza de Armas (it's the road to the left of the Cathedral when facing it). The Museo Inka provides visitors with a foundational knowledge of Cusqueñan history (see **Museums,** p. 234).

2 PLAZA DE NAZAREÑAS. Follow the road up to Plaza de Nazareñas. Avant-garde and refined, this is by far Cusco's classiest *plazoleta*, hosting the city's best art museum (**Museo de Arte Precolombiano,** p. 235), best restaurant/nightclub (**Fallen Angel,** p. 239), and best hotel (the one and only, five-star **Mirador**). The benches here provide solitude and respite from street peddlers.

3 HUAYNAPATA. Take Palacio up to Huaynapata, turn left, and walk up Huaynapata. The hike may be painful, but it is also peaceful and scenic. The only traffic on the road will be a few stray dogs, and the only noise a few high-school kids playing basketball. Meanwhile, you'll be able to gaze down upon the Plaza de Armas and the cathedral.

4 SAN CRISTÓBAL. Take the steep steps of Resbalosa uphill and turn around once you get to the top—the view from here is one of the city's best. Here's your chance to check out Iglesia San Cristóbal—or, if you've still got energy left in you, you can follow the road farther uphill toward the ruins of Sacsayhuamán.

ALTERNATIVE ROUTE: PANORAMIC PROSPECTS. If the Andes have whet your appetite for sublime vistas, consider taking this route instead: From the Plaza de Armas, walk up Sunturwasi (a.k.a. Triunfo) until you reach the Plazoleta San Blas. Turn left on Tandapata, then left on the pedestrian walkway Atoqsayk'uchi. Take a right on Choqechaka and a quick left on Ladrillos, joining the walking tour above at Huaynapata.

Tourist Ticket Executive Office, Sol 103 (☎22 7037). Open M-F 8am-6pm, Sa 8:30am-12:30pm.

Tours: Tranvía de Cusco, Parque Industrial G1 (☎22 3840; tinticusco@hotmail.com), on Huanchác, operates trolley tours (30min.) of the city's major sites. Tours leave from the Portal de Confitería on the Plaza de Armas. Adults s/7, students s/5, children and seniors free. For tours outside the city, see **Guided Tours from Cusco,** p. 241.

Consulates: UK: Urbanización Magisterial, 2nd fl. G5 (☎22 5571; brit-emb@terra.com.pe). Open M-F 9am-1pm and 3-6pm, Sa 9am-1pm. **US:** Tullumayo 125 (☎22 4112; consagentcuzco@terra.com.pe), inside the Instituto Cultural Peruana Norteamericano (ICPNA). Open M-F 8:30am-noon and 3-5pm, Sa 9am-noon.

Currency Exchange: Banks cluster 2 blocks down Sol from the Plaza de Armas. The walkways around the Plaza de Armas and along Sol harbor **casas de cambio.** Beware of false notes from the *cambios,* and never change money on the street. **Interbank,** Sol 380, at Puluchapata (☎23 2501), exchanges US dollars and euros, and cashes Visa and AmEx traveler's checks. Open M-F 9am-6:15pm, Sa 9:15am-12:15pm.

ATMs: Interbank, Sol 380, at Puluchapata, and **Banco de Crédito,** Sol 189, at Almagro. Both have 24hr. ATMs accepting all major cards. ATMs can also be found in many places around the Plaza de Armas, including **Gatos Market.**

Western Union: Santa Catalina Ancha 311 (☎24 8028). Open M-F 9am-7pm, Sa 9am-5pm.

American Express: Portal de Panes 123, of. 307 (☎08 005 0732), on the Plaza de Armas. Open M-F 9am-6pm, Sa 9am-1pm.

Language Schools: There are legions of language courses in Cusco, many of which combine language learning with homestays, sightseeing, and other activities. See **Alternatives to Tourism: Language Schools,** p. 90.

Other Alternatives to Tourism: Ecological and community development projects abound. See **Alternatives to Tourism,** p. 81.

LOCAL SERVICES

 Most businesses in Cusco close for lunch sometime between 12:30 and 4pm.

Outdoor Equipment: Shoe stores along Márquez between Heladeros and Plaza San Francisco sell hiking boots (s/139-390). For bicycle rentals, see **Guided Tours from Cusco** (p. 241). You can satisfy every other outdoor need at one of the following agencies; most rental companies do not accept credit cards.

Tatoo Outdoors & Travel, Plaza de Nazareñas 211 (☎24 5314). Enormous selection of outdoor clothing and gear, including major brand names. Prices in US dollars.

Quechua Campi, Procuradores 338 (☎80 7912). Small but well stocked. Sleeping bags (US$1-3 or s/4-10 per day), backpacks (US$1.50 or s/5 per day), tent (US$2-3 or s/7-10 per day), ponchos (US$1 or s/3.50 per day), binoculars (US$1 or s/3.50 per day).

Andean Travel Experts, Plateros 341 (☎24 4355). Inexpensive, quality rentals: sleeping bags (US$1.50 or s/5 per day), backpacks (US$1.50 or s/5 per day), tents (US$2 or s/8 per day), ponchos (s/3-4 per day). Open daily 8:30am-9pm.

Marle's Travel Adventure, Plateros 328 (☎23 3680). Rents cooking equipment (US$8 or s/28 per day) as well as tents (US$2.50 or s/9.50 per day) and sleeping bags (US$1.50 or s/5 per day). Open daily 8am-8pm.

Bookstores:

Genesis, Santa Catalina Ancha 307 (☎25 7971). Tourist information, non-fiction about Peruvian culture, and Peruvian literature. Open M-Sa 9am-10pm.

Jerusalén, Heladeros 143 (☎23 5428). Fiction and non-fiction in English and other languages. Open M-Sa 10am-9pm.

Los Andes, Portal de Comercio 127 (☎ 23 4231), on the Plaza de Armas. Tourist information and Spanish literature. Open M-Sa 10am-1:30pm and 5-9pm.

Market: Gatos Market, Portal de Belén 115, on the Plaza de Armas. Has all the essentials, plus public telephones and an ATM that takes all major credit cards. Open daily 8am-midnight. **Casa Ecológica Cusco,** Triunfo 393 (☎ 25 5646), sells organic foods and indigenous handicrafts. Jams and preserves s/6-15. Olive oil s/22. Bread s/2. Open M-Sa 10am-8pm, Su 4-8pm.

Laundromat: There are many along Procuradores, Suecia, and Teqsiqocha; most do not accept credit cards. **Laundry Servicio,** Teqsiqocha 450 (☎ 24 3698; open daily 9am-8pm), and **Lavandería Splendor,** Suecia 328 (☎ 80 6975; open daily 7:30am-7:30pm), offer 2hr. (s/4-5 per kg) and 4hr. (s/3 per kg) service, with free pickup and delivery from/to hotel or hostel. **Lava Lava Express,** Santa Catalina Ancha 345 (☎ 22 6651) or Recoleta 526 (☎ 24 7758), does dry cleaning. Open M-Sa 8am-8pm.

Film Processing: Foto César does the fastest film developing in the city (20min., s/12). Locations at Portal de Comercio 187 (☎ 22 9142), Sol 130C (☎ 22 5082), Sol 226, and Plaza San Francisco 116. Open daily 8am-9pm.

EMERGENCY AND COMMUNICATIONS

Police: Tourist police, Saphi 510 (☎ 24 9654), up Plateros from the Plaza de Armas, past Tigre. English spoken. Open 24hr.

24hr. Pharmacy: InkaFarma, Sol 210 (☎ 24 0167), 1 block down from the Plaza, at the Almagro intersection. Accepts all major credit cards. Smaller pharmacies are located at Heladeros 109 (☎ 38 0375), near the Mantas intersection, and Plateros 362, a short walk up from the Plaza.

Hospitals:

Clínica Americana, Infancia 508 (☎ 26 0101). Multilingual, tourist-oriented. Open 24hr. for emergencies.

Clínica Paredes, Lechugal 405 (☎ 22 5265). Specialists of all types. English spoken. Open 24hr. for emergencies.

Hospital Regional (☎ 23 1131, emergency 22 3691, clinic 24 3240), on Av. de la Cultura. Open 8am-noon for non-emergency consultations, 24hr. for emergencies.

Dentist: Dr. Virginia Valcarcel Velarde, Portal de Panes 123, 2nd fl. (☎ 23 1558 or 24 6220), on the Plaza de Armas. **Clínica Odontológica Franco,** Cachimayo F13 (☎ 93 2091, emergency 965 0179), down Av. de la Cultura. English, German, and Portuguese spoken. Available 24hr. for emergencies.

Telephones: Blue-and-gray **Telefónica** booths are ubiquitous. Local calls s/0.05 per min. SMS text messages s/0.20. Accept both coins and cards. Prepaid chip cards may be obtained at Telefónica stores (there's one at Sol 382, open M-F 8:30am-1:30pm and 3:30-6:30pm, Sa 9am-1pm) or at pharmacies and convenience stores. Booths list national and international phone codes, as well as numbers for information and emergency assistance. Instructions in English. Most Internet locations offer **international calling** (s/1 per min. to Europe, the UK, and the US).

Internet Access: Most cybercafes charge s/1.50 per hr. for Internet access, with standard 2MB connections. Many are equipped with printers, memory card readers, scanners, webcams, and international calling services. Bills over s/20 not accepted.

Cibernet Cafe, Plateros 326, 2nd fl. Chill while you check email in this cool cafe/bar. Open daily 6am-midnight.

Ink@net, Carmen Alto 113. Open daily 8:30am-1am.

Internet Station, Teqsiqocha 400. English and German spoken. Systems in a variety of languages. Open daily 9am-midnight.

Las Togas, Portal de Carnes 258. Open daily 8am-midnight.

Post Office: Serpost, Sol 800 (☎22 5232), at Av. Garcilaso, 5 long blocks from the Plaza de Armas. International mail (up to 20g) s/4.50 to the US and Canada, s/5 to the UK and Europe. Express mail (up to 100g) s/67 to the US and Canada, s/79 to the UK and Europe. Open daily 7:30am-8:30pm. No credit cards.

Express Mail: To the US, Canada, UK, and Europe in 3-5 days. All major credit cards.

FedEx: Pardo 978 (☎21 1101). Open M-F 8am-1pm and 3-8pm, Sa 8am-1pm and 3-7pm, Su 8am-1pm.

DHL: Sol 627A (☎24 4167). Open M-F 8:30am-1pm and 3-7pm, Sa 9am-1pm and 3:30-6pm.

World Courier del Perú, Sol 802 (☎22 2444). Open M-Sa 8am-8:30pm.

▐ ACCOMMODATIONS

Cusco swells with affordable places to stay. Nevertheless, it can be difficult to find vacancies during July, August, and late June's Inti Raymi festival. High-season reservations (and reservation confirmations) are recommended. Cusco hostels generally include luggage storage, security boxes, and 24hr. reception; however, most do not accept credit cards.

ACCOMMODATIONS BY PRICE

EPA East of the Plaza de Armas **SB** In San Blas **SC** Around San Cristóbal **WPA** West of the Plaza de Armas

UNDER S/11 (❶)		S/25-38 (❸)	
Hostal Tumi (224)	WPA	Hospedaje 250 (224)	WPA
S/11-24 (❷)		▨ Hospedaje Magnolia II (224)	EPA
Hospedaje Latino América (225)	SC	Hospedaje Sambleño (226)	SB
▨ Hospedaje Royal Frankenstein (223)	WPA	Koyllur (226)	SB
Hospedaje San Blas II (226)	SB	**S/39-59 (❹)**	
Hostal Resbalosa (225)	SC	▨ Amaru Hostal (226)	SB
Hostal Tullumayo (225)	EPA	Casa Hospedaje Sumaq T'ikaq (226)	SB
Hotel California (224)	WPA	El Condado de San Agustín I (225)	EPA
Hotel Royal Qosqo (225)	SC	Hostal Plateros (224)	WPA
Hotel Suecia (225)	SC	Hostal Qori Inti (225)	EPA
Hotel Suecia II (225)	SC	**S/60+ (❺)**	
		▨ Niños Hotel (223)	WPA

WEST OF THE PLAZA DE ARMAS

Around and beyond Plaza Regocijo, the Plaza de Armas's leafy counterpart, lies a colony of family-run, fairly quiet, and affordable places to stay.

▨ **Niños Hotel,** Meloc 442 (☎23 1424; www.ninoshotel.com), past Siete Cuartones. All revenues assist in the upbringing of 12 formerly homeless boys who now live with the Dutch owner. Each large, art-deco room bears the name of a boy and his sponsor. Family-like atmosphere and calm location let you escape the city's touristy tumult. 24hr. hot water, book exchange, flower-filled courtyard, chic cafe, and restaurant (breakfast s/6-10). Laundry (s/4 per kg; dry cleaning s/7). Check-out 11am. Single with shared bath US$12; double with shared bath US$24, with private bath US$30. ❺

▨ **Hospedaje Royal Frankenstein,** San Juan de Dios 260 (☎23 6999; characla_15@yahoo.com), off Plaza Regocijo. Lively lounges, hanging plants, assorted pets, and a social kitchen add zest to clean but cell-like rooms. Guestbook armed with useful advice left behind by fellow travelers. Sprightly owner speaks English and German. Lounge with cable TV, darts, boardgames, fireplace, and books. Laundry free if you do it

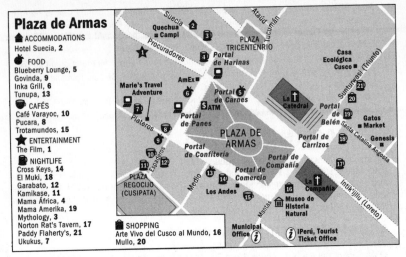

Plaza de Armas

ACCOMMODATIONS
Hotel Suecia, 2

FOOD
Blueberry Lounge, 5
Govinda, 9
Inka Grill, 6
Tunupa, 13

CAFÉS
Café Varayoc, 10
Pucara, 8
Trotamundos, 15

ENTERTAINMENT
The Film, 1

NIGHTLIFE
Cross Keys, 14
El Muki, 18
Garabato, 12
Kamikase, 11
Mama África, 4
Mama Amerika, 19
Mythology, 3
Norton Rat's Tavern, 17
Paddy Flaherty's, 21
Ukukus, 7

SHOPPING
Arte Vivo del Cusco al Mundo, 16
Mullo, 20

yourself (otherwise s/3 per kg). June-Sept. singles, doubles, and triples with shared bath s/20 per person; doubles with private bath s/55. Oct.-May dingles, doubles and triples with shared bath s/15; doubles with private bath s/45. ❷

Hospedaje 250, San Juan de Dios 250 (☎976 1169), off Plaza Regocijo. Basic and clean with warm blankets and an attentive staff, conveniently close to the Plaza. Singles with private bath s/25; doubles with private bath s/40. ❸

Hostal Plateros, Plateros 348 (☎23 6878; plateroshostal@hotmail.com). If you can't live without TV, this is the place to be: there is cable TV in each room, a 2nd-floor TV lounge, and an impressive 70-inch TV downstairs complete with comfy couches. Breakfast included. 24hr. hot water. Free laundry service. Private bathrooms. Singles s/40; doubles s/50; triples s/60. ❹

Hotel California, Nueva Alta 444 (☎24 2997), past Meloc. A lovely, quiet place, even if the rooms are average. 24hr. hot water. Laundry service (s/3 per kg). Check-out 10am. Private bathrooms. Singles s/20; doubles, triples, and quads s/15 per person. Discount for lengthy stays or large groups. ❷

Hostal Tumi, Siete Cuartones 245 (☎24 4413). As basic and affordable as they come. Clean bedrooms and not-so-clean collective bathrooms. Friendly staff. 24hr. hot water. Check-out 10:30am. Singles s/15; doubles s/20. ❶

EAST OF THE PLAZA DE ARMAS

Clean and friendly hotels turn up here and there as you make your way east of the Plaza de Armas. This part of the city is less touristy, emitting a more authentic vibe. Expect to pay more for the ambience and the often superior amenities.

Hospedaje Magnolia II, Regional 898 (☎22 4898), at Centenario. A 12min. walk from the Plaza de Armas; walk down Sol, take a right on Av. Garcilaso (which turns into San Miguel), then left on Centenario. In a circular, cornflower blue building. As authentic as Cusco gets and located near bus and train stations. Immaculate rooms with large windows. Kitchen on the roof with great views of the city. Breakfast US$1.50. 24hr. hot water. Laundry service (s/4 per kg). Check-out 10am. Singles US$8, with bath US$12; doubles US$15, with bath US$20; triples with bath US$25; quads with bath US$30. Discounts in the low season (Jan.-Mar.). ❸

El Condado de San Agustín I, San Agustín 415A (☎24 6299; www.condadohos-tal.com). Truly peaceful, this heated B&B may well be worth the price during Cusco's cold winters. Dimly-lit lobby with comfortable armchairs for lounging. 24hr. hot water. Laundry service (s/3.50 per kg). Heating, international telephone service, and cable TV in each room. Free access to Internet, printer, and scanner. Breakfast included. Kitchen access. Owner speaks English and German. Private baths. Singles US$15; doubles US$25; triples US$35. Extra bed US$5. All major credit cards. ❹

Hostal Qori Inti, Afligidos 120 (☎22 2220; www.qoriinti.com), half a block from Sol. The delightful staff keeps spacious rooms impeccable. Cable TV in every room. Internet lounge near lobby (s/2 per hr.). Continental breakfast included. Private baths. 24hr. hot water. Laundry service (s/5 per kg). Check-out 10am. Singles US$25; doubles US$35; triples US$45. Extra bed US$10. Discounts of US$10-15 Jan.-Mar. ❹

Hostal Tullumayo, Tullumayo 257 (☎24 8048). A truly amazing deal—spotless rooms with blankets and starched sheets. Private baths. 24hr. hot water. Laundry service (s/2 per kg). Heating. Check-out noon. Wood-floor rooms with continental breakfast s/20 per person. Carpeted rooms with American breakfast and cable TV US$10 per person. Singles, doubles, triples, and quads available. ❷

AROUND SAN CRISTÓBAL

It's a steep hike home in this neck of the woods, but a restful night awaits. The closer to San Cristóbal you get, the less oxygen fills the air and the more beautiful the view becomes. Farther down toward Procuradores, the location is more convenient, but the area's pulsing nightlife makes sleeping with earplugs a necessity.

Hostal Resbalosa, Resbalosa 494 (☎22 4839; hostalresbalosa@hotmail.com). Comfortable rooms with warm blankets, parquet floors, and big windows. Beautiful rooftop terrace with views of the entire city. Squeaky-clean bathrooms. Continental breakfast s/4, American breakfast s/5. 24hr. hot water. Laundry service (s/2.50 per kg). Check-out 10am. Singles, doubles, triples, and quads with shared bath s/5 per person. With private bath, singles s/15; doubles s/35; triples s/30. ❷

Hospedaje Latino América, Ladrillos 436 (☎24 0024; latinoamerica@peru.com), halfway between Choquechaka and Pumacurco. 3 floors with tiled rooms and bathrooms offer a good view of the hill above. The front desk will let you borrow the DVD player and DVDs for no charge. English spoken. 24hr. hot water. Laundry service (s/3 per kg). Communal kitchen. Singles s/15, with bath and cable TV s/25; doubles s/15 per person, with bath and cable TV s/35. ❷

Hotel Suecia II, Teqsiqocha 465 (☎23 9757). Turn left at the top of Procuradores and follow the street around the corner. Cushier than the original (see below), with welcoming rooms and a comfortable interior courtyard. Continental breakfast s/4, American breakfast s/5. 24hr. hot water. Laundry service (s/3 per kg). Check-out 10:30am. Singles s/20, with bath s/30; doubles s/30, with bath s/50; triples s/45, with bath s/70; quads s/70, with bath s/80. ❷

Hotel Suecia, Suecia 332 (☎23 3282; hsuecia1@hotmail.com). Simple rooms in a no-frills environment. Continental breakfast s/4, American breakfast s/5. 24hr. hot water. Laundry service (s/3 per kg). Heaters US$5 per night. Check-out 10am. Singles s/20; doubles s/35, with private bath s/50; triples s/45, with private bath s/70. ❷

Hotel Royal Qosqo, Teqsiqocha (☎22 6221), where the road bends. Neither royal nor hotel, but crammed with young backpackers, this very basic hostel is appropriately located atop so-called "Gringo Alley" (Procuradores). While the shared baths might seem dingy, the atmosphere is warm and fun-loving; a true "budget travel" experience. Internet cafe and movie theater adjoin the downstairs lobby. English spoken. 24hr. hot water. Check-out 11am. Reserve in advance for groups of more than 5. Singles s/20; doubles s/40, with bath s/70; triples s/70, with bath s/90. Jan.-Mar. prices lower by s/5. Student discount 10%. All major credit cards. ❷

IN SAN BLAS

This white-washed neighborhood on cobblestone streets behind the cathedral, a 5min. walk from the Plaza de Armas, is home to Cusco's hippest and most artistic residents. Recently, San Blas has welcomed many family-run hostels to its ranks, bringing hospitality at a slightly higher price. The side streets become deserted at night, so take a taxi if you're staying out of sight of the Plazoleta.

Amaru Hostal, Cuesta San Blas 541 (☎22 5933; www.cusco.net/amaru). This spotless wooden palace offers some of the most luxurious balconies, patios, and views in all of Cusco, and has a piano to boot. English spoken. Local TV and windows in each room. Breakfast included. 24hr. hot water. Laundry service (s/3.50 per kg). Heaters s/6 per night. Singles US$12, with bath US$20; doubles US$16, with bath US$30; triples with bath US$42. Additional bed US$10. ❹

Hospedaje Sambleño, Carmen Alto 114 (☎26 2979; sambleno@hotmail.com). The 3rd fl. yields awesome views of Cusco's hills. All rooms with have hardwood floors and private baths with showers. Breakfast s/4-6. 24hr. hot water. Laundry service (s/3 per kg). Check-out 9am. June-Sept. singles s/30; doubles s/50; triples s/80. Oct.-May singles s/25; doubles s/40; triples s/60. ❸

Casa Hospedaje Sumaq T'Ikaq, Tandapata 114 (☎22 9127). The endearing landlady takes exceptional care of her visitors, children, and many pets, all of whom run freely around the house. Large rooms, small baths, and wood-burning heaters in each room. Quiet garden patio. Breakfast included. 24hr. hot water. Kitchen access. Laundry service (s/3 per kg). Singles US$15; doubles US$30; triples US$40. ❹

Hospedaje San Blas II, Choquechaka 194 (☎24 9219; sanblascusco@yahoo.com). Standard and affordable, with clean beds and wooden floors. Breakfast included. 24hr. hot water. Laundry service (s/3 per kg). Singles US$7; doubles US$17, with bath US$22; triples US$24, with bath US$30; quads with bath US$25. ❷

Koyllur, Carmen Bajo 186 (☎24 1122; koyllur_cusco@hotmail.com). Dingy on the outside, but rooms are clean enough and bathrooms are private. A decent place to stay if you've got nowhere else to go. English spoken. Internet s/2 per hour. Continental breakfast s/5, American breakfast s/7. 24hr. hot water. Laundry service (s/3 per kg). Heaters US$3 per night. Checkout 11am. Double and triples US$10 per person. ❸

▢ FOOD

Cusco is known for its *cuy* (guinea pig), *trucha* (trout), *lechón* (roast suckling pig), and *rocoto relleno* (chili pepper stuffed with meat, vegetables, and spices, then wrapped in dough and fried). Picky eaters need not worry, however, as the streets around the Plaza de Armas tempt diners with international cuisine. Many a backpacker has been known to spend all his soles at these Mexican, Italian, and Japanese establishments. Should you grow tired of such pricey options, walking a few blocks down Loreto leads to local joints serving s/2-4 *menús*. Also, markets spring up on practically every block, and for pennies you can grab a can of soup, a couple pieces of fruit, and a box of crackers to make yourself a cheap, filling meal.

ON THE MENÚ. The *menú* is common fare in Cusco (as elsewhere in Peru), providing a multi-course meal (usually a salad/appetizer, entree, dessert, and drink) at a fixed, usually quite reasonable, price. Particularly in tourist-ridden Cusco, many restaurants offer *menús* that cater to international tastes. Some establishments have a pre-set meal-of-the-day, others work a la carte; in any case, if you want a square meal at a square deal, opt for a *menú*.

FOOD BY TYPE

PA Around the Plaza de Armas **SB** In San Blas

AMERICAN
Greens (229)	SB ❸
▨ Jack's (229)	SB ❷
Trotamundos (230)	PA ❷

BAKERIES
▨ Café Varayoc (230)	PA ❷
π Centro (230)	SB ❶

CAFES
El Arbolito (230)	PA ❶
Café Cultural Ritual (230)	SB ❷
▨ Café Varayoc (230)	PA ❷
Moni (230)	PA ❶
π Centro (230)	SB ❶
Pucara (230)	PA ❸
Sweet Temptation (230)	PA ❷
Trotamundos (230)	PA ❷

DELI AND SANDWICHES
Blueberry Lounge (228)	PA ❷
▨ Los Perros (227)	PA ❷

INTERNATIONAL
Al Grano (228)	PA ❸
Blueberry Lounge (228)	PA ❷
Govinda (228)	PA ❶
Greens (229)	SB ❸
Kin Taro (228)	PA ❷
La Granja Heidi (229)	SB ❶
▨ Los Perros (227)	PA ❷
▨ MAP Café (227)	PA ❹
Narguila (228)	PA ❷

NEW PERUVIAN
Inka Grill (228)	PA ❹
▨ Macondo (228)	SB ❷
▨ MAP Café (227)	PA ❷
Tupananchis (Meeting Point) (229)	SB ❷

TRADITIONAL PERUVIAN
El Sol (228)	PA ❶
Pacha Papa (229)	SB ❸
Pucara (230)	PA ❸
Los Toldos Chicken (228)	PA ❷
▨ Tunupa (227)	PA ❸

VEGETARIAN AND VEGETARIAN-FRIENDLY
Café Cultural Ritual (230)	SB ❷
Govinda (228)	PA ❶

AROUND THE PLAZA DE ARMAS

If you can briefly overlook your irritation with sidewalks full of pushy waiters, the Plaza offers some excellent dining options, some more expensive than others.

▨ **Tunupa,** Portal de Confituría 233, 2nd fl. (☎25 2936; zappa@terra.com.pe), on the Plaza de Armas upstairs from the Cross Keys Bar. With a beautiful balcony that overlooks the Plaza, Tunupa is a must for any Cusco traveler. An all-you-can-eat buffet (s/53) includes *pisco* sours, salad bar, soup, platters of hors d'oeuvres, dozens of entrees, and rich, elegant desserts. A la carte entrees s/16-35. Cocktails (alcoholic s/12-16; nonalcoholic s/8-12) and dessert buffet (s/18) make for a snazzy after-dinner affair. Try the Banana Backflip (s/12). Open daily 10am-3pm and 6-11pm. AmEx/MC/V. ❸

▨ **Los Perros,** Teqsiqocha 436 (☎24 1447), at Tigre. This "wine and couch" *tapas* bar is hip and funky (not to mention comfortable) and offers a small but delicious menu of fairly cheap eats. Try the vegetarian wontons (s/13) or the "I Smell India" (s/17). This gourmet deli by day transforms into a fun, crowded hotspot by night. If you're still twiddling your thumbs, there are board games and a book exchange. "Couch munchies" s/10-13. Sandwiches s/9-15. International entrees s/16-17. Beer s/5-11. Wine s/8-12. Open daily 11am-midnight. ❷

▨ **MAP Café,** Plaza de Nazareñas 231 (☎24 2476; mapcafe@amauta.rcp.net.pe), inside Museo de Arte Precolombiano. Tasteful ambience enhances a delicious dining experience at this contemporary "*novoandina*" gourmet" restaurant, where native Andean spices embellish the international cuisine. Vegetarians will like the rissoni with mushrooms (s/28). Crayfish and potato gnocchi are also popular (s/35). Dinner time is quite formal, so leave the frayed jeans at home. Coffee s/4-10. Smoothies s/7. Sandwiches s/22-32. Entrees s/19-50. Desserts s/14-21. Red and white wines s/66-120 per bottle. Open M-Sa 10am-10pm, Su 11am-10pm. All major credit cards. ❹

Blueberry Lounge, Portal de Carnes 236 (☎24 9458), on the Plaza de Armas. The plush couches, bright blue walls, elegant candlesticks, and hot pink lampshades lend a bohemian edge. The music is loud, the menu creatively tasty, and the open fireplace warm against the chilly Andean air. Deli menu by day, with baguettes (s/8-12) and tapas (s/6-8); box lunch takeout and delivery available (noon-8pm). In the evening, Blueberry serves up exotic entrees like Moroccan vegetable citrus salad (s/15), chicken and sesame curry (s/33), Thai fried rice (s/19), and Vietnamese summer rolls (s/17). Happy hour midnight-1am. Open daily 8:30am-2am. AmEx/MC/V. ❷

Inka Grill, Portal de Panes 115 (☎26 2992), on the Plaza de Armas. Taking inspiration from the legend of Túpac Turin, said to have traveled the world for 20 years before returning with none other than Christopher Columbus, Inka Grill offers locally inspired delights like Urubamba River salad (s/20) and Coca Leaf Crème Bruleé (s/26) to an international audience. The complimentary potato chips with creamy mint dipping sauce are a meal in and of themselves. English menus. Entrees s/25-39. Open M-Sa 10am-10pm, Su 11am-11pm. All major credit cards. ❹

Narguila, Teqsiqocha 405, up Procuradores and left on Teqsiqocha, tucked away in the bend of the road. Knowledge of Hebrew is not mandatory, but it can't hurt in this haven of quick and yummy food for the penniless traveler. Well known among the Israeli tourist crowd, many flock here for the authentic and fresh taste. Its walls are bizarrely decorated with everything from political posters to family photographs to enormous foam bunnies. Huge falafel and Ziva each s/8. Warm bread and spicy dipping sauce with every meal. Open daily 9am-11pm. No credit cards. ❷

Kin Taro, Heladeros 149 (☎22 6181), left off Plaza Regocijo when facing uphill. Ah, the scent of soy. Kin Taro has a splendid array of traditional Japanese dishes, notably sushi (s/12-25). Upstairs, kick off your shoes and dine Japanese-style, sitting on the floor. Teriyaki s/10-14. Noodle soup s/11-13. Open M-Sa 10:30am-3pm and 6:30-10pm. ❷

Govinda, Espaderos 128 (☎80 4864), near Plaza Regocijo. Hare Krishna in spirit, vegetarian in cuisine, and mellow in atmosphere. Tasty curried rice (s/7) and *subji govinda* (s/9), fruit salads (s/8-12), and soy concoctions (s/3-10) fill hungry tourists to the brim—and cheaply. The *samozas empanadas* (s/6) are probably the only samosas you'll find in Cusco. Open daily 8am-10pm. No credit cards. ❶

Los Toldos Chicken, Almagro 171 (☎22 9829; lostoldoschicken@peru.com), at San Andrés. Cheap, delicious, and enormous meals await. The house specialty—the mouthwatering *pollo a la brasa*—is already roasting over the fire as you walk in the door, and comes with a heaping pile of french fries and a visit to the well-stocked salad bar (s/7.50). Delivery available. Vegetarian pizzas and pastas (s/10-15). Open daily noon-11pm. No credit cards. ❷

Al Grano, Santa Catalina Ancha 398 (☎22 8032), at San Agustín. An experiment in pan-Asian cuisine, Al Grano rotates a healthy menu of international curries, identified by country. You can also choose from the owner's growing menu of "favorites from around the world." Excellent for family-style meals, and 2 spacious dining rooms easily accommodate large parties. Also claims "the best coffee in Cusco," a particularly strong blend of gourmet beans from Loreto and Quillabamba. Entrees s/20. Espresso s/3-5. Open M-Sa 10am-9pm. ❸

El Sol, Teqsiqocha 415 (☎22 7511). Cheap, simple fare. *Menú económico* s/7. *Menú italiano* s/10. 10% discount for ISIC and SAE. ❶

IN SAN BLAS

This is where backpackers-in-the-know settle down to eat. The hike is grueling, but the food is worth the effort.

▧ **Macondo,** Cuesta San Blas 571 (☎22 9415; macondo@telser.com.pe). The sign reads "Come into my world." Anything is possible in this magic realist's paradise, inspired by the mythical town in Colombian writer Gabriel García Márquez's *Cien años de soledad*. Trendy photographs are plastered to the tables, painted venus fly traps line the walls, and a dark woody crawl space provides upstairs seating. You can even sink into a bona fide bed of pillows. After you try the funky twist on Peruvian "jungle" cuisine, it may be hard to leave. Also doubles as a gallery for local artists. Try the *juane* (s/22), baked in a banana leaf from "deepest, darkest Peru," or for vegetarians, the flavorful *papas locas* (s/20). Alpaca, chicken, and veggie curries s/25-35. "Amazonic Salad" s/19. Breakfast s/7-15. Lunch s/6-18. Dinner s/18-35. Open daily 9am-10pm, after which the place transforms into a trendy bar. Dinner reservations recommended. ❷

▨ **Jack's,** Choquechaka 509 (☎80 6069), at Cuesta San Blas. Cave to your nostalgic cravings and order up a first-rate American meal. Takeout available. Breakfast all day (s/9-16), truly "super" sandwiches (s/8-13), and excellent milkshakes (s/5). Open daily 6:30am-10:30pm. Large groups reserve in advance. US dollars accepted. ❷

La Granja Heidi, Cuesta San Blas 525 (☎23 3759; www.geocities.com/naturefood). Crepes, omelettes, muesli, and yogurt (s/3-6) come in filling portions for breakfast, lunch, or dinner. For dessert, a slice of Heidi's famous cheesecake (made with milk from the owner's own cows) will keep you full for days. The scrumptious cakes are named after famous people—try the Marilyn Monroe or the Nelson Mandela (s/4). Open M-Sa 8:30am-9:30pm. ❶

Greens, Tandapata 700 (☎24 3820; greens_cusco@yahoo.co.uk), behind the church in Plazoleta San Blas. Steaks and curries for all palates. All-you-can-eat Sunday Roast has chicken, potatoes, vegetables, stuffing, wine, and desserts (s/35). The fireplace, couches, backgammon, and magazines ensure that diners linger. Appetizers s/7-16. Entrees s/20-28. Happy hour 6-7pm and 9-10pm. Food served 8:30am-midnight. ❸

Pacha Papa, Plazoleta San Blas 120 (☎24 1318), across from the Iglesia San Blas. Serves traditional Cusqueñan food in a romantic courtyard with a traditional stone fireplace, potted plants, white-washed walls covered in ivy, and classical music playing softly in the background. Alpaca s/30. Half *cuy* s/25. Appetizers s/10-16. Entrees s/15-30. Open daily 10am-9pm. No credit cards. ❸

Tupananchis (Meeting Point), Tocuyeros (☎74 1427). On a private road just off Cuesta San Blas, the cobblestone patio and wide umbrellas make it indeed a perfect meeting place. Tupananchis boasts that its cuisine is modern, contemporary, and "mystical," but it is perhaps more lucidly described as *novoandina*, as it adds new spice to traditional Andean fare. Appetizers s/10-17. Sandwiches and burgers s/8-13. Entrees s/18-30. Open daily 5am-10pm. ❷

THE LOCAL STORY

THE INCA TRILOGY

If you thought trilogies didn't exist until Star Wars or J.R.R. Tolkien, think again. As you explore Inca ruins and observe Peruvian art, both ancient and modern, it won't be long before you notice the pervasive presence of three symbols: the serpent, the puma, and the condor. Together, these three fundamental figures are known as the **Inca Trilogy.** An appreciation of the meaning of these symbols is essential to understa███ ██e Inca belief system and a█ ██

The **serpent,** or *hu████████,* was believed to dominate the underworld. He was the god of knowledge, symbolizing wisdom and intelligence. The **puma,** or *kaypacha,* dominated the earth and was the god of war, symbolizing force and hard work. The **condor,** or *hanacpacha,* dominated the sky and was god of peace, symbolizing the inner spirit and harmony. The Incas believed that these three divine beings must be in harmony in order for equilibrium to exist in the universe.

Such symbolism is one example of the larger trend among pre-Colombian Andean cultures to place divine significan██ upon birds, felines, and snake██ ██ fact, this symbolism is one of the most significant characteristics that the Incas shared with earlier cultures in the area.

Café Cultural Ritual, Choquechaka 140 (☎68 2223), off Cuesta San Blas. This simple cafe has become one of Cusco's most popular. The vegetarian-friendly menu varies daily. Moist banana cake makes a delectable dessert, as do the many ice cream specialties. The collection of boardgames and traditional handicrafts will entertain you while you wait. "Big healthy salads" s/8-10. Entrees s/8-15. Open daily 8am-11pm. ❷

▐ CAFES

Foreign invasion of Cusco has made java brewing, java selling, and java consumption a top priority—say goodbye to Nescafé. By day, cafes serve breakfast and sandwiches. At night, they transform into multilingual conversation parlors.

■ **Café Varayoc,** Espaderos 142 (☎23 2404), at Plazoleta Regocijo. Real espresso, and that's not to mention the cakes, pies, and pastries that will melt upon your grateful tongue. Chatty women behind the counter, "romantic rhythms" playing overhead, and stylish lampshades hanging above each table give quite a character to this "Swiss cafe." Named after the symbolic scepter *(vara)* of the Inca rulers (Varayocs), this cafe demands a visit. Espresso s/5. Fruit juice s/5. Sandwiches s/6-10. Crepes s/16. Specialty *Suisse Fondue* (s/35). Open daily 8am-midnight. AmEx/MC. ❷

Pucara, Plateros 309 (☎22 2027), off the Plaza de Armas. Pyramid-shaped hanging lamps, *ayahuasca*-inspired seat cushions, and an atmosphere of warm (as in, heated) quietude draw curious onlookers to this dimly-lit cafe and restaurant. A great place to go solo. Coffee s/3-4. Truffles Divine s/1 each. Appetizers s/8-10. Entrees s/10-26. Open M-Sa 12:30-10pm. ❸

π **Centro,** Atoqsayk'uchi 599, at Carmen Alto. This groovy pie palace makes phenomenal sweet tarts and savory quiches (s/5 per piece, s/35-40 per pie). The chocolate tart is to die for. Catering available, order 24hr. in advance. DJ jam session Tu 8pm. Open M-Sa 9am-10pm, Su 10am-10pm. ❶

Sweet Temptation, Herrajes 138A (☎24 4129). This flower shop with cafe is a small but charming tribute to nature's bounty. All organic ingredients. Try the "ecological" soup (s/8) or made-from-scratch lasagna (s/13). Take time to stop and smell (or buy) the roses (s/2 each). Open M-Sa 8am-9:30pm. ❷

El Arbolito, Sol 612. Let this chill cafe refresh you after the searing heat and endless commotion of Sol. Great for cool drinks and snacks. Breakfast s/7-9. *Empanadas* s/2. *Papa rellena* s/2.50. Banana or chocolate cake s/2. Open daily 7am-11pm. ❶

Trotamundos, Portal de Comercio 177, 2nd fl. (☎23 2387). This convenient establishment above the Plaza will serve you quick, cheap, and tasty snacks (s/2-12). Start your morning off with a satisfying American breakfast (s/6.50-15) and a quick email check (Internet s/1.50 per hr.). Open daily 8am-midnight. ❷

Moni, San Agustín 311 (☎23 1029; www.moni-cusco.com). Tucked away in the quieter east side of town, this humble joint has local and international dishes made to order. Tasty *papas a la huancaína* (s/6) and hot chocolate made from pure Quillabamba *cacao* (s/6). Open M-F 8am-3pm and 6-9pm, Sa 10am-3pm and 6-9pm. ❶

◔ SIGHTS

Most sightseeing in Cusco requires a **tourist ticket** (*boleto turístico*, US$10 or s/35, students and children US$5 or s/17.50). Paying individual entrance fees is not possible at most tourist ticket locations. Tickets are valid for 10 days only and are available at the Municipal Tourist Office and the Tourist Ticket Executive Office (see **Tourist and Financial Services,** p. 219), and at Casa Garcilaso.

CUSCO TOURIST TICKETS. Your *boleto turístico* gives you access to the Museo de Arte y Monasterio de Santa Catalina, the Museo de Arte Popular, the site museum at Qorikancha, the Museo Municipal de Arte Contemporáneo, the Museo Histórico Regional (Casa Garcilaso), and the nearby ruins of Sacsayhuamán, Qenco, Puca Pucara, Tambomachay, Pisac, Ollantaytambo, Chinchero, Tipón, and Pikillacta. The ticket does not include admission to the part of the Qorikancha that belongs to Convento de Santo Domingo, Convento de la Merced, or Museo Inka at the Casa del Almirante. It is also invalid for admission to Sacsayhuamán on the day of Inti Raymi, June 24.

A separate tourist ticket is required to visit certain **religious sites,** including the cathedral, Iglesia de San Blas, and the Museo de Arte Religioso del Arzobispado (s/10, students s/5; cathedral only s/5, students s/2). This ticket is valid for one day only. Tickets are sold at the window at the entrance to the cathedral (M-W and Sa 10-11:30am and 2-5:30pm, Th and Su 2-5:30pm, F 10-11:30am).

THE CATHEDRAL

On the Plaza de Armas; with the big steps. Open M-W and F-Sa 10-11:30am and 2-5:30pm, Th and Su 2-5:30pm. Ticket required, except during mass.

Built upon the foundations of the Inca Wiracocha's palace, construction on Cusco's cathedral was begun in 1550 and took nearly a century to complete. The church sustained serious damage in the 1986 earthquake; inside, some areas are still blocked off or obscured by scaffolding. Nonetheless, the cathedral is fascinating in its subtle incorporation of Inca symbolism, an element attributable to the large number of indigenous craftspeople who helped build it. Native flora and fauna adorn the carvings and paintings; look for triangular-shaped Madonnas, reflecting the mountains and Pachamama (Mother Earth). The cathedral also boasts a collection of several hundred paintings from the Cusco School.

CAPILLA DE LA SAGRADA FAMILIA (CHAPEL OF THE SACRED FAMILY). Visitors enter the cathedral through the Capilla de la Sagrada Familia. At the front lies a small altar, plated in silver taken from the grand silver mines discovered by the Spanish in Potosí, Bolivia. During Corpus Christi celebrations, this altar is mounted on a pickup truck as a parade float. Behind the altar lies a glittering wall covered in gold carving, with various holy figures embedded in it.

THE CUSCO SCHOOL

Many of Cusco's museums, no surprisingly, feature painting from the **Cusco School.** Thi prominent colonial school of ar spread throughout South Americ from the 16th to 18th centurie and included *mestizo* as well a indigenous painters. As a result o this mixed heritage, even paint ings on Christian themes incorpo rate a great deal of Andear symbolism: backgrounds are painted with local flora and fauna and biblical figures wear Inca cos tumes. Much of the *cusqueño* style focuses less on depicting scenes than on portraying specifi figures in specific detail; figures such as saints and angels are often richly adorned, wearing sumptuous gowns overlaid with gold to simulate brocade. Often the canvas carries an interna frame of flowers or iconesque epi sodes from the subject's life. Also on display is the gradual assimila tion of Catholicism into the indig enous consciousness. One anonymous painting features Jesus in a wine-press full o grapes, stamping the grapes and bleeding generously from his fiv wounds into the juice while hi overjoyed disciples wait greedil by the spigot.

Marcos Zapata, who is cred ited with the Last Supper painting in the Cusco Cathedral at whicl Christ dines on *cuy,* is one of th best known Cusco School artists many others remain anonymous.

VAULT. The main vault of the cathedral houses brilliant altars and ornate wooden gates. As you enter the chapel and walk counterclockwise in a circle, you'll encounter figures in this order: the Immaculate Conception, San José, Patrón Santiago, Virgen del Carmen, Virgen de los Remedios, La Santa Rosa, El Señor de la Sentencia, and El Señor de los Temblores (Lord of Earthquakes, the patron saint of Cusco). Passing into the nave, the silver-plated Renaissance-style main **altar** dominates, surrounded by mirrors intended to reflect candlelight and illuminate the room. Next to the altar, on the right, sits the oft-discussed **Last Supper,** attributed to Marcos Zapata of the Cusco School. A *mestizo* artist of the 18th century, Zapata borrowed inspiration from sacred Inca feasts when he made Christ's final meal a guinea-pig roast *(cuy)*. Opposite the altar stands the cathedral's finely carved wooden **choir,** considered one of the best in the Americas. The choir was used as a didactic tool for the evangelization of the natives. Each seat has an armrest supported by a pregnant-bellied carving of **Pachamama,** the Inca earth goddess—yet another example of indigenous artistry.

CAPILLA DEL TRIUNFO (CHAPEL OF TRIUMPH). Passing into the Capilla del Triunfo, next door, one encounters the **Altar del Señor de los Temblores** (Altar of the Lord of Earthquakes), a magnificent stonework covered in gold. According to legend, a procession that carried this Christ image through the Plaza de Armas brought a swift end to the 1650 earthquake. Blackened by centuries of candle smoke, el Señor repeats his performance (or at least his appearance) in the Plaza de Armas on the Monday of **Semana Santa** (Holy Week). A number of other altars incorporate painted carvings of Peruvian jungle fauna. In a **crypt** under the chapel, you can view the ashes of **El Inca Garcilaso de la Vega,** the *mestizo* chronicler of the Incas whose remains were returned to Cusco by Spanish royals in 1978. The El Triunfo chapel itself was the first Christian church built in Cusco. It was built on the site of **Suntur Wasi,** an Inca armory where Spanish troops took refuge during Inca Manco's 1536 attack, in which the Incas burned much of Cusco. Miraculously, the Spaniards survived and claimed to have visions of the Virgin Mary and St. James fighting back the flames (although it was probably just slaves with buckets of water). After the miracle, the Spanish subdued the Incas; in honor of their victory, they dragged stones from **Sacsayhuamán** (p. 245) to build El Triunfo. Later, the chapel was joined with the cathedral.

QORIKANCHA AND IGLESIA DE SANTO DOMINGO

On the grassy expanse 2 blocks down Sol from the Plaza de Armas, at Arrayaniyoq. Archaeological museum open daily M-Sa 9am-1pm and 2-5pm, Su 8am-2pm. Tourist ticket required. Santo Domingo and Sun Temple open M-Sa 8am-5pm, Su 2-4pm. s/4, with ISIC s/2; not included in tourist ticket.

THE STORY. When Atahuallpa was held prisoner in Cajamarca in 1533, the Incas promised his captor, Francisco Pizarro, rooms full of ransom in gold and silver from Cusco. Impatient, Pizarro sent three of his men to the Inca capital to expedite matters. The soldiers quickly found the Qorikancha (Court of Gold), a massive, gold-covered temple that extended from its present site to Sol's intersection with Tullumayo. The soldiers looted some 3150 pounds of pure gold plating from the walls. In subsequent trips, Pizarro and his army joined the mayhem, stealing tons of precious silver and gold objects. This obsession with gold baffled the Incas, who considered coca leaves more valuable. Years later, Dominicans built a Baroque church on the site. When a 1950 earthquake destroyed the church, revealing the Inca foundations, archaeologists cheered. Subsequent findings give an idea of the marvel that the Qorikancha must have been. It accommodated some 4000 priests and attendants, who made daily offerings to gods and deceased royal ancestors. A great golden disc deflected morning sunlight into the **gilded Sun Temple.** A **silver-lined Moon Temple** had its own silver disc. Other temples paid homage to thunder, lightning, the rainbow, and various stars. At least one room held the captured idols of conquered tribes, so that if subjugated peoples ever rebelled, the Incas could publicly desecrate their gods. The Qorikancha also acted as an **astronomical observatory** where *amautas* (priests of a learned caste) plotted the solstices and equinoxes and predicted eclipses, all of which were intricately tied to sacred and agricultural practices. Indeed, the Qorikancha was the center of a geographical zodiac wheel that encompassed 327 sacred sites.

THE TOUR. Enter through the underground museum on Sol to see a small collection of ceramics, tools, jewelry, photographs from the archaeological excavations, some old photos of Cusco, and models of Qorikancha. In some of the inner rooms, several **skeletons** and **craniums** from Inca times show how a forward-slanting deformation of the forehead was thought to be prestigious, and was induced upon birth. Exit past the bathrooms to the grounds upstairs, a **graveyard of Inca building blocks.** While the pre-Inca remains date from AD 800, without the historical background the sight looks more like a large yard filled with rocks. Far more interesting (but not included in the tourist ticket) is the part of the complex that belongs to the Church of Santo Domingo, up Arrayaniyoq and to the right, behind the church's main doors. This section is commonly called the **Sun Temple,** although its largest surviving shrines were probably dedicated to the moon and stars. Temples to lightning and the rainbow stand across the courtyard from these shrines. A large stone receptacle in the center of the courtyard, formerly covered in 55kg of gold, is said to have held *chicha* (a religious liquor) to quench the sun god's thirst. The church's sacristy also holds ornate religious vestments.

SAN BLAS

Up Sunturwasi (Triunfo) from the Plaza de Armas.

Known in Quechua as Tococache ("salt hole," suggesting that it might once have been a salt mine), San Blas is one of Cusco's oldest and most picturesque neighborhoods. It is also a thriving artistic community that produces both traditional and contemporary works. Winding streets and footpaths extend uphill from behind the cathedral; wandering through them yields numerous window-shopping opportunities and spectacular views of the city below.

JUL 17

FROM THE ROA

I CALL SHOTGUN

As an independent traveler, I'm always looking to make a friend out of a stranger, chatting it up with folks in cafes, clubs, street side—wherever I can. But some of my best conversations have been in transit, during that 5min. ride to the train station or on that 30min. rocky road to the ruins, with the fellow at the wheel. After all, who could know a place better than the folks who drive its streets daily (or dirt paths, as it may be the case)? Taxi drivers will tell you local stories, alternative histories, and legends you won't hear in museums. They'll tell you about all the esoteric and exceptional quirks of a place, if you just sit back and listen. In my six weeks of taxi chats, I discussed the virtue and folly of empire, compared the hay fields of the Sacred Valley to those in my backyard (in Missouri), debated the politics of India and Pakistan, uncovered multiple backwoods hikes and hidden trails, got updated on the latest in Latin pop, learned how to ride a motorcycle, swapped English lessons for Spanish tips, and listened to the stories of these men's lives—which often give the most insight of all. This isn't New York City, so don't be an estranged passenger—get in the front seat.

—Saritha Komatireddy

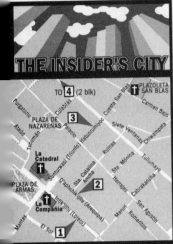

MAKE NEW FRIENDS BUT KEEP THE OLD

The arrival of the Spanish conquistadors spelled destruction for many of Cusco's original Inca walls and buildings. In the years that followed, the Spanish attempted to emulate Inca architectural styles in their own construction, but very little authentic Inca architecture remains in the city. The best of what's left can be seen by walking this route.

1 From the Plaza de Armas, walk down Intik'ijllu (a.k.a. Loreto; between Portal de la Compañía and Portal de Carrizos). Notice how the walls along Intik'ijllu have perfectly cut stones, assembled so ingeniously that they need no grout, mud, or cement between them. For years, scientists puzzled over how the Incas were able to cut stones so precisely without iron tools; researchers now suspect that they inserted wet wooden pegs into small holes in the rock, and as the wood absorbed the water, it expanded and split

ARTESANÍA. A walk up Sunturwasi from the Plaza de Armas will take you by various boutiques selling jewelry, ceramics, and textiles as well as paintings in the *cusqueño* and more contemporary styles. Small stores and workshops surround Plazoleta San Blas as well. The most notable artist is **Pancho Mendivil,** who produces beautiful painted woodwork, mirrors, and ceramics, including his trademark long-necked dolls. *(Plazoleta San Blas 619. ☎ 23 3247. Open daily 9:30am-9pm.)* The plazoleta itself hosts a small **craft market** on Saturdays, where you can watch as artists spin, weave, sew, whittle, and paint, selling their art as they make it.

IGLESIA DE SAN BLAS. A small, attractive church dating from 1562, the otherwise plain Iglesia de San Blas holds perhaps the best **wood-carved pulpit** in the Americas. The symmetrical pulpit is crafted from a single cedar trunk and features images of the Virgin Mary, apostles, and numerous angels and cherubs—all supported by the gut-wrenching efforts of eight heretics on the pulpit's underside. Legend has it that the carving was done by a leper named Juan Tomás Tuirutupa, and that his skull lies at St. Paul's feet. *(On Plazoleta San Blas. Open M-W and F-Sa 8-11:30am and 3-5:30pm, Th and Su 2-5:30pm.)*

OTHER CHURCHES AND MUSEUMS

■ MUSEO INKA (PALACIO DEL ALMIRANTE). The Museo Inka is a must-see for anyone curious about Andean civilization, transporting visitors from pre-Inca times through the rebellious years after conquest. Housed in the magnificent 17th-century Palacio del Almirante, the museum displays remarkably well-preserved ceramics and tools from the pre-Inca Nasca, Chimú, Mochica (Moche), Pucara, Tiahuanaco, and Huari cultures on the first floor. Some pieces of note include large Pucara monoliths and a funerary blanket dating from 900 BC. The center courtyard features a 3-dimensional stage scene depicting aspects of pre-Inca life. Alongside it lies the Textiles Center, dedicated to preserving ancient weaving techniques, where visitors watch as woolen scarves and shawls are created. On the way up to the second floor, visitors pass pictures and a model of the Queshwachaka Puente Inka, a bridge over the Apurimac River constructed entirely out of grass. The second floor is full of colorful dioramas depicting Inca agricultural practices, as well as Inca jewelry, clothing, weapons, and ceremonial vases. You can peek into a replicated burial crypt containing real mummies. Another room exhibits furniture from a salon that belonged to post-conquest Inca royalty, including wooden tables and chests inlaid with tortoiseshell and mother-of-pearl. Early copies of El Inca Garcilaso's *Comentarios Reales* introduce an exhibit on *inkaísmo*, a cultural preservation movement. *(Cuesta del Almirante 103, uphill and to the left of the cathedral. ☎23 7380. Open M-F 8am-6pm, Sa 9am-4pm. s/ 10; not included in tourist ticket.)*

■ **MUSEO DE ARTE PRECOLOMBIANO (LA CASA CABRERA).** Modern in design and exclusive in selection, the Museo de Arte Precolombiano presents ancient objects as art rather than relics. Housed within the renovated colonial mansion of Spanish Count Luis Jerónimo de Cabrera—prior to whose ownership the space served as a ceremonial Inca courtyard—the MAP's exhibits consist of a selection of 400 pieces from Lima's Larco Archaeological Museum, chosen for display here by an elite art critic and one of Peru's most famous painters. Galleries are organized by epoch and culture, each containing explanatory maps and histories, as well as intricate descriptions in both Spanish and English. Look at the antiquated works of the ancient Chimú and Virú peoples, witness the creativity of the prolific Mochicas, and, of course, gaze at the masterpieces of the late Incas. Other galleries showcase ceramic, wood, metal, and seashell creations. *(In the Casa Cabrera, Plaza de Nazareñas 231. ☎23 3210; amap@infonegocio.net.pe. Open daily 9am-11pm. s/16, students s/8; not included in tourist ticket.)*

MUSEO DE ARTE RELIGIOSO DEL ARZOBISPADO. Before this mansion belonged to the archbishop (who lives in the wing next to the museum), it was the home of the Marqués de Buenavista, built on the foundations of Inca Roca's palace. One of the palace's immense walls survives along Hathrumiyoq, or "Street with the Big Stone." This name refers to the great **12-sided stone** that fits harmoniously into the center of the wall. The exceptional courtyard is a sight in itself, with blue-and-white tiles from Seville, Spain, and beautifully carved wooden doorways and grilles. Well-preserved Cusco School paintings decorate the interior; one of the most interesting rooms is filled with paintings by **Zapata,** whose *Circuncisión* portrays baby Jesus facing the blade. *(At Hathrumiyoq and Herrajes. ☎22 5211. Open M-Sa 8-11:30am and 3-5:30pm, Su 2-5:30pm. Tourist ticket for religious sites required.)*

IGLESIA DE LA COMPAÑÍA. The other large church in the Plaza de Armas, La Compañía, was constructed over Amarucancha, the palace of Inca Huayna Cápac; one of the palace's walls still stands along Loreto. During the Jesuit church's

the stone. Their method for fitting the stones together so perfectly remains a mystery.

2 Take a left once you reach Maruri, and then take another left on Q'aphchik'ijllu (a.k.a. Arequipa), following it back to the Plaza. The walls of Q'aphchik'ijllu are authentic Inca; notice how joints between stones never overlap, and two joints are never placed atop one another.

3 Take a right on Sunturwasi (a.k.a. Triunfo) and follow it past Palacio. The walls of Hathunrumiyoq, between Palacio and Choquechaka, exemplify the differences between real Inca (on your right) and faux Inca (on your left) architecture. The perfectly fit stones on the right are all of the same grade and color, and go from large to small as the wall moves upward. The left side lacks such meticulous precision. Midway down the path, across from a colorful flag, you'll see on your right the famous stone with 12 corners.

4 Once you reach Choquechaka, take a left and follow the road to Choquechaka 339. The doorway of 339 is one of the last remaining genuine Inca doorways, marked by sides that lean inward at an angle and the precision-matched stones characteristic of the walls you saw earlier.

17th-century construction, a controversy broke out among local clergy when La Compañía's size threatened to match that of the cathedral. Eventually, even Pope Paul III turned against the building, but by then most of the church had been built. Along the main hallway are golden altars and gold-framed portraits of saints, with altars dedicated to El Señor de los Temblores (Lord of Earthquakes) and the Virgin Mary. Upon exiting the church, pause to look at the balcony mural depicting the crucifixion, and bid goodbye to the sculpted figure of St. Ignatius up above the archway. *(Church open for mass M-Sa 7am, noon, 6pm; Su 7:30, 11:30am, 6, 7pm. Free.)*

CONVENTO DE SANTA CATALINA. The convent currently houses nuns, but its foundations once supported a different kind of female residence: it was the **Acllahuasi** (House of Chosen Women). These women acted as the Inca's concubines or as virgin priestesses for Inti (the sun god) and were responsible for preparing the ruler's *chicha* and woven garments. Weaving clothes made out of alpaca and vicuña was an interminable affair, as the Inca tended to burn his garments after one wearing. The Sun Virgins also tended the Sun Temple (see **Qorikancha and Iglesia de Santo Domingo**, p. 232), prepared offerings to Inti, and served as liaisons to the Inca. Today, in addition to cloistering nuns, the convent shelters an **art museum.** A series of works on the ground floor captures the life of **Santa Rosa de Lima** and includes religious colonial paintings from the Cusco School, as well as an impressive conference room with beautiful Baroque frescoes. *(At Santa Catalina and Arequipa. Museum open M-Su 7am-6pm. Tourist ticket required.)*

IGLESIA DE LA MERCED AND MUSEO CONVENTO DE LA MERCED. This 16th-century church (rebuilt after the 1950 earthquake) maintains a small museum, housing notable works such as two paintings by the *cusqueño* painter Bitti and an image of the crucifixion by the Spanish Renaissance artist Zurbarán. Around the gorgeous courtyard are 25 paintings representing scenes in the life of Pedro Nolasco, founder of the Merced order. The roof is the original 320-year-old cedar carved in the baroque style by a *cusqueño* cabinet maker. Shiniest is the **Custodia de La Merced,** an 18th-century monstrance rendered from 22kg of gold and encrusted with 1518 diamonds and 615 pearls, including the second-largest pearl in the world. Most impressive is the crypt of **Padre Francisco de Salamanca,** covered in wall-to-wall frescoes. The story goes that Salamanca lived esconced in the crypt (painting to pass the time), except for Friday nights, when he'd walk around the main cloister of the church with a heavy cross tied to him. The cross now leans against a wall outside the crypt. Also notable is a 1738 painting by Basilio Pacheco—the second-largest oil painting in Cusco—representing third-generation Mercedians. The remains of **Diego de Almagro,** *conquistador* of Chile, rest under the church. *(On Mantas, off the Plaza de Armas. Art museum open M-Sa 8am-12:30pm and 2-5:30pm. s/3, not included in tourist ticket. Iglesia open M-Sa after 5pm, Su 10am-1pm. Free.)*

OTHER MUSEUMS. The **Museo Histórico Regional** is housed in the **Casa Garcilaso de la Vega,** former home of the important chronicler of the Incas. Within, there's a collection of pre-Inca ceramics, a mummy with braids that extend 1.5m, galleries of Cusco School paintings, and photos of the damage done by the 1950 earthquake that leveled Cusco. *(On Plaza Regocijo at Garcilaso and Heladeros. ☎ 22 3245. Open M-Sa 8am-5:30pm. Tourist ticket required.)* Across Plaza Regocijo sprawls the **Museo Municipal de Arte Contemporáneo** that displays regional handicrafts and modern painting. *(On San Juan de Dios. ☎ 24 0006. Open M-F 9am-6:30pm, Sa 9am-4pm. Tourist ticket required.)* **Museo de Historia Natural,** on the Plaza de Armas along Portal Compañía, displays several hundred stuffed animals and jars of formaldehyde filled with human embryos and animal oddities. *(Open daily M-F 9am-noon and 3-6pm. s/1.)*

OTHER SIGHTS

HISTORY OF CUSCO MURAL. Painted for Inti Raymi in 1992, the 500th anniversary year of Columbus's arrival in the New World, this colorful street mural portrays scenes from the history of Cusco. Depictions progress through time from left to right: agriculture, mining, and weaving, followed by war and enslavement, fortresses and cathedrals. Inca symbolism is incorporated throughout—see if you can find the puma, serpent, and condor, among others. *(On Sol, 5 blocks down from the Plaza de Armas, opposite the Ministry of Interior building.)*

TOWER OF PACHAKUTEQ. This shining monument, also created as part of the 500th anniversary of Columbus's discovery, serves as a tribute to the greatest Inca. Overachieving Inca Pachakuteq was largely responsible for the power of the glorious Inca empire, known for his daring defense against the invading Chancas, his subsequent conquest and expansion, his administration of the empire through the rule of law and a developing infrastructure, his establishment of a common religion (sun worship) and language (Runa Simi), and his construction of Cusco, the Sacred Valley monuments, and Machu Picchu. Climb the seven stories to the top of the monument—encountering historical depictions and artifacts along the way—for a spectacular 360-degree open-air view of the city and the surrounding mountains. *(On Sol, about 10 blocks down from the Plaza de Armas, halfway to the airport. Open T-Su 8:30am-6pm; tourist ticket required.)* Up on the hill behind the tower, a rival Pachakuteq tower lies unfinished, the abandoned remnants of competing political interests during the main tower's construction.

🎵 ENTERTAINMENT

MOVIES

Many restaurants and discos around the Plaza de Armas screen films in the afternoon and early evening. They aren't just 80s flops, either; somehow Cusco manages to snag recent releases. ▨**Sunset Video Cafe,** Teqsiqocha 2, 2nd fl., with its comfortable bench seats and theater-style snacks (juice s/3-7, milkshakes s/5), is as good as they come. Daily schedules are posted at 10am. (☎80 7434. Open daily 10am-11pm. Films at 3:30, 6:30, 9pm. s/3.) **Movie Net Cafe,** Santa Catalina Ancha 315, shows three movies per day (s/3) and rents DVDs and videos (s/4 per day). The weekly movie schedule is posted at the door. Internet access is in the back. (☎23 4651; www.freewebs.com/movienetcusco. Open daily 9:30am-10pm.) At **The Film,** Procuradores 389, 2nd fl., if you combine your movie experience with s/8 worth of food and drink, your ticket is free. The monthly schedule is posted at the door. (☎962 5898. Films at 1, 5, 9pm (s/2). Open M-Sa 1pm-midnight, Su 4pm-midnight.) **Mama África,** Santa Catalina Angosta 135 (☎24 1979) and **Mythology,** Portal de Carnes 298 (☎ 80 1744), each show two movies per day, free of charge; call to find out the schedule (see **Nightlife,** p. 239).

MUSIC AND THEATER

At night, restaurants and bars around the Plaza de Armas host live traditional music. For more formal dance performances, the **Centro Q'osqo,** Sol 604, has folk music and dances from Cusco and the surrounding region. (☎22 7901. Shows at 7pm. Tourist ticket required.) The **Teatro Municipal,** Mesón de la Estrella 149, also puts on occasional concerts, plays, and dance shows. (☎23 1847. Shows at 6 or 7pm. s/15.) Cusco's most authentic music and drama displays fill the streets during festivals, especially Inti Raymi (below), at the end of June.

JUNE: THE MONTH OF CUSCO

While the rest of Peru plods steadily along from day to day, every day is a party in Cusco, at least in the month of June. Each morning, a band marching through the streets awakens groggy tourists—cannon fire and firecrackers guarantee that no one sleeps too late. The Plaza de Armas empties of its normally ubiquitous taxis, only to fill with locals scrambling over each other to catch a glimpse of the day's parade (the luckier ones stake out spots on the balconies that overlook the Plaza). Huge stadium speakers in front of the main cathedral introduce each act as it passes by: choirs in traditional dress sing highland songs, children gleefully perform well-rehearsed traditional dances, actors interpret historical scenes and traditions, and families parade behind the crests of their saints. When the sun sets at the end of the day, fireworks light up the sky before the procession fizzles to a close and the blue-clad street cleaners begin their task of cleaning up for the night, prepared as always to do it all again tomorrow.

No one here needs a reason to party; if you ask a local what a particular procession is about, he'll likely respond with a simple "Es una celebración" ("It's a celebration, silly"). In reality, Cusco's celebrations are a mixture of religious and secular, historical and

▓ FESTIVALS

The most exciting festivals in Cusco are **Semana Santa,** the week before Easter, when El Señor de los Temblores (see **The Cathedral,** p. 231) parades through the Plaza de Armas; **Corpus Christi** (on the Thursday following Trinity Sunday), with its processions and abundant feasting; and, most importantly, **Inti Raymi** (June 24, around the winter solstice), the world-famous festival of the sun god. Cusco goes crazy as thousands of people fill its plazas to witness fireworks, dancing, parades, and hundreds of pounds of confetti strewn across the ground. Meanwhile, an elaborate pageant at Sacsayhuamán reaches new heights of revelry with song, dance, and the climactic sacrifice of a llama. Book accommodations well in advance.

 SAVE THE DATE. Inti Raymi is the well-known Inca celebration of the sun god, and it is widely supposed to take place on the day of the winter solstice. In fact, the festival takes place on June 24, three days late (the solstice falls on June 21). Is this the result of a miscalculation? Far from it: the Incas were impeccable astronomers. Rather, the fault lies with Spanish colonialists who, in an effort to coordinate Quechua traditions with Catholic ones, enforced a three-day postponement of Inti Raymi so as to coincide with the Spanish celebration of St. John's Day. Even after colonialism ended, the tradition stuck.

⬛⬛ SHOPPING AND ARTESANÍA

The immense **market** on the corner of Garcilaso and Huáscar is where locals shop and true bargains are found. (Open daily 8am-10pm.) A variety of specialty shops surround Plaza San Francisco, from the shoe-stocked stores along **Marqués,** between Heladeros and Plaza San Francisco, to **La Ibérica,** Plaza San Francisco 154-158, a full-fledged, fully-stocked candy store with imported sweets. (☎24 0810. Candy s/11-20. Soccer balls s/7. Open M-Sa 9am-1pm and 3:30-7:30pm.)

Cusco is the central exchange for handicrafts from all over Peru: carved gourds from Huancayo, tapestries from Ayacucho, weavings from the coast, sweaters and silver jewelry from all over the Andes, suggestive ceramic keychains from—well, no one will admit where. The enormous **Centro Artesanal Cusco,** on Ahuacpinta, off Sol, has hundreds of stalls to browse, and many vendors are eager to bargain. (Open daily 8am-9pm; cash only.) Likewise, jewelry craftsmen tend to set up shop along Procuradores, just off the Plaza de Armas. In the Plaza itself, adjacent to La Compañía, is the **Arte Vivo del Cusco al Mundo,** featuring work from a variety of Cusqueñan artists. (Open M-Sa 10:30am-1pm and 3:30-9pm. Free.) Stores in **San Blas,** the neighborhood uphill from and behind the cathedral, may be more expensive, but they often feature the work of neighborhood artists, including oil paintings, delicate ceramics, and lively painted masks and religious objects. **Mullo** offers by far the best collection of contemporary art in Cusco, at incredibly reasonable prices. Exquisite and stylish silver jewelry ranges s/20-300, equally affordable and far more beautiful than the jewelry that fills many a tourist shop around the Plaza. (☎22 9379. Open M-Sa 9am-5pm.) Mullo also displays and sells the work of 40 young Peruvian painters and printmakers, whose vibrant colors and styles convey powerful images of life in modern-day Peru. To get to Mullo, walk through **Another Planet,** Triunfo 120. Also, many restaurants and cafes simultaneously act as art galleries, displaying and selling pieces from up-and-coming local artists.

🗲 NIGHTLIFE

BARS

You'll never go thirsty for a beer in Cusco—that is, if your beer of choice is Cusqueña. Although the city's many foreign-owned pubs have brought international brews such as Guinness, Bass, Foster's, and Budweiser to the Plaza de Armas, only you can decide if a hometown high is worth the price. Maybe if you grab enough of the **free drink coupons** that local club promoters thrust at plaza-strollers, you'll be able to afford it. However, those suffering from altitude sickness should be careful; alcohol affects the body differently at higher altitudes, tending to make acclimation worse.

■ **Fallen Angel,** Plaza de Nazareñas 211 (☎25 8184; www.fallenangelincusco.com). As hip as any "in" spot in New York, London, or Paris, but at Cusco prices. Illuminated glass tables with fish swimming underneath, exquisite murals, and luxurious daybeds covered in pillows make for some of the best interior design in town. Walk through heaven, hell, and limbo, and choose to sit where you feel most comfortable. Excellent steak, salad, and pasta s/18-32. Martinis, cosmopolitans, and Manhattans galore s/12-20. VIP room available with reservation. Open daily 10am-late.

modern, indigenous and colonial—the essence of *mestizaje.* One day the people might celebrate their Quechua heritage and descendancy from the Incas; or the next, they will celebrate Catholic saints and the holiness of the Virgin Mary. It may be that an Inca ruler marches by shouting mandates and raising cheers from the crowd, followed by a group of miners shouting praise for the positive contribution that mining has made to Peruvian society.

The festivities reach their frenzied climax between June 16-24, building up to Inti Raymi. While finding a warm bed to sleep in isn't too hard, flights to and from Lima are filled to the brim in the last two weeks of June, so make your travel arrangements well in advance. The government publishes a schedule of the month's festivities, available at the municipal tourist office or at iPerú.

Of course, June isn't the only festive time in Cusco. Cusqueñans greet the new year with the symbolic **Entrega de Varas,** the passing of the wooden scepter of power *(vara)* to the Mayor, or Varayoc; at the end of March, Cusco and the surrounding areas host the **Fiesta de Sara Raymi,** or corn festival, and the celebration of the **Señor de los Temblores,** or Lord of the Earthquakes; on December 24, artisans on Cusco's main plaza celebrate **Santuranticuy** by selling religious figurines to liven up many a Christmas nativity scene.

Mandela's Bar, Palacio 121, 3rd fl. (☎22 2424; mandelasbar@yahoo.com). African tribalism is the theme of this tranquil lounge. Check out the rooftop seating area—if you thought you'd seen the best views in Cusco, think again. Sandwiches and snacks s/10. Entrees s/15-22. Drinks s/9-15. Happy hour 7:30-8:30pm and 10:30-11:30pm. DJ or live music after 9pm, best on Sa. Open daily 10am-late. No credit cards.

Fanáticos Pub, Santa Catalina Angosta 169 (☎24 0022; Jarot27@hotmail.com). This loud and lively pub has something for everyone. International music and music videos play in the background. Tacos (s/10-12). Multi-colored *Fanáticos* cocktail (s/12). Frequent, fun promotions and discounts. Happy hour M, Su after 5pm. Open daily noon-4pm and 7pm-late. MC/V.

Cross Keys, Portal de Confiturías 233, 2nd fl. (☎22 9227), on the Plaza de Armas. This established English pub fills nightly with expats and travelers. Munch on standard grub while you play pool or darts and enjoy the view. English Premier League shown every weekend. *Pisco* sour s/10. Assorted cocktails s/8-15. SAE discount 10% on beer. Happy hour 6:30-7:30pm and 9:30-10pm. Open daily 10am-1am.

Garabato, Espaderos 135, 3rd fl. (☎25 7740). Sidle up to the bar in this Peruvian version of the OK Corral, mount the saddle-topped barstools to sip the *garabato* (s/15) and fill up with some fast food (s/9-18) before you ride off into the sunset. Beer s/5. Live show nightly 10:30pm. Music varies daily (M rock, Tu Latin, W folk, Th and F rock, Sa *criolla*). Open daily 6pm-late.

The Muse, Tandapata 684 (☎24 6332; themusecusco@yahoo.dom), uphill off the Plazoleta San Blas. A hotspot for art-lovers, this fashionable conversation lounge also serves as a gallery, exhibiting contemporary works of art on its walls. Maybe after a few martinis (s/12) you'll think you can afford one. Drinks and snacks s/6-12. Happy hour 9:30-10:30pm and 12-1am. Live music each night after 10pm. Open daily 9am-late.

Norton Rat's Tavern, Intik'ijllu 115, 2nd fl. (☎24 6204), between Portal de la Compañía and Portal de Carrizos, on the Plaza de Armas. The tavern counts both Americans and Peruvians among its clientele. Spectacular balconies capture the nighttime lights. 3 dartboards and 2 pool tables. Tourists keep coming back for the Super Duper Norton Burger (s/10). Long Island iced tea s/7. "Aphrodisiac" drinks s/6-20. Beer s/5. Happy hour 7-9pm. Open daily 9am-3am.

Tangible Myth, San Juan de Dios 260 (☎26 0519; tangiblemyth@hotmail.com). This chill jazz bar draws a sizeable nightly crowd. Live jazz, funk, and blues bands at 9pm. Drinks s/5-18. Open M-Sa 3pm-late.

Paddy Flaherty's, Triunfo 124 (☎22 4663), to the right of the cathedral, off the Plaza de Armas. Always crowded, always fun. The faithful gather to watch rugby and other sports. English spoken, a lot. The famous shepherd's pie (s/12) is apparently made from a secret Irish recipe. Pint of Guinness s/15. Draft beer s/5-9. Happy hour 7-8pm and 10-10:30pm. Open daily 11am-1am.

Tierra del Sol, Carmen Alto 227 (☎24 9931), in San Blas. Brilliant hues of orange and yellow engulf you in every direction as you pore over Japanese comic books or browse the selection of handmade beaded necklaces (US$10-30). *Milanesa* (breaded fried cutlets) s/10-11. Drinks s/6-11. Beer s/6. Open M-Sa 9-1am, Su 7pm-1am.

Rosie O'Grady's, Santa Catalina Ancha 360 (☎24 3514; www.geocities.com/rosiesin-cusco), near Herrajes. This Irish watering hole eschews dark wooden interiors for light, upscale decor. Football and rugby fans gather around the TV. Live music every F-Sa at 9pm. Appetizers s/10-23. Entrees s/15-30. Drinks s/5-20. Guinness (when available) s/15. Cusqueña s/5. Discount for large groups. Happy hour 1-2pm and 8:30-9:30pm. Takeout available. Open daily 11am-2am. All major credit cards.

Jaguiga Bar Snooker, San Juan de Dios 268 (☎963 6438). A small billiards bar with 2 tables and alternative rock music in the background. Pool s/4 per hr. Drinks s/4-10. Open daily 1pm-2am.

CLUBS

Most nights of the week (especially June-Aug.), the streets around the Plaza de Armas thump to the beat of Cusco's discos. Some charge cover on Fridays and Saturdays, but free passes circulate on the Plaza. Leave the blue suede shoes at home—where foreigners hit the floor, Gore-Tex and fleece dominate the dress code. And don't expect to get to bed while it's still dark.

Ukukus, Plateros 316 (☎24 2951). Plenty of seating and floor space accommodate crowds at Plateros's hippest nightspot. DJs play rock, pop, salsa, and techno. Cusqueña s/5. Live music 11pm-midnight. Happy hour 8-9:30pm. Open late.

Kamikase, Plaza Regocijo 274, 2nd fl. (☎23 3865). The oldest disco-pub in town, Kamikase keeps on keepin' on. Standard reggae, disco, and 80s tunes play until dawn. Balcony over the Plaza. Fantastic Andean bar band plays 10:30pm-midnight. Beer s/5. Happy hour 8-10pm. Open daily 8pm-late.

Mama África, Portal de Harinas 191, 2nd fl. (☎24 1979), on the Plaza de Armas. Plays mostly house and hip-hop, and draws a much chiller crowd to its safari-themed space than some other *discotecas*. Celebrates festivals and holidays from around the world. English spoken. Pizzas s/12-15. Beer s/6. Drinks s/4-10. Happy hour 8:30-11pm. Salsa lessons nightly 9-11:30pm. Open daily 11am-late. All major credit cards.

Mama Amerika, Portal de Belén 115, 2nd fl., on the Plaza de Armas. The evening movie-goers morph into a lively night crowd at this modern cinema-disco. The decor includes a python that wraps around the ceiling to bite you at the bar. Sandwiches and other grub s/4-6. Beer s/5. Happy hour 3-10pm. Movies at 4 and 6pm. Free salsa lessons every night 9-10pm. Open daily 2pm-late. No credit cards.

Mythology, Portal de Carnes 298 (☎80 1744), on the Plaza de Armas. This disco plays mostly pop, hip-hop, and lots of Madonna for its largely American and Israeli clientele. Beer s/5. Drinks s/5-12. Happy hour M-Th, Su after 9pm. Open daily 9pm-late.

El Muki, Santa Catalina Angosta 114 (☎22 7799), near the Plaza de Armas. This favorite local hideaway is enormous and always crowded. El Muki plays everything from Britney Spears to Peter Tosh. F-Sa s/10 cover, includes a free drink. Women get 2 free drinks on Th. Open daily 10pm-late.

🏔 GUIDED TOURS FROM CUSCO

At the hub of the Peruvian travel network, Cusco tour agencies offer countless trips, ranging from easy and cheap (city and Sacred Valley tours) to more rugged (Inca Trail) and expensive (Parque Nacional del Manú). Prices vary—the following are high-season (May-Sept.) averages. Be forewarned that ever since the January 2001 Inca Trail restrictions (see p. 260), all tours of national parks and reserve areas in Peru have skyrocketed in price and continue to climb. In the last five years, Inca Trail prices have more than quadrupled. Shop around for the cheapest agencies, but remember that you get what you pay for. Cheaper tour agencies tend to be less kind to the environment and their workers; the companies listed below all have a good record of treating their surroundings and helpers with respect. Intrepid explorers can tackle some of these trips without an agency's help—look for maps, directions, and possible companions at the **South American Explorers** or the **tourist office** (see **Tourist and Financial Services,** p. 219). For more information on outdoor excursions, see **Trekking and Hiking,** p. 49.

THE INCA TRAIL

The standard 4-day, 3-night Inca Trail trek travels from Ollantaytambo to the gates of Machu Picchu (see **The Inca Trail,** p. 260, for day-by-day coverage of the trek). Recent government regulations have restricted the number of people on the trail each day to 500, including guides, porters, cooks, and staff. Reservations (at least with reputable agencies) must be made **at least 30 days in advance.**

A few agencies lead shorter or longer trips along the trail, and several "alternative" trails are rising in popularity in the face of regulations that limit Inca Trail travel. One such alternative is the 5- to 7-day **Salkantay** trek (p. 264) to Machu Picchu, offered by many of the same agencies for about the same price as the Inca Trail. The Salkantay trek avoids the conventional tourist path and skips the archaeological sites along the Inca Trail, but it is a quieter route with more exposure to the area's flora and fauna. Reservations for Salkantay can often be made as late as the day before departure.

No matter which trek you choose, bring your **passport** (and foreign-issued ISIC, if you have one) to the agency when making your reservation.

TIP

TRAVELING THE TRAIL.

Prices: Beware of agencies that offer cheap deals (under US$200); you'll get what you pay for.

Reservations: Confirm and reconfirm your reservations **at least one month in advance.** Check your agency's website for any changes, since prices and conditions can change unpredictably.

Guides: Ask if you will have the same guide for the Inca Trail and Machu Picchu. Some agencies save money by sending less experienced guides on the Inca Trail, then hiring a new one at Machu Picchu, since only certified guides are allowed into the ruins.

Porters and Cooks: Make sure that porters and cooks are given a place to sleep (a tent, not a cave), and tip well—they need and deserve it.

The agencies listed below are accredited, with guides certified for both the Inca Trail and Machu Picchu. They also all have agents and guides who speak English, and their cooks can even accommodate vegetarian preferences.

 Liz's Explorers, Calle de Medio 114 (☎24 6619; www.lizexplorer.com). Charmingly energetic Liz will put together a very well-structured trip for you. Guide Carlos Vásquez repeatedly earns rave reviews. Group size 2-18. US$250, students US$225. Also arranges ice-climbing. Open daily 8:30am-9:30pm. MC/V with 8% surcharge.

SAS Travel Peru, Garcilaso 256 (☎26 4249; www.sastravelperu.com), off Plaza Regocijo. Professional and personalized service. Group size 8-16. US$295, students US$270. Open M-Sa 8:30am-7:30pm, Su 4-8pm. AmEx/MC/V with 5% surcharge.

Q'ente Adventure Trips, Garcilaso 210 2nd fl. (☎23 3722; www.qente.com). High-season (June-Aug.) group size 8-18, low-season 8-12. US$270, students US$250. Salkantay US$570. Open M-Sa 8:30am-1:30pm and 3:30-7:30pm. All major credit cards.

United Mice, Plateros 351 (☎22 1139; www.unitedmice.com). Specialized guides. Inca Trail or Salkantay US$270, students US$250. Open daily 8am-8pm.

PARQUE NACIONAL DEL MANÚ

Most of the companies that head to Manú (see **Parque Nacional del Manú,** p. 422) offer similar packages, with tours ranging from 4-9 days. Some trips involve flying to Boca Manú, a town near the mouth of the reserve zone, or to Puerto Maldonado, on the opposite side of the reserve, but these save only time. Trips that bus in and out cost less and witness all the heights of Manú's forest.

Guides should be environmentally knowledgeable and conscientious. As you might expect from the name, beware of agencies claiming to be able to take you into the **impenetrable zone**—this is illegal and can be harmful to indigenous tribes. Heavy tourism, especially in the cultural zone, has led to a decrease in the number of sightings of endangered species, but with a sharp eye and the aid of an experienced guide, you'll still be able to see flora and fauna found nowhere else.

The companies below have fixed schedules from May to December; from January to April, the reserve zone often closes due to flooding. Expect to pay an entrance fee (US$50) and any airport taxes if you are flying, which are not included in the prices below. All these agencies employ English-speaking guides.

⚐ Pantiacolla Tours, Plateros 360 (☎23 8323; www.pantiacolla.com). Run by a biologist who worked in Manú, the (more) affordable and comparatively good Pantiacolla sends out camping tours as well as more posh, lodge-based tours. Pantiacolla also sponsors "Project Yine," a community-based program that organizes 3-day tours involving pottery-making, canoeing, and archery lessons with Manú natives (US$290). Camping tours: 9 days, 8 nights US$785 (in and out by bus); 7 days, 6 nights US$815 (in by bus and out by plane); 5 days, 4 nights US$745 (in and out by plane). SAE discount 10%, discount for large groups (20 people max.). Open M-Sa 9am-1am, Su 4-8pm.

Manú Ecological Adventures, Plateros 356 (☎26 1640; www.manuadventures.com), sends the most visitors to the park. Trips to the reserve zone leave 3 days a week. Trips to the cultural zone leave daily (2 people min.). 8 days, 7 nights US$640 (in and out by bus); 7 days, 6 nights US$640 (in and out by bus), US$726 (in by bus, out by plane); 6 days, 5 nights US$726 (in by plane, out by bus or vice versa); 5 days, 4 nights US$804 (in and out by plane). SAE or student discount 10%. Open M-Sa 8:30am-9pm, Su 8am-8pm. All major credit cards.

Vilca Expediciones, Plateros 363 (☎24 4751; www.cbc.org.pe/manuvilca). Vilca guides are both knowledgeable about the area and extremely eco-conscious. 8 days, 7 nights US$650 (in and out by bus), US$750 (in by bus, out by plane). 7 days, 6 nights US$770 (in by plane, out by bus), US$650 (in by bus, out by plane). 6 days, 5 nights US$750 (in by bus, out by plane). 5 days, 4 nights US$820 (in and out by plane). 4 days, 3 nights US$480 (in by bus, out by plane), US$780 (in and out by plane). SAE discount US$50. Open daily 8:30am-8pm. All major credit cards.

Inkanatura Travel, Plateros 361, 2nd fl. (☎25 1173; www.inkanatura.com). It may be expensive, but it's also incredibly organized, intellectually and physically challenging, and luxuriously accommodating—their "Cock-of-the-Rock" campsite is one of the few with flush toilets. 6 days, 5 nights US$1290 (in by bus, out by plane); 5 days, 4 nights US$1090 (in by bus, out by plane); 4 days, 3 nights US$950 (in and out by plane); 3 days, 2 nights US$450 (in and out by bus). Open M-Sa 10am-8pm, Su 4-8pm.

MISCELLANEOUS ADVENTURES

From the back of a horse to the back of a Harley, there are many ways to explore the area surrounding Cusco. Most adventure expeditions involve some advanced preparation and a guide, but others can be done spontaneously and independently.

WHITEWATER RAFTING

Of the various expeditions that run out of Cusco, **rafting** on the **Río Urubamba** (May-Sept. Class I-III; Oct.-Apr. Class III-V) is the most popular. The **Río Apurímac** offers lengthier expeditions (usually 4 days, May-Sept. only, Class IV-V). Be wary of companies that cut costs; they may also compromise safety. Raft only with reputable agencies, and make sure they cover the basics: life jackets and emergency preparations are a must. Rafting companies also often organize excursions on horseback and other outdoor adventures.

Swissraft, Plateros 369 (☎24 6414; www.swissraft-peru.com). 1-day trips on the Urubamba (Apr.-Dec.) US$20; 2-day trips on the Vilcanota (Jan.-Mar.) US$55-65; 3-day trips on the Apurimac (May-Dec.) US$175. Prices include transportation, food, and accommodations. No experience necessary. Open M-Sa 9am-8pm, Su 10am-8pm.

Eric Adventures, Plateros 324 (☎22 8475; www.ericadventures.com). Daily rafting trips on the Urubamba (US$25). 3-day kayaking lessons on the Apurimac in the dry season, Urubamba in the rainy season (US$100). See the website for information about many other excursions. Open M-Sa 9am-10pm, Su 9am-noon and 5-10pm.

CUSCO AND THE SACRED VALLEY

Instinct, Procuradores 50 (☎23 3451; www.instinct-travel.com), at the Plaza de Armas. Río Urubamba trips (1 day US$35), the Apurimac (4 days US$270), or into the Amazon (10 days US$700). Prices include transportation, food, and equipment. Instinct guides also lead treks on little-known trails through the Sacred Valley. 4 people min. All rafting guides are paramedics. SAE discount. Open daily 9am-1pm and 4-9pm.

HORSEBACK RIDING AND BIKING

Perol Chico (☎62 4475; www.perolchico.com). The Dutch owner saddles his mounts with traditional Peruvian riding equipment for treks through Quechua communities and trout farms. 1- to 12-day routes through the Urubamba Valley, including trips to Moray and Las Salineras. All leave from Urubamba. All experience levels. Many packages available, including: 1 day US$80; 2 days US$275-295; 12 days up to US$2500. Food and accommodations included. 10% SAE discount. Open daily 8am-8pm.

Loreto Tours, Medio 111 (☎22 8264). 1-day mountain-biking trip through Sacred Valley US$25 (chrome bike) or US$30 (aluminum bike). 1-day horseback-riding trip to Sacsayhuamán, Puca Pucara, and Tambomachay US$17 ("cultural route," includes Qenco) or US$20 ("mystical route," includes Salumpuncu). 1-day rafting trip on the Urubamba US$20. Rents 250cc motorcycles, US$45 per day. Open daily 9am-9pm.

Cusco Mountain, Plateros 394 (☎43 2454; www.mountaintours.com). Rents mountain bikes and leads biking tours through Moray, Las Salineras, and Urubamba. US$10 per day. Open M-F 9am-8pm.

Inversiones X-treme, Plateros 358 (☎22 4362). Rents specialized mountain bikes (US$15 per day). Open M-F 8:30am-8:30pm.

Rent-a-Harley, Garcilaso 265 (☎24 9348), off Plaza Regocijo. The noisy, wind-blowing-through-your-hair way to see the Sacred Valley. 4hr. US$79, 6hr. US$99, 24hr. US$139. Helmet, locks, and saddlebags included. Must be 28+ with a valid motorcycle driver's license. Open daily 9am-6pm. All major credit cards.

OTHER ADVENTURES

Learn the meaning of breathtaking as you glide, soar, climb, or swing through the awe-inspiring Andean scenery.

■ **Tandem Paraglider** (☎99 7333). Get a thrilling bird's-eye view of the Sacred Valley as you soar with Richard the Cloudwalker. No experience necessary. Half-day trips from Cusco (US$70). Call or email in advance.

Globos de los Andes, Casilla Postal 117 (☎23 2352; www.globosperu.com). Float above the Sacred Valley in a hot air balloon, up to 200m. US$50 per person. Price includes transport, drinks, live local Andean music, and 1hr. in the air.

Richard Sánchez (claveazulrsc@yahoo.com). Inquire at **Liz's Explorers** (p. 242) for this rough and highly experienced guide who leads ice-climbing expeditions on Chicón and San Juan (p. 254). US$60 per day.

Action Valley Cusco, Portal de Panes 123, of. 105 (☎24 0835; www.actionvalley-cusco.com), also field location 11km from Cusco on the Poroy highway. If you're itching for the extreme, try the bungee-jump (US$59), slingshot (US$59), or giant swing (US$15). Open daily 9am-6pm.

▶ DAYTRIPS FROM CUSCO

■ THE ROAD TO PISAC

Most sites in the Sacred Valley could qualify as daytrips from Cusco, but the area is so impressive in its own right that it gets its own section (p. 249). The following sites and sights are closer to the city, along the paved road to Pisac, and make excellent dayhike destinations. Prominent signs show the way to each. Some visitors like to view the ruins in reverse by taking a taxi (s/20) to Tambomachay, the farthest from Cusco, and then walking downhill. You can also catch a Pisac- or Calca-bound colectivo on Tullumayo, just south of Garcilaso in the lot on the left, and ask to get off at Tambomachay (30min., s/2). Agencies in Cusco offer horseback tours of the route (see **Horseback Riding and Biking,** p. 244); or you can rent horses at the Corcel Ranch just outside Sacsayhuamán or down the road from Cristo Blanco (5hr., s/25). If you leave Cusco around midday, you should be able to visit all the sights and return to the city by sundown.

SACSAYHUAMÁN

Sacsayhuamán is a steep hike from the town center, up either Choquechaka from San Blas or Resbalosa (a continuation of Suecia) from the Plaza de Armas (30min.). Open daily 7am-6pm. Tourist ticket required.

THE FORTRESS. Sacsayhuamán is arguably the most impressive ruin near Cusco (excluding Machu Picchu, of course), but half the fun may come from saying the name (pronounced, roughly, "sexy woman"). Legend says that the Incas created Cusco in the shape of a puma, and Sacsayhuamán is believed to form its head; the name may come from the words "sacsa uma," Quechua for "speckled head." While Inca Pachakuteq is credited with its construction as part of his imperial expansion, Sacsayhuamán is most famous as the site of a key battle during Inca Manco Cápac II's rebellion against the Spanish in 1536. The Incas claimed the fortress early in the struggle, garrisoning it with an estimated 5000 troops, and using it as a headquarters from which to attack Cusco. They seemed successful at first—conquistador Juan Pizarro (Francisco's half-brother) died from a slingshot wound in an attempt to win the area. But the bitter fighting that followed claimed thousands of lives and ended with a Spanish victory and Manco Cápac's retreat to Ollantaytambo. Many historians feel that this battle solidified the Spaniards' conquest and that Manco Cápac's loss of Sacsayhuamán sealed his empire's fate.

THE RUINS. Because of this grim history, people often think of Sacsayhuamán as little more than a fortress, but the original complex included many non-defensive buildings and towers. After the Spanish victory, most of these structures were demolished. The site then served as a municipal stone quarry until excavations halted this function in 1935, but by that point many of the structures had disappeared. Nevertheless, the parts that still exist are among the most remarkable Inca ruins around. Three tiers of giant zigzag stone ramparts were too massive to be carried off (the biggest stone was estimated at 8.5m and 361 tons) and now amaze visitors with their precise interlocking edges. Three towers—**Muyucmarca, Sayacmarca,** and **Paucarmarca**—once stood on the hill behind these ramparts, and the first two still have intact foundations. Only a few structures remain on the opposite hill, including the **Rodadero,** the site of an Inca throne formed from slick, carved volcanic rock. Just over the hill lies **Suchuna,** a round depression and a clearing that may have been a reservoir or water worship site. Short **tunnels** at the edge of the clearing dare tourists to stumble through their pitch-black interiors. At night, powerful lamps bathe the fortress in soft yellow light.

CRISTO BLANCO

Atop the hill, on the path between Sacsayhuamán and Qenco, visible from the city.

A replica of the larger, original Cristo Blanco in Brazil, this towering ivory statue of Christ faces the city, arms outstretched. The statue was a gift from the Palestinian Arab community in 1945, and a post nearby reads (in Quechua) "Alli n kay kaypacha wiñaypaqkachun," or "Peace prevails in the world."

QENCO

Near Km3 on the road to Pisac. Open daily 7am-6pm. Tourist ticket required.

Qenco ("zigzag") is a large limestone outcropping that the Incas altered for religious purposes, probably to serve as a shrine. It is one of the most interesting ruins because its former use is obvious. Inside, at the center of the structure (follow the side opening through the narrow tunnels) is a broad, flat rock—a **sacrificial table**—where the Incas sacrificed llamas to honor Pachamama (goddess of the earth). Steps cut into the side of the rock lead from the tunnels underneath to the top of the outcropping, where Inca priests poured animal blood down the **zig-zag channels** carved into the rock to predict the future by the path the liquid took: a turn to the right signified a good year, while a turn to the left gave cause for worry. Some interesting carvings on top of the outcropping include a small llama in relief and an even smaller headless condor, both located on the side closest to the road. Toward the center sits a small sundial, with lines in the stone indicating the equinoxes. Closer to the plateau's interior sits a mysterious stone topped by two fat cylinders and a small replica of a house. At the edge of the rock, a large 19-niche **amphitheater** surrounds a tall, decrepit rock, suspected to be a religious symbol of some sort, perhaps carved in the form of a sitting puma. The caves underneath the outcropping probably held **mummified remains** of Inca nobility.

SALUMPUNCU

About 1km past Qenco, off to the right from the main road that leads toward Puca Pucara.

This intricately carved Temple of the Moon is still used for rituals today. Inside the main cave sits the **mesa del templo,** an altar adorned with flower petals and ceremonial tokens. Some believe that the rock here—composed largely of quartz—emits positive energy, and small ceremonies are conducted every day throughout the year. A tiny speck of light falls onto the altar, entering through a small fissure in the rock high above. The **solstice moon** shines directly into the opening, and the speck of light grows until the altar is bathed in moonlight. The altar was also used as a sacrificial table: carved into the lower right side is a funnel leading to a narrow canal that drains into a hole below the stone archway—thus directing the animal's blood from the sacrificial table to the earth goddess Pachamama. Salumpuncu's stones are carved with several important animal symbols. The entrance is not so much an archway as it is a llamaway (entrance in the shape of a llama): looking at the entrance from inside the sacrificial space, it sits in profile facing right. As you exit, in relief along the upper-left of the tunnel, a serpent follows you out. Once you're back outside, a puma sits on the ground to your right and a condor perches on the ground front and center, facing you.

WAYACOCHA

Wayacocha can be reached by horseback or by car: the town lies on the horse trail between Salumpuncu and Puca Pucara and on the Cusco-Pisac road.

Wayacocha (pop. 500) is famous for absolutely nothing—perhaps that's what makes it so serene. In this town of highland farmers living in mud-and-brick houses, you'll likely be the only gringo within the village's 2km radius. Here's your chance to take it all in: unobstructed views of the hills meeting the horizon, the occasional cool breeze in the nearby eucalyptus trees, and sheep grazing along the "wet green" fields ("waya"=green, "cocha"=water).

PUCA PUCARA

About 6km beyond Qenco on the road to Pisac. Open daily 7am-5:30pm. Tourist ticket required.

"Puca Pucara" means "red fort," but the building more likely served as a kind of lodge. The site lies on what used to be a major commercial artery for the Incas, a roadway connecting Cusco with Pisac, Calca, and Urubamba. The buildings may have been both a resting place and an administrative center. Some also suspect that it could have been Inca Pachakuteq's hunting lodge. During wartime, the Incas used the fort for military purposes, quartering soldiers in the individual *tambos* (resting rooms) and basing reconnaissance missions within its walls. The messenger room has six windows carved into the rock. There was once also a lookout tower, but it fell during the battles with the Spanish. Much of present-day Puca Pucara is the product of reconstruction; due to the war with the Spanish, looting of rock for construction, and a devastating earthquake in the 1970s, very little of the original rock remains.

TAMBOMACHAY

About 0.5km beyond Puca Pucara on the road to Pisac. Open daily 7am-5:30pm. Tourist ticket required.

The misnamed Tambomachay means "cavern lodge," but is actually an ancient site of **water worship.** The cool, clear glacial water was believed to be the purest water in all the Inca Empire. A water cult directed the hillside's underground stream through a series of stone fountains, which still work today. There are four levels of fountains, each signifying one of the four natural elements (air, water, fire, earth). Ceremonies took place in December, at the beginning of the rainy season, to encourage the coming of the rain, and in April to entreat its halt. Below the main temple site (on the gravel path leading toward the road), a smaller fountain and stone bench were the site of **ritual bathing.** Most garden-variety ritual bathing took place here, while the upper fountains were reserved for rare ceremonial occasion and elite higher nobility. **Water cultists** still occasionally pilgrimage to Tambomachay, holding hands and calling upon the gods.

SOUTHEAST OF CUSCO

The sights this side of Cusco may not be as well known as others, but travelers hungry for more ancient ruins and untouristed towns will enjoy the trip. The highway southeast of Cusco is well paved and well used. Along the road, turnoffs to archaeological sites are marked by blue INC signs. The best way to travel the road is to catch a bus from Cusco's **Terminal de Sicuani,** on Av. de la Cultura (every 20min. 7am-7pm), hop off as you please to see the ruins, and then catch the next bus, combi, or taxi as it passes. Two small cities, Urcos (p. 248) and Sicuani (p. 248), can be visited along the way.

TIPÓN

Turnoff 23km past Cusco on the road to Sicuani (bus s/1). 4km uphill from the main road. Approx. 1hr. hike or 10min. taxi ride (s/5) up the dirt road. Open daily 7am-5:30pm. Tourist ticket required.

This vast collection of renovated mountainside terraces (elev. 3400m) is Inca agriculture at its most impressive. Water flows forcefully through the deep vertical irrigation channels, spattering and bubbling, giving rise to its Quechua name, *Timpuj* (boiling). The terraces' location protected them from floods and natural disasters, and their elaborate construction suggests that they may have been used for special crop strains or experimental agriculture. Climb the stone steps jutting out from the wall to traverse the path that runs alongside the right side of the fields. Several stone showers have been built alongside the path, fed by water that is diverted from the main irrigation canals. Near the upper terraces, the **zona urbana** contained housing for Inca farmers and field workers. At the very top, near the source canal, a series of fountains—the **fuente ceremonial**—served as a sacred site for water worship. The ruins of an old lookout tower loom on the opposite side of the fields, atop a hill. Behind it, a path called **El Camino Inca** leads uphill to more dwellings, unrenovated terraces, and a ritual site known as **Intiwatana**, to which the Incas ascended on ceremonial occasions to perform sacrifices to the sun god.

PIKILLACTA AND RUMICOLCA

About 7km past Tipón on the road to Sicuani, on opposite sides of the road from each other. Pikillacta is open daily 7am-5:30pm; tourist ticket required. Rumicolca is always open and free.

Pikillacta, or "Flea Town," is one of the rare ruins of the pre-Inca Huari culture (AD 600-950). Much of the old **fort** has now been destroyed or eroded, but fragments of wall are left here and there, and it is easy to imagine the barracks and storage rooms that once lined this labyrinthine complex. Some archaeologists believe that, rather than being used for military purposes, Pikillacta was a meeting place for rulers and thus hosted alliance-building feasts and rituals. The site is quite vast and is entirely enclosed by a long stone wall. **Rumicolca,** also constructed by the Huari, was once connected with Pikillacta and served as an aqueduct to supply the fort with water. The **water channels** can still be seen atop the large stone structures. The original construction was partially demolished by the Incas and then rebuilt as a large gateway and entrance checkpoint to the Inca capital at Cusco. These assorted uses across time and cultures explains the diversity of architectural techniques evident, with crude pre-Inca construction shored up by characteristically perfect Inca stonework.

URCOS   ☎ 084

The first major town on the road between Cusco and Lake Titicaca is tiny, isolated Urcos (pop. 25,000). The most notable sights are the **Laguna** (lake, always open and free) and the **Capilla Caninccunca** (open daily dawn to dusk, free) that lies on the shore opposite the town. Legend has it that a heavy gold chain lies at the bottom of the lake, frantically thrown in by the Inca Huáscar to preserve it from the rapidly approaching Spanish invaders. The small chapel is heavily decorated with valuable murals from the Cusco School.

Accommodations are lackluster, but if you're forced to stay here, **Hostal Amigo ❶**, Vallejo 321, uphill from the Plaza de Armas, provides basic accommodations. (☎30 7151. Singles and doubles with shared bath s/7 per person.) The main Plaza is lined with affordable *pollerías* and swarming with bread-sellers, for which Urcos is famous. If you happen to be in town on a weekend and are looking for something more formal, **Quinta Restaurante ❸** sits next to the lake on Prolongación Mariano Melgar and is blessed with panoramic views for diners to enjoy with their typical Andean food. (☎30 7334. Entrees s/15-20. Open Sa-Su 8am-6pm.)

Urcos lies 47km from Cusco on the road to Sicuani and is best reached by **bus** (45min., s/2). From Urcos, buses going on to Sicuani (2hr., s/5) or back to Cusco pass by the Plaza de Armas every 15-20min. There are **no ATMs** in Urcos. The **police station** (☎30 7021, emergency ☎30 7022) is in the uphill left corner of the Plaza de Armas. The **Hospital Centro de Salud** (☎30 7015) is three blocks away from the Plaza de Armas, up Tacna to Túpac Amaru. Along the same street there are several **Internet cafes. Serpost** is at the corner of Arica and Oropesa, one block down from the Plaza de Armas.

SICUANI   ☎ 084

If you're spending time in Sicuani (pop. 60,000), you're well off the beaten path. This market town's location on the main highway and railroad between Cusco and Puno makes it a convenient stopping point for travelers, though the city itself contains little of interest. The highlight of a stop here lies just outside the city, at the ruins of **Raqchi.** It is said that the Incas built this impressive temple to appease the god Wiracocha after the area was devastated by a volcanic eruption. The walls of the temple are composed of volcanic rock, and traces of ancient lava flows can still be found in some places along the stone. The architecture of the temple is unique among Inca ruins for its use of adobe and supporting columns. Take a combi from the city (15min., s/1) to reach the ruins. (Open daily 9am-5:30pm. US$2.) In the city center, the crumbling pastel **Catedral Antigua** (open daily dawn to dusk, free) dates from 1783. The inside is dimly lit (bring a flashlight if you want a good look at the paintings) and features a large dome above the main altar with images of El Señor de los Temblores. Near the front sits the old church bell, felled and never replaced, perhaps because it weighs in at 2000kg.

If you need to stick around for the night, **Hotel Obada ❸,** Tacna 104 at Garcilaso de la Vega, one block from the Plaza de Armas, is as good as it gets in this town. It's clean, carpeted, and spacious, with hot water in the mornings. (☎35 1214. Private baths. Singles s/25; doubles s/35.) A decent stay awaits at **Hospedaje Raqchi ❷,** on Manuel Callo Zevallos 145, 1.5km from the Plaza de Armas, along the railroad tracks. (☎35 1057. Shared baths. Singles s/10; doubles s/18.) Basic *menús* abound in Sicuani. **Wiracocha ❶,** Centro Cívico 142, next to the municipal office in the Plaza, has nice light sandwiches (s/1-3), meaty entrees (alpaca, trout, *cuy;* s/7-12), and delicious chocolate cake. (☎35 1293. Open daily 9am-1pm and 4-8pm.)

Sicuani is 138km from Cusco on the road to Lake Titicaca and is best reached by bus (3hr., s/6). Buses continue on to Puno (4hr., every hr., s/8) from **terminal terrestre** (mototaxi from the Plaza s/1). Transport within Sicuani consists of rickshaws and motorized three-wheelers (s/1-3 around the city). The central square is none other than the brilliantly named **Plaza de Armas.** Women in bright green vests stand along the streets offering **money-changing services.** The **police station** (emergency ☎105) is four blocks uphill from the Plaza de Armas, along Garcilaso de la Vega. The **city hospital** (☎35 1020) lies on Manuel Callo Zevallos, eight blocks from the Plaza de Armas, along the railroad tracks. **Internet cafes** abound. The **post office** is on the 3rd fl. of the municipal building on the Plaza de Armas.

PAUCARTAMBO ☎084

If you're in Cusco or heading toward Manú in mid-July, be sure to stop over in Paucartambo ("the top of the world" in Quechua). July 15-18 brings the **Celebración de la Virgen del Carmen** to this sleepy town 110km from Cusco, and streets explode with costumes, dance, music, and pageantry. This ancient festival makes the bumpy bus ride from Cusco well worth the effort. There are a few basic hotels in Paucartambo, but, without telephones, reservations are impossible. If you come during festival time, be ready to camp out in the freezing Andean night air, sleep on the floor of a public school, or find a room with a friendly local—Paucartambo locals are often eager to exchange food and a bed for some extra cash (s/5-10 per night). **Minibuses** (☎27 7255) to Paucartambo leave from Tullumayo off Garcilaso (4hr.; daily 9am, also Tu and Th 3pm and Su 5am; additional buses during festival time; s/7). You can continue on from Paucartambo to Parque Nacional del Manú or toward Tres Cruces (4hr., s/7), where you can see the spectacular rise of the "dancing sun" or "multiple suns," an effect of humidity and the meeting of weather fronts over a horizon that joins the Andes and the Amazon.

THE SACRED VALLEY

The Sacred Valley is a hiker's haven and a daredevil's playground, the ultimate cultural immersion and the ultimate archaeological dig. Remarkably intact ruins dot a landscape divided by a rambunctious river, lined with small-town markets that host disproportionately large festivals, and surrounded by towering peaks concealing hidden trails. Independent explorers can find ample solitude, or join one of the multitude of trekking, rafting, biking, riding, and roadtripping groups. In short, the Sacred Valley is a living "choose your own adventure"—and while each adventure has its own quirks, in every case the beauty and heritage of the Valley astound those who pilgrimage here.

An extensive exploration of the Sacred Valley inevitably involves many hours on the road. There are two main valley arteries, the **Pisac highway** (via Pisac, Lamay, and Calca) and the **Poroy highway** (via Chinchero and Maras), which meet in Urubamba. They are well paved and highly traveled, with buses, taxis, and colectivos happy to pick up passengers anywhere along the way, making spontaneous travel from town to town relatively easy.

PISAC   ☎ 084

If you're looking for quaint and rural, Pisac (pop. 9800; elev. 2972m) can satisfy your every wish. Competing with Cusco for the label of cultural center of the Sacred Valley, this *pueblo* centers around the Plaza de la Constitución, location of the one and only **Pisac Market.** The town's charms extend beyond its famous market, however. The **Fiesta de la Virgen del Carmen** (July 15-18) is celebrated with great pomp and show in this small town, in coordination with its sister city of Paucartambo. Last but far from least, one of the Sacred Valley's most popular day-hikes winds through the hills of the Pisac ruins.

▐▀ ▐ TRANSPORTATION AND PRACTICAL INFORMATION

Buses from Cusco (s/2) leave from the terminal on Tullumayo (Calca-bound) and Paputi (Urubamba-bound), and drop passengers off at the edge of town, next to the police station, just after crossing the Urubamba River. A 3min. walk uphill leads to the **Plaza de la Constitución** and the **market.** Buses return frequently to Cusco (1hr., every 10min. 5am-7pm, s/2) and Urubamba (35min., s/2) via Yucay (30min., s/2). On market days only, a money changer sets up shop at the corner of Bolognesi and Mariscal Castilla (the northeastern corner of the Plaza) and will exchange American dollars and traveler's checks for soles. The only **ATM** (24hr.) in town is on Manuel Prado in the Plaza, and accepts all major cards. A supermarket, **Sofis Market,** Bolognesi 564, is two blocks down from the Plaza. (☎20 3017. Open daily 6:30am-10:30pm.) The **police** are located where Manuel Prado intersects the river. (☎20 3074. Open 24hr.) A Centro de Salud **medical clinic** is half a block up from the Plaza on Intihuatana. (☎20 3157. Open 24hr.) A pod of public **telephones** is on Bolognesi, alongside the Plaza. An **Internet** cafe is on Manuel Prado, on the Plaza, and there's another on Amazonas, next to the bridge. Although there is no official post office, a **Serpost** pickup office for letters and small packages is inside Samana Wasi (see **Food,** below).

▐ ACCOMMODATIONS

Some of the most beautiful budget rooms in central Pisac belong to Southwestern US-inspired ◫**Hotel Pisaq ❸**, at Puno and Manuel Prado, on the Plaza, owned by two artists who have decorated to their hearts' content. Among the attractions are a sauna (US$2.50), all-day continental breakfast (US$3), and signature pizza on market days. (☎20 3062; www.hotelpisaq.com. English, French, and German spoken. 24hr. hot water. Laundry US$5 per load. Check-out noon. Rooms US$10 per person, with bath US$13. Restaurant open 7am-5pm. No credit cards.) For a quieter retreat from town, ◫**Paz y Luz ❹**, 1km east of the bridge, offers a homey B&B experience, complemented by the subtle sound of river rapids and amazing views of the valley peaks. Rooms are warm, well lit, and carefully coordinated. Breakfast is served in a glass gazebo overlooking cornfields. The owner also gives workshops in the Andean shamanic tradition in the B&B, which is supposedly strategically situated in the valley to absorb positive energy from the surrounding Apus (mountain spirits) and the Sacred River. (☎20 3204; www.maxart.com/window/gateway.html. 10min. walk or s/3 taxi ride from town. Continental breakfast included. US$15 per person.) **Samana Wasi ❷**, on Bolognesi in the Plaza, doubles as both a hostel and a restaurant. Lodgings boast beautiful dark wood floors, starched white sheets, and enormous windows that open onto the Plaza. Samana Wasi also has a downstairs money exchange and daily postal pickup, with stamps and postcards for purchase. (☎20 3018. Shared bathrooms with 24hr. hot water. Doubles and triples only; s/15 per person.)

◘ FOOD

🔲**Ulrike's Café ❷**, Manuel Prado 828, on the Plaza, has the best New York-style cheesecake in the Valley, made with milk from those same amazing cows at La Granja Heidi (see **Food**, p. 226). The restaurant is always bustling with international customers, lured by the colorfully painted walls, Saturday night showings of *Amelie* (7pm), and TV lounge with DVD collection. (☎20 3195; ulrikescafe@terra.com.pe. *Menú* with soup, entree, and brownie s/10, with cheesecake s/12.50. Open daily 7am-8pm.) 🔲 **Doña Clorinda ❷**, on the Plaza, directly across from the church, serves delicious Peruvian meals. Ask for an upstairs table and Doña will lead you past black-and-white pictures of the old (pre-earthquake) Cusco and up a narrow spiral staircase to a spacious dining room overlooking the Plaza. (☎20 3051. Entrees s/10-20. Andean buffet s/16. Open daily 7am-8pm.) Al fresco diners can enjoy the restaurant in the flower-filled courtyard of **Samana Wasi ❷**, complete with madly chirping parakeets and mountains looming in the distance. (Appetizers s/5-9. Entrees s/10-17. Open 7am-late.) **Valle Sagrado ❷**, Amazonas 116, one block from the bridge, has a neighborhood bar feel and the friendliest service in town. They serve seasonal specialties—try the fried trout (s/12). (☎20 3009; restaurantevallesagrado@hotmail.com. *Menú* s/5-10. Entrees s/10-14. Open daily 7am-10pm.) For a funky alternative hangout, go to **Mullu ❷**, Puno 352, on the Plaza, with a first-floor modern art gal-

THE BIG SPLURGE

A CONDOR'S VIEW OF THE VALLEY

Most visitors to the Sacred Valley spend much of their time crammed into colectivos or standing in buses for hours on end in order to make their rounds through the plethora of sights and towns. But nothing lets you see it all like the view from 5700m in the sky. Tandem paragliding requires no experience, and allows participants to gain an appreciation for the Sacred Valley as a whole, rather than bit by bit. With a swift takeoff from Cerro Sacro (elev. 3890m), the winds above the valley blow vigorously, and as the sun shines onto the ground below, thermal drafts carry you high into the sky. Glider flights reach altitudes of up to 5700m, above even the snow-capped peaks of the Urubamba mountain range, giving you a bird's eye view of the Sacred Valley's entire expanse. The hustle and bustle of daily life seems so far removed from these awesome heights, and everything below—towns, ruins, lakes, and rivers—seems small, distant, and beautiful. After 20-50min. of serene flight, you land softly in the farmers' fields below. US$70 is a small price to pay for this once-in-a-lifetime walk (or rather, glide) in the clouds. (See **Tandem Paraglider,** p. 244).

lery and chic second-floor cafe. (☎20 3073. Smoothies s/7-10. Appetizers s/3-12. Entrees s/12-18. Open Tu-Su 8am-8pm. The gallery accepts all major credit cards.

🞂 SIGHTS

The Pisac ruins constitute the largest standing Inca fortress—perhaps because, unlike their counterparts at Sacsayhuamán and Ollantaytambo, no famous battles took place here. Although this inaccessible fort city once occupied a key strategic point overlooking the valley, Pisac seems to have been abandoned before the Spanish Conquest. From the Plaza, two trails lead up to the ruins; both pass small native communities who still live in the hills. The path leading uphill from the right side of the Plaza (when coming from the bus stop by the river) leads to a paved road used by tour groups. Most hikers take the steep path that leads uphill from the Plaza's left side. The path is well marked and weaves through a number of complexes, the most impressive of which is the central Intihuatana (Temple of the Sun) sector, a triangle-shaped plateau that probably served as an astronomical observatory. There are four main parts to the ruins: the **Qantusraqay**—the upper fort with windows, guards' niches, and messenger rooms; the **water channels and ritual baths** that still function today; the **Qallaqasa**—a fortified complex and lookout point midway through the ruins; and **Intihuatana.** The entire area is flanked by agricultural terraces carved into the hillsides, which probably supported the entire fortress community. (1hr. ascent, 45min. descent; Cusco tourist ticket required 8:30am-4pm. Taxi 15min., s/10; with waiting time and descent s/20.)

On the hillside opposite the Pisac ruins, near the peak of the mountain, stands the image of La Ñusta, an Inca princess immortalized in stone. According to Quechua lore, La Ñusta's father banished her across the river, with the stipulation that she must walk straight away from the fortress and not look back, or she would be turned to stone. Her father decreed that the man who would marry his daughter would show his worth by building a bridge across the river, and only then could he reach the princess. The father's schemes were foiled when the princess turned to glance back at what she had left behind—in that instant, she was turned to stone, and her form can still be seen in the rock.

The interior of Pisac's colonial-era church, **Iglesia San Pedro Apóstol,** deviates from the standard model. Its walls, rather than being hung with elaborately framed paintings of the Cusco School, are decorated with brightly painted murals, depicting various angels, demons, and Biblical scenes. The main altar is dedicated to El Señor de los Temblores. Written in Quechua on the left wall, above a painting of Jesus, is the Quechua profession of faith "Qanmi Dios Kanki" ("You are God"). (Open M-Sa dawn to dusk, Su dawn-3pm.)

The weekend **market** remains the town's largest affair, brimming with canopied stands selling silver jewelry, ceramics, woven blankets, and old coins. Locals shop here, too, for vegetables and alpaca meat. Pisac's prices are comparable to Cusco's, but its selection is far superior. Bargaining is common. (Open Su, Tu, Th 8am-dusk.) Close by, uphill and off to the right of the Plaza on Mariscal Castilla, multiple galleries display the latest in contemporary Peruvian art.

LAMAY AND HUCHUY CUSCO   ☎084

Lamay (pop. 900; elev. 2930m) is an unremarkable little place, notable only perhaps for the underground **aqueducts** that run along its main roads, providing water throughout the town. The real attraction lies at the top of the hills across from town—the marvel-ous **ruins** of Huchuy ("Little") Cusco. A large royal hall, made partly of stone and partly of adobe, overlooks a group of terraces on the hillside. The estate is thought to have been the hideaway of Inca Wiracocha during the Chanca invasion, and legend has it that the Spanish found his mummy here after their conquest. The Spanish influence is evident at the ruins, in constructions such as the imperial-style reservoir. Lamay can be used as either a starting or ending point for the **hike** to Huchuy Cusco. A sign next to the town marks the entrance to a trail that leads up through the hillside (1hr., 4km); just follow the adobe-walled path, pass through the row of tall trees into the clearing, cross the creaky wooden-planked bridge, and you'll be on your way. Alternatively, you can make the long hike from Cusco (8hr., 24km)—an obscure trailhead is located near Puca Pucara (ask locals to point you in the right direction). This full day's hike travels past beautiful mountain lakes, Inca roads and irrigation channels, and excellent views of the snowcapped mountains on this side of the valley.

There are **no accommodations or restaurants** in Lamay. The town lies 11km from Pisac; **buses** and **colectivos** run along the highway (15min., s/0.50). The town's small **health clinic,** Puesto de Salud, is on the highway near the town entrance. Lamay has one public **telephone,** on Arequipa, a block up from the highway.

CALCA
☎ 084

Calca (pop. 15,000; elev. 2928m) claims to be the capital of the Sacred Valley, though it is more so in terms of commerce than sights and tourism. The town was once a temporary headquarters for Inca Manco Cápac II's rebellion against the Spanish, but was abandoned when Cusco was seized. A scenic 7km road up into the mountains from Calca leads to the **Baños Termales de Machacancha,** thermal baths originating from the mountains' hot springs, yellowish in color because of sulfuric emissions. To get to the baths, it's a 2hr. hike or a 30min. taxi ride (follow Grau uphill and the road leads right to them).

Tourist accommodations are few in this town, but are beginning to develop. **Hospedaje Villa María ❷,** Santos 388 at Lara, about 30m down from Plaza Sondor, has affordable, spacious rooms and a nice garden. (☎20 2110. Continental breakfast s/5. 24hr. hot water. Laundry s/3 per kg. Singles s/15; doubles s/25; add s/5 for private bath.) **Hospedaje San Francis ❷,** Bolívar 701 at Grau on the Plaza de Armas, offers basic budget accommodations, with breakfast in the downstairs cafe included. (☎80 1293. Singles s/10; doubles s/20, with private bath s/25.) While no place in Calca is particularly exceptional in its culinary selection, **Quinta Sol y Mar ❶,** Bolívar 812, just off the Plaza de Armas, has a decent courtyard restaurant. (*Menú* s/3-7. Entrees s/10-12. Open daily 10am-10pm.)

Buses drop off and pick up passengers along the main highway, Vilcanota (to Pisac s/1, Urubamba s/2, Cusco s/3). Follow Grau uphill to reach the town's central plazas, separated by the main church. On the right side of the church is Plaza Sondor, and on the left side the Plaza de Armas. The municipal **tourist office** sits next to the bank on Grau. There are **no ATMs** in Calca, but **Banco de la Nación,** on the corner of Grau and San Martín in the Plaza de Armas, has money changing services. The **police** are on Espinar, uphill from the Plaza de Armas (☎20 2223), and the **Centro de Salud** is on Grau at Pina Wasi, also uphill from the Plaza de Armas. **Public telephones** are located directly in front of the church. **Internet access** is available on Bolívar in Plaza Sondor and along San Martín between the two plazas. The **post office** is downhill from the tourist office on Grau, close to the Plaza.

YUCAY
☎ 084

Yucay (pop. 3000; elev. 2857m) was once the Inca Sayri Túpac's royal estate; his grounds occupied the sites of the present-day Plaza de Armas and Plaza Manco II. The **palatial walls** at one end of Plaza Manco II were his, while the walls across the

THE BIG SPLURGE

POSADA DEL INCA

Alongside Yucay's Plaza Manco, in a beautiful 300-year-old *hacienda*, lies the expansive and colorful **Posada del Inca Hotel** ❺, Plaza Manco II 123 (☎21 1107; www.sonesta.com). The hotel offers every conceivable amenity. While it may be a little pricey for the budget traveler (rooms start at US$78 per night), the posh hotel is not to be missed. Whether or not your wallet can survive an overnight visit, you can wander through lush gardens populated by alpacas and stop at the elegant **Inca Cafe** ❺ for a buffet lunch (US$10-14, 12:30-3pm) on the terrace. Dinner (appetizers US$4-9, entrees US$8-10; 6:30-10pm) is served inside, where patrons are warmed by open chimneys and soothed by the melodies of the Posada del Inca harpist after 6pm.

Best of all, the hotel features **Posada Aventura,** a tour group that provides biking and horseback riding opportunities all over the Yucay-Urubamba area. (Open daily 9am-5:30pm.)

The *hacienda* that houses the Posada del Inca Hotel also hosts an interesting chapel and the tiny **Museo Posada del Inca** on the second floor. The Museo features a collection of Inca artifacts, weapons, and ceramics from the Sacred Valley. Placards in English help explain the displays.

Plaza de Armas belonged to his princess. Nowadays the plazas are large green expanses, with wooden park benches around large blossoming *pisonay* trees; Plaza Manco II even has a small playground—a nice place to stop to picnic. Many dayhikes remain around the estate, including the beautiful trek that climbs through the mountains and ends with a glimpse of **pre-Inca petroglyphs.** The petroglyphs are nearly impossible to find on your own, so hiring a guide is the only feasible option. **Inkapusayuc Tours,** Plaza Manco II 103, offers guided hiking opportunities ranging from 1hr. to 1 day in length. (☎20 1099; inkapusayuc@hotmail.com. US$2-15 per person.) Tours can also be arranged with **Explore Perú,** inside the Sonesta Posada Hotel.

The best lodging is **Hostal Y'llary** ❺, Plaza Manco II 107, part of the same 300-year-old *hacienda* as the next-door **Sonesta Posada del Inca Hotel.** Y'llary offers a minimized version of Posada's grandeur at a (relatively) minimized price, with exquisite gardens and clean rooms. (☎20 1012. Continental breakfast included. Singles US$25; doubles US$30; triples US$40; additional bed US$10.)

To get from Cusco to Yucay, catch a **colectivo** (1¾hr., s/2) along Tullumayo or take a Caminos del Inca **bus** (1hr., every 20min. 5am-7pm, s/2.50) from the terminal at Tullumayo. Helicopters also occasionally land in the Plaza de Armas. From Yucay, you can travel to Urubamba by taxi (s/3), mototaxi (s/2), or colectivo (s/0.50), all of which pass frequently along the highway (4:30am-9:30pm). A small office next to the ruins in Plaza Manco II provides **tourist information**—a very knowledgeable local guide will regale you with interesting facts and legends. A **24hr. ATM** (accepts all major cards) is located in the courtyard of the Sonesta Posada, and **currency exchange** is available in the lobby. There is **no police station** in Yucay. A **medical clinic** sits across from the chapel, five blocks from Plaza Manco II. Yucay has a **public telephone** along the main highway, next to Plaza Manco II. **Internet access** is available in major hotels. A **Serpost** pickup location is in Plaza Manco II, next to the Sonesta Posada Hotel.

CHICÓN AND SAN JUAN GLACIERS

Most people never imagine that you can go ice-climbing in the Sacred Valley. But those white-topped peaks are indeed surmountable, and with the right equipment and a willingness to brave the cold, almost anyone can do the hike. While Ausangate and Salkantay tend to be highly technical peaks, a novice climber with the right guide can rough up his crampons with the more amicable (yet still thrilling) glaciers of Chicón and San Juan (sometimes called Chicón II).

AT A GLANCE

DISTANCE: 24km.	**TIME:** 2-3 days.
CLIMATE: Cool at the start, freezing at the end.	**ALTITUDE:** 2700-5300m.
	DIFFICULTY: Medium-Difficult.
FEATURES: Eucalyptus forests, ice-climbing, views of the Urubamba range.	**FEES:** None.

PRACTICAL INFORMATION

The trailhead begins at a small town near Huayllabamba along the Pisac-Urubamba highway, and continues through forest, lakes, and fields, relentlessly ascending to the snow and ice. The climb itself can be difficult if only because of the altitude (2000m up on the first day), but it's also important to keep seasonal climate in mind. On the glacier itself, there are several soft-zones in which avalanches are common—hikers should judge the safety of the climb when they reach the base of the mountain during the evening of the first day.

Maps: Topographical maps of the Sacred Valley are available in Cusco bookstores (see **Bookstores,** p. 221). Unfortunately, a map of the trail itself is not yet available.

Supplies: Crampons, snow gear (boots, ski pants, warm hat and gloves, etc.), and sunglasses are all essential, in addition to standard camping equipment (tent, sleeping mat and bag, cooking equipment). It's a good idea to bring harnesses and technical equipment. Everything is available in Cusco (see **Outdoor Equipment,** p. 221); technical equipment is provided by most guides, or for rent from some agencies.

Guides and Tours: A knowledgeable guide is crucial. Inquire at **Liz's Explorers** (p. 242) for the highly experienced Richard Sánchez (claveazulrsc@yahoo.com), a vibrant personality with a passion for the mountain. US$60 per day.

CAMPING

It's best to camp road-side at the trailhead the night before the hike so you can get an early start on the trail instead of worrying about morning transportation. The night is best spent on the **icchu** (firmly rooted, dry Andean grass) fields near the base of the mountain (4700m). The fields are next to plenty of lakes and snow, so water is readily available. Dry wood is plentiful in the area, making much-needed campfires easy enough to build.

THE TRAIL

GETTING TO THE TRAILHEAD. The trailhead is at **Huayakhari,** a small town between Huayllabamba and Calca. Take a bus, colectivo, or taxi from Cusco to Urubamba (s/2-5), and then catch a Pisac-bound colectivo from there, asking the driver to drop you off next to Huayakhari (s/3).

DAY 1. Following the dirt roads of Huayakhari toward the mountain (away from the road) and to the right (take a right at every fork), hikers approach the small town church. The trail continues past the church, on the left side. After about 40min. of following a small *riochuela* (stream) through potato and garlic fields, you'll enter a beautiful eucalyptus forest. The next 4hr. take hikers

FROM THE ROAD

NO PAIN, NO GAIN

The hike to Chicón is no walk in the park, but in all likelihood you'll notice something both inspiring and humbling during the first day's ascent (from 2700m to 4700m): you will repeatedly run into Quechua-speaking locals—mountain farmers—also doing the trek. In fact, they make this climb every day, to find grazing land for their cows and dry wood for their week's fires. They sometimes chuckle as they watch the tourists helplessly huff-and-puff their way through the altitude, but most often they're charmed that you've taken enough interest to climb at all. With warm words of encouragement, they'll race ahead, saying "see you at the top" in Quechua. Realizing the extraordinary daily endurance of these Andean natives makes your own burden seem a little lighter, even as the air becomes thinner and the terrain more forbidding.

If that doesn't do it for you, then the other thing you'll encounter along the trail—animal droppings—should. That's right, just when you think you can't go any farther, look at the turf around your feet and tell yourself that if a donkey can do this, you can too.

—*Saritha Komatireddy*

past farmers' houses, through riverbeds filled with hummingbirds, and into narrow and thorny thickets, until they reach **Yanaccocha** ("Black Lake"). This is a good spot to rest, have lunch, and scour the forest for birds and flowers. From here, hikers scale the hillside left of the lake (you can choose a slow and steady zigzag climb or a painfully steep but quick ascent) and continue upward. After about 1hr., you'll catch a glimpse of **Killuccocha** ("Yellow Lake"), another of the small lakes nestled in the mountains. The climb continues, and both the ascent over the foothills and the descent to the fields of the campsite are quite steep; be sure to have a good walking stick and take hold of the ubiquitous *icchu* for support. You should be able to reach the base of the ridge (4700m) well before nightfall (another 2hr. or so). From your campsite here, you'll be able to see the glistening crest of the glacier.

DAY 2, PART I. Hikers begin the 2hr. climb to the top of the ridge (5100m) at first light in order to catch the ice at its coldest. Once at the top, you can gaze at the peaks of the entire range—towering **Salkantay** (6264m), beautiful **Verónica** (5682m), rugged **Chicón** (5530m), and double-peaked **Pitusiray** (5049m). Outcroppings on top of the ridge make for some fun elementary rock climbing as well, allowing you to get higher and see even more of what is below. From here, hikers can decide whether to continue onto the glacier or not, taking into consideration weather and avalanche conditions. If you do go ahead, it's a 3-4hr. ascent along the ridge to the top of San Juan, and a comparable descent.

DAY 2, PART II. It's all downhill after lunch, although there are two paths to choose from. Across from the ridge, a trail on the other side of the mountain leads through the range and down to the town of **Urubamba.** This path is certainly the longer one (by about 2hr.), but it produces more breathtaking views of the range. The shorter route involves trekking across the *icchu* fields, which put you in view of the valley. From there, follow any of the dirt paths down past the agricultural terraces (the main path curves around the right side of the terraces) toward the farmers' houses below. The path continues past the houses into beautiful wet forests and runs along the **Río San Juan** (which originates from the glacier above). After about 2hr., you'll pass a small hydroelectric dam and come to a fork in the path. Both trails lead to the same destination: the small town of **Yucay** (p. 253). The left path is more direct, taking you to the main road in 20min. The right is more interesting, following an **Inca irrigation canal** (recently refortified with cement) through narrow forest passageways and expansive cornfields, and takes only 10min. longer. From Yucay, you can easily travel to anywhere in the valley.

URUBAMBA ☎ 084

In the heart of the Sacred Valley, Urubamba (pop. 14,000; elev. 2871m) feels more authentically Peruvian than many of its neighboring *pueblos:* you won't find any menus translated into English or overpriced llama rides in this town. Travelers most often land here after trekking through the Valley or following various trails within the Urubamba mountain range. Urubamba can serve as a starting point for treks, as well, and several local hostels, including **Posada del Chalán** (☎20 1541), at Km75, and **Posada Tres Marías,** Zavala 306 (☎22 5252; posada3marias@yahoo.com), offer adventure tourism excursions in the mountains. The town itself has very little to see, though if you follow Mariscal Castilla all the way uphill and take a right when the road turns to dirt, you'll find a modern cemetery, below which lies an ancient Inca ceremonial temple.

🔲**Hospedaje Macha Wasi ❹,** on Padre Barré, one block from Mariscal Castilla, across the street from Colegio Valle Sagrada, has elegant rooms, private baths, hot showers, thick blankets, and luscious gardens that make the charge seem a mere pittance. (☎20 1612. Breakfast US$2.50. Laundry s/4 per kg. Singles US$15; doubles US$20; triples US$25.) **Hospedaje Urubamba ❷,** on Bolognesi off the Plaza, offers basic dorm-style rooms with shared baths. (s/20 per person.) The best food in town is at **Pizzonay ❷,** Mariscal Castilla 205, where brightly colored walls, fascinating photography, and the scent of baking pizza will keep you cozy and entertained. (☎20 1611. Personal pizzas and lasagna s/9-14. Pancakes with peaches and sweet cream s/7. Open daily 5-10pm.) The cybercafe-bar-disco next door, **Connection,** Mariscal Castilla 203 at Manique, offers the hippest nightlife, with monthly exhibitions of contemporary painting and photography, occasional live concerts, and televised major sporting events. (☎962 6811. Full bar. Cosmopolitan s/8. Mai tai s/9. Drinks s/8-15. Internet s/2.50 per hr. Happy hour 5-7pm. Open M-Sa 10am-late.) **Pintacha ❶,** Bolognesi 523, off Palacio, is a chill sandwich bar and cinema cafe closer to the Plaza. (☎974 8525; cafepintacha@hotmail.com. Sandwich combos s/4.50-9. Coffee, cake, and ice cream s/2.50-5. Open daily 4pm-late.)

Buses arrive and depart from the bus station on the highway, 1km beyond Mariscal Castilla. From the station, walk uphill on the dirt road about five blocks to reach the **Plaza de Armas,** or from the Castilla/highway intersection, walk up Castilla to Comercio and turn left. **Combis** from the bus station go to: Chinchero (1hr., every 15min. 5am-7:30pm, s/2.50); Cusco (1¾hr., every 10min. 5am-7pm, s/3); Ollantaytambo (30min., s/1). To get to Yucay, catch a **taxi** (s/2), **mototaxi** (s/1), or **colectivo** (s/0.50) along the highway.

A surprisingly wide array of services revolves around **Mariscal Castilla,** perpendicular to the highway and inhabited by hordes of taxis and mototaxis. Urubamba has a **24hr. ATM,** on the highway, just past the Mariscal Castilla intersection. **AMAUTA** offers Spanish language classes (see **Alternatives to Tourism: Language Schools,** p. 90). On Tuesdays, a sprawling **market** lies just off the Plaza de Armas. Other services include: **Western Union,** at the corner of Mariscal Castilla and Comercio; **police** (☎20 1092), at Palacio and Bolognesi; **24hr. pharmacy,** on the Plaza de Armas, opposite the church; **24hr. medical clinic** (☎20 1334), along the highway at the end of Castilla; and high-speed **Internet service** at the corner of Grau and Belén. The **post office** is at 415 Plaza de Armas. (Open M-Sa 8am-12:30pm and 2-5:30pm.)

OLLANTAYTAMBO ☎ 084

In its day, Ollantaytambo's fortress witnessed many great conflicts and had its share of tragic tales. Today, the fortress enchants Ollanta's tourists with its colossal stone walls and fabulous valley vistas. As the best surviving example of Inca city planning,

Ollantaytambo village (pop. 8500; elev. 2846m) is a sight in itself. Grid-like streets are kept clean by waters diverted from the Río Patacancha into stone channels. Houses are arranged in enclosed blocks called *canchas*, and local men, who cherish their strong Quechua identity, wear the region's typical *poncho*.

☎ ⁊ TRANSPORTATION AND PRACTICAL INFORMATION. Buses arrive in Ollantaytambo's **Plaza de Armas.** The **fortress** lies at the end of **Principal,** which runs downhill from the Plaza and across the **Río Patacancha.** Walking out of the Plaza toward the river, **9 de Octubre** is the road to the left before crossing the river, and leads to the **train station** (10min. walk). **Trains** go to Aguas Calientes, better known as Machu Picchu Pueblo (1hr., 4 per day 7am-3pm, US$47-70) and Cusco (2hr., 3 per day 6-8pm, US$70). Schedules and prices shift constantly; ask for current information at the station, museum, or hostels. **Buses** to Cusco (2hr., every 20min., s/10) and Urubamba (30min., s/1) leave from the Plaza de Armas. **Tourist information, Internet access** (s/4 per hr.), and up-to-date train schedules are available at **Museo CATCCO** (see **Sights,** below). There is **no bank,** although local hotels and *boticas* are often able to exchange dollars. The **police** (☎20 4086) are on the Plaza. The Centro de Salud **health clinic** (☎20 4090) lies next to the river on 9 de Octubre. The **Centro Comunitario Telefónico** on the Plaza de Armas sells phone cards for its plethora of **telephones.** (Open daily 8am-10pm.) There is also a small **Internet cafe** on Aracama, across the bridge near the entrance to the ruins. Ollantaytambo has **no post office,** but many of the hotels on the Plaza have **Serpost** boxes for small letters. Packages and larger letters are best sent from Urubamba.

☎ ⛺ ACCOMMODATIONS AND FOOD. Ollantaytambo has some excellent lodging options. **KB Tambo ❷,** on Principal, just past the Plaza, is a bit dark, but the clean rooms have decent shared baths with 24hr. hot water. A sun-baked terrace yields fabulous views of the ruins. The owner also arranges mountain biking, horseback riding, and rafting tours in the area. (☎20 4091; www.kbperu.com. English spoken. Breakfast s/5-8 in the downstairs restaurant. Unlimited laundry s/5. Check-out 11am. Singles s/20; doubles s/30; triples s/35. MC/V.) Next to the train station, **Albergue Kapuly ❹** features handsome gardens, lovely decorations, and a sauna. (☎/fax 20 4016. Breakfast included. 24hr. hot water. Sauna US$5. Singles, doubles, triples, and quads US$10 per person.) **Hospedaje Los Andes ❸,** on Ventinerio, down the hill from the Plaza, has hot water, starched sheets, and warm blankets. The owners, a family of weavers, run a small workshop downstairs, selling home-made textiles fresh off the loom. (☎20 4095. Continental breakfast s/5. Singles, doubles, and triples s/15 per person, with bath s/25 per person.) The best eats in town are served at **Mayupata ❸,** on Convención, across the bridge. The menu ranges from traditional Peruvian cuisine to vegetarian options. (☎20 4009. Appetizers s/10-15. Entrees s/17-25. Open daily 6am-10pm.) **Gran Tunupa ❶** (☎20 4035), on Ventinerio, offers half-liter pitchers of fresh fruit juice (s/2-8), tasty banana pancakes (s/5), and the best view in town. A table on the porch overlooks the ruins, and notice the Inca-cut stone at the bottom of the stairway.

◰ SIGHTS. It's easy to imagine the Spanish soldiers' fright as they rode up to the **fortress** at Ollantaytambo. Perched atop a set of steep terraces, the Inca army rained arrows and dropped boulders on the helpless invaders below. During one battle, Inca Manco Cápac II flooded the courtyard at the foot of the fortress by diverting water from the Río Patacancha; Pizarro and his men retreated. To form the fortress's foundation, the Incas had dragged enormous granite blocks from the Cachicata quarry, 6km away. Three similar stones were abandoned mid-haul and now lie along the road into town. The stone courtyard (known as **Plaza Manyaraqui**) where Pizarro's men met watery failure, now holds a tribute to Inca engineering: a gushing channel that leads into the **Baño de la Ñusta** (Bath of the Princess), where locals sometimes soak their feet. From the bath, over 200 stone steps form the terraces in front of the fortress. At the top of the stairs to the left stands the unfinished **Temple of the Sun,** with several tremendous stones notable for their carved faces. Embedded in the mountain face across from the main terraces is the face of Inca Tunupa. Multiple trails run through and around the Ollanta ruins, each carefully delineated on the map inside the entrance, past the tourist ticket checkpoint. Official guides are also available to lead tourists through the ruins; the guide office is past the entrance. (Open daily 7am-7pm. Cusco tourist ticket required.)

Outside the entrance to the ruins, the Ollanta **tourist market** sells handmade dolls, Inca calendars, and stone sculptures, among the more common woolen garments and Andean textiles. **⬛Museo CATCCO,** on Principal, is small, but maintains captivating displays in English and Spanish. Each of its five excellently organized galleries includes murals or life-sized models depicting Inca customs and lifestyles, along with cultural, artistic, and archaeological artifacts. Also check out the museum's three-dimensional map of the valley with pre-Inca and Inca archaeological sites marked. (Open M-F 8am-10pm, Sa-Su 8am-8pm. s/3, students s/1.)

POROY   ☎ 084

There really isn't much to the small town of Poroy, the first village on the road from Cusco to Urubamba via Chinchero, except an interesting story. It is said that when Pizarro was making his way toward Cusco for the grand invasion, he decided to rest in this place for the night, saying to his troops, "Basta por hoy" ("Enough for today").

CHINCHERO   ☎ 084

Halfway between Cusco and Urubamba, Chinchero (pop. 9400; elev. 3762m) sits on a high plateau, far above the touristy mayhem. The town is quiet and peaceful, with plenty of space to wander and none of the anxious tour guides or pre-marked paths. With its excellent views of the surrounding plains and snow-capped mountain ranges of the *altiplano*, Chinchero makes an ideal daytrip from Cusco.

The town is known for its mysterious **Inca wall, vast agricultural terraces,** and **small Inca ruins.** The Inca wall lines one side of the main Plaza, and was probably the foundation of a large palace—once the country resort of Inca Túpac Yupanqui. The stonework tells of reconstruction, though certain beams and overhead tiles are evidently original. The palace once overlooked the vast terraces, which stretch alongside the Plaza and further northward beyond the church. Though most of the ancient canals have dried up, there are functional irrigation channels on the far side of the terraces, and farmers still cultivate these fields. Across the fields, a fascinating rock outcropping (approximately parallel to the church, but out of sight from the main Plaza) is believed to have been carved by the Incas. The monolith's slab-like outer faces, narrow inner stairways, and perfectly carved, box-like seats make it a rock-climber's playground. Scale its sides, explore its niches, shimmy through its crevices, and revel in the perfection of Inca construction. (To get to the ruins and the Plaza, follow the main cobblestone path, Manco II, uphill and left just before it becomes dirt. Cusco tourist ticket required.)

In the Plaza, the old Spanish **church** (built over an Inca temple) houses once-brilliant paintings of the Cusco School, now in the process of restoration. (Open M-F dawn-dusk. Free.) On the opposite side of the Plaza sits the town's **Museo de Sitio.** (Open T-Su 8am-5pm. Free.) The museum's collection comes entirely from excavations of the nearby ruins, and contains large (and largely unbroken) Inca pottery, stone mortars, ceremonial items, musical instruments, walking sticks, clay sieves, weaving looms, and an array of agricultural tools—all in remarkable condition. Every Sunday, an enormous **artisan market,** known for its unparalleled weavings, fills the ruins, as church services take place inside the reconstructed Inca temple. The market may still be a bit touristy, but here at least the tourists are Peruvian. (Open 6am-5pm.) Multiple trailheads around Chinchero lead hikers to **scenic paths** along the hills of the Sacred Valley.

Among them, a relatively easy 4hr. hike leads to Huayllabamba, passing an old Inca *tambo* (resting house) halfway. The trail can be spotted from the Plaza, on the opposing hill, leading up and to the right. Once you finish, you can catch a bus back to Cusco along the main highway next to Huayllabamba.

Chinchero lies 45min. from Cusco by **bus** (s/1.50). **Empresa de Transportes Interprovincial,** Grau 525 (☎80 5639), runs buses from Cusco to Urubamba via Chinchero (every 15min. 6am-7pm), which leave from the terminal at the beginning of Grau (taxi from the Plaza de Armas s/2). **Combis** also run between Chinchero and Urubamba (1hr., every 20min. 5am-7:30pm, s/3). **Taxis** line the main road to take tourists back to Cusco (s/15) or on to Maras (s/10).

■ MORAY AND LAS SALINERAS

Moray's **agricultural terraces** and the **pre-Inca salt pans** of Las Salineras (sometimes called Salinas) are a testament to human innovation. Moray consists of three sets of concentric **agricultural terraces** sculpted from natural depressions in the earth. The small changes in altitude among the steps create a variety of climate conditions—the lower levels are up to 15 degrees warmer than the ones above them—allowing an assortment of crops to be planted in one place. Archaeologists believe that Moray was a site of agricultural experimentation even before the Incas; earlier peoples may have used the terraces to develop corn that could grow at high altitudes. The terraces are still cultivated today, and visitors can see potatoes growing in some of the lower circles. Every August, the carnival of **Moray Raymi** takes place in the ruins—villagers and food-vendors perch along the agricultural terraces as over 100 dance groups take turns performing in the center throughout the day. A dirt path leads down into the largest set of terraces and circles around past the other two, returning to the site's entrance. (Entrance fee s/5, students s/3.)

Apparently ancient diners liked a dash of salt on the potatoes they grew at Moray, and nearby Las Salineras took advantage of another natural phenomenon to provide it. These pre-Inca salt pans, still used today, are forged from over 4000 *pozas* (shallow pools) dug into the hillside. Over time they fill with salty water from the mountain's underground stream (visible near the entrance to the pans), whose water is so saline that white salt crystals collect on rocks alongside the water, encrusting the entire hillside. In the dry season, the water in the pools evaporates, leaving a thick layer of sparkling salt. A local family collects and sifts the salt and packages it for national distribution. There is a small entrance fee to Las Salineras (s/3, students s/1).

Unfortunately, public transportation serves neither Moray nor Las Salineras. To reach the ruins, take a bus to the "desvío a Maras" (1¼hr., s/2.50). From this turnoff, it's a 1hr. walk on the same road to the tiny village of **Maras** (pop. 8200; elev. 3385m). During the high season (May-Sept.), taxis wait at the turnoff, heading to Maras (s/1), Las Salineras (s/10), and Moray (s/20). You can also negotiate a taxi tour of both Moray and Las Salineras with a taxi driver from Chinchero (s/35, waiting time included). If you'd rather hike it, the 2hr. walk to Moray from Maras is around 7km. Once on the trail, the path to Moray is very straightforward, but the initial trailhead is hard to find. Ask one of the villagers for directions. The same logic applies to locating the trail to Las Salineras, but the walk is even simpler and shorter, just a few kilometers down the hill. Alternatively, several agencies in Cusco and Yucay provide mountain biking excursions, horseback riding tours, and guided hikes to the sites.

THE INCA TRAIL

Peru's most famous hike, the Inca Trail, weaves up mountainsides and winds down into cloud forests like many other Inca highways throughout the Sacred Valley. But only this Inca Trail leads from the Inca imperial capital of Cusco to the stony gates of sacred **Machu Picchu,** the climax of the trek. For many, it is also the highlight of Peru, and one of the most incredible sites in South America. Few experiences could match

On January 1, 2001, the Peruvian government reformed the Inca Trail admission process in an attempt to reduce the number of hikers and damage to the trail. Prices skyrocketed, and new regulations stated that **all Inca Trail hikers must go with a licensed guide**. In 2004, the government restricted the number of hikers on the trail to 500 per day, making it necessary for hikers to reserve their place with a guide **at least 30 days in advance**.

the wonder of reaching the final pass at daybreak, then descending on the holy city to wander its temples and terraces. Spectacular moments fill the two to four days preceding arrival as well. The trail swings past diverse landscapes—jungle vegetation hung with moss, llama-dotted mountain stretches, rushing rivers, and potable streams—and a number of impressive ruins that build anticipation for what lies ahead. Any reasonably fit person should be able to complete the route, although the drastic altitude changes ensure a challenge; doing some preparatory hiking around Cusco is a good idea. Given the trek's awe-inspiring properties and supreme accessibility, it comes as no surprise that many attempt the Inca Trail, making crowds impossible to avoid from June to August. For information about hiking in Peru, see **Trekking and Hiking**, p. 49.

AT A GLANCE

DISTANCE: 18km or 48km.

CLIMATE: Extremely cold at high altitudes and temperate in low jungles.

FEATURES: Machu Picchu, numerous Inca ruins, jungle, vegetation, the Andes, breathtaking views.

TIME: 2-4 days.

ALTITUDE: 2400-4200m.

DIFFICULTY: Medium.

FEES: Vary according to the travel agency and time of year (see **Guided Tours from Cusco: The Inca Trail,** p. 241).

🛈 PRACTICAL INFORMATION

Traditionally, the Inca Trail begins at Qoriwayrachina (Km88), scales four mountain passes, runs through several stretches of jungle, and climbs up and down several thousand stone steps (a total of 48km). Most tours begin a bit earlier at Piscacucho (Km82), cover the trek in three nights, spend the fourth morning at Machu Picchu, and return to Cusco by train in the evening. An alternative to taking the Km88 route is to ride the train from Cusco as far as Huiñay Huayna (Km104), where the **Royal Trail** (a total of 18km) begins.

Maps: Good topographical trail maps (s/10) are available from the many bookstores in Cusco (see **Bookstores,** p. 221). Tour operators also supply them free of charge.

Supplies: Guided tours provide everything from tents to picnic tables (check before signing up). You will need to bring a warm sleeping bag (although many tours rent them for US$5-10), rain gear, a warm hat and gloves, wool socks, mosquito repellent, sunblock, a wide-brimmed hat, bottled water and/or iodine tablets, and a flashlight. Consider bringing toiletries and an extra change of clothes, as there are showers with hot water at the last campsite. Everything is available in **Cusco** (see **Outdoor Equipment,** p. 221). Even if your tour doesn't provide porters, they are available at an additional cost.

Guides and Tours: It is illegal to hike the Inca Trail without a licensed guide. Countless tours leave from Cusco (see **Guided Tours from Cusco: The Inca Trail,** p. 241).

🏕 CAMPING

Hikers must camp along the Inca Trail. Make sure to leave with everything you came with (including toilet paper), as the incredible number of hikers can result in substantial amounts of trash. The trail itself is well regulated, with campsite pre-registration for tour groups, trail watchmen, and guards, and eight official bathrooms along the way. Campfires (and fires in general) are prohibited on the trail. The large, fancy hotel that stands just outside the gates of Machu Picchu is the kind of place presidents and movie stars stay; budget travelers will want to spend the night in **Aguas Calientes** (p. 270) or just head back to **Cusco.**

◪ THE INCA TRAIL

DAY 1 (9-11KM). Most tours begin with an early bus ride to Km82, although others start later at Km88. Hikers cross Río Urubamba and pass the elegantly contoured ruins of **Patallaqta** ("Terrace Town"), which appear on the right. The ascent to this point is the first steep hike on the trail. The clearly marked path then crosses Río Kusichaca ("Happy Bridge River") and follows the river's bank before beginning the 2.5km climb toward the village of **Huayllabamba** ("Grassy Plain"), where many tour groups spend the night. There are some small ruins at Huayllabamba, including what is said to be a cemetery, but the main complex is now used to house the trail watchman. Some groups choose to camp 1.5km upstream at a smaller campsite. Others continue another 2hr. to a campground at **Llulluchapampa,** traveling up a stone stairway past a small patch of jungle with a green canopy. Llulluchapampa is the last site on the trail where you can purchase snacks and bottled water, at least until you reach Huiñay Huayna. Don't get too comfortable here—it's going to be a long, cold night. This may be a good time to hire porters (s/25-35 per pack per day) if you haven't already, to carry your stuff up the towering first pass you'll be facing on the second day.

DAY 2 (10-15KM). The main order of the day is scaling the steep incline to the **Abra de Huarmihuañusca,** better known as **Dead Woman's Pass,** the highest point on the Inca Trail. At a dizzying 4200m, the air feels much thinner than at the 3000m where most hikers woke up that morning. At Llulluchapampa, you can see the course of the daunting climb ahead, along the left flank of the mountain. The gentle U-shape at the top is the pass. The next 3hr. expose hikers to the elements: first scorching sun, then freezing winds closer to the pass. Hikers meet Huarmihuañusca with great celebration, although hail and snow sometimes cut the festivities short. With clear skies, you'll be able to see the major peaks of both the Urubamba (behind you) and Vilcabamba (in front of you) mountain ranges, as well as the ruins of Runkuracay in the distance across the valley. Past the summit, it's a 2hr. descent on stone steps to the **Pacamayo Valley** floor, where some groups spend the night. Other groups choose to continue up to the campsite just before the second big pass rather than staying in the valley. This does make the second day grueling, but it gets the hardest passes over with immediately.

DAY 3 (11-13KM), PART I. Halfway up the second pass lie the **Runkuracay ruins,** the only circular complex on the Inca Trail, consisting of what was most likely a watchman's tower and messenger room. Another 40min. uphill leads to the second pass, **Abra de Runkuracay** (4000m). Beyond this point, 80% of the Inca Trail is the real thing, original and unrestored. The footpath leads downhill through **a natural tunnel** and onward toward the **Sayacmarca** ("Inaccessible Town," 1hr.), an appropriate name given the sheer cliffs that surround the town on three sides. The lack of nearby agricultural terracing suggests that no one actually lived here. Given the four ritual baths—three of which are found across the middle of the complex—Sayacmarca may have been a sacred spot for meditating pilgrims. Walk to the far end of the ruins to a triangular **balcony** overlooking the **Aobamba Valley.** The sweeping view of the surrounding territory gives a hint at Sayacmarca's additional role as a control point for highway through-traffic. Behind Sayacmarca, on the other face of the mountain, are

The Inca Trail

▲ ACCOMMODATIONS
Machu Picchu Hotel, **11**
Visitor Center, **9**

▲ CAMPSITES
Cochapata, **6**
Conchamarca, **7**
Huayllabamba, **2**
Huiñay Huayna, **10**
Llulluchapampa, **4**
Pacamayo, **5**
Phuyupatamarca, **8**
Qoriwayrachina, **1**
Tres Piedras, **3**

traces of an abandoned (and now prohibited) Inca path that is supposed to have led toward Salkantay. Backtrack and rejoin the main trail as it passes **Conchamarca,** which probably once served as a resting house for weary travelers (it now serves as a watchhouse for trail guards). If you're feeling weary yourself, you can **camp** at the small site.

From Conchamarca the path descends into dense jungle, meandering past orchids, wild daisies, bromeliads, and hanging mosses. This section is among the best preserved parts of the Inca Trail. An hour later, the trail passes a 20m long **tunnel,** inside of which lies a map of South America that natural processes (so they say) carved into the stone. The trail then climbs very gradually to the third pass, **Abra de Phuyupatamarca** (3720m, 2hr.), which yields exceptional views of Aguas Calientes below, the backside of Machu Picchu mountain, and several snow-capped peaks including **Palcay** (5600m), **Salkantay** (6180m), and **Verónica** (5750m).

DAY 3, PART II. Descending, you arrive at the ruins of **Phuyupatamarca** ("Town in the Clouds") and pass its six working ritual baths. The surrounding terraces, too high up for crops, probably functioned as retaining walls. The top of the complex is dominated by a large slab of rock pocked with mysterious dents. Some think these held sacrificial offerings, but locals like to say that Hiram Bingham (discoverer of Machu Picchu) pitched his tent here on stilts for fear of snakes. More likely, this was the base of an important building that was never completed. Some groups choose to camp here, although the rocky plateau is very windy and cold.

From the ruins there are two trails: one bypasses the next two ruins and heads directly to Machu Picchu, the other tests your knees on a 2250-step stone staircase heading down to the terraces of **Intipata**. The right path descends to the ruins of **Huiñay Huayna**, which is next to a popular **campsite** and **hostel** that offers extremely popular **hot showers** (s/5), food, and beer. In the high season, however, the grounds can end up looking (and smelling) like something akin to a Lima shantytown. As an alternative, there are some coveted spots at the foot of Intipata, accessible from the main trail and from a short path that leads uphill from Huiñay Huayna. Huiñay Huayna ("Forever Young") was the last of the major complexes to be discovered (in 1941) and is named for the perpetually flowering orchid that grows nearby. Huiñay Huayna was most likely an agricultural center, as dozens of steep terraces cling to the mountainside.

DAY 4 (7KM). On your marks, get set, go! Groups attempt to wake at 3:30am in order to race the sun (and each other) over the pass to Machu Picchu in time for the legendary sunrise. To reach the pass, hikers must negotiate another hour of Inca stone pathways, which culminate in a brief but very steep set of 50 steps, probably a defensive measure to secure the vulnerable edge of this sacred city. **Flashlights** are essential when attempting to climb down near-vertical steps on the side of a cliff in the dark. It's a few minutes' climb to the fourth and final pass, **Intipunku** ("Sun Gate"), where one can watch the morning's first rays of sunlight fall on Machu Picchu below. (The sky starts getting light by 6am; Machu Picchu is illuminated 1hr. later.) On the morning of the summer solstice, the sun's rays shine directly through a large stone "gate" on the northern side of the ruins, and on the winter solstice they shine through an identical gate on the southern side. Now the celebrating begins as you, weary pilgrim, descend into the sacred city of the Incas—Machu Picchu.

ALTERNATIVE INCA TRAIL: SALKANTAY

As restrictions expand and prices rise for the Inca Trail, more independent (and spontaneous) travelers are choosing alternative paths. Growing in popularity among these alternatives is the trek through Salkantay: a 5-day, 4-night excursion that leads hikers along the other side of the Aobamba River Valley (the side opposite the Inca Trail), through higher passes, colder campsites, bigger waterfalls, and snowier paths, ending in the same glorious finale: Machu Picchu. Although there is only one archaeological site along this trail, flora and fauna abound, and many would argue that the more peaceful character of this road-less-traveled-by outweighs the fame of the original trail. Reservations for Salkantay can often be made as late as the day before departure; government regulations have yet to require guides, but guided tours are recommended. If you do go it alone, make sure you have plenty of food and supplies; on a given day, there may be only 30-100 people on the entire trail, so chances of running into other hikers are low.

AT A GLANCE	
DISTANCE: 52km.	**TIME:** 5 days.
CLIMATE: Extremely cold at high altitudes and temperate in low jungles.	**ALTITUDE:** 2400-4700m.
	DIFFICULTY: Medium-Difficult.
FEATURES: Machu Picchu, flora and fauna, waterfalls, thermal baths, the Andes, breathtaking views.	**FEES:** None.

🛈 PRACTICAL INFORMATION

The Salkantay trek begins with a bus ride from Cusco to Mollepata (3hr.). It follows the Río Blanco and the Río Santa Teresa through two mountain passes until it reaches the Hydroelectric Plant (near Km122), from which travelers take the local train to Aguas Calientes. Hikers can camp along the trail at the several designated campsites or along the forest or beach in between. Tour groups arrange for a hostel stay in Aguas Calientes on the fourth night, before the exploration of the Machu Picchu ruins on Day 5.

Maps: The best maps of the trail are available from the tour operators themselves, free of charge. Topographical maps of the valley region can also be purchased at Cusco bookstores (s/10; see **Bookstores,** p. 221).

Supplies: Guided tours provide food, tents, porters, and most necessary camping equipment. You should bring a sleeping bag, warm gear to survive the mountain chill (hat, gloves, several pairs of socks, etc.), a waterproof jacket and hiking boots, bottled water and/or iodine tablets, and a flashlight. If you're not going with a tour, remember to bring plenty of high-energy foods, coca tea (for the altitude), compact cooking equipment (5 days is a long time to go on cold eats), and a thermal sleeping mat, in addition to your standard camping gear. Everything is available in **Cusco** (see **Outdoor Equipment,** p. 221). Pack animals are available for rental near the beginning of the trail.

Guides and Tours: Many of the same agencies that offer tours for the Inca Trail also offer expeditions to Salkantay (see **Guided Tours from Cusco: The Inca Trail,** p. 241).

🏞 THE TRAIL

DAY 1. The first day begins with an early morning (5am) bus departure from Cusco to **Mollepata** along the Abancay road (3hr.). After a quick breakfast in Mollepata, the walking begins. It's a 4hr. trek till lunch at **Cruzpata,** and another few hours until **Soraypampa**—the first night's campsite. Along the way, hikers catch impressive glimpses of the **Salkantay, Umantay,** and **Soray peaks,** and pass through several ecological systems as the ascent toward higher terrain begins.

DAY 2. After a (hopefully) acclimating night's sleep, hikers begin the day's 8hr. of walking with a grueling ascent toward **Salkantay Pass** (4700m). Shortly after the pass is the beautiful **Laguna Salkantaycocha,** and a popular lunch spot follows at **Huayracpampa** (3600m). A bit more of a descent during the afternoon gets you to the campsite of **Challway.** This second day sees quite a change in scenery, hurtling from the majestic skirts of the Salkantay mountain to its snow-covered pass (from which you may be lucky enough to glimpse a condor or two) to the beginnings of the tropical forest.

DAY 3. Shortly after the beginning of the third day, hikers encounter the **Aguas Termales,** about 45min. out from Challway. From there, it's a 6hr. walk through wet forest, attractive waterfalls, diverse flora, and thickening jungle to the **beach of Sahuayaco,** upon which the third campsite lies.

DAY 4. The fourth day represents the last stretch of hiking—a 4hr. climb through the Paso a Inti Huatana to **Llactapata** (2700m), and then a 1½hr. descent to the **Machu Picchu Hydroelectric Plant.** After a filling lunch, hikers board the local train to **Aguas Calientes** and check into their hostel for the night. Tour groups usually enjoy complimentary wine at one of the small town's restaurants.

DAY 5. An early morning (6am) bus ride up to Machu Picchu allows hikers to catch the sunrise over the citadel. An afternoon of exploring follows the morning's extensive tour (2-3hr.), and most hikers leave for Cusco on the evening train.

MACHU PICCHU

*Open daily 5am-6pm. US$20, students US$10, children US$5. Repeat admission US$10. Even those coming off the Inca Trail must exit Machu Picchu and re-enter, getting their ticket stamped in the process. The nearest train station is in **Aguas Calientes** (p. 270). Shuttle buses depart for Aguas Calientes from the Machu Picchu Hotel (20min., 9am-5:30pm, US$4.50). Luggage storage (mandatory for backpackers fresh off the trail) is located near the admission booth (s/4 per bag, free for hikers with park ticket). Free maps are available in the administration office next to the luggage storage. English-speaking guides can be hired on site (US$15-20 per person). A terraced restaurant by the ticket booth serves overpriced, mostly American food (s/10-40) and a lunch buffet (US$22 per person). The only hotel is the luxurious Machu Picchu Hotel, outside the main entrance.*

Clinging to a vertiginous hillside, surrounded by towering green mountains, and bathed in a nearly constant stream of sunshine, the Inca ruins of Machu Picchu are among the most awe-inspiring sights in South America. The structures are as intact as Inca ruins come, for they had to contend only with natural forces; the invading Spaniards never knew Machu Picchu existed. Luckily for visitors, Machu Picchu's massive size comes close to absorbing the mobs of sunburnt tourists who visit annually. On average, 3000 people visit Machu Picchu each day; this number is much greater in July and August. Nevertheless, an early morning arrival at the citadel proves to be a peaceful, even spiritual, experience.

> **BORDER CROSSING?** Visitors to Machu Picchu can have their passports stamped in the administration office next to the backpack check by the entrance. It's not required, just a memento of your time in Inca Country.

A DISCOVERY LONG OVERDUE

US native **Hiram Bingham** is commonly touted as the discoverer of Machu Picchu, even though locals living nearby knew about the ruins long before Bingham explored the area and variations of the words "Machu Picchu" appeared all over property deeds and explorers' maps before the 20th century. Nevertheless, Bingham was the first with the resources to expose the city's significance to the rest of the world. On July 24, 1911, with the help and guidance of local farmer Melchor Arteaga, Bingham encountered the massive citadel. Ironically, he mistook it for the long lost Inca capital of Vilcabamba (p. 422; see **Bingham's Blunder,** p. 268).

What Bingham discovered turned out to be far more wondrous and enigmatic than even the lost city of Vilcabamba. Despite numerous excavations over the years, it is still unclear who built Machu Picchu, who lived there, or why. Nor can one say with any authority why it was abandoned or forgotten. Adding to the mystery, Bingham and others discovered several ruins near Machu Picchu—now part of the Inca Trail—which are similar in style. Like Machu Picchu, these were carefully constructed, inhabited, abandoned, and subsequently forgotten. Machu Picchu seems to have been the administrative center of this network of complexes, an entire region never preserved in Inca memory, despite the existence of royal oral historians whose duty it was to remember.

FIGURING IT ALL OUT

Machu Picchu was probably constructed under **Inca Pachakuteq** after the Incas defeated the rival Chanca people in 1438, an event that marked the beginning of the great Inca expansion. And yet, if one accepts that Machu Picchu had been abandoned before the conquest, that leaves less than a century for the city to have been built, populated, and left behind. Almost no one who has seen Machu Picchu's buildings, temples, and terraces is satisfied with this time frame, but few can offer an alternative account.

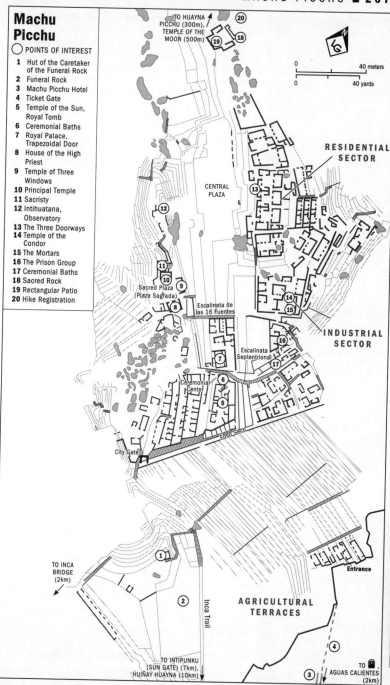

Machu Picchu

◯ POINTS OF INTEREST

1 Hut of the Caretaker of the Funeral Rock
2 Funeral Rock
3 Machu Picchu Hotel
4 Ticket Gate
5 Temple of the Sun, Royal Tomb
6 Ceremonial Baths
7 Royal Palace, Trapezoidal Door
8 House of the High Priest
9 Temple of Three Windows
10 Principal Temple
11 Sacristy
12 Intihuatana, Observatory
13 The Three Doorways
14 Temple of the Condor
15 The Mortars
16 The Prison Group
17 Ceremonial Baths
18 Sacred Rock
19 Rectangular Patio
20 Hike Registration

TO HUAYNA PICCHU (300m), TEMPLE OF THE MOON (500m)

0 — 40 meters
0 — 40 yards

RESIDENTIAL SECTOR

CENTRAL PLAZA

Sacred Plaza (Plaza Sagrada)

Escalinata de las 16 Fuentes

INDUSTRIAL SECTOR

Escalinata Septentrional

Ceremonial Center

Foso Seco

City Gate

TO INCA BRIDGE (2km)

Inca Trail

AGRICULTURAL TERRACES

Entrance

TO INTIPUNKU (SUN GATE) (7km), HUIÑAY HUAYNA (10km)

TO AGUAS CALIENTES (2km)

BINGHAM'S BLUNDER

n 1911, when locals showed ale professor **Hiram Bingham** kilometers of terracing and walls of Inca stonework now known as Machu Picchu, Bingham declared the site to be the long-lost Inca city of Old Vilcabamba.

After the Spanish Conquest, **nca Manco Cápac II** retreated to the jungle and built Vilcabamba as a military base. The Spanish ended the Inca resistance with a brutal 1572 invasion. They sacked Vilcabamba and executed the last Inca ruler, **Túpac Amaru,** n Cusco, extinguishing the Inca dynasty. In time, Vilcabamba was abandoned and forgotten, until Bingham's announcement centuries later that Old Vilcambaba had been found.

Or had it? Bingham's "discovery" stood unchallenged for 50 years, even though it didn't hold up to the simplest scrutiny. "Vilcabamba" means "Sacred Plain" n Quechua, but Machu Picchu is far from flat. Vilcabamba was attacked by the Spaniards, but Machu Picchu shows no signs of invasion. Vilcabamba was constructed in a hurry by a renegade set of Inca warriors, but Machu Picchu was no rush job.

Bingham's mistake was confirmed by **Gene Savoy** in 1964, when he discovered the true ruins of Old Vilcabamba at **Espíritu Pampa** (p. 422). Ironically, Hiram Bingham found part of these ruins n 1909, but passed over them.

Hiram Bingham's mistaken view that the city was built as a defensive post popularized the notion of Machu Picchu as a citadel. Its many lookout towers and drawbridge seem to support this view. However, archaeologists of late have considered Machu Picchu more a religious center than a fortress: Machu Picchu may have been a holy city at the end of a long walk of pilgrimage. Bingham's excavation studies of human remains revealed a large majority of women in Machu Picchu's population, initially suggesting the prominence of virgin priestesses (although later analyses of the human remains, with improved technology, deemed that the male-to-female ratio among the excavated population was about even after all). Evidence of habitation suggests that only around 1000 people ever lived there at one time. Yet the surrounding terraces—in Machu Picchu and nearby at Huiñay Huayna and Intipata—would have fed thousands. Perhaps Machu Picchu was a site of agricultural experimentation (intricately tied to sacred ritual), or maybe the city served as a jungle outpost guaranteeing a secure and constant supply of coca leaves. No one really knows.

LOCATION IS EVERYTHING

What makes Machu Picchu so breathtaking is its singular location high in the mountains—no wonder it was lost for so many years. Before construction, the site must have been a steep green mountainside blending into the rest of the valley. Finding and building on this site would have been an overwhelming task, but to Pachakuteq, the site's spiritual pre-eminence would have been worth the effort. Machu Picchu lies between the snow-capped peaks of the venerated Apus (mountain gods)—Salkantay to the west, Verónica to the east; beside the flowing waters of the most sacred river, the Urubamba; and below a clear view of the night sky, home of the Milky Way, which the Incas believed to be the celestial counterpart to the river. Machu Picchu was one of the holiest sites they could have chosen.

IT'S THE END OF THE WORLD AS WE KNOW IT

The mystery of the city's abandonment inspires even more speculation than its original purpose. Some believe the site's population was decimated by an epidemic disease. Others point to hypothetical sieges by the Antis tribe from the jungle. It is possible that Machu Picchu was a vacation estate for the Inca Pachakuteq and populated exclusively by his own clan—if true, the site's abandonment could be explained simply by the death of Pachakuteq. One theory conjectures that the entire region rebelled against the central authority of the empire, and that to prevent a major uprising, the ruling Incas based in Cusco swept in and moved the population out. Peruvian archaeologist Marino Sánchez offers a vivid narrative according to which Machu Picchu was struck by torrential rains, the gold-covered principal temple was hit by lightning, and everyone fled in fear of the bad omen. Guides to Machu Picchu will present these accounts with varying degrees of confidence, but it's all speculation.

EXPLORING THE RUINS

ABOVE THE MAIN CITY. Spread between two mountains, the sacred city sprawls along Machu Picchu mountain and faces Huayna Picchu mountain. The front entrance leads into what is called the **agricultural sector** of the city, great terraces that supported enough crops for the entire population. At the top of the terraces, there is a carved granite slab known as the **funeral rock,** which may have been used to prepare the dead for burial; this upper part of the city, into which hikers emerge from the Inca Trial, seemed to function as a cemetery. Those interested can follow the path in reverse to see **Intipunku** and the enormous terraces at **Huiñay Huayna.** Also from the cemetery hill, a road leads to the **Inca bridge,** a defensive drawbridge that has been restored with logs. Incidentally, those **llamas** munching on the grass have been installed for the tourists—they actually prefer to live at higher altitudes.

THE ELEMENTS. Back down the hill, starting at the front entrance, everyone walks across one of the large, flat terraces to reach 16 ritual baths in a row. On the left, just before the baths, is the Temple of the Sun, notable for its U-shaped wall that is nearly flawless in its fine masonry. On the winter solstice, sunlight shines through one of the windows and falls exactly on the center of the rock in the middle of the temple. This rock shares the Southern Cross's diamond shape, and many visitors hold their hands over it to glean energy from its supposed power source. A carved cave under the temple, which Bingham called the Royal Tomb, might have held human remains. Though no human remains have actually been found there, the high quality of the architecture does suggest some sort of ceremonial function. On the other side, next to the series of fountains, is a three-sided house, with a recently thatched roof. Inside the house are large pegs, upon which ceremonial items may have been hung. Together, it is suspected that these four buildings—the ritual baths, the Temple of the Sun, the open-air house, and the tomb—served as a tribute to nature's four basic elements: water, fire, air, and earth. It is said that the large buildings across the baths on the other side of the Temple of the Sun once housed Inca nobility.

THE SACRED PLAZA. Walk to the top of the staircase along the baths to reach the rock quarry. Near the piles of stones (some of which are used today for restoration) sits a large rock with several holes cut into it along a vertical line. Created by 20th century archaeologist Manuel Ballón, the rock is intended to serve as a model of how the Incas might have cut the large stones needed for construction. According to the model, dry wooden wedges were inserted into holes cut into the stone, and as the wood was moistened, it expanded to break apart the rock. Farther into the city, on the same terrace level, sits the beautifully symmetrical, three-walled **Temple with Three Windows,** carved from immense rocks. Opening onto the same plaza, the three-walled **Principal Temple** has one droopy corner that has partially sunk into an underground chamber. In one wall, an intricately-carved building block has at least 32 edges. Beyond this, on top of a small hill, resides the **Intihuatana,** another carved rock that may have been used to measure the sun's movements. Look over at the flat grassy area that divides the city like a parade ground.

THE INDUSTRIAL AND RESIDENTIAL SECTORS. On the other side of a grassy clearing stand dozens of stone complexes, most of which were probably ordinary housing. Within one of these buildings, two circular pans are carved into the stone floor. Bingham called these **mortars** because he thought they were used to grind corn; others have speculated that they were filled with water and used as mirrors to observe the night sky. A nearby staircase leads to the multilevel, intricately carved **Temple of the Condor.** Bingham incorrectly thought its inner chambers served as a jail, leading to the misnomer the "Prison Sector." The temple's more recent name stems from the triangular stone, thought to represent the condor's head, and a carved rock face that looks like an extended wing.

THE FAR SIDE. At the far edge of the city, en route to Huayna Picchu, another plaza with three-walled buildings centers on an erected rock. Called the **Sacred Rock**, it is shaped like the outline of the mountain behind it. Many visitors continue along this path in order to hike up the steep ■**Huayna Picchu** ("Young Mountain," 45min. ascent). A checkpoint near the Sacred Rock requires hiker registration; you must enter the path between 7am and 1pm, and return by 4pm. On the way up to Huayna Picchu (after about 20min.), a trail splits off toward the **Temple of the Moon** (45min. hike). One can also reach the Temple of the Moon from the top of Huayna Picchu by following the path that leads down the north face of the mountain, away from the Machu Picchu side (45min. descent). Be wary of stretches of steep stairs and missing rungs in wooden ladders; do not attempt this path in the wet season. Hikers who take this path can then return to the main trail along the easier lower path (45min. hike), but a thorough exploration takes about 3hr.

AGUAS CALIENTES   ☎084

This small town (pop. 2500; elev. 2060m), also called Machu Picchu Pueblo, was named for the **thermal springs** at the top of Pachacutec, but the springs would not receive nearly so much traffic were its railway station not the closest one to Machu Picchu. Tourists make up 90% of the town's daily population, prices are preposterously high, and hotels, restaurants, and souvenir shops abound. The hot springs and the temperate climate, however, make it a pleasant stopping point after a long day of exploring. When it comes to Machu Picchu and its *pueblo*, all good things (the most awesome views of the ruins, the best hotels and restaurants, the path to the train station) come with long sets of stairs, although the town (unlike the ruins) is wheelchair accessible, with stone and wooden ramps built alongside each cascade of steps.

◼ TRANSPORTATION

Train tickets from Aguas Calientes to Cusco can be purchased one day in advance at the **boletería,** on Imperio de las Incas (opens 8:30am), but most visitors reserve tickets through a tour agency in Cusco. Six trains leave daily from **Estación Nueva,** on Imperio de los Incas, but times and prices change very frequently; check local hostels and restaurants for up-to-date schedules (6am, US$10; later trains, US$25-70; last train leaves no later than 7pm). **Shuttle buses to Machu Picchu** (30min.; at least 1 per hr. 6:30am-5pm; US$4.50) leave from the lower part of the market.

◼◼ ORIENTATION AND PRACTICAL INFORMATION

From Estación Nueva, **Imperio de Los Incas** runs the gauntlet of souvenir booths downhill and continues along the local train tracks. When the road splits, a right turn leads to the **Plaza de Armas** and its large church. At the far end of the Plaza, **Pachacutec** leads uphill and to the right, filled with hostels and pizzerias. The hike to Machu Picchu is on the steep 2hr. trail (not the road).

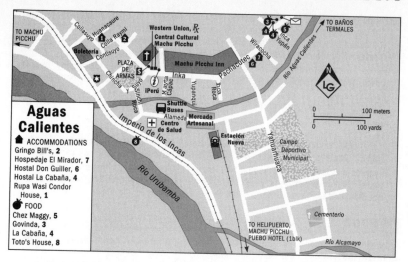

Aguas Calientes

▲ ACCOMMODATIONS
Gringo Bill's, 2
Hospedaje El Mirador, 7
Hostal Don Guiller, 6
Hostal La Cabaña, 4
Rupa Wasi Condor
   House, 1
🍎 FOOD
Chez Maggy, 5
Govinda, 3
La Cabaña, 4
Toto's House, 8

Tourist Office: iPerú (☎ 21 1204), half a block up Pachacutec from the Plaza, provides local and regional maps, a 24hr. tourist information and assistance line (☎ 574 8000), and consumer protection for tourist services. **Centro Cultural Machu Picchu,** on Pachacutec just off the Plaza, sells tickets to the ruins (6am-noon and 1-5pm) and has informative cultural displays.

Currency Exchange: Businesses on Pachacutec and Imperio de las Incas exchange dollars and traveler's checks. The **24hr. pharmacy** (☎ 21 1248), on the Plaza, gives **cash** in exchange for a credit card purchase, with a 15% commission fee. The pharmacy also has a **Western Union** service desk (☎ 422 0014).

Markets: Supermarkets are up and down Pachacutec and Imperio de Los Incas. You'll also find plenty of folks offering post-trail **massages,** which range from US$20 (from the local masseuse at Chez Maggy) to US$40 (with the Dutch professional at Machu Picchu Pueblo Hotel). A craft market, **Mercado Artesanal,** floods the area between the bus station and train station, but most goods (with the exception of "I survived the Inca Trail" t-shirts) can be bought much cheaper in Cusco.

Police: On Imperio de Las Incas (☎ 21 1178), next to the *boletería.* Open 24hr.

Medical Services: Centro de Salud (☎ 21 1037), at Alameda. Open 24hr.

Telephones: Public phone booths litter the streets.

Internet Access: Internet cafes are plentiful. s/5-10 per hr.

Post Office: Correo Central (☎ 21 1132), several blocks uphill on Pachacutec. Open M-Sa 10am-8pm.

🏠 ACCOMMODATIONS

Many housing options await you in Aguas Calientes; hostels fill quickly from June to August, so reservations are recommended. All but the most basic hostels have private baths, 24hr. hot water, and laundry service (s/5-6 per kg).

Hostal Don Guiller, Pachacutec 136 (☎ 21 1091). Clean, carpeted, simple rooms above a lovely restaurant (breakfast US$5). Singles US$15; doubles US$20; triples US$30. All major credit cards, with 20% surcharge. ④

Gringo Bill's, Colla Raymi 104 (☎21 1046), off the Plaza. You may cringe at the name, but you'll be pleased with your clean, well-decorated room. Newly built restaurant (breakfast included, 5:30-10am) and bar with game room downstairs. English spoken. Singles s/30; doubles s/35; triples s/55. All major credit cards. ❸

Hostal La Cabaña, Pachacutec 20-3 (☎21 1048; www.cabanahostal.com), farther uphill. Well-kept rooms. Restaurant has the best seating in town (see **Food,** below). English spoken. DVD rental available. Checkout 9am. Singles US$20; doubles US$25; triples US$35; additional bed US$10. All major credit cards. ❺

Rupa Wasi Condor House, Huanacaure 180 (☎21 1101; www.rupawasi.net), just off the Plaza. Tidy, compact, wood-floored rooms and a rooftop terrace, complete with hammocks, couches, and a unique view of the citadel. Breakfast included. Singles US$22; doubles US$32; triples US$47; additional bed US$12. No credit cards. ❺

Hospedaje El Mirador, Pachacutec 135 (☎21 1092). As basic as it gets, with small carpeted dorm-style rooms and clean baths. Some private baths. 24hr. hot water. Singles, doubles, and triples s/15 per person. ❷

🍴 FOOD

Countless restaurants line Pachacutec and Imperio de Las Incas, offering masses of pizza and some typical Peruvian dishes.

Chez Maggy, Pachacutec 156 (☎21 1006). This Cusco-based restaurant just opened a new Machu Picchu branch, offering a varied selection of Italian (s/14-19), Mexican (s/7-22), and Peruvian (s/14-35) entrees. Delivery available. All major credit cards. ❸

La Cabaña Restaurant, Pachacutec 20-3, in Hostal La Cabaña. The best seating in Aguas Calientes—each wooden table sits below a Japanese lantern and displays a huge bouquet of flowers. Entrees s/20-25. ❹

Govinda, Pachacutec 20 (☎21 1021), halfway up the hill toward the baths. This one's even better than the one in Cusco. Stone floors, thatched roof, and wide-open doors are refreshingly out of place amid all the pizzerias. All-vegetarian menu changes daily, but soups, salads, and soy are daily staples. Entrees s/10-20. Open daily 7am-10pm. ❷

Toto's House, on Imperio de Los Incas (☎22 4179; www.grupointi.com), across from the steps leading to the train station. A large, pleasant dining area overlooks exciting river rapids. Serves a filling lunch buffet (daily noon-4pm, US$13). Pizzas s/17-23. Entrees s/22-38. Open daily 10am-9pm. Reservations must be made in advance for the dinner buffet. All major credit cards. ❹

👁 SIGHTS

The **thermal baths** (*baños termales*) are Aguas Calientes's claim to fame, and they are good for relaxing sore muscles after the Inca Trail. (Open daily 5am-8:30pm. s/5 per person, towels and bathing suits for rental in neighboring shops s/2-3.) But they're not fooling anyone—Machu Picchu (p. 266) put this town on the map.

THE CENTRAL HIGHLANDS

At the heart of the Peruvian Andes lie the Central Highlands, a chain of rolling *sierras* swathed in vibrant green and gold. So close to the equator, few of the mountains in this region are snow-capped, but clouds often hang below the tops of the summits. Sadly, the stunning landscape holds a history far darker than its picturesque scenery would imply. In the 1980s and early 90s, this region was

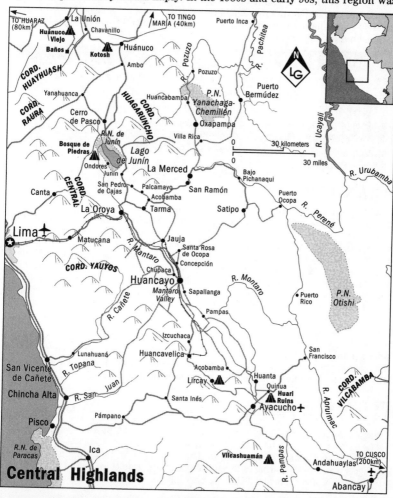

Central Highlands

struck from most travelers' itineraries, as it was overrun with peasant-based terrorist groups. For almost 20 years, the Sendero Luminoso and Túpac Amaru Revolutionary Movements used the area as a staging ground for their battle against the capitalist powers ruling the country. Recent government efforts to clean up the area have since forced most groups underground, culminating in July 1999, when then-president Alberto Fujimori appeared on public television leading the manhunt for and eventual apprehension of Oscar Alberto Ramírez Durand (a.k.a. Feliciano), the leader of the Sendero Rojo terrorist faction.

Today the lively towns of the central Andes are working to escape the shadow of their violent history. Although tourist offices have begun to spring up in an attempt to attract a bit of the lucrative tourist industry, the Central Highlands remain well off the beaten path. Here, the *sierra* is simply Peru being Peru. Markets are a place to buy potatoes, not souvenirs, and traditional clothing has yet to be choked out by legions of Adidas, Nike, and Puma. Transportation can be arduous and infrastructure remains a word reserved for Cusco. However, the region's casual nature is precisely its appeal—the Central Highlands are Peru at its most natural and genuine.

HIGHLIGHTS OF THE CENTRAL HIGHLANDS

ESCAPE the crowds at Peru's second-largest lake, the serene **Lago de Junín** (p. 281).

STROLL among graceful colonial mansions and world-renowned tapestry workshops in the Barrio Santa Ana under the highland sun of **Ayacucho** (p. 299).

HIKE through villages untouched by tourism, over mountains, past pre-Inca ruins, and across streams in the Mantaro Valley near **Huancayo** (p. 285).

SHIVER with cold and awe at the barren peaks that enclose the mountaintop town of **Huancavelica** (p. 296).

HUÁNUCO   ☎ 062

In an Inca-obsessed country, there is something refreshing about the (extremely) pre-Inca ruins that form Huánuco's biggest attraction. The earliest traces of civilization in the valley surrounding Huánuco (pop. 120,000; elev. 1912m) date back to 10,000 BC. In 1539, the Spaniards founded the city they called Huánuco on the site of what is today the nearby town of La Unión. Two years later the whole settlement was "moved" to its current location. A few colonial buildings still remind the modern visitor of a more aesthetically sensitive time in Huánuco's past, but such historical currents wield little influence over present-day Huánuco, with its video pubs, burger joints, and ubiquitous *tragamonedas* (slot machines). Only the ramshackle settlements climbing the hills on the outskirts seem like they could have been here long ago. Huánuco today is the capital city of a department of nearly one million people. Its streets are packed with fun-loving university students, villagers selling potatoes, and entrepreneurs whizzing by in taxis. But like the rest of Peru, Huánuco is always ready to take a break from work; the city's calendar is packed with festivals, beautifying the present by celebrating the past.

▐ TRANSPORTATION

Flights: Airport (☎51 3066), 6km north of the city center. **LC Busre,** 2 de Mayo 1355 (☎51 8113, in Lima 01 619 1313; www.lcbusre.com.pe). Open M-Sa 8:30am-7:30pm, Su 8:30am-12:30pm. Flies to **Lima** (45min.; M, W, Th, Sa 1:40pm; US$59). Flights may also be purchased through **Magenta Air,** 2 de Mayo 1253 (☎51 6580). Open M-F 8:30am-1pm and 3-7pm, Sa 8am-2pm.

Buses: Bus companies are scattered throughout the city, but prices and departure times fluctuate frequently. **Etposa,** Hermilio Valdizán 744 and Crespo Castillo 800 (☎51 2903) sends buses to **Lima** (9-10hr.; M-Sa 9, 10pm and Su 9am; s/25-30; buses leave from Crespo Castillo) and **Pucallpa** (12hr., 6:30pm, s/25; buses leave from Hermilio Valdizán). **León de Huánuco,** Malecón Alomia Robles 821 (☎51 2996), runs to **Lima** (9-10hr.; 10am, 8:30, 9:30pm; s/20-25; *bus cama* 10:30pm, s/32-40) and **Satipo** (10-11hr., 8pm, s/30) via **San Ramón** (6hr., s/25) and **La Merced** (7hr., s/25). **Transportes GM,** 28 de Julio 535 (☎51 9770) is the only other company running day buses to **Lima** (9-10hr.; 9am, 10, 10:15pm; also F 10:30pm; s/27-45). **Cómite de Automóviles 5,** General Prado 1097 (☎51 8346), sends colectivos to **Tingo María** (2hr., leave when full 5am-7pm, s/13). Colectivos to **La Unión** (5hr., leave when full 5am-2 or 3pm, s/20-25) leave from near Tarapacá and San Martín. Colectivos to other *sierra* towns such as **Cerro de Pasco** (2hr.), **Junín** (3½-4hr.), and **La Oroya** (4-5hr.) depart from the **Control de Cayhuayna** on the edge of town (taxi s/2-2.50).

Local Transportation: Huánuco is easily traveled by foot; nevertheless, colectivos (s/0.50) run along 2 de Mayo, 28 de Julio, and Abtao.

Taxis: Taxis in the city cost s/1.50-2; to the airport s/8-9. Mototaxis in the city s/1-1.50.

✴🛈 ORIENTATION AND PRACTICAL INFORMATION

Huánuco follows a grid pattern bordered by **Río Huallaga** to the east, **Río Higueras** to the south, and mountains all around. The principal streets border the **Plaza de Armas: Dámaso Beraún** and **General Prado** run (mostly) east-west, and **2 de Mayo** and **28 de Julio** intersect them. **Tarapacá,** a street of many bus stations, runs perpendicular to Río Huallaga, four blocks south of the Plaza de Armas. The street known as **Huánuco,** chock-full of budget accommodations, runs parallel to and one block behind General Prado. **Abtao** is parallel to and one block behind 2 de Mayo.

Tourist Office: 28 de Julio 910 (☎51 8345), on the Plaza de Armas. Offers a brand-new photo-brochure of the Huánuco department. Very helpful Spanish-only staff sell excellent town maps (s/1). Open daily approx. 7am-1pm and 2-10pm.

Currency Exchange: Money changers line 2 de Mayo on the Plaza de Armas.

Banks: Banco de Crédito, 2 de May 1005 (☎51 2213; open M-F 10am-6pm, Sa 9:30am-12:30pm) has a Plus/V **ATM,** as does **Banco Continental,** 2 de Mayo 1135, on the Plaza de Armas.

Markets: Mercado Modelo, bordered by San Martín and Huánuco, and the quieter **Mercado Antiguo,** 5 blocks away, primarily on Huánuco and Valdizan, offer similar staples: potatoes, meat, potatoes, juice, and potatoes. Both open during daylight hours.

Laundry: Lavandería La Primavera, Beraún 530 (☎51 3052). Wash and iron: shirts s/4, pants s/5, t-shirts s/2-3, socks s/1. Open M-Sa 8:30am-12:30pm and 3-8pm.

Emergency: ☎105.

Police: Constitución 501 (☎51 3115), at Abtao. Open 24hr. for emergencies.

24-Hour Pharmacy: Botica 24 Horas, Huánuco 613-A (☎51 6822). MC. Down the street is the larger **Inkafarma,** Huánuco 600 (☎51 6516). Open 7am-11:30pm.

Hospital: Hospital Regional de Huánuco, Hermilio Valdizan 940 (☎51 2400). Open 24hr. Includes pharmacy on premises.

Telephones: Telefónica del Perú, Beraún 765, on the Plaza de Armas, has offices throughout the city. Most have private booths and sell phone cards.

Internet Access: On nearly every corner, and sometimes several places in between. Speedy connections s/1 per hr.

Post Office: Serpost, 2 de Mayo 1157 (☎51 2503). Open M-Sa 8am-8pm.

ON THE MENU

TRY THIS AT HOME! RODENT STEW MADE EASY

The rumors are true. In Peru, rats are considered a delicacy. Well, not rats, rodents. Guinea pigs. *Cuy* (pronounced KWEE or KOO-weh). Even Jesus dined on a roasted *cuy* when he was in Cusco for his Last Supper.

The *cuy* has a long-established place in Andean culture. Evidence from the archaeological digs at Kotosh, near Huánuco, suggest that the raising of *cuy* belonged to the earliest stages of agrarian life here, more than 1000 years before the Inca heyday.

Cuy was sacred as well to the Inca, who considered its flesh to have special x-ray-like "sensitivities." To diagnose illnesses, the Inca rubbed a live *cuy* all over the body of the sick person, then sacrificed it to read and interpret its viscera, which would reveal its hidden answer to what ailed.

Cuy were also eaten in association with Kaymi, the August 1 festival which followed forty days after the Peruvian Winter Solstice on June 21. This day marked the earth's return to fertility, celebrated with songs, dances, animal sacrifices, housecleaning, forgiveness of one's fellow man, and of course, roasted *cuy*.

The following popular recipe for *picante de cuy*, or spicy *cuy*, can easily be made at home with rabbit or even chicken. Of course, made at home, it won't have those cute paws still attached...

■ ACCOMMODATIONS

There will be no bed shortage in Huánuco anytime soon. Fairly decrepit yet inexpensive lodgings choke the Mercado Modelo area; super-luxurious (and super-expensive) hotels overlook the Plaza de Armas. These little beauties fall somewhere in between.

■ **Hostal Huánuco,** Huánuco 777 (☎51 2050), between 28 de Julio and 2 de Mayo. Brimming with reminders of its glorious past as a sprawling mansion—art, manicured gardens, tile, and Greek columns. The funkiest—but somehow still the mellowest—place to sleep in Huánuco. Private baths have 24hr. hot water. Singles s/20; doubles s/25. ❷

Hotel Cusco, Huánuco 616 (☎51 7653), between 2 de Mayo and Abtao. It may be a little dark, but its 5 floors offer enough amenities to make it worthwhile. Cable TV, private hot baths, laundry service—even a parking lot (just in case you drove) and a *tragamoneda* parlor for when nothing's on TV. Singles s/35; doubles s/40. ❸

Hostal Las Vegas, 28 de Julio 934 (☎51 2315), on the Plaza. The simple rooms with telephone, cable TV, and private baths may not have sequin-suited dancers, but the casinos visible from the downstairs restaurant and the artificial plants help keep that Vegas feel alive. Avoid the rooms by the restaurant or facing the Plaza de Armas, if not to escape the noise, then for the splendid views of the *sierra* from the rooms upstairs in the back. Hot water mornings and evenings. Singles s/25; doubles s/37. ❸

Hotel Caribe, Huánuco 546, 2nd fl. (☎51 9708), next to the market. From the Plaza, walk 1 block down 2 de Mayo (away from the Cathedral), turn right and walk 2 blocks on Huánuco. Rooms facing away from the market and far from the pub are quieter. Cable TV s/5. Singles s/7; doubles with bath s/20. ❶

◖ FOOD

Restaurants proliferate on the streets radiating from the Plaza de Armas, but eat within a two-block radius and you'll be dining to the tune of jingling slot machines. Several good **bakeries** line 2 de Mayo south of the Plaza and **chifas** clump on Beraún to the west. Vendors cycle through town with fruit-laden "cart-mobiles."

■ **El Huapri,** 2 de Mayo 990 (☎51 2477), at the corner of 2 de Mayo and Huánuco, 1 block from the Plaza. This Peruvian-style diner knows the meaning of comfort food. Locals swear by this reliable grill and ice cream shop for *salchipapa especial* (sliced hot dogs, fries, and eggs with mayonnaise and ketchup; s/3) and milkshakes (s/3.50). Look for the giant yellow "D'Anafria" sign—it only says "El Huapri" inside. Hot dog or grilled cheese sandwich s/1.50. Ice cream s/3. Open M-Sa 8am-1pm and 4pm-midnight, Su 8am-1pm and 6pm-midnight. ❶

 Lookcos Burger Grill, Abtao 1021 (☎51 2460). Lookcos lives the American burger-joint legend with brightly-colored walls, pictures of Marilyn Monroe, and 30,000 songs on the karaoke machine. Burgers s/4-6. Tacos s/4-5. Really, really hungry? Dare to try the "Super Especial Lookcos" (s/8). Open daily 6pm-midnight. AmEx/DC/V. ❶

Pollería Shorton, Beraún 685 (☎51 2829), just off the Plaza near 2 de Mayo. Feel the burn as open flames roast giant chickens along the wall. Cheap *cerveza* and friendly owners make this a favorite. Entrees s/5-8. Open daily 11am-1am. AmEx/MC/V. ❶

Restaurant Central, 2 de Mayo 1275 (☎51 5240), toward the end of the 1st block after the Plaza. White-washed wooden booths and lots of kids give this old standby a down-home feel. Breakfast s/2.50. *Menú* lunch specials like *pollo a la cubana* with plantain, rice, and egg are s/3-5. A la carte s/4.50-8. Open daily 7am-10:30pm. ❶

San Felipe Panadería, Pastelería y Bodega, 2 de Mayo 1031 (☎51 4403), just before the Banco de Crédito. When the sight of chicken becomes just too much, duck in here for fresh-baked *empanadas* (s/1.50) and *torta de acelga* (s/1). Scrumptious *alfajores* (s/1) and brightly-colored cakes draw an evening crowd for sit-down dessert. ❶

Don Sancho Pizzería, General Prado 645 (☎51 6906). The delicious aroma wafting halfway down the street will whet your appetite for Don Sancho's oven-fresh garlic bread. With red plaid tablecloths reminiscent of traditional Italian checked ones, the only thing missing is the Verdi music in the background. Personal pizzas s/9-11. Fettucine alfredo s/9.50. Vegetarian lasagna s/11. Open M-Sa 6:30-11pm. ❷

Nature's Vid Restaurant Shop Vegetariana, Abtao 951 (☎51 6053). Owner Flora aims to please, and please she does; Nature's Vid serves Huánuco's burgeoning vegetarian population in this spacious, garlicky hideaway. Don't be fooled—Flora's *bistecs* are all made from soy protein. Large vegetable salad s/3.50. Delicious fresh-squeezed juices s/1.50-5. Entrees s/5-10. Open daily 7am-10pm. ❶

👁 SIGHTS

KOTOSH TEMPLES. Huánuco's claim to fame lies just 5km from the town's edge. The pre-Inca Kotosh Temples were built almost 4000 years ago, making

HUÁNUCO-STYLE PICANTE DE CUY

Serves four.

· 2 *cuy* (or substitute with appropriate portions of rabbit or chicken)
· 1kg yellow potatoes (new potatoes work well)
· 4 medium-sized yellow peppers (not too spicy; minced fine)
· spicy red pepper, dried, to taste (either powder or whole peppers may be used)
· 2 medium sized onions, diced
· 4-6 cloves garlic, pressed
· ½ cup (110g) roasted peanuts (ground to rough powder)
· oil for sautéing
· salt and pepper to taste
· beef stock (optional)

Peel and boil the potatoes and set aside. Pan-fry the *cuy* (or substitute) until browned and mostly cooked. Remove the meat from the pan and set aside. In the same pan, sauté onions, garlic, and pepper until they turn golden. Return the meat to the pan and let simmer covered 10-15min. or until the meat has cooked through, taking care not to let the mixture stick to the pot. Add water or beef stock as needed. Add the ground roasted peanuts. Serve over potatoes.

Note: Some recipes suggest marinating the *cuy* in a mixture of garlic, salt, and pepper for 2hr. as a first step.

them the oldest in Peru. The site, first identified in 1935 but only excavated beginning in 1960, reveals successive layers of evidence left by the *sierra*'s evolving societies, including more than 10 tons of pottery fragments. While little remains of the original structures, visitors can make out aspects of the temples' former statures. The complex's oldest structure rests at the top of the hill; its now-crumbled asymmetrical walls were once 3m thick. The **Temple of the Crossed Hands** ("Temple of Kotosh," 2000-1500 BC) is known for its sculptures of two sets of crossed hands, purportedly representations of the Southern Cross constellation. One set of sculptures represents males, with the right hand crossed over the left, representing strength; for the female hands, left over right symbolizes intuition. Both of the originals are now in the National Museum in Lima. The crossed hands may have symbolized friendship, but the temple also contained a series of niches used for less friendly purposes—the Kotosh placed animal sacrifices in the niches after they had baked them to death. *(Colectivos and camionetas can drop you off at Kotosh on their way to the mountains. Colectivos (s/1) depart from the corner of Aguilar and San Martín; camionetas (s/1) leave from the corner of Leoncio Prado and Aguilar. Taxi s/12 round-trip including waiting time. Open daily 8am-4pm. s/2.50, students s/1.50, children s/1.)*

CHURCHES. Huánuco is home to a surprising number of churches, several of which date from the colonial period. Although in differing states of preservation and maintenance, together they create a vision of Huánuco in a different era. The sight of brightly painted bell towers against the backdrop of rugged mountainside is striking. For a peek inside, visit in the early evening, around or just after the 6pm mass. Some also hold 6am services. The **Cathedral,** on the Plaza de Armas, built in 1965, preserves nothing of the original 1618 structure, which had become too dilapidated to be saved. However, the cathedral counts a venerated sculpture of San Juan de Burgos (see **Festivals,** below) among its colonial-era sculptures. To get from there to the **Iglesia San Cristóbal,** the first church the Spanish built in the town, face the Plaza, turn left, and walk all the way down Beraún to the corner of San Cristóbal, one short block from the river. Next you might walk to the **Iglesia San Sebastián,** which was built in the 17th century and holds the world's only sculpture of San Sebastián covered with smallpox. To get there from San Cristóbal, continue to the river, turn left, and pass the 1879 Calicanto stone bridge. Keep walking against the river current until you see a larger metal bridge; on the riverbank the imposing facade of San Sebastián fills the block between 28 de Julio and 2 de Mayo. The **Iglesia San Francisco,** built in 1560, has simple wooden benches leading up to a huge ornate golden altarpiece. From San Sebastián, take 28 de Julio away from the river, back to the Plaza. Turn left at its far side, following Beraún, and the church will soon appear on your left as San Martín opens on the right.

MUSEO DE CIENCIAS. This one-room museum houses a curious collection of stuffed animals native to Peru, all dissected and lovingly prepared by the curator, Nester Armas Wenzel, who learned taxidermy in Spain and Japan and loves to give tours. Watch for the case up front that displays a collection of deformed animals, including a cat with two mouths and a sheep with eight legs. *(General Prado 495. Open M-F 9am-noon, 3-6pm; Sa 10am-noon.)*

▣ NIGHTLIFE

Although Huánuco's only movie theater was converted into a Pentecostal Church a few years back, nightlife has shifted venues accordingly. Many of Huánuco's restaurants (and its slot machines) are open until midnight. Younger clubs are scattered around the corners of town by the river or in the newer settlements across it.

Billar Jumbo, General Prado 878, and its slightly quieter counterpart **Copacabana,** Tarapacá 636, are Huánuco's most popular pool halls, where teenagers and housewives alike cue up. (Tables s/2.40 per hr. 1L beer s/6. Open daily 10am-midnight.)

❄ FESTIVALS

Huánuco is at its best during its celebrations, and excuses to parade seem to come at least once a month. While many festivals are religious, all are deeply colored by the history and culture of the *sierra*. The **Fiesta del Señor de Burgos** (Oct. 23-28) celebrates a sacred sculpture of the saint now held in Huánuco's cathedral, brought to the city from Spain in 1593. Parades, music, traditional costumes, and a large fair light up the town. The 12th day of Christmas brings the **Fiesta de los Negritos** (Jan. 6-20), in which dancers fill the streets, dressed in costumes that borrow elements from both the Spanish conquerors and the black slaves they brought with them. In elaborately choreographed steps, they express their adoration of the newborn Jesus. **Semana Santa** (Holy Week, around Easter) is celebrated as it is all through the *sierra*, with costumed re-enactments of the Passion. The city also rallies around its **founding** and **Tourism Week** (Aug. 11-17) with big soccer matches.

LA UNIÓN

☎ **062**

Tucked away in the chilly *sierra*, La Unión (pop. 7000) is notable more for its fortunate proximity to nearby attractions than its own generic character. Ten kilometers from this sleepy mountain town lies under-appreciated Huánuco Viejo, fondly dubbed the "second-best Inca ruins" in Peru by the local tourist office. But the extreme difficulties of getting to this market town ensure that La Unión won't be a backpackers' mecca anytime soon. Of course, that's also part of its charm.

The ruins of **Huánuco Viejo,** known to locals as "Huánuco Pampa," sit at a lofty 3600m and are thought to have been one of the major administrative areas of the Inca Empire. At its height, Huánuco Viejo contained almost 4000 structures and extended more than 2½km. The first building in the complex, **Acllawasi,** was the primary textile production area. Farther along the deteriorating path is the **Plaza Central**—the large **Ushno** (pyramid) in the middle was the ceremonial center. Pass through the impressive doorways of the **Kallankas** to find the **Casa Inca,** where visiting Inca bosses enjoyed a lakeside view; sadly, only a stone outline of the artificial lagoon remains. To walk from La Unión (2½hr.), take Comercio past the market and turn left up Huánuco. Follow Huánuco uphill as it becomes a stone path; then take the trail that branches uphill to the left. Continue up this small, well-marked path for an hour after you cross the highway. At the top, walk straight ahead along the *pampa;* veer right to follow the wheel tracks. At the road (40min.), head right, toward the snow-covered mountains. Walk through the fields of grazing cattle, then go left toward the big blue sign and the entrance. Alternatively, the colectivo to **Isco-pampa** (s/5-8) can drop you off a 20min. walk away along the flat *pampa,* or a taxi (s/30, 35min.) can take you right to the entrance. (Ruins open daily 6am-6pm. Small fee.)

Visitors to the natural sauna of **Baños Termales de Tauripampa** descend into a large room, then climb into a tiny, pitch-black stone cave. The temperature rises dramatically along the 5m crawl to stone benches and small pools of near-boiling water—bring a bucket if you want to douse yourself. From town, walk 20min. south along the main road to Km139, where a large yellow sign marks the stone path to the baths. Or, snag a taxi (s/5) in the market; colectivos (s/1) en route to Huallanca can also drop you off. (Open daily Apr.-Dec. Small fee.)

Considering the conspicuous lack of tourists, La Unión has a surprising plethora of budget accommodations (singles s/10-20; doubles s/15-30), but none have telephone numbers. Finding food is also not a problem in La Unión. During the day, fresh fruit and bread appear everywhere, replaced after dark by vendors frying up potatoes and mystery meat. A few restaurants serve regional specialties.

Río Vizcara cuts through La Unión; everything of interest to a traveler lies east of the river. The main road, **2 de Mayo,** runs parallel to the river. The **Plaza de Armas** lies one block over, on **Comercio,** a central thoroughfare also parallel to the river. **Unión** bisects 2 de Mayo and Comercio before crossing the river via the town's major bridge. Streets are infrequently labeled, however, and addresses are mere technicalities. A **tourist office** on the Plaza de Armas is delighted to dust off the books and delve into La Unión's history. Other services include: **Banco de la Nación** (☎51 5213), at 2 de Mayo and La Unión; a **market,** near the intersection of Comercio and Ríos; and **police,** on Lourdes, near the Plaza de Armas. **Colectivos** to La Unión (5hr., leave when full 5am-2pm or 3pm, s/20-25) leave from near the corner of Tarapacá and San Martín in Huánuco. Several companies on the 12th and 13th blocks of Comercio in La Unión send return **buses** and **cars** to Huánuco. There are also buses to Lima from La Unión (12-14hr., afternoon departures).

JUNÍN ☎064

Junín (pop. 12,000; elev. 4115m) appears from a distance like a mirage shimmering on the *altiplano*. After its August 6, 1824 victory against Spanish forces, Junín was anointed a "heroic" city by Simón Bolívar. "Peaceful," however, is the word that comes to mind today; though it's located on the main highway, tiny Junín receives very few visitors. It's a shame, since Junín hasn't yet totally succumbed to concrete and corrugated iron; here and there, thatched roofs can be seen over garden gates, and grandmothers still sit on the Plaza, spinning wool while they gossip. Just 20km outside town, one of the world's highest altitude lakes offers a chance to see an as-yet undiscovered Titicaca—only even closer to the sky.

🖪🚆 TRANSPORTATION AND PRACTICAL INFORMATION. Buses and **colectivos** stop by the vendors lining **Manuel Prado,** what locals call the stretch of highway crossing the edge of town and dividing Junín in two. **Empresa Junín,** Manuel Prado 595 (☎70 4643), runs buses directly to Lima (6hr., 7 per day, s/10-20). Colectivos also arrive and depart here for equidistant Cerro de Pasco and Tarma (1hr., leave when full 7am-7pm, s/7-8). **Mototaxis** cost under s/1 in town.

Standing on Prado facing the food stalls, **Simón Bolívar** is on your left and **San Martín** is on your right. The central **Plaza de Libertad** lies between the two, four blocks down the gently sloping hill; the less focal **Plaza de Armas** is six blocks farther. **Banco de la Nación** is on the far-left corner, at the bottom of San Martín where the pavement becomes gravel, but the tiny bungalow keeps limited weekday morning hours. They may change dollars in a pinch. The **market** fills the huge building on top of the Plaza de Libertad at the uphill side, with a proper market on the bottom and shops and the post office upstairs. On Tuesdays it spills into the streets, taking over both San Martín and Bolívar. Other services include: **police,** Bernado Alcedo 170 (☎34 4008), two blocks away from the downhill Bolívar corner of the Plaza Libertad; **hospital,** Saenz Peña 650 (☎34 4159), turn right and walk three blocks to the end of the street from directly in front of the church in the Plaza de Armas; and **Serpost,** 2nd fl. of the market, of. 52, on Plaza de Libertad (☎34 4153; open M-Sa 8am-noon and 3-7pm).

🏠 ACCOMMODATIONS. Junín has only a few accommodation options, mostly without creature comforts such as hot water or showers. **Hotel Bolívar ❶,** Bolívar 248, on the Plaza de Libertad, is downhill on Bolívar to the Plaza. A sign above the *ferretería* (hardware store) across from the monumental column says only *"hospedaje."* Rooms are small and tidy, and the ones on the top floor facing away from the Plaza offer breathtaking views. (Singles s/10; doubles s/ 16.) **Hostal Leo ❷**, San Martín 251, also on the Plaza de Libertad, is far and away Junín's poshest hotel, delighting guests with not only hot water and homestyle (shared) bathrooms, but also with TVs. Alas, the windows in the rooms don't open fully, and reward prolonged gazing with cement-wall views. (☎34 4199. Large rooms with hot water and TVs s/25-30. Small rooms without hot water and black-and-white TV s/10.) **Hospedaje Libertad ❶**, Bolívar 294-296, is likewise on the Plaza de Libertad. Earnest and enthusiastic owner Juan Figueroa has one guestroom with private bath and shower. (Single s/12; double s/24.) Or, stay in one of his other rooms, and head back to the hallway toilet and sink. (Singles s/ 8; doubles s/16.) **Hostal San Cristóbal ❶**, Manuel Prado 550, is at the edge of town, on the left-hand side of the highway arriving from Cerro or looking across with your back to town. The simple rooms have concrete walls, piles of rough wool blankets, and showers down the hall, with hot water when the heater is working. (☎34 4215. Restaurant attached. Singles s/10; doubles s/15-18.) Since hot showers are a scarce commodity in Junín, those in desperate quest of one can visit the **Ducha de la Juventud,** Manuel Prado 363, on the right when facing town. Look for the mural of the showering woman. (☎34 4272. Shower s/2.50. Open daily 7am-9pm.)

❒ FOOD. Plaza de Libertad sports a couple places with cheap *menús* (s/2-5), and, starting around 6pm, often hosts food stalls by the market building. **Pollos a la Brasa "San Carlos" ❶**, San Martín 361, serves huge portions of standard but tasty *pollería* fare, letting you put a hearty meal in the old furnace before those famously cold Peruvian nights. *Menús* are s/3-5, or a whole chicken plus all the side dishes is s/20. (☎31 0588. Open daily noon-9pm.) During the late afternoon the **Fuente de Soda "Faedmilk" ❶**, Stall 53, on the second floor of the *mercado*, next to the post office, packs 'em in for hot chocolate and cake, cake, cake. (Hot chocolate s/.50. All kinds of cake s/.50. *Empanadas* s/1. Open M-F 2-8:30pm, Sa-Su 8am-8:30pm.) Excitingly, Junín now also boasts at least one alternative to diving under the blankets at nightfall. **▧La Cabaña,** Bolívar 597, at the Plaza, warms the local nightlife scene with drinks like *caliente de ron* ("hot rum," s/5) or, in a version made from the local brew, *caliente de maca* (s/3). There's also *mate* tea and coffee (s/.50), in case you're driving. The mixture of local hats and pelts on the walls makes it easy to imagine that little Junín has invented a hip New York spin on itself. (☎30 1670. Open daily 4:30-10pm.)

◙ SIGHTS. Keep an eye peeled for the now-defunct 1904 **railway station,** one block below the Plaza de Libertad, a few meters to the left of Bolívar. The recently restored local **church,** on the Plaza de Armas, also ranks high. The abundance and style of polychrome statues inside buoy local claims that the structure dates from the 16th century. Ornately carved Baroque-style floor-to-ceiling pillars on the left and in the altarpiece contrast with a graceful sky-blue roof painted with stars. Come around the time of evening mass for a look inside.

Junín's best-known sight, **▧Lago de Junín,** sits 30min. outside of town. It is the second largest lake in Peru (after Titicaca) and claims (erroneously, but not unbelievably) to be the world's highest (before Titicaca). The road through the **Reserva Nacional de Junín** passes traditional stone houses and grazing alpacas before reaching the lake, an ideal locale for strolling or lolling (provided you have warm clothing and are watching out for llamas). The entire journey, much of it over bird-rich wetlands, is stunning. The lookout point (near Km25) offers glorious views of the lake and landscape. Plenty of blue-billed, red-faced, and black-and-white spotted birds flap along the lake's periphery, but you should bring binoculars if you hope to glimpse one of the few remaining native *parihuana* birds. While the lake is renowned for its variety of feathered friends, non-birdwatchers can still appreciate the incredible scenery and remote villages along its banks. **Ondores** (at Km22) is the largest settlement on the shores of the lake and houses a lovely stone church. Reach Lago de Junín on Ondores-bound colectivos (35min., leave when full, s/2-3), which depart from the end of Bolívar at Prado. A taxi can then take you from Ondores to the lookout point, although it's a pleasant walk (3km, 30min.). Colectivos return to Junín every 20-30min. from Ondores.

TARMA ☎064

Spanish architecture *did* make it to Peru—and landed squarely in Tarma (pop. 72,000; elev. 3053m). From the arches that line Castilla to the city library on the modern Plaza de Armas, European influence is just the tip of Tarma's cosmopolitan iceberg. Tourists come to this "Pearl of the Andes" for its proximity to nearby religious sanctuaries and Peru's largest cave, but stay once they discover a surprisingly modern city in the midst of the Central Highlands.

ORIENTATION AND PRACTICAL INFORMATION

Downtown Tarma follows a standard grid pattern, making it fairly easy to navigate. The city's focal point is its **Plaza de Armas,** framed by north-south streets **Moquegua** and **2 de Mayo** and east-west streets **Lima** and **Arequipa. Av. Otero** runs alongside the river for most of the town's length. Where the river bends, it crosses that other water-view avenue, **Manuel Odria.** Moquegua, 2 de Mayo, and Lima have the greatest density of shops and restaurants.

Buses: Although agencies are scattered throughout the city, most buses and colectivos stop at the **terminal terrestre,** at Castilla and Vienrich. Connections to Oxapampa and Satipo can be made in La Merced. **San Juan,** Odria 219 (☎32 1677), near the stadium, goes to **Huancayo** (3hr., 12 per day, s/8); **La Merced** (1¼hr., every hr. 5:30am-8pm, s/5); and **Lima** (5-6hr., 11:30pm, s/10). **Transportes La Merced,** on Vienrich, 1 block below the archway, heads to **La Merced** (1¼hr.; 11:30am, 1:30, 11pm; s/5) and **Lima** (5-6hr.; 11:30am, 1:30, 11pm; s/15; *bus cama* 11:30pm, s/25). **Los Canarios,** Amazonas 694 (☎32 3357), goes to: **Huancayo** (3hr., 9 per day, s/8); **La Merced** (1¼hr., every hour 5am-6pm); **Lima** (5-6hr.; 10am, 10pm; s/12). Buses from Lima arrive on Callao, which leads to the center of town. Most buses from Huancayo arrive on Manuel Odria; to get to the Plaza from there, follow Manuel Odria toward the stadium, making a right to follow the Río Tarma. About 3 blocks later, make a left onto 2 de Mayo, which leads to the Plaza de Armas.

Tourist Office: 2 de Mayo 775 (☎32 1010; turistarma@hotmail.com), on the Plaza de Armas, facing the cathedral. Spanish only, though English-speaking personnel may be available on request. Provides city **maps** and information on local attractions. Open M-F 8am-1pm and 3-6pm, Sa 8am-2pm, longer during festivals such as *Semana Santa.*

Currency Exchange: Banco de Crédito, Lima 401 (☎32 2149). 24hr. Plus/V **ATM.** Open M-F 10am-6pm, Sa 9:30am-12:30pm.

Market: Mercado Modelo, 2 blocks toward the Río Tarma from the Plaza de Armas, bordered by 2 de Mayo, Moquegua, Amazonas, and Huánuco. Open daily 6am-7pm. Another **outdoor market** radiates out from the area surrounding Asunción and Puno at the bend in the river, particularly on Th and Sa.

Laundry: Lavandería Continental, Lima 582. Large items such as pants s/2.5, smaller articles by weight (s/3.50 per kg). Open M-Sa 8:20am-1pm and 3-8:30pm.

Emergency: ☎ 105.

Police: Callao 118 (☎ 32 1921). Open 24hr.

Hospital: Pacheco 362 (☎ 32 1400). Has a 24hr. pharmacy.

Telephones: Telefonía "Amira," Lima 320 (☎ 32 3166) and Moquegua 528, sell phone cards for long-distance calling. They also have phone booths for coin and card calls. Open daily 7:30am-10pm. Many *bodegas* and restaurants also have pay phones.

Internet Access: Scattered throughout downtown. **The Door,** Lima 892 (☎ 32 2568) has one of the fastest connections in town (s/1-1.50 per hr.). Open daily 8am-11pm.

Post Office: Serpost, Callao 356 (☎ 32 1241), between Moquegua and Paucartambo. Open M-Sa 8am-1pm and 3-6pm.

ACCOMMODATIONS

Lodging is readily available in Tarma. Quiet, clean, comfortable lodging is not. Although the trend toward hot water has caught up with most of the budget establishments, good values at prices counted in soles, not dollars, are still hard to come by. Prices rise 20% from those quoted during Semana Santa, during which time way-in-advance reservations are required. Think carefully about the choice between "windowless" or "streetside" rooms; when street noise is keeping you up at 3am, "windowless" begins to seem a lot more attractive.

■ **Hostal Albania,** Amazonas 534 (☎ 32 1399). The only carpeted joint around. As you check in, don't miss the practically pig-sized tarantula in a wall display case. All rooms have private bath and cable TV. Singles s/20; doubles s/30. ❷

Hospedaje el Caporal, Lima 616 (☎ 32 3636). Remember that old dream of opening a bed and breakfast in some enchanting, remote village? One family's dream came true with El Caporal, which opened in May 2004. Everything is new, from curtains to *colchones* (mattresses). Large rooms are good for families. All rooms come with private bath, cable TV, and continental breakfast. Singles s/40; doubles s/50; triples s/90. ❹

Residencial El Dorado, Huánuco 488 (☎ 32 1914), at Paucartambo. Clean rooms, high ceilings, and a pleasant courtyard. Hot private baths. TV s/5. Singles s/10, with bath s/15; doubles s/20, with bath s/35; triples with bath and cable TV s/45. ❶

Hostal Tucho, 2 de Mayo 561 (☎ 32 3483). Blue rooms lack windows but feature tidy, if cramped, bathrooms. The industrial motel complex has taken hold of Tucho and could get guests feeling blue (to match the walls), but Tucho is a reliable contender in a tough market. TV s/5; black-and-white TV s/3. Singles s/25; doubles s/35. ❸

Hostal Luna, Amazonas 393 (☎ 32 1589). For those whose budgets can't budge, this Versailles-sized collection of mismatched rooms includes hot water in outdoor shower stalls and 24hr. checkout. Singles s/10; doubles s/15. ❶

FOOD

Cheap restaurants with set *menús* crowd the streets around the Plaza de Armas. The following choices offer an alternative to the usual *pollerías* and *chifas*—or at least an improvement on them.

■ **Comedor Vegetariano Integral "Salud y Vida,"** Arequipa 676. Rejoice in vegan heaven. Even meat-eaters will be thrilled to discover the daily lunch *menús* (s/2.50) featuring dishes such as artichoke stew, soy steaks, and broccoli stir-fry, accompanied by hearty soups and herbal teas (s/.50). Carob coffee s/1. Whole grain breads s/.20. A welcome—and rare—escape from the *comida típica*. Open M-F and Su 7:30am-8:30pm. ❶

El Señorial, Huánuco 138 (☎32 3334), 2 blocks downhill from the Plaza on 2 de Mayo then right on Huánuco. With neon signs and lots of people, cafeteria-like El Señorial serves not only the typical *pollo a la brasa*, but pasta, steak (s/7-16), and sandwiches (s/1-3.50). *Menú* s/3.5-6. Entrees s/6-16. Open daily 8am-3pm and 6-11pm. ❷

Lo Mejorcito de Tarma, Arequipa 501, at Huaraz (☎32 3500), 2 blocks downhill on 2 de Mayo from the Plaza de Armas and 2 blocks to the right. The 12-page menu includes all manner of meat, seafood, and *comida criolla*. Vegetarian options include pasta, cooked vegetables, and potatoes with broccoli, all served on locally woven tablecloths in a classy salon decorated with fresh lilies. Sandwiches s/2-5. Gargantuan *menú* s/5. Entrees s/7-18. Open daily 7am-11pm. DC/V. ❷

Tradición y Buen Gusto, Moquegua 608-20. The name says it all ("Tradition and Good Taste"). Large tables are perfect for the extended families who crowd in here for home-style local favorites like *estufado de gallina* (chicken stew) and *patasca* (a corn-based soup). No surprises here, just fresh cooking and individually prepared standbys. *Menú económico* s/3.50; *ejecutivo* s/5. Open M and W-Su 8am-10:30pm. ❶

🔾 SIGHTS

WITHIN THE CITY. Although the majority of Tarma's sights are in the outlying hills, the city itself provides some entertainment. The town fills with Peruvian visitors during Tarma's **Semana Santa,** the week before Easter. In 2004, a publicity drive resulted in 7900 visitors, making Tarma the number-one destination for domestic tourism. The festival consists of a legendary procession over "the world's largest" **carpet of flowers,** meticulously woven into brightly colored patterns and pictures by hundreds of local craftsmen. Although flowers are one of Tarma's cash crops, the carpets use wildflowers gathered by the whole town. Every kind of blossom—including the potato flower—goes into the mix. The 1999 festival, which involved 12 tons of flowers covering 3200 square meters, was in the *Guinness Book of World Records,* and the festival has grown every year.

History books may say that Manuel Odria was a dictator (1948-56), but he was also a Tarmanian, and the city honors him with a **museum.** It has a better-than-usual collection of memorabilia, and three local pre-Inca mummies were recently added. *(On the 2nd fl. of the Municipalidad in the Plaza de Armas. Open M-F 8am-1pm and 3-6pm. Free.)* The beautiful **Iglesia Cathedral Santa Ana,** also on the Plaza, was constructed in 1954 in a Neoclassical style. *(Open daily until 10am.)*

SAN PEDRO DE CAJAS. San Pedro de Cajas (pop. 6000, sheep population 12,000; elev. 4000m) produces some of Peru's best-known **tapestries.** Each workshop dyes its own wool, and the tapestries often incorporate tufts of wool arranged to form pictures of rural scenes. Visit the Tarma tourist office (p. 282) for a beautiful example. The mass production of these tapestries is largely a development of the last 20 years, but the gender differentiation of weaving tasks goes back farther. Historically, men and women wove different kinds and qualities of cloth; today men do the principal weavings and finer work, while women act as shepherds and work small looms. Any weaver will show you his shop and work. *(Colectivos to Huagapo continue on to San Pedro, s/4.50.)*

LA GRUTA DE HUAGAPO. The water weeping from this cave's mouth may have given it its name—Huagapo means "to cry" in Quechua—and, after years of failed exploration, also offers its claim to fame. Huagapo is possibly the **largest cave in Peru.** However, it's hard to be sure, since no one has ever seen the end; even spelunkers using sophisticated underwater diving equipment have only managed to descend about 2800m into the cave. Legend claims that when the local men were preparing to defend against the invading Inca Pachacútec, they sent their women and children to hide in this cave, telling them not to leave until the men returned. All perished, still waiting for their vanquished soldiers to come, and the stalagmites and stalactites within are their crystallized tears. Amateur explorers can walk in about 300m to inspect stalagmites, stalactites, and an ancient cave painting. You'll need a flashlight and may want to hire a guide from the cave's mouth for s/5. *(Colectivos to Huagapo (1hr., leave when full, s/ 3.50) leave from both the corner of Otero and Moquegua and across from Grifo Ramón at Otero and Bermúdez. A leaflet for sale at the site (s/1.50; Spanish only) recounts local legends.)*

EL SEÑOR DE MURHUAY. An important site of pilgrimage near **Acobamba,** 9km from Tarma, the sanctuary of **El Señor de Murhuay** sits on a hill at the edge of town where an image of Jesus on the cross was etched into the rock, supposedly by a soldier during an independence battle. More religious locals hold that the carving appeared much earlier—around 1756—and that at various times it can be seen bleeding. Whatever the origin, paint now fills the holy outline, and the etching is enclosed in glass and surrounded by flowers in a giant church. Throughout May, elaborate dances and costumes celebrate the festival in honor of El Señor. *(Take a colectivo marked "Transrey" (15min., s/1) from the corner of Huánuco and 2 de Mayo. The white sanctuary is visible from town.)*

SHOGUEMARCA, MURALLA PUNTA, YAUMANPATA. The hills above Palcamayo (24km from Tarma) are dotted with a series of Inca-era ruins, primarily military in character. Cave paintings and small high-altitude lagoons can also be found nearby. These sites remain relatively unvisited but are in good condition. They can be seen as part of an extended, multi-day hike beginning from Palcamayo, although homestay in Cocón provides the only option besides camping for lodging. Alternatively, all can be visited in a day with a hired guide and car (s/70-100). Cars can approach to within a half-hour walk from each site. Ask at the Tarma tourist office for assistance in arranging transport or for hiking routes.

HUANCAYO
☎ 064

As the cradle of Huanca culture and the nucleus of the Río Mantaro Valley, the city of Huancayo (pop. 450,000; elev. 3240m) has recently gained a reputation as the mecca of Andean *artesanía*. During the 1980s and early 90s, tourism to the valley ceased as a result of rampant terrorism, culminating in the shutdown of the famed Lima-Huancayo rain line in 1991 (see **Natural Highs**). Huancayo served as a refuge for thousands escaping terrorist violence in the surrounding area, while thousands more fled the city and the region for Lima. But everything changed in the mid-1990s: as the violence subsided, those who had fled returned and those who had arrived remained. Modern Huancayo has emerged as one of the liveliest urban destinations in Peru—visitors today will find a thriving city with a booming nightlife. The area's abundant hiking trails lead from snowy mountaintops to the jungle's edge. In nearby villages, new generations of artisans continue to produce high-quality traditional art in wool, silver, and even vegetables (see **Artesanía Villages,** p. 294). Huancayo's hour as an international destination has come.

▐ TRANSPORTATION

Trains: The **train station,** Ferrocarril 461, Chilca (☎21 7724), is in the southeastern part of town. From Plaza Constitución, take Real to the right past Plaza Huamanmarca until you hit the train tracks. Turn right at the tracks and walk along the dirt road until the station appears on the left. Otherwise, take a taxi from Plaza Constitución (s/2).

NATURAL HIGHS

After being shut down in 1991, at the height of Shining Path activity in Huancayo, passenger service from Lima into the Andes has finally been restored in recent years. This extraordinary and famous trip—the highest altitude standard gauge railway in the world—was considered one of the great feats of engineering when it was constructed between 1870 and 1908.

The ride was stunning and severe, winding around rocky snow-capped peaks and traversing numerous ecological zones, from coastal desert to Andean sierra. Around the town of Ticlio, temperatures dropped far below freezing. The rail line reached its apex on the pass through the Galera tunnel—a startling 4829m above sea level. During its wild 12hr. journey to Huancayo, the train passed through 27 stations, 58 bridges, 66 tunnels, and 9 switchbacks.

Today, the Lima-Huancayo train carries passengers the last Sunday of each month during the dry season (Apr.-Oct.; US$30); the rest of the year, it is used only for cargo. After the line was privatized, the owners discovered that the transportation of artichokes and trout was more profitable than infrequent tourist trips. Increased political stability in the region is helping to reverse this, as more and more people rediscover this breathtaking journey.

Trains run to **Huancavelica** (*Expreso:* 5hr., M-Sa 6:30am, s/8.90-13; *Ordinario:* 6hr.; M-Sa 12:30pm, Su 2pm; s/7.80-13). Weekends (F-Su) get very crowded, so buy your ticket a day in advance. Other days, arrive at the station 1hr. early.

Buses: The cheapest way to get to **Lima** from Huancayo is to catch a bus (s/10) on the 15th block of Mariscal Castilla (Real turns into Mariscal Castilla northwest of the Plaza) at **El Tambo terminal terrestre.** These buses leave when full and have no schedule. Be aware that such companies have no agency offices in town, and their lower fares may indicate a lower level of bus maintenance, upkeep, and passenger insurance.

Cruz del Sur, Ayacucho 281-287 (☎23 5650). To **Lima** (7hr.; 8am, 1:30, 11, 11:30pm; s/35). No credit cards.

ETUCSA, Puno 220 (☎23 2638). To **Lima** (7-8hr.; 8am, 1, 11, 11:30pm; s/20-25; *bus cama* 11:45pm, s/40).

Expreso Molina, Angaraes 334 (☎22 4501). To **Ayacucho** (9-10hr.; 6:30, 10am, 8, 8:30pm; s/23-25).

Lobato, Omar Yalli 148 (☎23 1892). To **Satipo** (7hr.; 9, 10pm; s/20) and **La Merced** (6hr., 10:30pm, s/15).

Mariscal Cáceres, Real 1241 (☎21 6635). To **Lima** (7-8hr.; 10am, 10:30pm; s/16). *Autos* under the same auspices leave from the driveway next door for **Huancavelica** (3½hr., leave when full 3am-8pm, s/23).

Ormeño, Mariscal Castilla 1379 (☎25 1199), near the *terminal terrestre.* To **Lima** (7-8hr.; 1:30, 10:30pm; s/20; *bus cama* 11pm, s/40).

Turismo Central, Ayacucho 274 (☎22 3128). Has the greatest number of daily departures to: **Ayacucho** (11hr., 8pm, s/22); **Cerro de Pasco** (5-6hr., 2pm, s/12); **Huánuco** (8hr.; 2, 9:15pm; s/20); **La Merced** (6hr., 9pm, s/15); **Pucallpa** (24hr., 2pm, s/45); **Satipo** (10hr., 9pm, s/18); **Tingo María** (11hr.; 2, 7:30pm; s/25).

Local Transport: Taxis in the city cost s/2-3. Buses and urban colectivos cost s/0.80.

 Beware of **scam artists** and **thieves** throughout Huancayo, especially in the areas near the Mercado Mayorista and around the **terminal terrestre** in the El Tambo district.

◆ 🔢 ORIENTATION AND PRACTICAL INFORMATION

Most services revolve around the always-crowded **Plaza Constitución,** dotted with gardens and fountains, and permanently under attack by a swarm of blaring taxis. **Ancash,** to the north of the Plaza, and **Real,** to the south, contain banks, hostels, and restaurants. **Puno,** to the west, houses bus stations, and **Giraldez,** bordering the Plaza on the east, has a smattering of

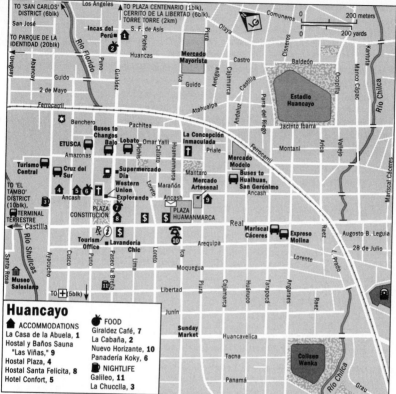

Huancayo

ACCOMMODATIONS
La Casa de la Abuela, **1**
Hostal y Baños Sauna
"Las Viñas," **9**
Hostal Plaza, **4**
Hostal Santa Felicita, **8**
Hotel Confort, **5**

FOOD
Giraldez Café, **7**
La Cabaña, **2**
Nuevo Horizonte, **10**
Panadería Koky, **6**

NIGHTLIFE
Galileo, **11**
La Chuccla, **3**

Sunday
Market

restaurants, Internet cafes, and nightclubs. About five blocks down Real from Plaza Constitución, **Plaza Huamanmarca** acts as a twin anchor to the downtown area, with phones, banks, and a post office.

Tourist Office: Tourism Office, Real 481 (☎20 0550), on the right inside the Casa de la Artesanía on Plaza Constitución. Limited usefulness due to no English, no excursion planning, and no maps (buy one at a news kiosk for s/3.50). Brochures in Spanish. Open M-F 8am-1pm and 2-5:30pm.

Tours: ☒ Explorando, Ancash 367 (☎21 7484; explorandoperu@turismoaventura.net), on Plaza Constitución, above Western Union. It's hard to say whether the otherwise laid-back guys at Explorando are more gung-ho about the mountains where they grew up or about sharing the central *sierra* and nearby jungle with visitors new to Peru. The purple walls of their tiny office are covered with photos and postcards from past trekkers. 2- to 8-day trips begin at US$10 per person. Some rental equipment available. Open M-Sa 9am-8pm. **Incas del Perú,** Giraldez 652 (☎22 3303; www.incasdelperu.org), attached to La Cabaña. Run by the charismatic Lucho Hurtado, who speaks near-flawless English and owns La Casa de la Abuela and La Cabaña (see **Accommodations,** p. 288). Dedicated to authentic cultural experiences in Huancayo and the Río Mantaro Valley. Open daily 9am-1pm and 3:30-7:30pm. Discounts for SAE members and students.

Alternatives to Tourism: Volunteering and Spanish language lessons are available in and around Huancayo. See **Alternatives to Tourism,** p. 81.

Currency Exchange: Banco de Crédito, at Real and Giraldez, where Giraldez becomes Paseo La Breña at the bottom of Plaza Constitución, has a 24hr. AmEx/Plus/V **ATM.**
Western Union, Ancash 367 (☎23 3705), on the Plaza. Open M-F 9am-1:30pm and 3-8pm, Sa 9am-2pm. There are other AmEx/Cirrus/Plus/V **ATMs** throughout town, including at **Interbank,** Real 640-642, and **Banco Wiese,** on Real, at Plaza Huamanmarca.

Market: Supermercado Día, Giraldez 277, 1 block above Plaza Constitución. Open daily 9am-10pm. AmEx/MC/V.

Laundromat: Lavandería Chic, Paseo la Breña 154 (☎23 1107), around the corner from Plaza Constitución. A spotless self-service laundromat. Washer and dryers s/5 each. Open M-Sa 8am-10pm, Su 10am-6pm.

Emergency: ☎105

Police: Ferrocarril 580 (☎21 9851), at Cusco.

24hr. Pharmacy: Boticas Arcangel, Real 467 (☎20 2200). AmEx/DC/MC/V.

Hospital: Clínica Ortega, Carrión 1124 (☎23 2921 and 23 5430), 2 blocks below Huancavelica.

Telephones: 20 public phones line the Ica side of **Telefónica,** Real 793, at Plaza Huamanmarca, but others are available throughout the city.

Internet: ALPH@net, Giraldez 242 (☎20 2906). s/1 per hr. Open daily 9am-10pm.

Post Office: Serpost (☎23 1271 or 23 2101), on Plaza Huamanmarca, on the left (look for a big sign), 3 blocks from Plaza Constitución on Real. Open M-Sa 8am-8pm, Su 9am-1pm.

⚑ ACCOMMODATIONS

Hotels line the streets of Huancayo's downtown area. Prices are slightly higher than in nearby Central Highland towns, but more amenities are also standard. Accommodations near marketplaces or above nightclubs tend to be less desirable.

▨ **La Casa de la Abuela,** Giraldez 691 (☎23 4383; www.incasdelperu.org), several blocks up from Plaza Constitución, past the train tracks. The delightful *abuela* (Lucho Hurtado's mother; see **Tours,** above) who runs this popular backpacker's hostel prepares glorious breakfasts and gossips with travelers in her garden while cats wander about. Immaculate rooms and communal baths with 24hr. hot water, game room, laundry service, kitchen, and cable TV. 6-bed dorms s/20 per person; doubles s/25, with bath s/30. Discounts for SAE, YHI, or ISIC, or for ownership of a guidebook that recommends the Casa (hint: you're looking at one). ❷

Hotel Confort, Ancash 237 (☎23 3601), to the west and 1 block from the cathedral next to Plaza Constitución. Convenient, if impersonal. This enormous hotel has over 100 rooms but remains fairly quiet, especially in the rooms at the back. All rooms have baths with 24hr. warm water. TV s/5. Singles s/20; doubles s/30. ❷

Hostal Santa Felicita, Giraldez 145 (☎23 5285), on the Plaza. Bright blue carpeting and a crucifix in every room are just 2 of the many amenities at the squeaky clean Santa Felicita. Private baths, 24hr. hot water, cable TV, personal phones, and laundry service make this an excellent value. The indoor-facing windows are a bit odd, but greatly reduce noise from the Plaza. Singles s/40; doubles s/60. ❹

Hostal Plaza, Ancash 171 (☎21 4507), 2 blocks from Plaza Constitución, behind the church. In a quiet neighborhood, with cable TV, personal phones, and reading lamps, this place is an information junkie's dream. All rooms with private bath and 24hr. hot water. Singles s/30; matrimonials s/40; doubles s/40; triples s/50. ❸

Hostal y Baños Sauna "Las Viñas," Piura 415 (☎23 1294), 1 block down Real from Plaza Huamanmarca and a block to the left, or follow Ancash away from the Serpost. The hotel is across the street from the far side of the *mercado artesanal*. Tiny rooms each with bath, cable TV, and telephone. Singles s/35; doubles s/45; triples s/55. ❸

🎯 FOOD

Cheap *pollo a la brasa* joints (¼ chicken s/2-3) and *chifas* line Real and Giraldez. For traditional meals, one must go farther afield. Particularly good *típicos* await in the El Tambo district, a s/3 taxi ride up Real. Huancayo is the birthplace of *papa a la huancaína* (potato smothered in cream sauce), and is also known for its *picante de cuy* (guinea pig) and *anticuchos* (cow heart). If a change of pace is in order, Huancayo's restaurant scene lives up to its burgeoning cosmopolitan status—authentic pizzas, vegetarian hideaways, and cozy art gallery/cafes can be found to suit every budget and palate.

Nuevo Horizante, Ica 578 (☎21 9370), around the corner from the Telefónica office at Plaza Huamanmarca. The crowds at this pure-vegetarian restaurant can't all be here because they don't eat meat—they keep coming back for the value, taste, and ambience. Skylights illuminate fresh asparagus soup (s/3.50) and salads (s/2-3) in one of 2 cheerful dining rooms. Bright yellow-and-green tile floor and live plants. Tucked away in the enclosed back porch, far from the maddening lunch crowd, regulars feast on the 5-course lunch *menú* (s/3.50). Smaller dinner *menú* s/3. Open Su-F 7am-10pm. ●

Panadería Koky, Puno 298 (☎23 4707), past the cathedral to the left and behind Plaza Constitución. The closest thing to an honest-to-goodness coffeehouse (coffee s/1.50; espresso s/2.50) you'll find in central Peru, this funky, glass-enclosed corner spot is known for its rich desserts (apple pie s/2.50; cheesecake s/3.50) and great people-watching. Also features cheap, tasty hamburgers (cheeseburger s/4) and *empanadas* (s/3). Continental breakfast s/6. Open daily 7am-10pm. ●

La Cabaña, Giraldez 652 (☎22 3303), across from La Casa de la Abuela. This swinging dinner spot fills nightly with foreigners and local families. It's pricey, but you're paying for the inimitable ambience (big tables and high-quality weavings on the walls) as well as the good food. Candles throughout the multi-room restaurant set the mood for La Cabaña's strong *sangría* (s/3 per glass). Sandwiches and hamburgers s/3-7. Pizzas s/18-25. Entrees s/20-35. Happy hour 5-7pm. Live folk bands Th-Sa at 9pm. Open daily 5pm-midnight. AmEx/DC/MC/V. ●

Huancahuasi, Mariscal Castilla 2222 (☎24 4826), in El Tambo, directly up Real (which changes into Mariscal Castilla). The extensive menu of *comida típica* at this local institution will satisfy any craving for *cuy* or *chicharrón* (s/9). Families dig into enormous servings of *pachamanca* (meat, beans, and grains wrapped in leaves and baked in an enormous oven; s/15) and *papa a la Huancaína* (s/5). Those who don't know where to begin will appreciate the *menú turístico* (taster's menu; s/10). Gallery of art and *artesanía* on the walls. Traditional music F-Su 1-5pm. Occasional literary readings. Open daily 8am-7pm. AmEx/DC/MC/V. ●

Giraldez Café, Giraldez 155 (☎23 5273), on Plaza Constitución. A hint of neon adds a brightening touch to the green faux marble decor at this kinder, gentler *pollería*, and all at greasy fast-food prices. *And* they deliver. Chicken *menú* s/5; *parilladas* s/5-18 per person; hamburgers s/3.50-6.50. Open daily 8am-midnight. ●

🔍 SIGHTS

Huancayo's vast array of daily **markets** provides constant novelties for the senses. Sellers hawk *everything* here, and an innocent Sunday stroll can result in a heavy pack indeed. If, when the shopping bag is full, a bit of culture calls, Huancayo has enough to pique the curiosity of the most blasé backpacker. A ramble through the downtown crowds gives way to hilltop views and solitary reveries. And beyond the city limits, the whole Mantaro Valley awaits.

MARKETS

MERCADO MAYORISTA. This is the best market in town, as you can weave through stalls of avocados and passion fruit, then visit herbal pharmacists selling large sticks of incense and herbs to help the prostate and liver. Enjoy freshly-squeezed juices and the best soups in the city. Keep a close eye on your belongings in and near the market area. *(Pass the railroad track on Giraldez and take a right on Huancas. The market is 2 blocks down. Open daily 6am-7pm.)*

SUNDAY MARKET. The Sunday market is Peru's largest market and Huancayo's best-known attraction. It began in 1572 as a trading fair between the Spaniards and the local Huanca people. More than 50,000 people still come weekly from throughout the Mantaro Valley to buy and sell here. Most stands sell ordinary goods, from cutlery to shoes, but more traditional items, such as blankets and sweaters, also abound. Food stands offer such delicacies as whole rodents (heads still attached). Most vendors arrive around 8am, making mid-morning the ideal time to visit. It may be easier to find higher-quality handicrafts here than at Huancayo's daily markets, since many artisans from surrounding towns only come once a week. *(The market stretches for dozens of blocks on Huancavelica. Head from the lower right-hand corner of Plaza Constitución down Giraldez, which immediately turns into Paseo la Breña. 5 blocks down, Huancavelica runs perpendicular—it's hard to miss.)*

MERCADO ARTESANAL. This small, winding market is filled with alpaca sweaters (s/25-40), brightly-colored socks (s/5), hats (s/5), scarves, belts, and blankets. Authentic, locally made crafts are sold alongside ugly synthetic weavings—make sure you purchase real alpaca or wool. To test the material, take a fuzz ball of the cloth and light it on fire. If it melts, your blanket was originally Tupperware. *(On the corner of Ancash and Piura, on the right from the upper right-hand corner of the Plaza Huamanmarca. Open daily 9am-6pm.)*

OTHER SIGHTS

■ **MUSEO SALESIANO.** Renovations and expansions to the Museo Salesiano de Historia Natural y Arqueología Padre Vicente Rasetto concluded in July 2004. The revamped museum features extensive dioramas showcasing the varied ecology and wildlife of Peru. For the bug-lovers among us, case after case of pinned six- and eight-legged critters line the museum's long hallways. The real show-stoppers, however, are the archaeological rooms, focused on Andean cosmology. Pavel Leira García and Judith Galicia Flores spent two years lovingly restoring and cataloguing newly transferred pieces from all over Peru. The highlights of the 2000-piece collection include a leopard in carved stone inset with quartz and lapis lazuli as well as numerous ritual figures in gold and silver, many of them from before the 5th century AD. *(Santa Rosa 299, El Tambo. ☎24 7763. Coming from the center of Huancayo on Real, turn left after the bridge/overpass. The Colegio Salesiano will be visible immediately. To enter the museum, follow the street's curve around to what seems to be the side of the building, where there is a smaller, open gate halfway down. Open M-Sa 9am-noon and 2-6pm. s/5.)*

PARQUE DE LA IDENTIDAD. It took four years to complete construction of the stone mosaic walls and *promenades* of this homage to Huanca (Quechua for "stone") culture. Every tree is of a native species, unlike the now-ubiquitous eucalypti growing outside the park walls. Even the decorative *chihuaco* birds perched on the lampposts are indigenous. Giant sculptures, such as a stone *mate burilado* (carved gourd), are monuments to native arts and customs. Surreal, gold-painted statues line the stone pathways, depicting painters, photographers, poets, and singers; opinionated locals proudly point out that there are no statues of politicians. In one corner, the mosaic floor shows the juxtaposed Huanca and European zodiacs. Across the street, a market (open daily 8:30am-9:30pm) dishes out *comida típica huancaína*; try the rich *picarones* (doughnuts) smothered in honey. *(In the San Carlos district, 2.5km from Plaza Constitución. From Giraldez at the Plaza, take colectivo #30 (10min., s/80), "directo Parque de la Identidad.")*

CERRITO DE LA LIBERTAD AND TORRE TORRE. A popular spot for family fun inside city limits, the park known as Cerrito de la Libertad actually encompasses a cluster of attractions, including a small municipal zoo *(usually open 9am-5:30pm; s/ 2)*, and behind it (a good scramble uphill or a longer, less-steep walk along the road) a church, playground, swimming pool, bandshell, and restaurant serving *anticuchos* (s/4) and the like, all mobbed with screaming children and their happy parents. In addition to the swingset, the unbeatable views of the city below make it worth confronting even Sunday afternoon crowds.

The subtly named geological formation of **Torre Torre** features erosion-formed sandstone towers that, from a distance, look like a fortress built into the mountainside. Taxis wait at the edge of the park. For the more rugged, it's a short (20-45min.) but uphill walk following the dirt road upwards and to the right. Don't despair if you get winded—the towers are visible from a few hundred meters below. *(To visit these sights on the upper edge of town, follow Giraldez upward from Plaza Constitución approximately 13 blocks to the Parque de Ajedrez (round-trip 5km, 2hr.), or take a taxi to the same point. Follow the stairs upwards to arrive at the zoo.)*

NIGHTLIFE AND ENTERTAINMENT

If the rest of the Central Highlands have gotten you hooked on karaoke and blinking neon lights, fear not: Huancayo's got it. But if you had a hankering to get dolled up and go dancing or just sip imported liquors, now's your chance.

La Chucclla, Ayacucho 316 (☎23 3888), 2 blocks from Plaza Constitución, between Ancash and Real, down the block from the Cruz del Sur offices, then down a little alleyway on the left. Chucclla (CHU-kla) is Quechua for "thatched roof," and, by extension, a home or gathering place. This particular thatched roof covers an enormous, high-energy round bar and nightclub. Onstage, a 6-person band cranks out popular Andean tunes on pan flute, saxophone, and electric guitar. It's hard to say whether the tables or the dance floor is more crowded. Most drinks come in pitchers, which just about says it all. Limited food menu includes *tamales* (s/3) and *anticuchos* (s/5) or pizzas to share (s/ 20-34). Beer and *calientes* s/6-8 per glass or s/16-20 for a pitcher. At midnight the floor clears for performances of regional dances. 18+. No cover. Open Th-Sa 9pm-3am.

Galileo, Paseo la Breña 378 (☎21 1101), 3 blocks below Plaza Constitución. If Huancayo had a yuppie bar scene, this would be it. Patrons munch on *alitas picantes* (hot wings, s/9) and *yucitas fritas* (jungle-style french fries, s/6) while sipping on cocktails (s/5-18) and grooving to rock-and-roll classics and classics-to-be beneath a ceiling painted with constellations. The excellent live band playing Spanish and English hits (Th-Sa) takes requests. 18+. No cover. Open M-W 6pm-midnight, Th-Sa 6pm-2am.

Cine Mantaro (☎25 3157), on the 9th block of Real in El Tambo. If all that hiking's just been too much for a rowdy night out, you can catch a Hollywood flick, complete with subtitles, at one of central Peru's only movie theaters. 3 showings daily (s/3-5).

DAYTRIPS FROM HUANCAYO

CHUPACA AND THE ARWATURO RUINS

Chupaca is 11km from Huancayo. Buses to Chupaca leave from around Parque 15 de Junio, at Amazonas and Pichis. From Plaza Constitución, hike 1 block up Giraldez to Ama-

zonas; Pichis is a block to the right (15min., s/1). To return to Huancayo from the ruins, first catch a passing colectivo back to Chupaca (s/1.50). Combis and colectivos for Huancayo (s/1-1.50) leave frequently from downhill of the Ahuac-bound departures.

Every Saturday, the population of Chupaca swells with visitors to its huge markets. For the complete experience, get off the bus at the **Plaza de Animales** on the way into town. Without crossing the paved road, follow the sounds of "baa" and walk down one block to a mindboggling **livestock fair,** which runs along the river's edge the remaining distance to the town. Successive zones of tethered sheep, pigs, donkeys, and cattle make strolling a bit challenging, but the expression "squeal like a pig" will take on new meaning. After reaching the last of the lowing oxen, climb to the left, straight uphill, and across the highway to reach Chupaca's **church** and the first of two main **plazas.** Every street fills with hawkers displaying pots, pans, or dining room tables. In one alleyway, twelve adjacent tables serve whole roasted pig, peeled fresh for each customer.

If pigs aren't your thing, alive or roasted, turn your sights toward the hills behind the church, where the **Arwaturo ruins** (also known as the Ahuac ruins, after the nearby village; s/1.50) can be seen high above. Colectivos, which can take you to where a new path climbs the hill, leave from the uphill corner behind the church. Alternatively, it's a 6km walk and slow climb if a morning walk sounds appealing. Begin by following the same road the colectivos take out of town. Where it forks, take the right-hand dirt path straight across the fields and to the base of the hill. The ruins are visible the whole time if you squint.

The name **Arwaturo** means "burnt bone" in Quechua, but the use of these buildings from AD 1200 remains disputed. Some believe them to have been regional granaries or storehouses, while others support the idea that they formed a military outpost. The breathtaking view of the entire valley stretched below doesn't rule out either possibility. One Quechua flood myth holds that this hilltop was where the surrounding peoples took refuge from the rising waters.

From Arwaturo, facing away from town, the view looks down on the tiny, underground-fed *laguna* of Ñahuinpuquio (Quechua for "eye of water"). Take the stone steps down toward it. Along the way is the **Recreo La Sirena ❷,** where entrees like fresh grilled trout from La Sirena's hatchery are s/5-7. Homemade *chicha* and the hearty corn soup *mondongo* are also on the menu. While lunch is being caught, one of the owner's children can take you out in a rowboat on the lake (s/1 per person, groups preferred) to see the ducks, some species of which are said to arrive yearly in February all the way from Canada.

CONVENTO DE SANTA ROSA DE OCOPA

*Take a bus from the corner of Calixto and Amazonas (see **Laguna de Paca,** below) to Concepción, then take one of the taxis that wait on the other side of the monument from the main road to the convent (15min., s/5). Ask the taxi to wait while you visit the convent if you're concerned about return transportation. The taxi will continue on to the town of Ingenio for another s/5. Office ☎21 0217. Offices open M and W-Su 9am-noon and 3-6pm, but the obligatory Spanish-only guided tours (s/4, students s/2 with valid ID) stop at 11am and 5pm.*

Near the town of **Concepción** is the Franciscan **Convento de Santa Rosa de Ocopa,** the first bulwark of 18th-century colonization and Christianization in the Peruvian Amazon. The convent's central **library** hasn't changed since it was built in 1725, and some of the 25,000 books date back to the 1500s. Almost a museum of the colonists' experiences, the convent holds various stuffed jungle beasts and birds and some paintings from the Cusco School. The church, built in 1905, has a lovely gilded interior and catacombs of deceased priests. The *comedor* (dining room), where every inch of wall and ceiling is brightly painted, is a bit more cheerful.

INGENIO

To get to Ingenio (30-45min., s/1.70), catch a bus or combi on the corner of Amazonas and Pichis in Huancayo, near Parque 15 de Junio. The blue-and-white trout farm is on the right at the top of the hill. Open M-Sa 8am-5pm, Su 8am-1pm and 1:20-5pm. s/1.

Ingenio is the altar at which Peru worships that most favorite fish, the trout. The village of Ingenio itself lies farther uphill, largely ignored by the throngs of hungry visitors who come to see its **trout farm**, or *criadero de trucha*, more formally known as the Centro Pisicola del Ingenio. The *criadero* produces 180,000kg of rainbow trout annually. It's fun to take a quick walk among the many channels of swimming entrees-to-be. Brightly painted murals describe the fascinating 360-day reproductive cycle of rainbow trout in exhaustive detail while the hearty aroma of the former inhabitants on grills all along the hillside wafts through the air.

Restaurants serving 1001 trout standards are packed shoulder-to-shoulder the whole length of the hill. Quality varies somewhat more than price, and ambience varies greatly. At the entrance into town, before the car toll, **Restaurante Avila ❸** (☎962 4253), is one of the bigger fish in the pond (entrees s/7-15). Such dubious dignitaries as Alberto Fujimori and Alejandro Toledo have both lunched here on delicacies like *trucha a la mexicana* (trout stuffed with cheese, onions, and peppers; s/10) and *trucha a la parilla* (grilled trout; s/7). The garden picnic area features a landscaped island with just one table for two. (Open daily 11am-5pm.) Far up, up, up only 50m below the *criadero*, **Recreo Arthur ❷** (☎968 0839), on the right just before the road curves, has a large garden with a small pool where you can catch your own lunch. The flowering trees between tables lend a festive air. (Trout dishes s/5-8. Open daily 8am-7pm. V.)

LAGUNA DE PACA

Buses and cars to Jauja leave from Calixto near Amazonas in Huancayo (45min., s/4); the cars leave when full but are worth the wait. From the Plaza, go up Giraldez 2 blocks, take a right on Amazonas, and the intersection with Calixto is 2 blocks farther. All transportation in and out of Jauja uses the Puente Ricardo Palma as an open-air hub. Jauja's Plaza de Armas is about 3 blocks farther down Junín. Taxis or mototaxis to the Laguna (5-8min., s/3-4) can be flagged down there. If your visit is during off-peak hours and you mind the 3km walk back town, drivers will often wait at the laguna (round-trip s/10-12).

Forty-five kilometers north of Huancayo, the tiny town of Jauja basks in its past glory as Peru's former colonial capital, and the current, though equally dubious, glory of its two main tourist attractions: the **Capilla de Cristo Pobre** and the gleaming **Laguna de Paca,** north of town. The Capilla, visible two blocks to the right from Junín (between Colina and Tarapacá, on San Martín) as you walk from the ad-hoc bus terminal to the Plaza de Armas, is doubly famous as an imitation of Paris's Notre Dame and as the first cement construction in the Mantaro Valley. As sights go, the Laguna de Paca is a whole different kettle of fish, mostly trout. Though the shore is home to many a gaudy umbrella and blaring hi-fi stereo, tranquility and peace await past the vacationing Peruvians. Cliffs on the left side of the road are criss-crossed with solitary, narrow paths. Be sure to carry a large stick or a couple of large stones, as the stray dogs here can be aggressive. Farther below, the small stretch of shoreline devotes itself to restaurants serving *trucha* (trout) and pitching boatrides (s/3-4; couples and families s/5) to the infamous **Isla del Amor,** where sirens reputedly lure visitors to their deaths. The restaurants are all essentially the same—daytime picnic places with gardens and outdoor tables—and nearly identically priced; **Las Olas ❷**, where the road begins to curve, is a touch swankier than its neighbors, and a sol pricier, too. (☎36 1119. *Trucha frita* s/7. *Ceviche* s/10. Large beers s/4-5.) **El Reflejo ❶**, the second on your right arriving at the *laguna,* also comes recommended.

Only slightly less fantastic—although perhaps significantly more scientific—than reports of the singing sirens are stories that the Laguna de Paca is connected underground to the Laguna Ñahuinpuquio, some 50km south, not far from Chupaca. Locals claim that objects lost in one *laguna* have surfaced in the other.

ARTESANÍA VILLAGES

To get to Hualhaus or San Gerónimo, take a bus marked "San Gerónimo" from the Parque de la Concepción Inmaculada in Huancayo. Get off on the right-hand side of the main road after 20min. for Hualhuas and 30min. for San Gerónimo. To get from one town to another, grab a bus on the main road.

About 20min. from Huancayo lies the tiny village of **Hualhaus,** famous for its fine alpaca goods. Tiny, family-run havens of *artesanía* offer the most beautiful and traditional pieces. Men do the traditional loom weaving; women make belts and spin yarn. Mentioning the names of the artisans below will prompt any town dweller to point you in the right direction. Worthy of a visit is **Slmeon Guevara,** whose house is about 100m to the left of the main road from Huancayo. His tiny shop, Perú-Inkaiko, has lovely blankets and bags. In the courtyard garden, watch heaps of knotted wool transform into incredibly fine skeins of yarn, then head upstairs to see the yarn woven on an old-fashioned loom into incredibly thick blankets. About 25m down on the right, **Faustino Maldonado** specializes in alpaca clothing, such as sweaters, hats, and soft leggings women wear under their thick skirts.

San Gerónimo, 10min. away by bus, is renowned for its silversmiths. **Sra. Nelly Vásquez** crafts intricate silver filigree earrings and rings in a tiny workshop with improvised tools. She'll gladly show you the secrets of her work. Her house has a white sign on the left—just walk through the courtyard to the back workshop.

🦅 HIKING NEAR HUANCAYO

The following dayhikes take 3-9hr., depending on their length and on your individual level of fitness and acclimation. None requires special equipment, but, as with any hike, be sure to carry adequate food, water, and first aid supplies, all of which can be purchased in Huancayo. Sunscreen and a walking stick also make excellent walking companions.

HIKE	DISTANCE	TIME	ALTITUDE	DIFFICULTY
Chongos Bajo-Ahuac-Ñahuinpuquio	10km	4-5hr.	3300-3400m	Easy
Chicche-La Esperanza	9km	3-5hr.	3400-3900m (descending)	Medium
Ingenio-Huahanca-Ingenio	14km	8-9hr.	3500-3800m	Medium

CHONGOS BAJO-AHUAC-ÑAHUINPUQUIO. The village of **Chongos Bajo** is proudly known as one of the best preserved in the Mantaro Valley, a place where the church dates from 1540 and the traditions and architecture of past centuries are still going strong. This hike leads from Chongos Bajo to the Arwaturo ruins and the Laguna Ñahuinpuquio at the edge of the village of Ahuac, not far from the town of **Chupaca** (p. 291). The trail toward Ahuac begins from behind the Iglesia El Copón, 7 blocks to the right as you face the main church on the Plaza. A hundred meters beyond this, the trail crosses a small irrigation canal, where the hike continues to the right. Not long afterward, the path will seem to split between a descending trail and a highway which climbs the mountainside. At this point, the hike begins to climb toward the village of **Tinyari,** passing a total of seven tiny underground-fed *lagunas* and the village cemetery. Neither climbing nor descending, the route follows the mountainside until reaching the next village, **Andamarca. Laguna Ñahuinpuquio** is approximately half a kilometer beyond Andamarca. Close by the Laguna, a recently constructed stone stairway brings the hike to a close at the **Arwaturo ruins.** A breathtaking view of the whole Mantaro Valley rewards the final effort of climbing those last meters. The village of **Ahuac** lies just below. *(Buses for Chongos Bajo leave from the corner of Giraldez and Amazonas (1¼hr., s/2). To return, taxis ply the route from Ahuac to Chupaca (8min., s/1.50). In Chupaca, numerous buses to Huancayo (40min., s/1) depart from the road below the church.)*

CHICCHE-LA ESPERANZA. This hike begins in the main park in the village of Chicche, from the spot where taxis arrive. Facing the park with the small news kiosk directly in front of you, take the path which heads to the left. The trail passes the **Laguna de Ataccocha** on the left. Continue downhill to the bottom of the mountainside, where a small river runs between the descending and rising slopes. Without crossing the river, follow the river's current along the bank. There are numerous small paths here, but all of them lead to the center of La Esperanza so long as you continue to follow the river's path. Just before arriving at the village, a giant round boulder known as **la piedra de Tulunco** will appear on the horizon. Climbing up it is relatively easy, but getting down can be a terrifying experience, as the round shape means a sheer drop and not being able to see the ground below. The altitude of this hike increases its difficulty, but the altitude change involved is primarily in passing to the lower elevation of La Esperanza. *(Taxis for Chicche leave from the corner of Calixto and Marañón in Huancayo (1¼hr., s/12). To return to Huancayo from La Esperanza, take a bus or taxi from the town plaza to Apata (10min., s/1), and from there take a bus for Huancayo (40min., s/3).)*

INGENIO-HUAHANCA-INGENIO. This route begins a few hundred meters before the toll for cars to go up Ingenio's hillside. Just before the first restaurants begin, a small bridge called the **Puente Inka** can be seen on the right from the road leading into town. This dirt road leads to the village of **Huahuanca** (elev. 3800m). As it crosses through town, the road traverses a park, where the road becomes a footpath. This path leads off from the right side of the park, climbing approximately 200m before reaching a sort of esplanade. This is the only point in the circuit at which the trail becomes less than absolutely clear. Stay to the right and the trail's well-marked character will return. The next landmark is the village of **Ancal.** At this point, the route hugs the

village cemetery and descends approximately 250m to the Río Chía. Following the river in the direction of its current, the hike's final stage (approximately the final 3km) reaches the village of **Ingenio**, eventually once again becoming a road rather than a path. The hike concludes by rejoining the main road at the top of Ingenio (p. 293), practically at the local **criadero** (trout hatchery). The descent to where the buses wait and to the hike's starting point is only a few hundred meters. *(Taxis and buses for Ingenio leave from the corner of Calixto and Marañón (40min., s/2-4) and return from the base of the hill along which Ingenio's criadero and many trout restaurants crowd. An early start is essential, as the frequency of return transport to Huancayo diminishes dramatically after 5pm.)*

HUANCAVELICA   ☎067

Beautiful Huancavelica (pop. 40,000; elev. 3676m), a small, remote city floating among the mountaintops, provides a peaceful alternative to the Cusco-Lima tourist track. Huancavelica got its start when mercury deposits were discovered here in the 16th century. The indigenous population was ruthlessly exploited in the Santa Bárbara "mines of death," where they were exposed to noxious gases on a daily basis. Today, the railway constructed to haul the fruits of this morbid industry provides one of the few ways to access the town, which is a great base for fascinating daytrips through the mountains.

■ ☎ ORIENTATION AND PRACTICAL INFORMATION

Exiting the train station, take a right and go two blocks downhill on **Grau** to the shop-filled main street, **Muñoz.** To the right lies the small **Plaza de Santa Ana,** where buses from Huancayo and other surrounding towns stop—look for the giant soccer ball. From the corner of Grau, turn left down Muñoz and walk 6½ blocks to the red, yellow, and green **Plaza de Armas.** Muñoz and **Virrey Toledo** run parallel to and border the Plaza, while **Manco Cápac** and **Ascensión Segura** run perpendicular. The **Río Ichu** lies more or less parallel to Muñoz. Townspeople think of the river as "down," and refer to locations like the market or the tourism office as "downhill," even though from the Plaza de Armas you'll feel like you're walking up an incline. Although Huancavelica is very compact, getting around at first can require patience, as street names—except for the major axes—are almost never used by the locals and even more rarely indicated by a sign.

Trains: (☎75 2898). Trains run to **Huancayo** (6hr.; 6:30am, 12:30pm; s/9).

Buses: There are many ways to get to **Ayacucho** from Huancavelica, but all involve either traveling on bad roads or going hours out of the way. For the most direct route, the only option is **Empresa San Juan,** Mariscal Cáceres 338 (☎75 1346); from the Plaza in front of San Sebastián and San Francisco at the end of Virrey Toledo, go right and then left at the traffic light. After you cross the river, a small plaza will appear on the left. The San Juan office is on the left side of the plaza. Early-morning **buses** go to **Puerte Rumichaca** (4-4½hr., 4:30am, s/10), where you can join the ranks waiting for a passing Ayacucho-bound vehicle at the side of the highway, near the weigh station. Wear layers for the trip, as the paved road from Rumichaca passes through snow-covered mountains (4500-5000m the whole way), and the cars don't have heat. **Autos (colectivos)** provide the fastest and most flexible means of getting to **Huancayo** (3½hr., leave when full 3am-8pm, s/23). Cars and their drivers wait on the Plaza de Armas at the corner with Muñoz, in front of the Hotel Presidente. **Ticllas,** Gonzales Prada 216 (☎75 1562), on the left halfway down, going down Muñoz from the Plaza de Armas to Plaza Santa Ana, provides the most frequent service to **Huancayo** and the only daytime departures by bus (5hr.; 8, 10am, 2:15, 3:45, 10pm; s/10). For **Lima** and other destinations, there isn't much difference between the various services lining Plaza Santa Ana, with the exception of the cushy

Transportes Lobato, O'Donovan 519 (☎ 75 2751), on the back corner of Plaza Santa Ana, left of the church, directly downhill from the train station. Sends buses to **Lima** (10-12hr., 7pm, s/25). **Oropesa,** O'Donovan 226 (☎ 75 3181), goes to: **Ica** (11hr., 5:45pm, s/28); **Lima** (10-12hr., 5:30pm, s/23); **Pisco** (8hr., 5:45pm, s/25).

Tourist Office: Dirección Regional de Industria y Turismo, Victoria Garma 444, 2nd fl. (☎ 75 2938), off the corner of Nicolás de Piérola. From the lower right-hand corner of the Plaza de Armas, walk away from the Plaza down Virrey Toledo. Take a right on Piérola and after 2 blocks go left on Victoria Garma. The Ministerio is on the right. The office has a free and very useful brochure on the town, including a street map. Spanish only. Open M-F 8am-1pm and 2:30-5pm.

Bank: Banco de Crédito, Virrey Toledo 383, on the corner of Piérola, 3 blocks to the left away from the lower right-hand corner of the Plaza de Armas. Open M-F 9:30am-3:30pm and Sa 9:30am-12:30pm. Plus/V **ATM.**

Markets: Mercado Central, on Piérola. With your back to the cathedral take a left on Toledo, walk 2 blocks, and turn right. The market is 2 blocks down on the left. Huancavelica also holds a significant **Sunday Market,** concentrated along Torre Tagle, the street parallel and uphill from Muñoz.

Police: Grau 173 (☎ 80 3078), in a green building on the left side of Plaza Santa Ana.

Hospital: Hospital Departamental de Huancavelica (☎ 75 3198), on Cáceres, uphill from the Instituto Nacional de Cultura, about a 15min. walk.

Telephones: Free-standing phones fill the city. **Telefónica,** Virrey Toledo 179 (☎ 75 3001), 1 block away to the right with your back to the cathedral, has phone booths and receives calls. Open daily 7am-10pm.

Internet Access: A dozen throughout town. **Sky@Net** (☎ 75 3552), on the Virrey Toledo side of the Plaza, is convenient and fast (s/1 per hr.). Open daily 8:30am-11:30pm.

Post Office: Pasaje Ferúa 105 (☎ 75 2750), off Muñoz on the right, 1 block past Plaza Santa Ana, coming from the Plaza de Armas. Open M-F 8am-8pm, Sa 8am-4pm.

▐ ACCOMMODATIONS

Variety is scarce in Huancavelica; look for the greatest number of blankets, since long nights are unimaginably cold.

Hotel Ascensión, Manco Cápac 481 (☎ 75 3103), on the Plaza. A variety of rooms for a range of prices. Recently remodeled, spacious rooms have 24hr. hot water in private baths with equally new mattresses and cable TV. Less recently spruced-up but still very well-kept rooms with half-bath (or singles with none) don't put quite as big a dent in the wallet, and they still have 24hr. hot water and a complete blanket-count. Singles s/10-35; doubles s/22-50. ❶

Hotel Camacho, Carabaya 481 (☎ 75 3298). Walk 5 blocks up Muñoz from Plaza de Santa Ana and Grau, and turn left uphill. Dwarf-sized rooms have toasty sheets. Communal showers. Some rooms with TV and ½ bath. Singles s/8, with ½ bath and TV s/20; doubles s/14, with ½ bath s/30. ❶

▐ FOOD

Chicken (s/2-5) in all its myriad disguises rules in Huancavelica, filling side streets with nameless hawkers of *caldo* and *saltado*. But there is another way.

Mochica Sachún Restaurante, Virrey Toledo 303 (☎ 75 2483), at the corner with Raimondi. Perhaps the warmest spot in all Huancavelica—take off that third sweater and smell the fake roses on each table. Breakfasts s/2.50-3. Entrees s/8-14; Nescafé (not *café pasado!*) s/1. If you're still not warm, pitchers of *calientes* are only s/10. Open daily 7:30am-10:30pm. ❶

Café Restaurant Joy, Toledo 216 (☎ 75 2860) right off the Plaza de Armas. A local watering hole featuring posters of John Lennon and an orange and black Mondrian interior deco scheme. Sandwiches s/1.50-4. Vegetarian omelette s/4.50. Entrees s/9-14. Open daily 7:30am-10pm. ❶

👁 SIGHTS

INSTITUTO NACIONAL DE CULTURA. The Institute, housed in a charming colonial building with a gurgling fountain in the courtyard, is dedicated to displaying the natural and cultural history of the region. In addition to an extensive cultural library, the institute houses two **museums.** The **Museo de Arte Popular** focuses on Huancavelican art and history, including traditional multicolored costumes. One display portrays the native *danza de tijeras* (scissors dance), in which outlandishly clothed people cavort with giant metal scissors to create a cacophonous clacking. The dance can be seen yearly during the festival preceding Christmas (Dec. 22-26). The **Museo Arqueológico** holds an impressive collection of Inca tools, weapons, and mummies. Other exhibits include paintings and a map of the Santa Bárbara mines. *(Plazoleta San Juan de Dios, at the corner of Arica and Raimondi, 1 block from the Plaza de Armas. ☎ 75 3420. Open M-F 9am-1pm and 2:30-6pm, Sa 9am-1pm. Free.)*

CHURCHES. There are eight churches within the town of Huancavelica; an inventory of the thirty-odd churches in area is in progress. Tourist visiting hours are unheard of here, so the curious sneak in with a curator or take a peek during mass. The yellow-and-red **Cathedral de San Antonio** was constructed in 1673 in the Baroque style and has a collection of paintings from the Cusco School. *(Directly on the Plaza de Armas. Mass daily 7am and 6pm. Open daily in the evenings and for Sunday mass.)* The squat **Iglesia de Santa Ana,** in the plaza of the same name, is Huancavelica's oldest church, built at the end of the 16th century. Much of the interior decor is similar to the style of El Greco. The **Iglesia y Convento de Santo Domingo,** on Virrey Toledo, two blocks to the left of the Plaza if looking at the cathedral, harbors the beautiful Virgen del Rosario y Santo Domingo that was brought from Rome. The Church is open only during festivals; speak with the resident priest to gain entry for a visit. At the end of Virrey Toledo, where it meets García de los Godos, the Plaza Francisco Bolognesi is home to the **Iglesia San Sebastián,** whose three-door, basilica-style construction is unique in the city. *(Open for mass at 5pm daily.)* Ask the Iglesia San Sebastián's Padre Raúl for permission to visit the adjacent 16th-century **Iglesia San Francisco,** home to statues carved from local wood and covered in gold leaf from nearby mines.

HOT SPRINGS. Huancavelica's own hot springs, **Aguas Termales de San Cristóbal** (22-25°C), are used as **thermal baths,** located in a blue-and-white building up a steep climb on Escalonda. The high sulfur content in the water is supposed to be good for skin ailments and rheumatism. Locals come to swim in the crowded pool or soak in private baths, but the under-appreciated perk is the view from the walk up. *(From the Plaza de Armas, walk down Manco Cápac on the same side as Hotel Ascensión until you reach the bridge at Río Ichu; epic stone steps continue to the baths on the other side, 4 blocks total. Open daily 6am-3pm. Pool s/1. Towel, bathing suit, and soap rental available s/0.50-1.50.)*

🏃 DAYTRIPS FROM HUANCAVELICA

MINAS DE SANTA BÁRBARA

From the Instituto Nacional de Cultura (on Raimondi, 1 block to the right of the cathedral in the Plaza de Armas), walk left down Juan García for 2 blocks and turn right on Agosto de Leguilla until you arrive at Colonial. Cross the bridge with two arches. From Leguilla, it's a lazy 4.5km, 1½-2hr. hike to the mines.

Discovered shortly after the Spanish arrival in the 16th century, the mines outside Huancavelica were exploited by the Spanish for their mercury deposits. With the help of natives, the Spanish dug so feverishly that the mines swelled large enough to fit streets, chapels, buildings, and a bullfighting ring within the walls and underground. At the peak of mining, more than 10,000 workers from all over Peru labored underground simultaneously. Life in the mines was so harsh and hazardous that once workers entered the mines, they often didn't see daylight again. To spare their children from the dangers of this life, mothers sometimes mutilated the legs of their newborn sons. The mines stand empty today, leaving behind an underground city and bitter memories of Spanish mistreatment. The first 170m of the mines remain open for exploration. Bring a flashlight, and be aware of very low oxygen levels within.

UCHKUS INKAÑAS

To get to the ruins, catch a cab or a combi to the village of Sachapite from Plaza Santa Ana (18km; s/2). From there, a 7km (1½hr.) hike downhill winds around the ruins of Qorimina, Incañan, and Chunkana. Incañan is the only site with an entrance fee.

A conflation of the Inca Empire and the lesser-known Tahuatinsuyo makes for some interesting and little-known ruins 25km from Huancavelica. Uchkus Inkañas was an important religious center and astronomical observatory. The irrigation canals that form **Qorimina** are shaped like a giant bird. Only 500m away, the giant arched doorway of **Incañan** greets the rising sun (entrance s/1). A little higher up, the houses of the Inca community are visible in the ruins of **Chunkana.** In the center, a geometrical figure (approx. 7m) engraved in the rock served as an astronomical clock to show the expected rainfall and most productive times for farming.

AYACUCHO ☎066

Packed with students, overflowing with colonial churches, and surrounded by artisan villages, Ayacucho (pop. 130,000; elev. 2800m) is the cultural center of highland Peru. During the day, the town center relaxes: students pack into one of the oldest universities in the Americas and businesses close their shutters for lunch breaks of epic proportions on the Plaza de Armas. However, the peacefulness that usually pervades Ayacucho, a name meaning "Corner of the Dead" in Quechua, is only a recent innovation. From AD 700 to 1100, the city was home to the ultra-violent Huari, who regularly decapitated prisoners of war and displayed their heads as trophies. In 1824, Ayacucho became the final battleground in the war for Peruvian independence, and the 1980s saw the Shining Path terrorist group spawned from Ayacucho's intelligentsia. The trauma of Ayacucho's past is largely invisible now, however, marked only by chunks of reconstructed buildings and the political bent of many conversations. Military occupation has dissipated, and the city's increased investment in colonial preservation has helped tourists once again find grandeur in this transformed city.

◉ TRANSPORTATION

Flights: Airport (☎81 2418), 4km outside of the town center. Taxi 15min., s/4-5. **Nuevo Continente,** 9 de Diciembre 160 (☎81 7504), 1 block from the Plaza de Armas, flies to **Lima** (35min.; M, W, F-Sa 4:30pm; US$59.50). Open M-Sa 8am-1pm and 3:30-8pm, Su 9am-1pm. **LC Busre,** Lima 178 (☎81 6012), 1 block up from the Plaza de Armas, has more frequent service to **Lima** (1hr., daily at 7am, US$69).

Buses: Except for the great dowager **Expreso Molina,** most bus companies have offices huddled together on **Pasaje Cáceres,** a small diagonal alleyway running from Mariscal Cáceres (between Tres Máscaras and Asamblea) off to the right until it rejoins Quinua, not far from the Molina offices on 9 de Diciembre. **Expreso Molina,** 9 de Diciembre 458 (☎80 2880), has service to **Huancayo** (9-10hr.; 6:30am, 8, 9pm; s/22-25) and **Lima** (9-10hr.; 9 departures daily, clustered in the early morning and after 8pm; s/25-45). **Chanka Express,** Pasaje Cáceres 150 (☎81 2391), departs for **Abancay** (16hr., s/35) and **Cusco** (22hr.; daily 6:30am, 7pm; s/40) via **Andahuaylas** (10hr., s/20). **Reybus,** Pasaje Cáceres 166 (☎81 9413), goes to **Lima** (9-10hr.; 8, 9pm; s/20). **Expreso Wari** (☎83 6323), Pasaje Cáceres across from Reybus, goes to **Lima** (9-10hr., around 7pm, s/20) and **Cusco** (22hr., daily 4am, s/45) via **Andahuaylas** (10hr., s/20) and **Abancay** (16hr., s/35).

Local Transport: Within town, mototaxis cost s/1 and *autos* s/2-3.

✴🛈 ORIENTATION AND PRACTICAL INFORMATION

Ayachucho's neatly gridded streets center on the Plaza de Armas and change names as they pass it. Reminiscent of Cusco, each street takes on yet another name beginning "Portal..." for the length of the Plaza itself. Almost everything of interest to tourists lies near this landmark. Most buses stop along **Mariscal Cáceres,** two blocks away.

Tourist Office: iPerú, on the Plaza de Armas (☎81 8305, 24hr. hotline 574 8000), toward Cusco from the cathedral. **Maps** and extensive local information in Spanish and English. Open daily 8:30am-7:30pm.

Currency Exchange: Banco de Crédito, at Portal Unión on the Plaza de Armas. AmEx/Plus/V **ATM.** Open M-F 10am-6pm, Sa 9:30am-12:30pm. Dollar **exchange booths** with good rates occupy an enclave directly across from the Plaza's cathedral. Most open daily 9am-11pm.

Market: Mercado Vivanco, on 28 de Julio, 3½ blocks from the Plaza de Armas, across from Iglesia San Francisco de Asís, sells everything from fresh fruit and bread to blankets and baskets. **Mercado Artesanal,** 4 blocks down 9 de Diciembre from the Plaza, sells handcrafted goods from nearby villages.

Emergency: ☎ 105.

Police: 28 de Julio 311 (☎81 9466), to the right of Iglesia San Francisco de Asís. Open 24hr. **Tourist police** (☎81 7846) are at 2 de Mayo and Arequipa on the Plaza. Open daily 8am-10pm.

24hr. Pharmacy: Pharmacies in town take the 24hr. shifts in turns. Each pharmacy should have posted outside the coordinates of the 2 pharmacies on duty that day.

Hospital: Hospital de Apoyo, Independencia 355 (emergency ☎81 2181). Also has a **24hr. pharmacy.**

Internet Access: Service of varying quality is available all over the city. **El Hueco Net,** Portal Constitución 9 (☎81 2596), off the Plaza, in the basement at the back, has the fastest connection in town (s/1.5 per hr.). They also offer Internet-based long-distance phone service. Open daily 8am-midnight.

Post Office: Serpost, Asemblea 293 (☎81 2224), at Cáceres. Open M-Sa 8am-7pm. **DHL,** Lima 273 (☎81 2826).

⌂ ACCOMMODATIONS

Hostels line Mariscal Cáceres, begging you to settle for a cheap, tawdry setup, but a few extra soles gets you something tall, dark, and handsome near the Plaza—with hot water to boot. Prices jump during Semana Santa (Holy Week), around Easter in March or April.

Ayacucho

ACCOMMODATIONS
Hostal Central, **4**
Hotel Huamanga, **6**
Hotel La Colmena, **5**
Hotel Los Alamos, **8**

FOOD
La Casona, **2**
La Pradera, **3**
Restaurante Los
Alamos, **8**

ENTERTAINMENT
Cine Cavaro, **1**

NIGHTLIFE
Los Balcones, **7**

Hotel Los Alamos, Cusco 215 (☎81 2782), at Tres Máscaras. It's hard to decide what's best about Los Alamos: the superb restaurant downstairs, or the spacious second-floor rooms with private bath, hot water, and cable TV. An orderly, comfortable place to stay, with red satin bedspreads for a touch of spice. Singles s/30; doubles s/40. ❸

Hostal Central, Arequipa 188 (☎81 2144), at Tres Máscaras. Though the large rooms scream "chain motel," the courtyard whispers colonial elegance. There's a nice view over the rooftops. A few rooms have private baths. 24hr. hot water. Singles s/12, with bath s/25; doubles s/22, with bath s/40. ❷

Hotel La Colmena, Cusco 140 (☎81 1318). Balconies fit for an aria overlook stunning courtyards, but aspiring Pavarottis ought not disturb patrons in the cheerful restaurant below. Cable TV and 24hr. hot water. Singles s/15, with bath s/25; doubles with bath s/30; triples with bath s/45. ❷

Hotel Huamanga, Bellido 536 (☎81 1871). Basic, clean, and cheap, and with that nice restaurant and garden outside, the blue-walled rooms don't seem quite so dim. 24hr. hot water. Singles s/10, with bath s/15; doubles s/15, with bath s/20. ❶

FOOD

Ayacuchan chefs take pride in delicately prepared meals of *mondongo* (lamb or pork soup boiled overnight with peeled corn) and *puca picante* (potatoes in a spicy red sauce with rice and fried meat). Most Ayacuchans supplement such light

CLASH AND BURN

At first I thought they were fire-crac█████Then the chant "El pueb███do, jamás será venc-ido" ███hed my window. I pushed the "light" button on my watch. 2:32am. I stuck in my ear-plugs and went back to sleep, vaguely connecting these sounds with the ongoing teachers' strike. Bright and early, I was ready to begin █y research in Ayacucho. Th█ streets were in ruins, lit-tered with chunks of concrete and smoldering heaps of burnt tires. Being the nonchalant gal I am, I exclaimed, "Wow, so I didn't dream it," and strolled off in search of coffee. But when I reached the Plaza de Armas, I realized my coffee would have to wait. A dense crowd was on the march. A line of policemen stood in front of the town hall, raising their riot shields as the crowd approac██d. The rhythmic shouts faltere█ ██ut soon the crowd of 300 (it was 7am) became a mob, shaking their fists with a single accusing roar, "Asesinos! Asesi-nos!" I figured it was time to go back to the hotel.

Fo███ he next few hours, I waite█ loitered around the hotel cafe. A visiting group of engineer-ing professors whose lectures had been cancelled sat drinking pisco sours from colored straws. "You can't have democracy without dis-cipline," said one. "But democ-racy almost always implies disorder," I answered. We were bored. Vague shouting reached us

fare with frequent visits to the numerous *heladerías* (ice cream shops) opposite the cathedral. **Top Market,** Asemblea 151, has supermarket goods. (☎81 4408. Open daily 8am-10pm.)

☒ **La Casona,** Bellido 463 (☎81 2733). Let the waiters in black waistcoats talk you into the 80-year-old special, *bistec a La Casona* (spicy cooked vegetables under brawny beef, a fried egg, and avocado strips; s/18). Lunch *menú* s/6. Entrees s/6-20. Open daily 7am-11pm. AmEx/DC/MC/V. ❷

Restaurante Los Alamos, Cusco 215 (☎81 2782), in the hotel of the same name. An attractive patio restau-rant where friends gather, pushing all the tables into one line and ordering round after round of *cerveza* while they feast on heaping portions of traditional fare: *pollo a la brasa, arroz chaufa,* and *sopa del día.* Tasty, abundant, reasonably priced, and friendly. Open daily 8am-9pm. ❷

La Pradera, Arequipa 170, 1 block from the Plaza de Armas, inside the courtyard, in the back and down the stairs. Vegetarianism's last stand, at least in Ayacucho, this tiny storefront restaurant serves those who manage to find it soy steaks galore (*bistec a lo pobre,* s/12), *tortillas* (omelettes) s/4-7, and daily lunch and dinner *menús* (s/3). Open M-Sa 7am-10pm. ❶

▣ SIGHTS

Tourist tickets, available at most churches and muse-ums, are a good value for those planning heavy-duty sightseeing; they cover most of the city's half dozen **museums,** the **Huari ruins,** and various other attrac-tions. If you're short on time, though, it may prove more economical to pay entrance fees (around s/2).

HUARI RUINS. Standing 22km from Ayacucho en route to Quinua, the ancient capital of the Huari Empire lies in disarray after its flourishing success in AD 700-1300, when some 50,000 people walked its streets and lived in its buildings. The site spreads 16 sq. km across cacti-studded mountain deserts and is divided into 15 districts, only three of which have been excavated. Within those three districts can be found a large rock, on which ani-mals might have been sacrificed, and the circular **Templo Mayor,** where offerings were left for the god Wiraccocha. In the same spot is **Monoachayoq,** funerary chambers that once held the Huari's headless prisoners of war. Entire noble house-holds were buried in the chambers of **Cheqo Wasi,** farther uphill along the highway. A small **museum** gives a chronology of the Huari civilization and its Tiahuanaco roots. *(Catch a colectivo (30-45min.) about 6* blocks downhill on the oval at Mariscal Cáceres. From the corner of Cusco and the Plaza de Armas, walk 2 blocks down Asamblea and turn right on Mariscal Cáceres. Open daily 8am-5:30pm. Small fee.

CHURCHES. In the 16th and 17th centuries, the Catholic Church built 33 outposts in Ayacucho (although the town officially has 37), supposedly to reflect the age of Christ at his martyrdom. The most important is the baroque **cathedral** on Plaza Mayor, first built in 1669, then rebuilt after being damaged in a 1719 earthquake. Silver artifacts in the small **Museo de Arte Religioso** (on the right side of the narthex) and gilded altars make the whole place shimmer. The intricately carved ceiling, constructed according to the Spanish-Arab *mudéjar* school, makes **Templo Santa Clara**, on Grau behind the market, a worthy destination. Built in the 1570s, the **Iglesia San Cristóbal**, six blocks west of the Plaza de Armas on 28 de Julio, was the first church in Ayacucho. Bask in the history of its modest adobe exterior, but the sanctuary is only open once a year on its anniversary. (*The best time to visit is during mass M-Sa 5 or 6pm, Su 10am. Free.*)

INSTITUTO NACIONAL DE CULTURA MUSEO HIPÓLITO UNANUE. This museum exhibits hefty monoliths recovered from the nearby Huari ruins, along with figurines, pottery, textiles, and other artifacts from cultures all over Peru. The creepier exhibits are the highlights of the collection—one display contains three mummies, including an intact infant. Another case is dedicated to the process of skull elongation, practiced from birth as a means of reinforcing class hierarchies. Finally, a collection of hole-riddled skulls explains how the Huari performed cranial surgery on injured warriors. Conclude your tour of the bizarre in the cactus garden next to the museum. (☎81 2056. *On the 5th block of Independencia, in the northern part of town. Head up Asamblea to Independencia, then go left 2 blocks and look for the sprawling white adobe complex on your right. Open M-Sa 9am-1pm and 3-5pm. s/2.*)

MUSEO MARISCAL CÁCERES. Once home to former President (1886-90 and 1894-95) and General Mariscal Cáceres (see **Growing Pains**, p. 65), the small mansion of the Museo Mariscal Cáceres is past its glory days. Still, it displays a (rather unkempt) collection of colonial paintings in the Baroque Cusco style. The series of religious scenes and bloody Jesuses proceeds through rooms full of colonial-era furniture and Cáceres's personal articles. Check out the series of photographs by which you can chart the growth of the great leader's signature mutton-chop whiskers. (*28 de Julio 508, at Chorro. Open M-Sa 9am-1pm and 2-6pm. s/3.*)

from the Plaza two blocks away. Tear gas wafted in under the door and we ran through the hotel courtyard looking for cold water to splash on our burning faces. Breathing hurt. From the rooftop we could see the columns of smoke growing darker—the mob was burning buildings now. We felt a mix of exhilarated curiosity, trepidation, and tense boredom.

In the evening it began to rain and the exhausted crowd dispersed. Every person had a different rumor: the strike would reconvene at 8pm; the army was on its way; a baby had been killed; the Interior Minister had declined to declare a state of emergency; there would be a curfew. The waiters at the hotel restaurant served a rushed dinner at 6pm, trying to make it home during the lull. The hotel guests sat in the dark courtyard, smoking and listening to the beginning rain.

The next morning, when I again stepped outside in search of coffee, all was quiet, but far from normal. Looters had sacked and burned every government building. The streets were charred. Police in combat uniforms with rifles and gas masks guarded the destroyed facades. People stood in awkward clusters, staring.

Confidence in renewal had been the identity of this town since the dispersal of the Sendero Luminoso in the 1990s. The tension I felt had as much to do with the past decade as the past 24 hours—Ayacucho was once again questioning its faith in itself.

—Irit Kleiman

ARTESANÍA

The prolific artisan community of **Barrio Santa Ana** spills down the city's southern hills. Narrow streets around the Plaza contain fascinating tapestry and sculpture workshops that open onto Plaza Santa Ana's concrete. The most extensive operation comprises the many workshops of the **Sulca family.** Their gallery, at Plaza Santa Ana 83, is covered with large, brightly colored tapestries depicting geometric riffs on Huari mythology, politics, poetic messages, and even a few works by M.C. Escher. **Alejandro Gallardo,** a few doors down from the Sulcas at Plaza Santa Ana 105-605, designs his tapestries based on Huari or Inca motifs, and his colors come from root- or fruit-based dyes. To the left and downhill from the Sulca gallery, the **Baljaguis** couple makes immense tapestries and small, attractive, decorative items of Huari or Inca design. All galleries are open roughly from 8am to early evening. *(To get to Santa Ana from the corner of the Plaza de Armas opposite the cathedral, walk 1 block up Lima and turn left on Grau. Follow Grau downhill through the market and uphill again until the streets turn to dirt. The small paths leading upward eventually meet Plaza Santa Ana, identified by numerous workshops peeking out of doorways.)*

ENTERTAINMENT AND NIGHTLIFE

Ayacucho's **Semana Santa** festival may draw giant crowds, but the rest of the year you're lucky to get a date for a movie: **Cine Cavaro,** 9 de Diciembre 361, plays subtitled American films on weekend nights. Ayacucho's eligible youth usually opt for dancing over movies; the wilder ones head for the salsa-heavy flashing-light affairs, while more Bohemian types sniff out the scarce hole-in-the wall bars. **Los Balcones,** Asambea 246, has live music F-Sa.

VILCASHUAMÁN   ☎066

Entering the mountainous village of Vilcashuamán, 120km from Ayacucho, is a step back in time. Townspeople accompany travelers to the many ruins of the Inca Empire's **Tawantinsayo,** scattered throughout town. This was the center of the Chanca empire when it was conquered by the Inca Pachacamac in the 1450s, marking the beginning of Inca expansion. The main ruin retains the foundations of its **Sun and Moon Temples** and has the only regional example of an *ushno*, or ceremonial pyramid, where the Inca ruler and his queen supposedly gave orders from their double throne. The entire town still exhibits Inca influence: small stores with Inca names peek out from between giant stone buildings, and ancient Inca holidays are celebrated with fervor.

An overnight stay at one of the **hostels ❶** on the Plaza will help you to appreciate the city's gorgeous surroundings. (About s/7.) **Restaurants ❶** operating out of private kitchens encircle the Plaza (soup and meat staples s/3-4). To get to Vilcashuamán from Ayacucho's Plaza de Armas, follow 2 de Mayo to Vivanco and walk 3 blocks downhill until Vivanco turns into Ramón Castilla. Just past the rotary, two companies send **combis** labeled "Vilcas" to the village throughout the day (4-5hr., leave when full). From the cathedral, walk 4 blocks down 2 de Mayo and turn left on Carlos Vivanco. To get back to Ayacucho, catch one of the combis circling the Plaza (the last ones leave around 4 or 5pm). Vilcashuamán centers around the Plaza, which is slowly being converted into a park. The cathedral, constructed on top of the Inca **Temple of the Sun,** stands next to the Plaza. The impressive **Temple of the Moon** lies to the right of the Plaza. Services include: **Banco de la Nación,** opposite the cathedral on the Plaza; **police,** next to the **Botica Jonathan,** on the Plaza; **Es Salud** medical clinic, in the blue-and-white building off of the Plaza; and two **public phones,** next to the police station.

ANDAHUAYLAS

On the long journey between Ayacucho and Cusco, all buses stop at the halfway point of **Andahuaylas** (pop. 35,000), famous as the birthplace of renowned author José María Arguedas. The quiet inhabitants are largely Quechua-speaking and host a huge Sunday market using the old system of bartering goods. Crammed between steep ridges, the city sits near a tranquil lake on whose banks the Chanca created an imposing temple and city, unearthed in 1997. If the thought of animal sacrifices atop an eight-level pyramid intrigues you, check out these **Sondor ruins,** the Chancas' last stronghold against the Incas. A trip to the top yields an unbelievable view of the mountains and nearby **Lake Pacucha. Combis** to the ruins leave five blocks down Peru from the Plaza, past the indoor concrete area. All of them stop at the lake in the small town of Pacucha and take various routes to the ruins (30-45min., about s/5). From the drop-off point, it's a short walk to the ruins. To return, catch a minibus before 4pm; many who miss the minibus hike to the town of Pacucha on the other side of the lake (3hr.) and catch a truck heading toward Andahuaylas.

Cheap hostels cluster around the Plaza, three blocks uphill from the river along Ricardo Palma. **Hostal Delicias ❷,** Ramos 525, is an ode to Robin Hood, with hunting-lodge decor and an overload of kelly green. Upscale rooms have 24hr. hot water and TVs. Posh **El Encanto de Oro Hotel ❸,** Casafranca 424 (☎72 3066), three blocks uphill and to the left of Los Celajes, in a brick building, has TVs, phones, immaculate hot baths, and brand-new furniture. *Pollo a la brasa* and other *comida típica* rule the Andahuaylas's restaurant scene, but a gem hides on Ramos just a block from the Plaza. **Restaurant Chifa El Dragón ❷,** Ramos 421, has the biggest selection of Chinese food in town. (☎72 1956. Entrees s/8-20.)

Malecón Grau, home to bus stations galore, lies at the bottom of a hill, along the river; the five parallel streets which lie uphill form most of the city. These are bisected by a dozen more: **Bolívar** and **Ricardo Palma,** to the left facing uphill from Grau, border the **Plaza de Armas** two blocks up; **Andahuaylas,** three blocks to the right, has more bus stations and restaurants; and **Martinelli,** two blocks farther, is the main drag. **Banco de Crédito,** on Peru, two blocks to the right of Martinelli, has a 24hr. AmEx/V **ATM.** A tiny **market** borders Ramos and Trelles, one street to the left of Andahuaylas. The **police,** Peru 198, are one block away from the bank. Most **buses** arrive and depart from Malecón Grau. A few more operate on the lower block of Martinelli, which intersects Grau by the main bridge. Several companies on Grau send buses to: Ayacucho (11hr., around s/25); Cusco (12hr., around s/30) via Abancay (5hr., around s/15); and Lima (20hr., s/50). Most buses leave around 6am or 6pm. Cramped **minibuses** often leave at the same time for half the price.

ABANCAY

The road from Andahuaylas emerges at a high mountain pass and begins its winding 3hr. descent to the valley town of **Abancay.** The narrow streets are surrounded by mountains framing the horizon with vertical cliffs, while deep canyons plunging into Río Pachachacua yield rugged hikes. About a 3hr. drive from Abancay on the road to Cusco, in a hidden valley 7km from the little town of **Curahuasi,** water from the Río Apurimac bubbles up into the **hot springs** of Cconoc. Although the springs are better described as "lukewarm," they are nonetheless a relaxing and popular spot for locals, who believe the waters have the power to cure ailments from arthritis to sterility. At night, people often stay up dancing and singing around bonfires by the river watching the stars. To get to the baths, take a Cusco-bound **bus** from Abancay and ask to be let off in Curahuasi (2hr.). Then hire a taxi (40min., s/5), or turn down the smaller road for a pleasant hike to the springs (1½hr.). To continue on to Cusco, hike up the dirt road from the springs to the highway. Buses to Cusco stop at the thatched bus stand (2½hr., s/6).

(Andahuaylas 1911—Lima 1969)

Walk through the high, narrow pathways of the Andes, cross one of the turbulent rivers that descend toward the Amazon, caress the Inca walls of Cusco, or note the poverty in which indigenous Peruvian people live, and you will experience the phenomena that moved one of Peru's foremost writers, José María Arguedas. There is nothing better than a short story, novel, or poem by José María Arguedas to introduce you to the Andean world.

Arguedas's own life experiences offered him first-hand knowledge of the social and cultural contrasts that divided his country. The son of a provincial lawyer who constantly traveled through the Peruvian highlands, Arguedas was left for long periods of time with his step-mother, who insisted that the young boy sleep and work with the indigenous servants. That is how Arguedas learned the Quechua language and came to identify himself wholly as a member of the indigenous people. Years later, as an anthropologist and a leftist militant, he learned much more about the native communities of the Andes by studying their customs, myths, and cosmovisions.

Arguedas's writings denounced the injustices of the *hacienda* system which had exploited and marginalized highland indigenous communities since the colonial period. At the same time, the imaginative richness of Arguedas's writing does not end with this conflict. An important aspect of Arguedas's work is that it goes beyond the descriptive realism of traditional *indigenista* writings. Before Arguedas, the majority of *indigenista* writers were only concerned with exposing the exploitative treatment that native people suffered at the hands of the *hacienda* owners, priests, and local officials. More than anything else, this early *indigenismo* was a literature of denouncement and protest. As such, it was destined not to transcend the political purposes of its historical moment. With Arguedas, however, *indigenista* writing takes on a whole new dimension. His preoccupation with the indigenous world is an internalized expression of solidarity. Arguedas's profound understanding of the indigenous culture allowed him to translate the mythology and the oral poetry of the Quechua peoples into modern, western literary form. Like no other writer before or since, Arguedas recovers the rhythms, metaphors, and animist meanings of the ancient beliefs of Quechua-speaking peoples, prolonging their presence in Peruvian culture.

As an example of this, in his most important novel, *Los ríos profundos* (1958), Arguedas uses a first-person narrative to recount the story of the adolescent Ernesto, an alter-ego who experiences various types of journeys: geographic, as he travels with his father through different Andean towns; social, as he participates in a social protest against local authorities; and personal, as the 14-year old protagonist begins to leave his childhood behind and take the first steps towards adulthood. This coming-of-age novel introduces Quechuan chants and narrative forms of a poetic character. One representative passage from the first chapter has the narrator-protagonist touching the Inca stones of a wall on Loreto Street in Cusco and feeling the stones transform into "a river of boiling blood." The novel is full of such beautiful moments of animism, poetic transformation, and dialogue with the landscape.

Arguedas also wrote many other important novels, including *Todas las sangres* (in more realist style), *El sexto* (about his horrendous experiences as a political prisoner), and *El zorro de arriba y el zorro de abajo* (about indigenous migration from the Andes and the shock of encountering the informal capitalist culture of the Peruvian coast). Arguedas's only collection of poetry, *Katatay* ("to tremble") appeared posthumously in 1972 and brings together seven poems in Quechua with Arguedas's own translations into Spanish. *Katatay* is a landmark in Peruvian poetry and Andean poetry in general, for it expresses the messianic and nature-inspired vision of several Andean myths. Of fundamental importance in this respect are the poems entitled "A nuestro dios-padre Túpac Amaru" and "Llamado a los doctores."

Arguedas had many literary and intellectual successes, but he could not tolerate the tremendous pain of seeing the marginalization of his people. Although a significant agrarian reform was carried out in Peru in 1969, it was not enough to prevent his suicide in December of that same year.

José Antonio Mazzotti, Ph.D is the Gardner Cowles Associate Professor in Romance Languages and Literatures at Harvard University.

In Abancay, cheap hostels line Arequipa on either side of the bus terminals. Quieter options are closer to the market, pricier ones on Días Bárcenas. **Hotel Imperial** ❷, Días Bárcenas 517 (☎ 32 1578), one block uphill and four blocks left of the terminals, has big beds and free breakfast. Abancay has endless inexpensive culinary options as well as a fair share of attractive, relaxing dining establishments. A surprisingly hip night scene boasts lots of bars, video pubs, and discos.

Abancay sits on a slope with the **Plaza de Armas** at the bottom. **Lima** runs across the top of the Plaza. **Cusco** and **Junín** run perpendicular to the Plaza, and **Huancavelica** and **Núñez** round out the downtown. Parallel to Lima and one block uphill is **Arequipa**, which turns into **Arenas** to the right of **Núñez**, where buses stop and cheap hostels congregate; one block further up is **Días Bárcenas**. A **tourist office** is at Arenas 121, 1st fl. (☎ 32 1664). **Currency exchange** is available at **Banco de Crédito**, Arequipa 218, two blocks from the buses. **Casas de cambio** flourish on Arequipa/Arenas, between Banco de Crédito and the stations. The **market** overflows onto the streets surrounding Arequipa, 2-3 blocks left of the Plaza. The **police** are at Lima 742, 7 blocks from the Plaza de Armas on the left, next to the statue of the Virgin Rosita. All **buses** to Cusco, Lima, and Andahuaylas stop in terminals on the left side of Arenas, 1 block up from the Plaza and 2 blocks to the right. **Expreso Wari** serves Cusco (5hr., 3 per day) and Lima (20hr., 5 per day) via Andahuaylas (5hr.).

THE NORTHERN COAST

Beyond the well-swept plazas and gleaming white churches of Peru's Northern Coast, tiny fishing boats mingle with cargo ships in the coastal currents that are the lifeblood of the Peruvian economy. Fishing industries account for 20% of the country's exports every year, second only to minerals. This dependence on the sea is evident in everything, from locals' professions to their culinary choices—it's hard to go 10 meters without running into a *ceviche* restaurant. But despite all the serious business being handled in these parts, the coast is known for its laid-back and friendly attitude. To the delight of surfers, the nourishing waters of the Pacific reach the shore as world-class waves that lap ruggved and pristine beaches.

However, the attractions of the Northern Coast extend beyond the maritime. Unlike most of Peru, the Northern Coast focuses on *pre*-Inca ruins—from Chan Chan to Sechín to Huacas del Sol y de la Luna, these relics by the sea preserve a piece of Peru's *really* ancient heritage. The icing on the cake is the fact that this area has yet to achieve the attention of most international tourists, meaning visitors here can experience Peru—past and present—at its most genuine.

HIGHLIGHTS OF THE NORTHERN COAST

EXPLORE the mud-and-brick ruins of **Chan Chan** (p. 320), the capital of the ancient Chimú Empire.

ADMIRE the gleaming colonial center and restored *casas antiguas* of **Trujillo** (p. 314).

SURF radical waves near the country's prettiest beaches: **Huanchaco** (p. 322), near Trujillo, and **Máncora** (p. 341), between Piura and Tumbes.

PONDER great literature in **Cabo Blanco** (p. 342), the town that inspired Ernest Hemingway's *The Old Man and the Sea*.

SAN PEDRO DE CASTA   ☎01

The simple Andean village of San Pedro de Casta (pop. 300) is the gateway city to the **Marcahuasi plateau.** An enigmatic collection of rock formations 90km east of Lima, Marcahuasi offers excellent camping and hiking, a rarity near Lima. These massive chunks of granite resemble sphinxes, tortoises, judges, and even the Egyptian fertility goddess Thueris (with the head of a hippo and the belly of a pregnant woman). Their source is unclear, but weekend pilgrimages often include crowds of Peruvians who speak of a powerful spiritual presence and "magnetic forces" coursing through their fingertips (cynics might call this altitude sickness). In any case, the plateau's dead silence provides silence and invites meditation. In the town itself, a 5min. walk south of the Plaza to the **mirador** provides stunning views of the valley. A small **museum** on the Plaza has a one-room collection of **mummies,** recovered from an ancient burial spot at Marcahuasi. They retain the fetal position in which they were buried, as well as the ghastly looks they had on their faces when they died. (Open M-F 9am-3pm.)

For those not wishing to camp, there are two main options: the **Hostal Marcahuasi ❹** has a nice courtyard and small restaurant, and rooms with private bath (singles s/25; doubles s/30-35). The **municipal hostel ❶** is much cheaper, but less

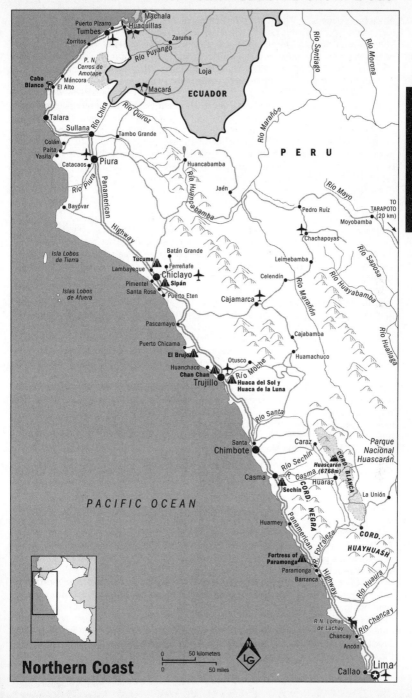

Northern Coast

attractive (beds s/5). The town's three **restaurants** are scattered around the Plaza and serve typical dishes (s/3-5). Because local restaurants often maintain unreliable hours, bringing food is wise. Ask around town for **Señor Manuel Olivárez** to obtain camping supplies, or if the tourist office runs out of maps—he sells a variety of practical supplies (tents s/30; sleeping pads s/10; sleeping bags s/5; maps s/1). Still, the best way to prepare is to bring your own from Lima. If camping at the top of the plateau, bring a compass in the rainy season to navigate in the dense fog.

Buses return to Chosica daily at 7:30am and 2pm. Arrive at the bus stop an hour early during the last weekends of June and July and the first week of October—festivals in town may mean you won't get a seat. All activity in San Pedro de Casta centers around the Plaza Principal, the town's transportation hub. The **tourist office** lies on the north side of the Plaza (opens when buses arrive), and you must register there to hike (s/10). Mules can also be rented there (s/15). Next to the tourist office, there is a convenience store with the town's only telephone (☎ 297 2344). A clinic lies on the same road, about a block away.

BARRANCA ☎ 01

Usually just a pit stop along the Panamericana Norte, Barranca is actually the perfect place to base yourself to visit the first major sight along the Northern Coast—the **Fortress of Paramonga**. Though its original purpose remains a mystery, there is little doubt that the **Fortress of Paramonga**, known locally as "la fortaleza," is one of the finest examples of Chimú ruins in all of Peru. Many speculate that the fortress actually did not serve a military purpose, but was used by the Chimú as a temple to the moon. With the arrival of the Incas, the site then became a temple of the sun prolonging its religious purpose. Others claim that this was a Chimú outpost to defend its empire. The lack of a sign at the under-guarded ruins unfortunately makes exploration more confusing than enlightening—something that may appeal to more hands-on travelers. To get there, take a cab from Barranca (round-trip s/12, including 1hr. wait). Don't get in a colectivo marked "Paramonga," as they all go to the town, not the ruins. (Open daily 8am-6pm. s/3; students s/2.)

The best place to stay in town is the pricey **Hotel Chavín ❺**, Galvez 222, with clean and very spacious rooms brimming with modern amenities—even if the retro decor is stuck in the seventies. (☎ 235 2253. Singles s/60; doubles s/65.) A much cheaper option is the **Hostal Colón ❶**, Galvez 407. Enter the semi-secluded hostel through the adjoining restaurant. (Shared-bath singles s/7; doubles s/12.) Locals flock to **La Unión ❸**, Galvez 159, for some of Barranca's finest *chifa* food. The wonton soup "La Unión" (s/13) is hearty enough for a lunch. (☎ 235 2340. Entrees s/15-25. Open daily 10am-11pm.) For a more international and varied menu, check out **La Estación ❷**, Galvez 364, where generous portions are a great value. (Entrees s/10-15. Open daily 9am-10pm.)

Turismo Barranca, Bolognesi 102 (☎ 235 3549), sends **buses** to Lima (4hr., every 15 min., s/8). **Tepsa,** Ugarte 305, off Lima (open daily 9am-midnight), sends buses to Chiclayo (8hr., 11:30pm, s/25) via Trujillo (5hr., s/16); Piura (10hr., 5pm, s/35); Tumbes (14hr., 3:30pm, s/50). Alternatively, stand at the *paraderos* on the corner of Lima and Ugarte and flag down buses heading either north or south—most will stop if they have empty seats. Barranca's bland **Plaza de Armas** divides the city into two distinct sections: a quiet residential coastal town, and a noisy transportation hub. Barranca's main streets are **Galvez,** home to most hostels and restaurants, and **Lima,** which doubles as the Panamericana and center of transportation activity. **Banco de la Nación,** Galvez 301, at the corner with Ugarte, exchanges AmEx traveler's checks. (Open daily 9am-12:30pm and 4:30pm-6:30pm.) The **police** (☎ 235 2136) are on the corner of Independencia and Zoraida, three blocks north of the Plaza de Armas. The **hospital** (☎ 235 2156) is at Nicolas de Pierola, and a **pharmacy**

is right across the street (☎235 3938; open daily 8am-9pm). **Internet** access is available at **Global Chip,** Galvez 453 (s/1 per hr.; open daily 9am-11pm). **Serpost** is at Ugarte 116, right off the Plaza de Armas (open daily 8am-8pm).

CASMA   ☎044

According to legend, Casma (pop. 27,000) gained its name from a small community of asthmatics who settled here to escape the thin air of the mountains. Apparently the Spaniards asked them why they had chosen this spot to settle but misheard their response, forever labeling the city "Casma." In more recent history, the city has been completely rebuilt since its utter devastation by a 1970 earthquake. Most tourists visit for the nearby beaches and important archaeological sights, including the 3500-year-old Sechín ruins, 3km from town.

▐ TRANSPORTATION. All north-bound **buses** traveling to and from **Lima** pass the Repsol gas station at the edge of town and will stop if they have empty seats. To get to the gas station, follow Nepeña up from the Plaza de Armas for about 10min. **Tepsa,** Ormeño 145 (☎71 2184, open daily 8am-midnight) goes to: Chiclayo (5hr.; 11am, 12:30pm; s/15); Lima (5hr.; 10am, 11pm; s/15); Piura (8hr.; 8, 10:30pm; s/25); Trujillo (3hr., 3pm, s/10); Tumbes (12hr., 6pm, s/35). **Los Casmiños,** on Nepeña near the Plaza de Armas (☎76 5083, open daily 8am-1am) has **colectivos** that head to Chimbote from the Plaza de Armas (50min., leave when full 6am-9pm, s/5). All south-bound buses go through Lima (usually 10am, 4, 8pm), departing from the many bus companies lining Luís Ormeño across from the gas station. **Mototaxis** around town should cost s/1.

▐ ORIENTATION AND PRACTICAL INFORMATION. The Panamericana splits when it passes Plaza Martín to form the town's two main streets: **Nepeña** (also called **Tarapacá** and **Luís Ormeño**) forms one side of the **Plaza de Armas,** and **Huarmey** lies one block behind the Plaza. **Banco de Crédito,** Bolívar 115-117, between the Plaza and Huarmey, accepts AmEx traveler's checks and gives cash advances on Visa cards. (☎71 1471. Open M-Sa 9:30am-12:30pm.) The **police** are at Magdalena 201 (☎71 2340), on Plaza Martín. **Hospital de Apoyo Casma,** Garcilaso de la Vega 658, is down Mejía from Plaza Martín. (☎71 1524. Open M-F 7:45am-1:45pm, 24hr. for **pharmacy** and emergencies.) **Internet access** is available at **Lucian@.com,** Huarmey 268 (☎71 1239; s/1 per hr.; open 9am-11pm), right off Plaza Martín. The **post office** is a block down Fernando Lomparte from Plaza Martín. (☎71 1067. Open M-Sa 8am-8pm.) Though there is no official tourist office, **▓Renato Tours,** Nepeña 370 (☎71 2528; renatotours@yahoo.com), run by Sandro Renato Córdoba, offers great tour packages of Casma and has tours in English.

▐ ACCOMMODATIONS AND FOOD. For a spacious, clean room with private bath and all the modern amenities, stay at **Hostal Montecarlo ❹,** Nepeña 403, where the fans in each of the 8 rooms provide a nice escape from the heat. (☎71 2065. Dorms s/25; singles s/35; doubles s/45; triples s/50. Discounts for longer stays.) Another comfortable option is the cheaper **Hostal Gregori ❷,** Ormeño 530, an elegant, labyrinthine establishment. (☎71 2019. Singles s/10-15, with bath s/20-25; matrimonials s/15, with bath s/30, with TV s/35; doubles s/25, with bath s/35; triples s/30, with bath s/50, with TV s/55. Extra beds s/10.) Those searching for true budget accommodations should head to **Hospedaje Central ❶,** on the south side of the Plaza de Armas, where beds in bland but clean rooms are the only option. (☎71 1249. Doubles s/10, with private bath s/15.) Get cheap eats (s/2-4) at the **outdoor market ❶** on Luís Ormeño, across the street from the Repsol gas station. (Open daily 6am-8:30pm.) For something a little nicer, **El Tío Sam ❷,** Huarmey 138, serves

ARCHAEOLOGIST FOR A DAY

Savvy travelers who want to escape the tourist circuit can check out **Renato Tours**. For US$10 per hr., Sandro Renato Córdoba reveals recently-discovered archaeological sites unknown even to many locals. Start the day off in Sechín, then speed away in a mototaxi to **Sechín Alto**. Broken ceramic pieces are everywhere—also look for the cone-shaped adobe bricks and stone walls. The **Lineas de las Pampa Colonada** are a northern version of the Nasca lines. About 45min. away is the expansive **Pampa de Llamas**, where Chimú travelers would exchange their tired llamas for fresh ones on their way north. Cotton, avocado, asparagus, and mango fields flank the road to the next **temple**, which is not for the faint of heart—the site was pillaged by graverobbers who, in a frenzy to find whole ceramics, left human bones scattered everywhere. The next stop, the huge city of **El Purgatorio**, was discovered in the last decade—you may see archaeologists at work here. Finally, a long walk through the *sierra* leads to the thirteen towers of **Tambo Incaico**, which represent the lunar calendar—ask Renato to show you the wooden roof that (incredibly) still stands. More impressive are the wide views of the entire **San Rafael Valley**.

Sr. Renato is in Casma at Nepeña 370 (☎71 2528; renatars@yahoo.com).

up generous portions of *comida típica* in a garage-like building covered with pictures from the Sechín ruins. (☎71 1447. Entrees s/6-17. Open daily 7am-10pm.)

◙ **SIGHTS.** Dating back 3500 years, the **Sechín ruins** are vitally important to archaeologists researching the region's ancient cultures. The two main buildings, one made of adobe and the other of stone, are connected to the rest of the complex by a series of passageways lined with over 300 carvings of half-naked warriors engaged in battle—one of the most fascinating and gruesome is the dismembered man whose spilled intestines continue onto another stone. The **Museo Mex Uhle,** at the ruins, has aerial photos of the ruins and a reconstruction of the front steps of the palace, as well as actual footprints of ancient Peruvians found at the site. Guides (s/8, Spanish only) are also available at the museum. To get to the ruins, take a mototaxi (s/2-3) and ask the driver to wait or return to pick you up. (Museum open daily 8am-6pm. s/5.)

The less frequented **Chanquillo ruins** consist of three enormous concentric oval walls built on a hilltop overlooking the Río Sechín. Their purpose remains enigmatic, but some archaeologists hypothesize that the geometric figures are related to astronomy. From the gas station at the edge of town, take a combi headed to San Rafael and ask to be let off "frente al castillo" (40min., s/2). From there, walk 1hr. to the ruins. Don't go alone since the place is often deserted.

Twenty years ago, wealthy vacationers from Lima and Chimbote adopted **Tortugas,** a fishing hamlet 20km north of town, as a getaway from the urban frenzy. Today, the area still claims a clean beach with plenty of swimming, water sports, fishing, and yachting from December to March. For most budget travelers, resort-level prices preclude stays of longer than a day. Tortugas-bound colectivos (20min., 4am-8pm, s/2) leave from Mejía, just off the Plaza, past the intersection with Nepeña.

CHIMBOTE   ☎044

The largest city between Lima and Trujillo, Chimbote (pop. 250,000) is admittedly more of an industrial center and transportation hub than a tourist mecca. Roughly 80% of the city is employed in fishing and related industries. Not only are there few sights, but a fishy odor permeates the air—so it is best visited only on the way to other more hospitable destinations.

E TRANSPORTATION. Most buses enter and depart from the new terminal, 8km south of the center on **Meiggs** (taxi s/4-5). **America Express** (☎35 3468; open daily 6am-midnight) runs buses to Trujillo (2hr., every 20min., s/6). **Ormeño** (☎35 3515; open daily 8:30am-1am) sends buses to: Chiclayo (5½hr., 12:30am, s/20); Lima (6hr.; 12:30am, 2:30pm; s/20); Piura (8hr., 12:30am, s/25); Tumbes (13hr., 8:30pm, s/50). **Linea** (☎35 4004; open daily 7am-11:15pm) goes to: Cajamarca (8hr.; 7:30am, 7:30pm; s/25); Chiclayo (7hr.; 9am, 3pm; s/16) via Trujillo (2hr., 6 per day, s/5); Lima (7hr., 11pm, s/20). **Transportes Yungay Express** (☎35 3642; open daily 6am-9:15pm) runs to Caraz (8hr., 9pm, s/20) via Huaraz (4hr., s/20). **Micros** (s/2) and **colectivos** (s/3-5) to Casma (50min.) leave from the intersection of Pardo and Tumbes, five blocks from the Plaza. **Taxis** within the city should cost s/3-4.

■⑦ ORIENTATION AND PRACTICAL INFORMATION. Chimbote's main street is **Victor Haya de la Torre** (also called **José Pardo**), two blocks from the water and parallel to the shore. The **Plaza de Armas** lies between Pardo and **Leonicio Prado** on the east and west sides, and **Enrique Palacios** and **Villavicencio** on the north and south sides. **Banco Wiese Sudameris**, Bolognesi 518, accepts AmEx traveler's checks, and has an MC/V **ATM**. (☎32 8880. Open M-F 9am-1pm and 4:40-6:45pm, Sa 9:30am-12:30pm.) Change money on Bolognesi and Pardo. Helpful city **maps** can be found at **Librería Minerva**, Manuel Ruíz 599, two blocks up Villavicencio and two blocks to the right. (☎32 5302. Open daily 9am-1:30pm and 4-9pm.) The **police** are at Prado 400 (☎32 1651), at Enrique Palacios on the Plaza. **Hospital "La Caleta"** sits on Malecón Grau. (☎32 3631. Open M-F 8am-1pm and 2-6pm, Sa 8am-1pm.) Call home from the **telephone office**, Pardo 420, on the Plaza. (☎32 8872. Open daily 9am-10pm.) **Internet** is at **Fun Planet Internet**, Enrique Palacios 505. (☎32 5922. s/1 per hr. Open daily 8:30am-1am.) **Serpost**, Enrique Palacios 441, is just off the Plaza de Armas. (☎32 3943. Open M-F 8am-1pm and 4-8pm, Sa 8am-1pm.)

⑥🖸 ACCOMMODATIONS AND FOOD. Hostal Chimbote ❶ Pardo 205, is one of the oldest hostels in town, and has a friendly staff and rooms with modern amenities or just the basics. Small windows offer little relief on warm nights. (☎34 4721. Singles s/12, with bath and TV s/20; doubles s/25, with bath and TV s/30; triples s/25.) **Hostal César's ❷**, Espinar 286, has furnished rooms with towels, shower curtains, baths and optional TV. (☎32 4946. Singles s/20; matrimonials s/25; doubles s/35; triples s/45.) For a night of luxury, stay at **Hotel Chifa Canton ❺**, Villavicecio 197. Each room includes a bathroom, cable TV, and a stocked minifridge. Fax service, laundry service, billiards, and ping pong are available. Ask for a room with an ocean view. (☎34 4388. Singles s/85; doubles s/110; triples s/129; suites s/155.)

In Chimbote, you're smelling fish all day, so you might as well eat some too. **Punta Sal ❷**, Villavicencio 104, serves some of the freshest and tastiest *ceviche* in town in a cheerful beach hut, appropriately located right near the harbor. (☎34 1556. Entrees s/10-20. *Ceviche* s/12-17. Open M-Sa 10am-6pm.) Enjoy some cheap eats at the **Mercado Central**, Manuel Ruíz between Espinar and Prado. (s/1-5. Open daily 8am-10pm.) With private wooden booths and authentic Chinese lanterns, **Chifa Canton ❷**, Bolognesi 498, is the most elegant restaurant in town, even if the food isn't incredible. (☎34 4388. Entrees s/10-24. Dine-in or take-out. Open M-F and Su noon-3pm and 6-11pm, Sa 11am-3pm and 6:30pm-midnight. **Restaurante Vegetariano Nuevo Era ❷**, at the corner of Pardo and Villavicencio, serves up a wide assortment of juices and dishes in a simple locale. (Juices s/2-4. Entrees s/6-12. Open daily 9am-9pm.)

SIGHTS. Most of Chimbote's sights lie outside of town. **Isla Blanca,** part of the Fauna Marina ecological reserve, provides opportunities to rock climb, admire marine wildlife, ponder the wind-sculpted stone formations, or simply relax on unspoiled beaches. Isla Blanca is difficult to access unless you are in a large group or with a tour company. **Antonella Tours,** Aguierre 388, of. 4 (☎32 7776), between Pardo and Prado, provides tours to Isla Blanca (s/10, min. 15-20 people) as well as to ruins in the Nepeña Valley, including Pañamarca (s/15, min. 15-20 people). Those wishing to stay on the mainland can relax at **El Buleuer "Isla Blanca,"** a pleasant walkway on the first block of Pardo with dolphin statues and colorful fountains, most beautiful at night.

For a break from the bleak *sierra* and constant monotony of Chimbote's modern buildings, a taxi from the Plaza de Armas (s/2-3) can take you to **El Vivero Forestal,** a virtual oasis and the town's equivalent of Central Park. Take a relaxing boat ride in the manmade lagoon (s/1) or a train ride all around the park (s/2). Perhaps the most interesting attraction is the Lancha Museo San Pedrito, a Chimbote fishing vessel open to the public. (Open Tu-Su 9am-6pm. Free.) For more adventure, find a taxi (30min., s/20-25) to ascend the nearby mountain, **Cerro de la Juventud.** Near the summit, the recently constructed **Santuaria Señor de la Vida,** an impressive church built into the mountainside, offers incredible views. You can reach the crypts beneath the sanctuary by walking 15m through a dark tunnel dug into the mountain. Residing there is a damaged statue, left in disrepair to symbolize terrorism's effects on Peru. From the church, it's a 30min. climb to the summit and the **Cruz de la Paz,** which affords even more spectacular views on clear days. To return, walk down the road to the highway (1hr.) and flag down a passing bus or taxi. Hiking from Chimbote to the church is not recommended without a guide, as the road is unmarked, and a wrong turn could quickly get you lost.

TRUJILLO ☎044

In Trujillo (pop. 690,000), the virtues of a sprawling metropolis sparkle without the vices: the pedestrian-filled plazas are safer, the streets less disorienting, and the scope less overwhelming. Colonial *casas antiguas* abound—much more charming than those in Lima Centro. But Trujillo, founded in 1534 by conquistador Diego de Almagro and named for the birthplace of Francisco Pizarro, was populated long before the arrival of the Spanish. The Mochica, Chimú, and Inca civilizations all inhabited these regions at one time or another. Remnants of their past splendor shine at archaeological sites like Huacas del Sol y de la Luna, El Brujo, and the enormous mud-brick city of Chan Chan.

TRANSPORTATION

Flights: Aeropuerto Carlos Martínez de Pinillos (☎46 4013; open daily 7am-9pm), 20min. from town. Taxi s/10 (from Huanchaco s/5). **Nuevo Continente,** Pizarro 470 (☎24 4042; open daily 9am-1pm and 3-6pm), flies to **Lima** (1hr.; daily 10:40am, 5:30pm, 8:40pm; US$64) and **Piura** (40min., daily 8:30am, US$34). **Lan Peru** (☎20 1859) flies to **Lima** (2hr., daily 6:25pm, US$73) via **Chiclayo** (30min., US$42). Prices and times change frequently. **Consorcio Turístico Del Norte,** Pizarro 478 (☎20 0412 or 26 2402; www.contunor.com.pe; open M-Sa 9am-8pm), on the Plaza de Armas, offers help finding flights out of Trujillo.

Buses: The majority of companies serving Lima and Tumbes have terminals around Ejército and Amazonas, north of the town center. **Continental/Ormeño,** Ejército 233 (☎25 9782; open daily 7am-11pm), goes to **Lima** (8hr.; 9am, 10pm; s/20) and **Tumbes** (11hr., 10:15pm, s/50). **CIVA,** Ejército 288 (☎25 1402; open daily 8am-10pm) runs

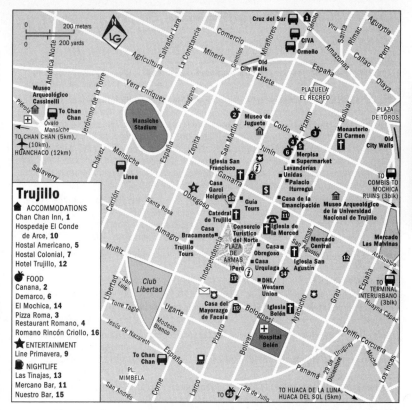

Trujillo

🏠 ACCOMMODATIONS
Chan Chan Inn, 1
Hospedaje El Conde
de Arce, 10
Hostal Americano, 5
Hostal Colonial, 7
Hotel Trujillo, 12

🍴 FOOD
Canana, 2
Demarco, 6
El Mochica, 14
Pizza Roma, 3
Restaurant Romano, 4
Romano Rincón Criollo, 16

⭐ ENTERTAINMENT
Line Primavera, 9

🌙 NIGHTLIFE
Las Tinajas, 13
Mercano Bar, 11
Nuestro Bar, 15

to **Lima** (8hr., daily 10:30pm, s/35) and **Tumbes** (11hr., daily 10:30pm, s/30) via **Piura** (5hr., s/20). **Cruz del Sur,** Amazonas 437 (☎26 1801; open 8am-noon and 1pm-8pm) travels to **Lima** (8hr., daily 9:45pm, s/30). **Linea,** Carrión 140 (☎23 5847; open daily 5am-10pm), serves **Chiclayo** (3hr., every hr. 6am-7pm, s/12). All other buses leave from the terminal at América Sur 2587 (☎29 7000; open daily 4am-11pm), southeast of town, to: **Cajamarca** (6hr.; 10:30am, 10, 10:30pm; s/18-30); **Chimbote** (2hr., 6 per day, s/5); **Huaraz** (8hr., 9pm, s/30); **Lima** (8hr., 5 per day, s/25-40; *bus cama* 10pm, s/50); **Piura** (6-7hr., 11pm, s/20).

Taxis: Within town s/2-3. To Huanchaco s/8. Prices go up after 11pm.

Car Rental: Casino Real Hotel, Pizarro 651 (☎25 7416), rents Daewoo cars (US$60 per day) and Toyota 4x4s (US$80 per day plus 18% tax). 150km per day, US$0.45 per extra km. Open 24hr.

🔧🛈 ORIENTATION AND PRACTICAL INFORMATION

Most plazas, hotels, restaurants, and colonial houses are enclosed in the **Old Town** by the circular **España,** which lies roughly in the location of the wall that encircled the town in colonial times. Remnants of the wall stand between the 11th and 17th blocks. At the center of the Old Town lies the busy **Plaza de Armas.** Crowds dodging taxis roam the shops and restaurants along **Pizarro,** between the Plaza and the **Plazuela El Recreo.** The main street out of the center, **Obregoso,** becomes **Mansiche** when it crosses España, and leads to the **Óvalo Mansiche,** where colectivos gather.

Tourist Office: iPerú, Pizarro 402 (☎29 4561; open M-F 8am-7pm, Sa 8am-2pm) has city maps and brochures. **Cámara Regional de Turismo,** Independencia 630, offers information on Trujillo's cultural history. Open M-F 9am-1pm and 4-8pm, Sa 9am-1pm.

Tours: Several companies offer tour packages for Trujillo's archaeological sights. All prices can be negotiated depending on group size and season. **Guía Tours,** Independencia 580 (☎24 5170; guiatour@amauta.rcp.net.pe), provides information-packed tours of Chan Chan (s/40), Huacas del Sol y de la Luna (s/35), El Brujo (s/60), and Trujillo itself (s/25) in English or Spanish. Independent travelers might have difficulty getting a tour if no group has bought a package. Grab some friends from your hostel and ask for legendary guide Pedro Puerta or his student Rubens Llacza. Open M-F 9am-1:30pm and 4-8:30pm, Sa 9am-noon. Tours depart at 9:30am and 2:30pm.

Bank: Interbank, Gamarra 463 (☎25 6725), 1 block up Pizarro from the Plaza. Exchanges AmEx/Citicorp/MC/V traveler's checks. AmEx/MC/V **ATM.** Open M-F 9am-6:15pm, Sa 9am-12:30pm. The **money changers** congregating on the Plaza have better exchange rates, but they also circulate high volumes of counterfeit currency.

Laundromat: Lavanderías Unidas, Pizarro 683 (☎20 0505). s/6 per kg, same-day service s/8 per kg. Open M-Sa 9am-2pm and 4-8:30pm.

Emergency: ☎105.

Police: Policía Nacional del Perú, Bolognesi 428 (☎22 2034) is the local police station. Open daily 8am-8pm. **Tourist police,** Independencia 630 (☎29 1705), provide tourist information when nearby offices close during the long lunch breaks. Open 24hr.

Hospital: Hospital Regional Docente, Mansiche 795 (☎23 1581 or 23 3102), at the corner of Roma, just past the Óvalo Mansiche, open 24hr. for emergencies. 24hr. **pharmacy. Hospital Belén,** Bolívar 350 (☎24 5281), fills the entire block at Bolognesi and Bolívar. Open M-Sa 8am-2pm, open 24hr. for emergencies. 24hr. **pharmacy.**

Telephones: Cabinas Públicas Pizarro, Pizarro 561 (☎23 1287). Accepts calling cards, but not collect calls. Open M-Sa 8am-10pm, Su 8am-2pm.

Internet: Nautilus, Pizarro 113. s/1.50 per hr. Sony PlayStation s/1 per hr. Open daily 8am-midnight.

Post Office: Serpost, Independencia 286 (☎24 5941), at Bolognesi. Open M-Sa 8am-8pm. **DHL/Western Union,** Almagro 579 (☎20 3689). Open M-F 9am-1pm and 4-8pm, Sa 9am-1pm.

■ ACCOMMODATIONS

Trujillo presents a bevy of accommodations for travelers. Places close to the Plaza are more secure and convenient but tend to be noisier and more expensive than outlying hostels. The best budget accommodations are in the nearby beach town of **Huanchaco** (p. 322). Even visitors more interested in sightseeing than sun bathing should consider staying there, as it's only a 20min. colectivo ride (s/1) from the city. Those who splurge and stay in Trujillo will find a good range of hostels close to more restaurants and will get a better sense of life in a dynamic and lively regional capital—you won't be disappointed either way.

Hospedaje El Conde de Arce, Independencia 577 (☎93 9258). Run by the descendants of the writer El Conde de Arce, this intimate *hospedaje* is an oasis of tranquility amid the bustle of Trujillo's center. Enjoy the courtyard, or rest in the enormous—and very tidy—rooms, for just a fraction of the cost of neighboring establishments. Kitchen use included. TV s/5, with VCR s/8. Laundry service (s/3 per kg). Singles s/15; matrimonials and doubles s/25; quads s/35. ❷

Hostal Colonial, Independencia 618 (☎25 8261; hostcolonialtruji@hotmail.com). Bright, clean rooms with Chan Chan-inspired designs and baths, TVs, and warm water. The incredibly personable César Arteaga leads a devoted staff. Colonial will go the extra mile to make sure guests get the best of everything in Trujillo, on or off their grounds, which include a cozy garden surrounding a seahorse sculpture. Singles s/45; doubles and matrimonials s/65; triples s/85. Low-season prices negotiable. ❹

Chan Chan Inn, Ejército 307 (☎29 4281 or 58 1565; mocheperu@hotmail.com), next to the Ormeño and CIVA bus stations. Bright orange walls enclose simple rooms right out of the 80s at this slightly remote spot. Owner Dante Voillus speaks English and French and can help arrange tours of the city's sights. The adjoining restaurant serves breakfast and lunch (s/3-6). Singles with shared bath s/20, with hot private bath, cable TV s/35; doubles with shared bath s/30, with hot private bath, cable TV s/50. ISIC discount s/5. ❸

Hotel Trujillo, Grau 581 (☎24 3921; fax 24 4241). This hotel's unintentional retro decor and the neon color combinations set the rooms aglow. Baths have hot water during specific hours: 6-9am and 4-6:30pm. Singles s/22; doubles s/35, with TV s/40; matrimonials with TV s/39; triples s/45. ❷

Hostal Americano, Pizarro 764 (☎24 1361). Americano's high ceilings, wall reliefs, hardwood floors, and antique furniture coax visitors to stay in one of its 150 rooms. Request a room with a balcony, as they are brighter than some of the rooms away from the street. Check-out 2pm. Hot water s/10. Singles s/16-20, with bath and hot water s/30; doubles s/26-30, with bath s/40. ❷

▌ FOOD

Trujillo presents great opportunities for culinary tourism. To sample the selection of upscale international cafes, with a wide range of vegetarian options, take a stroll along the seventh block of Pizarro. If you'd like to try local dishes such as *cabrito de leche* (goat cooked in milk), *arroz con pato* (rice with duck), or *shambar* (a wheat soup with beans and pork), head to the inexpensive restaurants lining Plazuela El Recreo at the end of Pizarro. The **Merpisa supermarket** at Pizarro 700 offers sustenance if your money belt is especially light. (☎25 7301. Open M-Sa 9:15am-1:15pm and 4:30-9pm, Su 9:15am-1:15pm.)

▨ Pizza Roma (☎20 6441), at the corner of Pizarro and Colón, has the tastiest pizza in town (large pie s/12-20). Grab a beer (s/3) and relax while watching Italian chef Cleto Leonardi work in the open kitchen or order to go. *Calzones* (s/14) are a specialty. Entrees s/8.5-13. Open M, W-Su 6-11pm, later on weekends. ❷

El Mochica, Bolívar 462 (☎29 3441). Locals flock to this joint to enjoy a wide range of *criollo* dishes. Take home more than just leftover *cuy* by purchasing the wall-art. Entrees s/10-22. Open daily noon-midnight. AmEx/MC/V. Or, for a quick bite, head to the adjoining **Salón de Té** (☎29 3440) for delectable sandwiches (s/3-4) and tea (s/1-3). Open daily 8am-noon and 5pm-9:30pm. ❷

Romano Rincón Criollo, Los Estados Unidos 162 (☎24 4207). Nestled in a nice residential area, this is where Trujillans go for the most important meal of the day: *el almuerzo* (lunch). With several traditional favorites, it may be hard to choose, but the *tacu tacu* (rice and beans) in a rich shrimp sauce stands out, and is enough for 2 (s/22). Budget travelers will appreciate the *menús* (s/10-13). Entrees s/14-35. Drinks s/2-13. Open daily 11:30am-5pm. MC/V. ❸

Demarco, Pizarro 725 (☎23 4251), tempts travelers and locals alike with its extensive menu in 5 different languages and its gorgeous desserts (s/4-9) perched in the window—the *suspiro a la limeña* (a *criollo* merengue) is exceptional (s/4.50). Entrees s/9-25. Wine s/10-35. Open daily 8am-11pm. AmEx/DC/MC/V. ❸

Restaurant Romano, Pizarro 747 (☎25 2251). The enormous menu explains why this small cafe fills up for lunch and dinner. Try the *chipe de camerones* (s/15) for a light yet delicious meal. A great selection of desserts (s/2-5) and some of Trujillo's best coffee (s/2-4). Entrees s/9-22. Open daily 8am-midnight. AmEx/DC/MC/V. ❸

Canana, San Martín 791 (☎29 5422). For tasty *comida criolla* (entrees s/15-30, salads s/7-8), traditional Peruvian dance, and *una jarra de cerveza* (a pitcher of beer; s/15), Canana is the place to go. Anyone can bust a move with Trujillo's best in the spectacular stage-and-dance area. Amazing variety of mixed drinks s/7-15. Traditional music F-Sa after 11pm. Cover s/10. Open Tu-Sa 6pm-5am. ❸

👁 SIGHTS

IN THE CITY CENTER

CHURCHES. Intricate artwork and fancy facades are the hallmark of Trujillo's churches and cathedrals. The **Basílica Menor** of the **Catedral de Trujillo,** on the corner of the Plaza de Armas, was built in the mid-17th century and remains the most important religious building in town. *(Visitors can enter nightly 5-8pm.)* The attached **Museo Catedralicio** has 1hr. guided tours that show you the exquisite wooden roofs, a cross with the relics of 32 different saints, and a statue of San Valentín that survived a 17th century earthquake. Creepy organ music plays as you descend to **crypts;** it complements the cheerful series of paintings depicting decapitated heads. *(Open M-F 9am-1pm and 4-7pm, Sa 9am-1pm; s/4.)* The gilded interior of the **Monasterio El Carmen,** Colón 609 at Bolívar, is breathtaking. Next door, **Pinacoteca Carmelita** houses religious paintings from the colonial era. *(Open M-Sa 9am-1pm. s/3.)* Many smaller churches around the center can be quickly visited. **Iglesia de la Merced,** Pizarro 550 was rebuilt after the 1619 earthquake, and has a typical baroque facade and 17th century colonial paintings on the side naves. *(Open M-Su 8-noon and 4-8pm.)* The gardens are also worth a look. The **Iglesia San Francisco,** on the corner of Independencia and Gamarra, has a story that is more interesting than its Baroque interior. It was here that San Francisco Solano predicted the 1619 earthquake that destroyed most of Trujillo. *(Open M-Su 8am-noon and 4-8pm.)* **Iglesia Belén,** on the corner of Ayacucho and Almergo, built from adobe and brick, boasts a 17th-century interior in the Trujillo style. *(No set hours.)*

CASAS ANTIGUAS. A number of beautiful colonial houses are scattered throughout Old Trujillo. Perhaps the most impressive, **Palacio Iturregui,** Pizarro 688, has been converted into a private club, but visitors are welcome in the art gallery. **Casa Bracamonte**—the oldest and most ornate house—now holds the administrative offices of Es Salud, a state health agency. Its picturesque gardens and intricate woodwork suit the decorative facade. *(Independencia 441. Open M-F 8am-3pm. Visits may be restricted without notice. Free.)* Trujillo's independence was declared in 1820 in the **Casa de la Emancipación,** Pizarro 610. Today it houses rotating exhibits of local artists and has a resplendent garden in back. *(Open M-F 9:15am-12:30pm and 4-6:30pm.)* The **Casa del Mariscol de Obregoso,** Obregoso 553, has an ornate interior typical of the viceroyal style, with both rotating exhibits and a permanent display of colonial furniture and silver. *(Open M-Su 9:30am-8pm.)* **Casa Calogne (Casa Urquiaga),** Pizarro 446, displays Republican relics such as the writing desk of former resident Simón Bolívar, and is an elegant neoclassical house. *(Open daily 9:30am-3pm.)* Find an extensive coin collection at the **Casa del Mayorazgo de Facala,** whose

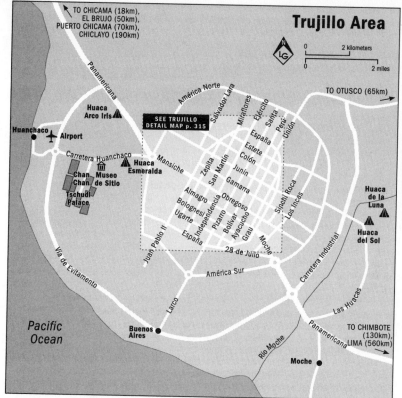

Trujillo Area

TO CHICAMA (18km),
EL BRUJO (50km),
PUERTO CHICAMA (70km),
CHICLAYO (190km)

TO OTUSCO (65km)

Panamericana

Huanchaco

Airport

Huaca
Arco Iris

SEE TRUJILLO
DETAIL MAP p. 315

América Norte

Salvador Lara

Miraflores

Ejército

Santa

Perú

Unión

España

Estete

Colón

Junín

Carretera Huanchaco

Huaca
Esmeralda

Mansiche

Zepita

San Martín

Gamarra

Chan
Chan

Museo
de Sitio

Almagro

Obregoso

Sinchi Roca

Los Incas

Tschudi
Palace

Bolognesi

Independencia

Pizarro

Bolívar

Ayacucho

Huaca
de la
Luna

Ugarte

Grau

Moche

España

Huaca
del Sol

Juan Pablo II

28 de Julio

Vía de Evitamento

América Sur

Carretera Industrial

Larco

Pacific
Ocean

Buenos
Aires

Rio Moche

Las Huacas

Panamericana

TO CHIMBOTE
(130km),
LIMA (560km)

Moche

NORTHERN COAST

exterior corner balcony is quite impressive. *(Open M-F 9:15am-12:30pm and 4-6:30pm, Sa 9:30am-noon.)* **Casa Garci Holguín,** Independencia 527, across from the cathedral, was recently restored. Plaques on the walls and an informational pamphlet (at the first cubicle on the left after you enter the offices across the courtyard) detail the house's turbulent history. *(Information desk open M-F 8:45am-12:45pm and 4:15-6:30pm.)* In general, the easiest *casas* to visit are those now occupied by banks, which are free and open to the public during business hours.

MUSEUMS. There are two archaeological museums in town worth visiting. **Museo Arqueológico de la Universidad Nacional de Trujillo,** Junín 682, at Ayacucho, has a varied collection of pre-Columbian artifacts displayed in chronological order, including a detailed exhibit on the restoration of Huaca de la Luna (p. 320), with informative displays in Spanish. *(☎ 24 9322. Open M-F 9:25am-2:30pm and Sa-Su 9:30-11:30am. s/5, students s/1.)* **Museo Arqueológico Cassinelli,** Piérola 601, behind the Mobil station, has a collection of over 2000 ceramic pieces spanning 2500 years, from the Paleolithic Age to the arrival of the Spanish. Relics from every culture that has occupied the area share space on the display room's cramped shelves. The fact that such a collection exists essentially in the basement of a gas station is mind-boggling. Ask the attendant for a description of the artifacts, some of which were unearthed by archaeologists and some by grave robbers. *(Open M-Sa 9:30am-1pm and 3-7pm, Su 9:30am-1pm and 3:30-6:30pm. s/5.)* For a break from ceramics, visit the offbeat **Museo de Jugete,** Independencia 705, which has a two-room collection of antique toys, including a few life-sized dolls and rocking horses. *(Open M-F 10am-6pm, Sa 10am-7pm. s/3, children s/1.)*

OUTSIDE THE CITY CENTER

The archaeological sites around Trujillo trace the rise and fall of two of the most important pre-Hispanic cultures on the northern coast: the **Mochica** (Moche) and the **Chimú.** While the Huaca Prieta and Cupisnique cultures lived in the Trujillo area some 3000 years ago, the first civilization to leave a significant mark was the militaristic Mochica culture, which extended its empire as far as modern-day Piura to the north and Chimbote to the south (100 BC-AD 800). The Mochica built the first major temples in the area, but they are most often noted for their artistic achievements in metalwork, weaving, ceramics, and pottery. After the Mochica's decline (AD 600-700), the burgeoning Chimú culture established itself in the Moche and Chicama Valleys, and by 1400 had expanded its territory from modern-day Tumbes to Lima. A confederation of dynastic families with their central capital at **Chan Chan** (below), the Chimú Empire was sacked and conquered by the Incas around 1460, 80 years before the Spanish arrived.

Several travel agencies in Trujillo offer **tours** (see **Tours,** p. 316), but guides can also be hired at the sites themselves for a fraction of the agency price (Chan Chan s/15-20, Huacas Arco Iris and Esmeralda s/6-8). Remember, however, that the quality of the visit (particularly to Huacas del Sol y Luna) varies with the quality of the guide. The ticket price at the Huacas del Sol y Luna includes the guided visit, while the ticket to see Chan Chan includes visits to Huacas Arco Iris and Esmeralda, and has a 2-day expiration date.

■ **HUACA DEL SOL Y HUACA DE LA LUNA.** Despite losing out to the Chimú, judging by their ruins, the Moche outshone their conquerors. Just 5km southeast of Trujillo, at the foot of Cerro Blanco, lie the mud-brick remains of the ceremonial capital of the Moche State. The site is defined by two massive structures, **Huaca del Sol** and **Huaca de la Luna,** which were once separated by the homes of the city's 15,000 nobles. Suburbs that housed 20,000 commoners fanned out from this central strip. Following the Moche's collapse, the area was used as an elite cemetery by later civilizations. The Huaca del Sol was partially destroyed by the Spanish, and has been eroding naturally over the past decades. One of the biggest temples of the era, it has yet to be fully excavated and thus is not open to the public—though one can only imagine what lies beneath this behemoth. To the west, the 30m high Huaca de la Luna was a burial ground for monarchs and is now the site's main attraction. The standard building technique, whereby each monarch's tomb was filled with adobe bricks, providing a foundation for the following ruler, has preserved the polychrome tomb decorations remarkably well. Of particular importance is the repeated presentation of anthropomorphic god **Aie-Paec,** known as the Decapitator, which appears frequently on the pottery and frescoes of other sites. Also look for the bricks that have the markings of clans that paid taxes by making a certain number of bricks. *(The temples are a 30min. combi ride (s/1) from the corner of Suárez and Los Incas in Trujillo, or a 20min. taxi ride (s/10). Guided tours are free with ticket. English/Spanish guidebooks s/10. Open daily 9am-4pm. s/5.)*

CHAN CHAN. Touted as the largest preserved **mud-brick city** in the world, Chan Chan was once the glorious capital city of the **Chimú Empire,** which extended 1000km along the coast from Tumbes to Lima. Today, visitors can explore the winding passages and interpret the symbolic carvings of the L-shaped **Tschudi Palace.** Informational signs in Spanish and in English make this palace highly navigable without a guide, so save your soles and just follow the fish-shaped arrows. Once you enter the main plaza of the complex, clap your hands and note the acoustics. The entire mud metropolis consists of 14 citadels, nine of which are believed to have been palaces of individual rulers. Following their deaths and a week-long funeral ceremony, rulers were elaborately interred in their respective royal underground residences—along with their wealth and some sacrificed subjects. Excavations have also turned up administrative, storage, metalworking, and residential sectors in the palaces, as well as an elaborate reservoir system that today is home to a few plants and *totora* reeds. Although Tschudi is definitely the main attraction for Chimú fans, other, smaller structures merit a visit and are accessible by combi and taxi. One-thousand-year-old **Huaca Arco Iris** (also referred to as "El Dragón") is named after the intricate depictions of rainbows and dragons that line the two-story structure. Many archaeologists believe that this was a ceremonial site devoted to the Arco Iris and fertility. The smaller **Huaca Esmeralda**, once an important temple, has detailed fish imagery in its friezes.

The Chan Chan admission fee includes access to these three sites and the small **Museo de Sitio de Chan Chan.** The museum highlights the advanced technology achieved by the Chimú and features a show explaining Chimú culture every 30min. Tickets for these shows are available at Chan Chan or the museum. The Spanish displays provide a history of the pre-Inca culture, while mannequins show the distinct facial features of these ancient people. A large ceramic, metal, and tools collection warrants a quick look. The ticket for all sites has a two-day expiration. *(From España and Independencia, or the Óvalo Mansiche, take a bus to Huanchaco (15min., s/ 1; taxi s/8). From there, either walk 1.5km to Chan Chan or take a taxi (s/3). To visit Huaca Esmeralda, take a cab from Chan Chan (10min., s/10) to the site or go back to the museum and flag down a passing bus (10min., s/1). Get off at the Iglesia de Mansiche and, facing it, take the road on the right up 3 blocks; turn right and go 1 more block. To continue to Arco Iris, hop on a combi back to the Óvalo Mansiche or the northern part of España. From there take a taxi (s/5) or a bus (s/1) to Esperanza. The Arco Iris area has an unsavory reputation—better to take a taxi and have your driver wait. Sites and museum open daily 9am-5pm. s/10, with ISIC s/5.)*

🎵 🎭 ENTERTAINMENT AND NIGHTLIFE

With the exception of Thursdays (which sees traditional music and dancing all over town in the different *peñas*), Trujillo's weekday nightlife is fairly quiet. On weekends, however, the city begins to show vital signs as Trujillans cut loose. For more sedate entertainment, check out one of the many movie theaters. The first-rate **Line Primavera,** Obregoso 239, has six screens that show English-language films with Spanish subtitles. (☎24 1277. Screenings M-Th s/5, F-Sa s/7.)

Mercano Bar, Gamarra 571, is one of the better options in town to enjoy a beer (s/4) or groove the night away. With a huge movie screen that shows music videos, live bands, a huge (and expensive) bar, and plenty of tables and floor space, the centrally located Mercano has it all. Drinks s/9-12, Th 2 for 1. Cover Sa s/15. Open Th-Sa 9pm-6am.

Nuestro Bar, Bolognesi 502 (☎960 0444 or 21 1620; nuestrobar@terra.com.pe). Grab a beer (s/5; pitcher s/5) or a mixed drink (s/8-15) and chill to alternative tunes in this relaxing bi-level bar. Open daily 7pm-late. AmEx/MC/V.

Las Tinajas, Pizarro 383-389 (☎29 6272), on the Plaza de Armas. Another chic upstairs-downstairs combo, housing a video pub, an eclectic mix of Baroque art, and an underground disco. Pitcher of beer s/15. Cocktails s/8-10. Cover for disco s/5. Pub open daily 8:30pm-3am; disco open Sa 9pm-4am.

🎭 DAYTRIP FROM TRUJILLO: EL BRUJO

Getting to El Brujo can be tricky without private transportation or a guided tour (s/50-70). Take a bus to Chocope (1hr., s/3) from the Terminal Interurbano (take Gamarra south, cross España, walk 2 blocks to Los Incas, and take the first left on Santa Cruz; it's on the right). From Chocope, take a combi to Magdalena de Cao (20min., s/1.3) then a mototaxi to the ruins (20min., s/3) or catch a taxi (25min., s/25) straight to the site. No guides, but the security guard will show you around. Spanish/English guidebooks s/20. A good choice on a Su, when most other places are closed. Open daily 8am-6pm. s/10.

Named after the witches of Chicama who use the surrounding area for their rituals—zealous travelers can see them every Friday night, but it is recommended that you go with a guide—"El Brujo" (the sorcerer) is a series of ruins and mounds dating back over 5000 years. Sixty kilometers from Trujillo in the Chicama Valley, this remote site remained relatively untouched by the grave-robbers and tourists who defaced many of the ruins closer to Trujillo. The scattered pieces of ceramics and human remains, however, suggest that some looters have indeed made it here in recent years. "El Brujo's" three pyramidal temples—**Huaca Prieta, Huaca Corta,** and **Huaca Cao Viejo**—are its main attraction, and Cao Viejo, consistently open to visitors, is the most impressive of the three. Inside, multicolored reliefs display scenes from Mochica, life such as prisoners, warriors, dancers, and human sacrifices. These impressive murals still retain much of their original colors. Don't miss the cross-section on the west side showing the temple's seven layers. Well-preserved human remains reveal the burial practices of the Mochica royalty. Servants and guards had their feet cut off and were placed in the burial vault with the corpse.

HUANCHACO   ☎ 044

Tourists passing through Trujillo frequently venture north to spend a few relaxing days in this serene beach town. Once a party hotspot, the Huanchaco of today only gets busy during high season (Jan.-Mar.) or when Trujillans flood its shores on weekends. A clean beach, good-sized waves (beware of sea urchins Jan.-Mar.), a bustling artisan market, magnificent seafood, and ample tourist facilities make Huanchaco the perfect place to spend a little time taking a break from all the ancient sights. You can still get a glimpse of Peru's more recent past here since it's one of the few places that uses *caballitos de totora* (fishing boats made from *totora* reeds). If you'd like to try this alternative method of "riding the waves," just approach any of the fishermen near the pier (40min. s/10, with instruction s/15).

Huanchaco doesn't suffer from a shortage of excellent accommodations; many of them line the beach. **La Casa Suiza ❷,** Los Pinos 451, two blocks up from the water near the town entrance, offers more options than a Swiss army knife: 24hr. hot water, a book exchange, laundry service, Internet access (s/2 per hr.), garage, cable TV, free boogie boards, wetsuit and surfboard rentals (s/18), and a rooftop terrace. (☎46 1285; www.casasuiza.com. Dorms s/40; singles s/20, with bath s/22; doubles s/34, with bath s/38.) **Naylamp ❷,** on the third block of the main beach road Victor Larco, (ask for "El Bocerón," which is near the end of the beach to the right when facing the water), has clean, bright rooms that vary in quality according to their age. Amenities include a communal kitchen, laundry, relaxing hammocks, and a dining room. (☎46 1022; naylamp@terra.com.pe. Dorms s/10; singles s/20-30; doubles s/30-45.) Naylamp also offers well-kept, safe **campsites ❶** with a view of the beach (s/6, s/8 with tent rental).

There is no shortage of fresh seafood in Huanchaco. The street along the beach is lined with inexpensive *picanterías*, but if you order a s/5 *ceviche*, you just might get what you pay for. **◼El Pisagua ❷,** Larco 400, may well serve the best *ceviche* (s/12) in Peru. Crowded solely by locals, this honest-to-goodness hole in the wall, should not be missed. (Open daily 10am-6pm.) For a more touristy location with better ocean views, visit **Lucho del Mar ❹,** Larco 600. The delicious *ceviche mixto* (s/20), containing at least five types of seafood, is worth the cost. The *Tiredito de Lenguedo* (s/20) is simply perfect. (Entrees s/18-30. ☎46 1460. Open daily 9am-6:30pm. DC/MC/V.)

All main activity in town is on Victor Larco, which becomes Tacna when you begin to leave town. To get to Huanchaco from Trujillo, take a **combi** from the Shell station at the Óvalo Mansiche (15-20min., s/1). To return, catch one headed back on Victor Larco Rivera. **Taxis** normally cost s/8, but prices skyrocket (s/12-15) after 11pm, when combis stop running.

PUERTO CHICAMA   ☎044

Surfing is Puerto Chicama's *raison d'être*—the beach (also referred to as **Malabrigo**) has one of the longest left-hand waves in the world. Huanchaco's waves may grant more consistency, but Puerto Chicama is the place where surfing legends are made, not to mention where many a world championship is held. Rides of almost 2km are not uncommon, starting at the cliffs on the left and ending at the pier. Mototaxis shuttle eager surfers down the beach when walk-time means less wave-time (s/10-20 per hr.). Bring your own board and wetsuit, as there are few places to rent equipment (though there are more in Huanchaco). At the Hostal El Hombre, you can rent a board for s/15-20. Be prepared for chilly water during winter months (Apr.-Dec.). Puerto Chicama itself is tiny, with little to do and few tourists around when the ocean gods are not smiling, but a walk down the **pier** where workers load barges with sardine fishmeal for export to China can be quite an experience. (Open daily sunrise to sunset. Permission to enter the pier must be granted by the municipality located on the Plaza de Armas, which is open sporadically; ask at the guard booth for information.)

Lodging options in Puerto Chicama have been transformed recently by **Hostal Los Delfines ④,** Lote 1 and 2 Mz. 86, up to the left and over the cliffs when facing the ocean. While a bit pricey, it includes all the amenities imaginable, including a pool with a swim-up bar, a restaurant with walls covered in surfer graffiti, and a spectacular view of the Pacific from the bay windows in each room. (☎65 0008 or 95 73720; losdelfineschicama@hotmail.com. Singles s/50; matrimonials and doubles s/80; triples s/120; suites with jacuzzi s/120. Jet ski rentals s/50 per hr.) **Hostal El Hombre ②,** Arica 803, next door to Los Delfines, was the first hostel in town and continues to be the budget surfer's hang-out. Great views, kitchen use, a relaxed atmosphere, and Alamiro Avanto García—"El Hombre" himself—have drawn surfers here since the 1960s. (☎64 0504 or 960 1027. Dorms s/10; surf equipment s/15-20.) Though it may have some of the most incredible waves this side of the Pacific, Puerto Chicama lacks many restaurants. If you walk down the road perpendicular to the roaring beach, you can find many similar establishments that serve *comida típica* (s/5-10). Bring a small stash of food from Trujillo just in case.

The main street, **Tacna,** is perpendicular to the Pacific, and leads to the accommodations at the end of town. The **Plaza de Armas** is one block up Tacna on **Grau,** where you will find the municipality and not much else. To get to Puerto Chicama, make sure your **bus** is going to Puerto Chicama (not the town of Chicama, 20min. outside of Trujillo). Take a bus from Terminal Interurbano in Trujillo (1½hr., every 30min., s/3; see directions for El Brujo, p. 321), or flag down a red bus (often with a sign saying "Paiján") as it passes the **Óvalo Mansiche.** From Paiján, take another colectivo down to Puerto Chicama (s/1.50-2). If you have a surfboard, take a **taxi** (1hr., s/70) from Huanchaco or Trujillo.

OTUSCO   ☎044

Just 73km from Trujillo, the small town of Otusco (pop. 8000) is home to one of Trujillo's (and Peru's) most important religious items, **La Virgen de la Puerta,** and is a beautiful example of a typical *sierra* town. Don't doze off on the 2hr. journey, or you'll miss some incredible views. Waterfalls, small roadside towns, wildlife, isolated fields, and wide ranges of agriculture provide breathtaking *vistas* of the Chicama Valley. During the winter, the different shades of brown blanket the mountains like a earthen patchwork quilt, and during the rainy season, you'll see a sea of green. Otusco is one of the better examples of *serrano* life, with the cobblestone walkways and the *teja* roofs that have been used in the town for centuries. The only sight in town is the **Cathedral,** home to the Virgen de la Puerta, famous for her reputed healing power. Every December, people all over the Northern coast head to Otusco to pray to this miraculous statue—on December 14th, just finding space to walk around town is a challenge. To see this important icon, go to the Cathedral on the Plaza de Armas, and before you enter, take the stairs to your left. Keep quiet on the balcony, as you will likely find many people praying. (Open M-Sa 11am-7pm and 9-11pm.) Attached to the Cathedral, the **Museo Religioso Cathedral de la Virgen** houses robes and capes worn by priests while visiting the Virgin. Also look for the cases of jewelry lining the left wall, all gifts given to the statue. (Open M and W-Su 8:30am-11:30am and 2-6pm, Su 8:30am-5pm. s/1.)

You shouldn't need to stay in Otusco for more than a few hours, but the **Hostal Santa Rosa ❶,** Tacna 325, has small clean rooms and is the best option in town, even if the stark white walls are unimaginative. (☎ 80 5952. s/8, with bath s/15.) **La Esquina ❶,** off the Plaza de Armas, serves some great *serrano* food; more adventurous eaters might enjoy the *cuy* (s/6), which is filling and quite tasty—just forget it's a rodent and you'll be fine. (Open daily 10am-9pm.)

You'll probably land on Obregoso when you arrive in town, but right near the stop is Tacna, Otusco's main street, where you will find a **hospital, Internet** (s/1 per hr.), and a **pharmacy.** Continue up Tacna to find the Plaza de Armas and Cathedral. **Buses** to Otusco (daily when full, s/5) depart from Unión 188 in Trujillo with **Nuevo Milgros** (☎ 42 5457; open daily 8am-6pm; s/5). Buses to Trujillo leave from Obregoso, but buy tickets on Tacna 308. (☎ 43 6357; open daily 8am-6pm; s/5.)

CHICLAYO ☎074

A stopover between the ancient cities of Zaña and Lambayeque, Chiclayo (pop. 620,900) began as a single mud hut next to the Cinto River. Now the capital of the Lambayeque district, it continues to act as a central hub for commercial and tourist activity in the area. Still, travelers often overlook Chiclayo, preferring instead to daytrip to the nearby sites from Trujillo. The highlight of the region's archaeological offerings can be seen at the Tumbas Reales museum, which holds the contents of the tomb of the Señor de Sipán, discovered nearby in 1987. Hailed as the "Peruvian King Tut," he is considered one of the most significant archaeological discoveries of the past century. Visitors who choose to spend time in the city beyond the tourist circuit will realize that, in addition to its ancient treasures and nearby beaches, Chiclayo lives up to its nickname, "La Ciudad de La Amistad" ("The City of Friendship"). The city's wide streets and well-maintained plazas buzz with amiable and outgoing locals who just want to welcome you to town.

▐▀ TRANSPORTATION

Flights: José A. Quiñones Airport (☎ 23 3192), 2km south of town. Taxi s/3-4. **Nuevo Continente,** San José 867 (☎ 20 9916; www.nuevocontinente.com.pe). Open M-Sa 9am-6pm. AmEx/MC/V. To **Lima** (1hr.; daily 7:30am, 5:30, 8:40pm; US$60) and **Piura** (30min., daily 6:40pm, US$40). **Lan Peru,** María Izaga 770 (☎ 22 3154). Open 9am-7pm. Flies to **Lima** (1hr., daily 7:25pm, US$65). AmEx/V. **TANS,** María Izaga 765 (☎ 27 1339). Open M-Sa 9am-9pm. MC/V. To **Lima** (1hr., daily 5:30pm, US$74).

Buses: Chiclayo's multiple **terminales terrestres,** each serving 1-10 bus companies, are mostly along Bolognesi, south of town. Call ahead for long distance trips, as times and prices change frequently. One of the few agencies not on Bolognesi is **Lit Peru,** Raúl Haya de la Torre 50 (☎ 23 4343; open daily 8am-10pm), which goes to **Chimbote**

Chiclayo

▲ ACCOMMODATIONS
Hostal El Pelegrino, **5**
Hostal Royal, **3**
Hotel Oasis, **2**

● FOOD
Café Cappuccino, **4**
Govinda, **1**
Parrillada Hebron Chicken, **6**
Sipán Restaurant, **7**

(6hr., 11am, s/15) via **Trujillo** (3hr., s/10). **Transportes Linea,** Bolognesi 638 (☎23 3497; open daily 6am-11pm), at Colón, serves: **Cajamarca** (5-6hr.; daily 1, 10pm; s/ 15-25); **Jaén** (6hr.; 1:15pm, s/15; direct 11pm, s/22); **Lima** (11hr., 8pm, s/70); **Piura** (3hr., 13 per day 6am-8pm, s/10); **Trujillo** (3½hr., 13 per day 7am-6:45pm, s/ 10). **TranServis Kuélap,** Bolognesi 536 (☎27 1318; open daily 7am-10pm), in Terminal Tepsa, has service to **Chachapoyas** (10hr., 6:45pm, s/30). Reserve in advance. **Transportes Chiclayo,** Leonard Baptiste Ortiz 010 (☎23 7984; open daily 6am-8pm), runs to **Piura** (3hr., every hr. 6am-8pm, s/10) and **Tumbes** (8hr., 9:30pm, s/20).

Taxis: s/1-2 around town, s/12-15 per hr.

🔌 🛈 ORIENTATION AND PRACTICAL INFORMATION

Locals refuse to refer to the central square as the Plaza de Armas, in recognition of the fact that the town was never conquered by the Spanish. The so-called **Parque Principal** is the focal point of most activity in town, with many banks and lots of traffic. Shopping and dining, as well as most other services, lie along **Balta** and **Agu- irre,** but the city is fairly spread out, and many people rely on the inexpensive taxis to get around. Most transportation options lie along **Bolognesi,** about five blocks from the Parque Principal. The busiest spot in town is the popular **Mercado Modelo** (see **Markets,** below), five blocks north of the Parque at Balta and Arica.

Tourist Office: Dirección de Turismo, Saenz Peña 838 (☎23 3132; lambayeque@mitinci.gob.pe). Ask for **maps** in English and other free literature. Open M-F 7:30am-4:30pm. Also, the small info booths of **PromPeru** are in the Parque Principal and on the corners of Balta and 8 de Octubre, or Balta Sur and Mangel María Izaga. Hours vary by season, but are usually M-Sa 9am-1pm and 3-7pm.

Tours: Tumi Tours, Aguirre 532 (☎22 5371; tumitours@terra.com.pe), has good packages for independent travelers. Full-day trips in a private car include Museo Sicán, Túcume, and Batán Grande (US$45). Tumbes Reales Museum or Sipán archaeological sight US$20. A trip on the Circuito de Playas (beach circuit) includes Pimentel and Santa Rosa (US$19). Guides speak English, French, Italian, and German. Tumi also books **flights** out of Chiclayo and provides **DHL** and **Western Union** services. Open daily 9am-1pm and 4-7:30pm. AmEx/DC/MC/V.

Banks: Interbank, Aguirre 641 (☎23 8361), on the Parque Principal. Changes AmEx/MC/V traveler's checks. 24hr. AmEx/MC/V **ATM.** Open M-F 9am-6:15pm, Sa 9am-12:30pm. **ViaBCP,** Balta 630 (☎23 4472), exchanges AmEx traveler's checks. Open M-F 9am-7pm, Sa 9am-1pm.

Markets: El Super, Luís Gonzales 881 (☎22 7580). Open daily 9am-2pm and 4-10pm. AmEx/MC/V. Mercado Modelo, on Balta between Arica and Pardo, 4 blocks north of Parque Principal, is large and lively. In the back, the **mercado de brujos** (witch market) has one of the best selections of traditional medicine in Peru. Open daily 8am-8pm.

Emergency: ☎105. **Fire:** ☎116.

Police: Vicente de la Vega 1182 (☎27 0751). Open 24hr. **Tourist police** are at Saenz Peña 830 (☎23 5181). Open 24hr.

Hospital: Hospital Regional Docente Las Mercedes, Luís González 635 (☎23 8232 or 23 7021). Open M-Sa 8am-1pm, 24hr. for emergencies and pharmacy. Private **Clínica Lambayeque,** Vicente de la Vega 415 (☎23 7961), is open daily 8am-8pm, 24hr. for emergencies.

Telephones: Telefónica del Perú, Elias Aguirre 631 (☎23 2225). Calling cards and collect calls accepted. Open daily 8am-11pm.

Internet Access: Most of Chiclayo's Internet cafes cluster around Plaza Aguirre. **Satellite,** Aguirre 127, is open daily 8am-11pm (s/1.50 per hr.).

Post Office: Serpost, Aguirre 140 (☎23 7031). Open M-Sa 8am-8:30pm, Su 8am-2pm.

ACCOMMODATIONS

Chiclayo has plenty of accommodations, but the most attractive are near the center of town, a fair distance from the bus terminals (taxi s/2).

Hostal Royal, San José 787 (☎23 3421; hroyalchiclayo@yahoo.com.es), right off the Parque Principal. In the heart of the city and packed with guests, this grand old building has a nifty winding staircase and large rooms with private baths and plenty of hot water. Some rooms have generous windows with street views. Singles s/23; matrimonials and doubles s/32; triples s/43. ②

Hostal El Pelegrino, Aguirre 476 (☎20 8969). Manages to pack a personal feel into the 80s motel decor. Large carpeted rooms have all the amenities—even writing desks. Request a room with a window. Cable TV. Private bath with 24hr. hot water. Singles s/40; doubles s/60; triples s/80. Discounts available. ④

Hotel Oasis, Lora y Cordero 858 (☎27 0339). The building is so tall you'll get a workout just getting to bed—request a room on the 2nd floor. Huge windows make the already spacious rooms feel even bigger. The 24hr. hot private baths are spotless. Cable TV. Singles s/40; matrimonials s/45; doubles s/55; triples s/70. ④

FOOD

Chiclayo's food options cater to all tastes and pocketbooks. A good sandwich can be had for a sol or two anywhere along Balta or the Parque Principal. Likewise, *criollo* restaurants abound, and there's always the ubiquitous *pollo a la brasa*. Folks with a sweet tooth will delight in the local specialty, **King Kong,** two cookies stuck together with *piña* (pineapple), *maní* (peanut), and *manjar blanco*.

Parrillada Hebron Chicken, Balta Sur 605 (☎22 2709). You can't miss this glowing 4-story, neon-lit local favorite. In this carnivore's paradise, the tasty and tender *pollo Hebron* comes with french fries and salad (s/12). Entrees s/8-15. Open daily 7:30am-midnight. AmEx/DC/MC/V. ❷

Sipán Restaurant, Izaga 900 (☎49 8970). This new corner eatery prides itself on its traditional northern *criollo* dishes. Enjoy fresh *chinguirito* (fried dogfish) on the 2nd floor loft, or be more daring and sample the *chirimpico* (boiled goat tripe). Entrees s/12-22. Open daily 11am-5pm. ❸

Govinda, Balta 1029 (☎22 7331), with a small, inconspicuous sign. One of the national Hare Krishna-run vegetarian consortiums, featuring "Hindu specialties" such as *alu panir sak* (a spinach and cheese dish, s/6). The fruit salad with all the trimmings is superb (s/3). *Menú* s/4. Entrees s/1-6. Open M-Sa 8am-9:30pm, Su 8am-4pm. ❶

Café Cappuccino, Federico Villarreal 115, (☎23 4911), attached to the Gran Hotel Chiclayo, about a 10min. walk east of the Parque Principal. Sip on the signature Café Cappuccino (s/8) or enjoy some tasty pizzas, hamburgers, and sandwiches, or even tacos. Entrees s/4-15. Coffee s/4-10. Open daily 10am-10pm. AmEx/MC/V. ❶

SIGHTS

Chiclayo itself has few touristy sights, though Mercado Modelo's **witch market** is interesting enough. The **Paseo de Las Musas,** at the end of Balta Sur, is full of somewhat cheesy statues and columns in the classical Roman and Greek style. The real attractions are in the surrounding towns. All are easily accessible by public transportation, but if you want to cram them all into one day you'll have to hire a taxi (s/12-15 per hr.). Give yourself two days to see all the museums and ruins without having to rush. Independent travelers may prefer to arrange a guided tour of all the sites (see **Tours,** p. 326). Groups will save money hiring guides on location and taking either taxis or colectivos to the sites.

LAMBAYEQUE

Combis to Lambayeque (20min., every 10min. 5am-11pm, s/1) leave from Vicente de la Vega and Angamos. Get off at Lambayeque's Plaza de Armas.

The main attraction in Lambayeque, 12km northeast of Chiclayo, is the outstanding ▓**Museo Tumbas Reales,** where the contents of the tomb of the **Señor de Sipán** are displayed (see **Sipán,** below). Three modern floors modeled after the Huaca de Sipán display the contents of one of the most important archaeological sites in Peru. Unfortunately all the displays are in Spanish, but the sheer beauty of the pieces makes them easy to appreciate, regardless of language barriers. The first floor is entirely devoted to Moche artifacts, mostly ceramics representing animals or deities. There is nothing spectacular about these pieces, so briskly walk through to see the pictures of the Huaca today and follow the arrows downstairs to see the gold and silver contents of the famous tomb itself. The artifacts on this floor are considered some of the most exquisite pieces in all of the ancient world, and it's easy to see why—stunning gold figurines stand alongside brilliant necklaces of gold and silver. As you descend to the third level, you'll see reproductions of the tomb and see pieces found in

NORTHERN COAST

the tomb of the **Viejo Señor,** an older dignitary thought to be a predecessor of the Señor de Sipán. If you can, skip the 7min. presentation at the end, which consists of a few mannequins dressed as the Señor de Sipán moving their upper bodies and blowing into conches—the one dull bit of the museum. (At the end of Viscardo and Guzmán, in a bright red building. Mototaxi from Plaza de Armas s/3. ☎28 3977. Open Tu-Su 9am-5pm. English and Spanish guides s/15. s/7, students with ISIC s/2.50.)

If you have more time in Lambayeque, make a quick trip to the **Museo Brüning.** Three amazing floors hold over a thousand ceramic pieces, mostly from the Chimú and Lambayeque cultures, as well as mummies, scale models, old tools, and a few textiles. Perhaps the best features of this museum are the displays in English and Spanish that explain the items. Before you go in, take a look at the colorful wall mosaic outside. (To get to the Brüning, turn left on Atahuallpa (next to Banco de Crédito) and walk one block; the museum is at the corner of Huamachuco. Mototaxi from the Plaza s/1. ☎28 2110; museobruning@epi.udep.edu.pe. Open daily 9am-5pm. English and Spanish guides s/10. s/7, students s/2.50.)

Still here? Check out Lambayeque's two mammoth architectural monuments: **Iglesia San Pedro,** built around 1700, on the Plaza de Armas at Bolívar and 2 de Mayo, and the 16th-century **Casa Monjoy** (also called the Casa de la Logia), one block down 2 de Mayo, which boasts what some claim is the longest colonial balcony in the Americas (64m). For a slice of local culture and a scrumptious lunch, head to ◼**El Rincón del Pato,** Leguia 270 (taxi s/2), a *criollo* restaurant full of local musicians singing their hearts out and a maitre d' who makes locals swoon as he croons classic northern Peruvian hits. The food is fresh, filling, and cheap. (☎28 2751. Entrees s/9-15. Open daily 11am-6pm.)

SIPÁN

Colectivos (50min., every 20min. 5am-6:30pm, s/1.50) leave from the Terminal Municipal Interurbano at Oriente (also called Carretera Ferreñafe) and Piérola (also called Agusto Belagia). Private taxis save time (round-trip s/40-50). Open daily 9am-5:30pm. Spanish-only guides s/15. s/7, students with ISIC s/2.50.

In early 1987, anthropologists realized that they had overlooked an important Moche burial site in the town of Sipán, 28km east of Chiclayo, when valuable artifacts from that area began popping up on the black market. Although many feared that the most important sites had already been looted, *huaqueros* (tomb robbers) somehow barely missed the richest tombs, including that of the warrior-priest known as **Señor de Sipán.** The Señor was the civil, religious, and military leader of the Moche people circa AD 300. Replicas of his tomb and nine others at the Sipán site provide a glimpse of what archaeologists first uncovered nearly 20 years ago. Although his grave measures only 5m to a side, it was packed with his finest regalia, offerings of food and drink, and the bodies of those who were sacrificed in order to accompany the Señor on his journey to the afterworld. Also at the Sipán complex are a small **museum** (inferior to those in **Lambayeque,** above, which house the actual contents of the tombs) that has a mannequin of the Señor and pictures from the excavation, and various **miradores** at the tops of ceremonial pyramids.

FERREÑAFE

From Lambayeque, take a taxi to Ferreñafe (15-20 min., s/6-8) and to the Museo Sicán, on the outskirts of town. You can also take a taxi from Chiclayo (round-trip s/25-30). ☎80 0048. Open Tu-Su 9am-5pm. Guides s/15. s/7.

About 20 km from Chiclayo, the small town of Ferreñafe happens to be home to the modern, huaca-shaped **Museo Nacional Sicán,** where gold pieces and artifacts from the tomb of the **Señor de Sicán** (not to be confused with the more impressive Señor de Sipán) are on display. Dr. Izumi Shimada, a Japanese anthropologist, was extremely interested in the Sicán culture, which existed at about the same time as the Chimú, but left few noteworthy pieces behind. In 1991, however, he found what he was looking for at the **Huaca Loro** in Batán Grande (below): two sets of tombs. The **eastern tomb** contained the body of a royal figure, the Señor de Sicán. For an unknown reason, he was decapitated and buried upside-down. All the striking artifacts from the tomb are now on display in the Sala de Oro, on the second floor of the museum. Modern facial reconstruction techniques were used to model a menacing clay head that approximates the ancient Señor's handsome face. The **western tomb** was discovered later; the Señor of this tomb was buried in the same way as the Señor de Sicán, but the virgin sacrifices buried with him were arranged in a unique hive-like configuration. When you enter the museum, head straight up the stairs and to the left, where a film in Spanish gives an overview of the museum. The next room houses life-sized replicas of the tombs—upside-down body and all. Mannequins demonstrate the making of impressive metallic objects in the next rooms, leading up to the Sala de Oro. A 10min. video in Spanish shows how DNA analysis revealed that the men in both tombs were related.

TÚCUME

Combis to Túcume (35-40min., 4am-9pm, s/1.30) leave when full from Angamos near Pardo in Chiclayo. The pyramids and museum are another 2km from town; mototaxi (s/1-3). Guides speak some English and French (1½hr., s/15 per group). Wear sturdy shoes for the hike up to the mirador. Open daily 9am-4:30pm. s/7, students with ISIC s/2.50.

Often called **El Valle de los Pirámides,** this complex of 26 ceremonial adobe pyramids was perhaps larger than Chan Chan when it was constructed between AD 700 and 1000. At 700m long, 280m wide, and 30m tall, the largest pyramid, **Huaca Larga,** is the largest adobe structure in South America. The site was once the capital of the Lambayeque civilization, whose history is outlined in the adjacent **Museo de Sitio Túcume,** interesting only for the detailed scale models of the site and the history of the region it provides. There are also temporary exhibits that change every few months in the far yellow building next to the museum. Most travelers come for the **miradores,** which can be reached via the direct route, or the more scenic one. The scenic route (30min.) winds through desert brush, far away from visiting school children, and leads you past the **Huaca Las Estacas** pyramid. Either route takes you to **Cerro Purgatorio,** where you can climb to *miradores* as high as 140m to get an awesome bird's-eye view of the unrestored complex. The Huaca Larga is closed for excavations, but opens occasionally for visitors.

BATÁN GRANDE

From Túcume or Lambayeque, take a taxi to Batán Grande (25min., s/8-10) and either have the taxi wait or pre-arrange a time for pickup. Many cyclists ride out to Batán Grande from Chiclayo (60km) and take a taxi back.

This ecological reserve in the Leche Valley draws visitors with a blend of archaeological and natural wonders. Among the site's 20 adobe pyramids are seven principal *huacas* that date from 500 BC. The tomb of the **Señor de Sicán** was discovered in the Huaca Loro only a decade ago and is now housed in the Museo Sicán in Ferreñafe (see **Ferreñafe,** above). But the main attraction at Batán Grande is its **Poma Forest,** with several rare plant and animal species. *Carob, sapodilla,* and *hurango* forests provide the natural habitat for bears, snakes, iguanas, and the endangered Aliblanca turkey, which was believed to be extinct 30 years ago. The **Millennium Tree,** over 1000 years old, draws witch doctors and superstitious tourists alike, who believe that the tree has mystical powers. With several pathways, the reserve provides a perfect spot for day-hikes, but the entire reserve closes at dusk.

NORTHERN COAST

BEACHES NEAR CHICLAYO

PIMENTEL

Combis to Pimentel (20min., every 5min. 6am-11pm, s/1) leave from the corner of Vicente de la Vega and Angamos.

In a city as hot as Chiclayo, few things are as refreshing as a day at the beach. Fortunately, the fishing town of **Pimentel** is a mere 14km away. In the summer (Jan.-Mar.), Pimentel is less a beach resort than a popular daytrip for locals, where lamppost speakers blast beachy tunes. Pimentel is dominated by its 630m-long pier, where fishermen reel in fresh fish each morning. A walk to the end over the precarious wooden slats (stay on the more stable parts along edge) costs s/1. When they're in a good mood, fishermen will rent their small motorboats and guide trips to the nearby islands of **Lobo de Afuera** and **Lobo de Tierra** (s/30 for 3-4hr., ask around the pier in the morning). The water is too calm for surfing, but in March the town hosts beach sport tournaments, fishing contests, and races with *caballitos de totora*, traditional fishing boats made out of reeds.

Pimentel is best seen as a daytrip from Chiclayo, as accommodations are limited. Fortunately, the one budget hotel fulfills its duties well. **Garuda Hostal ❷,** Quiñones 109, one block inland from the pier on the right, has clean, airy rooms in a big yellow house. The *comedor* serves breakfast, and guests are free to use the kitchen and body boards or to play with the pet dog. Request one of the two rooms with an ocean view. (☎45 2964. Cable TV. 24hr. hot water. Singles with matrimonial bed and bath s/35; doubles with bath s/55.) Restaurants line **Rivera Del Mar,** just off the beach, where locals serve seafood and *comida criolla* at solid prices (s/10-18). There are few services in town other than a basic **Banco de La Nación** (open M-F 8am-4:30pm, Sa 9am-1pm) and **police** on the Plaza de Armas.

OTHER BEACHES

Colectivos head to Santa Rosa (10min., s/1) and Eten (15min., s/1) from B. Leguin and Quiñones in Pimentel. In Eten you'll have to switch vehicles to get to Puerto Eten (5min., s/0.50; mototaxi s/1). Direct combis go from Puerto Eten to Chiclayo (50min., s/1.50).

South of Pimentel lie some smaller and more secluded shores. An easy walk leads to **Playa Las Rocas,** 2km south of town (taxi 5min., s/1), an empty stretch of beach with good waves for surfing. **Santa Rosa,** 6km from Pimentel, is a traditional fishing village dominated by a hectic public market. Colorful wooden fishing boats cover the sand, while fishermen in *totora* reed boats bob up and down on the water. About 18km from Pimentel, **Puerto Eten** may be remote (combis drive through a river to get there), but it's far from isolated—during the summer, sunbathers pack the seemingly endless 6½km of shoreline while a DJ pumps dance tunes from a makeshift stage on the beach.

PIURA   ☎073

Founded in 1532 by Francisco Pizarro, Piura (pop. 375,700) enjoys the distinction of being Peru's oldest colonial city. Originally located in the Tangarará Valley, Piura moved three times (evading pestilence and pirate attacks) before settling in 1588 at its present site. Today, as the department capital and the closest major city near the Macará border crossing, Piura is primarily seen as a convenient place to exchange money or catch a long-distance bus (an image the city is trying to shake). Unfortunately, the climate can be rather oppressive—the landlocked city shares the same debilitating heat as the coast, but lacks the relief of ocean breezes. Cool off with one of the many frozen treats sold by street vendors.

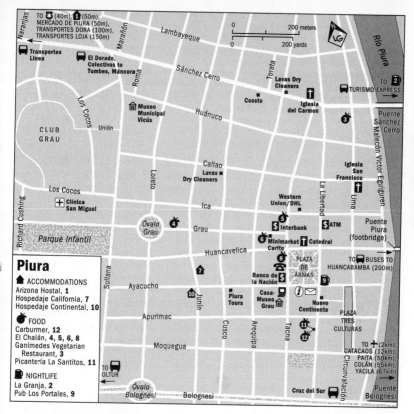

NORTHERN COAST

Piura

🏠 ACCOMMODATIONS
Arizona Hostal, **1**
Hospedaje California, **7**
Hospedaje Continental, **10**

🍎 FOOD
Carburmer, **12**
El Chalán, **4, 5, 6, 8**
Ganímedes Vegetarian
Restaurant, **3**
Picantería La Santitos, **11**

🍷 NIGHTLIFE
La Granja, **2**
Pub Los Portales, **9**

🖥 TRANSPORTATION

Flights: Airport (☎ 34 4505), 2km south of town. **Taxi** 10min., s/4-5. **Nuevo Continente** flies to **Lima** (2hr.; daily 9:40am, 7:40pm; US$74) via **Chiclayo** (20min., 7:40pm, US$40) and **Trujillo** (45min., 9:40am, US$30). AmEx/MC/V. **TANS** (☎ 31 1549), in the airport. Open M-F 8am-7:30pm, Sa 8:30am-6:30pm, Su 9:30am-12:30pm. Daily flights to **Lima** (2hr., 5pm, US$74) via **Chiclayo** (25min., US$32). AmEx/DC/MC/V.

Buses: Those arriving on the night bus from **Ecuador** should know that there are no buses to **Lima** until the following evening. Many choose to spend the day in **Chiclayo,** 3hr. south, where there are more sights and better bus options. In Piura, combis and micros head to **Sullana** from Sánchez Cerro (30min., every 30min. 4:30am-8pm, s/ 1.50). Colectivos to **Tumbes** and **Máncora** (3½hr., 5am-11pm, s/20) leave from outside the El Dorado terminal on Sánchez Cerro.

Civa, Ramón Castilla 101 (☎34 5421). Departs for **Huancabamba** (9hr., daily 8:30am, s/25).

Cooperativo de Transportes Loja, Sánchez Cerro 228-1B (☎30 9407), offers direct service to **Loja, Ecuador** (8hr.; 6am, 1, 10pm; s/25).

Cruz del Sur, Circunvalación 160 (☎33 7094), by Río Piura, just past the southern part of Lima. Open daily 7am-8:30pm. Goes to **Lima** (13hr.; daily at 6:15pm; s/74-110).

El Dorado, Sánchez Cerro 1119 (☎32 5875). Open daily 7:30am-midnight. Goes to **Trujillo** (6hr.; 1pm, midnight; s/20) via **Chiclayo** (2½hr., s/10), and also to **Tumbes** (4½hr., 8 per day 8:30am-12:15am, s/15).

Oltur S.A., Bolognesi 801 (☎32 6666). Open daily 8am-8pm. Sends luxury buses directly to **Lima** (14hr., 5:30 and 6:30pm, s/40-70).

Transportes Linea, Sánchez Cerro 1215 (☎32 7821). Goes to: **Chiclayo** (2hr.; 14 per day 5am-6pm, usually on the hour; s/12) and **Trujillo** (7hr., 11pm, s/25).

Turismo Express H y D, Tacna de Castillo 104 (☎34 5382), on the other side of the river. Open daily 6am-9pm. Goes to **Huancabamba** (9hr.; 7:30am, 6pm; s/23).

Taxis: Be aware—taxi drivers may try to scam unsuspecting gringos. The standard fare is s/1-2 within the city and s/4-5 to the airport. Drivers may also have deals with local hostels, so be wary of their recommendations.

BORDER CROSSING: INTO ECUADOR. The border is open 24hr. Previously, to officially enter or exit either country, you had to cross the bridge between the two countries by foot, passing through the immigration offices located on either side to receive **entrance** and **exit stamps** and to surrender or receive your tourist **T3 card.** Now, however, direct buses cross from Piura, Peru to Loja, Ecuador via Macará, Ecuador. Travelers who use these services often report less hassle at the border. **Cooperativo de Transportes Loja** (above) is one of a growing number of companies offering this service. If a direct bus isn't your style, it's also possible to make the trip in a series of shorter segments. From Sánchez Cerro and Sullana in Piura, catch a bus to the nearby town of Sullana (30min., every 30min. 4:30am-8pm, s/1.50). From José de Loma in Sullana, take a mototaxi (4min., s/1) to Calle 4 (or just ask for the *"paradero de autos para la frontera"*), where taxi-colectivos depart for the border ("la frontera") at **La Tina** (1¾hr., 4am-7pm, s/10). Once you cross the bridge, colectivos drive the 4km to **Macará** (5min., s/1 or US$0.25), where multiple buses leave for Loja each day. You can exchange soles and dollars on either side.

■ ♂ ORIENTATION AND PRACTICAL INFORMATION

Home to many banks and other businesses, busy **Grau** runs west from the **Plaza de Armas,** bordered by **Tacna** and **Libertad,** to the **Óvalo Grau.** The major north-south streets are **Loreto,** which intersects the Óvalo Grau, and **Sullana.** Most buses leave from **Sánchez Cerro,** west of Sullana. The **market** lies farther west, at the intersection of Sánchez Cerro and **M. de Uchuraccy. Puente Sánchez Cerro** sees the most traffic, while the pedestrian-only suspension bridge, **Puente Peatonal Piura** (also called **Puente Viejo**), lies to the south.

Tourist Office: Información Turística (☎31 0772; www.munipiura.gob.pe), at Ayacucho on the Plaza de Armas. Enormous office seems disproportionate to the number of tourists in the area. Friendly staff provides **maps** of the city and basic history of the region. Some English spoken. Open M-Sa 8am-1pm and 4-8pm.

Tours: Ask at the **Información Turística** office (above) for information on hiking, trekking, mountain biking, and kayaking. **Piura Tours,** Ayacucho 585 (☎32 8873; piura-tours@mail.udep.edu.pe), offers pricey tours of the city (3hr., US$25) and nearby towns (3hr.-2 days, US$20-70) in English, French, and German for groups of 6 people min. Open M-F 8:30am-1pm and 4-7:30pm, Sa 9am-1pm. AmEx/MC/V.

Banks: Interbank, Grau 154 (☎32 3201), changes AmEx/MC/V traveler's checks. 24hr. AmEx/Cirrus/MC/Plus/V **ATM.**

Markets: For daily goods, try **Cossto,** Sánchez Cerro 525 (☎33 7088; open daily 9am-9pm), or **Minimarket Carito,** Grau 165 (☎30 8906; open daily 8am-11pm; AmEx/V). **Mercado de Piura,** spreading out from Sánchez Cerro and M. de Uchuraccy, has everything you could ever want and a lot you never would. Open daily 6am-6pm.

Laundromat: Lavas Dry Cleaners, branches at: Arequipa 488 (☎303 809); Sánchez Cerro (☎30 8971); Callao 602 (☎30 4191 or 58 4135), at Cusco. Next-day service s/ 4.50 per kg, same-day service s/5.50 per kg. Open M-Sa 8:30am-2pm and 4-8:30pm.

Emergency: ☎105 or 30 7632.

Police: ☎30 7641, on the 13th block of Sánchez Cerro.

Hospital: Clínica San Miguel, Los Cocos 153 (☎30 2660 or 39 300). Open daily 9am-9pm, 24hr. for emergencies. **Hospital Reátegui,** Grau 1150 (☎33 1157). Open 24hr. for emergencies.

Telephones: Telefónica del Perú, Tacna 540 (☎/fax 30 7828). Sells and accepts calling cards; allows international collect calls. Open M-Sa 8:30am-2pm and 5-9pm.

Internet Access: Akasa, Tacna 642 (☎49 5577), off the Plaza de Armas. s/1.50 per hr. Open daily 8am-11pm.

Post Office: Serpost (☎32 7031 or 30 9393), on the Plaza de Armas. Open M-Sa 8am-8pm, Su 8am-2:45pm. **DHL/Western Union,** Ica 354 (☎30 4084). Open M-F 8:30am-1pm and 3:30-8pm, Sa 8:30am-1pm.

ACCOMMODATIONS

Apparently someone was expecting a lot of visitors—Piura today has a plethora of vacant budget hotels. Many offer rooms with views of the street and rooms with views of a cement wall for the same price, so be sure to specify what you want. Nighttime brings little relief from the heat, even during winter, so windows are a must, fans a bonus, and A/C a treat.

Hospedaje California, Junín 835 (☎32 8789). Bright and cheerful, this airy place sports: a sunny rooftop gazebo filled with polyester plants and lounge chairs to even out your farmer's tan; a large sink for doing laundry; and a much-needed fan in every room. Singles s/14; doubles s/25; triples s/33. ❷

Hospedaje Continental, Junín 924 (☎33 4531). The average-sized rooms are bare, but bearable. The lack of fans might make for a rough night. TV lounge. Singles s/14, with bath s/20; matrimonials s/20, with bath s/25; doubles s/20. Extra bed s/6. ❷

Arizona Hostal, Sánchez Cerro 1350 (☎306 904), 5 doors to the right of the police station. Amidst the insanity of Sánchez Cerro, this desert oasis awaits. Private bathrooms, hot water, cable TV, telephones, A/C, large closets. Reception open daily 7am-1pm and 4-8pm, with security service until 1am. Restaurant open daily 8am-4pm and 7-10pm. Singles s/30; matrimonials s/35; doubles s/40; triples s/55; quads s/70. ❸

FOOD

Piura exports its famous limes all over Peru, so chances are good that you've eaten one without knowing it. Since Piura lies far from the coast, there's less seafood served here than in most other towns, with the exception of *ceviche* made with local limes. Nearly-identical restaurants along Grau serve *comida típica*, but the colonial streets near the Plaza de Armas are home to some excellent eateries.

Picantería La Santitos, Libertad 1014 (☎33 2380). Locals pack this *criollo* restaurant at lunchtime. Enter through the creaky wooden doors to find a bamboo roof and subdued lighting that fit in with the relaxed, friendly atmosphere. For a hearty Peruvian meal, try the *tacu tacu con bistek* (s/16). Entrees s/12-24. Open daily 11am-4pm. ❸

El Chalán, with 4 locations: Tacna 520-6 on the Plaza (☎30 6483), Grau 453 (☎32 5167), Grau 173 (☎30 5000), and at the corner of Tacna and Ica (☎32 3818). A popular local chain reminiscent of a hometown diner—employees clad in striped shirts and chartreuse pants serve up sandwiches (s/5-11), burgers (s/8-12), and up to 30 flavors of ice cream. Open daily 7:30am-10:30pm. ❸

Carburmer, Libertad 1014 (☎33 2380), across the courtyard from Picantería la Santitos. If you're in the mood for a fine Italian meal, this is your best bet. Tasty large pizzas s/27-30. Entrees s/20-24. Open daily 6:30pm-1am. ❹

Ganímedes Vegetarian Restaurant, Lima 440 (☎329 176). A tropical hut stuck incongruously in the center of Piura. Pictures of tasty foods and natural landscapes prepare diners for Ganímedes's 25 kinds of fruit juice (s/1.5-2.50) and other natural fare. Entrees s/6.50-10.50. *Menú* s/5. Open M-Sa 7:15am-10pm, Su 11am-8pm. ❶

🅖 SIGHTS

A stroll down Lima starting at Sánchez Cerro passes several ramshackle colonial buildings. Piura's few real sights can be seen in a morning or afternoon.

CHURCHES. Piura's **Catedral,** Huancavelica 362, right off the Plaza de Armas, was built in the 16th century. The beautiful gold-leafed altar, believed to be one of the oldest in Peru, dates back about 350 years and depicts the beloved Virgen de Fátima. The pulpit is also covered in gold leaf, but only dates to the 17th century, with a high relief meant to depict the Immaculate Conception. *(Open M-F 7am-8am and 7pm-8pm, Su 8am-noon.)* The **Iglesia San Francisco,** on the corner of Lima and Callao, has sporadic hours but can be appreciated from outside. The oldest church in Piura, it was the site of the region's declaration of independence from the Spanish on January 4, 1821. The 18th-century **Iglesia Carmen,** Libertad 365, off Sanchez Cerro, is a national monument with a small religious museum. *(Open during mass. s/1.50, students s/1.)*

MUSEUMS. Piura's small museums may be a bit dry for those with little regional knowledge. **Casa-Museo Gran Almirante Grau,** Tacna 662, displays the photos, documents, and personal effects of Admiral Miguel Grau (1834-79), a naval hero from the War of the Pacific against Chile. The Admiral, who was born in this house, is Piura's pride and joy. (☎32 6541. Open M-F 8am-12:30pm and 3:30-6pm, Sa-Su 8am-noon. Free. Tours are also free, but tips are expected.) The **Museo Municipal Vicús,** on the corner of Sullana and Huánuco, hosts a variety of exhibitions with a local flavor on the ground floor. The basement area, Sala de Oro, features a collection of artifacts from the Vicús tribe, which inhabited the area from 200 BC to AD 600. *(Open Tu-Su 9am-5pm. Sala de Oro s/3, students s/2.)*

CATACAOS. This village, 12km from Piura, has an excellent **artesanía market** known for its *filigrana* (filigree; thin strands of gold and silver elaborately woven into delicate jewelry). Much of the metal is high quality (18-karat gold and grade 950 silver are common), and prices are surprisingly low—bargaining is expected. The market also sells other handicrafts, from wooden plates to Panama hats. Catacaos is also well known for its great selection of *picanterías* around the central plaza, which usually open for lunch. *(Combis to Catacaos leave from the mercado, near the intersection of M. de Uchuraccy and Sánchez Cerro (25min., every 15min. 7:30am-9pm, s/1). Open daily 9am-6pm.)*

🅝 NIGHTLIFE

Piura may not have the most exciting nightlife, but there are a number of discos and *peñas* (bars) in town. No matter where you go, take a taxi—peace of mind is worth a few extra soles. Most of the nightlife centers around the all-inclusive restaurant/*peña*/disco combinations on **Guardia Civil,** the eastern continuation of Sánchez Cerro on the other side of the bridge. **La Granja,** on Guardia Civil, draws a subdued set. (☎34 2800. Open daily 7pm-3am. AmEx/DC/MC/V.) If you prefer to stay close to the center of town, **Pub Los Portales,** at the corner of Libertad and Ayacucho, is a classy local bar with a wide variety of drinks and an upscale casino. (☎32 1161. Drinks s/8-13. Open daily 6pm-2am. AmEx/MC/V.)

DAYTRIPS FROM PIURA

PAITA

Transportes Dora, Sánchez Cerro 1387 (☎30 7949), 6 blocks up from Sullana, has frequent service from Piura to Paita (50min., leaves when full 5am-10pm, round-trip s/3.50).

The small town of Paita, 60km northeast of Piura, is landlocked Piura's port, a major fishing center in a natural bay and a stopping-point on the way to the beaches. In contrast to the port's prosaic present, its past was filled with drama and romance. British pirates, including adventurer Sir Francis Drake, repeatedly sacked Paita during the 16th century. Remnants of this tumultuous past can be seen throughout town, especially in the **Iglesia La Merced,** right off the Plaza de Armas (turn left at the Caja Municipal). This badly maintained church contains a slashed statue of the Virgen de la Merced, an important figure for the people of the region—a pirate tried to lop the head off, but obviously failed. (Open daily 9am-5:30pm.) Right across the street, the abandoned 18th-century **Edificio de la Aduana** (Customs House) has fallen into utter disrepair. Poorly preserved 200-year-old buildings line the streets north and south of the Plaza.

COLÁN

From Paita, it's a 45min. colectivo ride to Colán (s/1.50). Cars leave from San Francisco, 1½ blocks uphill from the market, across from the high school. Get there before 9:30am, or be prepared to wait. All returning combis pass by the Iglesia San Lucas, but it's quicker to take a colectivo up to the highway (6min., s/1) and catch a Piura-bound micro there (20min., s/1).

The entire Northern Coast is full of gorgeous beaches, and Piura has its fair share. The most notable is Colán, 15km north of Paita. Warm, calm waters make for relaxing beach-bumming at **Esmeralda** or **Palmeras.** All the houses nearby are built on stilts. The town is also famous for the **Iglesia San Lucas,** the oldest church in Peru, built by Dominican friars in 1536. **Bungalows Spilberg ❾,** on Costanera, to the right facing the water, is upscale, with shining white rooms, tiled floors, fridges, TVs, and hot baths. Other perks include garden hammocks, kayak rental (US$5 per day), and a pool. (☎961 5941; www.cpi.udep.edu.pe/CPI/spilberg. Doubles US$20. Group discounts.) Colán only has one public **telephone,** with spotty service, so don't expect too much contact with the outside world while in this village.

YACILA

From Paita, take a Yacila-bound colectivo from the market (60min., s/2). To come back, just hop on a Paita-bound combi.

The small beach is overshadowed by the more unique attraction: **sandboarding** on the dunes. You can also ask around town to visit the **Isla Foca,** the makeshift home of many birds and sea creatures, including Humboldt penguins.

HUANCABAMBA
☎073

As if consciously defying kilometers of coastal flatlands, the first towering peaks of the Andes shoot up with startling abruptness. Only by braving the narrow dirt road that winds up through a dense plain of clouds can one reach the lofty valley that cradles Huancabamba (pop. 8000), Peru's major traditional medicine center. It would be enough to visit Huancabamba for the landscape, but most come in search of spiritual and medicinal healing. Huancabamba is renowned for its **chamanes** (spiritual healers, a.k.a. shamans, *brujos*, *curanderos*, and *maestros*) and for the mystical **Lagunas de las Huaringas.** Whether you suffer from arthritis or unrequited love, financial difficulty or fevers, the *maestros* of the Huaringas promise to provide a cure in a long ceremony involving a variety of drugs and a hefty dose of shamanic spiritualism. While curious visitors are welcomed by locals, scorn or skepticism is not—these ceremonies are taken very seriously.

> *Let's Go* does not recommend recreational drug use.

Huancabamba's hostels never sleep, with people shuttling to and from the mystical lakes at all hours. **Hospedaje Danubio ❷**, Grau 208 (☎47 3200), on the Plaza de Armas, offers rooms with a wide variety of floor tiles and occasional mountain views. Common baths are reasonably clean. All rooms except those on the top floor have TVs. **Hostal El Dorado ❶**, General Medina 116 (☎47 3016), on the Plaza, also has a **restaurant ❸** specializing in *cuy*. Restaurants here are for the most part undistinguished, serving standard meat and rice dishes. *Rompopes*—a local libation made from *caña* (a strong sugarcane alcohol), egg, sugar, honey, lemon, and vanilla—is traditionally imbibed at midday.

The **bus terminal** is at the end of Centenario, three blocks uphill from the Plaza de Armas. There is a **tourist office** in the terminal with a list of registered *maestros*. The tourist office also arranges expeditions in the area. From Piura (see Buses, p. 331), **Civa** (9hr., daily 8:30am, s/25) and **Turismo Express H y D** (9hr.; 7:30am, 6pm; s/ 23) go to Huancabamba. Huancabamba's colorful **Plaza de Armas**, bordered by **Grau, General Medina, San Martín**, and the **Iglesia San Pedro**, sits about four blocks uphill from the **Mercado Municipal** (near the corner of **Unión** and **Choque Huanca**).

TUMBES   ☎072

In Tumbes (pop. 106,600), the sun shines, shines, and shines. It shone on Pizarro when he sacked the then-Inca city—although as proud locals will remind you, the Spanish conquistadors were unable to conquer it. It shone on the first prospectors to strike South American oil in 1862. It shone on the Ecuadorians who ruled the city for the first part of the 20th century, and it continued to shine on the Peruvians who took it back during the Border War of 1941. The shining sun is especially appreciated at the nearby beaches, which are among the continent's best. But the city is also pleasant. The center boasts lovely pedestrian walkways lined with pastel buildings and filled with shimmering, mosaic-covered fountains and monuments. What's more, Tumbes's fortuitous location makes the city a perfect base for trips south to the dry forest, north to the mangrove swamps, inland to the tropical rainforest, or nearby to the mineral mud baths.

⊏ TRANSPORTATION

Flights: Airport (☎52 5102 or 52 1262), 8km north of town. Taxi 15min., s/10. Travel agency shuttle s/5. **NuevoContinente**, Tumbes 217 (☎52 2350), flies to **Lima** (2hr., daily 4:20pm, US$74) via **Chiclayo** (1hr., US$40). Open M-Sa 8am-8pm. AmEx/MC/V.

Buses: Terminals cluster around the intersection of Tumbes and Piura, and the vast number of companies means you should have no trouble finding a way out of Tumbes, especially if you're headed to Piura or Máncora—just follow the shouts of the drivers announcing their destination. **Entrapesa**, Tumbes 391 (☎52 5850). Open 9am-9pm. Goes to **Trujillo** (8hr., daily 7pm, s/30) via **Chiclayo** (5hr., s/25) and **Piura** (3hr., s/ 18). **Ormeño**, Tumbes 314 (☎52 2288). Open daily 8am-1pm and 3-8pm. Goes to **Lima** (18hr.; daily 1pm, 7pm; s/75-120) via **Chiclayo** (5hr., s/30-55) and **Trujillo**

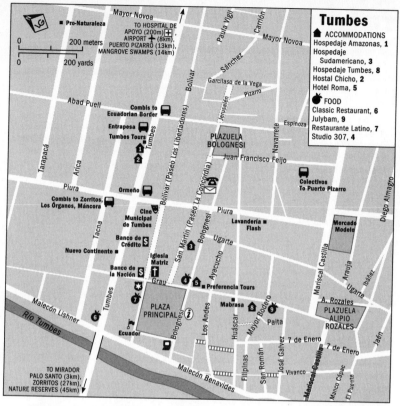

Tumbes

🏠 **ACCOMMODATIONS**
Hospedaje Amazonas, **1**
Hospedaje
Sudamericano, **3**
Hospedaje Tumbes, **8**
Hostal Chicho, **2**
Hotel Roma, **5**

🍎 **FOOD**
Classic Restaurant, **6**
Julybam, **9**
Restaurante Latino, **7**
Studio 307, **4**

(7hr., s/45-70). Also travels to **Guayaquil, Ecuador** (4½hr., daily 9:30am, US$15).
Combis to **Los Órganos** (2hr., leave when full 4am-8pm, s/6) via **Zorritos** (20min., s/1.50) and **Máncora** (1¾hr., s/5) leave from the intersection of Tumbes and Piura. **Terminal Tumbes,** Tumbes 306 (open 24hr.), at the corner with Piura, sends **colectivos** to **Piura** (3½hr., s/20) via **Sullana** (3hr., s/20).

Taxis: Mototaxis cost s/1-2 in town.

 BORDER CROSSING: INTO ECUADOR. Tumbes-Huaquillas is the most popular place to cross the Peru-Ecuador border. Consequently, there are often substantial waits and unpleasant hassles; it can be much easier (but less convenient) to cross between Sullana and Macará. If you still want to cross here, catch one of the **Aguas Verdes**-bound auto-colectivos (35min., 7am-7pm, s/1.50), either on Tumbes at Piura or on Mariscal Castilla at the northern end of the market, to **Peruvian Migraciones** (☎ 56 1178; open 24hr.). Get your **passport** stamped there, then take a mototaxi to the bridge (3km, 5min., s/1) and walk across to **Huaquillas, Ecuador.** You must then pass through **Ecuadorian Migraciones,** to the right after the bridge. Buses to **Guayaquil** leave from the far end of the main street (4hr., US$10).

ORIENTATION AND PRACTICAL INFORMATION

Finding Tumbes's social scene isn't hard: just stroll along the two pedestrian walkways, **Bolívar** (also called **Paseo Las Libertadores**) and **San Martín** (also called **Paseo La Concordia**), radiating from the ever-popular **Plaza Principal** at the town's southern end. The main vehicle thoroughfares are **Tumbes** and parallel **Mariscal Castilla**, home to **Mercado Modelo**. At night, stick to the Plaza and pedestrian zones; walkways and side streets are known for pickpockets.

Tourist Office: The **tourist office** (☎52 3699; tumbes@mitinci.gob.pe), in the Centro Cívico, on the Plaza Principal, room 204, dispenses free city **maps** and basic tourist information. Spanish only. Open M-F 7:30am-7pm. **Pro-Naturaleza**, Tarapacá 4-16 (☎52 3412; ptumbes@cosapidata.com.pe), an organization committed to conservation and sustainable development, gives tips about ecotourism in the area and organizes trips to nearby wildlife refuges. Open M-F 8am-1:30pm and 4-7pm.

Tours: Tumbes Tours, Tumbes 341 (☎52 4837; www.tumbestours.com), arranges city tours that include the mangrove swamps and the *miradores* (3-4hr., US$18 per person), trips to the nearby beaches and the Hervideros mud baths, trips to the mangrove forests or Hervideros mud baths (3-4hr., US$18 per person), and full-day tours of the Parque Nacional Cerros de Amotape (US$55) or the Zona Reservada de Tumbes (US$45) that include lunch. All tours (min. 2 people, though they'll take 1 if you pay double) are led by the enthusiastic Emilio Mendoza Feijo. Spanish only. Open M-Sa 8am-7:30pm. **Preferencia Tours**, Grau 427 (☎52 5518; turismomundial@hotmail.com), near the Plaza Principal, offers similar packages, including full-day trips to Cerros de Amotape (15hr., US$23) or the Zona Reservada (7hr., s/140). Also organizes visits to the mangrove swamps (5hr., s/140). Prices are set for groups of 3—if you have 1 or 2, the price is the same. Some English spoken. Open daily 8am-8pm.

Consulates: Ecuador, Bolívar 129, 3rd fl. (☎52 5949), on the Plaza Principal. Arranges tourist visas. Open M-F 9am-1pm and 3-5pm.

Currency Exchange: Banco de Crédito, Bolívar 261 (☎52 3150), on Paseo Los Libertadores, exchanges AmEx/CitiCorp/MC/V traveler's checks (US$12 commission for dollars). 24hr. Plus/V **ATM**. Open M-F 9am-1:15pm and 4:15-6:30pm, Sa 9:30am-12:30pm. **Banco de la Nación** (☎52 2355), on the corner of Bolívar and Grau. Open M-F 9am-1:30pm and 4-6:30pm. There's no MC ATM service anywhere in Tumbes.

Market: Mercado Modelo, on Mariscal Castilla between Ugarte and Piura. Open M-Sa 6am-5pm, Su 6am-1pm. **Street vendors** open until 7 or 8pm.

Laundromat: Lavandería Flash, Piura 1018 (☎52 3604). s/3 per kg; s/12 min. Open M-Sa 8:30am-1pm and 3:30-8pm.

Emergency: ☎52 3515 or 105.

Police: ☎52 2525 or 52 2800. On the 10th block of Tumbes.

Hospital: Hospital de Apoyo, 24 de Julio 565 (☎52 4275, 52 222, or 52 1703), at Tumbes. Open M-Sa 8am-1pm.

Telephones: Telefónica del Perú, San Martín 212, next to Serpost, sells phone cards and has public phones. Open daily 9am-9pm.

Internet Access: Modern Systems, Bolognesi 109 (☎52 2081), in the blue building on the corner of the Plaza Principal, behind the mural. s/1.50 per hr.

Post Office: Serpost, San Martín 208 (☎52 3866). Open M-Sa 8am-8:15pm, Su 8am-3:15pm.

ACCOMMODATIONS

Tumbes's safest budget hotels are near the Plaza Principal. Hot water comes at a price, and the cheapest hotels have even their cold water shut off at midday. Although hotel owners post prices at the front desk, many will negotiate for discounts. The heat can be unbearable, so get a room with a window or a fan. Make reservations in advance, as Tumbes receives heavy border traffic.

Hospedaje Tumbes, Grau 614 (☎52 2203). A friendly bargain. Not quite centrally located, but clean, spacious rooms come with fans and private baths. Cable TV in room s/5. Common TV lounge. Singles s/19; doubles s/29; triples s/39. ❷

Hotel Roma, Grau 425 (☎52 4137; fax 52 2494; hotelromatumbes@hotmail), at Bolognesi, on the Plaza Principal. Elegant interiors and bright bedspreads complement rooms with fans, cable TVs, and hot private baths. Staff provides basic tourist information. Singles s/40; matrimonials and doubles s/60; triples s/75. Extra bed s/18. ❹

Hospedaje Amazonas, Tumbes 317 (☎52 5266). Right by the major bus stations, this hostel is surprisingly calm and quiet. The large, comfortable rooms have fans, firm but snug beds, private baths, and clean wood floors. All rooms come with cable TV, but you can request to waive the fee (s/5) at check-in. TV lounge. Security box. Singles s/25; doubles s/35; triples s/45. ❸

Hostal Chicho, Tumbes 327 (☎52 2282), by the bus terminals. Rooms are tight, but have plenty of amenities: fans, TVs, fridges, hot water, and mosquito nets. Groups of 5 will revel in the *familiar* room (s/65), which has access to a pleasant balcony. Movies s/7. Singles s/25; matrimonials s/35; doubles s/40; triples s/45. ❸

Hospedaje Sudamericano, San Martín 130, 1 block from the Plaza Principal. Barebones rooms, but the location is convenient and the price a steal. Singles s/10, with bath s/15; doubles s/12, with bath s/17. ❶

FOOD

You'll have no trouble finding *comida típica* in Tumbes. The *conchas negras* (black clams, for which the region is famous), *ceviche*, and other seafood specialties are universally fresh. Vegetarian-friendly fare and dirt-cheap meals can be hard to come by, but *panaderías* like **Mabrasa,** Huáscar 245, at Grau, offer warm rolls for mere centavos. (☎52 2300. Open daily 6am-2pm and 4-9pm.)

Studio 307 (☎52 4052), at Grau and Bolognesi. Doubling as Tumbes's most popular nightspot, *"El Estudio"* is one of the best restaurants in town. Sandwiches and burgers s/4-10. Entrees s/8-15. Beer s/6. Open M-Th and Su 8am-midnight, F-Sa 8am-2am. ❷

Restaurante Latino, Bolívar 163 (☎52 3198), on the Plaza Principal. Pleasant outdoor tables, a huge menu in English and Spanish, and even larger portions of local specialties like *cau cau de mariscos* (s/15) and *ceviche* (s/12). Entrees s/11-13, specialties s/13.50-17.50. Live shows some nights. Open daily 7am-11pm. ❸

Classic Restaurant, Tumbes 179 (☎52 3188). In keeping with its name, these guys whip up Tumbes's classic dishes. Sandwiches s/2.50-3.50. Entrees s/11-16, including *conchas negras* (s/11). Open Su-F 11:30am-5pm. AmEx/V. ❷

Julybam (☎52 2288), on the corner of Grau and Bodero. Breakfasts (s/5-7), lunches (s/3-5), and dinners (s/5-7), or all 3 for s/8.50-10. Open daily 7am-9pm. ❶

SIGHTS AND ENTERTAINMENT

Four different ecological zones converge at Tumbes, making it a great place for all types of natural sightseeing. The **beaches** stretch south from the city. The *manglares* (mangrove swamps) begin north of Tumbes at Puerto Pizarro. The third and fourth regions comprise vast dry and wet forests to the southeast and east. To view all of these zones at once and get a sense of the abrupt contrast between them, check out the stunning 360° panorama from the **Mirador Turístico Palo Santo,** 2½km outside of town. On a clear day, the view stretches all the way to Ecuador's Isla Puná. (Taxi 10min., s/3. ☎ 52 4837. Open Th-Tu 10am-6pm. s/3.) The city streets near Grau and Huascar are full of colonial and 19th-century buildings, beautiful murals and fountains, and wonderful mosaics.

Residents emphasize that the city is *muy tranquilo*, which implies not only safe and clean (at least in the Plaza and on well-lit pedestrian paths) but also dead at night. The few small discos and karaoke bars near the Plaza Principal are lively only on weekends, and even then most empty out by 1am. You can watch American movies at the **Cine Municipal de Tumbes,** at Bolívar and Piura (Sa-Su 7pm; s/5), but most locals prefer a stroll through the Plaza.

◪ DAYTRIPS FROM TUMBES

NATURE RESERVES

*Tumbes Tours (see **Tours,** p. 338) offers great daytrips to both reserves that include transportation, lunch, and an informative Spanish-speaking guide (US$45 per person, less for larger groups). To visit both, you'll need at least 2 full days. If you want to visit the reserves on your own, you'll have to rent a 4×4 (US$65-85 per day), as the roads are unpaved and hard to navigate. The Tumbes tourist office strongly recommends hiring a guide and can make arrangements with any from their list (s/20-30 per day). Independent visitors also need a free permit from the Ministry of Agriculture (INRENA), Tarapacá 401 (☎ 52 6489), in Tumbes. The reserves are easiest to access March to November.*

The nature reserves near Tumbes offer a quick, inexpensive impression of South America's biological diversity. Two hours southeast of Tumbes await the orchids, butterflies, birds, and beasts (including jaguars, tigers, and armadillos) of the tropical rainforest known as the **Zona Reservada de Tumbes,** quite similar in flora and fauna to the Amazon Basin. Many wildlife enthusiasts come here to see two unique species: a breed of *mono coto* **(howler monkey)** much larger than those found around the Amazon, and the *cocodrilo americano,* a **freshwater crocodile** common in Río Tumbes. Across the river, lush vegetation turns to dry desert forest in **Parque Nacional Cerros de Amotape.** Spiny flora is less dense here, but the diversity of fauna is still impressive—**pumas, anteaters, red-headed monkeys, foxes, iguanas,** and **condors** all thrive in this arid ecosystem.

PUERTO PIZARRO

*Colectivos to Puerto Pizarro (20min., 5am-8pm, s/1) leave from Juan Francisco Feijo, half a block up from Mariscal Castillas and Francisco Ibañez, behind the market. Before you head out, check a tide book; while it's possible to visit the islands at low tide, high tide brings easier access to the islands and crocodile farms, not to mention better views. The Cómite Transportes Aquático (☎ 54 3018, ask for César Paredes or Miguel Velásquez) runs boats to the islands—no reservations necessary, just look for the few boats with outboards to the left facing the water. Alternatively, organize a tour (see **Tours,** p. 338) that will handle all that for you—including boat fees—and also visits the Mirador (US$18).*

Thirteen kilometers north of Tumbes, Puerto Pizarro is a fishing village so tiny that residents never bothered naming the few sandy streets. This poses no problem for visitors, however, as everything one needs lies along the main street to the water. Observing the fishing activity while munching on *ceviche* can be fun, but the **mangrove swamps** are the real attraction. The most popular destinations are the secluded **Isla del Amor** (5min., s/15), **Isla Hueso de Ballena** (10min., s/20), and **Isla de las Aves** (30min., s/30). The Isla del Amor is just a small beach, so named because locals claim that whenever two lovers go to the island, three people come back. The Isla Hueso de Ballena provides a view of the river as it joins the Pacific. The Isla de las Aves is particularly spectacular around 5 or 6pm, when its seemingly infinite avian residents, including **herons, frigates,** and **pelicans,** come home to roost. While it's possible to visit just one or two islands, the full tour, which can include a stop at the crocodile farm on **Isla Criadero de Cocodrilos** (entrance s/25 per boat), is much more satisfying (1-2hr., s/50 for groups of up to 8). In Puerto Pizarro, a few restaurants lie along the road to Tumbes.

BEACHES NEAR TUMBES

Two major marine currents intersect off the coast: cold Humboldt from the south and tepid El Niño from the north. This collision creates both sizable waves and a fertile marine habitat, featuring some of the largest fish banks in Peru, as well as numerous pelicans and egrets. Some beaches lie dormant during the winter (June-Sept.), but most pick up in the summer (Dec.-Mar.).

ZORRITOS

Zorritos, 27km south of Tumbes, is a fishing town with a clean beach and the most consistently warm water on the coast. Though its sizable waves pale in comparison to those farther south, the absence of a riptide makes Zorritos ideal for swimming. The lack of a sizable surfer scene actually works to Zorritos's advantage, making the beach safer than hotspots like Máncora. Other main attractions are the nearby **Aguas Termomedicinales de Hervideros.** The mud baths are famous for healing skin ailments—you can step into different pits for different problems: acne, warts, etc. There are no showers, so bring an old towel and some water to rinse with. Tour agencies in Tumbes (p. 338) charge US$20 for trips to the mud baths, but you can trek there on a marked trail that starts from Hostal Casa Grillo (3hr. round-trip). On the road from Tumbes, the village of **Caleta La Cruz,** 10km north of Zorritos, is of minor historical interest; it's the spot where Pizarro first landed on the Peruvian coast in 1532. Another popular bathing spot, **El Tubo,** a geyser created by a failed oil well, is 3km north of town and easily accessible by mototaxi.

To get to Zorritos from Tumbes hop on a southbound **combi** (s/1.50) from the intersection of Tumbes and Piura or get on any Piura-bound bus and ask the driver to drop you off (s/2). While there are a few small hotels and seafood restaurants in the village itself, **◪Hostal Casa Grillo (HI) ❷,** Los Pinos 563, at Panamericana Km1235, is 2km south. This eco-friendly ranch comes with lots of amenities and plenty of comfort. Spanish-born owner José León Millau also arranges tours (9 days, 8 nights US$260 all-inclusive) to nearby Cerros de Amotape, the Mangrove swamps, the mud baths, and the Bosque Húmedo de Tumbes. (☎/fax 54 4222; www.usuarios.lycos.es/casagrillo. Kitchen use. Laundry s/2 per kg. Horse rental s/15 per hr. Free bike use. Rooms US$6-7, with bath US$8-10. Discounts for *Let's Go* (US$1-2), HI (US$1), and ISIC (US$1).) Casa Grillo also allows **camping ❶** (US$2-3 per person, with tent US$5-5.50) and maintains an excellent, veggie-friendly **restaurant ❸.** Oven-baked pizzas (s/10-20) and the seafood *menú* (s/15) are favorites.

MÁNCORA   ☎073

Due to a fortuitous confluence of stunning scenery, killer waves, and an overall chilled-out attitude, Máncora's beaches have developed a legendary reputation. Attracted by hollow waves that reach heights of 3m in the summer (Nov.-Mar.) but are stellar year-round, **surfers** come in throngs to partake of this small town's most popular pastime. Although the Panamericana (called Piura) cuts through the center of town, the clean beach is completely isolated from the highway: one peaceful, seemingly endless strip of white sand. **Las Pocitas,** a series of tidepools worn into the underlying rock 2½km south of town, is a serene spot (mototaxi s/3).

Camping on the beach, while permitted and free, may be more worry than it's worth, especially since there are plenty of hostels in town. Several secluded beach hotels lie on a bumpy dirt road south, but most budget options are near the town. The most crowded is the beachfront **Sol y Mar ❸,** off the second block of Piura. All rooms have private baths, and the location can't be beat; guests relax on a huge patio facing the ocean or by the small pool. (☎85 8106; www.vivamancora.com/solymar. High season US$10 per person. Low season US$4.50.) **Casablanca ❷,** Piura 229, has similar, albeit slightly larger rooms with private cold baths. (☎85 8337. Singles s/15; doubles s/30, with ocean view, TV, and fan s/40; triples s/45.) Crowds hungry for seafood rush to **Restaurant Espada ❸,** Piura 655. The *ceviche* (s/16) is incredible. (☎85 8338. Entrees s/12-26. Open daily 8am-11pm.)

To reach Máncora, take a **colectivo** (s/5) from the intersection of Tumbes and Piura in Tumbes, or get on any Piura-bound bus and ask the driver to drop you off in Máncora (s/5). From Máncora, **Civa,** Piura 628 (open daily 10am-5pm), sends buses to Lima (15hr., daily 3:30pm, s/65-120). **Cruz del Sur** (☎49 6832; open daily 9am-7pm), at the end of Piura, also sends buses to Lima (16hr., daily 6:30pm., s/110-150). Using Piura or Tumbes as a transportation hub yields more options.

The **Panamericana** ("Piura") runs right through Máncora, and most of the restaurants and shops line the highway. If you walk just a few meters toward the ocean, you'll hit the gorgeous beach. Máncora's popularity has led to a surprising array of services. **Banco de la Nación,** Piura 527, exchanges dollars. (☎36 9235. Open M-F 8am-2:30pm.) A new 24hr. Plus/V **ATM** lies half a block south of the **Palacio Municipal,** where basic **tourist information** is available. The **police** are at Piura 645 (☎85 8098). **Telefónica del Perú,** Piura 509, allows collect and calling card calls. (☎/fax 85 8212. Open daily 7am-11pm.) **Internet** is at **Surf@Net,** Piura 605. (☎67 2459. s/1.50 per hr. Open daily 10am-2pm and 4-11pm.) If you come unprepared for the waves, **Soledad,** across from Sol y Mar, rents bodyboards (s/10 per day) and longboards (s/15 per day) and sells the latest surfing gear. (Open daily 8am-10pm.)

CABO BLANCO

Most backpackers probably recognize Cabo Blanco from the labels on Peru's most popular economy rum, but in an unexpected union, surfers and literature buffs alike revere this fishing center 109km south of Tumbes as something more. **Ernest Hemingway** made frequent visits here in the 1950s and supposedly wrote *The Old Man and the Sea* in the **Cabo Blanco Fishing Club Hotel;** the 1955 movie version was also filmed here, not in Cuba. Unfortunately the Cabo Blanco Fishing Club has been closed for a few years. You can visit the remnants of this once grand hotel by asking locals for directions, but the visit to the sight may prove more of a hassle than it's worth. With all the oil pumps crowding the water nowadays, Cabo Blanco hardly looks like a place that inspires great novels, but its radical waves (Nov.-Dec., 2.50-3m) bring a flood of surfers every year. Camping on the beach is free; pitch your tent above the tide line. To reach Cabo Blanco from Tumbes, simply stand by the highway and look for a Cabo Blanco- or Piura-bound **colectivo.** Get off at the El Alto turnoff (45min., s/2), and take a **camioneta** to the beach (30min., s/2).

THE NORTHERN HIGHLANDS

The Cordillera Blanca is the most spectacular expanse of mountains in Peru and the second highest range in South America—19 of its summits are over 6000m in elevation. Towering from the center, Nevado Huascarán (the country's highest peak, at 6768m) lends its name to the 3400 sq. km Parque Nacional Huascarán, which holds jagged, glacier-crowned peaks, brilliant alpine lakes, sprawling mountain passes, and unlimited opportunities for outdoor adventure. Between the Cordillera Blanca and the smaller Cordillera Negra lies the Callejón de Huaylas, a beautiful glacial valley that stretches some 15km across. There are countless treks to be made and mountains to be climbed in this area, all of them best attempted during the dry season (May-Sept.). Crossing the Río Marañón, travelers witness a distinct change in climate and vegetation; its waters mark the end of the Cordillera, the beginning of the elevated jungle, and the edge of the northern highlands.

In the highland outskirts of the north, farmers continue to work the fertile lands as they have for centuries. As one of the relatively undiscovered areas of the country, this swath of mountainous terrain is host to a plethora of rural villages and remote cities that serve as gateways to spectacular hikes through the pristine Andean surroundings. In these far-flung regions, the concept of urban stress is as foreign as laptops and cell phones.

HIGHLIGHTS OF THE NORTHERN HIGHLANDS

TREK the awe-inspiring slopes of the **Cordillera Huayhuash** (p. 359).

CONTEMPLATE the symbolism of the ancient engravings at the 3000-year-old **Chavín de Huántar** ruins (p. 352).

STROLL along the **Pastoruri Glacier** (p. 353) near Callejón, where the famous Puya Raymondi plant grows.

DELVE into the stunning mountain scenery of **Parque Nacional Huascarán,** a UNESCO Mankind Heritage Site (p. 349).

THE CORDILLERA BLANCA

HUARAZ   ☎ 043

As the primary gateway to the Cordillera Blanca, Huaraz (pop. 114,000; elev. 3100m) buzzes with constant chatter about Andean adventures. Surrounded by snow-capped mountain peaks, Huaraz sees more and more Goretex- and polar-fleece- clad tourists every year. It's never hard to find great climbing, hiking, rafting, and traveling companions in Huaraz. It is, after all, the jumping-off point for the best hiking in Peru. Among older locals, however, talk is not always so light-hearted: Huaraz residents refer to events in the region's history as *"antes de"* (before) or *"después de"* (after) the catastrophic earthquake that shattered all but one street and killed half the city's population in 1970. Huaraz is still rebuilding,

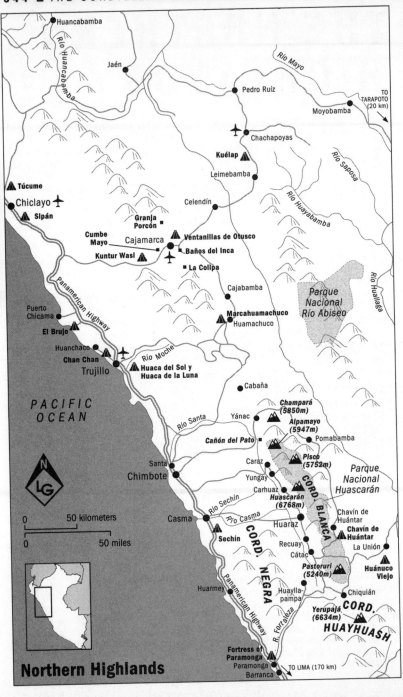

Huancabamba

Río Huancabamba

Jaén

Río Mayo

Pedro Ruíz

TO TARAPOTO (20 km)

Moyobamba

Chachapoyas

Río Saposa

Kuélap

Leimebamba

Río Huayabamba

Túcume

Chiclayo

Celendín

Sipán

Granja Porcón

Cumbe Mayo

Cajamarca

Ventanillas de Otusco

Kuntur Wasi

Baños del Inca

La Collpa

Río Huallaga

Cajabamba

Parque Nacional Río Abiseo

Puerto Chicama

Panamerican Highway

El Brujo

Marcahuamachuco

Huamachuco

Huanchaco

Río Moche

Chan Chan

Trujillo

Huaca del Sol y Huaca de la Luna

Cabaña

PACIFIC OCEAN

Río Santa

Champará (5850m)

Yánac

Alpamayo (5947m)

Cañón del Pato

Pomabamba

Santa

Caraz

Pisco (5752m)

Parque Nacional Huascarán

Chimbote

Yungay

Carhuaz

Huascarán (6768m)

CORD. BLANCA

Río Sechín

Huaraz

Chavín de Huántar

Casma

Río Casma

Chavín de Huántar

Sechín

Recuay

La Unión

CORD. NEGRA

Cátac

Pastoruri (5240m)

Huánuco Viejo

Huarmey

Huaylla-pampa

Chiquián

Yerupajá (6634m)

CORD. HUAYHUASH

Panamerican Highway

R. Fortalza

Fortress of Paramonga

TO LIMA (170 km)

Paramonga

Barranca

Northern Highlands

50 kilometers

50 miles

but urban splendor—or lack thereof—isn't what draws tourists. It's the city's prime location in the Callejón de Huaylas (Río Santa Valley) and the countless companies catering to their needs that make it so popular with outdoorsy types.

TRANSPORTATION

Buses: Bus companies flank Raymondi, Bolívar, and Lucar y Torre. **Cruz del Sur,** Lucar y Torre 573 (☎58 7722; open daily 8am-9pm), goes to **Lima** (7hr.; 11am, 10pm; s/35). **Transportes Línea,** Bolívar 450 (☎72 6666), goes to **Trujillo** (9hr., 9:30pm, s/35) via **Chimbote** (7hr., 9:30pm, s/30). **Móvil Tours,** Bolívar 452 (☎72 2555; open daily 7am-11pm), sends buses to: **Chimbote** (6hr.; 9, 9:30pm; s/25-30); **Lima** (8hr.; 9:30am, 12:30, 10, 11pm; s/25-45); **Trujillo** (8hr., 9:30pm, s/35). **Chavín Express,** Cáceres 338 (☎72 4652; open daily 4am-9pm), goes to **Chavín** (4hr.; M-F 4, 9:30am, 2, 8pm and Sa-Su 8, 9:30am, 2, 8pm; s/10). **El Rápido,** Bolognesi 261 (☎962 6361; open daily 5am-8pm), sends buses to: **Huallanca** (4½hr., 6am, s/15); **Llamac** (5hr., 5:30am, s/20) via **Chiquián** (2½hr., 5:30am, s/10); **La Unión** (6hr., 12:30pm, s/18). **Combis** depart from the bridge over the Río Quilcay and head north to **Caraz** (2hr., every 30min. 5am-8pm, s/3.50) via **Carhuaz** (1hr., s/2) and **Yungay** (1½hr., s/3). For eastern and southern Cordillera Blanca destinations, look for **combis** on Cáceres and 27 de Noviembre.

Taxis: Taxis cruise up and down Luzuriaga (s/2 in town).

Bike Rental: Chacraraju Mountain Shop (see **Outdoor Equipment,** below).

ORIENTATION AND PRACTICAL INFORMATION

Snug between the Cordillera Blanca and the Cordillera Negra, Huaraz rests in the Río Santa Valley, also known as the **Callejón de Huaylas.** The majority of Huaraz's tourism industry is centered on the main thoroughfare **Luzuriaga,** between **Raymondi** and the **Plaza de Armas.** Other businesses radiate out from the Plaza and are concentrated within the rectangle created by **Gamarra, 27 de Noviembre, Raymondi,** and **28 de Julio.** Beyond these boundaries, the number of backpackers thins noticeably, and Huaraz goes back to being just another mountain town.

TOURIST AND FINANCIAL SERVICES

Tourist Offices:

■ **Casa de Guías,** Parque Ginebra 28 (☎72 7545 or 72 1811), 1 block from the Plaza, through one of the tunnels from Luzuriaga. In addition to running Peru's only accredited school for mountaineering guides, the Casa also provides guides, maintains a list of accredited and in-training guides, and sells hiking **maps.** The bulletin board outside posts trekking info. Dorm-style **accommodations ❷** are also available here (s/15). Open M-Sa 9am-1pm and 4-8pm.

iPerú, Luzuriaga 734, Pasaje Atuspariá (☎72 8812), on the Plaza. Provides assistance to tourists and has info on Huaraz. They also accept and keep on file complaints against local guide agencies. Open M-Sa 8:30am-6:30pm and Su 9am-5pm. The **tourist police** keep an office on the mezzanine (see **Police,** below).

Oficina Central del Parque Nacional Huascarán, Federico Sal y Rosas 555 (☎72 2086). Sells **tickets** to the park and has **maps** that can be photocopied. They also provide up-to-date information about park conditions and advice about hiking routes. Open M-F 9am-1pm and 3-5pm.

Tours: For information and a list of agencies, see **Guided Tours from Huaraz,** p. 351.

Banks: These banks are all located on or just off the Plaza, and all have **24hr. ATMs.**

Banco Continental, on the Plaza. Plus/V ATM.

Banco de Crédito, Luzuriaga 691 (☎72 1170). Open M-F 10am-6:30pm, Sa 9:30am-12:30pm. Plus/V ATM.

Banco Wiesse, Sucre 760 (☎72 1500). Open M-F 9am-1:30pm and 4-6:30pm, Sa 9:30am-12:30pm. Cirrus/Plus/V ATM

Interbank, Sucre 687 (☎72 3015 or 75 1502). Has a **Western Union** office. Open M-F 9am-1pm and 4-6:15pm, Sa 9:15am-12:30pm. AmEx/Cirrus/Plus/V ATM.

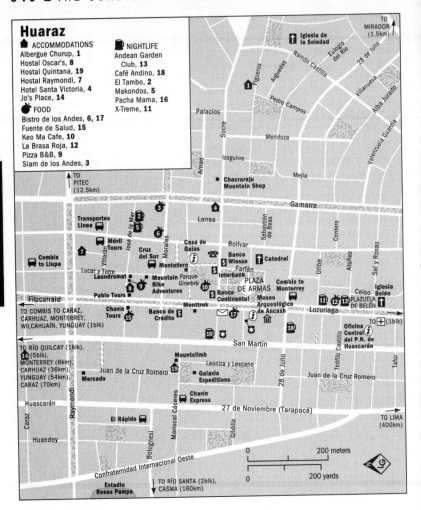

Huaraz

⌂ ACCOMMODATIONS
Albergue Churup, **1**
Hostal Oscar's, **8**
Hostal Quintana, **19**
Hostal Raymondi, **7**
Hotel Santa Victoria, **4**
Jo's Place, **14**

🍴 FOOD
Bistro de los Andes, **6, 17**
Fuente de Salud, **15**
Keo Ma Cafe, **10**
La Brasa Roja, **12**
Pizza B&B, **9**
Siam de los Andes, **3**

🍷 NIGHTLIFE
Andean Garden
  Club, **13**
Café Andino, **18**
El Tambo, **2**
Makondos, **5**
Pacha Mama, **16**
X-Treme, **11**

LOCAL SERVICES

Outdoor Equipment: Bargaining is expected, especially if you're renting more than 1 item, or for more than 1 day. Many equipment rental places also provide guides.

Chacraraju Mountain Shop, Sucre 959 (☎72 7241; rommel667@hotmail.com), ½ block uphill from Gamarra. This general equipment rental store has the nicest bikes around (US$20 per day) as well as equipment for skiing, snowboarding, trekking, and climbing. Open daily 8am-10pm.

Galaxia Expeditions, Cáceres 428 (☎72 5691; galaxia_expedition@hotmail.com). Rents trekking and climbing gear, boots, and coats. Prices are similar to Mountclimb's. Full gear for 2 US$50 per day. Organizes treks and climbs, and guides speak English, French, and German. A small cafe and climbing wall hide behind the equipment racks. Open daily 8am-2pm and 4-10pm.

Monttrek, Luzuriaga 646 (☎72 1124; fax 72 6976; monttrek@terra.com.pe). Hiking equipment, ski, and snowboard rentals. Climbing wall available. Open daily 8am-2pm and 4-10:30pm.

Mountclimb, Cáceres 421 (☎72 6060; www.mountclimb.com). Top-notch equipment. 2-person tents from US$2 per day. Stoves US$2.50 per day. Sleeping bags US$2-3 per day. Also arranges tours (see **Guided Tours from Huaraz,** p. 351). Open daily 9am-1pm and 5-10pm.

Markets: Indoor market, at Raymondi and Juan de la Cruz Romero. Has all the fruit, dry food, and shoe repair specialists you could ever need. Open daily 7am-7pm. The **Feria Artesanal,** on the Plaza de Armas, sells local handicrafts. Open daily 9am-9pm.

Laundromat: A dozen or so full-service laundromats dot the downtown area. Many hotels also offer laundry service. Standard rate s/3 per kg. **Lavandería Tintorería B&B,** José de la Mar 674 (☎72 1719), specializes in cleaning items like sleeping bags and coats (s/20) and backpacks (s/8-15). Open M-Sa 9am-1pm and 3-8pm.

EMERGENCY AND COMMUNICATIONS

Emergency: ☎105.

Police: Regular **police** are at Sucre, Mz. 1 (☎72 1330), just below the Plaza. **Tourist police** are at Luzuriaga 734, Pasaje Atusparía, on the Plaza. On the mezzanine of the iPerú tourist office. Open M-F 8am-1pm and 5-8pm.

Hospital: Hospital de Apoyo "Victor Ramos Guardia" (☎72 1861, ext. 47), on Luzuriaga near Pedro Villón. Open daily 7am-1pm, for emergencies 24hr.

Telephones: Public phones are all over Huaraz. For more privacy, try a booth in **Telefónica,** Sucre 729-797 (☎72 2020). Open daily 7am-11pm.

Internet Access: Plentiful throughout Huaraz. s/1-1.50 per hr.

Post Office: Serpost, Luzuriaga 702 (☎72 1030), on the Plaza de Armas, at the corner of Sucre and Luzuriaga. Open M-Sa 8am-8pm.

▐▛ ACCOMMODATIONS

Huaraz sees a wide variety of travelers, and the smorgasbord of comfortable, affordable accommodations reflects this. Lodgings here come in two varieties: hotels and backpacker hostels with dorm rooms. There is a kind of symbiosis between lodgings and tours: many expedition companies have a few guest rooms, and many backpacker accommodations can help to arrange expeditions. Everywhere in Huaraz, bargaining is common from October to April.

▨ **Albergue Churup,** Amadeo Figueroa 1257 (☎72 2584). Popular, and rightly so. Airy and well-furnished lounges, a spacious backyard, book exchange, trip advice, equipment rental, laundry service (US$1 per kg), and 24hr. hot water make this a weary traveler's dream come true. Large breakfasts s/8. Reservations recommended. No singles. Dorm beds US$4. Upstairs rooms with bath and breakfast, US$8-10 per person. ❷

Jo's Place, Daniel Villazaín 276 (☎72 5505), 2½ blocks past the bridge at Fitzcarrald (the continuation of Luzuriaga), then 2 blocks to the right. Backpackers compare trekking tales as they picnic in the tent-filled garden of this out-of-the-way hostel. British owner Jo and his wife Vicky make visitors of all nationalities feel at home with tasty breakfasts (s/3.50-6) and trekking advice. TV room/lounge with fireplace. Kitchen. Dorms US$3; singles US$4, with bath US$5. ❷

Hostal Quintana, Mariscal Cáceres 411 (☎72 6060), 2 blocks down from Luzuriaga, through the merchant tunnel, next door to Mountclimb. A nondescript exterior belies the clean, comfy interior. The rooms with bath are a particularly good value. The roof deck offers a place to sunbathe. Rooms s/15 per person, with bath s/20. ❷

Hotel Santa Victoria, Gamarra 694 (☎72 2422). A 3-star escape when you need a little luxury in your life. All rooms come with cable TVs, private baths, and monogrammed bedspreads. Breakfast included. Singles s/45; doubles s/70. Prices are eminently negotiable, even in the high season. ❹

Hostal Oscar's, José de la Mar 624 (☎72 2720), off Luzuriaga. Comfortable rooms have private baths, hot water, and color TVs. Choose a room on a high floor or at the back to avoid early morning noise. Singles s/25; doubles s/40; triples s/50. Prices drop by s/5-10 during the low season. ❸

Hostal Raymondi, Raymondi 820 (☎72 1082), very close to the long-distance bus companies and not far from transport (i.e., combis). Basic but well-furnished rooms with baths surround an expansive reception area. The walls of each room sport a different hand-painted design. Hot water 8-11am and 6-8pm. Singles s/25; doubles s/30. ❸

🍴 FOOD

Huaraz has enough restaurants to satisfy any cravings and every budget. In the evenings, numerous elegant establishments fill with hungry trekkers just back from the mountains. Authentic Thai, French, Italian, and steak dinners will be a welcome break for many and a dent in the wallets of others. For cheaper, regional fare, look for local hangouts tucked between the trekking storefronts. Around Luzuriaga, numerous eateries offer lunchtime *menús*; be sure to try the Cordillera's signature dishes, *llunca* (wheat soup) and *charqui* (dried pork).

■ **Bistro de Los Andes,** two locations: on the Plaza de Armas (☎72 9556), above Serpost, and Morales 823 (☎73 6703). The meeting place of French and Peruvian cuisine. If you're up early, come for excellent brewed coffee (s/3). Later in the day, *trucha a la almendra* (almond trout s/22) is the house specialty. Other hits include giant salads (s/10-15) and the captivating *aji de quinoa* (s/10) or *de pollo* (s/17). Plaza de Armas location open daily 7am-11pm; Morales storefront open daily 11am-11pm. ❸

■ **Keo Ma Cafe,** Parque Ginebra 628 (☎72 8915), through the passage above Interbank, off the Plaza at Sucre. This honest-to-goodness coffee shop gets absolutely packed on rainy afternoons. Everything is delicious—the fresh cakes (s/1.50-4.50), breakfast (s/5-8), *empanadas* (s/2), and quiches (s/3). Chocolate truffles s/0.50-1.50. Keo Ma also prepares box lunches for dayhikes. Open 7am-9pm daily. ❶

Pizza B&B, José de la Mar 674 (☎72 1719). The massive eucalyptus-burning wood oven warms chilled travelers and cranks out crispy-crusted pizzas with your choice of toppings (personal s/9, s/0.80 per topping; large s/17, s/1.80 per topping). Even the sauce is made from scratch. Garlic bread s/3.50. Pasta s/11-15. Argentine steak s/24-29. Open daily noon-midnight in high season, 5pm-midnight in low season. ❷

Siam de los Andes, Gamarra 560 (☎72 8006), 3 blocks up Julián de Morales from Luzuriaga. Thai-American climber-chef Naresuan prepares exquisite curries and stir-fries. Set *menú* only (s/25-35). Great food justifies high prices. Open daily 6-10pm. ❹

Fuente de Salud, José de la Mar 562 (☎30 3028), just below Luzuriaga. True to its name, this is the perfect place to cure whatever might be ailing you. Common prescriptions include hearty breakfasts (s/5-11), vegetable soup (s/7), and the house specialty yogurt (s/3-9). Entrees s/8-20. Open daily 7am-11pm. ❷

La Brasa Roja, Luzuriaga 919 (☎72 7738). This joint is packed with trekkers and locals enjoying finger-lickin' chicken, pasta, and sandwiches. Entrees s/10-13. Open daily noon-midnight. ❷

🔆 SIGHTS

The main attractions here are of the outdoor variety; nevertheless, many of Huaraz's tour agencies offer **city tours** encompassing several primary sights (3-5hr.), although it's easy to see them on your own.

PARQUE NACIONAL HUASCARÁN. The world's highest tropical mountain chain is home to over 650 glaciers, nearly 300 lakes, and 26 mountain peaks that top 6000m. Established in 1975, the park was declared a UNESCO Mankind Heritage Site ten years later. Dozens of pre-Inca ruins nestle against the hills, and the descendents of ancient native peoples still herd animals and inhabit tiny towns within the park's boundaries. *(The park office, Federico Sal y Rosas 555 (☎72 2086), sells tickets and has maps. They also inform visitors about park conditions. Open M-F 9am-1pm and 3-5pm. Numerous tour companies arrange trips into the park ranging from daytrips to multi-day excursions; see **Guided Tours from Huaraz**, p. 351; and Hiking Near Huaraz, p. 353.)*

MUSEO ARQUEOLÓGICO DE ANCASH. This museum courageously attempts to represent all the cultures who have lived in the Ancash department over the past 12,000 years. Of particular interest are the nearly 100 Recuay **monoliths** that decorate the garden. Other exhibits include models of various sites (Cueva de Guitarreros, Wilcahuaín) and displays on music, metallurgy, and mummification. *(Luzuriaga 762, on the southwest corner of the Plaza de Armas. ☎72 1551. Open M-Sa 9am-5pm, Su 9am-2pm. s/5, students s/2. Guided tours available.)*

MONUMENTO ARQUEOLÓGICO DE WILCAHUAÍN. Dating back to AD 800-1000, these two Huari ruins, Chico and Grande, were used as food storage facilities and ceremonial centers. Three principal stone structures, impressive for their squat symmetry and obvious strength, mark the two locations. Of course, if you've been to the nearby Chavín ruins (p. 352), these might be a bit of a let-down. It's also possible to combine a visit to Wilcahuaín with a good bath at Monterrey. *(Combis marked "Wilcahuaín" leave from the bridge over Río Quilcay to Chico (30min., s/1) via Grande. Visit Chico first, then walk down to Grande and catch a combi home. Alternatively, it is possible to walk the 6km to the ruins, either on the main road or through the town of Huanchac. Open daily 8am-6pm. s/4, students s/2.)*

LOS BAÑOS DE MONTERREY. Two large pools and 19 smaller *pozas* (private chambers for one or two people) lure both locals and tourists. The water is brown, but don't worry—it's just minerals. *(7km north of Huaraz. Catch the green-and-white bus at the corner of Luzuriaga and 28 de Julio, or flag it down along Alameda Fitzcarrald (30min., s/ 0.50). Open daily 7am-6pm. Larger pool s/3. Private bath s/3 for 20min.)*

NIGHTLIFE

Nightlife booms in Huaraz, where hopes of cashing in on the tourist influx increase every year. For cheap drinks to get the night started, numerous bars and smaller discos at the end of José de la Mar offer competing specials. If you've got extra energy (and extra soles), party the night away at the following clubs.

El Tambo, José de la Mar 776 (☎72 3417), 3 blocks up from Luzuriaga. Smoky, crowded, and the music is always pumping. The DJ spins a mix of Top-40 hits, salsa, merengue, and technocumbia. Popular with travelers and locals alike. Beer s/5. Open daily 8pm-dawn. V.

X-Treme, at Luzuriaga and Uribe. A relaxed bar popular with backpackers, featuring rock music. Artwork left over from the previous owner, combined with chalk graffiti done by guests, creates an atmosphere where darts, checkers, and leather couches fit right in. Open daily 7pm-late.

Andean Garden Club, at Luzuriaga on the Plazuela de Belén. An open-air bar that captures the dual passions of the Huaraz backpacker scene—cold beer and rock climbing. A professional bouldering wall, the occasional bonfire, live bands, burritos, and excellent chili-burgers (s/8) create a friendly atmosphere from the afternoon on. Beer s/5. Sandwiches s/3-10. Open daily noon-midnight.

Café Andino, 28 de Julio 562 (☎72 8354), near Luzuriaga. This coffee house roasts its own beans and isn't afraid to add liquor. The travel advice, multilingual library, book exchange, and board games keep travelers entertained. Open daily 8am-10pm.

Pacha Mama, San Martín 687 (☎72 4200). An airy cafe and bar complete with fireplace, pool table, and big chess board. Mixed drinks s/8-10. Open daily noon-midnight.

Makondos, José de la Mar 812. Although next door to Tambo, Makondos is still able to pack the club's maze-like dance floors and cavernous side rooms. Upstairs bar has large windows good for both a view and a welcome gust of cold, fresh Andean air. Beer s/5. Open daily 8pm-dawn.

⚑ GUIDED TOURS FROM HUARAZ

Companies offer everything from driving tours to hang gliding adventures. Beware of agencies without credentials. Prices are more negotiable October through April, but even during peak season, comparison shopping is worthwhile. The following agencies offer an array of adventures.

Pablo Tours, Luzuriaga 501 (☎ 72 6384; pablotours@terra.com.pe). Tours of **Cañón del Pato** and **Laguna Parón** (2 person min., s/25-30), **Chavín de Huántar** (s/35), **Huaraz** (s/25), the **Lagunas Llanganuco** (s/30), and **Pastoruri** (s/30). Tours in English, French, German, and Italian, but call ahead and expect to pay extra. Prices drop slightly Oct.-Apr. Open daily high season 7-9pm, low season 7am-1pm and 4-9pm.

Chavín Tours, Luzuriaga 502 (☎72 1578; fax 72 4801; chavint@telematic.edu.pe). Tours to **Chavín de Huántar** (8hr., s/25-35), **Laguna de Llanganuco** (7hr., s/20-30), **Pastoruri Glacier** (7hr., s/20-30), and the city (4hr., s/20). Additional s/5-10 for entrance fees. Reservations preferred. Open daily 7:30am-noon and 4-9pm.

Montañero, Parque Ginebra 30 (☎72 6386). Works closely with the *Casa de Guías* and offers trekking, climbing, mountain biking, and conventional tours. Their shop offers equipment for sale and rental (2-person tents US$3-6 per day). The owners speak English, French, and German. Open daily 9am-1pm and 4-8pm.

Monttrek, Luzuriaga 646 (☎72 1124; fax 72 6976; monttrek@terra.com.pe). The place to go for extreme sports, with hang gliding, rafting, rock and ice-climbing, trekking, and horseback riding. Hiking equipment, ski, and snowboard rentals. Climbing wall available. Open daily 8am-2pm and 4-10:30pm.

Mountain Bike Adventures, Torre 530, 2nd fl. (☎72 4259; www.chakinaniperu.com), between José de la Mar and Julián Morales. Focuses on bike tours (US$20 per day) of Huaraz and the Cordilleras Blanca y Negra, but owner Julio Olaza provides other services too: dorm-style **lodging** ❷ (s/15), laundry (s/3 per kg), tons of regional **maps,** a well-stocked book exchange, and nightly info sessions (6-7pm). All tours include bikes, gloves, helmets, and English-speaking guides. Open daily 9am-1pm and 4-8pm.

Mountclimb, Cáceres 421 (☎72 6060; www.mountclimb.com). Trekking, climbing, rafting, and horseback riding expeditions. Open daily 9am-1pm and 5-10pm.

⚑ OUTDOOR ACTIVITIES

Hiking in and around **Parque Nacional Huascarán** is just one of many outdoor opportunities near Huaraz. For agencies that lead these expeditions, see **Guided Tours from Huaraz,** p. 350. For equipment rentals, see **Outdoor Equipment,** p. 345. For information on trekking and mountaineering, see **Hiking Near Huaraz,** p. 353.

BY LAND

Horseback riding (s/70 per day) provides a (relatively) comfortable way to admire the scenery north of Huaraz. Monttrek and Mountclimb lead popular trips such as Quebrada Quilcayhuanca (2-3 days) and Vicos to Laguna Lejiacocha (2 days).

Mountain biking expeditions can give you a new take on a traditional trek. Mountain Bike Adventures does rides in the Cordillera Negra; Chacraraju Mountain Shop (see **Outdoor Equipment**, p. 345) covers Blanca and Negra.

BY SEA

The Río Santa presents great **rafting** opportunities year-round. From November to May you can enjoy a "mellow" float from Jangas to Macará (1hr., Class I-III) or tackle either the Yungay-Caraz route (2hr., some Class V) or the toughest stretch of all, Carhuaz-Taquero (1hr., Class IV-V). Water levels are low the rest of the year, but the Río Santa is never tame. Many companies lead rafting excursions, but with 18 years of river experience, Monttrek is the granddaddy of them all. Arrange tours at least one day in advance (US$15-25 per person, 4 people min.).

BY AIR

If you'd rather soar than swim, consider getting a bird's-eye view of things while doing a little **hang gliding.** Only experienced fliers can attempt morning runs in the Callejón—the climatic changes are too dangerous for novices. If you're interested in gaining experience, contact **Jorge Chávez** in Lima. (Cell ☎ 01 444 5004; www.peru-fly.com.) If there's not time to learn, novices can fly tandem with a guide (30min.-2hr., US$40). Contact Monttrek to make arrangements.

BY SNOW

If you'd rather slide than ride, it's possible to trek up to Pastoruri Glacier and squeeze in some downhill action. **Skiing** and **snowboarding** equipment is available for rent at either Monttrek (US$15 per day for full gear) or Chacraraju Mountain Shop (US$20 per day for full gear). Transportation can be arranged with Pablo Tours or Huaraz Chavín Tours for around s/25 round-trip. When you feel like going vertical, check out a **rock or ice-climbing** course. Monttrek offers day-long ice-climbing at Pastoruri Glacier (s/70-80; includes transport, equipment, and guide) and 2- to 3-day rock climbing near Monterrey (US$20 per day, includes equipment and guide). Monttrek also takes experienced rock climbers to the Big Walls in the region, 300-1000m granite faces. Quebrada Llaca, Torres de Rurec, and Torres de Parón (a.k.a. the Sphynx) are the most popular climbs (3-4 days, US$25 per day).

🌿 FESTIVALS

The most important of Huaraz's several regional festivals is **Fiesta de Mayo** (May 2-9), which features dance festivals (showcasing *shacshas* and *huancillos*), fireworks, and the traditional procession of the Señor de la Soledad, normally kept in the Iglesia del Señor de la Soledad. Other significant celebrations include the **Semana de Huaraz** (July 22-25), the **Fiestas Patrias** (July 27-29), and the **Semana de Andinismo** (dates variable, check with the regional tourism office). Andinismo involves rock climbing, biking, kayaking, rafting, hang gliding, golfing, and skiing competitions. During festivals, transportation and lodging prices rise dramatically.

▶ DAYTRIPS FROM HUARAZ

The city's prime location makes short excursions to either of the Cordilleras easy. Many daytrips enter **Parque Nacional Huascarán**, a 340,000 hectare park created in 1975 to preserve the beauty of the Cordillera Blanca. Visitors should expect to pay a fee (day pass s/5, month pass s/65). For more daytrips, inquire at any of the aforementioned tour agencies or at the park office. (*Federico Sal y Rosas 555.* ☎ *72 2086. Open M-F 9am-1pm and 3-5pm. See* **Tourist Offices***, p. 345.)*

FLOWER POWER

The Puya Raymondi plant grows at altitudes of 3800-4200m and is found in only a few places in the world, including the Peruvian Andes. Among the distinctions of the Puya Raymondi plant are its immense size (up to 12m) and its status as the plant with the largest flowering stalk in the world. The plant is the largest member of the bromeliads, or pineapple family, though it looks more like a cactus than a pineapple plant.

Puya Raymondi live up to 100 years before coming to a brief, flashy end: they suddenly put forth thousands of flowers, which bloom for 2-3 months before the plants die. May is the best month for viewing this flowery swan song.

The latter half of the plant's name honors the Peruvian naturalist Antonio Raymondi, who first described it scientifically. "Puya" is derived from the Quechua word *pua* (spine), referring to the sharp, inward-pointing hooks on each stalk. The spines are so sharp and strong that it's not uncommon for animals to get inextricably stuck, leading to periodic attempts by herdsmen to burn the plants out. The Puya Raymondi have survived though, and remain an interesting and unique sight of the Andes. Just don't look too closely...

■ **CHAVÍN DE HUÁNTAR.** The intricate, 3000-year-old Chavín ruins stand as a testament to the extraordinary culture which came to influence people as far north as the Ecuadorian border and as far south as Ica. The Chavín lived here from about 1300 to 200 BC, and their stone ceremonial center managed to endure on its own until its formal protection by UNESCO in 1985. In order to build the temple, workers flattened a steep hill and constructed labyrinthine **galleries** (four of which are open to the public). A visit begins in the Plaza Cuadrangular (the Square Plaza), the larger and relatively younger of the central square spaces at the ruins. The nearby **Portico de las Falcónidas** (Arcade of the Eagles), with its male figure carved on black stone and female figure carved on white stone, demonstrates the Chavín's philosophy of duality. Large canals that once carried rushing water are visible beneath; some speculate that their purpose was to cool and ventilate the temple, or mimic the sound of thunder, which the Chavín revered. The most important artifact at Chavín is the beautiful **Lanzón**, still in its original site inside a gallery. The tall, white granite carving of a humanoid figure almost certainly represents a deity, adorned with fangs and serpentine carvings. Two other famous relics, the **Estela Raymondi** and the **Tello Obelisk**, were moved to the Museo Arqueológico in Lima (see **Museums**, p. 119); replicas lie near the start of the trail.

Although technically the whole complex is called the **Museo Arqueológico Chavín de Huántar,** the actual museum building, which houses other notable examples of Chavín carving, can be found near the entrance on 17 de Enero Sur, a 5min. walk uphill from Chavín's Plaza de Armas. *(Open daily 8am-5pm. s/10, students with ID s/5.)* A guide or an informational pamphlet (s/3, at the gate) can be helpful in understanding the culture behind this site—if your Spanish is adequate. Next to the museum grows a hearty San Pedro cactus, a plant whose juice induces a hallucinogenic trance, consumed regularly by Chavín priests to aid in divination. There are a few hotels in Chavín, but most visitors choose to daytrip here rather than spend the night. *(The majority of visitors come to Chavín with tours from Huaraz (2hr., around s/35), arriving around noon and leaving around 4pm. To reach Chavín independently, catch a bus on Chavín Express, Cáceres 338 (☎72 4652), from Huaraz (4hr.; 4 per day; s/10). Chavín Express, 100 Manco Cápac, on the Plaza in Chavín, sends buses back to Huaraz (4hr., 3 per day, s/10).)*

■ **LAGUNA 69.** It may have an unoriginal name, but this deep blue glacial lake at the foot of Nevado Chacraraju (6112m) is anything but bland. The hike leads up from the valley of the Lagunas

Llanganacu and provides panoramic views of glaciated giants such as Huascarán, Pisco, and Huandoy. *(From Yungay, take a Yanama-bound combi and ask to be let off just past Km31 at Cebollapampa (1½hr., s/5). Follow the trail branching off the left side of the road past the base camp and stay to the right of the river. The trail traverses cow and donkey pastures, then narrows and climbs up to the lake (16-17km, round-trip 6hr., elev. 3900-4600m). If you go with a guide, ask to start the hike from Km42, where a ridge provides even more impressive views from a poorly marked trail. Park fee s/5.)*

LAGUNA CHURUP. Lying at the foot of Nevado Churup (5495m), the turquoise lake of the same name provides newly arrived trekkers and climbers with a great hike for altitude adjustment before more lofty endeavors. The hardy can also begin this dayhike in Huaraz—ask at a tour agency or the Park office for where to catch the trail from Huaraz. Walk up the footpath to Pitec (1hr.), always choosing the rockier narrow path when it forks. *(Take a combi from the corner of Caraz and Vallunaraju in Huaraz to Llupa (30min., s/2). Park fee s/5 for daytrippers. From Pitec, the uphill hike takes 3hr. with significant rock scrambling toward the end. Return to Llupa by 5pm or risk a 30min. walk to Unchus, where combis to Huaraz run until 5pm.)*

LAGUNAS LLANGANUCO. On a clear day, two spectacular Andean lakes at the base of Huascarán shimmer, appearing to stretch themselves toward the Cordillera Blanca's highest peaks. Tourists most often visit the lower lake, Chinacocha, where tours from Huaraz (s/20-25) provide an hour of free time to rent rowboats (20 min., s/2.50), stroll along an interpretive nature trail (20min.), or simply sit back and admire the view. *(To travel the 60km to the Lagunas Llanganuco independently, start in Yungay (p. 363). Park fee s/5.)*

PASTORURI GLACIER. This popular excursion brings visitors to a flat Andean glacier (5240m). Although no special equipment is necessary, it's best to be acclimated before you attempt a visit. Tours climb to the top (45min.), then take an hour to explore a beautiful ice cave, stroll along the glacier, and admire the view. Tour agencies often combine this trip (9hr., s/20-25 per person) with a visit to Callejón's famous **Puya Raymondi plants** (see **Flower Power**, p. 352). Other stops include **Pumapampa** (where oxygen, trapped in ice and forced underground, bubbles to the surface in a cold spring) and **Pinturas Rupestres,** the site of cave paintings from 10,000 BC. *(Park fee s/5.)*

WILCAHUAÍN TO MONTERREY. More impressive than either of these two Huaraz sights is the easy hike (1½hr.) that links them. The mainly downhill hike passes through several Quechua villages and features dramatic views of both mountain ranges. It's best to travel in groups. *(From Wilcahuaín, follow the path behind the ruins down to the soccer field and up the next hill to the small community. Turn left at the aqueduct and follow it to Monterrey.)*

HIKING NEAR HUARAZ

It's the prospect of adventure in the Cordillera Blanca that calls people to Huaraz; such adventure can take many forms, but among the most exhilarating are multiday trekking and mountaineering expeditions. Although novices should leave Huascarán to the experts, anyone in decent shape can trek with a guide and appropriate equipment. Some treks are easy enough to do independently or with an *arriero* (mule driver), but you should always at least discuss your plans and route with a tour operator or guide before embarking. Keep in mind that rain, snow, and hail storms blow in throughout the year, although much less severely from May through September. In addition to the costs of equipment rental, initial transportation, and a guide, there is an admission fee (1-month pass s/65) for excursions in Parque Nacional Huascarán (p. 349.) For more information, see **Trekking and Hiking**, p. 49, or **Guided Tours from Huaraz**, p. 351.

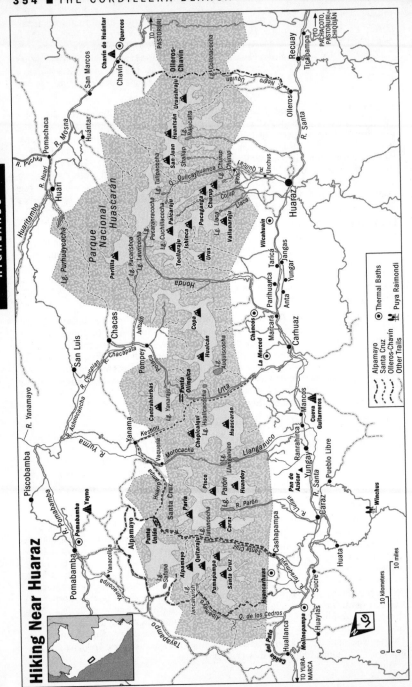

Hiking Near Huaraz

NORTHERN HIGHLANDS

Legend:
- Thermal Baths
- Puya Raimondi
- Alpamayo
- Santa Cruz
- Olleros-Chavin
- Other Trails

0 | 10 kilometers
0 | 10 miles

DON'T LEAVE HOME WITHOUT IT. Huaraz is full of renegade guides offering their "services" at a "discount." Such shady characters rarely possess the proper training or equipment to face the mountains safely. When hiring a guide, ask to see his state-issued, photo-bearing badge. Certified tour guides carry blue cards. **Guías de alta montaña** (high mountain guides) have orange cards. If you are in doubt about the validity of a guide's credentials, check with the **Casa de Guías** (p. 345), which keeps files on all certified mountain guides.

HIKE	DISTANCE	TIME
Olleros-Quebrada Rurec-Quebrada Rajucolta	70km	4 days
Collón-Pariahuanca	36km	3-4 days
Huaraz-Laguna Llaca	27km	2 days
Huaraz-Laguna Palcacocha	30km	3 days
Huaraz-Laguna Rajucolta	33km	3 days
Los Cedros-Alpamayo-Vaquería	100km	9 days
Pachacoto-Carpa-Pastoruri	28km	2 days
Pitec-Laguna Cuchillacocha	30km	2 days
Pitec-Laguna Shallap	26km	2 days
Pitec-Laguna Tullpacocha	25km	2-3 days
Quebrada Quillcayhuanca-Quebrada Cojup	60km	4 days
Collón-Valley Ishinca-Quebrada Aquilpo	50km	3-4 days
Collón-Joncopampa Ruins-Pariahuanca	25km	2 days

TREKS. At the **Casa de Guías** (p. 345), you can find certified mountain guides who have completed a rigorous three-year course to gain accreditation from the Peruvian Mountain Guide Association (UIAGM; US$40-50 per day), as well as *aspirantes* (those working toward certification; US$30-40 per day). The Casa also maintains a list of trained *arrieros* (US$10 per day, US$5 per day per mule). Licensed guides, *aspirantes*, and porters are usually called upon only for more serious mountaineering endeavors (see **Climbs,** below). Rent basic gear from the numerous travel agencies in Huaraz. (Average prices per day: headlamps US$1, sleeping mats US$0.50, pairs of walking poles US$2, warm jackets US$2-3, and cooking pots US$1.50.)

Of the more than 35 circuits around Huaraz, the treks in the chart enjoy current popularity. The more difficult **Los Cedros to Alpamayo** trek (9 days) allows a glimpse of the fourth face of Nevado Alpamayo, considered to be one of the most picturesque in the world. The journey begins at Cashapampa (2hr. from Caraz by camioneta, s/5), traverses six mountain passes along Quebradas Alpamayo and Yanacollpa, and ends in Pomabamba. To see nearly all of the Cordillera Blanca, extend this trek into a mammoth 17-day excursion by also taking in Punta Yanacu (4850m), Punta Olímpica (4850m), Jiutush village, and the Portachuelo de Honda (4750m), ending in Marcara.

CLIMB	ALTITUDE	TIME
Alpamayo	5947m	6-8 days
Chopicalqui	6354m	4-6 days
Huascarán	6768m	6-8 days
Ishinca	5534m	3 days
Nevados Pisco	5752m	3-4 days
Tocllaraju	6034m	4-5 days
Urus	5420m	3 days

CLIMBS. For serious technical climbing trips, head to the **Casa de Guías** (p. 345) for advice. They can pair you with either an accredited guide (US$70-100 per day) or an *aspirante* (US$40-60 per day) according to your needs. The most popular climbs are sometimes also the easiest, so inexperienced climbers shouldn't feel discouraged. **Nevados Pisco** (5752m), **Ishinca** (5534m), and **Urus** (5420m) require little more than a sense of adventure, well-acclimated lungs, the proper gear, and a qualified guide. Moreover, these 3-day climbs can provide the necessary knowledge and experience to tackle greater heights—like the mammoth **Huascarán** (6768m; 6-8 days). The smaller peaks needn't be just stepping stones—many people combine Ishinca and Urus into a 4-day trip for multiple peak-bagging; others add two more days and climb **Tocllaraju** (6034m) as well. Keep in mind, however, that climbs are much more dependent on weather conditions than is trekking. Even during the dry season, storm fronts can make summitting impossible. As a result, many agencies are reluctant to organize climbs without some conditional payment agreement if weather prevents a successful summit. If this is your first experience climbing but you still aspire to scale more challenging mountains, you can take a 3-day ice-climbing course (US$160) that will prepare you for both the technical and safety aspects of the climb.

SANTA CRUZ (VAQUERÍA)

The **Llanganuco to Santa Cruz Valley** trail is the most popular trek in Parque Nacional Huascarán. Traversable in either direction, the 4-day route never takes more than 6hr. per day—and sometimes only half that. Fast-movers can complete the route in three days. As a 4-day hike, the route is best approached from Chashapampa as it gives a little more time to acclimate before the pass, and offers the option of a practice run to the Alpamayo base camp. To finish in three days, begin in Vaquería so you camp below the pass on the first night and then spend the next afternoon and following day walking downhill. An alternative 6-day hike approaches **Ulta.**

AT A GLANCE	
DISTANCE: 45km.	**TIME:** 3-4 days.
CLIMATE: The best time to go is during dry season (May-Sept.).	**ALTITUDE:** 2900m-4750m.
	DIFFICULTY: Easy-Medium.
FEATURES: Amazing Andean views of glacial peaks, narrow gorges, diverse vegetation.	**FEES:** Entrance fee for Parque Nacional Huascarán s/65, good for 1 month.

🛈 PRACTICAL INFORMATION

Transportation: Camionetas from Caraz run to the **Cashapampa starting point** (2hr., s/5). Combis from Yungay go to the **Vaquería starting point** (3hr., before 10am, s/8).

Camping: Camps lie near picturesque alpine lakes. Park officials have recently equipped the main trail with outhouses and designated campsites.

Maps: Maps are available for photocopying at trekking agencies throughout Huaraz, including Monttrek and Mountain Bike Adventures (p. 345), and at Pony's Expeditions in Caraz (p. 365).

Supplies: See **Camping and Hiking Equipment,** p. 48. Bring an extra tent and food if using an *arriero*. There are a number of grocery stores in Huaraz on Luzuriaga.

🥾 THE HIKE

Day 1 starts you right off with a steep climb (600m) before reaching a more gentle slope that will lead to the campsite, Llamacorral. **Day 2** continues the relatively easy march uphill but with the option of venturing out on a side trip to the Alpamayo base camp for an amphitheater-like view of the Alpamayo and the surrounding mountains. Signs point to the turnoff, which is less than 1hr. before the Tuallipampa campsite right below the pass. **Day 3** requires you to rise early to ascend the pass (1-2hr.) before adverse weather sets in. Then, ease your way down the long, steep descent on the other side of the pass to Puria for the final night's camping. **Day 4** is an easy hike (3hr.) to Vaquería, where combis wait sporadically and buses pass through unpredictably.

The alternative **Santa Cruz Ulta** is an extension of the classic Santa Cruz, tacking on two days, another high pass, and unparalleled views of Mount Chopicalqui (6354m), Contrahierbas (6036m), and the jagged Mount Ulta (5875m). The first three days progress the same as the classic Santa Cruz trek except that on the evening of the third day, you camp a little closer to Cachinapampa. **Day 4** begins the brief respite between passes as you descend to Colcabamba and then begin hiking back uphill to your camp, Molinopampa. **Day 5** is tough, as you complete your climb uphill to the spectacular Punta Yanayucu Pass (4850m) before descending to Cashapampa and a well-deserved night's sleep. **Day 6** is the comparatively restful continuation of the descent into the Ulta Valley, where you can find transportation back to Caraz.

ALPAMAYO (FULL LOOP)

This hike is significantly harder than either variation of the Santa Cruz, both for its length (12 days), as well as the terrain, which features more than a half a dozen passes, with many above 4700m. But your effort is rewarded with some of the most spectacular views of the entire Cordillera Blanca. Proper acclimation is needed before beginning, and a guide or at least an *arriero* should be considered.

AT A GLANCE	
DISTANCE: 92km.	**TIME:** 10-12 days.
CLIMATE: The best time to go is during dry season (May-Sept.).	**ALTITUDE:** 2900m-4860m.
	DIFFICULTY: Medium-Difficult.
FEATURES: Numerous passes, lakes, and mountains—most notably Alpamayo.	**FEES:** Entrance fee for Parque Nacional Huascarán s/65, good for 1 month.

🛈 PRACTICAL INFORMATION

Transportation: Hualcayán is most easily reached from Caraz by combi (s/7) or shared taxi (s/30-40).

Camping: There are several designated sites, but hikers can camp where convenient.

Maps: Maps are available for photocopying at trekking agencies throughout Huaraz, including Monttrek and Mountain Bike Adventures (p. 345), and at Pony's Expeditions in Caraz (p. 365).

Supplies: See **Camping and Hiking Equipment,** p. 48. Bring an extra tent and food if using an *arriero*. There are a number of grocery stores in Huaraz on Luzuriaga.

🛈 THE HIKE

Day 1 is part transport day and part gentle introduction to the upcoming trek. Arrive in Hualcayán (the site of some small pre-Inca ruins) and hike to either Huyshcash or Calamina, depending on how you feel. **Day 2** takes you to the beautiful Cullicocha lakes before a steep climb to the Osururi Pass (4860m), and then a descent to Osururi for camp. **Day 3** doesn't give you much time to rest, as you go straight up to the Vientona Pass (4770m) and then down to the Alpamayo Valley, ending the day with a gentle climb to Jankarurish Lake. **Day 4** is for either rest or exploration of the Alpamayo base camp. **Day 5** picks things back up with a climb to the Caracara Pass (4830m), a descent to the meadows of Quebrada Moyobamba, an easy climb to Mesapata Pass (4460m), and then a final descent to the Safuna lakes for camp. **Day 6** brings you to the Pucacocha Lake, right at the base of Mounts Alpamayo and Pucachira, before camping at Huillcapampa. **Day 7** begins four consecutive days of passes, with the Pucachirca Pass (4610m) and then descent to Jankapampa. **Day 8** is the lower Tupa Tupa Pass (4360), with a descent to Huecrucocha Lake. **Day 9** continues the trend with the Alto Pucaraju Pass (4640m) and descent to Tuctubampa. **Day 10** joins you with the Santa Cruz trek as you join the crowd over the Punta Unión Pass (4760m) and down to Tuallipampa. **Days 11-12** are the same as the beginning (or end) of the Santa Cruz, leading you out to Cashapampa and transportation back to Caraz.

OLLEROS TO CHAVÍN

This fairly easy and uncrowded 3-day trek, beginning near Huaraz, winds through open fields and wide valleys, providing views of snowy peaks along the way. The icing on the cake, the Chavín de Huántar temple, awaits at the trail's end.

AT A GLANCE	
DISTANCE: 33km.	**TIME:** 3 days.
CLIMATE: The best time to go is during dry season (May-Sept.).	**ALTITUDE:** 3140m-4700m.
	DIFFICULTY: Easy.
FEATURES: Views of snow-capped peaks from Punta Yanashallash, Chavín de Huántar temple.	**FEES:** Entrance fee for Parque Nacional Huascarán s/65, good for 1 month.

◪ PRACTICAL INFORMATION

Transportation: Take a colectivo from Huaraz (s/1.50) to the trailhead in Olleros, 27km south of Huaraz. To return to Huaraz from Chavín, see **Chavín de Huántar,** p. 352.

Accommodations: Camp along the route; hotels are available at the end in Chavín.

Maps: Maps are available from the South American Explorers in Lima (p. 101) and from trekking agencies throughout Huaraz. The route is well marked.

Supplies: See **Camping and Hiking Equipment,** p. 48. Bring an extra tent and food if using an *arriero*.

Guides: See **Guided Tours from Huaraz,** p. 350. The well-marked trail does not require a guide. *Arrieros* are available in Olleros to help carry heavy packs (US$10 per day, US$5 per mule per day).

◪ THE HIKE

Day 1 consists of a gradual ascent to Sacracancha (4-5hr.). **Day 2,** the longest day, begins with a 5-6hr. climb to the traditional picnic spot at Punta Yanashallash (a 4700m pass between two glaciers) and a 2-3hr. downhill walk to the campsite. **Day 3** passes several Quechua villages (2hr.) before culminating at spectacular **Chavín de Huántar,** near the town of the same name. From there, buses go back to Huaraz.

CHIQUIÁN ☎ 044

Nestled deep in the Andes, the village of Chiquián (pop. 5000; 3350m) is a place where roads see more feet and hooves than tires, where traditional dress still fends off chilly mountain nights, and where traditional architecture has miraculously survived the region's seismic activity. Most visitors to Chiquián use it as a gateway for treks into the Cordillera Huayhuash, a range more rugged and isolated than its famous northern counterpart, the Cordillera Blanca. Due to the completion of a new road, though, the town of Llamac has recently displaced Chiquián as the traditional starting point for excursions into the Huayhuash, so many trekkers now just pass through, perhaps only stopping to change buses.

TRANSPORTATION AND PRACTICAL INFORMATION. Chiquián lies on a hill, sloping gently down from south to north. Most buses arrive uphill from the center of town and depart from the **Plaza de Armas.** The two main streets, **2 de Mayo** and **Comercio,** run parallel and connect the Plaza de Armas to **Plaza Bolognesi,** at the north end of town. **Long-distance buses** go to either Huaraz or Lima, but will let you off at smaller towns along the way, where you can make connections to more remote areas. **Cavassa,** Bolognesi 421 (☎74 7036), on the Plaza, sends buses to Lima (8hr., 10pm, s/16). **El Rápido,** Figueredo 218 (☎74 7049; open daily 7am-8pm), below the Gran Hostal Huayhuash, goes to Huaraz (2¾hr.; 5am, 2pm; s/7). A **combi** leaves every morning for Llamac (45min., 8:30am, s/5).

Banco de La Nación, on the Plaza, exchanges currency but won't accept traveler's checks. (☎74 7021. Open M-F 8am-2:30pm.) There are **no ATMs** in town. The **police** (☎74 7124) are several blocks uphill from the Plaza on Comercio. **Centro de Salud** is down Comercio and to the left at Plaza Bolognesi. (☎74 7085. Open 24hr. for emergencies.) Find **Internet** on the Plaza, but be prepared to wait in line. (s/0.50 per 15min.) **Serpost** is on the second floor of the large white building on the Plaza. Enter beneath the antennae, turn right at the top of the stairs, and go the second door on the right, labeled "RENIEC." (☎74 7085. Open M-F 8am-1pm and 2-4pm.)

ACCOMMODATIONS AND FOOD. For a small town, Chiquián offers plenty of good accommodations. The best bargain is the ◙**Gran Hostal Huayhuash** ❶, 28 de Julio 400, upstairs from the El Rápido bus office. Hot private baths, cable TV, and amazing views grace every room. Other features include laundry, cash exchange, a restaurant, and steep stairs to help get you in shape for your trek. Owner Freddy García can help arrange all your travel plans, whether you are staying here or not. (☎74 7049. Dorms s/10; singles s/20; doubles s/30; triples s/40.) **Hostal Los Nogales** ❶, Comercio 1301, lies three blocks uphill from the Plaza. In a large colonial house surrounding a flower-filled courtyard, Nogales boasts hardwood floors, hot baths, and plenty of spots to relax. The handsome, wood-oven-heated dining room adds yet another element of rustic comfort. The owner and his son also organize treks and have a limited supply of equipment for rental. (☎74 7121. Singles s/10, with bath and TV s/20; doubles s/20, with bath and TV s/40; triples s/30, with bath and TV s/60.)

If you're hungry after a long day of hiking, the two hotels above both offer the best—but also the most expensive—food in town. Cheaper eateries abound, but **Chifa Pollería "Menacho"** ❶, Comercio 660, two blocks below the Plaza, offers the greatest variety, with Chinese dishes, regional plates (s/5-8), and local trout. (*Menú* s/3. Open daily 6am-9pm.) **Restaurante Jerupoja** ❶, two blocks past Cassava's office, also serves a good selection of dishes (s/4-8) with the flexibility to cater to your tastes with advance notice. Owner Bernobé Ybarra also works as a cook on treks. (☎74 7232. Open daily 6am-9pm.)

HIKING NEAR CHIQUIÁN

PRACTICAL INFORMATION. The **Cordillera Huayhuash** is deceptively large, encompassing 1400 sq. km, 115 glaciers, three regional departments (Ancash, Lima, and Huánuco), more than six rivers, and **Yerupajá,** the second tallest moun-

CORDILLERA HUAYHUASH

AREA: 1400 sq. km.

CLIMATE: Best time is June to mid-September. The rest of the year sees more rain and wind.

FEATURES: Yerupajá (Peru's 2nd highest peak), mountain lakes, Andean wildlife.

TIME: 3-12 days.

ALTITUDE: 3250-4800m.

DIFFICULTY: Medium-Difficult.

FEES: None.

tain in Peru (6634m). The principal trekking route is an 8- to 10-day circuit of the entire Cordillera Huayhuash, beginning and ending in Llamac, but there are many possible variations. Hikers and guides alike reverently describe the beauty of the Cordillera's soaring peaks and crystal lakes, but those looking for the empty hiking trails of several years ago may be disappointed.

Despite its growing popularity, Huayhuash can pose a challenge for the independent traveler. The new road to Llamac, though shortening the trek by two days of comparatively uninspiring scenery and low-impact walking, has also removed without replacement what had been a good place to search out and find hiking partners—Chiquián. The most viable option now for meeting companions is the endless labyrinth of hotels and travel agencies of Huaraz. If you make enough inquiries and leave enough messages on billboards, your efforts will usually be rewarded, but this process can be long and aggravating. If you have all your gear and food, it is most effective to just wait at the trailhead in Llamac and offer to split guide fees with any larger group that passes through. If you prefer a bit more luxury, you can also wait at Chiquián and scour the bus that stops there on the way to Llamac. Solo travelers and smaller groups, especially ones without mules and guides, are much easier targets for bandits, so travel in large groups.

The two treks listed here offer suggestions for routes of varying length and difficulty for seeing the Cordillera Huayhuash. However, new treks and different routes for old ones are constantly being added. Weather changes also sometimes permit the use of otherwise ignored passes. It is best to consult travel agencies in Huaraz or guides in both Chiquián and Llamac before selecting a specific path. (For more information, see **Trekking and Hiking**, p. 49)

Maps: The best **map** of the region is available from the South American Explorers in Lima (US$5; p. 101), but others can be found in Huaraz at the **Casa de Guías** (s/35), and locally at **Mountain Bike Adventures** in the Gran Hostal Huayhuash (p. 359).

Supplies: Most trekkers hire an **arriero** (mule driver; US$8-10 per day) and at least one **burro** (mule; US$5 per day). Make sure that your *arriero* is licensed by the Chiquián Provincial Tourist Service Association of the High Mountains (Auxiliar de Alta Montaña); all members should have a photo ID card. **Porters** (US$15 per day) can help carry equipment from base camp during peak ascents. Porters and *arrieros* may or may not double as **cooks** (US$5-10 per day). **Guides** (Spanish-speaking US$30 per day, bilingual US$40 per day) can be found in Chiquián. Tents, sleeping bags, stoves, and dry camping food can be obtained in Huaraz (see **Outdoor Equipment,** p. 345) or at the **Gran Hostal Huayhuash** in Chiquián (in limited quantities; p. 359). Water, cheese, milk, and fish can be acquired from communities along the trail, but don't depend on these sources. Bring warm clothing, as the nights are extremely cold.

Tours: To bypass dealing with the details, ask for a full package deal: tent, sleeping bag, *arriero, burros,* cook, food, emergency horse, and bus tickets to and from **Lima** (prices vary by group size and tour length). Any or all of this can be arranged with the **Gran Hostal Huayhuash** (p. 359) in Chiquián or various tour agencies in Huaraz (p. 350).

■ **8- TO 10-DAY HIKE.** The principal route is an 8- to 10-day hike that winds around the Cordillera Huayhuash and begins and ends in Chiquián. **Day 1** begins in Llamac after an early morning bus ride. You then continue down to the beautiful Laguna Jahuacocha, where some guides advise spending a day both to acclimate and to explore one of the most inspiring points of the entire trek. **Day 2** brings you to Rondoy, where you can psych yourself up for the next day's 4700m pass. **Day 3** is the first true test, as you pass over Cancanán Pass (4700m). Camp that night near the beautiful Laguna Mitucocha. The next few days have more intense altitude increases, rewarded with incredible panoramic views as you pass the eastern side of the Cordillera, including several of Yerupajá. After a 5hr. walk, **Day 4** brings you to Laguna Caruacocha, another good place to take a rest. **Day 5,** is the hardest, with a stiff 7hr. walk to Huayhuash. **Day 6** takes you to Lake Viconga where there are some soothing hot springs. (If thermal waters aren't enough to rejuvenate you, you can hike one or two more days to Cajatambo, where there are daily buses to Lima.) It's another mountain pass on **Day 7** to reach Huanacpatay. For some excellent day trips, climb the mountains parallel to Río Pumarinri. Heading downhill on **Day 8** will take you to Huayllpa. **Day 9** begins the high point (literally) of the journey when you arrive at Tapush, a peak of 4800m. Finally, on **Day 10,** you conclude with the long walk back to Llamac.

■ **3- TO 4-DAY HIKE.** Choose this for a more brief introduction to the Cordillera Huayhuash, but one that still affords a glimpse of one of its highlights, Laguna Cahuacocha. **Day 1** from Llamac follows the Quebrada Caliente to Rondoy. On **Day 2** you climb to the Sambunya Pass and then drop down to the sublime Laguna Jahuacocha. On **Day 3** you have the recommended option of exploring the Solterococha and Rasaccocha Lakes. **Day 4** takes you across the smaller Pampa Llamac Pass (4300m) and back to Llamac for transport out.

POMABAMBA

Though serene and in a stunning locale, the town of Pomabamba (pop. 4400) is often overshadowed by its role as terminus to a number of memorable journeys, including various hikes and a long bus ride from Huaraz that weaves through the heart of the Cordillera Blanca. Locals often refer to their town as "La Ciudad de Los Cedros" for the two long-standing cedars in the Plaza, but visitors will be more impressed by the regionally famous **alpaca wool ponchos** and **rings of intertwined silver cords** if they are in the market for material memories. Just outside the city are seven **thermal baths** to help soothe aching muscles from either the arduous trek or the cramped bus ride that brings people to town. The **Caminata Cerro Curayacu** leads to a panoramic view of the area and provides a nice vantage-point to watch the local artisans in action. For those for whom no visit to a Peruvian town is complete without an excursion to the local ruins, the pre-Inca **Ruinas de Yaino** (4hr. round-trip) should fill the void. **Hospedaje Estrada ❸,** on Lima, is a clean and quiet spot to spend the night. (☎ 75 1048; s/15 per bed.) Plenty of undistinguished and indistinguishable restaurants populate the Plaza and serve all the local favorites. **RENZO** runs a **bus** to Pomabamba from Huaraz (daily 6:30am, s/20), and early-morning buses make the return trip.

CARHUAZ ☎ 043

Known as "Carhuaz Borrachera" ("Intoxicating Carhuaz"), this sleepy hamlet 33km north of Huaraz lives up to its moniker. Boasting enthusiastic nascent tourism and a climate milder than that of Huaraz, Carhuaz (pop. 13,000; 2650m) rewards visitors with tranquil lodgings and an ice cream shop on almost every corner. Although for most of the year it's a great place to escape the comparative hustle and bustle of Huaraz, this town tends to get a bit tipsy itself during its yearly patronal **fiestas,** which take place throughout September.

TRANSPORTATION. Combis to Huaraz (1hr., s/2) leave from the corner of La Merced and Ucayali, half a block downhill from the Plaza. Those to Caraz (1hr., s/2) via Yungay (30min., s/1.50) leave from the corner of La Merced and Progreso, on the ice cream side of the Plaza. **Móvil Tours** keeps a sort of office with the woman who runs the Bazar Fortune Shop, across from where the combis to Huaraz depart (☎79 4048; open daily 7am-1pm and 4-9pm). **Buses** leave nightly for Lima (8hr.; 8:30am, 9pm; s/25-30) via Huaraz (1hr.). Bus prices rise during festival times.

ORIENTATION AND PRACTICAL INFORMATION. Carhuaz's **Plaza de Armas** lies four blocks above **Carretera Central,** the main road in the Callejón de Huaylas. The four streets which frame the Plaza and radiate outwards are home to nearly everything of interest to a visitor. Beginning on the north side of the Plaza at the row of ice cream shops and moving clockwise, they are **Progreso, Comercio, Buin,** and **Merced.** Street numbers, especially away from the Plaza, do not always follow consistent sequential order.

For **tourist information,** talk to **Felipe Díaz,** who owns the Café Heladería El Abuelo and the eponymous Hostal El Abuelo (see **Accommodations and Food,** below), and who also designed the definitive tourist map of the region. Sr. Díaz has also written an impressive and very thorough guide to the Cordillera Blanca. **Banco Continental,** on Merced on the Plaza, changes dollars. (☎79 4122. Open M-F 8am-2:30pm.) Other local services include: **police** (☎79 4197), on Buin just south of the Plaza; **Farmacia Señor de Lurén,** Buin 557, just north of the Plaza (☎79 4392; open daily 7am-10pm); and a **hospital,** 5 blocks down Progreso from the Plaza and 2 blocks to the right on Tacna (☎79 4106; open M-Sa 7:30am-1:30pm). Coin-operated **pay phones** are scattered throughout the center of town. **Internet access** is available at **Internet Adonai,** Progreso 769, on the Plaza near Comercio. (☎79 4313. s/1.50 per hr. Open daily 9am-10pm.) The **post office** is on Buin on the Plaza de Armas. (☎79 4118. Open M-Sa 8am-1pm and 2-6pm.)

ACCOMMODATIONS AND FOOD. Carhuaz harbors several under-visited but decent hostels. **Las Torrecitas ❷,** Amazonas 412, four blocks uphill on Comercio and two blocks to the right from the Plaza de Armas, rents spotless modern rooms with parquet floors, TVs, and private baths with hot water and good water pressure. (☎79 4213. Continental breakfast s/3. Singles s/15; doubles s/30.) True to its name, the comfortable and tranquil **Las Bromelias ❷,** Brazil 208, three blocks up Comercio and one block to the right from the Plaza, has a beautiful flower garden with baby chicks and ducklings waddling around, chased by abundant kittens. (☎79 4033. Singles s/20 with bath; doubles with bath s/30.) If you need a break from the travails of traveling (and are willing to pay for it), **Hostal El Abuelo ❺,** 9 de Diciembre 257, two blocks up Merced and one-and-a-half blocks to the left, is the place to go. This sparkling new addition to town has every convenience, right down to packets of shampoo and bedside chocolates. (☎79 4456. Continental breakfast included. Singles US$30; doubles US$40. All major credit cards.)

While Carhuaz may not be the culinary epicenter of Peru, there are a few places to get a good meal. **Café Heladería El Abuelo ❶,** at Progreso and La Merced, on the Plaza, may well be the only restaurant in Peru (or the world) with *pisco* sour or beer milkshakes (s/5.50). They specialize in ice cream snacks (s/5-8) and tourist information, but also offer a complete menu, with breakfasts (s/8-13), sandwiches (s/3-10), and main dishes like *pollo a la naranja* (s/19) and trout with creamy mushroom sauce (s/20). (☎79 4149. Open daily 8am-7pm. AmEx/DC/MC/V.) For something more conventional, try **Helados Huascarán ❶**, Progreso 757, on the Plaza, home to traditional ice cream flavors made in-house. (☎79 4239. Double scoop s/1. Open daily 6am-8pm.)

◙ SIGHTS. A few unusual sights and several pleasant part- or full-day strolls set Carhuaz's offerings apart. Several years ago, in the Cordillera Negra, American anthropologists discovered the **Cueva de Guitarreros,** a cave supposedly inhabited over 12,000 years ago. To get to the cave, take a combi north to Tingua (15min., s/1). From Tingua, cross Río Santa and walk north (1hr.). The **Chancos hot springs** are famous for caves that have been converted into private saunas. Take a colectivo to Marcará, 7km south of Carhuaz, and then walk or take a colectivo (4km, s/1) uphill. (Open daily 6am-6pm. s/5 for 15min.) Closer to town (45min.), a short hike in the foothills of the Cordillera Negra provides stunning views of the snow-capped range. Follow La Merced downhill from the Plaza and continue 3km on the road past the bridge. A popular but challenging dayhike to **Laguna Auquiscocha** (4319m) offers spectacular views of a waterfall plunging into a mountain lake surrounded by non-native cyprus trees. A Chacas-bound combi from the corner of Progreso and La Merced can let you off at the trailhead where Quebrada Ulta and Quebrada Catay merge (1hr., leave when full 6am-5pm, s/1.50). From there, it's a 5-6hr. round-trip hike. Finally, a trip to **Punta Olímpica** (4890m) yields breathtaking vistas from the high pass on the road to Chacas from Carhuaz. Chacas-bound combis (2hr., s/15) go right by the pass, where you can get off and wait for the return combi after you explore.

YUNGAY ☎044

Yungay (pop. 10,000) got a tragic 15 minutes of fame on May 31, 1970, when an enormous earthquake brought a cascade of rock and ice down Nevado Huascarán, smothering the tiny town below and killing 25,000 residents. Today, the rubble is something of a tourist attraction, and the town has moved; the few survivors rebuilt their homes 1km north of the original location. Now cowering in Huascarán's massive shadow, quiet Yungay has yet to assign names to most of its streets. Otherwise, the town's catastrophic past seems to have faded from memory. At the Tuesday market, the streets fill with enthusiastic villagers whose vibrant dress crowds out the bland concrete facades looming over the town. Younger women in green or purple leggings with layers of skirts and silky, sparkling florescent tops recall the gaudy-glam of 80s rockstars. At the end of the day, though, Yungay is just another quiet town tucked away in the midst of the towering Andes; only its status as a regional crossroads distinguishes it from neighboring mountain villages.

◩⊅ TRANSPORTATION AND PRACTICAL INFORMATION. Combis to Caraz (30min., every 20-30min., s/1) leave from the lowest corner of the Plaza de Armas; those to Carhuaz (30min., s/1.50) and Huaraz (1½hr., s/4) depart slightly less frequently from the corner of Graziani and 28 de Julio, 1 block south of the Plaza. Alternatively, you can hail combis going either way on the Carretera Central (6am-8pm). **Buses** on Graziani at the Plaza (open daily 7am-8pm) run to Chimbote (9hr., 7pm, s/18) and Lima (9½hr., 4 per day, s/20).

Banco de la Nación, on the north side of the Plaza, exchanges dollars but not traveler's checks. (☎79 3104. Open M-Sa 8am-2:30pm.) Other local services include: **police** (☎79 3300), at Graziani and 28 de Julio; **mountain rescue police** (Unidad de Salvamento de Alta Montaña; ☎79 3292), on Jaime Gonzales, the first right after Hostal Gledel from the Plaza; a **pharmacy** at Botica Santa Teresa, on Graziani on the Plaza (open daily 7am-9pm); and a **hospital** (☎79 3044), on República de Cuba,

1½ blocks north of the Plaza de Armas, between the blue brick walls. **Telefónica del Perú** is in the Región Norte office, next to the municipality on the Plaza. (☎ 79 3283. Open daily 8am-1pm and 2-8pm.) The **post office** is on Graziani just south of the Plaza. (Open M-Sa 8am-noon and 2-4pm.)

🖪🖪 ACCOMMODATIONS AND FOOD. 🖪**Hostal Gledel ❶**, on Graziani, two blocks down from the Plaza de Armas, caters shamelessly to tourists and does so well. It offers 24hr. hot water, free luggage storage, and tasty traditional breakfasts and dinners, though meals require advance notice. (☎ 79 3048. Internet access s/5 per hr. Singles s/10; doubles s/20.) **Hostal Pan de Azúcar ❷**, La Merced 32, two blocks up and to the left of the Plaza, is new and comfortable, though a little hard to find. Soft and low-lying beds occupy plain but comfortable rooms. (☎ 73 0571. Tourist information and laundry-service available. 24hr. hot water. Singles s/18; doubles s/30; triples s/50.) **Hostal Yungay ❶**, on Santo Domingo at the Plaza, is pretty basic—they offer 24hr. hot private baths, laundry service (s/3 per kg), *menú* (s/3), and kitchen use. (☎ 79 3053. Singles s/10; doubles s/20.)

Restaurant Progresso ❷, Arias Giazziazi, on the way to the Pueblo Antiguo, is a bit out of place with its ascetic interior. It stocks all the usuals, as well as *ceviche de trucha* (s/10), and good ice cream. (☎ 80 4818. Open daily 8am-8pm.) The outdoor **El Alpamayo ❷**, on the highway in the northern outskirts, tends to fill up around lunchtime with various bus tours. *Pachamanca* (tamales, meat, corn, potato, and yams cooked in an underground oven; s/10) is available on weekends. (☎ 79 3090. *Menú* s/3.50. Open daily 7am-7pm.) **Café Pilar ❷**, right below the Plaza, has hip red walls with blue splashes and mirrors, as well as the closest thing to a European cafe atmosphere in all of Yungay. (Cheap fruit juices and sandwiches s/2.50.)

🖪 SIGHTS. Just south of the new city lies **Campo Santo**, burial site of the former Yungay. Amazingly intact, the facade of the **old church** presides over what was once the Plaza de Armas. At the other end of the former town, a **statue of Christ** dominates the old cemetery, where many townspeople fled to escape the 1970 mudslide. The two remnants overlook rosebushes that form a cross through the town center. (20min. walk or colectivo ride (s/0.50) from the new Plaza de Armas. Open daily 8am-6:30pm. s/2.) Far less depressing, the dazzling **Lagunas Llanganuco** (see **Daytrips from Huaraz**, p. 351), sit nearby; the access road begins in Yungay. Many tourists visit the lakes with a tour group from Huaraz, but it's easier to get there from Yungay. Take a Yanama-bound combi to **Llanganuco** (1hr., leave when full 6-10am, s/5) from the intersection of Graziani and 28 de Julio. To return, simply flag down one of the combis after 2pm (s/3-4) on the way back from Yanama. Travelers can also get off the combi halfway to the lakes and hike to the pre-Inca ruins of **Keushu** (30min.). Another hike (6hr.) goes from Yungay to Caraz on a 17km trail bowing toward the Cordillera Blanca from the main highway, offering fantastic views of both mountain ranges.

CARAZ ☎ 044

Lying 67km north of and almost 1000m lower than Huaraz, Caraz (pop. 11,000) enjoys a climate far sweeter than the bitter cold of the high Andes. Maybe that's why locals call it "Caraz Dulzura" ("Sweet Caraz"). Or perhaps the sugary *sobrenombre* (nickname) takes root in the region's renowned *manjar blanco*, a scrumptious milk, sugar, and cinnamon spread. In any case, this tranquil terminus of the Callejón de Huaylas, the glacial valley between the Cordilleras Negra and Blanca, serves well as either a resting place or a more convenient launch pad than Huaraz for exploring the northern reaches of Parque Nacional Huascarán.

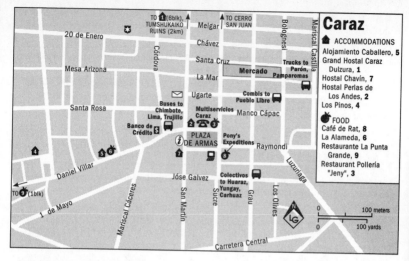

Caraz

■ ACCOMMODATIONS
Alojamiento Caballero, **5**
Grand Hostal Caraz
Dulzura, **1**
Hostal Chavín, **7**
Hostal Perlas de
Los Andes, **2**
Los Pinos, **4**

● FOOD
Café de Rat, **8**
La Alameda, **6**
Restaurante La Punta
Grande, **9**
Restaurant Pollería
"Jeny", **3**

TRANSPORTATION

Buses: Companies cluster near the corner of Córdova and Daniel Villar. Open daily 7am-7:30pm. To: **Chimbote** (9-10hr.; 8:30am, 6:30pm; s/20); **Lima** (9-10hr., 5 per day 8am-8pm, s/20-25); **Trujillo** (12hr.; noon, 6pm; s/25). **Camionetas** to **Parón** leave from the corners of Mariscal Castilla and La Mar (1½hr., 4:30am, s/5), and Mariscal Castilla and Santa Cruz (1hr., 1pm, s/3). **Colectivos** and **combis** leave from the corner of Grau and Galvez to **Huaraz** (2hr., leave when full 6am-6pm, s/3.50) via **Yungay** (20min., s/1) and **Carhuaz** (1hr., s/2).

Taxis: Rides in town cost s/1-2.

ORIENTATION AND PRACTICAL INFORMATION

Sucre (the main thoroughfare) and **San Martín** run parallel to each other and form two sides of the **Plaza de Armas**. **Daniel Villar** forms the Plaza's northern (uphill) side and also connects to the **Carretera Central**, which curves around to define the southern and western edges of town. **Córdova** runs parallel to San Martín, one block off the Plaza de Armas. **Grau** is another main street parallel to Sucre, one block on the other side of the Plaza.

Tourist Offices: Pony's Expeditions (below) has the best tourist information. The **Oficina de Información Turística** (☎ 79 1029), on San Martín, next to the Municipalidad, dispenses photocopied city **maps**. Open M-F 8am-1pm and 2:30-5pm.

Tours: Pony's Expeditions, Sucre 1266 (☎ 79 1642; www.ponyexpeditions.com), on the Plaza de Armas. Rents top-name **bikes** (US$25 per day with guide) and all necessary hiking, climbing, and fishing gear. Owner Alberto Cafferata speaks English and arranges personalized tours, treks, and climbs. Open daily 9am-1pm and 4-9pm.

Banks: Banco de Crédito, Villar 217 (☎ 79 1012), near the Plaza de Armas, takes AmEx traveler's checks. Open M-F 9:30am-1pm and 3:30-6pm, Sa 9:30am-12:30pm. There is an **ATM** at the Banco de Crédito on the street intersecting the square by Pony Expeditions, right off the Plaza.

Market: The indoor market at Sucre and La Mar spills east along La Mar and Santa Cruz to Castilla. Merchants sell everything from bread to bicycle parts. Open daily 6am-6pm.

Police: (☎79 1335), on 20 de Enero, near Córdova.

Hospital: San Juan de Dios Caraz (☎79 1026), 1 block down Circunvalación Norte from its intersection with Mariscal Castilla. Open M-Sa 8am-2pm, emergencies 24hr.

Telephones: Multiservicios Caraz, Sucre 809 (☎79 1918), allows calling card and collect calls. Slot machines available while you wait for a booth. Open daily 7am-11pm.

Internet: Several near the Plaza. s/3 per hr.

Post Office: San Martín 909 (☎79 1094). Open M-Sa 8am-6pm.

ACCOMMODATIONS

Caraz sees only a fraction of the travelers that tramp though Huaraz, yet there are still plenty of good beds awaiting weary travelers.

Hostal Perlas de Los Andes (☎79 1130), on the Plaza de Armas. Recently built with immaculate modern furnishings, tiled bathrooms, and large comfortable beds. Though lacking the character of some of the other options in town, Las Perlas has a perfect location, cable TV, a downstairs restaurant (one of the best in town), and views of the Plaza in some rooms. Singles s/35; doubles s/50. ❸

Los Pinos, Parque San Martín 103 (☎79 1130; lospinos@terra.com.pe), 6 blocks down Villar from the Plaza. Rooms are quiet, clean, and have 24hr. hot water. Bonfires and folk music every F. Kitchen, laundry, ping-pong, restaurant (entrees s/5-10), and nightly movies. Owner runs an in-house travel and adventure tour agency. **Camping** US$2.50. Singles US$8, with bath US$10; doubles US$16, with bath US$20. 5% discount for HI and significant discounts during the low season. ❸

Grand Hostal Caraz Dulzura, Saenz Peña 212 (☎79 1523), 10 blocks uphill from the Plaza, along Córdova and then Saenz Peña. A comfortable hostel with all the amenities: lounge, full bar, restaurant (entrees s/3-10, *menú* s/4), 24hr. hot water, and common TV. The tranquil location, sunny patio, and green decor make it a relaxing refuge from the busy city center. Dorms s/17; singles s/25; doubles s/45. MC. ❷

Hostal Chavín, San Martín 1135 (☎79 1171), on the Plaza de Armas. It may be a bit dark, but the beds are comfy, all rooms have newly refurbished hot private baths, some have cable TV, and check-in/check-out times are extremely flexible. Owner Señor Walter Sotelo gives lectures on the 1970 earthquake, complete with photos of Yungay before, during, and after. Singles s/25; doubles s/35; triples s/45; quads s/60. ❸

Alojamiento Caballero, Villar 485 (☎79 1637). It's got 3 things going for it: a nice view of the Cordillera Negra, front door keys for guests, and its status as the cheapest place in town. Shared electric hot showers. Dorms s/10; matrimonials s/20. ❶

FOOD

As noted above, sweets—*manjar blanco*, delectable pastries, Inca Kola—are extremely popular in Caraz. A bevy of *pollerías* and restaurants specializing in highland cuisine await those avoiding premature tooth decay.

Café de Rat, Sucre 1266 (☎79 1642), above Pony's Expeditions. Luckily the name has nothing to do with the interior of the restaurant or the food. Nibble on a crepe, salad, or pasta on the quiet balcony overlooking the square. Book exchange and extensive CD collection. Breakfast s/3.50-10. Pasta s/9. Crepes s/6. Sandwiches s/2.50-4. Open M-Sa 7am-1pm and 4-9pm. ❶

Restaurant Pollería "Jeny" (☎79 1101), on the Plaza de Armas. Serves breakfast (s/3.50-6) and sandwiches (s/1-2), but the main focus is *comida típica* (s/8-12) and the house specialty, *pollo a la brasa* (¼ chicken s/6). It's also the place to go to have a beer and watch the big game. Open daily 6am-11pm. ❷

Restaurante La Punta Grande, Daniel Villar 595 (☎79 1320), at the Carretera Central. Sit on the garden platform as you enjoy traditional foods like *cuy, lomo saltado,* and fresh trout. *Menú* s/4. Entrees s/9-11. Open daily 8am-8pm. ❶

La Alameda, Daniel Villar 412 (☎79 1935), 3 blocks off the Plaza. For a taste (or a bucketful) of the famous *manjar blanco,* La Alameda has a wide variety of sizes and sugary by-products.

⊙ SIGHTS

Excavations at the **Tumshukaiko Ruins** have revealed some impressive pre-Chavín architecture, but most structures remain concealed. Still, visits reward travelers with great views of the Callejón de Huaylas. *(Take San Martín north from the Plaza, and bear left on 28 de Julio. Cross the bridge, take the third left, then bear right, and go uphill 30min.)*

▶ DAYTRIPS FROM CARAZ

Most hikers and climbers base themselves out of Huaraz (see **Hiking Near Huaraz,** p. 353), but Caraz also has its share of worthwhile excursions. Whether on foot, horse, or bike, these excursions traipse through beautiful countryside and help you acclimate before moving on to bigger (or at least higher) things.

PASO DE WINCHUS

Paso de Winchus offers more than amazing views of the Cordillera Blanca and the Pacific Ocean: it's also a great place to spot the Puya Raymondi plant in bloom (see **Flower Power,** p. 352). Keep your eyes peeled for the giant hummingbirds that have evolved as the sole pollinators. *(To reach the pass, either go with a private tour (see Pony's Expeditions, p. 365) or catch a Pamparomas-bound colectivo (2hr., 9am, s/5) from the corner of La Mar and Castilla. To get back, catch a colectivo or head down to Pueblo Libre, where colectivos return to Caraz until 3pm. Be forewarned—it's 33km from the pass to Pueblo Libre, a journey perhaps best made by bike.)*

DAYHIKES

HIKE	DISTANCE	TIME	DIFFICULTY
▨ Laguna Parón	28km	5-7hr.	Medium
Cerro San Juan	16km	6-8hr.	Medium
Pueblo Libre to Caraz	9km	2-3hr.	Easy
Cañón del Pato	Variable	Variable	Easy

▨ **LAGUNA PARÓN.** Laguna Parón (4200m), the largest and deepest of the mountain lakes in the Callejón de Huaylas, lies at the end of a sweaty 900m climb. During some parts of the year, drainage diminishes its grandeur, but nothing can abate the magnificence of the numerous snow-capped peaks that tower over the lake. The trail begins with beautiful views of the Cordillera Negra and just gets better as you trek into the canyon. The rest of the path has plenty of vegetation and small, roaring rivers. Nothing beats the culmination, though—the shimmering turquoise waters of Laguna Parón. For those with extra time, a longer trek (4hr. round-trip) around the left side of the lake brings hikers to pleasant **Laguna Artesancocha.** *(Colectivos run to Parón (1hr.; 4:30am, 1pm; s/3-5) from Mariscal Castilla and La Mar in the morning and Mariscal Castilla and*

Santa Cruz in the afternoon. Ask the driver to let you off at the Parón road sign. From there, it's a 3-4hr. hike to the lake. It's possible to walk up and return to the descending colectivo (2pm) in a day, but staying overnight allows more time at the lake. Alternatively, you can rent bikes from **Pony's Expeditions** (p. 365) and ride the 32km back to town or take a taxi (round-trip s/70).)

CERRO SAN JUAN TO YUNGAY. Also called "Vuelta al Huandoy," this 6-8hr. (20km) hike climbs up to 3400m and provides both nice views of mountain ranges and an introduction to local flora. **Maps** are available from either Pony's Expeditions or the Oficina de Información Turística (see **Tourist Offices**, p. 365). (From the Plaza, go uphill on Sucre and continue past its intersection with 28 de Julio. The trail eventually descends to Puente Ancash, a bridge on the Carretera Central near Yungay. From there, simply flag down a combi heading back to Caraz (15min., s/1).)

PUEBLO LIBRE TO CARAZ. Helpful for acclimating, this hike displays the Callejón's drier side. You'll see nine types of cacti over the 9km mostly downhill walk through the Cordillera Negra. The journey yields Cordillera panoramas and ends with a walk across the suspension bridge over the Río Santa. (Catch a combi to Pueblo Libre from the corner of Bolognesi and Ugarte (30min., s/1.50). From the town, follow the old highway through the Guadalupe community back to Caraz (2-3hr.).)

CAÑÓN DEL PATO. A product of constant wear by the Río Santa, the canyon is the meeting place of the Cordilleras Blanca and Negra. Their peaks, an average distance of 16km apart through the rest of the Callejón de Huaylas, suddenly appear to be a stone's throw apart. For a good view, take the trail that splits off from the road near Túnel Mellizo and runs past Bocatoma ("the mouth that drinks"), the inlet for the hydroelectric plant at Huallanca. The canyon is so narrow that the road has 35 tunnels. (To get to the far end of the Cañón del Pato, take a colectivo to Huallanca (2hr., round-trip s/10) from the corner of Grau and Manco Cápac, or grab a taxi (round-trip s/30). Or, get off halfway at Túnel Mellizo and walk until you catch a return colectivo (s/5). Guided tours are available (5hr., s/40-50 per person; see **Pony's Expeditions**, p. 365).)

NORTHERN HIGHLANDS

HUAMACHUCO ☎ 044

Between the coast and the highlands, tranquil Huamachuco (pop. 20,000; elev. 3200m) is a good spot to literally catch your breath while you prepare to climb in altitude. Travelers embarking upon the arduous route to Cajamarca up the Río Moche Valley will be rewarded with spectacular canyons, sparkling mountain lakes, and jagged Andean peaks, but the stop in Huamachuco has little more to offer than a crowded Plaza pinned in by a beautiful church and the surrounding mountainside. In recent years, Huamachuco has experienced a revival of sorts following the discovery of gold in the surrounding areas. Unfortunately, such newfound wealth has been somewhat slow in translating to improved accommodations and inventive restaurants, nor has it really found its way into the hands of most citizens. Perhaps its most visible manifestation is in the immaculately manicured topiaries that animate the Plaza—local classics such as alpacas and donkeys mingle with a more mysteriously conceived elephant sporting a sombrero.

▐▌ TRANSPORTATION AND PRACTICAL INFORMATION

The life of this small town centers around the **Plaza de Armas**, the **market**, and **Balta**, the artery which connects the two and borders the Plaza with **Castilla, San Ramón**, and **Carrión**. Most bus companies arrive and depart from Balta, near the market.

Aviación Líder, Balta 264 (☎44 1248), uphill from the Plaza, has **flights to Trujillo** (20min.; M, W, F 11am; US$45). **Transportes Agreda,** Balta 887, has **buses to Trujillo** (7hr.; daily 8am, 6pm; s/15). **Transportes Horna** has similar offerings but leaves a bit later (8:40pm, s/23) so that you arrive at the more reasonable hour of 6am. **Transportes Anita,** Pasaje Hospital 109, leaves for **Cajabamba** (4hr.; 4, 11:30am, 12:30pm; s/6). The **Municipalidad,** Castilla 564, functions as a tourist office and provides pamphlets, brochures, and colorful posters. (☎/fax 44 1022. Open M-Sa.)

ACCOMMODATIONS

Surprisingly, a place to sleep can sometimes be hard to come by, as technicians, managers, prospectors, and other personnel from the mines frequently snatch up the best rooms in town. The supply of adequate lodging, however, is growing.

Hostal Huamachuco, Castilla 354 (☎44 1393), on the Plaza de Armas. Clean, spacious rooms with 24hr. hot water, laundry service, phones for international calls, and a small cafeteria next door. TV s/5. Singles s/13, with bath s/25; doubles s/22, with bath s/34. ❷

Hostal San José, Balta 324 (☎44 1044), also on the Plaza de Armas, facing the cathedral. Clean and cozy rooms and particularly spotless bathrooms with 24hr. hot water. Most rooms have TV. Receptionists offer helpful information about the town and the surrounding area. Singles s/15; doubles s/25. ❷

Noche Buena Hostal, San Ramón 401 (☎/fax 441 435). Lives up to its name, as ever-smiling owners provide tidy, comfortable rooms with TV and hot private baths. The nicest of all Plaza hotels. Singles s/30; doubles s/35. ❸

Colonial Hotel, Ramón Castilla 537 (☎44 1334). An intricate tile fountain in the courtyard screams "upscale," but prices remain affordable. Singles s/15, with private bath and TV s/25; doubles s/25, with private bath and TV s/45. ❸

FOOD

In Huamachuco, dining can be challenging—no one wins points for originality, as chicken appears to be the dish of choice everywhere. Newly found affluence has contributed a little zest to this standard option; several *pollerías* on the Plaza now advertise with giant, flashing neon chicken signs. A few restaurants deviate from this pattern, but don't expect anything too far removed from *saltados* and *chifa*.

Restaurante Colonial, part of the hotel of the same name, serves a steady fare of *comida típica* as well as a few pasta and salad dishes. The wooden bar and exquisite artwork of locals establishes El Colonial not only as perhaps the most inventive local cuisine but also the most distinguished. Open daily 8am-10pm. ❷

Doña Emilia, San Martín 790 (☎58 6910; donaemilia@hotmail.com). Quiet and quaint with only a few tables, all overlooking the Plaza. Scrumptious cakes, pies, and cookies. The loyal clientele and friendly servers will discuss anything from the injustices of development to Latin American poetry. Entrees s/5-10. Open daily 9am-8pm. ❷

Restaurante Brasa Chicken, Balta 533 (☎44 1079). Locals agree that this is one of the best *pollerías* in town, and it even serves a few other dishes. Chicken s/5. Open daily 8am-midnight. ❶

Juguería Renatos, Balta 264 (☎44 1248), just up from the Plaza. Serves a variety of sandwiches (s/3-5) and fresh juices. Open M-Sa 8am-9pm. ❶

◎ ♫ SIGHTS AND ENTERTAINMENT. The impressive pre-Inca ruins of **Marcahuamachuco** reside on a hillside (elev. 3595m) 9.5km from the city. Among the circular fortresses at the crest of the mountain are **Cerro del Castillo** and the impenetrable **Cerro de las Monjas,** thought to have housed the Inca Virgins of the Sun. The stonework indicates that these triple-walled stone structures once reached at least three stories high. To reach the site, walk down Bolívar, turn right after the bridge, and follow the highway to the summit (3hr.). Taxis (round-trip s/30 from the Plaza de Armas) also make the trip. **Wiracochapampa** is closer and can be reached on foot (1hr.) or by taxi (10min., s/7); head downhill from the Plaza along San Román. The **Baños de Yanazara** make an ideal spot for rest and relaxation. Combis (2hr., 4am, s/5) leave from the hospital and return at 3pm. Cheap lodging is available at the baths upon consultation with the priests. The beautiful **Laguna Sausacocha,** along the way to the baths, is not to be missed. The lake can be visited on foot (round-trip 4hr.) or by combi (30min., every hr. 7am-3pm, s/2).

Huamachuco is annually jostled awake by its greatest tourist attraction, the festival honoring the **Virgen de la Altagracia.** Streets buzz, prices soar, and courageous (or drunk) men take on bulls in the town bull ring during the week around August 15. The best of Huamachuco's limited disco scene is **Aruba Discoteca,** Lara 535. It's kickin' on the weekend but a little slow earlier in the week. (☎441 181. Cover s/2. Open daily 9pm-6am.) Those wanting to catch a movie on the big screen should head to the **Cine Municipal,** at Balta on the Plaza, for nightly showings of slightly dated movies (s/1).

CAJABAMBA   ☎044

Another unintended, but often required, stop on the scenic route from Trujillo to Cajamarca, Cajabamba (pop. 5000) comes as a pleasant surprise. While following the road past the marketplace ends at a breathtaking *mirador,* any spot in the city serves as a great viewpoint for the surrounding Andean peaks. On Sunday, Cajabamba really comes alive, with a market that attracts villagers from all over the region. When the sun beats down, try on some of the local *sombreros* and maybe take in a street show with an astrologer or one of the many marching bands.

■♪ **TRANSPORTATION AND PRACTICAL INFORMATION.** Buses leave from Grau or Bolognesi from the side of town nearest their destinations, but most companies can be found on the Plaza or across from the market. **Transportes Rojas,** Bolognesi 700 (☎85 1394), sends **buses** to Cajamarca (5hr.; 3am, 12:30pm; s/10). **Transportes Horna,** Prado 165 (☎85 1397), on the Plaza, serves Trujillo (12hr.; 4:30, 6pm; s/20). **Transportes Anita,** Grau 1170 (☎44 1535), across from the market, connects to Huamachucho (2hr.; 4am, noon; s/6). As always, the **Plaza de Armas** is the center of the action, bordered by Prado, Ugarte, Grau, and Bolognesi. Facing uphill, Grau turns into a pedestrian mall to the right for three blocks before leading to the market and eventually the road to Huamachuco. **Banco de la Nación,** Bolognesi 549 (☎85 1059), just off the Plaza, exchanges currency and may change traveler's checks. Use calling cards at **Telefónica,** Grau 876, on the pedestrian mall just off the Plaza. (☎85 1509. Open daily 6:30am-10:30pm.) The **police** (☎85 1088) are located on Grau, three blocks downhill from the market, and the **Hospital Señora del Rosario** (☎85 1099) is at La Torre and Juaréz. **Internet** can be found all around the Plaza and on Grau (s/1.50 per hr.). **Serpost,** La Torre 701, is two blocks up Ugarte from the Plaza. (☎85 1393. Open M-F 8am-noon and 2-6pm, Su 8am-4pm.)

■◖ **ACCOMMODATIONS AND FOOD. Hostal La Casona ❷,** Ugarte 586, on the Plaza, has some of the nicest rooms in town, with TV, comfy beds, private bath and even a jacuzzi. The sitting room has plush red couches overlooking the Plaza. (☎85 1300. Singles s/10; matrimonials s/15; doubles s/30.) Also on the Plaza, **Hostal Flores ❷,** Prado 137, offers basic rooms; those on the second floor have private baths, bucket showers, and great balconies overlooking the Plaza. (☎85 1086. Singles s/10, with bath s/15; doubles s/25, with bath s/30.) At **Hostal Caribe ❶**, Cardenos 784, three blocks down Grau away from the Plaza and the pedestrian mall, on the right, find cheap, clean, comfortable accommodations with hot water. (☎80 1486. Singles s/10; doubles s/20.) If you've had it with *pollo a la brasa*, there are two other options. **Restaurante La Casona ❶**, next to the hotel of the same name, serves oldies but goodies including trout and pastas. (Open daily 8am-9pm.) For a little more variety, **Restaurante Don Luco ❶**, down Prado toward the cemetery until a big sign points the way, has daily specials such as rabbit, goat, and fresh trout. (Open daily 7am-10pm. Bar open until 1am F-Sa.)

◨ ◪ SIGHTS AND ENTERTAINMENT. Beyond the Sunday market, Cajabamba itself has few sights, but a closer look reveals several points of interest. The town **museum,** one block from Hostal La Casona on the left, houses a rather impressive collection of dinosaur bones, as well as some extremely large beetles that the curator promises were not culled from any of the hotels. The curator can also help organize trips to some of the archaeological sites where these bones and other artifacts were found. For the more morbid, the **cemetery** down from the Plaza at the end of Prado sits below a cliff—the site of numerous suicides by forlorn lovers. In between the morbid and the celebratory, Cajabamba is currently building a **bullfighting ring** for *fiestas*, most of which occur in October.

On Friday and Saturday nights, the tables are pushed to the side at **Restaurante Don Luco,** and disco balls fulfill their purpose. **The Video Pub,** one block down Prado from the Plaza and to the right, plays an eclectic selection of Spanish pop and American rock hits. Its interior resembles a converted gymnasium with an impressive number of black lights, but it still draws crowds on weekends.

CAJAMARCA ☎076

The city of Cajamarca (pop. 115,000; 2750m) has been the feather in many a warrior's cap. First home to various pre-Inca civilizations, the area was conquered in 1465 by the Incas. Sixty-seven years later, it witnessed an epochal moment: the imprisonment and execution of the great Inca Atahuallpa by Francisco Pizarro, an event that sparked a chain of battles ultimately leading to the Spanish conquest of the region in 1534. Although remnants of pre-Hispanic societies linger and can be explored in the surrounding valley and mountains, the town itself displays far more Spanish influence, earning Cajamarca a reputation as one of the finest colonial cities in Peru. Amazingly, the search for precious metals continues to drive the local economy—the largest gold mine in South America ensures that Cajamarca does not rest on its historical laurels. It also means that Cajamarca is home to great cuisine, luxurious hotels, and upscale shopping.

▣ TRANSPORTATION

Flights: Airport (☎82 2523), 3½km east of town. Taxis from town (s/5), or catch a combi line "C" (10min., s/0.50) from El Batán (see **Food,** p. 374). **Aero Cóndor,** at Cajamarca Tours (see **Tours,** below), serves **Lima** (1¼hr., 8:15am, US$72).

Buses: Most bus companies are stationed on Atahuallpa's 3rd and 4th blocks. This is not the same Atahuallpa that appears on the map; it is 2km east of the center of town, about 4 blocks past La Recoleta. Take a **taxi** (s/2) or a **colectivo** (s/0.50) headed toward the **Baños del Inca. Transportes Línea,** Atahuallpa 318 (☎82 3956), has the nicest (and most expensive) buses to: **Chiclayo** (6hr.; 11pm, s/20; *bus cama* 10:45pm, s/25); **Lima** (12hr., 7pm, s/70); **Trujillo** (6hr.; 10:30am, 10pm; s/

20; *bus cama* 10:30pm, s/30). Other, less expensive companies run to **Chiclayo** (s/15) and **Lima** (s/25) via **Trujillo** (s/15). **Transportes Perú Bus,** Atahuallpa 405 (☎83 0431), runs to **Cajabamba** (5hr.; 1am, 2:30pm; s/10). **Empresa de Transportes Atahuallpa,** Atahuallpa 299 (☎82 3075), serves **Celendín** (4-5hr.; 7am, 1pm; s/10), where you can catch buses to **Chachapoyas** (12hr., Su and Th 12:30pm, s/10) via **Leimebamba** (8hr., s/8).

✦ ⓴ ORIENTATION AND PRACTICAL INFORMATION

At the heart of it all, the **Plaza de Armas** is home to most hotels and restaurants. The bustling Plaza is the choice location for a variety of activities, including concerts, handicrafts displays, and romantic liaisons.

Tourist Office: The enthusiastic but only moderately helpful **ITINCI** (☎/fax 82 2903), in the 6th block of Belén, on the 1st fl. of the Conjunto Monumental Belén, has a few brochures (some in English) with city **maps.** Open M-F 7:30am-1pm and 2:30-5:15pm.

Tours: Tours are often the only way to see the sights outside of town. Choice of agency makes little difference, as they all share minivans and guides. Groups go to Cumbe Mayo, Granja Porcón, Otusco, La Collpa, Baños del Inca, or on **city tours** (normally 2 per day, 9am and 3pm, s/15-20). Many agencies also arrange trips to Kuntur Wasi for groups of at least 5 (around s/70 per person). In addition to leading tours to nearby sights, **Cajamarca Tours,** 2 de Mayo 323 (☎82 5674), sells airline tickets and has **Western Union** and **DHL** service. Open daily 7am-7pm. **In God We Trust Tours,** Amalia Puga 673 (☎/fax 82 4687), gives guided tours of all popular destinations in English and French, offers **currency exchange** services for AmEx/MC/V, and cashes traveler's checks (20% commission). Open daily 7am-11pm.

Currency Exchange: Interbank (☎82 2460), on 2 de Mayo 546, at the Plaza, has an AmEx/MC/V **ATM.** Open M-F 9am-1pm and 4-6:15pm, Sa 9:15am-12:30pm.

Laundry: Lavandería Dandy, Amalia Puga 545 (☎82 8067). s/5 per kg. Open M-Sa 8am-7:30pm.

Emergency: ☎105.

Police: (☎82 2165). The giant green edifice on Plazuela Recoleta, just off Amalia Puga.

24hr. Pharmacy: Check any pharmacy's *en turno* schedule, posted outside, for the one on 24hr. duty.

Hospital: Hospital Regional MINSA, Mario Urteaga 500 (☎82 2156).

Telephones: Telefónica del Perú, 2 de Mayo 460 (☎82 1008), on the Plaza de Armas. International calls. Open daily 7am-11pm.

Internet Access: Around the Plaza de Armas and on Amalia Puga between the Plaza and La Recoleta (s/2 per hr.).

Post Office: Serpost, Amazonas 443 (☎82 4065). Open M-Sa 8am-9:30pm. **Cajamarca Tours** (see **Tours,** above) offers **DHL** and **Western Union** service.

⌂ ACCOMMODATIONS

The best values are found on the Plaza de Armas, and searching for a room with a balcony overlooking the Plaza is worth the effort. However, streets in all directions abound with hotels, and a quiet corner of solitude is not hard to come by.

Hostal Residencial Atahuallpa, Atahuallpa 686 (☎82 7840), 1 block from the Plaza, off El Comercio. Sunrise-yellow indoor courtyard. Large rooms with baths and electric hot water. Some rooms have big windows overlooking a quiet pedestrian street. Singles s/20; doubles s/35; triples s/45. ❷

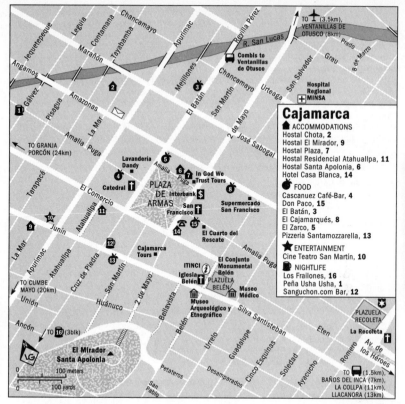

Cajamarca

🏠 **ACCOMMODATIONS**
Hostal Chota, 2
Hostal El Mirador, 9
Hostal Plaza, 7
Hostal Residencial Atahuallpa, 11
Hostal Santa Apolonia, 6
Hotel Casa Blanca, 14

🍴 **FOOD**
Cascanuez Café-Bar, 4
Don Paco, 15
El Batán, 3
El Cajamarqués, 8
El Zarco, 5
Pizzeria Santamozzarella, 13

⭐ **ENTERTAINMENT**
Cine Teatro San Martín, 10

🍸 **NIGHTLIFE**
Los Fraliones, 16
Peña Usha Usha, 1
Sanguchon.com Bar, 12

Hostal Santa Apolonia, Amalia Puga 649 (☎82 7207), on the Plaza. Surrounding a quaint courtyard filled with plants, the carpeted rooms boast cable TV, stocked mini-fridges, and pristine hot baths. Rooms are rather small, but comfortable, as most of the floor space is lost to big beds. Reservations recommended. Singles s/50; doubles s/80. AmEx/MC/V. ❹

Hostal Plaza, Amalia Puga 669 (☎82 2058), in a huge building above 2 busy courtyards and a treehouse-like system of wooden stairwells. Some of the spacious rooms have balconies, but those fill up fast. Hot baths. Singles s/15, with toilet s/20, with shower and Plaza view s/25; doubles s/28, with toilet s/35, with shower and Plaza view s/45. ❷

Hotel Casa Blanca, 2 de Mayo 446 (☎/fax 82 2141), is the most upscale hotel on the Plaza and a great place to splurge. Posh, spacious, and situated in an ideal location, it has every amenity imaginable. Breakfast included. Singles s/70; doubles s/100; triples s/130. Smooth-talkers may be able to finagle a discount. AmEx/MC/V. ❺

Hostal El Mirador, La Mar (☎82 4149), near the movie theater. Colonial stylings define El Mirador—the walls are the classic white of the rest of the town, and the beautiful wooden staircase maintains a sense of dignity. Rooms have 24hr. hot water. Singles s/50; doubles s/70; triples s/90. ❹

Hostal Chota, La Mar 637 (☎82 8704). Chota transcends its less-than-ideal location off the Plaza and common baths by charging half the price of Plaza hotels. Singles s/10; doubles s/20. ❶

FOOD

Because of the high number of dairy farms in the area, Cajamarca specializes in products such as fresh butter, yogurt, and *manjar blanco* (a sweet spread made with milk, sugar, and egg whites). Predictably, Cajamarca is a cheese-lover's paradise; *queserías* (cheese shops) market traditional and exotic Swiss varieties. **Los Alpines**, on Junín, behind the Plaza, sells many kinds of cheese (many sold only in 1kg wheels, s/30-70) and also arranges visits to the store's farm (about 15min. away) where the cheese is made. (Open daily 8am-6pm.) Buy local cheeses, along with other packaged and canned goods (s/1-5), at **Supermercado San Francisco ❶**, Amazonas 780. (☎82 2128. Open M-Sa 8am-9:30pm, Su 8:30am-1pm and 4-8pm.) For non-Peruvian food, check out the pizzerias and Mexican eateries uphill from the Plaza on San Martín.

▨ **El Batán,** El Batán 369 (☎82 6025; anabufet@hotmail.com). Eat in the courtyard decorated with plants and paintings, or move inside the restored 18th-century house, There, find a fireplace and small stage where groups perform both traditional and modern Peruvian tunes, as well as some international Spanish favorites, F-Sa 10pm (s/7). Choose from the fancy set *menú* (s/29-35), the more modest lunch *menú ejecutivo* (s/12), or traditional *criollo* and original vegetarian a la carte items (s/12-19). Open Tu-Th and Su 10am-11pm, F-Sa 10am-1am. ❸

Pizzeria Santamozzarella, Junín 1128 (☎80 1966), near Cruz de Piedra. Owner "Che" Ruben spins the pies himself and tops them with his special Argentine recipes (personal pizzas s/8-10). English and Latin rock hits keep people swilling beers well into the night. Open Tu-F 8:30am-11pm, Sa-Su 5pm-11:30pm. ❷

Cascanuez Café-Bar, Amalia Puga 554 (☎82 6089). This down-home cafe has the best mousse, chocolate cake, and fruit pie in town (slices s/4), as well as cappuccino (s/5), omelettes (s/5-7), and heartier entrees (s/14-22), but get there early if you want a slice of cheesecake. Open daily 8am-11pm. ❷

Don Paco, Amalia Puga 726 (☎83 0911), across the street from Iglesia San Francisco. The woodwork and Andean pottery in this intimate restaurant are simple but elegant. The lunchtime *menú* is a bit pricey (s/15-20), but the food is excellent. Fresh pasta, fish, and meat entrees (most s/10-25) complement the surprisingly well-stocked bar. Open daily 8am-11pm. ❸

El Cajamarqués, Amazonas 770 (☎82 2128). Pass under the arches into the regal dining hall smacking of medieval Europe, complete with weaponry and stuffed animal heads. Proceed into a garden courtyard and watch the toucans pad around while you enjoy succulent *comida típica* and international dishes. Entrees around s/14. Open daily 8am-11pm. AmEx/MC/V. ❷

El Zarco, Batán 170 (☎82 3421), just of the Plaza. A popular restaurant with an airy dining room, extensive and inexpensive menu, and wonderfully well-dressed waiters. Open daily 8am-11pm. ❶

SIGHTS

Although most tourist attractions lie outside Cajamarca, the town is interesting in its own right. The beautiful 17th-century **Iglesia de San Francisco** on the Plaza de Armas is covered with volcanic rock carvings and contains a museum of Peruvian and Ecuadorian religious art. (Museum, galleries, and underground crypts open daily 3-6pm. s/3.) On the opposite side of the Plaza, the smaller, though still impressive, **cathedral** houses a breathtaking, ornate golden facade behind the altar.

EL CONJUNTO MONUMENTAL BELÉN. A complex of colonial buildings in downtown Cajamarca, the Conjunto includes the **Iglesia Belén** (built in the late 17th century), the small **Museo Médico** inside the Instituto Nacional de Cultura, and the **Museo Arqueológico y Etnográfico** across the street. While vestiges of religious art might suggest that the Medical and Archaeological Museums were once churches, the eighteenth-century buildings were actually used as hospitals with small chapels for the infirm. The highlight of the Conjunto is **El Cuarto del Rescate,** the room where the Spanish held Atahuallpa (the last Inca emperor) prisoner. According to legend, the room was to be filled with his ransom—once with gold and twice with silver. He was ordered to stretch his hand as far up as possible to determine the required height of the treasures; the spot he touched, exactly 2.4m high, is still marked on the wall with a red line. Once part of Atahuallpa's palace, the room is the only remaining example of Inca architecture in Cajamarca; the rest of the Inca city was torn down by the Spanish conquistadors to make space and provide building material for their new colonial city. (*El Cuarto del Rescate is at Amalia Puga 750, across from the Iglesia de San Francisco. The rest of the complex is around the corner, surrounding the intersection of Belén and Junín. Open M-Sa 9am-1pm and 3-6pm, Su 9am-1pm. General entrance ticket to all buildings in the complex s/7.50; tickets good for 3 days. Spanish-speaking guides can be hired at the complex for about s/10 per site. For an English-speaking tour, go to a travel agency (see **Tours**, p. 372); prices are comparable, but guides are less specialized.*)

EL MIRADOR SANTA APOLONIA. For an excellent view of Cajamarca, visit this lookout looming high above the city. It lies in a trim garden park at the crest of a mountain just above the Santa Apolonia cathedral. Ascending the roughly 100 steps is not difficult, but may take a little longer than expected for those not adjusted to the altitude. The vista overlooks the vast, flat valley, set 2700m above sea level amid somewhat puny peaks. Supposedly, Atahuallpa used to review his subjects here. A natural rock formation resembling a throne is known as the Inca Chair. (*Stairs begin at the end of 2 de Mayo. Open daily 8am-11pm. s/1.*)

LOS BAÑOS DEL INCA. Just beyond Cajamarca's borders lie Los Baños del Inca, a typical Peruvian natural hot springs where Atahuallpa supposedly bathed shortly before his capture. Today, guests may enjoy private indoor baths with water drawn from the springs (s/4), sit in the sauna (s/8), or go for a swim in the outdoor pool (s/2). The actual springs are a scalding 78°C, but bathers can alter the temperature with knobs. (*Take a taxi (s/5) or a colectivo (15min., s/0.50) from Amazonas in Cajamarca. ☎82 1563. Open daily 5am-7:45pm.*)

▮ NIGHTLIFE

For a town with many students and lots of new wealth, Cajamarca's nightlife is slow, but things do pick up on weekends. First-run US and international movies can be seen nightly at the **Cine Teatro San Martín,** Junín 829. (☎82 3260. s/5-7.)

Peña Usha Usha, Amalia Puga 142, 4 blocks from the Plaza. Small and intimate, Usha Usha is the ideal place to seek out traditional *criolla* music. Weekends feature live bands; on weekdays, the owner often breaks into song when the mood is right. Cover s/1.50. Open M-Sa 9pm-late.

Sanguchon.com Bar, Junín 1137 (☎83 2097). It's not a cybercafe, but they do serve all sorts of cocktails, including the perfect *pisco* sour and Brazilian *caipirinha*, dubbed the strongest drink in the world. Open M-Th 6pm-1am, F-Sa 5pm-4am.

Los Frailones, Perú 701, at the corner with Cruz de La Piedra, about 6 blocks uphill from the Plaza. Perhaps the most popular disco in Cajamarca, with all of the usual flashing lights, thumping Spanish pop, and strong drinks made even stronger by the altitude. Cover s/15 for men, s/10 for women. Open Th-Sa 9pm-4am.

⚡ DAYTRIPS FROM CAJAMARCA

▨ CUMBE MAYO

There is no public transportation to Cumbe Mayo, 20km southwest of Cajamarca. The easiest way to visit is with a guided tour (4hr., s/15-20). It's also possible to walk there along the winding mountain road from Cajamarca (3-4hr.); signs at Santa Apolonia mark the road. Take a jacket, since it's cold at 3600m.

These rolling green hills, dotted with mammoth rock formations, derive their name from the Quechua "humpi mayo" or "thin river." Actually a 9km-long **aqueduct** built by the pre-Inca Cajamarca culture around 1500 BC, this "river" is the oldest known manmade structure in South America. It forms a series of perfect right angles at various junctures along its route; according to one theory, this geometric configuration was intended to symbolize the sacred staircase leading to the afterlife. The site also contains a number of **ceremonial caverns** and **sacrificial altars** oriented to the rising sun in the east, where pre-Inca petroglyphs, including snakes, crosses, skulls, and surprisingly, even a bona fide smiley face are etched into the floor and walls. Dominating the tranquil landscape are the **bosques de piedra** (rock forests), gigantic volcanic rocks eroded by rain into shapes resembling mushrooms. Try to spot the dinosaur, contemplative iguana, military general, horny toad, seahorse, and priest reading a book. **Camping** is permitted everywhere in these scarcely populated hills, though you'll either have to walk to and from town or make arrangements with a tour company.

GRANJA PORCÓN

Agencies charge s/15-20 for a 4hr. tour. Open daily 5:30am-7pm. If you want to stay in the albergue, the cooperativa can arrange for a private car.

Founded in 1975, this 12,000 hectare communal ranch (formally called the **Cooperativa Agraria "Atahuallpa Jerusalén"**) is part of one of the world's largest reforestation projects. Technically, "reforestation" is a misnomer, since the co-op's 10,500,000 trees (mostly pine, eucalyptus, and cypress) do not grow naturally at this altitude and are not indigenous to the Andes; instead, these trees are used, in place of native trees, for paper and furniture. With funding from the Peruvian government, the Universidad Nacional de Cajamarca, and various international environmental organizations, 60 families live here in a self-sufficient town that runs on hydroelectric and solar power. Going from rags to riches in barely a quarter century, this *cooperativa* is a rare success story (many similar projects around the country have failed) and a source of Cajamarcan pride in demonstrating how the cold, seemingly uninhabitable *sierras* can be transformed into a veritable gold mine of renewable resources. Regrettably, the real gold deposits that lie beneath the forests may one day jeopardize their existence. Guided trips include a hike through the hilltop forests and a tour of the town and endangered animal sanctuary (which houses wildly-plumed rare birds, monkeys, *tigrillos*, leopards, a puma, and freely roaming vicuña). Guests who just can't leave can stay at the comfortable, hot-water **albergue ❻**. (☎/fax 82 5631. Singles US$20; doubles US$40.) Eat in the **restaurant,** where food is prepared exclusively with home-grown ingredients.

VENTANILLAS DE OTUSCO

Tours cost s/15, but Otusco is easily reached on your own. Take a combi from where El Batán becomes Revilla Pérez, 4 blocks downhill from the Plaza de Armas (20min., s/1). Hardier souls may also venture to Otusco by foot; it's a pleasant 2hr. walk from the Baños del Inca. From the Baños, follow the river heading away from Cajamarca. There are no signs, but friendly locals will point you in the right direction. Open daily 8:30am-6pm. s/3.

This necropolis consists of hundreds of niches or *ventanillas* (small windows), built in AD 800 by the Cajamarca as tombs for the most important members of their society. All of the bones, along with any treasures that may have been inside, were sacked by the Incas when they conquered the land around AD 1470. A few of the *ventanillas* (on the left side) have been restored. Children may approach you, eager to show (and sell) you the fruits of their labors (fossils of ancient seashells collected from the nearby mountainsides, evidence that these lands were once submerged under the ocean). Guided tours usually combine Otusco with a trip to a **flower farm** that grows some of the world's largest *hortensias* (guaranteed to be taller than you) and a Swiss-style **cheese factory.**

LA COLLPA AND LLACANORA

5hr. tours cost s/15-20, and include a visit to the Baños del Inca. Other options include taking a taxi (20min., s/25) to the hacienda (s/1.50) or catching a combi to Jesús and then retracing the road back 1½km to La Collpa.

Hacienda La Collpa is a cattle ranch situated in a gorgeous pastoral setting with an artificial lake. It is best known for **"cow calling"**—late every afternoon, ranch hands round up the cattle by summoning each animal by name. The nearby town of Llacanora has 7000-year-old **cave paintings** and is a 20min. walk from an impressive **waterfall.** A second, even larger waterfall is tucked back about a 15min. walk from the first. However, rain occasionally washes out the usual route, doubling the duration and level of difficulty of the hike.

KUNTUR WASI

4hr. from Cajamarca. Full-day tours with an agency cost s/80 per person for a group of 5.

Less frequently visited because of the distance, but well worth the effort, this 3000-year-old stone complex consists of ceremonial plazas, terraces, and enormous petroglyphs with representations of anthropomorphic gods of pre-Inca civilizations. The gold crowns and breastplates discovered in tombs here now reside in the nearby **Museo La Conga,** about a 10min. walk from the ruins.

LEIMEBAMBA ☎ 041

The discovery of over 200 mummies in the nearby archaeological site of **Laguna de los Cóndores** has attracted a great deal of attention to this peaceful town (pop. 5000), where foreigners are still the objects of curious glances, and where cargo-laden horses have the right of way. Leimebamba is in the beginning stages of adopting a more extensive tourist network to cope with the surge of visitors interested in exploring the multitude of ruins left behind by the Chachapoyas culture.

⌨ ☎ TRANSPORTATION AND PRACTICAL INFORMATION. Combis head to Chachapoyas (4hr., 3:30-4:30am, s/7) via Tingo (2hr., s/5). Register with the drivers parked in the Plaza after 7pm and they'll pick you up on the way out of town. **Buses** from Celendín bound for Chachapoyas (5hr., Su and Th 7:30pm) pass through town briefly, as do buses going the other way (7hr., F 2pm). From Celendín there is regular bus service to Cajamarca (4-5hr., s/10). A **tourist office,** San Agustín 407, on the Plaza, contains a small **museum** and provides tourist passes to the various sights nearby. (Open M-F 8am-noon and 2-8pm.) Leimebamba has **no bank,** but individuals are usually eager to **exchange dollars** for soles. This includes the **police,** Sucre 115, on the Plaza. **Centro de Salud,** La Verdad 480, three blocks from the Plaza, provides 24hr. emergency medical services. **Telefónica del Perú,** Amazonas 426, on the Plaza, has the only two telephones in town. (Open daily 7am-10:30pm.)

🛏️🍴 ACCOMMODATIONS AND FOOD. While the accommodations and food options in Leimebamba are rather sparse, the few that do exist are very good. A sign on the Plaza points the way to **Laguna de los Cóndores ❷**, Amazonas 320, half a block up the street on the left. Knowledgeable owners offer comfortable rooms with incredibly clean bathrooms, a relaxing first-floor lounge, and tourist information galore. (Singles s/15, with bath s/30; doubles s/25, with bath s/40.) A little farther down Amazonas on the right is the poorly marked **Hostal La Casona ❷** (☎77 0261), recently renovated, with surprisingly luxurious rooms next to a large and peaceful deck and lounge. (Rooms s/20 per person.) **Restaurante Celis ❶**, a block off the Plaza, entices with gorgeous apple pies (s/3) in the window. Give the *lomo saltado* a try. (Entrees s/5-10.) **Restaurante El Caribe ❶**, 16 de Julio 712, offers select dishes of *comida típica* (beef anyone?) as well as a *menú* (s/3) for lunch. Sandwiches and snacks are available all day. (Open daily 6am-11pm.) **Panadería Jovita**, La Verdad 514, has good bread and a few sweets—ideal for daytrips.

🔲 SIGHTS. You'd better be both interested and energetic if you want to see the original resting place of the hundreds of mummies recovered from **Laguna de los Cóndores**. The one-way trip takes 9hr. walking or 8hr. on horseback. A full three days are recommended for the trip—two days of transport and one for exploring the lake and its surroundings. The site contains seven stone towers, four polychrome *chullpas* (stone tombs), and about 200 circular structures near a beautiful lake. Well-preserved mummies were first interred in the *chullpas* over 1000 years ago, but it is believed that these individuals underwent secondary burials as later cultures made room for members of their own societies. By the time archaeologists visited the site in 1997, *huaqueros* (tomb robbers) had already sifted through the mummies and carelessly moved them from their original position. Ceramic remains indicate the influence of the Chimú and Cajamarca cultures, and the discovery of *quipus* (strings used for communication) emphasizes the presence of Inca administration. To visit the ruins, tourists must be accompanied by a guide (s/25 per day, with horse s/45 per day). Tourists also need a permit (s/10) from the tourist information office on the Plaza. Basic accommodations (straw mattresses) are available at the summit (s/6 per person).

If mummies are not quite worth a 3-day journey, check out the **Museo Leimebamba**, on Austria from Leimebamba. On display are some of the lake's 220 mummies, as well as textiles and artifacts found at the sight that show the evolution of culture in the area after the Inca invasion. Unfortunately, Incas destroyed much of what pre-dated them, which greatly limits current knowledge of earlier cultures. Most of the mummies are held in canvas sacks for preservation, but you can still easily make out their shape, as well as some features. Some of the damaged mummies are kept on display and depict (graphically) the burial position, as well as unique physical features preserved through mummification, including ear piercings and hair styles. A portion of the museum is devoted to the consequences of grave robbing and archaeological looting. There is also an orchid garden and an exhibit about the climate and ecology of the region. (20min. by taxi from the Plaza. http://centromallqui.org.pe/ley_ubicacion_en.htm. Open M-Sa 10am-4pm. s/5.)

La Congona is a much more accessible site that can be easily visited in a daytrip. The circular structures at the summit exhibit the three frieze types identified with the Chachapoyas culture. Apart from the archaeological ruins (a 3hr. walk from the end of Bolívar), the hilltop offers beautiful vistas of the nearby countryside. A free pass from the tourist office is required. To go with a Spanish-speaking guide (s/25 per day), make reservations at least one day in advance. The less-explored region of **Tajopampa** also requires an overnight stay, but is well worth it. The ancients buried their dead in the caves of this area's 500m cliff. Among the numerous red arches and rock paintings, the image of a man holding a bleeding head supports theories concerning the bellicose nature of the Chachapoyas. Other nearby residential compounds can also be explored. To get to the site (5hr.), hire a guide (s/20 per day) and obtain a free permit from the tourist office prior to departure. Accommodations are available and prices are negotiable.

CHACHAPOYAS   ☎ 041

As the capital of the Amazonas department, Chacha (as it is affectionately called) is home to some of the most impressive but least visited ruins in Peru. The extraordinary pre-Inca fortress of Kuélap, 4hr. away by combi, is one of the largest architectural works in the Americas. Due to its remote location in the Northern Highlands, Chachapoyas (pop. 20,000; 2335m) sees relatively few foreign visitors, nor the shoeshine boys and money changers that inevitably follow. Even getting there is an adventure. Most opt for the bumpy 8hr. bus from Chiclayo, but true thrill-seekers take on the 16hr. journey from Cajamarca via Celedín, a spectacularly scenic ride not for the faint of stomach. If you're still thirsting for adventure, the crossroads to the jungle is only 2hr. away.

▐ TRANSPORTATION

Buses: Combis and **taxis** are concentrated around the market on Grau, and most buses arrive on or leave from Salamanca and Arrieta. The road to Chiclayo is much more comfortable and much quicker than the route via Celendín. As a result, most bus service runs through Chiclayo, where there are connections to most major destinations. **Trans-Servis Kuélap,** Ortiz Arrieta 412 (☎77 8128), has bus service to **Chiclayo** (11hr., 7:30pm, s/35). **Movíl Tours,** Libertad 464 (☎77 8545), also has comfortable service with a small meal to **Chiclayo** (11 hr., 8pm, s/40). **Civa,** La Libertad 812 (☎77 8048), goes to **Lima** (22hr.; M, W, F noon; s/65). **Viaje del Carmen** sends a microbus along the mountainous highway to **Celendín** (F 7am, s/30). From Celendín it is possible to catch a bus to **Cajamarca** (5hr., s/10-12). **Combis** (1½hr., 5am-6pm, s/6) and shared **taxis** (s/10) leave from the 3rd block of Grau for **Pedro Ruíz,** where it is possible to flag down a bus headed to **Tarapoto** (9hr., s/20-25).

▐✱▐ ORIENTATION AND PRACTICAL INFORMATION

The main landmark in town is the **Plaza de Armas,** bordered by **Ayacucho, Grau, Amazonas,** and **Ortiz Arrieta.** The commercial center and **mercado** are on **La Libertad,** one block north of Ayacucho, between Grau and Ortiz Arrieta. Most combis to nearby towns leave from Grau between La Libertad and **Salamanca** (also called **San Juan de la Libertad**). Most essential services can be found around the Plaza.

Tourist Office: Arrieta 1250 (☎/fax 77 8355), on the Plaza. **Maps,** up-to-date combi schedules, and an interactive CD-ROM. Open M-F 7:30am-1pm and 2:15-5:15pm. The **Instituto Nacional de Cultura,** Ayacucho 904 (☎77 7045), has information about area sights. Open M-F 10am-5pm.

Tours: Café de Guías, Ayacucho 755 (☎77 7664), in the Gran Hotel Vilaya, has loads of brochures, books, **maps,** guide referrals in English, and coffee. Open daily 7am-1pm and 3-10pm. **Amazon Tours,** Arrieta 520 (☎77 8294; amazon_tours@starmedia.com), on the Plaza, is another valuable source of information and tour packages. Offers guided trips in Spanish or English (s/50) to Kuélap, Karajía, or Revash. Also offers a 5- to 7-day trek through the mountains to Kuélap (US$200). Min. 4-5 people required for trips. Open M-Sa 7am-1pm and 2:30-9pm, Su 7am-1pm. **Hostal Revash (see Accommodations,** below) also offers tours to Kuélap, Revash, and Karajía (s/30), as well as trekking excursions. Local expert **Carlos Burga** (via Hostal Revash) offers his services as a Spanish-speaking guide (s/100-150 per day). **Luís Castañeda** is a knowledgeable English- and Spanish-speaking guide (US$25 per day).

Currency Exchange: Banco de Crédito, Arrieta 580 (☎77 7430), on the Plaza. AmEx/V ATM. Open M-F 9:30am-1pm and 3:30-6pm, Sa 9:30am-12:30pm.

Market: The busy indoor **market,** at the corner of La Libertad and Grau, provides a cheap dining option. The *mercados* at Arrieta on the Plaza, and **Comercial Tito,** La Libertad 860 (☎77 7123, open M-Sa 7:30am-1:30pm and 3-6:30pm), are good places to stock up before daytrips.

Laundromat: Lavandería Clean, Amazonas 817 (☎77 7078), 1 block from the Plaza, offers same-day service for s/3 per kg. Open M-Sa 8am-1pm, and 3-6:30pm.

Emergency: ☎105.

Police: National Police, Ayacucho 1040 (☎77 7176).

Medical Services: Hospital Apoyo de Chachapoyas (☎77 7016), on the 3rd block of Triunfo, is open 24hr. for emergencies. **Es Salud** is 2 blocks from the Plaza down Arrieta.

Telephones: Telefónica del Perú, Ayacucho 924 (☎77 8089 or 77 8094), on the Plaza. Accepts international calling cards. Open daily 7am-11pm.

Internet: Ciber Club, Triunfo 769 (☎99 9231), charges s/2 per hr. Open daily 8am-midnight. **Amazon Tours** provides web service (s/3 per hr., s/1 discount for clients).

Post Office: Serpost, Grau 553 (☎77 7019), on the Plaza. Open M-Sa 8am-8pm.

ACCOMMODATIONS

Due to the recent increase in ecological and archaeological tourism, a number of comfortable hotels have sprung up to counterbalance the town's more basic accommodations. Many are willing to drop prices without much bargaining.

▨ **Hostal Revash,** Grau 517 (☎77 7391), on the Plaza, has large rooms with cable TV, comfy beds, and 24hr. hot water in what may be the greatest showers outside of Lima. Small cafeteria, gift shop, and laundry service (s/5 per kg). Owner Carlos Burga is an expert on the region and eagerly helps arrange travel plans. Singles s/35; doubles s/50. Discount Dec.-Mar. s/5-10. ❸

Hotel El Dorado, Ayacucho 1062 (☎77 7047), 1 block from the Plaza, in a colonial house. 2nd fl. rooms all have electric hot baths, TVs, and wooden or tiled floors. Laundry service (s/5 per kg). Singles s/25; doubles s/30; triples s/35. ❸

Hostal El Tejado, Grau 534, 2nd fl. (☎77 7654), on the Plaza. Comfortable and immaculate rooms with hot private baths. Nice restaurant overlooking the Plaza; breakfast included. TV s/5. Singles s/30; doubles s/45. ❸

Hostal Johumaji, Ayacucho 711 (☎77 7279; fax 77 7819), 2 blocks from the Plaza, offers day-, week-, or month-long rates. All rooms have electric hot showers. Comfortable (and cheap) enough to warrant longer stays. TV s/5. Singles s/15; doubles s/25. ❷

FOOD

Due to Chacha's location, there is a strong jungle influence in the otherwise highland cuisine. Rice-covered *juanes* (rice, chicken, black olives, and egg wrapped in a banana leaf) are considered a tropical delicacy, but at higher altitudes, yucca is substituted for the water-needy grains. *Purto mote* (a mixture of beans and corn) is another Chacha favorite. For a light snack, there are a couple of small cafes with juices, desserts, burgers, and *juanes* at Arrieta on the Plaza. *Anticuchos* are grilled late into the night beside the market on Grau.

Chacha, Grau 545 (☎77 7107), on the Plaza. Serves heaping platters of *comida típica*—the *bistec a lo pobre* is nearly enough for two. The open dining room, right on the Plaza, can get chilly at night. Lunch *menú* s/3. Entrees s/7-12. Open M-Sa 7am-10pm, Su 7am-3pm and 7-11pm. ❷

Eden, Grau 448, down from the Plaza toward the Mercado. A brilliant little vegetarian restaurant, serving all the same *comida típica* without the meat. Some menu items even include broccoli, a rarity in Peru. Tofu is substituted in saltados and other typically *lomo*-dominated dishes. Entrees s/5-12. Open daily 8am-9pm. ❷

Las Rocas, Ayacucho 932 (☎77 8158), on the Plaza. Dim lights and close-packed tables let you dig in and feel like one of the gang. Chicken, beef, and tortilla entrees are a king's portion at a pauper's price (s/3-7). Open M-Sa 7:15am-9pm, Su 6-9pm. ❶

Mataleche, Ayacucho 616 (☎77 8325), 3 blocks off the Plaza. Despite serving what locals consider the best beef, chicken, and *cuy* dishes in town, Mataleche's location keeps tourist numbers and prices down. Entrees s/6-10. Open daily 7am-9pm. ❷

NORTHERN HIGHLANDS

👁 SIGHTS

Although sights within town are limited, several lookout points provide brilliant views of Chachapoyas and the surrounding countryside. The **Mirador de Huancuarco** is a 1hr. walk on Arrieta, going uphill from the Plaza past the bus companies (taxi 20 min., s/2.50). You can reach another *mirador* by walking up Salamanca, turning left and winding up the hill five blocks past Arrieta (30min.). **El Pozo** (fountain) **de Yana Yacu** is a large, crumbling stone building about six blocks up from the Plaza. Legend has it that anyone who drinks from these waters is destined to live in Chachapoyas until he or she dies—an experience you might want to save until you know what you're in for. At the **Instituto Nacional de Cultura** (p. 379), there is a small **museum** with a couple of mummies and a smattering of artifacts that whet the appetite for future excursions and provide a (somewhat scanty) introduction to the history of the region.

The most exciting times to be in Chachapoyas are during the **Fiestas Patronales** (the first two weeks of August) and the **Semana Turística** (the first week of June), when an exposition of local foods and dances culminates with a procession of representatives from nearby villages.

🎵 NIGHTLIFE

For a small town, Chachapoyas has a surprisingly active nightlife, but don't expect much early in the week. And if you go alone, don't expect to be left to ponder the bottom of your glass. Dancing is a requirement, and Chachapoyans, both men and women, will make sure you do. For drinks before hitting the disco, there are numerous small bars along Ayacucho that serve carafes of local liquors (s/3.50-5) in flavors from grape to apricot. All discos play roughly the same mix of salsa and Latin and American pop. Because there is generally no cover, many people do a circuit of clubs in one night.

Los Troncos, 2 de Mayo 561, behind Hostal Revash. The most happening place in town. The dance floor is like a stage, bordered by a jumble of tables and chairs. As a matter of etiquette, the dance floor usually clears after every song and is repopulated by different pairs right away. Beer s/3. Large pitcher s/10. Open daily 9pm-late.

La Noche, Triunfo 1061, several blocks off the Plaza. La Noche is more bar than club, but it still has plenty of energy. Beer s/3. Open daily 9pm-3am.

El Ritual, Ayacucho Mz. 11, a bit farther out of town. Gringos stick out in this flashy joint. Open daily 9pm-3am.

DAYTRIPS FROM CHACHAPOYAS

Most people don't come all the way to Chacha just to stay in town. While you can reach most of the outlying sights on your own, the **Instituto Nacional de Cultura** (p. 379) recommends venturing out in groups, preferably with a guide, since some of the paths in remote areas are a bit treacherous. Check out their archaeological displays as a preview to local trips. Tours not only provide more information, but also offer better access to many sights. While all are fairly close to Chachapoyas, the many archaeological sites and ruins in the surrounding area aren't arranged along any easily navigable circuit. Slow public transportation and poor roads further limit the area you can cover in a few days. Tours, however, will often combine major sites with less visited attractions a bit more off the beaten track.

KUÉLAP

To get to the ruins, catch the early-morning combi with Transportes ROLERS at the first block of Grau (3hr., 4am, s/10), and return on the same bus later in the day. Alternatively, the more fit can trek to the ruins from Tingo, a 1½-2hr. bus ride from Chachapoyas. The path, marked by red arrows, starts in Tingo near the bridge and follows a level plain along the river before turning and becoming a steep 4hr. mountain climb. It's possible to do the hike alone, but a guide is recommended. If you do the hike, you will almost certainly need to stay for the night around Kuélap. Basic accommodations (without electricity and running water) are available in the INC dorm ❶ (s/10 per person). Slightly more comfortable stays can be had in Kisango by walking 30min. down the road leading to Kuélap, or you can continue a full 2hr. away to Pueblo de María. Bring your own food, water, and rain gear. Kuélap's gates open daily 8am-5pm. s/10, students s/5.

A massive pre-Columbian fortress built atop a mountain, Kuélap inevitably draws comparisons to Machu Picchu. Though it doesn't receive nearly as much attention as the latter, Kuélap was built earlier (between AD 800 and 1300 by the Chachapoyas peoples), "discovered" earlier (in 1843), and lacks Machu Picchu's hordes of camera-toting tourists. Surrounded by a wall 30m high, this defensive fortress measures 584m by 100m, and its 3000m altitude results in a commanding position over the surrounding valleys. Archaeologists are still puzzled about whom the Chachapoyas were defending themselves against and where the massive quantity of stone came from, but the sheer distance they had to lug the rocks implies that it was someone unfriendly. While the stonework is not as fine as that of the Incas, the complex remains amazingly intact despite the passage of time.

Shrouded in thick cloud forest vegetation, Kuélap is comprised of three distinct levels containing over 450 circular structures. The fat cats lived in **Pueblo Alto** (the second level), surrounded by thick, fortified walls and plazas believed to have served some public ceremonial function. The masses resided in **Pueblo Bajo** (the first level), in more modest dwellings built closer together. Some theories suggest that these masses were not comprised of run-of-the-mill peasants but were limited to military personnel. The peasants, rather, lived outside the gates and cultivated the land in the hills around Kuélap, only seeking shelter inside the walls when attacked. The **torreón** marks the northern tip of the third level, where warriors are believed to have resided in preparation for a quick defense. The recovery of axes and other weapons from the *torreón* has led archaeologists to theorize that it was a military lookout, and indeed this watchtower provides one of the most spectacular views. Back toward the first level, elaborate friezes are cut into the sides of structures in the form of serpents, deer eyes, and other cloud forest fauna. Near the southern end of the complex lies **El Tintero** (The Inkwell), a 6m-high inverted cone whose function remains a mystery. The interior bowl is aimed east toward the rising sun, and bones recovered nearby suggest it was used for human sacrifice. Others theorize that its structure has astronomical significance as a kind of calendar. Only four round edifices on the lowest level have been fully excavated. The artifacts uncovered there indicate that they served as residences before the Incas invaded and started using them as burial chambers. One of these residences has been "restored" to show how archaeologists believe the fortress looked before it was conquered and abandoned.

OTHER RUINS NEAR CHACHAPOYAS

KARAJÍA. Another spectacular funerary site, Karajía contains 3-4m anthropomorphic wooden coffins that were carefully deposited under a cliff overhang between AD 800 and 1300. Crouched mummies were placed inside each coffin and skulls were perched atop each sarcophagus. The mummies have since been removed by archaeologists, but the coffins remain. *(Buses go to Luya (every hr. 5am-5pm, s/5) from Arrieta near the market in Chachapoyas. From there, walk to the ruins (2½hr.) or take a taxi from Luya to Cohechán (1hr., s/5), cutting the walk to 1hr. The last combi from Luya to Chachapoyas leaves at 3pm. Luya has a modest hospedaje if you miss it.)*

Near Karajía, there are several other minor sites that can easily be incorporated into a daytrip with a tour. **El Pueblo de Los Muertos,** above the town of Lamud, is the site of several tombs and sarcophagi. You can also visit **Kiocta,** a subterranean cavern with gigantic stalactites and stalagmites. Be sure to bring rubber boots (s/3) and a flashlight for every member of the group. A 1hr. walk from the town of Tinkas leads to another group of mausoleums at **Wangli.**

REVASH. This impressive location consists of red, rectangular edifices built into the side of a cliff. The structures were erected as tombs and decorated with rock paintings. Although you cannot enter the mausoleums, the view from below is still worth the visit (even better with binoculars). One building inexplicably has what appears to be a Christian cross. *(Take a combi going to Leimebamba as far as Yerbabuena (2hr.). From Yerbabuena, take a combi toward Santo Tomás and ask to be let off at the path to Revash (20min.). From there it's a 1hr. climb to the site. As you walk, look up at the cliff to see smaller collections of tombs sporadically inserted in the rock face. The last combi from Yerbabuena to Chachapoyas leaves at 4pm, but Yerbabuena has a hospedaje if you miss the bus.)*

JALCA GRANDE. This small town is the site where Chachapoyas was originally founded in 1538, 74km from its present location. Today, it is a popular folklore center that attracts tourists to its stone colonial tower and the nearby **Ollape ruins** (40min. walk). The circular structures at Ollape are believed to have been erected between AD 1150 and 1300, and display diamond friezes. **Laguna Mamacocha** (3hr. walk) makes a good daytrip from Jalca Grande. *(Combis travel daily to Jalca (3½hr., 2pm, s/8) from Salamanca in Chachapoyas. Tuleo Culqui is a popular Spanish-speaking guide. ☎89 0242. s/20 per day. Visitors usually stay overnight in one of Jalca Grande's hospedajes.)*

OLÁN. Of all the Chachapoyas residential complexes in the region, this is by far the most extensive. With approximately 600 circular homes, this is the best site to see the three traditional frieze types: rhombus, zig-zag, and Greek-stepped. The site is remarkable for both the quantity and the quality of its well-preserved friezes and pre-Inca decorations. *(From Chachapoyas, take a combi from Salamanca to Montevideo (4hr., noon, s/8). Trek 1½hr.; ask locals to point the way. The return combi from Montevideo to Chachapoyas leaves at 4am, so visitors must wait at the hostel in Montevideo.)*

LEVANTO AND YÁLAPE. Levanto and Yálape are 22km from Chachapoyas. Yálape was constructed between AD 1110 and 1300, and contains pre-Inca circular buildings with diamond friezes. The Colla Cruz ruins, near the town of Levanto, consist of an Inca foundation wall topped by a round structure. This construction typifies the perplexing relationship between the Inca and Chachapoyas peoples that archaeologists are still trying to resolve. *(Combis go to Levanto daily (2hr., noon, s/8-10) from Salamanca in Chachapoyas. Combis return to Chachapoyas at 2pm, so you'll have to walk 3hr. back along a pre-Inca trail or spend the night.)*

HIKING NEAR CHACHAPOYAS

If you're tired of hours on bumpy roads, there is yet another option for exploring the Chachapoyas region. A number of travel agencies, including Hostal Revash and Amazon Tours (see **Tours,** p. 379), offer several treks through the cloud forests that separate the archaeological highpoints of the region. A sample 4-day itinerary might includes transportation on **Day 1** to Karajía, then to the gorgeous **Valle Belén,** where you spend the first night in a cabin. On **Day 2,** walk 6hr. through the cloud forests and visit **Piriquilla,** an archaeological site still being excavated. That night, sleep with a family in Congón. On **Day 3,** a 4hr. ride on horseback takes you to the village of Lanche, and another 2hr. by horse brings you to Yumal, where you hop back on motorized transport to spend the night at Choctamal. On **Day 4,** you visit Kuélap and return to Chachapoyas. *(US$40 per person per day, all-inclusive; the price drops to US$25 for groups of six or more.)*

THE AMAZON
BASIN

If there's an off-the-beaten track to be found, it's in the heart of South America's steamy rainforests. The Amazon is home to 23% of the world's freshwater supply, 800 species of mammals, 2500 species of fish (more than the entire Atlantic Ocean), and 25,000 species of plants (more than 50% of those identified). It is the most diverse ecosystem in the world, and many of its secrets remain unrevealed.

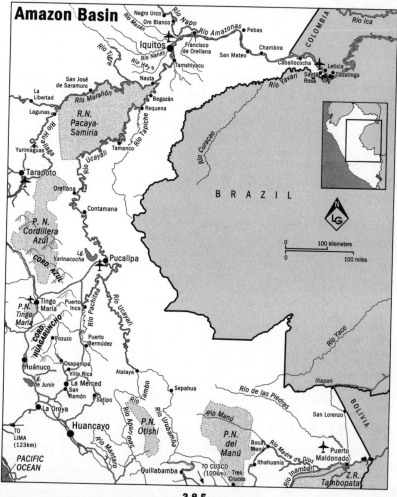

Visitors soon discover that the jungle is not the local zoo—you're not going to encounter certain elusive animals regardless of how or with whom you see the rainforest; there's simply too much vegetation for them to hide behind. Countless insects, yes. Incredible vegetation, yes. Many large mammals, no. Despite the millions of tourist dollars circulating, the forest will not cater to the whims of passing visitors. In fact, dispersed throughout this hot, sticky paradise, dozens of native tribes remain unaffected by outsiders, living as they have for centuries.

The most popular way to visit the Amazon is through a tour. Unfortunately, while jungle tours cater to a variety of tastes and levels of adventure, few fall within the realm of budget travel. Cheaper options, often with freelance guides, do exist, but it's nearly impossible to tell the gems from the con men, and signing up—not to mention handing over any money—can involve substantial risk. Yet for those willing to follow the road less traveled, other possibilities exist. Hopping aboard a cargo boat, stringing up your hammock, and disembarking at one of the myriad small villages along the riverfront is one of the most authentic and cheapest ways to explore the region. Those seeking wildlife of a different variety will be pleased to discover that jungle cities are the party capitals of Peru, with fancy discos raging until the sun comes up. Whether you pound the pavement of the unique urban centers, peruse unexplored vegetation, or cruise the busy waterways, your tour of Peru will not be complete until you make a stop in the jungle.

HIGHLIGHTS OF THE AMAZON BASIN

STROLL along **Iquitos**'s boulevard on the Amazon at sunset—then hop on the nearest boat heading toward the surrounding untouched rainforest (p. 386).

DAZZLE your senses with a colorful visit to the **Pilpintuwasi Butterfly Farm** (p. 393).

SWAT mosquitos while exploring the wildlife-filled waterways of the **Reserva Nacional Pacaya-Samiria (p. 399)**.

DISCOVER a new plant in **Parque Nacional del Manú** (p. 422), one of South America's most pristine parks—it's only got 12,000 species so far.

IQUITOS

☎ 094

Perched at the mouth of the majestic Amazon River, Iquitos (pop. 350,000; elev. 106m) immediately conjures wistful notions of adventure and the unexplored. Tourists travel for days to observe the incredibly diverse Amazonian wildlife and the increasingly assimilated indigenous tribes continuing to survive in the lowland forest. Yet travelers who come so far to see the forest in all its glory make a mistake if they overlook the jungle hotspot. While the looming and highly visible rainforest no doubt contributes to this inspiration, Iquitos itself has an undeniable, almost magical allure. Although it is the largest city in the world unreachable by road, every street and dirt path within its limits screams with the constant passing of motocars. Lush meadows are transformed into throbbing open-air *discotecas*, while suburbs like the shantytown of Belén reach beyond land and float upon the rivers themselves. Shamans help the devout or the merely curious explore the very essence of their soul through a drug-induced state of intense reflection using *ayahuasca*. Iquitos is not merely the gateway to adventure, but is an adventure in itself—the heartbeat of Loreto province.

🚆 TRANSPORTATION

Flights: Aeropuerto Francisco Secada V. Iquitos (☎26 0147), 7km south of the city center. City buses stop outside the airport gates, then run up Aguierre-Huallaga-Condamine and down Ocampo-Tacna-Grau (s/0.50). Mototaxi s/7. **Nuevo Continente,**

Próspero 232 (☎24 2995), just past the Plaza de Armas, offers flights to **Lima** (1½hr.; 8:55am, 8:40pm; US$64). Open M-Sa 9am-6:30pm. AmEx/MC/V. **TANS**, Arica 273 (☎22 1599; www.tansperu.com), is across the street from its competitor. Open M-Sa 8:30am-1pm and 3:30-7pm. To: **Lima** (2½hr., 11:30am) via **Tarapoto** (1hr.); **Lima** (2½hr., 6pm) via **Pucallpa** (1hr.). All flights to every location are US$64, including flights to stopover points. **Airport tax** of s/12 on all domestic flights. International service to Iquitos from the US and Europe may begin in the near future.

The Iquitos airport is full of **con men**. Mototaxi drivers have been known to offer prices as low as s/1; however, they receive a commission when they take you to a hotel with which they have contracted. Similarly, tour operator representatives often swarm like piranhas, pushing tourists to commit before they have had time to shop around for the tour that suits them best. Have a destination in mind before you arrive (or head straight to the tourist office) and be suspicious of taxi drivers who say that your hotel of choice has burned down.

Buses: The paved Iquitos-Nauta road has been "nearly complete" for several years. Currently, only a small patch of about 20km remains to be paved. When dry, buses can still make the journey, but after rains the road is treacherous and often impassable. Unfortunately, there is no reliable way to predict the condition of the road ahead of time, making any attempt a somewhat risky endeavor. When the road is finished, travelers will be able to cut their travel time upriver from Iquitos considerably: a 2hr. bus ride will replace the 12hr. boat ride to Nauta, where travelers will be able to board a boat heading upriver to Yurimaguas.

Boats: Depending on the height of the river, boats depart M-Sa from either **Puerto Masusa** or **Puerto Servicio**—both are off La Marina in the north of the city. Aguierre-Huallaga-Condamine bus s/0.50. Mototaxi s/3. Boats accepting passengers display signs to announce their destination and time of departure, but few boats leave on schedule. Most depart around 6-7pm and go to: **Lagunas** (1-2 days, s/25-30); **Pucallpa** (4-6 days, s/65); **Yurimaguas** (3-4 days, s/45-80); **Leticia, Colombia** and **Tabatinga, Brazil** (1-3 days, s/80). Prices negotiable. **Speedboats** also leave M-Sa for **Tabatinga** (10hr., 6am, US$50) courtesy of speedboat agencies located along Raimondi between Pevas and Loreto, including **Transtur**, Raimondi 344 (☎23 1278), and **Rápido Expreso Loreto**, Raimondi 384 (☎23 3157). Speedboats also depart from the small port of **Bellavista** for destinations along the Río Nanay. Any Huallaga bus with "Nanay" on the side stops at Bellavista (20min., s/0.50). Mototaxi s/3.

Local Transportation: Plaza 28 de Julio is the best place to catch buses. During the day and evening, red *"rápido"* buses run down Ocampo-Tacna-Grau to the airport (although they deviate briefly to the west) and then back up Aguierre-Huallaga-Condamine to La Marina, the Masusa port, and Bellavista Nanay (s/0.50).

OLD MAN RIVER. A boat ride along the Ucayali offers as good a view of the jungle as any tour. However, the boat stops innumerable times en route. Each of the three largest villages houses at least one basic hostel: **Contamana** lies 14-36hr. from Pucallpa; **Orellana** is about halfway between Iquitos and Pucallpa; and **Requena** lies 18-22hr. from Iquitos. Inconveniently located control stations in the first two towns often demand a look at foreigners' passports; your caption should inform you if this is necessary and point you in the right direction. (For more on boat travel, see **Essentials: Getting Around**, p. 35.)

Taxis: Motorcycle rickshaws known as *motocarros* or *motos* are everywhere downtown. To anywhere in the town center s/1.50, to the port s/3, to the airport s/7.

Motorcycle Rental: Park Motors, Tacna 621 (☎23 1688), near Palma, rents motorcycles (but not helmets). s/6-12 per hr. Limited cars (s/20 per hr.) and trucks (s/25 per hr.) are also available. Open daily 8am-2am. Visión Motos, Nauta 309 (☎23 4257), near Fitzcarrald. s/7-8 per hr., s/80 per day. Open daily 8am-midnight. Both require a driver's license, which can be from your country of origin.

BORDER CROSSING: INTO BRAZIL AND COLOMBIA. Crossing the border at **Tabatinga, Brazil** or **Leticia, Colombia** is a laid-back—if slightly disorganized—process. The entire area is a neutral, tri-national zone, so if you are not delving farther into Colombia or Brazil, it is acceptable to explore both cities without officially entering either country or getting your passport stamped. The two cities are so close together that they could easily pass as one; colectivos run between them (10min.; frequent until 7pm; 1000 Colombian pesos or 1 Brazilian real, about US$0.40). Leticia and Tabatinga share one port, in Tabatinga, and one airport, in Leticia. Boats from Iquitos stop in the Peruvian border town of Santa Rosa, where foreigners disembark, get their passports stamped, and turn in their tourist cards. The port in Brazil has no tourist facilities, but a taxi (10 reals) can take you to change money and to get your passport stamped at the police office. US citizens need a visa to enter Brazil; most other western nationals need only a passport. Visas (US$40) can be purchased at the Brazilian consulate in Leticia. People entering also occasionally must provide proof of inoculations, particularly for yellow fever. Health officials at the Peruvian border often give shots and inoculation cards to those without them. Everyone must go to the Departamento Administrativo de Seguridad office in Leticia, Calle 9, No. 962. (☎592 7189. Officially open daily 8am-noon and 2-6pm, but usually 24hr.)

ORIENTATION

Approximately 1860km northeast of Lima and technically an island, Iquitos is encompassed by rivers: **Río Itaya, Río Nanay,** and—most conspicuously—**Río Amazonas** to the east. **Malecón Tarapacá** (the **Boulevard,** as it is commonly called) is the pedestrian walkway that fronts the Amazon. One block inland, the main drag called **Próspero** runs from the **Plaza de Armas** eight long blocks south and downriver to the massive **Belén Market.** Most shops, services, and accommodations lie in the area between these landmarks and **Plaza 28 de Julio,** south of the Plaza de Armas, north of the market, and two blocks farther from the river. Avenues running north-south, parallel to the river, change names as they pass the two plazas. Regardless of the direction, block numbers increase as streets move away from the Plaza, Calle Napo, and the river. Streets signs are rare at most intersections.

PRACTICAL INFORMATION

TOURIST AND FINANCIAL SERVICES

Tourist Office: Napo 232 (☎23 5621; turismo.mpm@tvs.com.pe). Hidden in the center of the Plaza de Armas, the tourist office offers friendly but sometimes overly objective advice. It has a listing of guides, information on local attractions, free city **maps,** and a folder of brochures for the many camps and lodges outside of Iquitos. Open M-F 8am-8pm; Sa 9am-1pm; most Su 9am-1pm. For more comprehensive and boisterous council, American Gerald Mayeaux, ex-director of tourism, can typically be found at his restaurant, **The Yellow Rose of Texas** (p. 391). All tourists should consult one or both of these authorities before signing on to any jungle trip, as some companies and private guides have been criticized for cheating tourists. Report any such activities to the tourist office or the police.

Iquitos

🏠 **ACCOMMODATIONS**
The Hobo Hideout, **5**
Hospedaje La Pascana, **10**
Hospedaje Perú, **17**
Hostal Alfert, **25**
Hostal Ambassador (HI), **2**
Hostal Libertad, **16**
Hotel El Sitio, **18**
Hotel Lima, **21**
Sandalo Hotel, **22**

🍎 **FOOD**
Chez Maggy, **8**
El Huasi, **7**
Iron House Regal
   Restaurant, **12**
Restaurant-Cevichería
   Paulina, **20**
Restaurant El Rico
   Tacachu, **24**
Shambo, **15, 19**
Snack Bar Antojitos, **6**
The Yellow Rose of Texas, **13**

🎭 **NIGHTLIFE**
Agricobank, **1**
Amauta Café-Teatro, **9**
Arandú, **11**
Club Adonis, **23**
Jungle Jim's Pub, **14**
La Paranda, **4**
Noa Noa, **3**

TO AMAZONIA ART
GALLERY CAMU CAMU
(2km)

TO 1 (1blk)

Tavara

Yavari

TO ⚓🚌 PUERTO SERVICIO (2km),
PUERTO MASUSA (3km),
BELLAVISTA (4km),
PILPINTUWASI BUTTERFLY FARM

Pevas

Nauta

Callao

Napo

Putumayo

Nanay

Araujo

Lores

Morona

Brasil

Bolognesi

Moore

Cáceres

Tacna

Huallaga

Fitzcarraid

San Martín

Grau

2 de Mayo

Aguirre

Abtao

Arica

Ugarte

José Galvez

Condamine

Loreto

Fitzcarraid

Raimondi

Pevas

Nauta

Napo

Maldonado

Ocampo

Putumayo

Universidad Nacional
de las Amazonas

Visión
Motors

Yacuruna
Lodge Office

Museo
Municipal
ⓘ

PLAZA
DE ARMAS

La Iglesia
Matriz

Iron
House

Mad Mick's Trading Post/
Cumaceba Lodge Office

Banco de
Crédito $

Lavanderia
Imperial

Telefónica
del Perú ☎

Nuevo
Continente TANS

Muyuna
Lodge Office

Loving Light
Lodge Office

Banco del
Trabajo $

Supermercado
Los Portales

Museo
Amazónico
de Loreto

Lavacenter
Lavandería

Ricardo Palma

Heliconia
Lodge Office

Park Motors

Paucar
Tours

Prospero

PLAZA
28 DE
JULIO

Bermúdez

Ucayali

García Saenz

Araña

9 de Diciembre

TO ✈ SAN JUAN (5km),
SANTO TOMÁS (8km),
PUERTO ALMEDRA (12km),
QUISTACOCHA (13km)

Hurtado

Malecón Tarapacá

Río Amazonas

MERCADO
DE BELÉN

C. 1
C. 2
C. 3
C. 4

Venicia

Canoes

TO ✚ HOSPITAL
APOYO IQUITOS (2blk)

TO COMBIS TO
QUISTACOCHA

16 de Julio

N

0   200 meters
0   200 yards

AMAZON BASIN

Currency Exchange: Banco de Crédito, Próspero 200 (☎23 3115), on the Plaza de Armas. 24hr. V **ATM.** Changes AmEx traveler's checks for dollars or soles with a US$11.50 min. commission. Open M-F 10am-6pm, Sa 9:30am-12:30pm. **Banco del Trabajo,** Próspero 223 (☎22 3134), has **Western Union** service. MC/V **ATM.** Open M-F 9am-1:30pm and 3:45-7pm, Sa 9:15am-12:45pm. **Paucar Tours,** Próspero 648 (☎23 2131), has **DHL** service. Open M-Sa 8am-12:30pm and 3:30-7pm. If you're in a hurry, avoid street money changers, who have been known to cheat tourists; instead, look for those with actual storefronts near Lores and Próspero.

Alternatives to Tourism: See **Pilpintuwasi Butterfly Farm,** p. 84 and p. 393.

LOCAL SERVICES

English Newspaper: American Robert Goodier publishes the monthly **Iquitos Review,** an English paper with articles on the city and its citizens, the Amazon, current events, and things to do in the area. Pick one up at hostels and restaurants around town.

Market: The ▒ **Belén Market** (see **Sights,** p. 392) sprawls for blocks between the river and Arica, south of Saenz. Open daily dawn-late in the evening. **Supermercado Los Portales,** Morona 185 (☎23 1552), at Próspero, has canned goods great for jungle trekking, and a huge selection of toiletries and other staples, as well as a diverse liquor shelf. Open daily 6:30am-midnight.

Laundromat: Lavandería Imperial, Putumayo 150 (☎23 1768), between Próspero and Tarapacá. s/10 per 4kg, iron s/4. Open M-Sa 8am-7pm. **Lavacenter Lavandería,** Próspero 459 (☎24 2136). Wash, dry, and fold s/2.90 per kg. Open M-Sa 7:30am-9pm.

Outdoor Equipment: Mad Mick's Trading Post, 184B Putumayo, next to the Iron House (see p. 392). Sells rubber boots, ponchos, hammocks, mosquito nets, hats, fishing gear, and everything else necessary for a jungle excursion. Mick will buy equipment back when you're done using it. Book exchanges and sales. Open daily 8am-8pm.

EMERGENCY AND COMMUNICATION

Police: Morona 126 (☎23 3330), near Tarapacá.

Emergency: ☎105.

24hr. Pharmacy: Medisel, Arica 130 (☎24 3453), on the Plaza de Armas. AmEx/MC/V.

Hospital: Hospital Apoyo Iquitos, Portugal 1710 (☎26 4710), between Libertad and Leticia. Open 24hr. for emergencies.

Telephones: Telefónica del Perú, Arica 297 (☎23 2324), at Sargento Lores. Open daily 7am-10:30pm. Telephones throughout town accept calling cards, but require a refundable 50-centavo coin (or higher denomination) before dialing the calling card number.

Internet Access: Throughout town, especially near the Plaza de Armas. Most charge s/2-3 per hr. and are open 8am-2am.

Post Office: Serpost, Arica 402 (☎23 4091), at Morona. Open M-F 7:30am-7:30pm, Sa 7:30am-6:30pm.

▟ ACCOMMODATIONS

As tends to be the case with many prices in Iquitos, room rates are a bit inflated, but during the low season (Oct.-May) prices are highly negotiable. When selecting a room, bear in mind that the incessant buzz of mototaxis makes streetside rooms especially noisy. Most hotels offer only tepid water in their showers, but Iquitos's hot climate makes this a refreshing break. Guides often approach travelers in Iquitos hotels; consult the tourist office before trusting anyone, even guides recommended by hotel owners.

▧ **The Hobo Hideout,** Putumayo 437 (☎23 4099), near Condamine. Run by an American with a zest for Amazon wildlife, Iquitos's newest hostel is rapidly becoming a backpacker favorite. Rooms are clean and comfortable, and the popular 3-story bungalow provides an excellent oasis from the urban jungle. As a licensed tour operator, the company specializes in fishing trips and overnight Amazon adventures. Kitchen access. Dorms s/15; singles s/25, with bath s/35; doubles s/30, with bath s/40; bungalow suite s/100. MC/V. ❸

Hospedaje La Pascana, Pevas 133 (☎23 1418; pascana@tsi.com.pe), between Raimondi and the Amazon River. Catering to a backpacker crowd, Pascana has 18 simple, quiet rooms, several thatched picnic tables, a book exchange, travel agency, luggage storage, and some English-speaking staff. Breakfast s/4. Singles US$9; doubles US$12; triples US$15. ❸

Hostal Ambassador (HI), Pevas 260 (☎23 3110). Clean, modern rooms with A/C, cable TV, bedside lamps, phones, and hot baths. Breakfast included for non-discounted guests. Reservations recommended. Singles US$20, HI members US$11; doubles US$30/$22; triples US$40/$33. AmEx/MC/V. ❺

Hotel Lima, Próspero 549 (☎23 5152), between Brasil and Palma. A narrow corridor leads from the hectic marketplace to a shady and relaxing common area. Clean rooms with private, though slightly dank, bathrooms, hot bath, and fan. Singles s/25; doubles s/25; triples s/35. ❸

Hostal Libertad, Arica 361 (23 5763). In a great location right off the Plaza de Armas. Guests enjoy large and spacious rooms with good views of the commotion below. The open-air cafe is especially good for people-watching. All rooms have cable TV, private bath, and hot water. Minifridge s/5; air conditioner or extra bed s/10. Singles s/25; doubles s/40. ❸

Hostal Alfert, Saenz 01 (☎23 4105), off Hurtado by the Amazon. Not in the ritziest area, but where else could rooms have such panoramic views of the surrounding area? To take full advantage, request a room on an upper floor. All rooms have hot baths and fans. Luggage storage available. Singles s/15; doubles s/25; triples s/35. ❷

Hotel El Sitio, Palma 545 (☎23 4932), between Tacna and Moore. Quiet but often full. Placid, plant-lined outdoor corridors lead to impeccably kept (but screenless) rooms, complete with bath, fan, and TV. Singles s/25; doubles s/35. ❸

Sandalo Hotel, Próspero 616 (☎23 4761 or 22 1996; sandalo@iquitos.net), near Palma. With A/C, cable TV, hot baths, and minifridges in every room, Sandalo's luxuries facilitate a post-jungle splurge. Airport transportation and continental breakfast included. Singles US$15; doubles US$25; triples US$30. *Let's Go* discount. ❹

Hospedaje Perú, Próspero 218 (☎23 1616), near Lores. Almost disguised by the neighboring bakery, this spot keeps you close to the action. Cable TV, fan, and hot clean private bath await guests who don't mind the commotion. Singles s/25; doubles s/35. ❸

◘ FOOD

Chifas line Grau on the blocks south of the Plaza 28 de Julio and cheap *comida típica* abounds on Condamine north of the Plaza de Armas, while on La Marina. Additionally, many stalls in the Belén market offer jungle specialties like *paiche* (giant river fish), amazing mixed-fruit juices (s/0.50-1), and *juanes* (rice, chicken, black olives, and egg wrapped in a banana leaf), all at their best in Iquitos. Opening hours are highly flexible and depend on the number of patrons.

▧ **The Yellow Rose of Texas,** Putumayo 180 (☎24 1010), near the Iron House. High-tail it over to the newest addition to Gringo Alley, where Tex-Mex, Cajun, and local specialties are cooked up all day long (s/10-15). Tourist info and advice on jungle trips available in Texas-sized portions. *Menú* s/8-10. Open 24hr. ❷

AMAZON BASIN

Restaurant-Cevichería Paulina, Tacna 591 (☎23 1298), at Palma. Around lunchtime, Paulina's charming 2-room restaurant hosts an eager crowd, most awaiting her famous *ceviche* (s/10-20). Soups s/7-18, steaks s/16-20, noodles s/10-15, juices s/2-4. The best deal by far is the *menú* (s/6-10). Open M-Sa 7am-10pm, Su 7am-5pm. ❸

Chez Maggy, Raimondi 181 (☎23 2566), near Nauta. The prominently displayed wood oven prepares the tastiest pizzas in town, and several pasta dishes (s/12-18) add variety to the menu. Forget the rigors of the road while sipping a glass of wine (s/28-30 per bottle), and regarding the Cubist paintings. Pizza s/10-12. Open daily 6pm-midnight. ❷

El Huasi, Napo 326 (☎24 2222), just off the Plaza de Armas. Buzzing with lunchtime activity as locals and travelers alike come to enjoy an unbeatable *menú* (s/6-7). Tasty *ceviche*, fish, and vegetarian dishes (s/10-12). Open daily 7am-4:30am. ❷

Snack Bar Antojitos, Napo 380 (☎23 4631), near Condamine. Plain but popular with the locals, Antojitos serves salads (s/5-6), sandwiches (s/2-5), and fresh juices (s/2-3) for a fraction of the plaza prices. At night, the front develops into a makeshift roadside stand serving large sloppy plates of a mountainous french-fry salad. Lunch *menú* s/6. Open daily 9am-1am. ❶

Iron House Regal Restaurant, Putumayo 182 (☎22 2732), at Próspero. Feel like a rubber baron seated on the famous balcony overlooking the Plaza de Armas. Then return in the evening to quaff beer at their British pub, run by an Englishman. Local deer, alligator, and *paiche* dishes, as well as less exotic fare (s/17-35). Open daily 8am-3am. ❹

Restaurant El Rico Tacachu, Hurtado 873, between Ucayali and Saenz. With tidy tables, a reasonably clean cooking space, and a view of the marketplace, this is the best place to get the Amazonian fish and meat dishes you saw in nearby Belén but were afraid to try. Entrees s/5-7. Open daily 6am-2:30pm. ❶

Shambo, Morona 394 (☎24 3487), at Huallaga; also at Grau 1048, Tacna and Palma, Jáuregui and 28 de Julio, and Morona 204 at Próspero. A city-wide chain serving amazing popsicles (s/0.50-1) made from local and more common fruits. Also available in beer flavor. During evening *fútbol* matches, it hosts mass gatherings of sticky-fingered spectators. Open M-Sa 9am-11pm, Su 9am-9pm. ❶

🜄 SIGHTS

■ **BELÉN.** One of the most vibrant (and poor) areas in Iquitos, the impoverished neighborhoods of Belén sit on the Amazon where the community and its residents literally try to stay afloat. Some houses rise and fall with the river on rafts that must be replaced every two years; others stand on longer-lasting stilts that are tree-house high during the dry season. An intricate—though disorganized—system of planks, logs, and ladders connects the houses with one another. Just wandering around aimlessly, you might very well innocently and unknowingly stumble into someone's living room. Don't worry too much, as in a community where privacy is a concept as foreign as cable TV, such trespasses are generally overlooked, and residents will simply point you in the right direction.

Touring is best done in boats, as even the most sure-footed traveler is likely to plunge into what is optimistically imagined to be mud. A less intrusive and more dramatic way of viewing Belén is to hire a canoe to paddle you around the port and the narrow waterways that infringe upon the village. At times (generally Aug.-Nov.) the settlements rest on mud alone, making travel by canoe impossible.

Besides the fanciful architecture, the main reason to visit Belén is its crowded **market,** which ideally functions as a kind of buffer between urban Iquitos and residential neighborhoods. In reality, however, the cacophony of shouting, laughing, hawking, and screeching (mostly from the monkeys) from the market, as well as the pungent and hardly alluring aroma blanket the entire area and render all of Belén one great marketplace. With a careful eye, you can find anything from dried fish to turtle or crocodile meat to spectacular exotic fruits. Ask around for *guanábana*, a large prickly green fruit that somewhat resembles an artichoke heart, but whose white, pulpy center tastes like juicy cotton candy. At **Pasaje Paquito,** in the center of the market, herbalists sell jungle remedies reputed to cure everything from cancer to arthritis. If you appear confused or overly curious, the vendors will likely diagnose you with one or any number of diseases in order to make a sale. The market is also a great source of snacks, as booths abound with freshly grilled fish, chicken, steak, and plantains. Juice stands are always nearby to help wash it down. *(To hire a canoe (s/5 per hr.), head down Ugarte, through Belén market and past the small circular plaza to Puerto Itaya. The market lies 8 blocks from the Plaza de Armas, with the Amazon on your left.)*

■ **PILPINTUWASI BUTTERFLY FARM.** Austrian Gudrun Sperrer's butterfly farm shows off over 40 species of the most colorful (and least dangerous) insects of the Amazon. A tour of the grounds follows the life cycle of a butterfly, displaying the insects' transition from egg, to caterpillar, to several months in a pupa shell, before finally emerging and spreading their wings. The varieties are impressive and the coordination truly astounding—especially considering that the butterflies only live for about a week. Look for the giant iridescent blue Morpho, spotted owl, and transparent species. The farm releases almost 80% of their butterflies into the wild. If you don't see anyone around when you arrive, just bang on the drum at the entrance, and relax in one of the hammocks overlooking a small lake. As you wait, a couple of overzealous monkeys will arrive to comb through your hair for any insects you might have acquired on the walk over. The farm also has a tapir, a puma, and an anteater (all of whom have been rescued or donated) and plans to introduce a crocodile into the lake next year. Opportunities are available for **volunteers** (see p. 84) to help and learn more about raising the insects. *(From Bellavista Port take a colectivo boat to Padrecocha (25min., s/1). Turn left at the top of the dock stairs, continue parallel to the river, and follow the signs. The walk is about 15min. ☎23 2665; pilpintuwasi@hotmail.com. Open Tu-Su 9am-5pm. US$5, students s/10.)*

BORAS Y YAGUAS. From the small port of Bellavista on the Río Nanay (see **Boats,** p. 387), speedboats (round-trip s/20-25) take groups to see the Boras and Yaguas, two indigenous groups who perform traditional dances for tourists. Alternatively, a small canoe can take visitors to the Boras (30min., s/2) and wait to bring them back. A cheaper option is to take a colectivo boat from the port to Padrecocha (25min., s/1), from which the Boras are a 30min. walk. Follow the trail leading away from the river and bear right halfway there at the large metal sign for San Andrés. For a more realistic vision of integrated indigenous culture, try to stick around after the show, when ceremonial garb is shrugged off for the now more traditional t-shirt and blue jeans. The dancers usually expect payment (around s/10) for their performance.

INSTITUTO DE MEDICINA TRADICIONAL (IMET). A government-funded and operated hospital specializing in the application and development of traditional medicines, IMET is the perfect alternative for those who wish to sample the curative powers of the Amazon but don't feel comfortable entrusting themselves to the care of a shaman. But it need not be merely a destination for the ill; even the most spry traveler could benefit from a walk through the impeccably kept gardens which house more than 600 species of vegetables and 800 species of herbs, all with unique medicinal properties. If not otherwise occupied with patients, the staff may be happy to walk you around and explain some of the plants' uses. *(San Lorenzo 205, in Guayabamba. ☎09 426 5669; imet@ddm.com.pe. Mototaxi ride from city center s/1.50.)*

PUERTO ALMENDRA. With its own botanical garden and arboretum, the harbor has an extensive collection of leaves and wood from the Nanay Basin. The staff also offers walks through the surrounding forest. Home to the Puerto Almendra Research and Forest Teaching Center. *(12km from the airport and about a 30min. drive from the city.)*

AMAZON BASIN

IRON HOUSE. A symbol of the city's short-lived affluence, the Eiffel-designed Iron House was brought across the Atlantic in pieces by a rubber tycoon with grand ambitions for a cosmopolitan city center. Fully assembled in 1889, the much-hyped structure looks today like a house made out of tin foil. When tapped, the walls emit a deep, hollow sound. Ascend to the upstairs restaurant in the late afternoon for an unparalleled (some might say imperial) view of the Plaza. *(On the Plaza de Armas, at Putumayo and Próspero.)*

MUSEO AMAZÓNICO DE LORETO. This relatively new museum (opened in 1996) has already amassed a considerable collection of weapons, paintings, and turn-of-the-century pictographs. Highlights include more than 70 detailed fiberglass sculptures of tribespeople from throughout the Amazon Basin. The exquisitely restored 1863 government building with its finely carved wood ceilings, ornate dining hall, and historic meeting room is a sight in itself. *(Malecón Tarapacá 386, at Morona. Look for the "Prefectura Loreto" sign. ☎ 23 1072. Open M-F 9am-1pm and 3-7pm, Sa 9am-1pm. s/3; university students s/2; children, grade-school students s/1.)*

BIBLIOTECA AMAZÓNICA. The beautiful Biblioteca Amazónica is more a working library than a tourist attraction, but the tiled, carved-wood reading room and view of the river are worth a look, even if you're not here to do research. Look for an old copy of Columbus's journal as well as a collection of literature and traditional stories from the region. *(Malecón Tarapacá 354, 2nd fl., next door to Museo Amazónico. ☎ 24 2353. Open M 3:30-6:45pm, Tu-F 8:30am-12:15pm and 3:30-6:45pm. Free.)*

ASOCIACIÓN ARTESANOS IQUITOS SAN JUAN DE BAUTISTA. Just beyond the hustle and bustle of downtown Iquitos, San Juan vends a wide collection of *artesanía* more authentic than what you'll find in town. Over 20 booths sell necklaces, wooden butterflies, wood carvings, paintings, and hammocks, among other items. Most vendors craft the goods themselves, so visitors can ask questions and, often watch them work. *(Take an airport-bound bus along Tacna-Grau and ask to be let off at "los artesanos de San Juan" (10min., s/0.50). Open daily 8am-7pm.)*

AMAZONIA ART GALLERY CAMU CAMU. This small gallery houses the work of Peruvian artist Francisco Grippa, who paints with a spatula. Unfortunately, most of the original pieces have been moved to Grippa's home in Pevas and what remains resembles less a museum than a private collection of sundry smaller works piled in a corner. There are, however, some especially good examples of Grippa's work with indigenous peoples and the wildlife of the Amazon. Grippa's nephew is still happy to show you around and cut you a deal on a signed lithograph. *(Trujillo 438. Mototaxi s/1.50. ☎ 25 1081. Open daily 10am-1pm and 4-8pm. Free.)*

◗ NIGHTLIFE

BARS

While locals need neither special occasion nor venue to drink, most tourists and well-to-do *Iquiteños* stay pretty close to the breezy and expensive joints overlooking the Amazon on Tarapacá between Nauta and Napo, or to those on Puntumayo (a.k.a. "Gringo Alley," the expat section of town near the Plaza de Armas). Most bars serve all the usual favorites with alcohol imported from across the world, as well as a selection of hometown brews like *chuchuhuasi*—a strong wine-like drink with a kick added by *aguardiente* (the equivalent of moonshine).

Amauta Café-Teatro, Nauta 250 (☎ 23 3109), between Raimondi and Fitzcarrald. A lavish, artsy enclave watched over by a mammoth portrait of poet César Vallejo, this bar/theater/gallery hosts live *criollo* music every night at 10pm. The enormous drink menu includes *Iquiteño* classics such as *chuchuhuasa*, *clavohuasca*, and *siete raíces* made with local liquor, not to be taken lightly for the uninitiated. Shots s/3.50. Mixed drinks s/6. Open M-Sa 6pm-5am. AmEx/MC/V.

Arandú Bar, Maldonado 113 (☎24 3434). Popular with travelers in town between jungle trips, the bar's patio overlooks the Amazon as American rock music blasts in the background. Pilsner beer s/4-9.50. Open daily 4pm-2am. DC/MC.

La Paranda, Pevas 174 (☎93 7880), near Raimondi. The Amazon murals and Choza hut interior provide the feeling of a jungle lodge, until the mirror ball and 80s rock music bring you back to the city. Locals come out in full force to see rock cover bands on weekends. 1L pitchers of beer s/15. Open Th-Sa 10pm-3:30am.

Jungle Jim's Pub, Putumayo 168 (☎23 5294), near the Plaza de Armas. This Gringo Alley mainstay serves up cold beer in frozen glasses (s/5) amid waterfalls and leafy plants. When playing darts, try not to hit the green parrot, Jungle Jim himself. Open M-W and Su 7am-late, Th-Sa 24hr.

CLUBS

Nighttime is no relief from the Amazonian heat. *Iquiteños* love to dance—many save as much cash as possible for weekend splurges lasting well into the night. The best information about hot happenings comes via the fluorescent banners around town. Two popular bands, **Explosion** and **Kaliente,** play current Latin hits at Iquitos clubs.

Agricobank (☎23 7113), at Condamine and Pablo Rosell. On weekends, live bands turn this modest outdoor venue into a throbbing jumble of limbs and bodies. Cheap beer (s/3.50) turns any gringo into a salsa/merengue dance *aficionado*. For those still not confident enough to venture out on the floor, picnic tables on the side provide a great place to people-watch and maybe learn a few moves. Cover s/5. Open F-Sa 9pm-4am.

Noa Noa, Pevas 298 (☎23 2902), at Fitzcarrald. The most popular indoor establishment in Iquitos, Noa Noa plays a mix of Latino beats and American pop classics. Flashing lights, smoke machines, and a multilevel dance floor provide a great setting to dance up a storm. The cover varies but is usually s/5-10. Women typically get in for free. Open Tu-Su 9pm-3am.

LGY, Punchara district (mototaxi s/4), is full of surprises. Walking in from yet another dusty street you'll swear you've been transported to some exclusive European disco. Flashing lights, green lasers, and disco balls set the mood. Don't worry if you're solo, as the bar staff can be counted on for a dance between drinks. Cover s/5. Open Th-Sa 9pm-3am.

Club Adonis, Jercito, Mz. 17, has a huge dance floor that gets crowded F-Sa, with a sizeable turnout on Su as well. Colorful paintings fill the walls and an airy 2nd floor allows a respite from the fast-paced dance floor. Cover s/5. Open Tu-Su 8pm-4am.

FESTIVALS

Although *Iquiteños* seem to need no excuse to party, the city has festivities several times a year. **La Feria de San Juan** is held on the days surrounding June 23 and features parades, fairs, and concerts dedicated to the city's patron saint. Consumption of *juanes* (see **Food,** p. 391) is especially popular during this festival. In recent years, Iquitos has developed its own unique brand of **Carnaval,** celebrated during the week leading up to Shrove Tuesday, as in Brazil and New Orleans. Water balloon fights, colorful parades with Amazonian themes and costumes, and a culminating dance around the *Húmisha* tree are all part of the merriment.

AMAZON BASIN

⚡ DAYTRIPS FROM IQUITOS

QUISTOCOCHA

Frequent combis (25min., s/2) leave from Próspero, just downhill from José Galuez, beyond Belén. Mototaxi s/10. Open daily 7:45am-5pm. s/3, children s/1.

Located 13km south of the city, the attractive waterside Quistococha resort offers rest, relaxation, and a chance to see all the animals you missed on your jungle trip. The main attraction at this complex is a pleasant **beach** with a roped-off swimming area—the water may be reddish, but it's considered safe. Stories abound in Iquitos about an escaped crocodile that now resides in the lake, though rumors remain unsubstantiated. Picnic tables, walking trails, lawn chairs, rowboats (s/5 per hr.), and volleyball courts make for a full day of play away from the buzz of Iquitos. Meanwhile, in a well-maintained **zoo** (no additional fee), monkeys frolic, a giant river otter flips for visitors, gargantuan *paiche* fish lurk just underwater, and pumas and jaguars yawn and pace in unfortunately small cages. The snake house may inspire second thoughts about jungle expeditions. Make sure that you follow all paths to their end because the zoo is deceptively large. Beyond the monkey cages and tapir pen are a beautiful lake and small botanical gardens. A restaurant waits inside, but the booths just outside the complex gate serve less expensive fare. Watch out for weekend crowds. Other local swimming holes include Morona Cocha, Rumococha, and Sungarococha (mototaxi from the city center s/10).

SANTO TOMÁS

To reach Santo Tomás, take any bus marked "aeropuerto" heading down Tacna/Grau and ask the driver to let you off at the road to Santo Tomás (s/0.50). Taxi colectivos wait to take you the rest of the way to the village (15min.; s/1 per person, private taxi s/3).

This village is home to a coalition of 20 **potters** and other clay-molders who produce magnificent *artesanía* in their home studios according to the traditions of the Cocamas tribe. Behind thin wooden walls, these talented artists mold intricate pots in under 5min. The organization's current president, the knowledgeable Emerito Pacaya Aricari (☎ 67 6704), can point visitors to interesting crafts. To find him, follow the main street several minutes to the school; he lives and works in the house directly to the left (Lote 08). You can also walk down the street and peek into any open front door, as most artists set up their work in their front rooms. The craftspeople see few visitors, so most will gladly sell a pot (s/3-50) or knick-knack (s/2). Santo Tomás also has a gorgeous **lake** that, during the wet months, becomes a haven for water-sports lovers. (Canoe rental s/5 per hr.) There are a number of other lakes in the area with similar potential for relaxation and frolicking. **Santa Clara** has beautiful white sand beaches during the dry season. **Rumococha's** (3.8km from the airport) still waters make it an ideal place for fishing.

⚡ INTO THE JUNGLE FROM IQUITOS

The Iquitos tourist office delights in pointing out that Loreto, the jungle province of which Iquitos is capital, occupies an area roughly equivalent to the size of Germany. Smart advertising, since this promise of vast virgin forest brings the city most of its visitors. Despite the crowds, the lay of the land ensures that Loreto's most pristine areas stay that way—virtually inaccessible. Of the various protected areas near Iquitos, the **Reserva Nacional Pacaya-Samiria** and **Tamshiyacu-Tahuayo Community Reserve** provide the best looks at rainforest. As a general rule, the farther you travel from Iquitos along smaller tributaries, the more diverse the flora and fauna. Both independent guides and tour agencies abound in Iquitos.

When the call of the wild finally takes hold, the most popular option remains a 3- to 4-day stay at one of the many jungle lodges located both upstream and downstream from Iquitos. These lodges follow a set format that allows maximum exposure to both plant and animal life in a minimal amount of time. Four days may seem like a long time, but given the difficulties of jungle travel and the awesome vastness of the jungle, it is barely enough to scratch the surface. The other option for jungle excursions is to hire a private guide for a more personalized, adventure-oriented experience. Essentially, the difference between the two forms of travel is the degree to which the trip will be of your own planning and cater to your own preferences—that, and, of course, the number of mosquito bites that you can expect to take home as souvenirs.

PRIVATE GUIDES

Much more so than a lodge, your choice of a guide will define your jungle experience. Most guides have established (though generally unique) routes, specialized knowledge of a particular region, and relationships with certain tribes that can help inform your selection. But you should have some idea about where you want to go or what you want to see, as well as what degree of "adventure" you want to have before seeking out a guide. You will spend a lot of time in close quarters with your guide—you must feel comfortable enough with whomever you choose to enjoy yourself and learn from him. Be sure to meet your guide directly before committing to a trip. For more information, see **Jungle Tours,** p. 50.

 Numerous guides wait in Iquitos to take tourists into the jungle. Unfortunately, many have received complaints for lack of knowledge, stealing money, sexual harassment, and, most commonly, for not completing the trip as planned. Visitors arriving by plane enter an airport crammed with tour guides shouting for their attention. Before committing to one, visit the **tourist office** (p. 388) for access to records on all of the guides in town.

Richard Fowler, Chinchilejo Travel Agency (☎67 7645; www.geocities.com/aukcoo). If you think lodges are for wimps and want to get down and dirty in the jungle, you've come to the right place. As a naturalist specializing in reptiles, an 8-year resident of Loreto, and a former US Army Ranger, Richard knows the Amazon and knows how to provide a unique jungle experience. Whether you want to follow jungle cats, shrink monkey heads with the Jivaro, or kiss anaconda heads, he will tailor a trip just for you. His specialty trips include a 2-week survival course and a journey through sandy cat country, where Richard sets up blinds and hides for viewing, and points out tracks from the more than 5 species of jungle felines that prowl through the area. He also teaches his patented cat-calling technique. Most recently, Richard has added a trip to the practically unexplored and as-yet unexplainable Pyramids of Pusharo, near Manú. Trips generally cost US$50 per person per day, but prices vary by trip duration and group size.

Carlos Grandes has 46 years of jungle experience and leads trips down the Ucayali and on 5-day walks toward the Brazilian border and the Río Yavari. This area is home to the Matse Indians, who are known for their hunting skills, as well as their facial tattoos of black flares meant to mimic the appearance of a puma. Carlos speaks some English. He can shape personalized tours, but the trips get more interesting and cheaper as they get longer (3 days min.). Trips usually cost US$40 per person per day; cost decreases with larger groups. Find Carlos at the **Iron House** or **The Yellow Rose of Texas** (see **Food,** p. 391), or in the nearby town of Begazán (15hr. via Pucallpa-bound boat, s/20) The **tourist office** (p. 388) can also contact him.

JUNGLE LODGES

The most important thing to keep in mind when choosing a lodge is to make sure you understand what's included in your stay—and what languages your guides speak—before you sign up; food (with vegetarian options), speedboat transportation, daytrips, and lodging are all usually included, but get a written contract. A typical visit might include any or all of the following: a nighttime search for alligators *(caimanes)* and tarantulas, excursions into the jungle to find examples of local fauna and wildlife, canoe trips to go bird-watching, a visit to a native village, swimming with dolphins, day hikes, or even sessions with a shaman. Most lodges can also organize overnight camping trips into the jungle. You should confirm and request this prior to leaving, or they may try to charge you extra. As almost all companies can provide similar services, the feature that will most distinguish one from the next for the budget traveler is the price. Often the prices quoted in Lima or overseas are more than double what will be available to walk-in customers. To get the absolute best deal, go around to each of the different agencies (which are all conveniently located next to each other on Putumayo) and press them for a discounted price—don't hesitate to tell them rival lodges' quotes. If you are a walk-in customer, be sure the operator understands that no one brought you there so would-be tour pirates won't receive commission.

▨ **Muyuna Amazon Lodge and Expeditions,** Putumayo 163, 1st fl. (☎24 2858 or 264 2906; www.muyuna.com). Muyuna, 130km from the city on the Río Yanayacu, is right next to the native village of San Juan de Yanayacu. Lodge activities are standard (bird-watching, native community visits, shaman ceremonies, piranha fishing), but flexible. George, Neycer, and Eduardo are among the highly-praised guides working exclusively for the lodge. For more info, ask for Analía or her husband, Percy. Accommodations in rustic yet comfortable bungalows with bath, mosquito nets, kerosene lamps, and balconies to watch for dolphins in the river. US$80 per day; discounts for large groups, SAE or HI members. Open 24hr. AmEx/MC/V.

Heliconia Lodge, Palma 242 (☎23 1959; www.heliconialodge.com). In Lima: Las Camelias 511, of. 402 (☎442 4515). Resort-like accommodations at mid-range prices, just 80km from Iquitos, on the Amazon and Maniti Rivers. Activities include bird-watching and native village visits. US$50 per day. Camping excursions into the Yanayacu river section of the Reserva Nacional Pacaya-Samiria US$120 per day. Their **Zungarococha resort,** only 20km from Iquitos on the Nanay River, has a pool, charges lower prices, and is more oriented toward rest and relaxation than jungle adventure. US$30 per day. Office open M-F 8am-12:30pm and 3:30-7pm, Sa 7:30am-3pm. AmEx/MC/V.

Yacuruna Lodge and Expeditions, Pevas 225 (☎22 3801; www.yacuruna.com). A relatively new lodge 60km from Iquitos on the Yanayacu River, in a swath of primary forest. English- and Spanish-speaking guides take guests through the thick of it to ensure they learn as much as possible about jungle flora and fauna. They can also help explain the lodge's impressive collection of wild orchids. Choose between rustic bungalows and camping trips in the Pacaya-Samiria Reserve. US$50 per day, negotiable. Group discounts. Open daily 7am-10pm.

Loving Light Amazon Lodge and Expeditions, Putumayo 128 (☎24 3180; www.junglelodge.com). Rustic bungalows and a hammock lounge 140km from Iquitos make this both a comfortable and authentic jungle experience. Outstanding indigenous cuisine with vegetarian options available on request. Well connected with local shamans. US$40-50 per day. Open daily 7:30am-8:30pm.

Explorama, La Marina 340 (☎25 2526 or 25 2530; US contact ☎800-707-5275; www.explorama.com). The granddaddy of jungle trips from Iquitos. Organized, well run, and expensive, Explorama takes visitors to the ACTS environmental laboratory and the largest canopy walkway in the world. Each of their 5 lodges varies in price and offers a slightly different program; they can be combined to fit travelers' needs. The farthest is 160km from Iquitos. Rates vary by lodge and group size. US$100-200 per day. Open daily 7:30am-6pm. AmEx/MC/V.

Cumaceba Lodge and Expeditions, Putumayo 184 (☎23 2229), next to the Iron House. The main lodge is 36km from Iquitos on the Amazon, in a wide swath of relatively untouched forest. Provides many of the comforts of the more expensive lodges for a lower price. In the Bonbonaje Camp, 80km from the city, Cumaceba offers camping in the middle of primary jungle chock full of animals. The covered, elevated sleeping platform and mosquito nets help keep guests bite-free. US$40 per day for either location or a combination of the two. Open daily 7:30am-8:30pm.

INDIGENOUS COMMUNITIES

Travelers who come to the Amazon hoping to spend time with indigenous tribes untouched by the outside world will probably be disappointed. Tourists have nearly always been preceded by Christian missionaries, government representatives seeking to move people from protected forests and petroleum reserves, or scientists aiming to discover the jungle's secrets. That said, many partially assimilated indigenous people have preserved elements of their heritage which they are eager to share with visitors (often for a fee). Personalized trips to these communities can be arranged through private guides or the tourist office in Iquitos (p. 404).

A daytrip from Iquitos to the village of San Andrés takes visitors to the **Boras** and **Yaguas** communities (see **Boras y Yaguas,** p. 393), where locals are eager to temporarily discard their jeans and baseball caps for more traditional jewelry and reed-based clothing. Many jungle lodges include brief visits to Yaguas communities for similar cultural exchanges. For a more authentic visit, the **Cocamas** people living at the entrance to the Pacaya-Samiria Reserve welcome travelers to their town, San Martín, as part of a reserve tour run entirely by community members. San Martín offers visitors a vivid glimpse of how Peru's indigenous people are dealing with globalization. Through hard work, the Cocamas language is being preserved, as are traditional fishing methods and general jungle knowledge. Soccer and volleyball games are almost a constant, however, and churches and Coca-Cola signs remind visitors that the world keeps getting smaller.

Indigenous communities having little or no contact with the outside world do exist in Peru, but visitors must be prepared to spend a good deal of time (at least 12-15 days) on an excursion deep into the Amazon in order to find them. American guide Richard Fowler (p. 397) has developed extensive contacts with tribes throughout the Amazon Basin. Visits to the **Jivaros** focus on one of their clans, such as the Shuar, Achuar, and Moratos, located between the Tigre and Paztaza rivers in southern Ecuador and northern Peru. Among other things, these fierce warriors are known for their expertise in shrinking the heads of vanquished enemies. With a trusted guide they will show you the process using a monkey head in place of a human's. Another remote tribe, the **Matses,** are among the greatest hunters on the planet. They have incorporated some modern technology into their techniques, but maintain their proven tracking and trapping methods. The Matses are also known for an extremely painful ritual in which poison from frog sweat is smeared onto burned skin to cleanse the system and leave a permanent mark of toughness. Though by no means obligatory during a visit, these lifelong scars may serve as an excellent souvenir of a jungle trip. Participation in this ritual is not for the faint of heart, however. If you're looking for a souvenir a little less permanent, head down to the Río Ucayali to **the Shipibo** Indians, renowned for their pottery and colorful fabrics.

RESERVA NACIONAL PACAYA-SAMIRIA

Although not as well known as Parque Nacional del Manú to the south, Pacaya-Samiria is gradually becoming the jungle destination of choice for those wishing to escape the oppressive crowds and prices of more popular national parks. At 20,800 sq. km, Pacaya-Samiria is the largest protected area in the country, representing 1.5% of the nation's total land area. Only limited zones have been opened to tourism in recent years, guaranteeing that the park remains a bastion of pristine jungle. Some 450 bird species, 100 different mammals species, 69 reptiles species,

58 amphibians species, and countless scores of insects species still reside within. The remote location between the Marañón and Ucayali rivers, the strict regulations on visitors, and the absence of park amenities should ensure that the reserve remains unspoiled—accessible only to travelers who don't mind roughing it.

AT A GLANCE

AREA: 20,800 sq. km.	**GATEWAYS:** Iquitos (p. 386) and Lagunas (p. 401).
CLIMATE: Humid tropical lowland forest.	
HIGHLIGHTS: Largest protected reserve in Peru, crocodile-hunting, swimming, bird-watching, piranha-fishing.	**CAMPING:** Permitted, either in tents or in hammocks.
	FEES AND HOURS: Entrance fee s/100, plus licensed guide fee (required).

▐ TRANSPORTATION

Visitors must come with a guided tour, and one of the major distinctions between the various operators is the way they move through the park—there is some disagreement regarding the best way to view the most animals. ASIENDES usually travels on boats with limited motors known as *peke-peke* (for the sound they make), which allow them to take visitors deep into the reserve. They operate under the conventional wisdom that the bigger, rarer animals like anacondas, sloths, jaguars, etc. are more easily viewed farther away from the periphery, where there is less human presence. Operators out of Lagunas travel by paddled canoe. They argue that motors scare away animals, and that by floating in silence close to the shore, animal-watchers can spot just as many creatures without venturing into to the reserve's deepest corners.

✳ ▐ ORIENTATION AND PRACTICAL INFORMATION

Pacaya-Samiria has three main areas from which the primary forests and wildlife within can be accessed: the Yanayacu River, the Samiria River, and the Tibillo River. The Yanayacu section is the most accessible from Iquitos, and is the destination for most of the jungle lodges and guides. Pacaya-Samiria, home to the Cocama Indians and their community-based lodge ASIENDES, is the most difficult to get to, but houses perhaps the richest array of plants and animals within the portions of the reserve open to visitors. The Tibilo, easily reached from Lagunas, has almost as much wildlife as the Samiria region, but with more varied terrain.

Supplies: Iquitos has the closest thing to outdoor equipment (see **Outdoor Equipment,** p. 390). Bring insect repellent, a hammock, mosquito net, long-sleeved shirts, rain jacket, and tall boots. Both Lagunas and Iquitos have markets with good camping food.

Tours: The only way to enter the reserve is with a licensed tour operator. Many of the Iquitos jungle lodges are authorized to take visitors to the Yanayacu River section. Two main organizations specialize exclusively in Pacaya-Samiria. Though each conducts tours into different areas of the park, both guarantee sightings of dolphins, birds, reptiles, caimans, and monkeys. Gamaniel Sánchez of the Empresa de Servicios Turísticos y Protección Ecológica Lagunas, runs the only tours on the Tabillo River.

ASIENDES (☎251 1854; asiendesperu@hotmail.com). An alternative to the traditional jungle lodge. Run by Cocama Indians living in the Pacaya-Samiria Reserve, ASIENDES is a community-based and community-run development project. All visitors will spend their first afternoon exploring the community, talking with its extremely friendly members, and maybe even taking in a soccer game or concert. Accommodations with the community in the village of San Martín are extremely basic, but the guides make it as comfortable as possible. Jungle trips are generally flexible, with options ranging from 3-7 days, or longer if you want to explore the farthest regions open to tourists (US$50 per day). One of the major advantages of ASIENDES is the guides' knowledge of the region. Their tribe has been living in this area for centuries, and they are the only ones able to (successfully) navigate the area. Most days include some sort of combination of both river travel and jungle walking. If you arrange your trip from Iquitos, ASIENDES will even have someone ride with you on the ferry to pitch your tent and make sure you get off at the right spot. Proceeds support the community and conservation efforts.

Empresa de Servicios Turísticos y Protección Ecológica Lagunas, Fitzcarrald 530 (☎40 1007). Gamaniel Sánchez, Lagunas's head honcho, has maps and books on the reserve, as well as access to Spanish-speaking guides (US$30 per day). Brothers Kleber and Edinson Salda, and Genaro Mendoza, have excellent reputations. To properly enjoy the abundance of monkeys, birds, caiman, and river dolphins on the reserve, go for 5-6 days. Those looking for an extended adventure can make the 15-day (round-trip) journey to the remote Pastacocha Lake. Trips are mostly by *peke-peke* canoe, but you can hike as well, depending on water levels. Gamaniel is currently working with park rangers to build monkey-proof viewing stations at a 1-2 day journey from the park entrance. If you don't have much time or can't stomach paying the s/100 park fee, Gamaniel can also arrange some minor exploration in the region before the park's entrance.

⛺ CAMPING

Official campgrounds do not exist within the reserve, but guides are usually able to locate dry ground on which to pitch tents. Often, however, these spots are disconcertingly close to where you go at night to look for crocodiles. Alternatives include tying hammocks to trees (make sure no dead branches lie above). If the rain becomes too much, many of the ranger stations have extra bunk and floor space which they'll loan out temporarily. Regardless of where you lay your head, the most important thing to remember is to secure your mosquito nets. At sunset, the blood-sucking beasts descend in a cloud and will bite through clothing. Bring plenty of repellent, and bring your own water or be prepared to treat river water.

LAGUNAS ☎094

Buried deep in the Peruvian Amazon, accessible only by river boat or puddle-hopping plane, the small *pueblo* of Lagunas (pop. 3000) is a cheaper and less-developed jumping-off point than Iquitos for exploring the immense expanse of rainforest known as the **Reserva Nacional Pacaya-Samiria** (p. 399). The town is within walking distance of the park entrance, but unfortunately, the flexibility afforded by its proximity to the park can be countered by the difficulty of getting there, and by the even greater difficulty of getting away.

Accommodations in Lagunas are scarce and basic. For those who do spend the night here, **Alojamiento Miraflores ❶,** Miraflores 249, one block off the Plaza de Armas and parallel to Lores, has a clean common bathroom (complete with some of the only toilet seats in town) and one shower. All rooms have screens, and other perks include luggage storage, meals, and purified drinking water. (☎40 1001. Singles s/10; doubles s/15; triples s/22.) Bucket showers are the norm at **Alojamiento "Farmacia" de Marciano Escobedo Álvarez ❶,** Huallaga 140, next to some scenic marshy waterways. The clean, basic rooms are above the downstairs **pharmacy.** (☎40 1009. Singles s/7; doubles s/14.) From there, it's a 15-20min. walk toward the park entrance to a *paiche* pond that will become part of the small lodge under construction. It's a good place for monkey-watching or renting a pole to catch fresh fish for dinner. If you'd rather not kill your own food, **Dona Dani ❶,** a block down from the Plaza, serves up reliable meals all day. Another good option (if you have the foresight) is to go to the market in the morning or to the port around 5pm to buy fresh fish and vegetables. The ladies in the restaurants by the water will cook them up any way you like for a minimal charge. For entertainment in the evenings, follow the crowds to any of the few locales around town that have TVs.

LOVE BOAT?

After a few weeks of traveling in Peru, you get pretty accustomed to seeing displays of bravado as Peruvian men seek the attention of *gringa* women. But every once in a while, you are treated to a scene of such fantastic romantic absurdity that you can't help but notice.

While on the ferry from Iquitos to Lagunas, I was sharing the large cabin on the third deck with, among others, a girl from Holland by the name of Anna. Occasionally we would venture out together onto the open deck for some fresh air and a nice view of the river. During one such survey, a Peruvian man nearly ten years Anna's senior fell instantly and madly in love with her—or so at least was his refrain for the next 30hr. He would make unsolicited visits to our cabin, bumbling protestations of his love before being rebuffed by Anna or one of the attendants on the boat.

Eventually, distraught and confounded, Anna's would-be knight in shining armor came to me and asked if Anna liked birds. Intrigued, I told him I wasn't sure, but I imagined that she did. At every stop for the next 10 hours, he jumped out to talk to the villagers who lined the shore trying to sell snacks, crafts, and jungle animals to passengers. I quickly realized that he was searching for a yellow-headed parrot or parakeet to match Anna's blond hair.

After many failed attempts, he

To reach Lagunas, take an Iquitos-bound **boat** (12-13 hr., 1 per day, s/10) from Puerto Able Gerry in Yurimaguas or a Yurimaguas-bound boat (2 days, usually 1 per day, s/30-40) from Iquitos. Leaving Lagunas is much the same as getting there. Hop aboard the daily Iquitos- (2 days, usually 1 per day, s/30) or Yurimaguas-bound boat (12-16 hr., usually 1 per day, M and W-Su, s/10). The schedule for departing boats is so variable sometimes that the only option is to wait alongside the river for a boat going in the right direction. You can pay for shopowners to call up- or downstream for the time of arrival, but these projections are not always accurate. Occasionally, **lanzadores** (speed boats) will pass by with an extra seat or two (s/40) and make the journey to Yurimaguas in 4-6hr. rather than the 12hr. large passenger boats require. The port is located almost 1½km (**mototaxis** shuttle back and forth for s/2) from the Plaza, which means that unless you are willing to gamble with the unpredictable transportation schedule you will have to stay at one of the many ramshackle hotels that line the waterway (s/5). In a subtle admission of the inherent difficulties of river travel, the few good general shops sell *aguardiente* (moonshine) by the liter. Just ask someone to throw a bucket of water on you when your boat arrives.

The town of Lagunas can be confusing to navigate, as the Plaza de Armas is more of a reference point than it is the center of activity. To get there, follow the road from the port past the cemetery and turn right. The Plaza is lined by **Carrión, Lores Vásquez,** and **Jarequi.** In town, services are few. They include: the **police,** Carrión 388 (☎ 40 1044), on the Plaza de Armas; a **hospital,** Centro de Salud, Fitzcarrald Mz. 9 (☎ 40 1018, open 24 hr. for emergencies); **Mercado de Abastecimiento,** Fitzcarrald Mz. 7 (open daily 4am-8am, surrounding shops open daily until 9pm); and a **post office,** Padre Lucero 911 (☎ 40 1031).

YURIMAGUAS   ☎ 065

Known as the "Pearl of the Huallaga," the port of Yurimaguas (pop. 10,000) is a place many pass through, but few come to stay. Ubiquitous and thriving outdoor markets are the primary hubs of action, while the Plaza remains eerily quiet. Caught in a flux of constant transition caused by developing regional transportation networks, Yurimaguas seems to find itself in that awkward stage of being too big to be quaint and too small to be urban. Nevertheless, it prides itself on two redeeming features: the manifold European influences still apparent in its architecture and decorative wall tiles, and its vital role as a gateway to the more remote regions of the lowland Amazon Basin. But if the subtle stylings of fading architectural distinction do not pique your interest, then try to organize your visit around a festival, when Yurimaguas plays host to a more vivacious form of aesthetic exhibition: beauty pageants. Held in the community gymnasium, these pageants even attract international contestants. Despite the swimsuit contest, however, Yurimaguas maintains traditional values—a nun presides as one of the judges.

TRANSPORTATION

Buses: Transportes Paredes Estrella, Cáceres 220 (☎35 1307), and **Transportes Huamanga** (☎35 1416), on the 2nd block of Cáceres, head to: **Chiclayo** (24hr., s/50); **Lima** (36hr.; 6, 7am; s/70) via **Tarapoto** (6hr., s/10); **Trujillo** (28hr., s/60). To reach Cáceres, walk 6 blocks down Jáuregui from the Plaza and take a left. **Transportes New Image,** César López 623 (☎35 1483), sends **autos** (shared taxis) to **Tarapoto** (4-5hr., leave when full 3am-5pm, s/25). To reach Transportes, walk 3 blocks down Jáuregui from the Plaza, take a right onto Tacna, and the first left onto López. **Yurimaguas Express** (☎35 2727), and **Oriente Express** (☎35 2122), near the intersection of Huallaga and Tacna, send **trucks** to **Tarapoto** (5-6hr., leave when full 3am-5pm; cab seat s/20, backseat s/10). The abundance of potholes on the road to Tarapoto can make for a nauseating journey, so pack some motion sickness medication.

Boats: Yurimaguas has several ports. Boats to **Iquitos** (3 days; s/30-40, cabin s/60) via **Lagunas** (12-13hr., s/10) leave from the main port, **Puerto La Boca,** 11 blocks down Castilla from the Plaza de Armas. Boats leave M-Sa, usually in the afternoon, but few leave on schedule (some can leave as much as a day late). Other ports, such as **Puerto Abel Guerra,** between La Boca and the Plaza, and **Puerto Garcilaso de la Vega,** to the right from the Plaza when facing the river, send boats to more local destinations, such as **Lago Culpari.**

ORIENTATION AND PRACTICAL INFORMATION

Ríos Shanusi, Paranapura, and **Huallaga** form Yurimaguas's borders. The **Plaza de Armas** sits next to the Río Huallaga. **Castilla** and **Bolívar** are parallel, extending to the left from the Plaza when facing the river. **Comercio** and **Lores** are parallel, extending to the right from the Plaza when facing the river. **Jáuregui,** the main drag, extends from the Plaza, perpendicular to the river. After five blocks, the street divides—Jáuregui heads to Tarapoto, while **Libertad** passes the **airport.** The **market** lies on Jáuregui, two blocks from the Plaza away from the river.

finally located one for the reasonable price of 10 soles, and for the next hour he stood expectantly below the passenger deck waiting for Anna. His patience fading, he began to call to her until she finally appeared.

In a scene loosely reminiscent of the balcony scene in Romeo and Juliet, she leaned over the railing to receive the wooden stick to which the little bird was tethered. Obviously moved, she brought the bird close to her face and put out her hand in order to stroke the bird's head. But as her fingers extended, the bird hopped from its perch and bit her.

Anna's piercing scream as she dropped the stick drew the rest of the passengers out from the cavernous holds within the boat. Anna cursed the man (impressively, in Spanish) and then ran back into the cabin, refusing to reemerge or speak to her suitor at all for the rest of the trip. It seemed that there was an irreconcilable difference in roots—she was a natural brunette.

—Max Arbes

Tourist Offices:

Manguare Expediciones and Centro Artesanal Manguare, Lores 126, just off the Plaza. The best source of information. Run by Orlando Zagazeta—the heart and soul of Yurimaguas tourism—it's stocked with **maps**, magazines, photos, 4 pet monkeys, and a river otter.

Oficina de Cooperación Técnica, Plaza de Armas 114 (mpaacooptec@usa.net), in the Municipalidad. Offers **maps** and advice. Open M-F 8am-2:30pm.

Tourist Office, Lores 100 (☎35 2676), in the large blue building on the Plaza. Open M-F 7am-1pm and 2-4:30pm.

Currency Exchange: Banco Continental, Lores 132 (☎35 2070), just off the Plaza. US$10 commission on traveler's checks. Has a Visa **ATM.** Open M-F 9:15am-12:45pm and 4-6:30pm, Sa 9:30am-12:30pm.

Market: Mercado Yurimaguas, 2 blocks from the Plaza. Meat and produce sold daily 3am-noon. Household goods available daily 6am-9pm.

Emergency: ☎105.

Police: (☎35 2627), on the 2nd block of Condamine.

Pharmacy: Botica Milagro, Jáuregui 123 (☎35 1586), at Arana. Open daily 7am-10pm. For the **24hr. pharmacy** on duty, consult the *el turno* schedule in the newspaper or in other pharmacy windows.

Hospital: Hospital Apoyo Santa Gema, Progreso 307 (☎35 2135, emergency 35 2142), 1 block down Jáuregui from the Plaza, then 3 blocks to the right.

Telephones: Telecomunicaciones y Servicios Yurimaguas, Bolívar 122-24 (☎/fax 35 2020), 1 block from the Plaza. Long distance calls, but no calling card calls. Open daily 7am-10pm. **Telefónica del Perú** booths around town accept calling cards.

Internet Access: JC's Systems, Plaza de Armas 113 (☎35 2267). M-F s/5 per hr., Sa-Su s/4 per hr. Open daily 8am-midnight.

Post Office: Serpost, Arica 439 (☎35 2172). Open M-Sa 7:30am-1:30pm and 3-5pm.

ACCOMMODATIONS

Quintas and *hostales* line the streets in Yurimaguas, but quantity does not ensure quality. Most options leave something to be desired—usually toilet seats.

Porta Péricos, San Miguel 720 (☎35 2009), near the San Miguel port. More a resort than a hotel, Péricos has breezy rooms with cable TV, minifridges, hot baths, and table fans. When foosball tires you out, cool off under the *choza* umbrellas overlooking the river valley. Continental breakfast served on a breezy upstairs patio is included. Doubles US$20; triples US$30. ❸

Hostal de Paz, Jáuregui 431 (☎35 2123), 4 blocks down from the Plaza. Rooms include a ceiling fan, cable TV, and bath. Mosquito screens on windows keep you bite-free, though windows between bedrooms and the hallway limit your privacy. Singles s/20; matrimonials s/26; doubles s/28. ❷

Hostal Luís Antonio, Jáuregui 407 (☎35 2065). A vast array of amenities and price levels ensures something for everyone—take the spotless courtyard and inviting pool, for instance, or the floor-to-ceiling windows of the adjoining restaurant. Singles US$5, with TV s/40; doubles US$10, with TV s/60, with TV and air conditioning s/80. ❷

Hostal César Gustavo, Atahuallpa 102 (☎35 1585), 4 blocks down Jáuregui and 1 to the left. Fully equipped with ceiling fans, firm mattresses, and a wing with spotless new private baths (but no toilet seats). Singles s/15; doubles s/20. ❷

FOOD

The majority of food options in town blend together. At night, small booths selling cheap hamburgers and jungle food line Cápac between López and Huallaga.

La Maloka, San Miguel 520, by the San Miguel port. A short mototaxi ride from the center (s/1). Salivate over savory river fish, wild boar, and even ants (in season in Aug.), while enjoying a panoramic view of the Paranapura River. The jungle lodge layout adds just the right ambience. Entrees s/8-10. Open daily 10am-midnight. ❷

La Prosperidad, Progreso 107 (☎35 2057), at Jáuregui. Preferred by locals, this double-decker snack bar serves up tasty morsels all day. Multicolored lights and handmade signs celebrate the latest *fiesta.* Trekkers-on-the-go can stop by the road-side bar for some Peruvian "walk-thru." Hamburger s/3. *Pollo a la brasa* s/7. Juice s/2. Open daily 8am-1pm and 4pm-midnight. ❶

Trucho Pizza, Plaza de Armas 137-139 (☎35 2072). Can't stomach another bite of *comida típica?* Find solace in a personal pizza piled with toppings (s/6-10). *Pollo a la brasa* (s/7-14) available if you change your mind. Open Tu-Su 4pm-midnight. ❷

♫ ❀ ENTERTAINMENT AND FESTIVALS

On weekends, live bands sometimes give salsa and merengue concerts in the fields on the outskirts of town. Look for the poster advertisements or ask a mototaxi driver for the dates and times. Other festivities include the **fiesta patronal,** in early August. During these 11 days, a different neighborhood holds a *fiesta* each night. The dancing, food, *artesanía,* and an occasional reenactment of Pamplona's running of the bulls culminate in a big party on the final day. Aside from this madness, most entertainment comes from surrounding jungle trips.

LAGO CUIPARI

At the beautiful lake town of Lago Cuipari, visitors can visit orchid gardens and experience some of the most beautiful sunsets in Peru. The lack of electricity or running water gives visitors the impression that this peaceful village (pop. 800) has escaped the complications of 21st-century life—that is, until the occasional (battery-powered) stereo pierces the solitude. Village life revolves around the lake, as fishermen undertake the daily ritual of casting and collecting their nets. In August, over 100 species of orchids are in full bloom. Those thirsting for even more jungle flora and fauna can take multi-day excursions from the lake into the depths of the jungle to see the entangled vines of the **Templo de Los Renacos,** where, according to local superstition, tiny people live at the bottom of the trees—residents leave them small offerings to ensure their health and prosperity. A man named **Orlando** (a.k.a. *el hombre con el mono,* "the man with the monkey"), an ardent advocate of regional tourism, knows the lake well (ozjungle@ole.com; US$15 per day). If Orlando can't make it, he has reliable guides with in-depth knowledge of the lake who can accompany you and arrange accommodations. Orlando's office is in the Centro Artesanal Manguare (see **Tourist Offices,** p. 404), just off the Yurimaguas Plaza.

Lago Cuipari

If you'd rather go it alone, **colectivo boats** to Lago Cuipari (2½hr., 3 per day 7am-noon, s/2.50) depart from Yurimaguas, on Puerto Garcilaso de la Vega, at the end of Garcilaso, to your right from the Plaza when facing the river. Return boats leave in the morning, so prepare to stay overnight. There are no hotels in Cuipari, but you can **camp** along the ample green space by the lake, or stay in people's **homes ❶** (s/.7.50-10 including meals). In the dry season (May-Sept.) boats stop at La Libertad or Las Mercedes, both a 2hr. walk to the lake. From La Libertad, head to the village walking perpendicular away from the river and turn left at the lakeside village of San Isidro. Follow the curve of the lake to Cuipari. After heavy rains, these paths can turn into mud, making the hike twice as difficult.

TARAPOTO   ☎ 042

Tarapoto's lush vegetation has earned it the tag "Ciudad de las Palmeras" (City of Palm Trees). The mountainous high-jungle terrain, laden with waterfalls and pot-hole-filled roads, contrasts sharply with the arid *sierra* to the west and the flat lowland jungle to the east. For most travelers, Tarapoto (pop. 116,000; elev. 330m) serves as a traffic hub to and from the jungle, but those who breeze through town miss a chance to see one of Peru's fastest growing cities in action. Businessmen career through the streets in revved mototaxis, while market vendors hawk everything from the latest bootleg to homegrown herbal remedies.

⌐ TRANSPORTATION

Flights: Guillermo del Castillo Paredes Airport, Pimentel 1 (☎52 2278), a few blocks downhill from the Plaza in Barrio Huayco. Mototaxi s/.2. **Nuevo Continente,** Moyobamba 101 (☎52 7212 or 52 4332), on the Plaza. Open M-F 8am-1pm and 3-7pm, Sa 8am-1pm and 3-6pm. AmEx/MC/V. Flies to **Lima** (1hr., 4:50pm, US$64). **TANS,** Plaza Mayor 491 (☎52 5339), on San Martín. Open M-F 8am-1pm and 3-7pm, Sa 8am-1pm and 3-6pm, Su 8am-noon. Flies to: **Iquitos** (50min., daily 10:40am, US$50); **Lima** (1hr., 7:10pm, US$50); **Pucallpa** (70min., daily 10:40am, US$50).

Buses: Companies are concentrated on Salaverry, near Morales. Mototaxi s/.2. **Paredes Estrella** (☎52 1202), on the 8th block of Salaverry; **Turismo Tarapoto,** Salaverry 705 (☎52 6161), and **Expreso Huamanga,** Salaverry 935 (☎52 7272), run to **Lima** (26hr., s/.65-70) via **Chiclayo** (15hr., s/.35-40) and **Trujillo** (18hr., s/.45-50). These buses all pass through **Pedro Ruíz** (8hr., s/.25), where it is possible to catch a **truck** (2hr., s/.6) or shared **taxi** (1½hr., s/.10) going to **Chachapoyas. Expreso Huamanga** and **Paredes Estrella** go to **Yurimaguas** (6hr., s/.10-12) via the **Cataratas Ahuashiyaku** (1hr., 10-11am, s/.3). Trucks (6hr., s/.12) and shared taxis (5hr., s/.25) to **Yurimaguas** leave when full from Jorge Chávez in the Banda de Shilcayo neighborhood.

Cars: Autos leave from the Paradero de Moyobamba, a few blocks before the bus companies, on Salaverry. They run to **Moyobamba** (1¾ hr., s/.20), from where you can get another *auto* to **Rioja** (30min., s/.5) and then one to **Pedro Ruíz** (2¾ hr., s/.20) before catching a final *auto* to **Chachapoyas** (1¾, s/.10). Autos are significantly faster and more comfortable that buses, and they depart much more frequently. If you find yourself waiting a while for the car to fill, it is sometimes effective to threaten to leave.

✳ ⓘ ORIENTATION AND PRACTICAL INFORMATION

In most cities, the hub of activity is the Plaza de Armas, but in Tarapoto, it's the **Plaza Mayor.** All streets bordering the Plaza change names as they pass it. Facing uphill, the street at the bottom of the Plaza running east-west is **San Martín** to the left and **Maynas** to the right. Parallel, at the top of the Plaza, **Grau** runs left and **Moyobamba** runs right. Perpendicular, uphill **San Pablo de la Cruz** turns into **Pimentel** as it goes downhill. **Hurtado** also runs uphill and becomes **Compagnon** as it goes downhill. Most services line San Martín, Pimentel, and the Plaza Mayor.

Tours: Fomentours, San Martín 148 (☎52 2257), 1 block from the Plaza, gives tours of the **Cataratas Ahuashiyaku** (s/80 per car), **Lamas** (s/80 per car), and **Laguna Sauce** (s/70 per person), and can arrange **rafting trips** (US$25 per person) on the Río Mayo, as well as hikes to the more remote waterfalls. Request English-speaking guides in advance. Open M-Sa 8am-8pm, Su 8am-1pm. V.

Banks: Interbank, Grau 118 (☎52 2942), 1 block from the plaza, has an AmEx/MC/V **ATM** and changes AmEx traveler's checks for a US$5 commission. Open M-F 9am-1pm and 4-6:15pm, Sa 9:15am-12:30pm. **Banco del Trabajo,** Hurtado 155 (☎52 7000), provides **Western Union** services. Open M-F 9am-1:30pm and 4-7pm, Sa 9am-1pm.

Markets: Large, open-air **Mercado 2,** a few blocks downhill from the plaza on Lima, between Rosa and Cáceres, has jungle food, handicrafts, and everything in between.

Laundromat: El Churre, San Pablo de la Cruz 140 (☎69 0599), 1 block from the Plaza. Machine dried s/7 per kg, line dried s/3 per kg. Open daily 8am-10:30pm.

Emergency: ☎105.

Police: Hurtado 298 (☎52 2141).

Pharmacy: Check the sign behind the counter of **Farmacia Popular,** San Martín 220 (☎52 2079), to find the 24hr. pharmacy on duty.

Hospital: Clínica San Marcos, Leguía 604 (☎52 3838). Open 24hr. for emergencies.

Telephones: Telefónica del Perú, Castilla 128 (☎52 8430). Open daily 7am-10pm.

Internet Access: Cafes crowd the streets near the Plaza. s/3 per hr.

Post Office: Serpost, San Martín 482 (☎52 2120), 5 blocks from the Plaza. Open M-Sa 8am-8pm.

ACCOMMODATIONS

Tarapoto has a fair number of cheap *hospedajes* (s/10-15 per person) on streets around the Plaza, but most travelers opt for a slightly more expensive hostel, as quality improves dramatically. Mototaxi drivers often tell visitors the hostel they want is full, in order to get a commission from another. Ask to see for yourself.

Alojamiento El Mirador, San Pablo de la Cruz 517 (☎52 2177). As close as you can get to the jungle while still near the center of town. Tranquil environment encourages rooftop hammock-napping. 1st fl. singles with private bath, TV, and fan US$13; doubles US$16. Simpler 2nd fl. singles s/35; doubles s/45. ❸

Hostal San Antonio, Pimentel 126 (☎52 5563), just off the Plaza. Standard rooms surround a garden with plenty of seats in which to relax. Rooms have large beds, hot baths, fans, and cable TV. Singles s/25; doubles s/35. ❸

Hotel Monte Azul, Camla Morey 156 (☎52 2443; fax 52 3636), not Manuela Morey or Arias de Morey. Minibars in every room. Breakfast at the rooftop restaurant included. Singles s/75, with A/C s/109; doubles s/109, with A/C s/159. AmEx/MC/V. ❺

Hostal Edinson, Pimentel 105 (☎52 4101), at Maynas, half a block from the Plaza. Party at the disco, casino, or karaoke bar, then crash in a spacious, comfy room. Electricity, hot water and cable TV. Breakfast s/2.50. Singles s/25; doubles s/35. ❸

FOOD

Tarapoto's fusion of highland and jungle cuisine has produced fabulous fruit juices and filets made with *cecina* (beef) rather than *trucha* (trout). Locals devour *anticuchos* (grilled cow hearts) right off the stake. Street vendors selling these and other savory grilled meats appear after sundown throughout town. If you really want to eat like a local, join the hordes at one of the myriad *pollerías*. Vegetarians should stick to the tourist restaurants on the Plaza.

JJM Café, San Martín 202 (☎52 7452). This cafe has all the right touches to make you feel at home, not the least of which are freshly-squeezed juices (s/2), tasty sandwiches (s/2.50-5), and scrumptious cakes (s/3.50). Open M-Sa 8am-1pm and 3-11pm. ❶

Helados La Muyuna, Castilla 271 (☎52 1085), near Leguía. From *aguaje* and *maracuya* to the staple vanilla and chocolate, this creamery serves so many mouth-watering flavors you'll want to skip dinner. About s/1 per scoop. Open daily 9am-10pm. ❶

Las Terrazas, Hurtado 183 (☎52 6525), on the Plaza. Delicious dishes, including *paiche* (s/15) and *juanes* (s/5). *Menú* s/5. Open daily 8:30am-midnight. ❷

Banana's Burger, Arias de Morey 102 (☎52 3260), at San Martín. Popular with locals, who rock out at the upstairs disco. Specializes in burgers (s/3.50), chicken (s/4), and sandwiches (s/4). Open 24hr. ❶

👁 🌿 SIGHTS AND FESTIVALS

MUSEO UNSM. The entrance to this one-room museum displays some startling examples of jungle wildlife, including anaconda skins. Inside, exhibits cover Tarapoto's long history in a circular fashion—first the fossilized shells, dinosaur bones, and mastodon jaw; followed by archaeological remains and colonial arti-facts; and finally newspaper clippings and photographs of Tarapoto from 1940 to 1960. *(Maynas 179. ☎52 2544. Open M-F 7am-8:45pm. s/1.)*

FESTIVALS. Highland customs are still practiced by descendents of the Chancas *(Motilones)* who live in Tarapoto. Travelers lucky enough to arrive during Tarapoto's main festival, in honor of the **Patrona de la Santa Cruz de los Motilones** (July 7-19), can witness these highland influences first-hand. Tarapoto's other major celebration is the week-long remembrance of its **anniversary** (Aug. 14-22), which includes traditional *pandilla* dances.

🎷 NIGHTLIFE

Even after the sun sets on Tarapoto, this jungle town keeps hopping, especially on weekends. In addition to the tourist trap *recreos* (restaurant/bars) sprinkled along Río Cumbaza, the outskirts of the Morales neighborhood (mototaxi 20min., s/5) is the unlikely location of several posh dance clubs, especially right near the bridge.

Discoteca Papillón, Peru 208 (☎52 2574), in the Morales neighborhood, has an out-door pool and patio area for midnight dancing breaks. Popular with foreigners and locals alike. Live salsa on F. Cover s/5. Open F-Sa 9pm-6am.

Bajú (☎52 5320; bajudisco@yahoo.com), on the 6th block of Manco Cápac, next to the Río Cumbaza. Bajú opened in 2002, and the Tarapoto dance scene hasn't been the same since. Fog machines and light shows keep 'em partying until the sun comes up. Cover s/5. Open F-Sa 9pm-6am.

🏞 DAYTRIPS FROM TARAPOTO

LAMAS. The descendants of the ancient Chancas (known as *motilones*) who inhabit the small town of Lamas are renowned for their highland traditions and handicrafts, seemingly out of place in the jungle. The waterfalls **Cascada de Chapawanki** and **Cascada de Mishquiyacu** lie nearby. *(To get to Lamas, take a combi (20min., leave when full 3am-9pm, s/3.50) from a bus company on Salaverry.)*

AQUATIC ADVENTURES. The spectacular **Cataratas Ahuashiyaku** waterfalls make for an easy daytrip. Look for the **Laguna Venezia** recreation area (s/1) on the way to the cascade. *(A 2hr. walk uphill along the highway toward Yurimaguas. Alternatively, take a Yurimaguas-bound bus (1hr., 10am, s/3-5) or a mototaxi (round-trip s/30-40).)* **Laguna Azul** (Blue Lake), a beautiful lake also called Laguna Sauce (Willow Lake), requires a longer excursion. *(To get to the lake, take a mototaxi (s/1.50) to the Sauce bus stop in the Shilcayo district, then hop on a Sauce-bound combi (3hr., s/12). Lodging (s/15) is available at the lake.)* During the dry season (June-Nov.), various tourist agencies in Tarapoto organize **rafting** trips (US$25 per person) down the Río Mayo during the dry season. *(See Tours, p. 407.)*

MOYOBAMBA   ☎042

Once thought to be enticingly near a rich source of profitable cinnamon, Moyobamba never quite lived up to expectations. Still, it remains a quaint town, where the end of every boulevard has distant views of the jungle. Just outside the city limits are several hot springs. The most popular are the **San Mateo springs,** 5km from town, a 1hr. walk or 15-20min. mototaxi ride (s/7-10). The sulfur baths of **Oromina** are 6km from town and are reputed to have healing powers.

Due to Moyobamba's proximity to Tarapoto, it shouldn't be necessary to spend the night, but **Hostal Celis ❸,** Callao 845 (☎56 2457), has rooms with hot private baths and a lounge with TV. (s/25). Plenty of other accommodations line Alonso de Alvarado. Find cheap eats and fruit juices (s/1) at the **indoor market** across the street. **Olla de Barro ❷,** at the corner of Pedro Canga and Serafín Filomeno, dishes up local specialties amid tiki hut decor. Autos run from Tarapoto to Moyobamba (1¾hr., s/20), leaving from the Paradero de Moyobamba, on Salaverry.

PUCALLPA   ☎061

Pucallpa (pop. 314,000; elev. 154m) oozes energy. Mototaxis crowd the streets, vendors push and pedal goods, and even shoe-shine boys seem in a rush to be somewhere. Meanwhile, by the port, cargo ferries continue their endless cycle of loading and unloading, while vultures circle overhead, waiting to dive at any scraps left behind. As Peru's largest jungle town accessible by road, Pucallpa's port forms an important link between the rainforest's resources and the rest of the country's markets. Left largely untouched by the rubber boom that proved so profitable in other jungle cities, Pucallpa today uses a combination of native crafts and modern technological advances to forge its own funky personality.

▐ TRANSPORTATION

Flights: Airport (☎57 2767), 5km west of the city center. Mototaxi s/3; taxi s/5. **Nuevo Continente,** 7 de Junio 861 (☎57 5643), flies to **Lima** (55min., daily 1:30pm, US$64). **LC Busre,** Tarapacá 805 (☎57 5309), at San Martín, flies to **Lima** (1¼hr., daily 11am, US$65). **TANS,** Arica 500 (☎59 1852), at Arana, flies to **Iquitos** (50min., daily at 3pm, US$65) and **Lima** (45min., daily at midday, US$65).

Buses: Bus and *auto* (colectivo) companies cluster on 7 de Junio near Raimondi and San Martín. **Selva Express,** 7 de Junio 804 (☎57 9098), and **Turismo Ucayali,** 7 de Junio 799 (☎59 3002), run autos to **Tingo María** (6hr., leave when full 4am-2pm, s/40). **TransRey,** Raimondi 677 (☎57 2305), goes to **Lima** (22hr., 5pm, s/35) via **Tingo María** (8hr., s/20) and **Huánuco** (11hr., s/25). **Turismo Central,** 7 de Junio 955 (☎57 7168), goes to **Lima** (23hr., 9am, s/35) and to **Huancayo** (21-22hr., 6:30am, s/45) via **Tingo María** (9hr., s/20) and **Huánuco** (12hr., s/25). **Transportes Palcazú,**

Raimondi 715 (☎57 1273), half a block from 7 de Junio, sends daily pickup **trucks** to **Palcazú** (8hr., 7:30am, s/35) and **Puerto Inca** (6hr., 8am, s/30). Trucks leave every other day for **Puerto Bermúdez** (11hr., 7am, s/50); call ahead for departure days.

Boats: Chalkboards announcing destinations and departure times adorn passenger vessels, although few leave on schedule. Even so, boats leave every few days for **Iquitos** (3-8 days, s/70-100) from the ports at **La Hoyada** (Dec.-Mar.), **Cruze el Mangual** (Apr.-July), and **Pucallpillo** (Aug.-Nov.). The exact location of each port shifts from season to season and year to year. Rubí, at the Tourist Office (below) will help visitors quickly locate the next departing boat and its correct port.

Public Transportation: The most popular **colectivo** route runs south down 7 de Junio toward the swamp and north up Ucayali (s/0.80-1).

Taxis: Mototaxis cost under s/2 within town and s/5 to Yarinacocha.

■ 🛈 ORIENTATION AND PRACTICAL INFORMATION

Pucallpa sits on the west bank of the **Río Ucayali,** 860km northeast of Lima. Its principal avenues include **Ucayali** and **7 de Junio,** the latter of which runs parallel to Ucayali and houses the town's largest **market.** These streets are intersected by **Raimondi** and **San Martín.** The **Plaza de Armas** is a block toward the river from Ucayali, between **Independencia** and **Sucre,** which run perpendicular to Ucayali. **Tarapacá,** on the northish side of the Plaza de Armas, forms the last of Pucallpa's major cross-town thoroughfares, packed with shops, restaurants, and of course, mototaxis. Most **buses** arrive on 7 de Junio or Ucayali. At the far north end of town, many streets change names as they cross **Inmaculada.**

Tourist Office: Dirección Regional de Comercio Exterior y Turismo, 2 de Mayo 111 (☎57 1303; fax 57 5110), near Inmaculada. From the Plaza, walk down Tarapacá toward the river and turn left on Portillo, which becomes 2 de Mayo. English-speaking Rubí and her staff are friendly, knowledgeable, and happy to show you the jungle themselves. Rubí will also help independent travelers locate and arrange passage on the next boat bound for Iquitos. Open M-F 8am-1pm and 2-4:30pm.

Currency Exchange: Banco de Crédito, Raimondi 404 (☎57 1364), at Tarapacá. 24hr. Plus/V **ATM.** Open M-F 9:30am-6:30pm, Sa 9:30am-12:30pm. **Banco Continental,** Ucayali 699 (☎57 5123) at Raimondi. 24hr. Plus/V **ATM.** Open Jan.-Mar. M-F 9:15am-1pm and 4:30-6:30pm; Apr.-Dec. M-F 9:15am-12:45pm and 4-6:30pm; year-round Sa 9:30am-12:30pm. **Interbank,** Raimondi 569 (☎57 1711), across from Banco Continental, has a 24hr. AmEx/Cirrus/MC/Plus/V **ATM** and will also receive **Western Union** payments and transfers. Open M-F 9am-1pm and 4-6:15pm, Sa 9:15am-12:30pm.

Outdoor Equipment: HS&E Supply, Portillo 561 (☎57 4360). A range of equipment for sale, from hard hats to tents. Open M-Sa 8am-1pm and 3-8pm.

Markets: Pucallpa's 4 markets are known by number. **Mercado 2,** the largest, stretches along 7 de Junio. **Mercado 1,** bordered by Tarapacá, Portillo, Huáscar, and Alameda, sells unique items such as hammocks (s/10-40).

Laundry: Lavandería Gasparín, Portillo 526 (☎59 1147). Self-service washing machine s/7, includes detergent; dryer s/8. Open M-Sa 9am-1pm and 4-8pm.

Emergency: ☎105.

Police: San Martín 466 (☎57 5257), near Tacna. Open 24hr.

Hospital: Augustín Cauper 285 (☎57 5209), between Diego Delunadro and Mariscal Cáceres. Open 24hr. with pharmacy for emergencies.

Telephones: Com TeleAmerica, Tarapacá 639 (☎57 6444), on the Plaza. Has several phone booths and also sells phone cards. Open daily 7am-10pm.

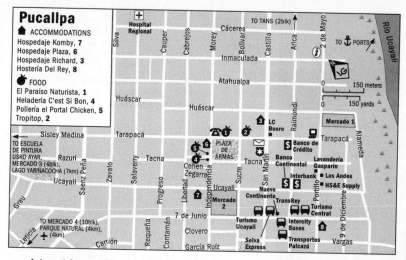

Pucallpa

🏠 ACCOMMODATIONS
Hospedaje Komby, **7**
Hospedaje Plaza, **6**
Hospedaje Richard, **3**
Hostería Del Rey, **8**

🍴 FOOD
El Paraíso Naturista, **1**
Heladería C'est Si Bon, **4**
Pollería el Portal Chicken, **5**
Tropitop, **2**

Internet Access: Many access points scattered throughout the city, but none match **Trial Cabinas de Internet,** Portillo 396 (☎59 2833), at Tarapacá. Fast Internet s/1.50 per hr. Surf 5hr., get 1hr. free. Open daily 7:30am-11:30pm.

Post Office: Serpost, San Martín 418 (☎57 1382). Open M-Sa 8am-6:45pm.

🏠 ACCOMMODATIONS

Pucallpa's wide variety of accommodations will fit anyone's budget and everyone's expectations. The cheapest lodgings cluster on 7 de Junio near Sucre. In this heat, a fan is an absolute must. None of these hotels have hot water, but you probably won't miss it. For an alternative splurge—no, not cable TV—the jungle lodges outside Yarinacocha (see **Into the Jungle from Lago Yarinacocha,** p. 414) are worth considering. They're close enough that you can still spend the day in Pucallpa.

Hospedaje Komby, Ucayali 360 (☎ 57 1562; fax 59 2074), 1½ blocks up from the Plaza. With private baths, cable TV, telephones, and helicopter-sized fans in each room, the Komby is komfortable. The fabulous pool doesn't hurt, either. Only the price tells you that this is still Peru. Singles s/25-30; doubles s/35-40; triples s/45. ❸

Hostería Del Rey, Portillo 747 (☎57 5815), down 7 de Junio toward the river and right on Portillo. High-ceilinged rooms with baths and fans strong enough to rival hurricane season. Check your bath first—plumbing isn't the same everywhere. TV s/5. Singles s/15; doubles s/20. ❷

Hospedaje Richard, San Martín 350 (☎48 5283). If the room fans can't beat the heat, at least the front desk has ice-cold drinks for sale (s/1-2.50). Go for the rooms with large windows and private baths to counteract the aesthetic void created by the unappetizingly orange walls. Singles s/10, with bath s/15; doubles with bath s/25. ❶

Hospedaje Plaza, Independencia 420 (☎59 2118), right off the Plaza. For those in search of an authentically rustic experience right in the center of town, this 2nd-story hostel sports slatted wood-plank walls. A few rooms have partitioned private baths and fans to complement the noise from the Plaza. Rooms at the back have none of the above. Singles s/10, with bath s/15; doubles s/20. ❶

AMAZON BASIN

THE LOCAL STORY

JUNGLE TRIPPING

All over the Peruvian jungle, locals report that the hallucinogenic plant *ayahuasca* is the recreational drug of choice. The Incas used Ayahuasca centuries ago for purification rituals and dream interpretation. Traditionally, only shamans drank *ayahuasca*, which supposedly gave them the ability to solve the problems of their followers. In recent years, however, some people interested in the plant's powers have started imbibing the substance themselves.

Ayahuasca is so potent that those who use it follow a special diet for two days before ingesting the drug and seek counsel from other users. Even then, the drug's potency makes usage extremely risky. Some users of the drug report developing a "third eye," through which they can view the past and present united, the philosophy of nature, and the meaning of paradise.

Painter Pablo Amaringo, whose neo-Amazonic pieces are inspired by his experience with *ayahuasca*, said that the plant puts you in contact with beings from other worlds and dimensions. Amaringo gave up *ayahuasca* in 1976 after he found himself injured by an emissary of the spirit world.

Groovy.

Let's Go does not recommend recreational drug use.

🍴 FOOD

Fruit juices and fish dishes are never hard to come by in Pucallpa. A **fruit market** appears daily along Ucayali between Independencia and Sucre. Farther along, at the intersection with San Martín, vendors sell overwhelmingly sweet coconut patties (s/0.50). Another block down, Raimondi (between Ucayali and Tacna) hosts multiple burger joints. For Italian food, head to Inmaculada between San Martín and Independencia. Street stands serving a multitude of grilled meat and fish, *juanes*, and corn (s/1-4) appear nightly near the corner of Ucayali and Independencia, one block from the Plaza. **Los Andes**, Portillo 553-557, is a well-stocked supermarket. (☎57 1290. Open M-Th 8am-1pm and 3-9pm, F-Sa 8am-9pm, Su 10am-1pm.)

- **Heladería C'est Si Bon**, Independencia 560 (☎57 1893), off the Plaza. From the first bite, this restaurant and dessert shop lives up to its name. You'll regret not trying the ice cream—do it with a banana split (s/12). Breakfast s/6-8. Hamburgers s/5-8. Pastries and cakes s/1-3.50. Milkshakes s/6. ❶

- **El Paraíso Naturista**, Tarapacá 653 (☎962 1151), on the Plaza. If it's hard to find a seat in a vegetarian restaurant during the lunch rush in meat-and-potato Peru, you know the place is doing something right. Entrees include Peruvian favorites served vegetarian-style. The yogurt with honey (s/1.50) is out of sight. Lunch *menús* s/3.50 and s/6. Entrees s/3-9. Open M-F and Su 7am-9pm. ❶

- **Tropitop**, Sucre 401 (☎57 2860), at the corner of Tarapacá, on the Plaza. With 5 breakfast *menús* to choose from (s/3.50-6), there could hardly be a better place to start the day. Extra-cheerful waitresses make anyone feel like a regular from the very first visit. Outside breakfast hours, the menu blends local specialties like *yucca rellena* (s/3) with more exotic dishes like lasagna (s/8). Open daily 7am-11:30pm. ❶

- **Pollería El Portal Chicken**, Independencia 510 (☎57 1771), on the Plaza. This triple-decker joint, with speedy service and a neon green glow, is the best of the city's many chicken restaurants. ¼ chicken s/6. Entrees s/6-24. Open daily 5pm-midnight. ❷

🧭 SIGHTS

PARQUE NATURAL Y MUSEO REGIONAL. Most notable for its extensive **zoo**, the park features some beautiful animals in rather small cages. There's also a small island on which a collection of monkeys cavort uncaged, in something resembling their natural habitat. Sometimes the animals allow visitors to touch them. Beyond the zoo and over the shark-head bridge sits the **museum.** Four small huts outline aspects of local culture: one contains pottery from the Shipibo Conibo Indians; another, an assortment of pelts and skins; the third, bones, shells, and fossils; and the last, a collection of sculpture from the local Escuela Tahua. It's also possible to float around one of the park's small lakes in a rowboat or take the resident horse for a short ramble (both s/3 per hr.). *(To get to the complex, take any northbound combi marked "Pista," and ask to be let off at the "zoológico." Then walk down the dirt road until you arrive at the park entrance. 15min., s/0.80-1. Open daily 9am-5pm. s/5, children s/1.)*

ARTESANÍA. Internationally renowned painter **Pablo Amaringo** runs the **Escuela de Pintura Usko Ayar,** whose name is Quechua for Spiritual Prince. Don Pablo has developed a style he calls "neo-Amazónico," which consists of jungle landscapes inspired by shamanic visions he had while under the influence of the hallucinogenic *ayahuasca* plant (see **Jungle Tripping**). Today, students continue to study his style and the symbolism in his drug-induced paintings, and friendly teachers show off students' work between classes. Amaringo's work is also on display, but he no longer endorses use of the drug. *(Sánchez Cerro 465-67. ☎ 57 3088. Mototaxi s/2. Generally open daily 8-10am and 2-5pm. Free.)*

🎵 🍸 ENTERTAINMENT AND NIGHTLIFE

Pucallpa's primary festival, the **Fiesta de San Juan,** takes place June 17-25, with the festivities reaching their peak June 24. To honor San Juan, Pucallpa's patron saint, locals head to the river or lake to bathe in purifying water, then celebrate with traditional dances, music, boat and swimming races, and lots of beer. The city's **anniversary** (October 1-18) provides another occasion to party with parades, traditional dances, music, and *artesanía* displays. Pucallpa's disco scene is extensive but not particularly distinguished; salsa-dancing 20-somethings and San Juan *cerveza* rule the night. The majority of Pucallpa's clubs are tucked away in residential neighborhoods near the road to the airport (mototaxi s/2).

LAGO YARINACOCHA ☎ 061

Constantly in flux, the Amazon's mercurial waterways seem to delight in playing mind games—or hide-and-go-seek, at the very least. It is common for a river to drastically shift its course over the span of just a few years. In the process, it may leave a "footprint" of its former course in the form of an **oxbow lake** that sometimes re-floods during the rainy season. Such is the case with Lago Yarinacocha, a footprint left by the mighty Río Ucayali. Seven kilometers northeast of Pucallpa, Lago Yarinacocha and its anchoring settlement, Puerto Callao (which everyone refers to simply as Yarinacocha), serve as a weekend retreat for the city's residents and a potential jungle gateway for foreign wanderers.

🚍 TRANSPORTATION. To get to Puerto Callao and the lake, take a **colectivo** marked "Yarina" (15min., s/1) from Ucayali in Pucallpa. All transport between Pucallpa and the lake breezes through the Puerto Callao Plaza de Armas, stopping two blocks down at the waterfront, where all the action is. Colectivos in Puerto Callao come in two breeds—those with outboard motors and those with engines under the hood. Boats leave from the port, ferrying groups to any destination on the lake (1½hr. to San Francisco, 30min. to the botanical gardens, 15-20min. to jungle lodges; leave when full; s/1-1.50). Colectivos with four wheels or **mototaxis** can also be taken to San Francisco (1hr., s/2) and the Botanic Gardens (40min., s/2).

AMAZON BASIN

🔳🔢 ORIENTATION AND PRACTICAL INFORMATION. The center of activity in Puerto Callao is right along the water's edge. Although for most services Pucallpa provides a better option, a few conveniences can be found in Yarinacocha. The **Mercado Modelo** is one block back from the waterfront, above where the colectivos stop and turn uphill. The **police** are uphill in a dark green building on the Plaza de Armas (☎59 6417; 105 for emergencies). **Farmacia Melchorita,** at Ahuatiya 286 (☎59 6580), stays on duty 24hr. **Pay phones** are scattered through town, especially away from the water. **Internet access** is available at **Charapitos.net,** which stays open 8am-10pm daily, long after the boatmen have gone home (s/2 per hr.).

🔳🔲 ACCOMMODATIONS AND FOOD. There is little reason to sleep in Puerto Callao, so close to Pucallpa, but **Hospedaje Los Delfines ❶,** on Ahuatiya at Circunvalación, has gigantic rooms with fridges and fans. To get there, face the water, then follow the waterfront road all the way to the left. Turn away from the water at the end of the road; the *hospedaje* is one block up on the left, across from the electric company. (☎48 5517. Knob-tuned TV s/2. Singles s/15; doubles s/15-25.) At lunchtime everyone emerges to cook fresh fish along the street (s/3-6), and countless restaurants line the waterfront. The pricey **Balsa Turística Anaconda ❸,** to the right when facing the water, gives new meaning to the term "lakefront property" by literally floating on the lake. (☎59 6950. Delicious seafood entrees s/13-17. Live music Su 2pm. Open daily noon-6pm.)

◻ SIGHTS. Multiple destinations around the lake tempt visitors. Just to the north (left if you're facing the water from Puerto Callao) sits **San Francisco** (pop. 1200), and farther along, smaller **Santa Clara**—both are traditional Shipibo villages. Women sit outside their houses selling *artesanía* at unbelievably cheap prices. Closer to Puerto Callao, **Isla del Amor** is the best place to swim, with volleyball courts and shady trees nearby. Unlike many spots on the river, it's actually considered safe (fauna-wise) to swim in Lago Yarinacocha, if the muddy-colored water beckons. To be on the safest side, though, it's best to skip that dip if you have any kind of appetizing cut or sore that could attract piranhas. Though popular in the dry season (June-Sept.), the resort simply doesn't exist summer (Nov.-Jan.)—it's all covered up. Boats to Isla del Amor (20min., s/1) depart frequently from the port area. On the right side of the lake (if you're facing the water from Puerto Callao) sit the **Botanic Gardens,** 1hr. by boat from Puerto Callao, which house over 2300 plants and the peaceful sound of hundreds of birds. (Open daily 7am-3pm. s/2.)

🔳 INTO THE JUNGLE FROM LAGO YARINACOCHA. Tour boats provide guided tours to anywhere on the lake (s/15 per hr.). The stated price is normally per group, so larger groups get a better deal.

Beyond daytrips, guides lead excursions (3-5 days) around the lake and environs, which include direct aquatic connections to the Río Ucayali and nearby virgin jungle. Guides around Yarinacocha charge around US$35 per person per day, and sometimes have a 2-person minimum. Choose your guide carefully, and make sure he has adequate equipment—meet him personally before you hire. **Gilbert Reategui Sangama** (www.sacredheritage.com/normita) has 35 years of jungle experience, speaks English, and gives personalized trips; look for his boat, "Normita," in the shore line-up. **Mauricio Sende Icoa,** whom everyone knows as "Boa," is another helpful and informative guide. He does not have his own boat, but he often works with Gilbert. Another recommended guide is **Gustavo Paredes Polonio,** whose boat is called "Poseidon." It is hard to find a boat around *siesta,* after dark, when it's raining, or during soccer games. **Santa Clara** is a 30min. walk from San Francisco, but only from November to April—much of the area floods during the winter months (May-Oct.) and is only accessible by boat. For specifics on what to look for in a guide or lodge, see **Jungle Tours,** p. 50.

Jungle lodges in the area differ from those near other jungle towns in both location and price. Although they are undeniably in the jungle, Yarinacocha's lodges are all within a 20min. **colectivo** boat ride of Puerto Callao (s/1) and are thus entirely connected to modern society. Perhaps more importantly, these jungle lodges are significantly cheaper than equivalents to the north and south. ▓**La Perla ⑤,** between La Cabaña and Nueva Fátima, on the far side of the lake, takes travelers in as one of the family. Its German and Peruvian owners house visitors in rooms bedecked with indigenous artifacts and animal skins. The upper half of the outside walls in each guest room are just screens, so visitors fall asleep and awake to the sounds and sight of surrounding wildlife. Citrus and banana trees run amok behind the house. (☎961 6004; www.eproima.net/laperla. Rooms US$30 per person, includes 3 meals and transportation to and from the Pucallpa airport.) **Nueva Luz de Fátima,** actually a small village, lies just beyond the jungle lodges. There, **Silvia Morales** and **Gilbert Reategui Sangama ③** open their home to travelers who wish to experience real life in a 45-family lakeside town (s/50 per person, includes 3 meals). Accommodations are extremely spartan—tourists stay in partitioned bedrooms in a wood hut—but you can't get much more genuine than this. The entire village shares the common bathrooms out back, and showering means dumping buckets of river water over your head. (No telephone; www.sacredheritage.com/normita. s/25 per person, includes 3 meals.) For a completely different experience, head to **La Cabaña ⑤,** a lakeside resort with individual cabins, each with its own outdoor patio. A flashy sign and giant deck with lounge chairs overlooking the river make this resort easy to spot. If all those jungle beasts and bugs freak you out, never fear: La Cabaña mows its lawn and hangs swings from its tree branches. (☎57 9694, cell 961 5364. Cabins US$35 per person, includes 3 meals.)

TINGO MARÍA   ☎064

Where the Andes give way to the jungle, little Tingo María (pop. 52,400; elev. 649m) bustles, known for its bottomless cave and comparable cocaine supply. Steamy weather and ubiquitous greenery cloak the town's already mysterious exploits. Aside from its slightly scandalous reputation, Tingo María has a splendid mountain backdrop, not to mention one of the grandest caves in the country. Give it a point for originality, too; it's one of the only cities without a Plaza de Armas.

▐ TRANSPORTATION

Buses: Most buses arrive at the southern end of Raimondi near the corner of Callao and downhill away from the market toward where it turns into Enrique Pimentel. The large bus companies are mostly useful for trips to Lima. **Leon de Huánuco,** Enrique Pimentel 164 (☎56 2030) has service to **Lima** (12hr.; 7:30am, 7, 7:30pm; s/25-30; *bus cama* 7:45pm, s/35), as does **Transrey,** Raimondi 201 (☎54 2565; 12-13hr., 7pm, s/35-40). Operated by a variety of companies, **colectivos** are the best way to get between Tingo María and Huánuco or Pucallpa. Those to **Huánuco** (2hr., leave when full 5am-7pm, s/13) leave from the corner of Raimondi and Callao, diagonally across from the gas station. To catch one for **Pucallpa** (8-9hr., leave when full 5am to mid-afternoon, s/35-40) go to Tito Jaime at Cayumba, diagonally across from the *mercado*.

Local Transport: Mototaxis should not cost more than s/1-1.50 within town.

✴ 🔢 ORIENTATION AND PRACTICAL INFORMATION

Cradled in a curve of **Río Huallaga**, Tingo María lies 545km northeast of Lima. Wide and grassy **Alameda Perú** runs the not-so-lengthy length of town and bisects the city's primary square, **Plaza Leoncio Prado.** The side where buses and colectivos arrive is the site of most businesses and hotels. There are more restaurants along **Tito Jaime** (1 block away), while **Raimondi** (2 blocks away) is home to banks, bus companies, and the police. **Veayali** is the first street on the other, primarily residential, side of Alameda Perú.

Tourist Office: Alameda Perú (☎56 2351), right off the Plaza. With a bit of luck they'll have free but hard-to-read maps in stock. Open M-F 8am-1pm and 3-3:45pm; Sa-Su 8am-1pm.

Currency Exchange: Banco de Crédito, Raimondi 249-251 (☎56 2110), and **Banco Continental,** on Raimondi between Lamas and Pucallpa. Both have Plus/V **ATMs.**

Market: The **Mercado Modelo** fills the block between Alameda Perú and Tito Jaime and between Callao and Cayumba.

Emergency: ☎105.

Police: Raimondi 413 (☎56 2533), at Prado. 24hr. emergency service.

Hospital: Ucayali 114 (emergency ☎56 3075). 24hr. emergency attention.

24hr. Pharmacy: Botica Flores, Ucayali 101 (☎56 1316).

Telephones: Telefónica del Perú, Tito Jaime 421 (☎56 3426). Open daily 7:30am-10pm.

Internet Access: Increased bandwidth has brought an Internet boom to Tingo. **Rock@sInternet,** Tito Jaime 101 at Callao (☎56 3351 and 56 1910), stands out for the number of ports and long hours. s/1 per hr. Open daily 8:30am-midnight.

Post Office: Serpost, Alameda Perú 451 (☎/fax 56 2100), on the Plaza. Open M-Sa 8am-8pm.

🏠 ACCOMMODATIONS

Cheap lodgings around s/7 are numerous, but many are downright frightening. Those listed below are far better values. Unless otherwise stated, none have hot water and checkout is at noon.

Hospedaje Palacio, Raimondi 158 (☎56 2055 or 56 2319), near Callao. The giant central courtyard doubles as a zoo. Squawking parrots may act as 6am wake-up calls, but they're easy to forgive after a delicious breakfast at the adjacent cafe (s/5). Decor is minimal but spotless. Rooms with private baths have fans and TVs. Singles s/10, with bath and TV s/25; doubles s/25, with bath and TV s/42. ❶

Hotel Nueva York, Alameda Perú 553 (☎56 2406), on the Plaza. Practically a skyscraper on Tingo's understated skyline, this modern hotel does its best to be cheerful with potted plants, laundry service, and restaurant. The rooms feature 24hr. hot water (ask them to turn it on) and smell freshly cleaned. Singles with bath and TV s/30; doubles s/40; triples s/55. ❸

Hotel Las Palmeras, Callao 283 (☎56 1338). Recently renovated, this mecca of tile and tall ceilings is by far the fanciest in Tingo. Complete with fans, hot water, and cable TV (s/5). Singles s/12, with private bath s/20. ❷

Hospedaje Viena, Lamas 252 (☎56 2194), between Tito Jaime and Raimondi. This rambling hostel could host an army. Keep looking until you find the best room. Singles s/10, with bath s/15; doubles s/15, with bath s/20; triples s/18, with bath s/25. ❶

Hostal Falcón, Sucre 245 (☎56 1817). From the Plaza, with the river to your right, walk down Alameda Perú and take a left on Callao; take the first right on Olaya, then a quick left onto 9 de Octubre; Sucre is the next right. Comfy rooms in a slightly deserted residential neighborhood come with mirror, towel, soap, and toilet paper. The rooms on the balcony overlooking the street are the nicest, but be wary at night—there are no street lights. Singles with bath s/15; doubles with bath s/20. ❷

FOOD

At day's end, most locals eat at the outdoor stands that seem to sprout at every intersection. Fortunately, the restaurant-bug endures: from pizza to *pollo*, Tingo has tasty eats to be discovered.

▨ **El Mango,** Lamas 232 (☎56 1671). For a classy treat, check out the absolute best pizzas around (personal s/7-12) or savor sandwiches (s/2.5-3.50) and Peruvian entrees (s/10-12) while relaxing in the shade of the giant mango tree sheltering the stylish garden courtyard. Open M-Sa 8am-3pm and 7-11pm. ❷

El Chascl, José Prado 213 (☎01 9809 9223), at the corner of Prado and Raimondi across from the police station. To find this island of delights, don't look for a sign—there isn't one. Instead, look for the crowds filling every terrace table and counter tile. They're after the home-cooked goodness of fried *trucha* (trout; s/5), roasted stuffed peppers (s/3.50), and fresh-squeezed pineapple juice (s/2-3). Open daily 7:30am-9pm. ❶

La Tía Julia, Alameda Perú 374 (☎56 1257). Wearing a chef's *toque*, surrounded by murals of the *selva*, Tía Julia cooks up some of the best *comida típica* around. Her specialty is *tacachas* (mashed fried plantains and meat; s/6-8). Don't miss the *juanes* (egg, rice, olives, and meat wrapped in a giant leaf; s/6) or the fruit juices (s/0.50). ❶

Trigale, Tito Jaime 542 (☎56 1638). Perhaps the only place in Tingo with mood lighting. Couples and families enjoy pizza (s/8-10) and lasagna (s/12) to the sound of subdued Latin hits. Open daily 6-11pm. ❷

SIGHTS

PARQUE NACIONAL TINGO MARÍA. Reclining on the outskirts of the city (6km outside the city, cave less than 1km from the entrance), the **Bella Durmiente** (Sleeping Beauty) mountain—named because its curves resemble those of a woman in repose—marks the location of **Parque Nacional Tingo María.** The 18,000 hectare reserve maintains a few wooded trails and a refreshing river, but its most popular attraction is the **Cueva de las Lechuzas (Cave of the Owls).** So immense that it's rumored to be bottomless, this cave could inspire a full day of exploration, (although the extreme heat, bats, and cockroaches make most visitors turn back well before that). Even the most amateur spelunker can explore the cave's mouth, where wooden walkways provide security. There, magnificent rock formations hide flocks of **parrots.** Beyond the walkways, seemingly countless **oil birds** make their nests, and deeper still live the infamous **owls.** Bring a flashlight and hat to keep droppings off your head. If you plan to travel beyond the walkway, wear sturdy shoes. *(Mototaxi s/1.50 per person. For s/5-10 the driver will wait for the return trip to town. Guides are not required, but can be hired in Tingo. Park open daily 8am-5pm. s/5.)*

PUERTO BERMÚDEZ   ☎063

If Cusco is the tourist heart of Peru, then Puerto Bermúdez is the belly-button, or so the locals claim, pointing out that their tiny village (pop. 4000) sits at Peru's exact geographical center (a plaque in the ground marks the spot). People travel to Puerto Bermúdez in search of a small *albergue* that has become the hottest budget jungle lodge in the country. The lodge runs excursions into the jungle, where an authentic, unspoiled world of lush vegetation, indigenous communities, and rolling hills awaits. After you've sated your craving for adventure, the lodge offers tempting spots to kick back, relax, and recover from all those mosquito bites.

The **▨Albergue Humboldt ❸** is all the way down Castillo. Follow the road downhill and along the river; Humboldt's gate is on the left, marked by a small sign on the streetlight (mototaxi s/1). In addition to trekking, the *albergue* arranges rafting trips and ethnological, archaeological, and ecological tourism excursions. Backpackers staying at the *albergue* (Spanish for "community house") discuss travel experiences in the library, comfortable hammocks, and spotless rooms. Humboldt's personalized trips range from a one-day waterfall visit to a 10-day boat trip to Cusco. Ashaninka natives act as guides, as they know the jungle better than anyone else, and Jesús can also provide information to arrange your own expedition. (☎72 0267, frequently out of service; www.geocities.com/puerto_bermudez.)

Alameda Ramón Castillo is the town's main artery, running parallel to the river two blocks inland from the waterfront. **Oxapampa** and **Remigio Morales** run perpendicular to the river, intersecting **Castillo** and **Capitán Larry**—between which lies the town's **airport.** Getting to Puerto Bermúdez is not for the faint of heart. **Trucks** and **combis** leave from the main bus terminal in La Merced (Oct.-Mar. 10-12hr., Apr.-Sept. 8-10hr.). From Puerto Bermúdez, companies on Castillo send trucks and combis back to La Merced (Oct.-Mar. 10-12hr.; Apr.-Sept. 8-10hr.). Castillo shelters most of the town's services, few of which have addresses or telephone numbers. There is **no currency exchange** in Puerto Bermúdez. Services include: a **market,** on the third block on the right heading down Castillo; a **hospital,** 200m beyond the bus companies heading up Castillo; the **police,** 200m past the hospital after turning left off Castillo at the hospital's intersection; and **telephones,** on Morales.

LA MERCED ☎064

Forced into isolation by decades of regional terrorism, La Merced (pop. 26,000) cultivated oranges and coffee rather than hiking trails or tourist lodges in the surrounding Chanchamayo Valley. Today, although official tourist services are still developing, everyone seems to have symptoms of tourism fever. From restaurant owners to mototaxi drivers, offers for freelance guides are as plentiful as the citrus trees blanketing the nearby hills; fully half of the businesses facing the airy Plaza de Armas are tour agencies. Even so, while motos race through the narrow, curvy streets and the market swirls with activity, travelers have yet to beat a path through La Merced. They're missing out—those now trickling in find a lively, orange-scented community on the jungle border, amid hills awaiting exploration.

There are many inexpensive hotels in La Merced but no great values—just solid, clean rooms sprinkled throughout town. (Singles s/10-30; doubles s/15-40; triples s/20-55). La Merced's restaurant situation resembles that of its hotels: many contestants, but no prizewinners. Chicken places are scattered on Tarma, and a few touristy places offer good, clean traditional food on the Plaza. Cheaper, less professional meals await at the **jueguerías** (small booths selling juice; most open daily 6am-midnight) in the **market,** one block down Tarma from the Plaza (with the hill on your left).

Several buses depart daily for La Merced from Lima, including **Empresa La Merced** and **León de Huánuco** (2-8hr., several daily 8am-10pm, s/15-20; see **Intercity Transportation,** p. 94). In La Merced, **buses** run from the **terminal,** seven blocks down twisty Tarma, to: Huancayo (4½-5hr., several per day); Huánuco (7hr., 1 per day); Lima (8hr., several per day, s/20) often via Tarma (1½-2hr., s/5-6); Palcazú (10hr., 2 per day 3:30-4:30am), the place for connections to Pucallpa; and Puerto Bermúdez (8hr., 3 per day 3:30-4:30am). Frequent **colectivos** go to Huancayo (5hr., leave when full, s/13) via Tarma (1½hr., s/5-6), and to Oxapampa (2½-3hr.). **Colectivos** to San Ramón cluster on

Junín, toward the hill and outside the main gate of the terminal. **Mototaxis** around town cost about s/1. La Merced sits on hills overlooking the Río Tambopata. The **Plaza de Armas** lies four blocks up from the river and is bordered by **Tarma** and **Palca** (parallel to the river) and **Junín** and **Ancash** (perpendicular to the river). Many services lie along **2 de Mayo,** one block from the Plaza, parallel to Junín. Services include: **Banco de Crédito,** on the plaza at Tarma and Junín, with a Visa **ATM** and money changers clustering outside; a **market,** three blocks down from the Plaza on Tarma, toward the bus station (open daily 6am-midnight); **police** (☎53 1292), on Pirola, two blocks up Junín from the Plaza; **Serpost** is on 2 de Mayo between Arica and Pirola.

SAN RAMÓN ☎064

A 12km jog down the road to Lima, La Merced's sibling city (pop. 22,000) is much like its bigger sister. A visit to the **Tirol Waterfall** provides a welcome excuse for a walk in the jungle, albeit not a solitary one—the falls are popular among foreigners and Peruvians alike. A beautiful 30min. walk takes you along a marked path next to the river (which can get prohibitively muddy during the rainy season). A mini-waterfall foreshadows Tirol, but you'll know when you reach the actual 60m-high falls. It's possible to **swim** in the pool below. To reach the starting point, take a mototaxi to *"Catarata Tirol"* (15min., about s/4). An small admission fee is collected on the path. For more aquatic fun, **Centro Recreacional Miguel Ángel,** at the end of Paucartambo, has a sparkling **swimming pool.**

Colectivos to San Ramón (15min., leave when full, about s/8) from La Merced depart from Junín and Arica, one block uphill from Banco de Crédito, and from the bus terminal gate; **autos** return from San Ramón's Plaza de Armas (s/1-2). San Ramón's **tourist office,** Pardo 110, provides information about other area attractions. To reach the **police** (☎33 1222), on Pachitea, walk up Progreso one block from the Plaza, turn right and continue for two blocks. **Banco de Crédito,** Pardo 201, on the Plaza, has a Plus/V **ATM** around the corner.

OXAPAMPA ☎063

Although perched amidst the mountains, seemingly in the middle of nowhere, Oxapampa (pop. 13,000) is no backwoods town, with its cruising combis, elegant clothing stores, and—showing the influence of the German-Austrian settlement nearby—sporadically Teutonic architecture. Still, while the urban center may not jive with its rural surroundings, the two are linked. Farming and cattle industries support Oxapampa, providing the backbone of the town's prosperity: its delicious yogurt and cheese. Oxapampa's greatest tourist

asset, the 122,000-hectare **Parque Nacional Yanachaga-Chemillén,** is also Peru's largest cloud forest. Host to countless waterfalls, birds, and flowers, the park is excellent for bird-watching or hiking. For better or worse, this is an area for independent exploration, as it has no tourist resources. Camping is allowed. The INRENA **park office** at the corner of San Martín and Pozuzo in Oxapampa can provide more information. (☎76 2544. Open M-F 8am-1pm and 2:30-6pm.) Pozuzo-bound **colectivos** leaving from Oxapampa pass through the park (1½hr., about s/5), shortly after passing through the village of Agua Salada. A sign marks the beginning of the park and the village of Yulitunqui marks the end. To get out of the park, flag down a passing colectivo.

Several companies send **buses** to: La Oroya (6hr.); Lima (12hr., 4:30pm, s/25) via La Merced (3hr.); Tarma (5hr.). **Colectivos** go to Pozuzo (3hr., 3 per day) and La Merced (3hr., leave frequently throughout the day). **Cars** run to Huancabamba (1hr., leave when full). From the terminal, **combis** leave for Villa Rica (4hr., 3 per day), where there are connections to Puerto Bermúdez. The **Río Chontabamba** and the **Río La Esperanza** border Oxapampa. Commercial **Bolognesi** runs past the **Plaza de Armas** and across the Chontabamba, while perpendicular **Bolívar** and, farther from the river, **Mariscal Castilla,** carve the Plaza's other borders. Wandering **San Martín** bisects the corner of Bolognesi and Castilla. Accommodations and dining options in Oxapampa lack any standouts, but food is relatively easy to find, especially in the Plaza de Armas. The **tourist office,** Bolívar 464, 2nd fl., has **maps** and sells slick guidebooks. Services include: **Banco de Crédito,** Bolívar 310; a **market,** one block down Bolognesi toward the river, on the right; **police,** 338 Bottger (☎76 2217, 24hr. emergency ☎105); and **Serpost,** Castillo 205.

QUILLABAMBA ☎084

Locals refer to Quillabamba (pop. 10,000) as "La Ciudad de Verano Eterno," the City of Eternal Summer. Indeed, it is a slice of paradise amidst the immense, untamed jungle, and the closest rainforest town to Cusco.

⌐ TRANSPORTATION. Quillabamba was once the last stop on the Cusco rail line, but can now be reached only by bus as the train tracks were wiped out by a recent landslide. **Buses** (8hr.; 8am, 1, 7:30, 8:30pm; s/15) leave from Cusco's **Terminal de Quillabamba** on Antonio Lorena (☎24 9977; taxi from the Plaza de Armas s/2.50). It's a long, rough ride on an unpaved road through the highlands—as always, *Let's Go* discourages nighttime bus travel. To get to Quillabamba's **bus terminal** from Plaza Grau, walk past the market and make the first left on Convención; the station is two blocks ahead on **28 de Julio.** Buses run to: Abancay (5hr.; 7am, 8pm; s/13); Arequipa (20hr., 8:30pm, s/40); Cusco (9hr.; 8am, 8pm; s/15); Kiteni (5hr., 7:30pm, s/10); Ivachote (6hr., 6pm, s/12); Ollantaytambo (7hr.; 8am, 8pm; s/12); Tinti (9-10hr., 4pm, s/12). **Taxis** and tricycle taxis cost s/1-2 within town.

◪◩ ORIENTATION AND PRACTICAL INFORMATION. Two central plazas orient the town of Quillabamba: the irregularly shaped **Plaza Grau,** and the beautifully shady **Plaza de Armas,** three blocks downhill and to the left. To arrange **tours** in and around the Quillabamba area, try **Kiteni Tours,** Libertad 577 (☎28 2477), at Bolognesi, or the small transportation agencies that sit along Ricardo Palma, one block from the Plaza. **Banco de Crédito,** Libertad 545, one block uphill from the Plaza de Armas, cashes traveler's checks and has an AmEx/Plus/V **ATM** (open M-F 9am-1pm and 4-6:30pm, Sa 9:30am-12:30pm); **Banco Continental,** on Bolognesi, has a Cirrus/V **ATM.** The **police** are on Libertad at the Plaza (☎28 1327; open 24hr. for emergencies), and the **hospital** (☎28 1695), on Gamarra between Grau and San Martín, is open 24hr. for emergencies. A well-stocked **supermarket,** Taurus, is at Libertad 513, uphill from the Plaza (open daily 6am-9pm), and a **pharmacy** is further up the street at the corner of Libertad and Bolognesi (open daily 8am-10pm). **Public telephones**

lie around the Plaza. **Internet access** can be found at **Juegos en Red** (Espinar 235) on the Plaza, as well as at several places along Grau. The **post office**, Libertad 511, is on the Plaza. (☎28 1086. Open M-Sa 8am-8pm, Su 9am-12:30pm.)

⌂🍴 ACCOMMODATIONS AND FOOD. The best lodging options begin with **Hostal Alto Urubamba ❷**, 2 de Mayo, between Mario Concha and Espinar, one block from the Plaza de Armas. Enthusiastic service, a delicious restaurant (continental breakfast s/7; best coffee in town s/1), and spacious wood-floored rooms make it quite a find for the budget traveler. (☎28 1131; altourub@ec-red.com. Singles s/19, with bath and cable TV s/36, with 24hr. hot water s/40; doubles s/26, with bath and cable TV s/45, with 24hr. hot water s/50; triples s/36, with bath and cable TV s/66, with 24hr. hot water s/70.) **Hostal Quillabamba ❹**, Grau 590, has a swimming pool and even a miniature zoo. Snubbing animal rights activists the world over, they hold cockfighting competitions every year between May and July (call for exact schedules, which vary each year). All rooms come with telephones, cable TV, private baths, and 24hr. hot water. (☎28 1369. Reception 9am-midnight. Singles s/45; doubles s/65; triples s/85; quads s/105. All major credit cards.) Uphill from the Plaza de Armas sits **Don Carlos ❸**, Libertad 556, with a lovely restaurant (open daily 6-10pm) and clean rooms with telephones, cable TV, private baths, and 24hr. hot water. (☎28 1150. Check-out 1pm. Rooms start at s/45 (singles) and climb s/20 with each additional person. V.)

Quillabamba is no gourmet haven, but excellent pizza (s/9-12) and pasta (s/7-9) can be found at **Pizzería Venecia ❹**, Libertad 461, between the post office and the police station. (☎28 1582. Free delivery. Open daily 6pm-midnight.) Cheap deli-style sandwiches (s/1.50-3) and *empanadas* (s/1) are served at **Café La Esquina ❶**, Espinar 201, at Libertad in the Plaza de Armas. (☎28 1224. Open daily 7:30am-11pm.) With delicious ice cream (s/4-9) and milkshakes (s/2-7), **Gelatería Italiana ❶**, on the corner of Libertad and Espinar in the Plaza, will keep you cool in the jungle heat. (Open daily 10am-10pm.)

◎ SIGHTS. The **park** at the base of Libertad affords a glimpse of the Río Urubamba, but for a closer look, try the **Sambaray complex**, 2km north of town (s/1). This recreational area has an outdoor swimming pool, volleyball court, soccer field, and a restaurant, not to mention access to the nearby rapids of the Urubamba, in which adventurous travelers can either **swim** or go **tubing**. Colectivos to Sambaray (15 min., s/1) leave continually from Plaza Grau, or take a taxi (s/2). A bit farther outside town lie four different **waterfalls** (each in a different direction): Urusayhua, Yanay, Cañon de Mesa Pelada, and the most impressive, ■**Siete Tinajas**—a series of seven stone pools carved out by the falling water. Wear sturdy shoes and be careful, as there is no longer a trail to the top of the falls. Take a colectivo or combi from Grifo Tinoto (45min., s/3) or an express taxi (30min.; s/20, round trip s/30). Each year on July 25, the town celebrates its own history and heritage with **Fiesta Quillabamba**; the Plaza de Armas is packed with processions, performances, and bus-loads of tourists from Cusco and elsewhere.

EL PONGO DE MAINIQUE

El Pongo, often heralded as the most awe-inspiring waterfall in South America, is "near" Quillabamba in the sense that it's 300km farther into the jungle. El Pongo's whitewater rapids are some of the wildest in Peru, but take only 15min. to navigate. Rent a canoe to take you through the rapids and bring you back up (round-trip 6hr.; fuel s/200, US$30-40 per person for the boatman's services). Keep in mind that El Pongo is dangerous at any time of year (prohibitively so in the rainy season) and that boats in Ivachote are unlikely to provide helmets or life jackets. Undeterred? Well, the gorge—30m at its widest point with 60m rock walls overhung with jungle flora—is stunning indeed.

There are **no accommodations** in this riverside village, but many groups camp on the beach. The nearest hostels lie in Kiteni, between Quillabamba and Ivachote. The cheapest place to find **boats** to El Pongo is Ivachote, 200km from Quillabamba and 90km from El Pongo. To reach El Pongo, take a Tinti-bound **bus** (9-10hr., 4pm, s/12) from Palma, just off Grau, to the dock, where you can catch a morning boat (45min., s/30) to Ivachote. Most returning canoes leave Ivachote in the morning as well, and buses and trucks to Quillabamba depart from Tinti around noon.

OLD VILCABAMBA

The long sought-after city of Vilcabamba—the last refuge of the Incas—was finally located in the middle of the jungle near Quillabamba. The lost city, which Hiram Bingham was searching for when he stumbled across Machu Picchu (p. 266), served as the base from which Inca Manco Cápac II launched the second rebellion, and his descendants—the last remnants of the rebel Incas—lived in the city until the assassination of Túpac Amaru in 1572. The remaining ruins were part of a massive fortress city, characterized by classic Inca construction as well as post-conquest features such as Spanish roof tiles. **Colectivos** and trucks from Quillabamba go to San Miguel (10hr., s/12-15), from which you can hike or take horses to the ruins—it's a half- to full-day's trip, depending upon the mode of transportation.

PARQUE NACIONAL DEL MANÚ

Situated at the confluence of the Manú and Alto Madre de Dios Rivers, Parque Nacional del Manú has been declared a World Biosphere Reserve (by UNESCO in 1977) and a World Heritage Site (by the International Union for Conservation of Nature in 1987), and is one of the largest parks in South America. First set aside in 1973, its nearly 4.5 million acres of largely untouched primary and secondary forests contain 13 species of monkeys, 1000 species of birds, 100 types of bats, 200 different mammals, and an astounding 3228 named species of plants (with another suspected 17,000 species yet to be labeled). Manú is a refuge for many endangered animals, among them jaguars, black caimans, giant otters, harpy eagles, and seven species of macaws The altitude spans from 300 to 3450m, encompassing lowland rainforest, cloud forest, and the scrubby vegetation of the Andean *páramo*. As a result of such incredible biodiversity, Manú has become a jungle hotspot, and during July and August even the remote waterway gets downright crowded. Although Manú probably offers the best opportunity to see animals in the Peruvian rainforest chances remain slim even here. Choice of tour guide is extremely important, as more knowledgeable guides will know where to spot wildlife. Most visitors will see macaws, monkeys, and caimans, and the lucky ones might see a jaguar or two.

AT A GLANCE	
AREA: 18,418 sq. km.	**GATEWAYS:** Cusco (p. 215) and Puerto Maldonado (p. 424).
CLIMATE: Humid sub-tropical forest plus humid tropical forest makes for stickiness year-round.	**CAMPING:** Permitted in some locations, but bring a tent to avoid vampire bats.
HIGHLIGHTS: Bird-watching, vine-swinging, animal-spotting, canoeing, zip-lining, mosquito-swatting.	**FEES:** Entrance fee US$50 plus licensed guide fees (required) if you're entering the reserve zone.

◪ TRANSPORTATION

Most visitors come with a guided tour. For those brave enough to venture independently, boats are the preferred mode of transport. **Gallito de las Rocas** (☎27 7255) sends **buses** from Cusco's Huarcuropata Station to Shintuya (12hr., M-F 10am, s/15), where you can hop a cargo canoe to Boca Manú (8-10hr., 1 per week, s/50). But that's as close to the reserve as you're likely to go if traveling independently, since permits into the reserve are generally issued only to organized tour agents only. It is usually faster and more cost-effective to travel to Manú with a guided tour anyway, whether or not you decide to stay on for the tour itself.

ORIENTATION AND PRACTICAL INFORMATION

Today, three "zones" combine to form Manú: the **cultural zone,** the **reserve zone,** and what is commonly referred to as the **impenetrable zone.** This last area occupies the space of the original national park, and only people native to the area and scientists with special permission may access it. Aerial photographic evidence suggests that it houses two tribes who are isolated from the outside world. The other two zones joined Manú as buffer states at the time of UNESCO's 1977 declaration of the area as a World Biosphere Reserve. In the inhabited cultural zone, there are few restrictions; residents may live as they please. Though uninhabited, the reserve zone welcomes visitors and offers what could be the best chance in all of the Peruvian jungle (the accessible parts, anyway) to see animals.

Supplies: If you travel with a guided tour, supplies are generally provided. If you're exploring on your own, acquire all supplies before leaving for Manú. Cusco has many supply stores (see **Outdoor Equipment,** p. 221) to meet your needs (see **Camping and Hiking Equipment,** p. 48).

Tours: The only way to enter Manú's reserve zone is with a registered tour operator (see **Guided Tours from Cusco,** p. 241), but they're expensive. Travelers who come with expectations of glimpsing big game at every turn will be disappointed. However, the plant life in Manú is fascinating from a biological standpoint, and there are monkeys and birds aplenty to satisfy eager eyes.

CAMPING

Tour groups provide their own accommodations. For independent travelers, none of the gateway towns possess very desirable (if any) accommodations; it's best to have a tent and sleeping bag. **Beaches** are an attractive place to camp, but **vampire bats** live in this region, so it's not wise to sleep outside without a tent.

HIKING

Jungle hiking is done with a machete and a general sense of direction. Be sure to bring a compass if you aren't going with a guide. At **Blanquillo,** a few hours

IN RECENT NEWS

MONEY DOES GROW ON TREES

Peru's national debt may be the salvation of the rainforest. In June 2002, Peru and the US signed a historic "debt-for-nature" exchange. This savvy swap saw the US cancel US$5.5 million of Peru's debt (an amount that would have cost over US$14 million after interest) in exchange for the Peruvian government's creation of a US$10 million conservation trust fund.

The deal has stuck. Money from the trust fund is channeled annually into the Peruvian conservation network, providing a stable source of funding for conservationists and wildlife researchers. The funds help to maintain 27.5 million acres of protected jungle; fend off destructive logging, hunting, and clearing; and educate and support indigenous peoples. Various US-based NGOs, including Conservation International, the World Wildlife Fund, and Nature Conservancy, together committed more than US$1 million to the Peruvian initiative. These groups now lend their expertise to advise local groups on conservation strategies.

For Peru, intact rainforests are no longer of purely aesthetic or even biological value; now, they are also a much-valued political and economic asset.

downriver from Boca Manú, a series of trails winds through the jungle. Some lead to **Cocha Camungo,** a lake that houses a catamaran similar to the one in the reserve zone at Cocha Salvador. Blanquillo is unregulated, so anyone with a few paddles can take this catamaran for a spin. Swimming here has its dangers: Camungo hosts both hungry piranhas and territorial giant otters. Discerning the entrance to the trails can be difficult, but you may be able to find a boatman in Boca Manú who can point it out.

THE MANÚ TOUR

Of course, your itinerary will depend upon the tour company you choose to travel with, but this might be a sample excursion.

DAY 1. Leave Cusco early in the morning by bus. The winding roads that lead to Manú pass several historical sites on the way. The funeral towers of **Ninamarca** are usually the first stop, where visitors receive a tour of the tombs. Next comes **Paucartambo,** a small colonial town high in the mountains. Here you are close to the highest point in Parque Nacional del Manú, at 3800m. The descent from Paucartambo goes through extensive **cloud forest;** here you'll get your first glimpse into the wonderful world of tropical flora and fauna. **Orchids** and **ferns** bloom alongside **epiphytic plants** (plants which depend on others for structural support). Visitors might see the American or **Spectacled bears** that roam this area or witness the peculiar mating rituals of Peru's national bird, the **cock-of-the-rock.** Before the end of the first day, you will have crossed the **Acjanacu Pass,** which marks the entrance into the Cultural Zone of Manú.

DAY 2. Most groups arrive at the port of **Atalaya** and board a motorboat. The day is spent traveling on the **Alto Madre de Dios** river, watching for birds along the way: **kingfishers, egrets, herons,** and the condor of the jungle, the **King vulture.** Here also visitors have the chance to go **river rafting** (Class I and II rapids) down the **Koshñipata river** and catch a spectacular view of the **Koñeq Canyon.**

DAY 3. Most groups make their way up the river into the reserve zone and around the village of **Boca Manú,** home of the famous **Macaw clay lick,** where visitors can observe hundreds of parrots gathering to eat clay (an integral part of their diet). The birds are loud, colorful, and spectacular to observe. There are also many **trails** in this area, explorable late in the day with a machete in hand.

DAY 4. Catamarans take visitors out on the Río Manú toward **Cocha Otorongo.** This particular trip allows for **fishing** and the exciting opportunity to see **larger wildlife,** including groups of turtles, white caimans, capybaras, and even jaguars. Near Otorongo is a 20m high observation platform from which **giant otters** are visible.

DAY 5. Across the way from Otorongo is **Cocha Salvador,** the popular next stop on the tour, an oxbow lake best visited on catamaran. Travelers silently observe giant otters, black caimans, and other avian and marine life. The animal population in this area is unique in that it has never been subjected to hunting by humans.

DAYS 6-9. Groups wake up to the calls of the **Red Howler monkey,** then begin their return trip. While some return directly to Boca Manú and fly back to Cusco, others paddle past the village toward the beaches of **Blanquillo** for more wildlife observation. Some will boat back down to Atalaya or spend additional time exploring the cloud forest. In the end, all trips return to Cusco.

PUERTO MALDONADO   ☎082

Making its name in rubber, then gold, and now as the "Biodiversity Capital of the World," Puerto Maldonado (pop. 34,400; elev. 183m) has created quite a niche for itself in the tourism industry. The town's position as the primary jumping-off point for the vast Reserva Nacional Tambopata and Parque Nacional Bahuaja-Sonene, which har-

Puerto Maldonado

🏠 ACCOMMODATIONS
Hospedaje Bahía, 9
Hospedaje El Astro, 16
Hostal Cahuata, 18
Hotel Rey Port, 11

🍴 FOOD
Carne Brava Grill & Bar, 17
El Califa, 4
El Hornito, 6
El Tucán, 1
La Casa Nostra, 14
La Cocina de Mi Abuela, 15
Refrigerio Mi Frontera, 13
Tu Dulce Espera, 12

⭐ ENTERTAINMENT
Arcade, 10
Billar, 8

🍸 NIGHTLIFE
Anaconda, 3
Coconut, 7
Discoteca Witite, 2
El Boulevard, 5

bor such wonders as the world's largest macaw *colpa* (clay lick), enables it to draw a larger proportion of visitors than any other border town of the Peruvian jungle. This heavy traffic, however, affects the 25km of park trails far more than the town's four paved streets; many companies whisk their clients straight from the airport to waiting boats, ensuring that Puerto Maldonado's humid languor remains largely undisturbed.

TRANSPORTATION

Flights: Aeropuerto Internacional Padre Aldamiz Puerto Maldonado (☎57 1531), 7km outside the city.

Nuevo Continente, Velarde 584 (☎57 2004; pem@aerocontinente.com.pe), south of 2 de Mayo. Open daily 10am-10pm. Daily flights to **Lima** (2hr., 9:50am, US$64) via **Cusco** (30min., US$34).

Lan Peru, Velarde 503 (☎57 3677), at 2 de Mayo. Open M-Sa 8am-8pm, Su 9am-1pm. Flies to **Cusco** (30min.; Tu, Th, Sa 12:40pm; US$44) and **Lima** (90min.; M, W, F, Su 1:10pm and Tu, Th, Sa 12:40pm; US$64).

TANS, Velarde 147-151 (☎57 3861), between Loreto and Billinghurst. Open M-Sa 8am-1pm and 4-8pm, Su 8am-1pm. Flies to **Lima** directly (90min.; Th, Su 5pm; US$70) and also to Lima (2hr., daily 11:30am; US$70) via **Cusco** (30min., US$40).

Buses: Buses to **Laberinto** (2hr., every 15min. 5:30am-6pm, s/7) leave from Ica, near Ernesto Rivero. From Laberinto, boats run to **Boca Colorado** (6-8hr., several per week, s/60) and from there to **Boca Manú** (4¾hr., 1-2 per week, s/30-40).

Trucks: Trucks to **Cusco** (2-4 days, daily between noon-1pm, s/20-30) leave from Ernesto Rivero, half a block south of the market.

Boats: An occasional boat heads from the **Puerto Capitanía**, at the end of Arequipa and down the stairs, to **Puerto Pardo** at the **Bolivian border** (2hr. with outboard motor, 8hr. in motorized *peke-peke* canoe). Groups can also hire a private boat at the port (US$300 per boat, up to 12 people).

Taxis: Mototaxis and tricycle taxis cost s/4-6 to the airport, s/0.70-2 anywhere in town.

Moped Rental: Take your pick on Prada, between Velarde and Puno. s/4 per hr.

BORDER CROSSING: INTO BOLIVIA. If you're planning to cross into Bolivia at Puerto Pardo/Puerto Heath, you need to get an exit stamp on your passport from the immigration officials in Puerto Maldonado. (Ica 727 at 28 de Julio, on Plaza Bolognesi. ☎57 1069.) From Puerto Maldonado, it's a 6-8hr. *peke-peke* canoe ride down the Río Madre de Dios to Puerto Pardo. There is little bureaucracy (or infrastructure) at the Puerto Pardo crossing; just wait for the next canoe to Puerto Heath, Bolivia and then cross the border. If you're planning to cross back into Peru, however, you must continue upriver to Riberalta, Bolivia (10-12 days) and get your passport stamped there.

✦ 🖍 ORIENTATION AND PRACTICAL INFORMATION

Puerto Maldonado's streets form a grid; the major roads are paved. **León Velarde** runs from **Río Madre de Dios,** through the **Plaza de Armas,** past the post office, several kilometers southeast to a port on the **Río Tambopata.**

Tourist Office: MINCETUR (municipal office), Fitzcarrald 252 (☎57 1164; madrededios@mincetur.gob.pe). Also has a tourist info booth at the airport. Maps of the city with major sites and establishments, hostel recommendations, and independent guides.

Tours: See **Into the Jungle from Puerto Maldonado,** p. 429.

Consulate: Bolivia, Loreto 272, 2nd fl. (☎57 1290), on the Plaza de Armas. Open M-F 9am-1pm.

Currency Exchange: Banco de Crédito, Carrión 201 (☎57 1001), at Arequipa, on the Plaza de Armas. Exchanges traveler's checks. Open M-Sa 10am-4pm, Su 9:30am-12:30pm. Also has a 24hr. AmEx/Plus/V **ATM. Banco de la Nación,** just up the street on Carrión, exchanges cash. Open M-Sa 8am-5:30pm.

Market: Mercado Modelo, bordered by Ica, Ernesto Rivero, Fitzcarrald, and Piura, 8 blocks from the Río Madre de Dios.

Outdoor Equipment: Supersport on 2 de Mayo and **Armugue** on 28 de Julio provide supplies for excursions, as do many of the tour agencies offering trips into the jungle (see **Into the Jungle from Puerto Maldonado,** p. 429).

Emergency: ☎105.

Police: On Billinghurst (☎57 1022), at the end of Velarde. Open daily 8am-1pm and 5:30-8pm.

Pharmacies: Farmacia, Velarde 590 (☎57 3554), at Prada. Open M-Sa 24hr., Su 9am-2pm and 5-11:30pm. **Botica Beatrize,** Velarde 510 (☎57 1612). Open daily 7am-11pm.

Hospital: Hospital Santa Rosa, Cajamarca 171 (☎57 1127), off Velarde. **Es Salud clinic,** on Cáceres (☎57 1074), at Km3 on the airport road.

Telephones: Phone booths cluster around the Plaza de Armas. There is no calling center with direct international lines, though a phone store at Carrión 273, on the Plaza, sells international calling cards (to US, 5min. s/5). Open daily 10am-11pm.

Internet Access: Internet cafes line the paved roads. s/ 2.50 per hr. everywhere. **Zona Virtual,** on Velarde just inland from the Plaza, offers Internet as well as Playstation 2 (s/2 per hr.). Open daily 8am-12:30am. **Juegos en Red,** on Loreto in the Plaza, has memory card capability and laser printing (s/0.50 per page). Open daily 8:30am-11pm. **Pedriño,** Velarde 718 (☎57 1379), between Troncoso and Tacna, boasts the fastest connections in town. Open daily 8am-midnight.

Post Office: Serpost, Velarde 675 (☎/fax 57 1088), at Troncoso. Open M-Sa 8am-8pm, Su 8am-2pm. **Western Union/DHL,** Loreto 224 (☎55 2328), is on the Plaza. Mail to the US/Canada in 3-4 days, to UK and Europe 4-5 days. Open M-Sa 8am-1pm and 4-8pm.

ACCOMMODATIONS

Those who choose to stay a night in the city rather than rush right to the jungle are rewarded with low prices, as hostels here serve as many (if not more) Peruvian tourists as internationals. The sweltering heat and suffocating humidity make some sort of fan a necessity for visitors—consider bringing your own just in case.

Hotel Rey Port, Velarde 457 (☎57 1177). Clean rooms with powerful fans in each one. Lovely views. Laundry service (s/4 per kg). Singles s/10, with bath s/25; doubles s/20, with bath s/35; triples s/30, with bath s/50. ❶

Hospedaje Bahía, 2 de Mayo 710 (☎57 2127), between Piura and Lambayeque. Airy rooms with standing fans. Nice staff. Laundry service s/2-4 per piece. Singles s/15, with bath s/25; doubles s/20, with bath s/40; triples s/30; additional bed s/10. ❷

Hostal Cahuata, Fitzcarrald 517 (☎57 1526), between Rivero and Piura. Removed from the Plaza, but next to the main market. Rooms are small but tidy. Large windows and balcony on each floor. No fans. Cable TV s/ 5. Singles s/10, with bath s/20; doubles s/20, with bath s/30; triples s/30, with bath s/40. ❶

Hospedaje El Astro, Velarde 617 (☎57 2128). Basic rooms are clean and have tiled floors. No fans. Singles s/12, with bath s/20; doubles and triples s/22, with bath s/28. ❷

FOOD

Cheap eats (*menús* s/2) cluster around the market, especially near the Piura-Ica intersection. Between Velarde and Puno, **2 de Mayo** hosts numerous chicken joints. Look for jungle-fresh fruit juice like the yummy *cocona* (passion fruit).

THE LOCAL STORY

LIAR, LIAR, ANTS ON FIRE

Most people's jungle phobias revolve around lions and tigers and bears—or at least jaguars and pumas, at any rate. However, contrary to tour propaganda, your chances of encountering a giant feline strolling through the rainforest are about as great as a sudden cold spell.

But don't breathe easy yet; there are dangers in the jungle you never dreamed of. The skinny **Tangarana tree,** long used medicinally by indigenous groups, looks innocuous enough from afar. Get closer, though, and you may notice an eerie clearing, perfectly circular, around its base. Just don't get *too* close: a mere tap on its trunk will call out legions of **fire ants.** These tiny, sting-packing red critters live on the fungus that grows inside the hollow Tangarana, and they work hard to protect it. They'll attack—and usually kill—any parasite or animal that dares scale their tree. It's wise to bring along a tube of menthol cream, available in pharmacies, to treat the wounds if you stumble upon these little devils unawares. In years past, the fire ants served as juries for indigenous communities, who would strap accused criminals to a Tangarana. If a criminal lived, he was considered guilty (and therefore needed to be executed). If the fire ants killed him (it's said to take 100 stings), alas! He was innocent, but also dead.

🔲 **El Hornito,** Carrión 271 (☎57 2082), on the Plaza. Munch on complimentary garlic bread and listen to live Andean tunes as your personal pan pizza bakes in the wood-fire oven. The back room doubles as a nighttime hotspot (see **El Boulevard,** p. 429). Delivery available. Pizzas s/12-15. Open daily 5:30pm-midnight. All major credit cards. ❷

🔲 **Tu Dulce Espera,** Velarde 469 (☎38 9034). An enticing array of cakes, pies, and *flan* (s/1-3), as well as hot snacks like *empanadas* and french fries (s/1.50-6). Open daily 7am-1pm and 5-11pm. ❶

Carne Brava Grill & Bar, Fitzcarrald 539 (alimansourmali@hotmail.com), across from the market. The best grilled meat in town (s/17-30). A wide selection of drinks, including local beer (s/4), whiskey (s/10), Brazilian *sangría* (s/17), and French and Chilean wines (s/27-47). Jungle juices for the sober s/3. Open daily 4pm-midnight. ❸

La Casa Nostra, León Velarde 515 (☎57 2647), south of 2 de Mayo. Jugs of juice (s/2-3) and excellent breakfasts (s/4-6.50). American breakfast s/6.50. Sandwiches and omelettes s/3-6. Open daily 7am-1pm and 5-11pm. ❷

El Califa, Piura 266 (☎57 1119), between Cusco and Carrión. A popular lunch spot with friendly service and a neighborhood feel. Entrees s/9-13. Open M-Sa 9am-5pm. ❷

La Cocina de Mi Abuela, Prada 341 (☎961 2744). Tasty, authentic meals. Lunch *menú* s/4. Open M-Sa 11am-10pm. ❶

Refrigerio Mi Frontera, 2 de Mayo 552. A small street cafe with hot *empanadas,* cold sandwiches, and delicious fresh cake (all s/1-5). Open 6am-1pm and 5-10:30pm. ❶

El Tucán (☎57 2290), inside Wasaí Lodge at Billinghurst and Arequipa, toward Río Madre de Dios from the Plaza. This open-air riverside gazebo offers the town's calmest dining; a mesh-screened dining area is available for mosquito-filled nights. Try the fresh fish straight from the river (s/14-18). Entrees s/15-20. Open daily 7am-3pm and 6-10pm. All major credit cards. ❸

🄶 SIGHTS

The music and merriment of the annual **Feria Agropecuaria, Agroindustrial, y Artesanal** is constant background noise in Puerto Maldonado July 23-28. Live music, merry-go-rounds, rows of foosball tables, and the latest fruit and vegetable harvests pack the fairgrounds a few kilometers from the city (taxi s/2). But you can enjoy Puerto Maldonado's other sights any time of the year.

OBELISCO. A glass tower at the intersection of Fitzcarrald and Madre de Dios becomes a shining blue beacon at night. Built in 1997 along with Plaza Centenario (which sits nearby on Madre de Dios), the tower has metal sculptures of miners at its base, recognizing the long history of rubber and gold mining around the river banks. Climb the 22 flights of stairs to the top for a lovely view: during the day you'll see the city surrounded by the rainforest; at night, you'll have to peer over the cuddling couples to glimpse the grid of lights below in the midst of a greater darkness. *(Open daily 8am-10pm. s/1.)*

BIODIVERSITY CENTERS. These non-profit projects operate in the Puerto Maldonado area and provide informative displays on the wildlife of the nearby reserve areas and the Amazon Basin as a whole. Not only are these centers interesting to visit, but there's another incentive—profits are put toward conservation education and sustainable development projects in local communities. **Japipi** can be visited on the way into town from the airport. This center takes its name from the native Ese-Eja word for "butterfly." Dedicated to the Amazon Basin's world record for butterfly diversity— more than 1200 species of butterflies have been recorded in an area of 5½km in the Tambopata Reserve—this center features more than a thousand butterflies in different stages of life, in both laboratory and natural settings. *(On Faucett, at Km6 on the airport* *road. A 3min. (200m) walk from the airport.* ☎57 3534; *japipi_peru@yahoo.com. Open daily 8am-2pm. US$5.)* The **Tropical Fish Export Aquarium** manages a changing collection of approximately 100 species of fish on any given day, reminding visitors that the Amazon Basin hosts a suspected 3000 distinct species of fish—15 times the number of species in all of Europe. Profits support local fishing communities. *(At Km4 on the airport road.* ☎57 1874; *www.gonewildperu.com. Guided tours US$3.)*

📻 🎵 NIGHTLIFE AND ENTERTAINMENT

Puerto Maldonado comes alive beneath its beautiful sunsets. The obelisk dons its garlands of blue lights, the yellow ice cream tricycle begins circling the Plaza, balloon vendors and popcorn sellers hover around the clocktower, and many establishments open their doors for the first time all day. Pedestrians meander about the Plaza and its sidestreets as late as midnight on weeknights. Friday and Saturday nights in particular bring out a crowd of youngsters. Clubs play great Latin music, there's no cover, and most spots party until dawn.

Discoteca Witite, on Velarde, 2nd fl. (☎57 2219), between Billinghurst and the Plaza. When it comes to dancing, this is most partiers' first choice. Open F-Sa 10pm-late.

El Boulevard, Carrión 271 (☎57 2082), behind the pizzeria on the Plaza. A foosball table, checkers set, and giant TV accessorize this chill video pub. Food available from the pizzeria (see **El Hornito,** p. 428). Cocktails and hard liquor s/6-14. Beer s/3.50. Open daily 6pm-late. All major credit cards.

Anaconda, on Loreto, on the Plaza de Armas. A "pub discotek" that stays alive every night of the week. Open daily 8:30pm-late.

Coconut, Carrión 263 (☎57 3063), on the Plaza de Armas. Large dance floor and American pop tunes. Open daily 8pm-late.

Billar, Velarde 347. Rack 'em up! Billiards s/3 per hr. Open daily 8am-midnight.

Arcade, Velarde 373 (☎982 9993). Plenty of digital distractions. s/1 per video game. Open daily 8:30am-midnight.

🎨 ARTESANÍA

Several boutiques in town feature jungle *artesanía*, direct from the Ese Eja and Machiguenga tribes that live in the nearby protected reserve areas (Tambopata and Manú). This is the real thing—the style of these handicrafts is unique to the region. **Souvenirs Manú,** Carrión 291, at Velarde on the Plaza de Armas, sells beaded jewelry (s/3-10), bow and arrow sets (s/20-30), and of course t-shirts (s/30). (☎57 3962. Open daily 8am-12:30pm and 4-10pm.) **Nativo,** Lambayeque 1050, has maps and books in English, native art, and indigenous instruments. (☎57 1663; ripamontti@mixmail.com. Open daily 8am-10pm.)

🌴 INTO THE JUNGLE FROM PUERTO MALDONADO

The **Reserva Nacional Tambopata,** whose 6000 square kilometers include ⬛**Lago Sandoval,** the Parque Nacional Bahuaja-Sonene, and Las Pampas de Heath National Sanctuary, serves as a prime area for jungle exploration. You probably won't see any large mammals, but during most park tours it's not uncommon to see **monkeys, caimans,** many **brilliantly colored birds,** and perhaps a **giant otter.** The reserve contains more than 575 species of birds, 1200 species of butterflies, and 135 species of ants. The Tambopata and other reserves in the area charge entrance fees (US$10-30). Most excursions into the rainforest include hiking, canoeing, and observation of flora and fauna, with additional activities depending on the length of the tour.

THE LOCAL STORY

CHULLACHAQUI

The worst of all worst-case scenarios would be to become lost in the depths of the fierce, untamed Amazon Basin. That's why it's crucial to keep your focus while hiking through these forests, and not become distracted by Chullachaqui, the deviant spirit of the jungle.

Chullachaqui lives in the largest tree of the jungle, the Lupuna tree, which has in the middle of its trunk a belly-like wooden formation; it is in the belly of this "pregnant" tree that locals believe the spirit resides. Appearing in the form of a close friend or family member, Chullachaqui emerges from the depths of virgin forests to confuse innocent explorers and make them lose their way. Chullachaqui plays to the interests of the ambitious—it tempts with promises of undiscovered patches of forest or rare bird sightings, cunningly convincing us to deviate from the path well traveled by.

The sure way to know if you're being conned by the spirit is to look at its feet—if one foot is in the form of a jaguar, ocelot, or bear paw, then it's Chullachaqui you're talking to, and you should get away as fast as you can. If both feet are human, then it really is just your friend or family member, and you need to stop being paranoid.

Prices include food, accommodation, transportation, and all relevant park fees. Reservations can often be made the day before departure, but reserve farther in advance to ensure availability.

TOUR AGENCIES

Green Nature Expedition, 2 de Mayo 298 (☎30 0027; greennature001@hotmail.com), at Velarde. Excellent service in the office, and knowledgeable English-speaking guides in the field. 1- and 2-day excursions to Lago Sandoval (US$60-100) and longer (4-6 days) trips to Tres Chimbadas, Bello Horizonte, and the Macaw clay lick (US$60-70 per day). Open daily 8am-8pm.

Peru Tours & Travel, 2 de Mayo 400 (☎80 3064; perutoursytravel@hotmail.com), at Puno. Full-day (US$50) and 3-day, 2-night (US$150) jungle trips to Lago Sandoval and Tres Chimbadas. Professional service; English spoken. Min. 2 people for all trips. Open M-Sa 8am-9pm, Su 8-11am.

Tribe Expeditions, 2 de Mayo 601 (☎57 2832; tribeexpeditions@hotmail.com). Touting profound "local knowledge," Tribe's bilingual guides will take you hiking and camping in the jungle (1-3 days, prices vary with excursion and duration). Option of extended stay without guide. All equipment included except sleeping bag.

Inka EkoTour Peru, Velarde 543 (☎57 2338; inkaekotourperu@hotmail.com). Offers 1-, 2-, and 3-day jungle trips to Lago Sandoval and Tres Chimbadas (US$48 per day). Flexible itineraries. Open daily 8am-1pm and 3:30-9pm.

INDEPENDENT GUIDES

Victor Yohamona (☎57 2613; fax at Hotel Cabaña Quinta 57 1045). Well-established and English-speaking Victor leads 1-day rainforest expeditions and visits to indigenous communities, 4-day trips to Lagos Sandoval and Valencia (2-3 people US$30 per day), excursions deeper into the Tambopata Reserve (2-3 people US$50 per day), and 8-day trips up the Río Las Piedras (2-3 people US$50 per day). Includes food, most accommodations (though not tents for camping), and transportation, but not reserve fees.

Beti Montero Saamona (☎961 2320; betis_tours@hotmail.com). English-speaking Beti will apply his jungle expertise to a tour that's right for you. Meet in advance to customize your itinerary. Trips run US$40-50 per day.

JUNGLE LODGES

Although there are more affordable ways to experience the area's 1000+ species of butterfly and the clay lick, a slew of expensive lodges provide an opportunity to see the jungle in style.

Rainforest Expeditions, Arequipa 401 (☎57 1056; pdaza@rainforest.com.pe). In Lima: Arambaru 166, Miraflores (cell ☎01 421 8347; fax 421 8183). Maintains the large and luxurious **Posada Amazonas** lodge in conjunction with the local Ese Eja community. The fact that a native group owns half the lodge and makes up the majority of its employees sets Posada apart. They can also arrange stays at the small **Tambopata Research Center** (☎57 2575), 4-5hr. upstream and just 500m from the *colpa*. Both have private baths and transportation to and from the airport. 4 days, 3 nights all-inclusive at the Posada US$280; 5 days, 4 nights (3 nights at Posada and 1 at the Research Center) US$565.

Tambopata Jungle Lodge (☎22 5701; fax 23 8911; www.tambopatalodge.com). A few hours from the clay lick on the Tambopata. Organizes 3- to 5-day tours of the forest (US$170-250) and clay lick (US$450-610). Tours include transportation, food, lodging, and guides. They also have a **lodge** in town for easy access to nearby daytrips.

Wasaí Lodge & Expeditions, on Billinghurst (☎57 2290; maldonado@wasai.com), at Arequipa. In Lima: Higueras 257 (☎96 37665; lima@wasai.com). In Cusco: Plateros 320 (☎22 1826; cuzco@wasai.com). Organizes daytrips and expeditions from and between its **Maldonado Lodge** in the port city and the **Tambopata Lodge** a few hours upstream from the clay lick. Excursions range from 1-7 days (US$70-700) and can include hiking, fishing, gold mining, mountain biking, canoeing, and swimming. 2 person min. for all trips. Open daily 5am-10pm.

DAYTRIP FROM PUERTO MALDONADO: LAGO SANDOVAL

Formed long ago by the Río Madre de Dios, this oxbow lake (3km long, 800m at its widest, 6m deep in the middle) is surrounded by dry, tropical, and swamp forests. The wildlife includes several endangered species, and the area's animals don't seem alienated by the humble human presence here. Giant otters, monkeys, and macaws can be seen hunting, playing, basking in the sun, and generally making noise. Visitors should not fish or swim in the lake, and as you walk through the forest, it's best to walk in silence—you'll see more, and happier, animals. From Puerto Capitanía in Maldonado, the lake's port is a 40min. ride downriver (s/40-60 in a *peke-peke* canoe). There is a checkpoint and visitor sign-in near where the boat drops you off, and a trail leads past it to the lake (5km, 1hr.). A jungle guide or fieldbook will identify vegetation along on the way. A small boatman's house sits lakeside, where you can rent canoes for the day (s/20). From there, it's a 1hr. row to the lookout tower. Leave another couple of hours to explore, float aimlessly, and finally return to the port.

The entrance fee for the Reserva Nacional Tambopata (US$10) must be paid at the INRENA office, Cusco 165 (☎57 3278), prior to departure. Maps of the Tambopata reserve are available from tour agencies and the tourist office (p. 426). Also bring sunblock, bottled water, a flashlight, and powerful insect repellent. Rubber boots are highly recommended (and a necessity in the rainy months), though in the dry season (June-Aug.), one can get by with normal shoes. Day-trip necessities as well as camping equipment are available at stores in Puerto Maldonado (see **Outdoor Equipment,** p. 426). Some lodges and agencies also rent equipment. Several agencies and free-lancers in Puerto Maldonado lead trips to Lago Sandoval (see **Into the Jungle from Puerto Maldonado,** p. 429). Lago Sandoval is easily done as a daytrip, but staying overnight has its benefits—more animals come out in the evenings. There are two lodging options near the lake: one is the high-end **Sandoval Lake Lodge ❺** (US$60-70), and the other is the more affordable *hospedaje*-like **Albergue ❸** (s/25). **Camping** is also possible in the area near the boatman's house.

APPENDIX

SPANISH QUICK REFERENCE

PRONUNCIATION

Each vowel has only one pronunciation: A ("ah" in father); E ("eh" in pet); I ("ee" in eat); O ("oh" in oat); U ("oo" in boot); Y, by itself, is pronounced the same as Spanish I ("ee"). Most consonants are pronounced the same as in English. Important exceptions are: J, pronounced like the English "h" in "hello"; LL, pronounced like the English "y" in "yes"; and Ñ, pronounced like the "ny" in "canyon." R at the beginning of a word or RR anywhere in a word is trilled. H is always silent. G before E or I is pronounced like the "h" in "hen"; elsewhere it is pronounced like the "g" in "gate." X has a bewildering variety of pronunciations: depending on dialect and word position, it can sound like English "h," "s," "sh," or "x."

Spanish words receive stress on the syllable marked with an accent ('). In the absence of an accent mark, words that end in vowels, "n," or "s" receive stress on the second to last syllable. For words ending in all other consonants, stress falls on the last syllable.

The Spanish language has masculine and feminine nouns, and gives a gender to all adjectives. Masculine words generally end with an "o": *él es un tonto* (he is a fool). Feminine words generally end with an "a": *ella es bella* (she is beautiful). Pay close attention—slight changes in word ending can cause drastic changes in meaning. For instance, when receiving directions, mind the distinction between *derecho* (straight) and *derecha* (right).

Quechua was the official language family of Tawantinsuyu, the Inca Empire. Several of its languages are still spoken by an estimated 12 to 16 million people in the Andean region, primarily in Peru and Bolivia, but also in Colombia and Argentina. On the *altiplano*, Aymara is the primary indigenous language group. Quechua and Aymara have only three vowels, and, as in Spanish, the stressed syllable is normally the next-to-last one. The link between Quechua and Aymara is rather slim. While they share 190 words, it seems more likely that this resulted from geographic interaction rather than common origin.

LET'S GO SPANISH PHRASEBOOK

ESSENTIAL PHRASES

ENGLISH	SPANISH	PRONUNCIATION
Hello.	Hola.	OH-la
Goodbye.	Adiós.	ah-dee-OHS
Yes/No	Sí/No	SEE/NO
Please.	Por favor.	POHR fa-VOHR
Thank you.	Gracias.	GRA-see-ahs
You're welcome.	De nada.	DAY NAH-dah
Do you speak English?	¿Habla inglés?	AH-blah EEN-glace
I don't speak Spanish.	No hablo español.	NO AH-bloh ehs-pahn-YOHL
Excuse me.	Perdón.	pehr-DOHN
I don't know.	No sé.	NO SAY
Can you repeat that?	¿Puede repetirlo?	PWEH-day reh-peh-TEER-lo

SURVIVAL SPANISH

ENGLISH	SPANISH	ENGLISH	SPANISH
Again, please.	Otra vez, por favor.	I'm sick/fine.	Estoy enfermo(a)/bien.
What (did you just say)?	¿Cómo?/¿Qué?	Could you speak more slowly?	¿Podría hablar más despacio?
I don't understand.	No entiendo.	How are you?	¿Qué tal?/¿Comó está?
What is your name?	¿Cómo se llama?	Where is (the center of town)?	¿Dónde está (el centro)?
How do you say (dodge-ball) in Spanish?	¿Cómo se dice (dodge-ball) en español?	Is the store open/closed?	¿La tienda está abierta/cerrada?
Good morning/night.	Buenos días/noches.	I am hungry/thirsty.	Tengo hambre/sed.
How much does it cost?	¿Cuánto cuesta?	I am hot/cold.	Tengo calor/frío.
Why (are you staring at me)?	¿Por qué (está mirándome)?	I want/would like...	Quiero/Me gustaría...
That is very cheap/expensive.	Es muy barato/caro.	Let's go!	¡Vámonos!
What's up?	¿Qué pasa?	Stop/that's enough.	Basta.
Who?	¿Quién?	What?	¿Qué?
When?	¿Cuándo?	Where?	¿Dónde?
Why?	¿Por qué?	Because.	Porque.

YOUR ARRIVAL

ENGLISH	SPANISH	ENGLISH	SPANISH
I am from (the US/Europe).	Soy de (los Estados Unidos/Europa).	What's the problem, sir/madam?	¿Cuál es el problema, señor/señora?
Here is my passport.	Aquí está mi pasaporte.	I lost my passport.	Perdí mi pasaporte.
I will be here for less than six months.	Estaré aquí por menos de seis meses.	I have nothing to declare.	No tengo nada para declarar.
I don't know where that came from.	No sé de dónde vino (eso).	Please do not detain me.	Por favor no me detenga.

GETTING AROUND

ENGLISH	SPANISH	ENGLISH	SPANISH
¿How can you get to...?	¿Cómo se puede llegar a...?	Is there anything cheaper?	¿Hay algo más barato/económico?
Does this bus go to (Lima)?	¿Va este autobús a (Lima)?	On foot.	A pie.

APPENDIX

ENGLISH	SPANISH	ENGLISH	SPANISH
Where is (Mackenna) street?	¿Dónde está la calle (Mackenna)?	What bus line goes to..?	¿Qué línea de buses tiene servicio a...?
When does the bus leave?	¿Cuándo sale el bús?	Where does the bus leave from?	¿De dónde sale el bús?
I'm getting off at...	Bajo en...	I have to go now.	Tengo que ir ahora.
Can I buy a ticket?	¿Podría comprar un boleto?	How far is...?	¿Qué tan lejos está...?
How long does the trip take?	¿Cuántas horas dura el viaje?	Continue forward.	Siga derecho.
I am going to the airport.	Voy al aeropuerto.	The flight is delayed/cancelled.	El vuelo está atrasado/cancelado.
Where is the bathroom?	¿Dónde está el baño?	Is it safe to hitchhike?	¿Es seguro pedir aventón?
I lost my baggage.	Perdí mi equipaje.	I'm lost.	Estoy perdido(a).
I would like to rent (a car).	Quisiera alquilar (un coche).	Please let me off at the zoo.	Por favor, déjeme en el zoológico.
How much does it cost per day/week?	¿Cuánto cuesta por día/semana?	Does it have (heating/air-conditioning)?	¿Tiene (calefacción/aire acondicionado)?
Where can I buy a cellphone?	¿Dónde puedo comprar un teléfono celular?	Where can I check e-mail?	¿Dónde se puede chequear el email?
Could you tell me what time it is?	¿Podría decirme qué hora es?	Are there student discounts available?	¿Hay descuentos para estudiantes?

DIRECTIONS

ENGLISH	SPANISH	ENGLISH	SPANISH
(to the) right	(a la) derecha	(to the) left	(a la) izquierda
next to	al lado de/junto a	across from	en frente de/frente a
straight ahead	derecho	turn (command form)	doble
near (to)	cerca (de)	far (from)	lejos (de)
above	arriba	below	abajo
traffic light	semáforo	corner	esquina
street	calle/avenida	block	cuadra

ACCOMMODATIONS

ENGLISH	SPANISH	ENGLISH	SPANISH
Is there a cheap hotel around here?	¿Hay un hotel económico por aquí?	Are there rooms with windows?	¿Hay habitaciones con ventanas?
Do you have rooms available?	¿Tiene habitaciones libres?	I am going to stay for (four) days.	Me voy a quedar (cuatro) días.
I would like to reserve a room.	Quisiera reservar una habitación.	Are there cheaper rooms?	¿Hay habitaciones más baratas?
Can I see a room?	¿Podría ver una habitación?	Do they come with private baths?	¿Vienen con baño privado?
Do you have any singles/doubles?	¿Tiene habitaciones sencillas/dobles?	Can I borrow a plunger?	¿Me puede prestar una bomba?
I need another key/towel/pillow.	Necesito otra llave/toalla/almohada.	My bedsheets are dirty.	Mis sábanas están sucias.
The shower/sink/toilet is broken.	La ducha/pila/el servicio no funciona.	I'll take it.	Lo tomo.
There are cockroaches in my room.	Hay cucarachas en mi habitación.	They are biting me.	Me están mordiendo.

EMERGENCY

ENGLISH	SPANISH	ENGLISH	SPANISH
Help!	¡Socorro!/¡Ayúdeme!	Call the police!	¡Llame a la policía/los carabineros!
I am hurt.	Estoy herido(a).	Leave me alone!	¡Déjame en paz!
It's an emergency!	¡Es una emergencia!	They robbed me!	¡Me han robado!
Fire!	¡Fuego!/¡Incendio!	They went that way!	¡Fueron en esa dirección!
Call a clinic/ambulance/doctor/priest!	¡Llame a una clínica/una ambulancia/un médico/un padre!	I will only speak in the presence of a lawyer.	Sólo hablaré en presencia de un abogado(a).
I need to contact my embassy.	Necesito contactar mi embajada.	Don't touch me!	¡No me toque!

MEDICAL

ENGLISH	SPANISH	ENGLISH	SPANISH
I feel bad/better/fine/worse.	Me siento mal/mejor/bien/peor.	I have a stomach ache.	Me duele el estómago.
I have a headache.	Tengo un dolor de cabeza.	It hurts here.	Me duele aquí.
I'm sick/ill.	Estoy enfermo(a).	Here is my prescription.	Aquí está la receta médica.
I'm allergic to...	Soy alérgico(a) a...	I think I'm going to vomit.	Pienso que voy a vomitar.
What is this medicine for?	¿Para qué es esta medicina?	I haven't been able to go to the bathroom in (four) days.	No he podido ir al baño en (cuatro) días.
Where is the nearest hospital/doctor?	¿Dónde está el hospital/doctor más cercano?	I have a cold/a fever/diarrhea/nausea.	Tengo gripe/una calentura/diarrea/náusea.

INTERPERSONAL INTERACTIONS

ENGLISH	SPANISH	ENGLISH	SPANISH
What is your name?	¿Cómo se llama?	Pleased to meet you.	Encantado(a)/Mucho gusto.
Where are you from?	¿De dónde es?	I'm (twenty) years old.	Tengo (veinte) años.
This is my first time in Peru.	Esta es mi primera vez en Peru.	I have a boyfriend/girlfriend/spouse.	Tengo novio/novia/esposo(a).
Do you come here often?	¿Viene aquí a menudo?	I love you.	Te quiero.
Do you have a light?	¿Tiene fuego?	What a shame: you bought Lonely Planet!	¡Qué lástima: compraste Lonely Planet!

NUMBERS, DAYS, AND MONTHS

ENGLISH	SPANISH	ENGLISH	SPANISH	ENGLISH	SPANISH
0	cero	20	veinte	last night	anoche
1	uno	21	veintiuno	weekend	fin de semana
2	dos	22	veintidos	morning	mañana
3	tres	30	treinta	afternoon	tarde
4	cuatro	40	cuarenta	night	noche
5	cinco	50	cincuenta	month	mes
6	seis	100	cien	year	año
7	siete	1000	un mil	early/late	temprano/tarde
8	ocho	1 million	un millón	January	enero
9	nueve	Monday	lunes	February	febrero
10	diez	Tuesday	martes	March	marzo
11	once	Wednesday	miércoles	April	abril
12	doce	Thursday	jueves	May	mayo
13	trece	Friday	viernes	June	junio
14	catorce	Saturday	sábado	July	julio
15	quince	Sunday	domingo	August	agosto
16	dieciseis	today	hoy	September	septiembre
17	diecisiete	tomorrow	mañana	October	octubre
18	dieciocho	day after tomorrow	pasado mañana	November	noviembre
19	diecinueve	yesterday	ayer	December	diciembre

EATING OUT

ENGLISH	SPANISH	ENGLISH	SPANISH
breakfast	desayuno	lunch	almuerzo
dinner	comida/cena	drink (alcoholic)	bebida (trago)
dessert	postre	bon appétit	buen provecho
fork	tenedor	knife	cuchillo
napkin	servilleta	cup	copa/taza
spoon	cuchara	Do you have hot sauce?	¿Tiene salsa picante?
Where is a good restaurant?	¿Dónde está un restaurante bueno?	Table for (one), please.	Mesa para (uno), por favor.
Can I see the menu?	¿Podría ver la carta/el menú?	Do you take credit cards?	¿Aceptan tarjetas de crédito?
This is too spicy.	Es demasiado picante.	Disgusting!	¡Guácala!/¡Qué asco!
I would like to order the eel.	Quisiera el congrio.	Delicious!	¡Qué rico!
Do you have anything vegetarian/without meat?	¿Hay algún plato vegetariano/sin carne?	Check, please.	La cuenta, por favor.

MENU READER

SPANISH	ENGLISH	SPANISH	ENGLISH
a la plancha	grilled	kuchen	pastry with fruit
al vapor	steamed	leche	milk
aceite	oil	legumbres	vegetables/legumes
aceituna	olive	lima	lime
agua (purificada)	water (purified)	limón	lemon
ajo	garlic	limonada	lemonade

SPANISH	ENGLISH	SPANISH	ENGLISH
almeja	clam	locos	abalone (white fish)
arroz	rice	lomo	steak or chop
arroz con leche	rice pudding	macedonia	syrupy dessert
ave-palta	sandwich with chicken and avocado	maíz	corn
Barros Luco	sandwich with beef and cheese	mariscos	seafood
Barros Jarpa	sandwich with ham	miel	honey
bistec	beefsteak	naranja	orange
bundín de centolla	crab with onions, eggs, cheese	nata	cream
café	coffee	paila marina	soup of various shellfish
caldillo de congrio	eel and vegetable soup	pan	bread
caliente	hot	pan amasado	a common heavy bread
camarones	shrimp	papas	potatoes
carne	meat	papas fritas	french fries
cazuela	clear broth with rice, corn, and chicken or beef	parrillas	various grilled meats
cebolla	onion	pasteles	desserts/pies
cerveza	beer	pastel de choclo	corn cassarole with beef, chicken, raisins, onions, and olives
ceviche	raw marinated seafood		
chacarero	sandwich with beef, tomato, chili, and green beans	pebre	mild or spicy salsa eaten with many foods
chupe de marisco/locos	sea scallops/abalone with white wine, butter, cream, and cheese	pernil de chanco a la chilena	braised fresh ham with chili sauce
churrasco	steak sandwich	pescado	fish
chorizo	spicy sausage	picoroco	dish using barnacle meat
coco	coconut	pimienta	pepper
congrio	eel	pisco sour	drink made with pisco (from grapes) and egg whites
cordero	lamb	plato	plate
curanto	hearty stew of fish, chicken, pork, lamb, beef, and potato	pollo	chicken
dulces	sweets	porotos granados	cranberry beans with squash and corn
dulce de leche	caramelized milk	puerco	pork
empanada	dumpling filled with meat, cheese, or potatoes	queso	cheese
ensalada	salad	sal	salt
entrada	appetizer	tragos	mixed drinks/liquor
gaseosa	soda	vino tinto/blanco	red wine/white

APPENDIX

QUECHUA AND AYMARA PHRASEBOOK

ESSENTIAL PHRASES

ENGLISH	QUECHUA	AYMARA
hello	napaykullayki	kamisaraki
good bye	ratukama	jakisiñkama
how are you?	allillanchu?	kunjamaskatasa?
please	allichu	mirá
thank you	yusulpayki	yuspagara
yes	arí	jisa
no	mana	janiw
where?	may?	kawki?
distant/close	karu/sirka	jaya/jak'a
down/up	uray wichay	aynacha alaxa
how much?	maik'ata'g?	k'gauka?
what?	iman?	kuna?
why?	imanaqtin?	kunata?
water	unu	uma
food	mihuna	manq'a
lodging	alohamiento	qurpa

NUMBERS

ENGLISH	QUECHUA	AYMARA	ENGLISH	QUECHUA	AYMARA
1	uc	maya	20	iscay-chunca	pätunca
2	iscay	paya	30	qimsa chunca	qimsa-tunca
3	quimsa	quimsa	40	tahua chunca	pusi-tunca
4	tahua	pusi	50	phichcca chunca	phichcca-tunca
5	pichcca	pisca	60	soccta chunca	suxta-tunca
6	soccta	sojta	70	ccanchis chunca	paqalqu-tunca
7	Ccanchis	pacallco	80	pusacc chunca	qimsacalcu-tunca
8	pusacc	qimsacallco	90	isccon chunca	llatunca-tunca
9	isccon	Llallunca	100	pachac	pataca
10	chunca	tunca	1000	huarancca	huaranca

SPANISH GLOSSARY

aduana: customs
agencia de viaje: travel agency
aguardiente: strong liquor
aguas termales: hot springs
ahora: now
ahorita: "now in just a little bit," which can mean anything from 5 minutes to 5 hours
aire acondicionado: air-conditioned (A/C)
a la plancha: grilled
al gusto: as you wish
alemán: German
almacén: (grocery) store
almuerzo: lunch, midday meal
alpaca: a shaggy-haired, long-necked animal in the cameloid family
altiplano: highland
amigo/a: friend
andén: platform
anexo: neighborhood
arriero: muleteer
arroz: rice
arroz chaufa: Chinese-style fried rice
artesanía: arts and crafts
avenida: avenue
bahía: bay
bandido: bandit
baño: bathroom or natural spa
barato/a: cheap
barranca: canyon
barro: mud
barrio: neighborhood
biblioteca: library
bistec/bistek: beefsteak
bocaditos: appetizers, at a bar
bodega: convenience store or winery
boletería: ticket counter
bonito/a: pretty/beautiful
borracho/a: drunk
bosque: forest
botica: drugstore
bueno/a: good
buena suerte: good luck
buen provecho: bon appétit
burro: donkey
caballero: gentleman
caballo: horse
cabañas: cabins
cajeros: cashiers
cajeros automáticos: ATM
caldera: coffee or tea pot
caldo: soup, broth, or stew
calle: street
cama: bed
camarones: shrimp
cambio: change

caminata: hike
camino: path, track, road
camión: truck
camioneta: small, pickup-sized truck
campamento: campground
campesino/a: person from a rural area, peasant
campo: countryside
canotaje: rafting
cantina: drinking establishment, usually male-dominated
carne asada: roast meat
capilla: chapel
caro/a: expensive
carretera: highway
carro: car, or sometimes a train car
casa: house
casa de cambio: currency exchange establishment
casado/a: married
cascadas: waterfalls
casona: mansion
catedral: cathedral
centro: city center
cerca: near/nearby
cerro: hill
cerveza: beer
ceviche: raw fish marinated in lemon juice, herbs, veggies
cevichería: ceviche restaurant
chico/a: boy/girl, little
chicharrón: bite-sized pieces of fried meat, usually pork
chuleta de chancho: pork chop
churrasco: steak
cigarillo: cigarette
cine: cinema
ciudad: city
ciudadela: neighborhood in a large city
coche: car
colectivo: shared taxi
coliseo: coliseum/stadium
comedor: dining room
comida típica: typical/traditional dishes
con: with
consulado: consulate
correo: post office
cordillera: mountain range
corvina: sea bass
crucero: crossroads
Cruz Roja: Red Cross
cuadra: street block
cuarto: a room
cuenta: bill/check
cuento: story/account
cueva: cave
curandero: healer

damas: ladies
desayuno: breakfast
descompuesto: broken, out of order; spoiled/rotten food
desierto: desert
despacio: slow
de turno: a 24hr. rotating schedule for pharmacies
dinero: money
discoteca: dance club
dueño/a: owner
dulces: sweets
edificio: building
email: email
embajada: embassy
embarcadero: dock
emergencia: emergency
encomiendas: estates granted to Spanish settlers in Latin America
entrada: entrance
estadio: stadium
este: east
estrella: star
extranjero: foreign/foreigner
farmacia: pharmacy
farmacia en turno: 24hr. pharmacy
feliz: happy
ferrocarril: railroad
fiesta: party, holiday
finca: a plantation-like agricultural enterprise or a ranch
friajes: sudden cold winds
frijoles: beans
frontera: border
fumar: to smoke
fumaroles: hole in a volcanic region which emits hot vapors
fundo: large estate or tract of land
fútbol: soccer
ganga: bargain
gobierno: government
gordo/a: fat
gorra: cap
gratis: free
gringo/a: North American
guanaco: animal in the camelid family
habitación: a room
hacer una caminata: take a hike
hacienda: ranch
helado: ice cream
hermano/a: brother/sister
hervido/a: boiled
hielo: ice
hijo/a: son/daughter
hombre: man
huaquero: graverobber
iglesia: church

impuestos: taxes
impuesto valor añadido (IVA): value added tax (VAT)
indígena: indigenous, refers to the native population
Internet: Internet
isla: island
jarra: 1L pitcher of beer
jirón: street
jugo: juice
ladrón: thief
lago/laguna: lake
lancha: launch, small boat
langosta: lobster
langostino: jumbo shrimp
larga distancia: long distance
lavandería: laundromat
lejos: far
lente: slow
librería: bookstore
lista de correos: mail holding system in Latin America
llamada: call
loma: hill
lomo: chop, steak
madre: mother
malo/a: bad
malecón: pier or seaside thoroughfare
maletas: luggage, suitcases
máneje despacio: drive slowly
manjar blanco: a whole milk spread
mar: sea
mariscos: seafood
matas: shrubs, jungle brush
matrimonial: double bed
menestras: lentils/beans
menú del día/menú: fixed daily meal often offered for a bargain price
mercado: market
merienda: snack
mestizaje: crossing of races
mestizo/a: a person of mixed European and indigenous descent
microbus: small, local bus
mirador: an observatory or look-out point
muelle: wharf
muerte: death
museo: museum
música folklórica: folk music
nada: nothing
niño/a: child
norte: north
obra: work of art/play
obraje: primitive textile workshop
oeste: west
oficina de turismo: tourist office
padre: father

pampa: a treeless grassland area
pan: bread
panadería: bakery
panga: motorboat
parada: a stop (on a bus or train)
parrilla: various cuts of meat, grilled
paro: labor strike
parque: park
parroquia: parish
paseo turístico: tour covering a series of sites
payaso: clown
pelea de gallos: cockfighting
peligroso/a: dangerous
peninsulares: Spanish-born colonists
peña: folkloric music club
pescado: fish
picante: spicy
pisa de uvas: grape-stomping
pisco sour: a drink made from pisco, lemon juice, sugarcane syrup, and egg white
plátano: plantain
playa: beach
población: population, settlement
policía: police
pollo a la brasa: roasted chicken
pueblito: small town
pueblo: town
puente: bridge
puerta: door
puerto: port
queso: cheese
rana: frog
recreo: place of amusement, restaurant/bar on the outskirts of a city
refrescos: refreshments, soft drinks
refugio: refuge
reloj: watch, clock
río: river
rodeo: rodeo
ropa: clothes
sabanas: bedsheets
sabor: flavor
sala: living room
salida: exit
salto: waterfall
salsa: sauce (can be of many varieties)
seguro/a: lock, insurance; adj.: safe
semáforo: traffic light
semana: week
Semana Santa: Holy Week
sexo: sex
shaman/chamán: spiritual healer

SIDA: the Spanish acronym for AIDS
siesta: mid-afternoon nap; businesses often close at this time
sillar: flexible, white, volcanic rock used in construction
sol: sun/Peruvian currency
solito/a: alone
solo carril: one-lane road or bridge
soltero/a: single (unmarried)
supermercado: supermarket
sur: south
tarifa: fee
tapas: bite-size appetizers served in bars
telenovela: soap opera
termas: hot mineral springs
terminal terrestre: bus station
tienda: store
tipo de cambio: exchange rate
trago: mixed drink/shot of alcohol
trekking: trekking
triste: sad
trucha: trout
turismo: tourism
turista: tourist
valle: valley
vicuña: a llama-like animal
volcán: volcano
zona: zone

INDEX

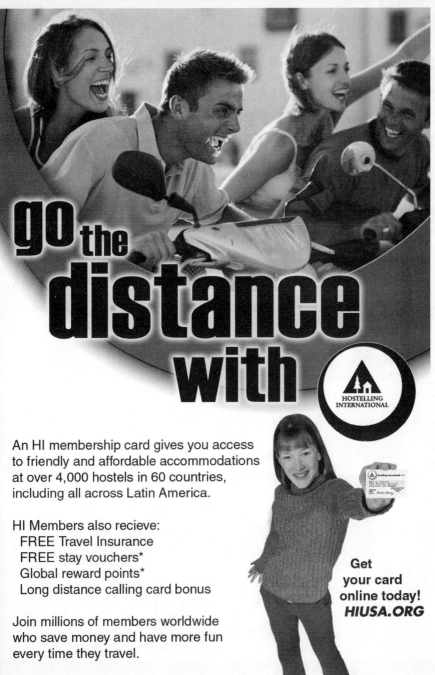

MAP INDEX

MAP LEGEND

Hotel/Hostel	Library	Building
Camping	Beach	Park: city, other
Food	Hospital	Plaza/other area
Nightlife	Police	Beach
Cafe	Post Office	Water
Entertainment	Tourist Office	Glacier
Museum	Point of Interest	Swamp
Church	Embassy/Consulate	Pedestrian Zone
Theater	Telephone Office	Steps
Internet Café	Airport	Trail
Bank	Bus Station	Metro Line/Stop
Pharmacy	Train Station	
	Ferry Line/Landing	

Thermal Bath	
Cave	
Waterfall	
Pass	
Peak	
Mountain Range	
Ranger Station	
Archaeological Site	
Monastery	
Wildlife Preserve	
Border Crossing	

ABBREVIATIONS:

C.	Cerro, Capo
Lg.	Laguna, Lago
PL.	Plaza
Pq.	Parque
P.N.	Parque Nacional
Q.	Quebrada
R.	Río
R.E.	Reserva Ecológica
R.F.	Reserva Forestal
R.N.	Reserva Natural
Z.R.	Zona Reservada

The Let's Go compass always points NORTH.